The Meaning of Literature

BY THE SAME AUTHOR

Toward Dramatic Illusion: Theatrical Technique and Meaning from Hardy to "Horace"

Tragedy and Truth: Studies in the Development of a Renaissance and Neoclassical Discourse

The Discourse of Modernism

The Uncertainty of Analysis: Problems in Truth, Meaning, and Culture

Timothy J. Reiss

The Meaning
of Literature

Cornell University Press

Ithaca and London

First published 1992 by Cornell University Press.

Excerpt from *Archy and Mehitabel* by Don Marquis, copyright 1927 by Doubleday, a division of Bantam, Doubleday, Dell Publishing Group, Inc. Used by permission of the publisher.

International Standard Book Number 0-8014-2646-4 (cloth)
International Standard Book Number 0-8014-9947-X (paper)
Library of Congress Catalog Card Number 91-23344
Printed in the United States of America
Librarians: Library of Congress cataloging information
appears on the last page of the book.

⊗ The paper in this book meets the minimum requirements
of the American National Standard for Information Sciences—
Permanence of Paper for Printed Library Materials, ANSI Z39.48-1984.

For Patricia J. Penn Hilden

frail gestures and small hands
jars in Tennessee
a cabin, nine bean-rows
and a hive

Contents

i am the artist
a creator and a demi god
it is ridiculous to suppose
that i should be denied
the food i need in order
to continue to create
beauty i tell you
plainly mister fly it is all
damned nonsense for that food
to rear up on its hind legs
and say it should not be eaten

you have convinced me
said the fly say no more
and shutting all his eyes
he prepared himself for dinner
and yet he said i could
have made out a case
for myself too if i had
had a better line of talk

of course you could said the spider
clutching a sirloin from him
but the end would have been
just the same if neither of
us had spoken at all

boss i am afraid that what
the spider said is true
and it gives me to think
furiously upon the futility
of literature
                    archy

—Don Marquis, *Archy and Mehitabel*

Acknowledgments

Most of the research work for this book was done on two occasions, made possible by three awards: a fellowship from the Social Sciences and Humanities Research Council of Canada in 1983–84, one from the American Council of Learned Societies in 1986–87, and an Emory University Faculty Award in the same year. In the summer of 1989 I was able to complete the European research, thanks to a New York University Research Challenge Fund Grant. New York University also helped with final preparation. I am most grateful to all the funding bodies.

Some bits and pieces of the work have appeared in print before. A few pages of Chapter 2 are taken, not entirely verbatim or unadulterated, from "Montaigne and the Subject of Polity," in *Literary Theory/Renaissance Texts*, ed. Patricia A. Parker and David Quint (Baltimore: Johns Hopkins University Press, 1986), pp. 115–49. Material now scattered among Chapters 3, 5, and 6 appeared in "Power, Poetry, and the Resemblance of Nature," in *Mimesis: From Mirror to Method, Augustine to Descartes*, ed. John D. Lyons and Stephen P. Nichols, Jr. (Hanover, N.H.: University Press of New England, 1982), pp. 215–47, 269–73. An earlier version of what is now Chapter 4 was published in *Renaissance Drama*, n.s. 18 (1988), and has since appeared in *Renaissance Drama as Cultural History: Essays from "Renaissance Drama," 1977–1987*, ed. Mary Beth Rose (Evanston, Ill.: Northwestern University Press, 1990), pp. 171–209. A different version of Chapter 9 appeared in *Gender and Theory: Dialogues on Feminist Criticism*, ed. Linda Kauffman (Oxford: Blackwell, 1989), pp. 11–50. The earliest version of Chapter 10 was given as a lecture at Camrose Lutheran College in Alberta in late 1984 and will appear in the Acts of the colloquium of which it was a part. All have been substantially rewritten even in those cases in which the frame remains essentially the same. I thank all the presses concerned for permission to use these materials here.

All translations are my own, except as noted.

The staffs of many libraries have been generous with their facilities and their time. Particularly, I must thank those of the Ashmolean, the Bodleian, and the Taylorian in Oxford; the Archives and Bibliothèque Nationales in Paris; the Bibliothèque Royale in Brussels; and the various libraries of the Katholieke Universiteit Leuven. In the last case, I thank José Lambert for the liberality of his friendship. The staffs of the Emory and New York University libraries have been equally forthcoming. In the former, Julia L. Jones and Margaret Whittier were helpful far beyond the call of their jobs. I thank them both.

Almost all the primitive versions of these chapters were given as lectures at various institutions in North America and Europe. I thank the audiences for their frequently generous feedback. I cannot possibly acknowledge all those who intervened on such occasions (even if I knew them), but I would like to thank Julio Rodríguez Luis for a question that made me rethink parts of Chapter 1; Mary Beth Rose and Jacques Dubois for remarks about Chapter 4 (and the latter for his warm hospitality in Liège); Joan DeJean for reading that same chapter and Chapter 7; Robin Howells for correcting some errors in Chapter 7; Wlad Godzich, Vladimir Krysinski, Perry Meisel, and Walter Moser for comments on Chapter 10; and Marc Angenot, Frances Ferguson, Patricia J. Hilden, Darko Suvin, and George Szanto for pushing me on Chapter 9. What is now Chapter 8 was first a response to an invitation by Christie McDonald. Patricia Hilden was further gracious enough to take time from her own work to read the Introduction and Epilogue. In writing or in collegial exchange, more people gave generously of their time and thought: I would like to record my gratitude particularly to Daniel Javitch, for divers moments of wisdom and pieces of information, and Eugene Vance, for conversations over many years. I further thank Donald R. Kelley and the other Press reader, both of whom gave a long typescript exquisitely careful attention. Much of the material now in this book has provided grist for graduate seminars at Emory University, the Graduate Center of the City University of New York, the State University of New York at Binghamton, and New York University. The students in those seminars have a share in what that material has now become. As usual, I am sincerely grateful to Bernhard Kendler, Kay Scheuer, Kim Vivier, and the staff of Cornell University Press.

One person above all is present in these pages, in the thought and debate behind them, in some of the arguments their conclusions record, in the calm and equability that makes concentrated writing possible at all, and considerably in their style. Though she surely disagrees with some of their detail and even, it may be, with their principal contention, I trust she will accept their dedication.

TIMOTHY J. REISS

New York, New York

The Meaning of Literature

Introduction

In 1972 René Wellek wrote that the "political attack on literature is a foolish generalization."[1] He was dismissing those who would depreciate literature on the grounds that it is an ideologically conservative and socially repressive instrument of bourgeois capitalism. Certainly such simplistic assertions do deserve to be refuted by the superficially obvious counterclaim put forward by Wellek himself that historically literature has as often served subversive and revolutionary goals as it has those of established authority. As Wellek presents them, these two activities are often simultaneous but neither, therefore, particular to literature nor defining of it. That the opposition is possible at all, and in these terms, hints that those on both sides of the argument are neglecting a few aspects of the question. A major one is that they take for granted that they know what *literature* is. And of course, they do. They know what it is in their culture, whatever difficulty they may have in providing any seriously and generally acceptable definition. They also know what authority and subversion and reaction are.

No one, I take it, would disagree with the thought that literature serves some purpose, like all other human activities. If human activities are necessarily social, simply because they are human, we can agree that literature serves some social purpose. Literature is, then, a socially purposive discursive activity (sign practicing and organizing) that we suppose to serve some specifiable role within the totality of different discursive practices composing what we call society (and how any society understands itself).

[1] René Wellek, "The Attack on Literature," in *The Attack on Literature and Other Essays* (Chapel Hill, N.C., 1982), p. 5. The essay first appeared in 1972.

But societies change. Human activities develop. We may even presume that humans in (and of) society themselves change with the transformations of the societies that mold and define them, whatever the common substrate. The concepts of person, of will and intention, of mind and knowledge did not, for instance, have the same meaning for Aristotle that they had for Descartes. Should we for that reason suppose the one offers a false description of reality, while the other gives a true one? Should we not rather assume that their descriptions themselves formed part of an overall social and conceptual environment that provided the functioning framework for effective action? That environment is what we call reality. Environments, then, change in some degree with the societies whose actions form them as they simultaneously form those societies (the definitional separation is both awkward and false). It follows that literature alters its role, its action, its forms of practice as the environment of which it is a part evolves.

This is the assumption behind the title of this book, which might otherwise seem at once impossibly imprudent, presumptuous, and unconscionably arrogant. It indicates the argument that what we know as "literature" has occurred in a particular time and place.

This is not to deny the obvious. No human society seems to be without art. From the very earliest times we have an abundance of visual evidence, in caves, on dwellings, of innumerable artifacts. Spoken forms may be extrapolated from an equal diversity of evidence: from visual depictions, from tradition, from various known oral cultures, from the timeworn existence of myth and legend, from the immediate committing of such tales to writing as soon as the medium and materials were available. We may also add, therefore, that most, if not all, societies with writing may be said to have something we could call literature. I rehearse these tired and perhaps trivial matters deliberately. For I wish to deny what is often taken as a self-evident corollary: that literature is a human behavior common to all societies, a means of communicating universally similar feelings, thoughts, and so forth which crosses ages and spaces.

All sociocultural environments are composed of innumerable discursive types (literature, philosophy, forms of work, practices of law, economic exchange, and the rest) whose mutual coherence depends to some extent on one dominant mode of comprehension, or way of understanding what a given society is in particular and all societies are in general (when a society is at all interested in others). That is not to say other modes of comprehension are absent, whether competing or not, but that to become common currency they need to pass, as it were, through the dominant mode.[2] Nor is it to say that societies are doomed to mutual incomprehension. But it is to say that comprehension takes effort, takes listening to

[2]I have rehearsed these issues in more detail in *The Discourse of Modernism* (Ithaca, N.Y., and London, 1982), *The Uncertainty of Analysis* (Ithaca, N.Y., and London, 1988), and "Société, discours, littérature: De l'histoire discursive," *Texte*, no. 5/6 (1986–87), 151–79.

wholes before extrapolating the meanings of parts. Nor is it to say that all values and meanings are relative. But it is to say that we must know the detail of difference before foolishly clamoring the relativeness of all values. It is to say that absolutes need understanding beyond the differences of time and place. That, too, requires effort. Nor, finally, is it to say that one should not love the art of one's culture and tradition. It is to say that such love does not inevitably require a belief in the universality of that art.

To say that all cultures have "art" is, therefore, not to say very much. Not only do we need to know what any given culture did, does, or would understand as "art," but we also need to know what particular sociocultural role is played by *that* discourse among all those others surrounding it. Understanding what societies other than our own take written or spoken art to be requires an effort that cannot start by taking for granted our own assumptions about the matter. David Summers remarks: "It is important not only that the meaning of art has changed but also that the meaning of what was always called 'art' was always changing. The simple continuity of terms indicates the continuity of a tradition, and the transformation of the meaning of those terms indicates the transformation of the tradition."[3] To catch both continuity and change is a challenge that must involve an attempt to understand the questions that seemed most urgent to the culture as a whole in which occurred the literature or art that we seek to understand.

What *we* have called "literature" is part of an environment in which we are able so to name it. I argue, here and elsewhere, that that environment developed out of a moment of fairly abrupt discursive transformation occurring in Western Europe during some of the years traditionally known as the Renaissance, between roughly the mid-sixteenth century and the early seventeenth. The transformation was consolidated by the turn of the latter century, or at least by the end of the first two decades of the eighteenth. This is not to deny further development, but to claim that there were no more immediate fundamental changes of assumption. By and large the discursive class by then dominant (what I call the *analytico-referential*) stayed so at least to the end of the nineteenth century. Despite increasing unease, it may be thought largely to be so still.

The thinker most evidently behind these arguments is Michel Foucault, although I would deny (as he came to do, at least implicitly) that anything took place in the nature of a "rupture." Elements of new dominant practices gradually developed within a previously quite different order of thought and action. The works mentioned in note 2 offer elements for an analysis of this phenomenon, but Hans Blumenberg has done it more punctiliously and with far greater learning.[4] By illustrating at once the

[3]David Summers, *The Judgment of Sense: Renaissance Naturalism and the Rise of Aesthetics* (Cambridge, 1987), p. 17.
[4]Hans Blumenberg, *The Legitimacy of the Modern Age*, trans. Robert M. Wallace (Cambridge, Mass., and London, 1983), and *The Genesis of the Copernican World*, trans. Robert M. Wallace (Cambridge, Mass., and London, 1987).

logic of the transformation and how its elements were inherent in medieval and Reformation thought, he has sought to answer those who claimed the European Renaissance and Enlightenment to be an "illegitimate" about-face in human development (notably in his German context, Georg Lukács, members of the Frankfurt School, and Martin Heidegger, but others too: Claude Lévi-Strauss, Jacques Derrida, and Jean-François Lyotard, to mention only a few). He has also tried to show how certain continuities have stayed essential in modern thought.[5] Whether showing that Enlightenment argument and metaphor evolved from earlier aporia, contradiction, and development, and have remained live practices, can answer the "legitimacy" claim should perhaps be left for those involved in the debate to decide. There the issues are philosophical, requiring a post-Hegelian or post-Marxian teleological view of history: for what, otherwise, can it *mean* to speak of an "illegitimate development of human history"?

If, however, the point is well taken that these transformations are entirely explicable, that the guiding norms of what we call Enlightenment were aspects of a "natural" development, there is a social and political consequence. Those who saw twentieth-century events and political orders as largely disastrous, and who accepted the debate's premises and the claim that Enlightenment was ultimately pernicious in its results, could logically plead for a return to something more naturally human supposed to have preceded the about-face. The lost community or wholeness they claimed to glimpse would not simply counter the individualistic fragmentation taken to inhere in Enlightenment, but would show how it was in fact a "betrayal" of true humanity. The answer to disaster thus lay in a rediscovery of that numinous time. Such a response reveals its inherent absurdity once the misapprehension of its foundation has been shown. Not wholly indifferent to Blumenberg's analyses, therefore, are the political arguments of Jürgen Habermas as to the "legitimation" of the modern state. Allowing that the dialectic of Enlightenment may produce abuse, he seeks to draw its corrective from within (in rational debate among individuals in the public sphere, for example), affirming that in any case societies have only the instruments of order that their history has given them.[6] Together, Blumenberg and Habermas make a powerful argument about the continuity, the transformation, and the use of history.

This book argues that literature took a specifiable role in the particular history of which both Blumenberg and Habermas are writing. It denies literature any claim to represent such deep permanencies of human being as might let it be identified with some false nostalgia for that numinous "wholeness" of nature. It tries to show the reasons for our literature's

---

[5]Hans Blumenberg, *Work on Myth*, trans. Robert M. Wallace (Cambridge, Mass., and London, 1985).
[6]For his place in the debate: Jürgen Habermas, *The Philosophical Discourse of Modernity: Twelve Lectures*, trans. Frederick G. Lawrence (Cambridge, Mass., 1987).

establishment, the nature of its development, and finally its own under-standing of a fragmentation simultaneously found problematic in the political sphere. The book thus follows literature from its instauration in the seventeenth century to a term in mid-nineteenth-century Romantic aesthetic analysis. It suggests that since then literature—in respect of any active social role—has suffered from a kind of repetitive inertia, as it has also been changing its meaning and cultural role. The book also infers, of course, that such new role and such new meaning can come only from what literature already was. It is, however, not my purpose to explore what they may be.

In particular, I argue that the concept and practice of literature and of literary criticism were elaborated during this period as the fulfillment of a multiple problematic: at once epistemological, aesthetic (as it would eventually be called), moral, and political. I contend that this elaboration occurred as part of a social solution to a crisis viewed explicitly at the time as at once logico-linguistic and sociopolitical. That literature was, of course, not alone as a solution is not to make its activity any less vital, or any less self-conscious. Such self-consciousness meant that it was ini-tially hesitant. My first two chapters describe all those hesitations and doubts, both in the realm of art and in that of political practice and theory, as a conceptual consensus and a social order broke down—or appeared to everyone to be doing so. The consensus had been based chiefly on a theological discourse. It was replaced by a political one: having to do, that is to say, with the ordering and actual relations of power between recog-nized government authority and citizens, between citizens, and between governments. This replacement itself demanded that such notions as those of "authority" and "citizen" themselves be worked out. That oc-curred at the same time. The second chapter discusses these changes by relating the remarkable display of hesitancy in any number of political theoretical texts to the facts of war and revolt.

Because my topic here is the nature of literature, the first chapter starts with the felt loss of purpose in what were called poetry and rhetoric. Although that will soon be seen as complementary to a more widespread sense of crisis, my aim in this volume dictates that art be the starting point. Loss of purpose showed itself at once in quarrels over poetic goals, in disputes about language, in arguments about the relation between poetry and the public sphere, in a growing hesitancy of debate itself. It was also shown in discussions about the connection between contemporary writing and past writing, in an increasingly dismayed sense of difference of quality, materials, and sociocultural security. To some extent I have em-phasized Sir Philip Sidney's *Arcadia*, because it brought all these issues together. I am aware that the association of pastoral and politics is a familiar one. In the first place, however, it allows me to play off continuity and change against each other throughout the book, because the associa-tion recurs continually. In the second place, one cannot simply ignore the fact that pastoral did play a fundamentally important part in the sixteenth-century debate about letters. We are obliged to look in such places if we wish to grasp thoroughly those issues that contemporaries found most pressing.

I have also emphasized the cases of Spain, France, the Low Countries, and England because they were increasingly the major political and cultural Western European powers. Italy and the Empire are not wholly neglected, but they do not play a major role in my argument—even though Italy had earlier supplied much, if not most, of the material for the developing artistic debate, while the Empire was a principal player in the political maneuvering. I have downplayed certain optimisms, not because they were not important at the time, but because they would not be in the future: those expressed, for example, in such movements as hermeticism, humanism, Neoplatonism. They offered forms of discourse, modes of thought, that were ultimately overwhelmed by the analytico-referential. None of this, whatever the occasional unfamiliarity of detail, may give a specialist reader any particularly novel understanding of the age. But Chapters 1 and 2 provide the essential foundation for understanding the subsequent instauration. It is against the background of a combination of artistic and political dismay that the specific nature of the new literary establishment may be understood.

The third chapter collects these strands, to show how, particularly now in France and England, literature was developed for its fourfold purpose, especially at first for a political one. It claims this purpose to be deliberate and complex. It shows how literature came to correspond to a specific form of political authority, debate, and practice. It also argues that the theoretical premises of apparently differing political orders were the same. These points are pursued in Chapter 5, and 6 shows how imbricated the other three functions—the epistemological, the ethical, and the aesthetic—had become. Yet I do not wish to imply that literary artifacts were related in any obscure way to historical events and political decisions. On the contrary, the relation, however complex, was also evident. That is why I occasionally relate in some detail familiar decisions and events—apart from the obvious fact that recounting is always interpretation and so demands a few such details. That is also why I look at works that contemporaries saw as most important. Of major interest are the reasons for that evaluation. (What is now mostly *unfamiliar* is the nature of the constraints producing these familiarities and importances of literature.)

Chapter 4 brings in what I see as the other principal aspect of this inception of literature: not only its role in debate about reason (what I call its *epistemological function*), but its role in debate about the gendering of reason. A gender question was also embedded in political discussion, so this chapter picks up on the preceding one as it feeds this new debate into following ones. This issue comes to a head, though, in Chapter 7, pursuing the ways in which the debates about gender, literature, and politics, about taste and reason, about writer and public, were wholly one by the end of the century. These chapters seek to examine in detail and separately several complex issues integral to what literature was becoming. These issues could not well be analyzed as a whole, however much they might be such in actual practice. I hope Chapter 7 succeeds in weaving them together.

Chapter 8 then discusses how literature, in creating a tradition for itself, was able to make itself the universal embodiment of ubiquitous values and so be removed from the constraints of a particular culture and history (thus giving it the potential to become that privileged site of a future nostalgia for the numinous, that conscience of a flawed society, grasped by future theoretical claim). Its representatives accomplished this by defining its name, adjudicating its past in particular authors and writings, and establishing its current producers. The following chapter, using mainly the example of Mary Wollstonecraft so as to keep in hand the various strands of our debate, argues the subsequently confining nature of the now-dominant discourse by the end of the eighteenth century. The case of women's status and role was an especially acute test for the constraints imposed by such dominance.

The last chapter analyzes certain strands of literary development (notably that of the sublime) through the eighteenth century, to show how the idea of literature came to a head (and a sort of "end") by the mid-nineteenth. Previous chapters have increasingly pointed toward a "summation" of many of their issues, with Hegel's name becoming its marker. This is not to imply he was alone or even that his work did signal either a new beginning or a closure. That work may be taken, however, as a particularly strong moment, marking a watershed whose consequences are still being felt. Hegel was at once typical and exemplary.

He was typical in summing up this entire history of aesthetic and political debate and doing so in terms supplied by the group of his near contemporaries. Wellek has suggested that Hegel's writing on aesthetics was "the culmination of the whole astonishing development of German speculation on art."[7] Although Wellek adds that in naming such as Kant, Schiller, and Schelling, he is mentioning "only his most obvious predecessors," my claim is the broader one that Hegel's work partly closed debates begun three centuries before. His work was exemplary in that it discussed the literature and art of that history with quite special complexity and fullness. Moreover, by founding its discussion on the identification of terms of literature's development and elements of its nature with those taken to explain other cultures and such of their aesthetic artifacts as had been brought into its tradition, his analysis underscored the expansion of literature's universalist claims.

---

[7] René Wellek, *A History of Modern Criticism, 1750–1950*, 6 vols. (New Haven, Conn., 1955–86), 2:318.

Typicality and exemplarity do not have to do with how well acquainted writers in (say) France and England may have been with Hegel's work and that of his German contemporaries. Such acquaintance remains in any case a matter of some scholarly debate. They have rather to do with what Hazlitt called "the spirit of the age." My discussion aims to show how Hegel does embody that spirit. As a philosopher, he became influential in Britain and Italy only sometime after his death, in France not until more than a century later. That his work has in recent years become a principal subject of debate in many areas may be taken to indicate something of the lasting importance of the issues with which it dealt. Chapter 10 is intended to show, too, both the place of Hegel's work in its time and the seriousness with which his idea of literature needs to be taken in our current debates.

To follow these later developments in the detail they really require would demand several volumes, particularly since one clearly implicit assumption in what I have just described is that what we call "Romanticism" is a continuation, not a rupture. Although that is hardly an original idea, many readers will no doubt raise objections. Length prevents me from assuaging these here, but I have throughout, chiefly from Chapter 6 on, used the device of referring forward extensively to future statements that seem to me to repeat the same premises as earlier debate. It is, of course, true that analogies of this sort *prove* nothing. Still, they can well be more than just indicative. When Plato's young Theaetatus said he found them absurd, his Eleatic respondent took a gently mocking example to suggest otherwise. And he opined that "the spirit of rational enquiry" should respect such analogies, for its object "in its efforts to discover affinity and the lack of it throughout the range of the arts is understanding."[8] Here my aim is to signal continuities, affinities, and maybe identities, of which only a few can be thoroughly explored in later chapters. The examples proposed are anyway not simple analogies. I always indicate the nature and implications of their parallels. More important, Chapters 9 and 10 do give some of them a little of the attention they deserve. That the German case is then silently drawn into discussion until this point mainly about France and England involves a claim about the general cultural development of Western Europe. That the Slavic is not involves merely a lack of competence.

I am aware of the many kinds of resistance an argument of this sort is likely to encounter. My Epilogue seeks to respond to some of them, as well as to follow up on a few of the many loose ends. I also recognize that my choice to emphasize dominance at the expense of subsidiary strands will strike some as merely setting aside whole fields of endeavor and practice and, perhaps worse (for I suppose most critics would allow that one cannot cover everything), as denying nuance. I can only answer that the choice

---

[8]Plato, *Sophist*, 227B, in *The Sophist and The Statesman*, trans. and intro. A. E. Taylor, ed. Raymond Klibansky and Elizabeth Anscombe (London, 1961), pp. 108–9.

has been deliberate. I know other strands may not be only residual (as I implied sixteenth-century optimisms were), but may provide emergences responding to some of the questions raised in the Epilogue. My object was to pursue not these, but affinities and dominance.

This book is not, then, a history of modern literature or literary criticism. Wellek's multivolume work on that topic has fulfilled its aim admirably—quite apart from any number of books that do it for national literatures. The present book is predicated on the assumption that through whatever places criticism and literature may have passed since the European seventeenth century, they have not changed in any basic way: in the sense that they are always struggling with the same tensions, the same fundamental elements, and the same claims as to purpose, means, and effect. The familiarity of those tensions, elements, and claims results from literature's having been a response to a particular set of issues, embedded in a history that by and large remains ours. The book indicates the reasons for this familiarity of what we call literature and of the analyses we make of its artifacts. It may also show why the nineteenth-century institutionalization explored, for instance, by Peter Hohendahl—schools, publishing, criticism, journals, and so forth—was perhaps *necessary.*[9] Maybe it implies, too, that physical institutionalization of that sort marked the end of a socially "organic" development, the moment when active process became sealed tradition, echoing therefore the end indicated at the conclusion of this volume.

Wellek's (and Hohendahl's) work is a detailed description of the creation specific to a given era and culture. This book is rather a contentious element in a wider argument about historical patterns and development. This aim involves some simplifications, but I nonetheless believe it is urgent that we understand our discursive operations and organizations as the creation and establishment of certain historical needs. Literature and its criticism compose one such cultural creation. This book traces their history only as a factor of the whys, wherefores, and consequences of that creation.

[9]Peter Uwe Hohendahl, *Building a National Literature: The Case of Germany, 1830–1870*, trans. Renate Baron Franciscono (Ithaca, N.Y., and London, 1989).

Chapter 1

A Poetics of Cultural Dismay

Shall I ever again, within my country's borders,
With wonder see a turf-heaped cottage roof,
My realm, at last, some modest ears of grain?
Think of these fields in a soldier's cruel hands!
These crops for foreigners! See how discord leaves
Countrymen wretched: for *them* we've tilled and sown!
   —Virgil, *Eclogues*, trans. Paul Alpers, I. 67–72

Virgil's Meliboeus lamented a pastoral Arcadia entirely disturbed by the depredations of the veterans of Philippi. The countryside had gone to soldiers ignorant of its needs, alien to its older population, and "barbaric" in their relation to the land. Written probably between 42 and 37 B.C., the *Bucolics* were both plaintive regret for that lost Arcadia, knowing it to have been ever but a fiction, and recognition that the post-Philippi (42 B.C.) military settlement had been essential to the reestablishment of social order. The celebrated passage in the fourth Bucolic, foretelling the return of the "Virgo," predicted the advent of some universal justice.[1] Less than ten years later, just two years after Actium (31 B.C.), the *Georgics* provided an instruction appropriate to such new farmers—with doubtless exiguous success. It is no surprise to read in Suetonius that Augustus enjoyed a complete rendering of this poem by Virgil and Maecenas as he was returning victorious from the East. The *Aeneid* was to culminate this series of poems reflecting the establishment of political order: from Arcadia lost to Rome triumphant.

Sixteen hundred years later Rome had once again yielded to Arcadia, whose age of wonder was to be equally short-lived this time. By the late 1570s Sir Philip Sidney could readily draw the magic land into a poetics of despair. King Basilius has incomprehensibly abdicated his charge as prince of Arcadia, under the suasion of the illiterate churl Dametas. Believing the voice of untutored ignorance to be that of sagacious innocence, of an Erasmian wise Folly, and persuaded that the entirely hermetic prophecy of

---

[1] Justitia (Greek *Diké*) had left the earth after the Saturnine age had yielded to the iron. She had been incorporated into the heavenly pantheon as Astraea-Virgo or Themis. On this (especially as it applied, later, to Elizabeth I), see, e.g., Frances A. Yates, *Astraea: The Imperial Theme in the Sixteenth Century* (1975; rpt. Harmondsworth, 1977), pp. 29–38.

an in fact irrational Delphic oracle could be interpreted distinctly as a clarion call of reason (shades of Rabelais's "dive bouteille" and of Hythlodaeus's reference to the Delphic "know thyself" in *Utopia*), Basilius has withdrawn from public life into what he takes for a place of private welfare.

Deprived of their clear head of order and literate reason, the state and society have fallen into anarchy. The illiterate Dametas is supposed to complete the upbringing of Basilius's daughters, Pamela and Philoclea. The herdsman's own daughter, Mopsa, thinks to wed the courtly shepherd Dorus, actually Musidorus prince of Thessalia, so disguised that he may penetrate the lowly new world in which Basilius fancies he may protect himself and his family from the slings of fortune, from the predicted onslaught of the world. At the same time, Pyrocles, prince of Macedon, has concealed himself as the Amazon Zelmane, that he may have access to his beloved Philoclea.

Ranks have been wholly inverted. Order has become anarchy. Sexes have been confused. Illiteracy has been directed to teach literacy. Basilius's own family (a bad sister-in-law, Cecropia, and her better son, Amphialus) revolts, kidnapping his two daughters and the disguised Zelmane. Peasants rebel. Foreign powers fret at the borders of Arcadia. The world obeys the whim of a spinning top's whip, plaything of Montaigne's "branloire pérenne." Euarchus, the well-named Macedonian king, brought as judge to reestablish order, will justly remark: "Although long experience hath made me know all men (and so princes, which be but men) to be subject to infinite casualties, the very constitution of our lives remaining in continual change, yet the affairs of this country . . . , makes me abashed with the strangeness of it."[2] Indeed, when we arrive at this final moment of judgment, the King is apparently dead, his wife dishonored, the two princes guilty of various criminal activities. Only a comedic coup de théâtre could avoid an entirely tragic catastrophe. The constant implicit references to humanist ideals mark here only their failure. (This failure of conceptual models reflected in the novel was countered—not surprisingly, since it suggested the dismissal of past error—by the success of the book itself, which by the late eighteenth century had become the most widely read prose fiction in the English language. The readers of Samuel Richardson's *Pamela* would readily recognize his eponymous heroine's aristocratic forebear.)

Arcadia *had* been a very different place. Jacopo Sannazaro, in the earliest Renaissance text to use the setting (written between the 1480s and 1504), had portrayed an unalloyed "country of the mind," dedicated "to poetry, to pleasure, to love, to contemplation."[3] Sincero, the author's persona, re-

---

[2]Sir Philip Sidney, *The Countess of Pembroke's Arcadia*, ed. Maurice Evans (1977; rpt. Harmondsworth, 1987), p. 794.

[3]Introduction to Jacopo Sannazaro, *Arcadia and Piscatorial Eclogues*, trans. and intro. Ralph Nash (Detroit, 1966), p. 23.

counted and shared a world where shepherds cultivated the Muses; appreciated love (quite physically embodied); contemplated beauty, whether in poetry, in nature, or in women; and enjoyed an ambivalently separate world of tranquil indolence. Sincero may finally have viewed this inactual world with some irony, but he never questioned it in any fundamental way. Poetry could present a realm of ideal pleasure and indeed realize it, at least for a space, within a literate community.

Nor should we think of this claim as simply escapist. It echoed the humanist social ideal of a community linked by mutual bonds of amity and exchange of duty, as we find it in Erasmus, More, and Castiglione, who presented his model court as an urban version of Arcadia. Sidney indeed deliberately recalled *The Courtier* in making his major protagonist the son of a king of Macedon. Pyrocles, disguised throughout most of *Arcadia* as an Amazon warrior, was also the very embodiment of courtly virtue. In Castiglione's Urbino, when Cesare Gonzago had asked how one learned that grace essential to courtliness, Ludovico de Canossa had replied that one must look and learn from those epitomizing such qualities. "How important this seemed to King Philip of Macedon," he had said, "can be seen from the fact that he wanted it to be Aristotle, the eminent philosopher, and perhaps the greatest ever, who should teach the elements of letters to his son Alexander." For "what the courtier especially requires in order to speak and write well . . . is knowledge."[4] This union of Arcadia and Urbino, of country and city, of letters, arms, and sensibility, provided Sidney and others with a principal symbol of a world destroyed.

The author of *The Courtier* was to die in Spain, where the same topos had received a no less influential treatment in the *Églogas* of Garcilaso de la Vega, published posthumously in 1543 (Garcilaso was killed fighting in Italy). In his 1580 commentary on this poetry, itself a monument of poetic theory, Fernando de Herrera wrote:

> The matter of this poetry is the affairs and deeds of shepherds, above all their loves; but loves that are simple and harmless, neither deadly from the fury of jealousy, nor soiled by adulteries; struggles between rivals, but without death and blood. The gifts they give to their loved ones are valued more for the thought than for the price, for they send golden apples or doves taken from the nest.
>
> Their way of life represents the golden age; speech is simple, elegant; feelings are affectionate and delicate; words savor of the countryside and the rusticity of the village; but not without grace, nor with profound ignorance and aged peevishness; for rusticity is tempered with the purity of diction proper to its style.[5]

Herrera specifically placed Garcilaso in the tradition now represented by Sannazaro, whom he congratulated on being the "only one worthy of

---

[4]Baldesar Castiglione, *The Book of the Courtier*, trans. George Bull (Harmondsworth, 1967), pp. 66, 76.
[5]"Comentarios de Fernando de Herrera (1580)," in *Garcilaso de la Vega y sus com-*

being read among all those writing eclogues since Virgil."[6] But the commentator had by then read a quite different kind of text using the material, one of equal importance in literary history, Jorge de Montemayor's *Siete libros de la Diana* (1559). Of this fiction, López Estrada has used strikingly similar language: "The shepherds have eyes, ears and mouth busy only with seeing, hearing and singing such beauty. And they love love for itself, with no hope of favor."[7] It was this that provided the context for Herrera's commentary-as-poetic, whose purpose was to improve the vernacular language and its knowledge, and only then to instruct in the various kinds of poetry.[8] And Herrera felt that, like the teachings of *The Courtier*, this poetic inhered in the arcadian topos: his was simply a (long) gloss drawn from the *Églogas* themselves. Some sad years later (1617), Miguel de Cervantes offered Garcilaso as the poet/soldier who had indeed established Arcadia in reality, fixing it on the banks of the Tagus by the "holy city" of Toledo: "Here his shepherd's flute trilled, the waters of this river paused to hear it, the leaves of the trees ceased fluttering, and the winds grew calm to give news of his astonishing song a chance to go from tongue to tongue and from one nation to another through all the world." In a familiar literary cliché, the Tagus itself, with its "golden sands," became almost the image of a new age: "But did I say golden? Made, rather of pure gold!"[9]

This Arcadia (a nostalgic memory by Cervantes's time) clearly represented an ideal of social stability, linking a civil and linguistic community through a kind of aesthetic politics of amity and a graceful exchange of duty. It provided the exemplary *locus amoenus* for an idea of politics considered not in terms of power relations but "as the theory and practice of social consensus," at the same time as it embodied a matching notion of rhetoric and philology as "the theory and practice of linguistic consensus."[10] Such copiousness of meaning may suffice to explain the huge

---

entaristas. Obras completas del poeta, acompañadas de los textos íntegros de los comentarios de El Brocense, Fernando de Herrera, Tamayo de Vargas y Azara, ed. Antonio Gallego Morell, 2d ed. (Madrid, 1972), p. 474.

[6]Ibid., p. 475.

[7]Prólogo to Jorge de Montemayor, *Los siete libros de la Diana,* ed. Francisco López Estrada (1954; rpt. Madrid, 1970), p. lxxviii.

[8]Herrera, "Comentarios," p. 307. Ignacio Navarrete has argued that Herrera's remarks in fact attacked a canon that had made the courtier-poet (and the imperial ideology he enacted) an ideal: Herrera wished to make Garcilaso an epitome of learned humanism ("Decentering Garcilaso: Herrera's Attack on the Canon," *PMLA,* 106, no. 1 [1991], 21–33).

[9]Miguel de Cervantes Saavedra, *Los trabajos de Persiles y Sigismunda* (1952; rpt. Madrid, 1980), p. 204; *The Trials of Persiles and Sigismunda: A Northern Story,* trans. Celia Richmond Weller and Clark A. Colahan (Berkeley, Los Angeles, and London, 1989), pp. 234–35: III 8. The cry bordered the proverbial: Juvenal already warned of the corrupting allure symbolized by "shady Tagus and its gold rolled down to the sea" (Satire III, ll. 54–55).

[10]Victoria Kahn, *Rhetoric, Prudence, and Skepticism in the Renaissance* (Ithaca, N.Y., and London, 1985), p. 27.

influence rapidly acquired by Ludovico Ariosto's *Orlando furioso* (1516, 1532). It became a "classic" in a few years.[11] With whatever irony Ariosto may have used his material, the arcadian elements still enacted an ideal of social grace, aesthetic pleasure, and literate intercourse. In this respect little was changed by Torquato Tasso's *Aminta* (played with enormous success in 1573) or by Battista Guarini's *Pastor fido*, completed in 1584 and published in 1590. Nor would that ideal be seriously challenged even by a later text such as Honoré d'Urfé's *Astrée* of 1607, although Arcadia had become a more real Forez and signs of disturbance had begun to appear.

All these landmarks fully echoed the arguments of literary critics and political commentators. By the 1570s, however, something was already giving way. The world had now become all too solid. The calm fabric of Arcadia had been most rudely torn. Literary device could no longer remain separate from the real world in which it dwelt. No longer could it be an ornament, a recreation, or even a commentary, however ethical or political, let alone a portrayal of some separate realm of imagination. The world was sundered, and with it the arts and the sciences of divers kinds of writing. Not only Sidney's *Arcadia* would reflect such dismay. In *Gerusalemme liberata*, Tasso (whom Sidney may well have met in Paris in 1572)[12] made the pastoral interlude a moment of misguided indolence, a springe set to divert the hero from the business of war. Yet he still related the gladsome success of the First Crusade, the victory of Goffredo over the pagans. In Spain, Lope de Vega would soon write a *Jerusalén conquistada* (1609), whose material, the Third Crusade, told only of disaster (his title thus becoming wholly ironic): the death of Barbarossa, followed by the quarrels and failures of three other Christian kings, Richard the Lionheart, Philippe-Auguste, and, anachronistically, Alfonso VIII of Castile. Elements drawn from Ariosto and Tasso merely added to an unutterable confusion.[13]

In 1598 Lope had dealt similarly with Arcadia itself, making it in truth a pastoral version of Castiglione's court: here, that of Alba de Tormes, then ruled by Antonio Alvarez de Toledo, grandson of the Netherlands's most brutal governor. But however much its occupants might discuss poetry, virtue, beauty, or love, and however their actions might reveal the elements of gracious behavior, this Arcadia had become a place of hopelessness ("Adiós, dueño mío," says the heroine to the hero at the end, "que esperar no puedo [Farewell, my love . . . , for I can have no hope]"). The final departure "del verde valle" was supposed to herald the advent of

[11]On this matter, see Daniel Javitch, *Proclaiming a Classic: The Canonization of "Orlando Furioso"* (Princeton, 1991). I am most grateful to the author of this work for the opportunity of reading it in manuscript.
[12]John Buxton, *Sir Philip Sidney and the English Renaissance*, 2d ed. (London, 1964), p. 44.
[13]Lope Félix de Vega Carpio, *Jerusalén conquistada, epopeya trágica*, 3 vols., ed. Joaquín de Entrambasaguas (Madrid, 1951–54).

knowledge—at least for the hero, Anfriso, and his masculine friends (the heroine, Belisarda, was herself condemned to the despair of an unhappy marriage). Yet the "ciencia" was the worn knowledge of trivium and quadrivium, and the hero was finally left to understand that "un hombre / tan ciego y tan perdido / su vida escribe y llora arrepentido (so lost and so blind a man, writes his life and weeps in regret)." Gone was "la verde primavera / de [sus] floridos años (the green spring of his flowered years)," now was only the "triste estado" of bereavement. The steady tone of quiet pessimism could seem a response to the chiaroscuro of Cervantes's earlier *Galatea* (1582), torn between familiar pastoral quiet and moments of bloody violence.[14] Unsurprisingly, such Arcadias were soon to become the bitterly decaying Mancha of *Don Quijote* (1605/1615), whose hero at the last fell victim to sympathetic cynics (themselves profoundly ambiguous) and died on waking from his not happy but at least contented and often fruitful illusion. With Cervantes would come Luis de Góngora, whose pastoral *Soledades* (1613–18) told its tale of retreat and bitterness in a language whose extreme difficulty emphasized that very retreat.

The pessimistic sense of despair, as these various texts suggest and as we will soon see again, was not limited to one country or to one area of influence. The power of writing and of thinking, the sense of order, and the certainty of being were everywhere in doubt. Decay, dissolution, and generalized catastrophe seemed universal. The question might soon become how to put it all together again. But it was not yet easy to see how it could even be asked. And in the meantime, *we* need some idea of what it was that had fallen apart. That is the matter of this chapter and the next.

The forms and concepts of writing whose efficacity had been shattered (writing being what is chiefly at issue in the present work) corresponded to three ways of acting and being in the world. All three had offered a

[14]Lope Félix de Vega Carpio, *Arcadia,* ed. Edwin S. Morby (Madrid, 1975), pp. 377, 449–52. Miguel de Cervantes, *La Galatea,* ed. Juan Bautista Avalle-Arce (Madrid, 1987). It is true that in England and elsewhere such plays as *Histrio-Mastix* (c. 1589) and a wide variety of royal pageants appeared to offer hopes of glory. Similarly, so abnormal a poem as Michael Drayton's *Poly-Olbion* (started in the late 1590s, but whose first part was published only in 1612, its second in 1619) exhausted its one hundred thousand alexandrines in praise of an England whose real and mythical geography and history it rather bluntly catalogued (to the joy of later antiquarians). But Drayton was the first to agree that his long tour of England and Wales, with John Selden's learned commentaries, would garner little success (he was right): the time, he said in his preface, was "a disadvantage against" him (*Poly-Olbion,* in *The Works,* ed. J. William Hebel [Oxford, 1961], IV.v). At the same time, the "optimistic" tradition of the "Byzantine" novel (most famously represented in the sixteenth century by Longus's *Daphnis and Chloe,* Heliodorus's *Theagenes and Chariclea,* and Achilles Tatius's *Clitophon and Leucippe*) perhaps culminated in Cervantes's *Persiles* (1617), leading on, it may be, to the French romances of the later seventeenth century. But when these were not narratives of conventional fictive illusion—explicitly unreal—they were, like *Persiles* itself, novels of deeply disturbing violence. None of this in any way alters the *dominant* expression of profound pessimism and hopelessness—or the fact (more important for my present purpose) that writers were increasingly feeling the futility and uselessness of writing itself.

complete, a global comprehension. Let me call them *scholastic, humanist,* and *courtly.* The first had viewed all writing as a stage in understanding and participating in the divine, whatever the exact form of such activity.[15] The second took writing as helping to create an equitable human community. The third saw it as enhancing an established monarchical power structure. I want to suggest that in many ways they came together in sixteenth-century argument, that one element eventually common to all, the question of the poet's authority, will survive and play a powerful role in the later invention of modern literature, while a second common aspect, distance and isolation, will lead by the end of the century to a widespread feeling of utter impotence.

By the mid-sixteenth century all three ideas of writing turned in fact on a perception of "distance." For secular writers, the divine was increasingly thought of in terms of transcendence, and to recall earlier claims of immanence merely emphasized these writers' own remoteness from such claims. Christian Rome was now losing its central authority. For its part, the courtly idea of writing was that of recreation, a gracious trope supervenient to the business of power. Humanist authors, on the other hand, tended to see writing either as a commentary, however serious, on the real duties of social intercourse or as a persuasion to the necessary offices of community. In each case, writing was clearly divided from religious, social, ethical, and political activity. The affirmative force of poetic *distance* was entire. Poets and their poetry were not, and could not be, integral to the body politic. That was often given as the reason why it was so difficult to justify writing in the vernacular: while Latin, said Juan de Valdés (sometime between 1534 and 1541) was the language of "arte" and books, Castilian was "por uso," for everyday use. The *afetación* that was a normal part of writing would twist the relations essential to social and political intercourse. Valdés was thus not altogether unhappy to condemn the *Amadis de Gaula* for affectation and anachronism: it demonstrated his point.[16]

---

[15]See, e.g., Reiss, *Discourse of Modernism,* pp. 58–94; Bruno Sandkühler, *Die frühen Dantekommentare und ihr Verhältnis zur mittelalterlichen Kommentartradition,* Münchner Romanistische Arbeiten, no. 19 (Munich, 1967); Brian Stock, *The Implications of Literacy: Written Language and Models of Interpretation in the Eleventh and Twelfth Centuries* (Princeton, 1983). Need I observe that little is new in the idea that the hopes of the early Renaissance yielded to despairing dismay? Wittingly or not, Franco Simone's groundbreaking work implied that the change marked the path from South to North. I argue that it related to changing sociopolitical context, regardless of place. Simone later came to a similar view: see *La coscienza della rinascita negli umanisti francese* (Rome, 1949), esp. pp. 91–161; *Il rinascimento francese: Studi e ricerche* (Turin, 1961); and an edited anthology, *Culture et politique en France à l'époque de l'humanisme et de la Renaissance* (Turin, 1974). Donald R. Kelley has explored this trajectory in France: *The Beginning of Ideology: Consciousness and Society in the French Reformation* (Cambridge, 1981).
[16]Juan de Valdés, *Diálogo de la lengua,* ed. Juan M. Lope Blanch (Madrid, 1976), pp. 43, 154, 47.

Castilian could indeed best be kept for such letters as Valdés's friends wished him to discuss and for those "refranes castellanos" circulating in Rome, defined by Valdés as "proverbs and adages" for the rule of everyday life.[17] In such writing the Erasmian Valdés could emphasize the needs not of poetry and poetics but of *uso:* "The whole of good Castilian speech consists in your saying what you wish with as few words as you can, in such a way that by clearly setting forth the concept in your mind and making what you wish to say understood, you could remove none of the words from a sentence or a statement without damaging either its meaning, or its emphasis, or its elegance."[18]

Valdés, like Pietro Bembo (whose *Prose della volgar lingua* of 1525 was explicitly Valdés's rival), was clear that these demands were wholly different from those of *arte y libros.* Bembo's point had been that the vernacular should help *overcome* distance and *not* lead to further confusion. The issue, that is to say, was the same for both of them, although their solutions were radically at variance. Both Bembo and Valdés were writing at a time before the sense that society's fabric was entirely rent had become overwhelming. Both thought proper use of language could resolve such difficulties as might have appeared. In this sense, and although she was ironizing at Sidney's expense, Virginia Woolf was quite right to remark of such writing that it had to "be careful to turn away from what [was] actually before it," that it was "made for slow, noble, and generalized emotion."[19]

Her irony would have been lost on humanists and courtiers alike. For them, such ideals and abstractions formed the entirely expected boundaries and limitations of poetic writing. Any further claim would have been at once overweening, unseemly, and uncouth—showing just that lack of measure and sure taste that made certain English aristocratic writers sometimes laugh at poor, low-bred Gabriel Harvey. Only the sad, deluded

---

[17]Ibid., p. 48.

[18]Ibid., p. 158. We should perhaps remember here that Latin and the vernacular were not simply split between an educated elite and a broader mass audience. It is certainly the case that those professionals who had Latin were thought superior to those who did not, but neither group "was likely to belong to the highest estates in the realm," says Elizabeth L. Eisenstein. The vernacular movement appealed, perhaps, "to pages as well as apprentices," but also "to landed gentry, cavaliers, and courtiers" (*The Printing Revolution in Early Modern Europe* [Cambridge, 1983], p. 31). Eventually, the vernacular movement would merge with what will be literature, while Latin will remain the language of "science," of more specialized domains of knowledge. Literature would then bind the social estates, becoming the cement and guarantor of a new political order and social fusion. Valdés's distinction between Latin, "por arte y libros," and the vulgar tongue, "por uso," was therefore rather important.

[19]Pietro Bembo, *Prose della volgar lingua,* in *Prose e rime,* ed. Carlo Dionisotti (1960; rpt. Turin, 1966), pp. 73–309. This three-part dialogue was begun probably as early as 1500, two parts being sent to a Venetian friend in early 1512 (*Prose,* pp. 16, 34). Woolf's remark is from "The Countess of Pembroke's Arcadia," in *The Second Common Reader* (1932; rpt. New York, 1960), p. 38.

Caballero de la Triste Figura could argue, even in 1615, that authors should use the language they "marmaron en la leche (sucked with their mothers' milk)": although in his world, innkeepers and travelers will indeed listen to the public readings this made possible. Yet he found himself saying, as he spoke of acquiring language through childhood nourishment, that so "natural" a poet was immeasurably improved by art, an art still equated with a learned Latin, rather than the vernacular "poesía de romance."[20] Woolf's irony tells us, of course, how far such taste has receded into the past, how writing of art has yielded to an entirely more sober instrumentality.

In fact, such separation had not been new to the sixteenth century, and the problem of situating writing within the solely human or the separate sphere of commentary and recreation had long since become a perplexing issue. Among major middle English poets, John Lydgate is certainly considered the most socially minded, closest to actual political life. Ending a chapter on his *Troy Book* (1412–20) and *Siege of Thebes* (c. 1420–22), Lois Ebin has noted how such interest was Lydgate's particular contribution, "as a poet concerned with order in the world rather than the transcendental journeys of Dante, Langland, and Chaucer" (although several recent commentators would dispute at least such a judgment of Chaucer).[21] Poetry, all art, always responds somehow to social constraints. The statement hardly bears repeating. But the real questions concern the matters of how it does so, of how it is perceived as doing so, of what are the constraints, and what the public's expectations. When Lydgate averred in the *Siege of Thebes* that Amphion was the exemplar of the poet as civilizing agent and then represented eloquence as a more powerful tool for social order than brute force,[22] he may well have foreshadowed Marco Vida, George Puttenham, or Sidney, but his views cannot be compared with those of William Davenant, Nicolas Boileau, or John Dryden.

These later writers saw the poet/*littérateur* caught in the actual political *process* in some entirely intimate way. For them, literature was an integral part of that process. For Lydgate and his contemporaries, the poet could be an actor in the social and political environment only as commentator, observer, as mere ornament even on the body politic. Lydgate actually intended his rather doubtful praise of poetry to persuade princes that they should inspire love rather than fear, and he used the particular case of Amphion's Thebes to make the general point that "elloquence" was better than "violence." The task was to "transform occasional events into works of a more permanent nature," to draw wide ethical principles from histor-

[20]Miguel de Cervantes Saavedra, *Don Quijote de la Mancha*, ed. Angel Basanta, 2 vols. (Barcelona, 1985), 2:850–51, 1:473–78; *The Adventures of Don Quixote*, trans. J. M. Cohen (1950; rpt. Harmondsworth, 1970), pp. 569, 277–80: II.xvi, I.xxxii.
[21]Lois A. Ebin, *John Lydgate* (Boston, 1985), p. 59.
[22]John Lydgate, *Siege of Thebes*, ed. Axel Erdmann, *Part I: The Text* (London, 1911), pp. 10–14.

ical or contemporary action. The poet was "an 'enluminer' and an orderer" whose goal was that "of ennobling and civilizing" humankind.[23] Alain Renoir has similarly remarked how the *Thebes* poem served to show the mutual dependence of social rules and people, not in specific detail, but as a kind of general abstraction. Such demonstrations may have controlled "the organisation of the entire poem,"[24] but they were still, and emphatically, a commentary from without. They were on a par with the kind of semiproverbial *sentences* one would still find later in the theater of Robert Garnier, for example, at the end of the sixteenth century.

The poem remained a mirror of princes, whose intent was to provide general advice and proverbialization rather than any kind of precise, situational analysis. The writer was considered entirely outside actual events, distant from them, a servant of patrons whose actions poetry served to embellish. That is why in the early sixteenth century Thomas Feylde saw the earlier poets as rhetoricians. Chaucer, he wrote, was the "floure of rethoryke eloquence"; John Gower was an "experte in seyence" who "wrote moralytyes herde and delycyous"; Lydgate produced "workes" both "fruytefull and sentencyous," for which he would ever be known as "a famous rethorycyne."[25] Indeed, following Boccaccio's explanation of the Theban myth ("this derkë poysye"), Lydgate himself undermined any idea that the poet might have some direct involvement in events, writing that Amphion was not a poet, but a man to whom Mercury had given great excellence in the "craft of Rhetorik." The King's "song" was not that active poetry whose powerful and direct effect was to raise the walls of Thebes. It was "no thyng but the crafty speche" by which he persuaded the population to build the city.[26]

This genre of political gloss and counsel continued through the Middle Ages and into the Renaissance. To it belonged Lydgate's *Fall of Princes* ("translated" from Boccaccio), the seventh book of John Gower's *Confessio amantis* (c. 1390), and Christine de Pisan's *Livre des fais et bonnes moeurs du sage roy Charles V* (1404). Such texts were "poetry" only in the sense they were in verse, and they were "literature" in the very broad meaning then ascribed to the term: "The expressions *litteratura* and *bonae litterae* are coterminous with the humanist concept of a *respublica litterarum* broad enough to comprehend the commentaries of Budé, the poems of Macrin, Dorat and Du Chesne, the public oratory of Muret and Sorbin, and the *Essais* of Montaigne," pertaining, that is to say, to a very general learning.[27]

[23]Ebin, *Lydgate*, p. 142. I return briefly to the *difference* between Renaissance and neoclassical concerns at the end of Chapter 6.

[24]Alain Renoir, *The Poetry of John Lydgate* (London, 1967), pp. 126–27.

[25]Thomas Feylde, prologue to the "Contrauerse bytwene a Louer and a Jaye," quoted in Ebin, *Lydgate*, p. 140.

[26]Lydgate, *Siege of Thebes*, p. 11, ll. 214, 219; p. 12, ll. 225–39.

[27]Grahame Castor and Terence Cave, eds., *Neo-Latin and the Vernacular in Renaissance France* (Oxford, 1984), intro., p. xiv.

In the late fifteenth century Polydore Vergil defined "literas" precisely as the letters of the writing needed to record all knowledge. A few years later Christophorus Mylaeus noted that "letters" were invented to supplement memory, leading to writing and thence to poetry, story, history, and the divers kinds of *sapientiae*. Logically enough, the last book of his work on "universal history" was about the manifold written products of those letters, "literatura." Listing then by names ranging from Aaron to Trismegistus, Homer to Aristarchus, Cicero to Justinian, Augustine to Erasmus, Galen to Budé, Mylaeus covered the varieties of written sapience.[28] Within such an encyclopedic science, writing of public counsel, in verse or prose, properly belonged to oratory and rhetoric (to which, too, belonged political satire). Indeed, only to rhetoric was any *public* function of this kind granted at all, for poetry was a matter of entertainment, and its learning an agreeable supplement. Pierre Fabri noted this in the first lines of his 1521 *Grand et vrai art de pleine rhétorique:*

> Rhetoric is thus a politic science, of how to talk credibly and speak according to the teaching of the art of persuading or dissuading in its matter, of how to dispose it in its parts, to embellish each with fine terms, to memorize it in proper order and pronounce it well. And just as the physician makes his medicines in likelihood of curing his patient, and yet may not cure him, so it is not required that one always obtain what one asks when persuading or dissuading. It suffices that in obeying the rules, language be beautifully ordered.[29]

The orator was the physician of the body politic. The point was a perfectly traditional one, coming down from Cicero and Quintilian: the purpose of rhetoric was public persuasion. Not yet was this the task of what *we* think of as literary texts. Now, although the first-mentioned writings were much earlier than the beginnings of humanism as we generally think of it, at least in England, such a view of writing would not be at all foreign to such as Erasmus and More, Elyot, Castiglione, or Budé. All wrote texts of this kind, while the English *Mirror for Magistrates*, a series of didactic tragic verse tales by William Baldwin and others, first published in 1559 and gradually accruing further ethico-political narratives in subsequent editions, finally appeared in an entirely new version as late as 1609. Such texts had long since lost their glow and their earlier force, however, partly from changes in the notion of the writer and partly from uncertainties about social and political order and authority. The earlier poet of this kind had held a readily recognizable relation to the collec-

---

[28]Polydorus Vergilius, *De rerum inventoribus libri octo . . .* (Basel, 1532), pp. 27–32; Christophorus Mylaeus [Christophe Milieu], *De scribenda universitatis rerum historia libri quinque* (Basel, 1551), pp. 201–6, 245–305. I thank Donald Kelley for drawing my attention to these two encyclopedists. The first part of Chapter 8 discusses the development and meanings of the word "literature" in more detail. See also Chapter 2, note 38.

[29]Pierre Fabri, *Le grand et vrai art de pleine rhétorique*, ed. A. Héron, 3 vols. in 1 (1889–90; rpt. Geneva, 1969), 1:15.

tivity. He or she (we may recall that Christine de Pisan was Lydgate's exact contemporary) was commonly thought to exercise wholly rhetorical skills to produce an abstracting and generalizing commentary on events from without, whose goal was to help forge a broad social consensus.

Some fifty years before Lydgate, in chapters 6 and 7 of the fourteenth book of the *De genealogia deorum* (1350s–70s), Boccaccio had similarly praised poetry for its exhortatory and ornamental capacities and qualities, situating its origins in a form of "exquisite discourse" whose initial purpose had been to laud the divine. In no sense was it considered socially constitutive. Poetry was rather an essentially *useful* "facultas" whose goal was to tell truth, to exhort, to aid in the well-being of social order and understanding in ways more agreeable and seductive than those of "locutionum" less "exquisitarum."[30]

Boccaccio was very much a transitional figure, and when speaking of the writer's telling, he still has in mind that divulging of truths, whether sacred or secular, that was the particular task of all those who glossed authoritative texts. Their original aim had been to bind the human to the divine presence, to forge a passage from the world to the domain of the sacred. Augustine had long since argued that secular as well as profane writings were such an instrument. In the *De doctrina christiana*, he concluded that because profane writings could be beautiful, because "beauty is a means by which the mind is led to perceive an underlying truth," because beauty itself depended on the presence of some deep "significatio," and because such *significatio* ultimately embodied something of the divine, even "pagan literature" might be read for profitable truths as well as pleasure.[31]

In his *Life of Dante*, Boccaccio took this equation yet further, ascribing properly anagogical aims to the interpretation of profane writings, both post- and pre-Christian ones. The writer would show "the causes of things, the effects of virtues and vices, what we ought to flee and what we ought to follow; in order that we may attain by virtuous action the end that they, although they did not rightly know the true God, believed to be our supreme salvation." (Hence, for example, the sacred interpretation of Virgil's fourth Bucolic.) Thus, as Alastair Minnis concludes, "the end of poetry is not incompatible with the superior end of theology," even in cases of poetry written by those who knew neither Christ nor the true God and which of necessity failed therefore "to understand the nature of our supreme salvation."[32] In fact, such a view of the purposes of poetry led

---

[30] Charles G. Osgood, ed. and trans., *Boccaccio on Poetry: Being the Preface and the Fourteenth and Fifteenth Books of Boccaccio's "Genealogia Deorum Gentilium"* (1930; rpt. Indianapolis, 1956).

[31] Concetta Carestia Greenfield, *Humanist and Scholastic Poetics, 1250–1500* (Lewisburg, Penna., 1981), pp. 33–35.

[32] Alastair J. Minnis, *Medieval Theory of Authorship: Scholastic Literary Attitudes in the Later Middle Ages* (London, 1984), p. 217. The quotation is from Boccaccio's *Vita di Dante*, in *The Earliest Lives of Dante*, trans. and ed. J. R. Smith, Yale Studies in English, no. 10 (New York, 1901), p. 51.

quite directly to humanist objectives and understanding of the poet's role as interpreter and counsel. Nor was it entirely foreign to some aspects of the courtly view of the poet. Indeed, it may well be a memory of this "sacred" function that explains the endurance of that tradition of "radical 'prophetic' protest" which David Norbrook has sought to follow from More to Milton.[33] But by now the theology was that of an *absent* Divinity, increasingly replaced by urgencies of a secular, political kind: and the writer could come to embody an otherwise lost authority.

In many ways the more strictly "poetic" genre of the theater had taken over the rhetorical and moral function of writing by the mid-sixteenth century. Here "religious politics was virtually the whole substance of drama." The fact was, of course, that actual political dispute was willy-nilly pervaded with theological argument, and to the extent that humanist drama was commentary, it could not avoid religion. And yet, as David Bevington has added, it always did so "in terms of ideas and platforms."[34] The writer, that is, remained an absent god. And such were indeed frequently the terms applied. Sangsup Lee has claimed that the Elizabethans viewed poetry as "in some way or other related to the Divinity," as "an instrument of Divine Grace." It was certainly the case that J. C. Scaliger saw the poet with his creative powers "almost as another God."[35] Yet there was nothing very unusual in these claims, save only, as Marvin Herrick has remarked, their "extreme glorification of the poet." Otherwise, they reflected everything learned "from Plato, Aristotle, Cicero, and Horace."[36] One could well add that they also echoed fundamental medieval claims about authorship.

The point is not idle. For, then, the supposedly radical oppositional stance taken by such as Sidney, Spenser, and Greville will be seen to sit firmly within a familiar tradition. Neither their argument nor their style was "radical." They may have questioned Elizabeth's policies, they may have fought for a Continental Protestantism, but in neither case was any opposition at all clear: what was at stake was not principle, but degree and manner of implementation. Greville's and Sidney's encomia of Elizabeth may often have been tempered with dismay at her caution, but they were no less wholehearted for all that. Further, writing of art remained outside the world on which it commented. Were it to bring civility, it would do so "not literally but by prophetic vision, by imagining the world as it might

---

[33]David Norbrook, *Poetry and Politics in the English Renaissance* (London, Boston, and Melbourne, 1984).

[34]David M. Bevington, *Tudor Drama and Politics: A Critical Approach to Topical Meaning* (Cambridge, Mass., 1968), pp. 3, 25.

[35]Sangsup Lee, *Elizabethan Literary Opinion: A Study in Its Variety* (Seoul, 1971), p. 180; Julius Caesar Scaliger, *Poetices libri septem* . . . , 2d ed. (n.p., 1581 [1st ed. 1561]), I. 1.

[36]Marvin T. Herrick, *The Fusion of Horatian and Aristotelian Literary Criticism, 1531–1555.* Illinois Studies in Language and Literature, 32, no. 1 (Urbana, Ill., 1946), p. 33.

be and encouraging people to remake it."[37] Indeed, their apocalyptic vision was itself profoundly conservative politically (whether in Estienne de La Boétie or elsewhere), essentially dependent on a passage out of the *polis*, away from real political engagement. It had its counterpart in the mid-1580s in Henri III's penitential and Counter-Reform Gallican movement, strongly influenced by St. Charles Borromeo, which hoped to appease divine wrath and bring tranquility back to France. That it led directly to the Ligue's accusing Henri of practicing sorcery, to the violent destruction of its center at Vincennes in early 1589, and to the king's assassination merely underscored its political irrelevance—even its counterproductivity.[38]

Such authors and actors differed little, in intent, from the later Jesuit Pierre Le Moyne, who, writing an avowedly Aristotelian and scholastic work, asserted that the poets' task was to discover eternal and universal principles: "They will contemplate the Beauties of the Divinity; / They will imbue themselves with its qualities; / They will see through the Light to its very Principle." We can readily see how this conservative claim was rooted in the Middle Ages. The arguments that "poetry is celestial" and that the poet limned such qualities as tended toward "the Sovereign Good" refer us straight back to Boccaccio, Dante, and beyond them to Augustine and others.[39] No less was this the case for such as Sidney and Greville.

This interpretative and commentative ideal of the poet, derived in part from medieval argument, also owed much to the ongoing debate between humanist and courtly objectives. Daniel Javitch has shown that late Tudor claims about the poet were largely derived from Castiglione, him of our urban Arcadia. They provided a basis for courtly behavior, an ornament in the service of princely power, going far beyond the mere requirements of writing. At the same time, this ideal was in most ways at odds with a set of humanist educational goals that modern criticism has tended to view as the principal, if not only, thread leading toward later literary and artistic achievement. We have already seen that the thread was anyway more complicated, but Javitch has shown, as has Glending Olson for the late Middle Ages, that court poetry should be understood as a "literary entertainment" whose primary goal was the search for "beautiful effects."[40]

[37]Norbrook, *Poetry and Politics*, p. 147.

[38]Francis A. Yates, *The French Academies of the Sixteenth Century*, Studies of the Warburg Institute, vol. 15 (1947; rpt. Nendeln [Liechtenstein], 1968), pp. 154–74, 213–24.

[39]Pierre Le Moyne, *Les peintures morales, où les passions sont representees par Tableaux, par Characteres, & par Questions nouuelles & curieuses* (Paris, 1640), pp. 252, 270, 325–49. On Le Moyne, and this text in particular, see Timothy J. Reiss, "Problems in Logic and Rhetoric," in *A New History of French Literature*, ed. Denis Hollier (Cambridge, Mass., 1989), pp. 278–84.

[40]Daniel Javitch, *Poetry and Courtliness in Renaissance England* (Princeton, 1978), pp. 3, 29; Glending Olson, *Literature as Recreation in the Later Middle Ages* (Ithaca, N.Y., and London, 1982).

The Tudor ideal of poetry became that of a leisured supplement to life, although it simultaneously learned to satisfy "the court's encomiastic needs," a task it was most definitely to keep.

Such a "playful" view was clearly foreign to the "purposeful and political" ends of humanistic schooling. There texts were put to "social and political uses" rather "than esthetic ones."[41] The distinction was not entire, of course, and Fulke Greville could praise Sidney's *Arcadia* for its hortatory benefits: "This representing of virtues, vices, humours, counsels and actions of men in feigned and unscandalous images is an enabling of free-born spirits to the greatest affairs of states."[42] Spenser similarly asserted his "*Faerie Queene*, to represent all the moral vertues," and, in the context of a conversation recorded by Lodowick Bryskett, seems to have considered the poem equal to a treatise providing "knowledge of Morall Philosophie."[43] Still, Javitch is right to observe that whatever overlap there may have been, the two views remained fundamentally split. Comparing the texts basic to both, Castiglione's *Courtier* and Cicero's *De oratore*, he sees an opposition between "court" and "camp," between the leisurely art of poetry and the useful conflict of oratory: "The orator owes service to the individual or to the case he is defending and, more broadly, to the public good of his state; the courtier owes service to his sovereign and then to his lady, or ladies in general."[44]

There had been many attempts to bring the two differing views together. In France the most outstanding instance had been that of Pierre de Ronsard. His poetic career had begun unambiguously as that of a courtier. Between 1555 and 1565, faced with a decaying political and religious situation, he turned toward a poetry of political exhortation and commentary. By the mid-1560s he had come back to a courtly poetry of "communication between superior souls," of scorn toward the *vulgaire*, and of decorative excellence. The attempt to combine a courtly and a politically aware poetry ended "in a sort of defeat." The effort to resolve "the conflict between poetic ideal and political requirement" sank into "the sands of courtly makebelieve."[45]

---

[41]Javitch, *Poetry and Courtliness*, pp. 3–4, 9. Anthony Grafton and Lisa Jardine have emphasized, however, that the stated humanist goals were just that: goals. The ideological import of their practice was usually more in evidence than the pedagogical ideal: *From Humanism to the Humanities: Education and the Liberal Arts in Fifteenth- and Sixteenth-Century Europe* (London, 1986).

[42]Fulke Greville, "A Dedication to Sir Philip Sidney," in *The Prose Works*, ed. John Gouws (Oxford, 1986), p. 3.

[43]Lodowick Bryskett, *A Discourse of Civill Life [1606]*, ed. Thomas E. Wright (Northridge, Calif., 1970), pp. 21–22.

[44]Javitch, *Poetry and Courtliness*, p. 27. Cf. Marc Fumaroli, *L'âge de l'éloquence: Rhétorique et 'res literaria' de la Renaissance au seuil de l'époque classique* (Geneva and Paris, 1980), p. 597. A useful brief summary of humanist views on art and culture (pre-sixteenth century) may be found in Lauro Martines, *Power and Imagination: City-States in Renaissance Italy* (1979; rpt. Harmondsworth, 1983), pp. 262–300.

[45]Francis M. Higman, "Ronsard's Political and Polemical Poetry," in *Ronsard the Poet*, ed. Terence Cave (London, 1973), pp. 277, 285.

Cervantes made the issue central to *Don Quijote*, by and large to the advantage of arms and surely in favor of their separation. "Away with those," cried his *hidalgo*, "who say that letters have the advantage over arms." The aim of the humanities, certainly, was "to maintain impartial justice, to give every man his rights, to make good laws, and to see that they are kept." Yet those goals were less than those of "the profession of Arms, whose aim and object is peace, the greatest good which men can desire in this life." There might well be no place that did "not allow room for arms and learning—especially if arms and letters bring beauty as their pilot and guide"; arms and letters offer "two roads to honour," yet arms "win you more honour." "For though Letters may have been the foundation of more estates than Arms, still soldiers have an indefinable superiority over men of letters, and a certain splendour about them that puts them above everybody."[46]

Cervantes used the theme more briefly in *Persiles y Sigismunda*. Early on, the "Spanish Barbarian" Antonio told how, after completing *la Gramática*, he was "inclined by the stars somewhat to letters, though much more toward arms." Certainly, however adept the hero, Periandro/Persiles, may be at both, the action clearly gives entire preference to arms. Still, when Cervantes put himself in the novel in this very context (as "an attractive pilgrim"), it was perhaps to favor letters, although the two were no less separate: "For some years I was dedicated to the practice of war, and now for others, the more mature ones, I've been a man of letters. In the war years I earned something of a good reputation, while in my years as a writer I've been more or less respected. I've published some books that weren't condemned by the ignorant as bad and didn't fail to win the approval of the wise."[47] The ironic tone, however, refuses conclusion.

In these same years Greville chose Sidney as alone potentially able to overcome that opposition, bringing "the affection and true use [of letters] both into the court and camp." Sidney died before such a union could be consolidated: "It pleased God, in this decrepit age of the world," wrote his friend, "not to restore the image of her [the Golden Age's, Arcadia's] ancient vigour in him otherwise than as in a lightning before death."[48] A generation later Cervantes bewailed a like loss of confidence: "Now sloth triumphs over industry, idleness over labour, vice over virtue, presumption over valour, and theory over the practice of arms, which only lived and flourished in the golden age and among knights errant."[49] Sidney was widely seen as the signal epitome of the courtly poet, the very embodiment of the commentative *and* ornamental ideal. His death at Zutphen, direct result of the futile courtesy of removing his thigh armor to avoid

---

[46]Cervantes, *Don Quijote*, 1:554, 606, 2:768, 930; *Adventures*, pp. 340, 382, 506, 628: I.xxxvii, xlii, II.vi, xxiv.
[47]Cervantes, *Trabajos*, pp. 33, 263; *Trials*, pp. 33, 303: I.v, IV.i.
[48]Greville, "Dedication," pp. 21–22, 23.
[49]Cervantes, *Don Quijote*, 2:728; *Adventures*, p. 477: II.i.

any unfair advantage over a companion who had neglected to wear his own, marked the end of hope with respect to a particular kind of literacy, as it also symbolized with quite spectacular harshness the vanity and unreality of a specific aesthetic (and political) model. Henri III's destruction was to do the same in the realm of religion.

One could indeed say of this model, as of Castiglione's *Courtier*, that it turned "aside from the realities of life to its idealization."[50] No doubt Sidney would have argued, as Greville did later for him, that such diversion clarified the elements and issues whose distinct comprehension then allowed one to live life better, more virtuously, with greater courage and more exact understanding. Yet the fact remained that the life then lived was divorced from the knowledge taken to enable that living. The gesture of emulating a friend, himself simply forgetful, by fighting without his cuisses, may have been chivalrous but bore no relation to the real perils of war (as many lamented at the time).[51] The price of this idealization of the poet, by the late sixteenth century, was further to exaggerate poetic writing's distance and isolation from social and political activity in the world. In doing so, it reinforced the sense of pain and dismay with which people observed a world in apparent dissolution. For it suggested that painstaking learned writing could have no effect on activity in that world. In tearful desperation Sancho Panza urged Quijote back into his chivalric fantasies or into a new pastoral fiction, rightly understanding that failure would indeed mean his master's death. In vain. Like Sidney, Quijote will die, "pues ya en los nidos de antaño no hay pájaros hogaño": "Let us go gently, gentlemen, for there are no birds this year in last year's nests. I was mad, but I am sane now. I was Don Quixote de la Mancha, but to-day, as I have said, I am Alonso Quixano the Good. May my sincere repentence restore your former esteem for me."[52] Verse, fiction, the imaginary were all quite

[50]George Bull, introduction to Castiglione, *Courtier*, p. 16. For a good discussion of the sense of Sidney's gesture (whether anachronistic courtliness or military efficiency), see Rosanna Camerlingo, "Matters of Honor: Knights and Courtiers in Sidney's Two *Arcadias*," Ph.D. diss., New York University, 1991, pp. 1–12. This study analyzes the *Arcadias* in light of these differing interpretations. My own point depends not on Sidney's intention (which one could anyway never know), but on the interpretation that became the common myth about Sidney and his life.

[51]Writing in the 1620s about the Jan. 1577 siege of Marmande, the Protestant poet, soldier, and diplomat Agrippa d'Aubigné made the point. He attributed an exactly similar gesture to mere vanity—unworthy, he said, to be recorded in his public *Histoire universelle:* "When he saw that he was the only man in his troop who was wearing brassards, he took them off before the attack" (Théodore-Agrippa d'Aubigné, *His Life, to His Children: Sa vie à ses enfants,* trans. and ed. John Nothnagle (Lincoln, Neb., and London, 1989), p. 34. His point was that however privately satisfied he might be with this behavior, such vanities were (at best) strictly for private consumption, not for public histories: for they actually wronged the public interest. Sidney was a very belated example of the poet/soldier, whose ancestor was doubtless medieval. Closest to him in time were such exemplars as Garcilaso, mortally wounded near Fréjus in 1536, or the Greek-Italian Michael Marullus, drowned in 1500 near Volterra while fighting against the French with Caterina Sforza. Such figures belonged to an older dispensation, one now long gone.

[52]Cervantes, *Don Quijote*, 2:1348; *Adventures*, p. 938: II.lxxiv.

incommensurable with the world. To believe otherwise was to tilt at windmills.

Such a view was not simply widespread. It was almost monolithic. Certainly, as an expression of one viewpoint among a few, it was not entirely new. The century-long debate about the writer's authority had not infrequently seen the claims of detached commentary teeter on the edge of isolation. As early as his 1517 *De arte poetica*, Vida was so far from understanding poetry and the *polis* as even minimally allied that he urged his contemporaries at least to "excel in the arts and pursuits of learning," just because political authority and all hope of intervention had failed. Even the vision of power that might have been had Leo X not died did not provoke Vida into any encomium of poetry's hortatory or commentative potency, although he did seem to make one possible exception in the sole case of Virgil, "holiest of poets," whom all should aspire to follow. But more or less at the same time (1531), when Juan Luis Vives wrote of the collapse of letters in his *De disciplinis*, it was to show just how education and practice could repair that loss. Of course, too, his understanding of *litterarum* was that of Polydore Vergil and Mylaeus.[53]

In England (where Vives had spent some of the 1520s) and a generation later Sir Thomas Elyot likewise argued the poet's solitude and necessary separation from the commonweal. The favored protagonist of his 1545 dialogue, *The Defence of Good Women*, started by impugning the reputation of the poetic authorities on whom his antagonist Caninius had chosen to base his commonplace criticisms. Thus the pure Candidus:

> The authors whom ye so muche do set by, for the more part were poetes, which sort of persons among the latines and grekes wer neuer had but in smal reputacion. For I culd neuer rede that in any weale publike of notable memory, Poetes were called to any honorable place, office, or dignity. Plato out of the publike weale which he had devised, wolde have all poetes utterly excluded. Tulli, who next unto Plato excelled all other in vertue and eloquence, wolde not haue in his publike weale any poetes admitted. The cause why they were soo litell estemed was, for as muche as the more part of their invencions consisted in leasinges, or in steryng up of wanton appetites, or in pouryng out, in railynge, their poison of malice.[54]

What matters here is not that some poets may in fact have been called to public service or have written sincerely and decently. The point is the *perception* that they should not be and have not. (Of course, since one

---

[53]Marco Girolamo Vida, *The De arte poetica*, trans. and ed. Ralph G. Williams (New York, 1976), pp. 80–83 (Bk. II, esp. ll. 561–66), 125 (III. 588); Juan Luis Vives, *De disciplinis libri XX* (Antwerp, 1531). On the argument about writerly authority and its effect on the very nature of writing, see, e.g., Terence Cave, *The Cornucopian Text: Problems of Writing in the French Renaissance* (Oxford, 1979); and Thomas M. Greene, *The Vulnerable Text: Essays on Renaissance Literature* (New York, 1986).

[54]Sir Thomas Elyot, *The Defence of Good Women*, in *The Feminist Controversy of the Renaissance*, ed. Diane Bornstein (Delmar, N.Y., 1980), f. Bv[ro-vo] (mispaginated for Av).

issue here was the misspeaking of women, Elyot might well have been referring to Christine de Pisan's *Book of the City of Ladies*, newly translated into English in 1521, whose goddess Reason made the point to the narrator at the outset that poets always wrote fiction and usually meant the opposite of what they wrote.) The point is that they were seen not as participants in the state and community but as peripheral ornaments. Elyot's Candidus added, therefore, that although he set small store by poets "whan they excede the terms of honestie," yet "if they make verses, conteynyng quicke sentences, void of ribauldry, or in the commendacion of vertue some pratie allegory, or do set forth any notable story, that do I set by them as they be well worthy." Elyot echoed here Feylde's commentary or the view of a Lydgate. It was wholly different from what we will find a century later, when literary writers will have become an integral part of state authority and intimate partners in the political process. A poetry glorifying and magnifying for posterity the deeds of some monarch or other patron was a very different matter indeed from a literature wrought to spread a political message throughout the society with access to it.

It is the case that the imbrication of court poetry and princely power did become extremely close, such that, as Jonathan Goldberg has shown, for instance, James VI (of Scotland) could request that Elizabeth punish Spenser for comments in the *Faerie Queene* about his mother, Mary Queen of Scots. This "circulation of power" (as Stephen Greenblatt calls it) yet remained wholly within court life and discussion—besides the fact that the kind of sovereignty in question was quite different from what will be developed half a dozen decades later. Indeed, that James could expect such punishment might imply that Spenser was understood *not* to represent government views. In any case, the king's complaint implied nothing about the *nature* of the relation between poetry and politics. It may be argued that this court poetry contained the seeds of later "literature," but for the moment the growing separation of the court itself from noncourtly life, its ever more solipsistic turn (as revealed in court festivals in Italy, France, and England), was itself an aspect of the distancing process under discussion, whose consequences, at least in England, would explode forty years later.

Poetry surely disseminated an ideology (as when does it not?). But its efficacity depended exactly on its *not* saying what was *behind* such ideology: it created a broad abstraction about the events and nature of princely authority (although it evidently in some sense "contained" them, for otherwise no generalization would be possible). Poetry could include ambiguities and even apparently "subversive" effects, it might disseminate "an iconography of state" (as Leonard Tennenhouse has put it), but it necessarily referred to a distant king, a "*deus absconditus*, hidden beneath the mask" (Goldberg). Such writing relied on separation and distance from the acts themselves of polity and the daily functioning of authority; on an absence, indeed an inability, of intervention. This poetry was, as all is, profoundly ideological in aim, but it was not, as later literature would be, specifically political: formative of and active in the actual performance of sovereignty and political order (see the end of Chapter 3).[55] By the end of the sixteenth century the "Platonic" argument had swollen to a noisy chorus. Greville noted in his *Treatie of Humane Learning* that poetry and music were "things not pretious in their proper kind," but rather a "pleasing sauce to dainty food; / Fine foyles for iewels, or enammel's grace, / Cast vpon things which in themselues are good." Replying in the same last decade of the century to Thomas Campion's argument in favor of classical quantitative verse, Samuel Daniel picked up identical metaphors: "Eloquence and gay wordes are not of the substance of wit; it is but the garnish of a nice time, the Ornaments that doe but decke the house of a State, and *imitatur publicos mores:* Hunger is as well satisfied with meat serued in pewter as in siluer." It was not, he wrote, "the contexture of words, but the effects of Action, that giues glory to the times."[56]

In France the poet François Malherbe famously remarked to Honorat de Racan that "a good poet [was] no more useful to the State than a good player of ninepins." Back across the Channel this same view was captured with scornful accuracy in Lord Treasurer Burghley's contemptuous response to Walter Raleigh's efforts to obtain a royal recompense for Spenser in 1591: "What, all this for a song?"[57] More seriously, Greville remarked that before his death Sidney had come to see "that even beauty itself, in all earthly complexions, was more apt to allure men to evil than to fashion any goodness in them."[58] Such were the predominant conclusions of an argument whose lines we can follow through the century. We do not, I

[55]This kind of ideological imbrication has been argued by (apart from some already mentioned) Jonathan Dollimore, *Radical Tragedy: Religion, Ideology, and Power in the Drama of Shakespeare and His Contemporaries* (Brighton, 1984); Jonathan Goldberg, *James I and the Politics of Literature: Jonson, Shakespeare, Donne, and Their Contemporaries* (Baltimore and London, 1983); Stephen Greenblatt, *Shakespearean Negotiations: The Circulation of Social Energy in Renaissance England* (Berkeley, Los Angeles, and London, 1988); Stephen Orgel, *The Illusion of Power: Political Theater in the English Renaissance* (Berkeley, Los Angeles, and London, 1975); Graham Parry, *The Golden Age Restor'd: The Culture of the Stuart Court, 1603–42* (Manchester, 1981); Leonard Tennenhouse, *Power on Display: The Politics of Shakespeare's Genres* (London and New York, 1986). The references are to Goldberg, pp. 1–6, 112, and Tennenhouse, p. 186. On the festivals, see Orgel, *Illusion of Power;* Margaret McGowan, *L'art du ballet de cour en France (1581–1643)* (Paris, 1964); Aloïs Maria Nagler, *Theatre Festivals of the Medici, 1539–1637,* trans. George Hickenlooper (New Haven, 1964). Most magnificently, see Stephen Orgel and Roy Strong, *Inigo Jones: The Theatre of the Stuart Court,* 2 vols. (London, 1973).

[56]Fulke Greville, *A Treatie of Humane Learning,* in *The Works in Verse and Prose Complete,* ed. A. B. Grosart, 4 vols. (1870; rpt. New York, 1966), 2:48 (St. 113); Samuel Daniel, "A Defence of Ryme," in *Elizabethan Critical Essays,* ed. G. Gregory Smith, 2 vols. (1904; rpt. Oxford, 1937), 2:372, 371.

[57]Malherbe's remark is quoted in François Malherbe, *Oeuvres poétiques,* ed. Marcel Simon (Paris, 1972), p. 233; Burghley's is given in E. K. Broadus, *The Laureateship: A Study of the Office of Poet Laureate in England, with some Account of the Poets* (Oxford, 1921), p. 45. (Spenser was in fact awarded £50: see p. 35.)

[58]Greville, "Dedication," p. 11.

think, need much more detail here, but four important writers will enable us to sum up the issue: Estienne Pasquier in France, Sidney in England, Cervantes and Góngora in Spain.

In 1560, Pasquier tells us, he wrote his "Pour-parler du prince," a work about the characteristics, abilities, knowledge, and actions appropriate to the good monarch. This late "Mirrour" took the form of a dialogue among a scholar, a philosopher, a man of law ("le curial"), and a politician ("le politic"). The scholar was the first to speak at length and expressed the familiar view that without "Lettres" there would be no human society:

> You [Letters], when the world was still raw, polished our minds. You first led us to virtue, drew humans yet scattered hither and yon, erring like beasts, into mutual intercourse. For this reason, you were singled out for preeminence and named humane Letters, acknowledging thereby that you had called humans to their due humanity. You alone made us choose homes, when we yet had, in our first nature, only caves and grottos in which to hide ourselves. You taught us to build houses, to contract marriage with one another, to prosper in alliances and families, which gradually grew to villages, and began to swell into cities.[59]

Eventually, a "perpetual union" was created among people, who then placed themselves under the rule of the wisest and most learned "in the knowledge of Letters." Orpheus and Amphion were the exemplary cases. (Here, of course, letters were eloquence, rhetoric, history, philosophy, written laws: everything taught in the universities and contained in Polydore Vergil's and Mylaeus's sort of "encyclopedia.")

Even this quite traditional and generously vague notion of letters as culturally foundational was dismissed without ado by the "curial" (the philosopher had come second but barely addressed the issue). This was a practical man, insisting on law and military might. He spurned the "scholar's rubbish": "While you amuse yourself in telling us such tales, the common and ignorant populace, because it doesn't understand you, pays you no attention." The poet is, added the curial for good measure, a "poor idiot." Thus did he reject a humanist view of letters. But the last speaker, the one Pasquier said expressed his own view, was the "politic." By using this name, Pasquier may just possibly have been directing attention to the group of *Politiques:* those who sought a middle, secular, and political path between the extremes of Catholic and Huguenot opponents. If so, the utter isolation of writers from the real world and the ineffectuality of letters was simply further emphasized. For the "politic" also held the view that the scholar was quite wrong. All letters were at best useful to the prince only as a "passetemps" requiring to be "taken with ripe judgment." More often than not, princes who so amused themselves

---

[59]Estienne Pasquier, "Pour-parler du prince," in *Les oeuvres*, 2 vols. (1723; rpt. Geneva, 1971), 1:1017–44. This quotation, p. 1020.

left their peoples "in great suffering." Even when letters were not positively bad, he concluded, they were "matters of indifference, for with or without them many good Republics have endured for many years." At their worst, letters gave "a trivial floss of words" (*un fleuretis de paroles*) from which no one could draw any "well-founded maxims."[60]

Against a background of debate such as Pasquier's dialogue typified, one can readily understand why only twenty years later Sidney rested the case for the *Defence of Poesie* on the writer's isolation. For though he echoed the view of Pasquier's scholar (and of so many others, including the more-or-less contemporary George Puttenham)[61]—an encomium of poets as the earliest communicators of knowledge—he immediately went on to insist on poetry's separateness, its difference from "the scope of all the other sciences." Indeed, its specificity lay precisely in its distinction from all such literate knowledge as resided in material reference: "Only the Poet disdeining to be tied to any such subjection, lifted up with the vigor of his own invention, doth grow in effect into an other nature: in making things either better than nature bringeth foorth, or quite a new, formes such as never were in nature." Poetry was the highest kind of human activity precisely because entirely separate from them all: "The *Poet* onely, onely bringeth his own stuffe, and doth not learn a Conceit out of matter, but maketh matter for a Conceit."[62] Truly, one could say that Sidney's death was very precisely the result of turning literary conceit into military matter.

The poet was to portray even human greatness by showing such humans as humans never were in reality nor could ever be; forging aspiration, not painting the actual. This was so even though poetry fulfilled this function as "an Art of *Imitation*." In order to "imitate," poets "borrow nothing of what is, hath bin, or shall be, but range onely reined with learned discretion, into the divine consideration of what may be and should be."[63] A similar view of wit would be expressed in the mid-seventeenth century by such as Baltasar Gracián in his *Agudeza y arte de ingenio* and Emanuale

---

[60]Pasquier, "Pour-parler," pp. 1026–32. The group known by the 1580s as the *Politiques* did not exist in 1560. The word *politique (politicus)* had long meant anyone concerned with the *polis*. It was used pejoratively by the 1570s, notably after the Saint Bartholomew massacre, to name those who sought to exclude religion from political affairs. But the term's use to name a "party" of moderation dated at least to the ecumenical Colloque de Poissy of 1561. Pasquier's own views remain a subject of scholarly debate. See E. M. Beame, "The Limits of Toleration in Sixteenth-Century France," *Studies in the Renaissance*, 13 (1966), 250–65; Kelley, *Beginning of Ideology*, pp. 203–10; Nicolai Rubinstein, "The History of the Word *Politicus* in Early-Modern Europe," in *The Languages of Political Theory in Early-Modern Europe*, ed. Anthony Pagden (Cambridge, 1987), pp. 41–56.

[61]George Puttenham, *The Arte of English Poesie, 1589*, ed. Edward Arber (London, 1869), pp. 22–23.

[62]Sir Philip Sidney, "The Defence of Poesie," in *The Prose Works*, ed. Albert Feuillerat, 4 vols. (1912; rpt. Cambridge, 1968–70), 3:4, 8, 26.

[63]Sidney, "Defence," pp. 9–10.

Tesauro in *Il cannocchiale aristotelico*, works in which primacy of language and its manipulation over material reference were urged with dazzling joy and lengthy brilliance. That the view was finally to disappear from serious literary argument (these texts themselves being once again credited with importance—significantly—only in our own time) signals the "victory" of a different kind of argument. In the meantime, however, the isolation of the poet and the inability of poetry to affect (let alone effect) worldly activity led to a verbal dismay captured to perfection in Sidney's *Arcadia*.

Even when Cervantes seemed to suggest (in 1606) that a proper novelistic art could in some way mediate precisely between the real and the reader of "fiction," he concluded in doubt:

> Fictions have to match the minds of their readers and to be written in such a way that, by tempering the impossibilities, moderating excesses, and keeping judgement in the balance, they may so astonish, hold, excite, and entertain, that wonder and pleasure go hand in hand. None of this can be achieved by anyone departing from verisimilitude or from that imitation of nature in which lies the perfection of all that is written. I have never seen a book of chivalry with a whole body for a plot, with all its limbs complete, so that the middle corresponds to the beginning, and the end to the beginning and middle.

Some authors, he allowed, may be quite accomplished in certain genres, but on the whole modern poetry, drama, and prose were in complete decay and disarray.[64] Panza and Quijote themselves inhabited a world where fact and fiction, reality and fantasy, truth and falsehood were utterly inseparable. Even commentary was awry.

The writer's distance from the world, the voice speaking commentaries on more urgently public figures, was marked by an Erasmian copiousness of diction. Woolf wrote of "Sidney's sheer delight in wandering. The syllabling of the words," she went on, "even causes him the liveliest delight. Mere rhythm we feel as we sweep over the smooth backs of the undulating sentences intoxicates him. Look, he seems to cry, as he picks up the glittering handfuls, can it be true that there are such numbers of beautiful words lying about for the asking? Why not use them lavishly and abundantly?" A later, less exuberant age, one for which "the dew is off the language," would consider such verbal luxury to be an "unformed babble of sound." Such leisured verbal opulence would become the "drone to the bagpipe" of reasonable action that Thomas Rymer later accused Shakespeare of indulging.[65] Such exuberance reflected Bembo's, Valdés's,

[64]Cervantes, *Don Quijote*, 1:661–69; *Adventures*, pp. 425–31: I.xlvii–xlviii.
[65]Woolf, "Countess of Pembroke's *Arcadia*," p. 35; Thomas Rymer, "A Short View of Tragedy [1692]," in *The Critical Works*, ed. Curt A. Zimansky (New Haven, Conn., 1956), p. 86.

Joachim Du Bellay's, Roger Ascham's, or Herrera's call to make the literary vernaculars, as well as their ambivalence about them. In England it perhaps reached its paroxysm in Euphuism—of which John Lily's 1578 *Anatomy of Wit* remained no doubt the most sparkling example. Yet by definition no end could be set to such copiousness, no term of final, or at least settled, order. And in that, it matched the uneasy political tempests of the times, the feared vicissitudes of social change. Could Sidney, had he lived, ever finish revising *Arcadia*? Any more than Montaigne his *Essays*? Small wonder, perhaps, that Spenser never completed the *Faerie Queene*.[66] For his part, Cervantes put an abrupt end to Alonso Quijano el Bueno's tilting by killing him off, preventing any future writer from bringing "him out of the tomb," putting him through "a third journey," and embarking him "on any new expedition."[67]

As Cervantes was finishing the second part of *Don Quijote* and (presumably) his *Persiles*, Luis de Góngora was writing and circulating his *Soledades* (1613–18). On the one hand, this unfinished poem was a retreat into a pastoral (and piscatorial) domain where depictions of quotidian realities were inseparably mingled with poetic and mythical device, in a language of distorted syntax, obscure tropes, largely concealed mythology, and almost private invention. Its readership was therefore among a small elite. On the other hand, the two *Soledades* offered a quite bitter—if not savage—reflection of current crisis. Halfway through the *Soledad primera*, more or less without preparation or provocation, an old shepherd makes of navigation and the conquest of America a tale of greed and misfortune, of misery and catastrophe for Spain. The glory and the wealth, like the memory of the old man's drowned son, "es buitre de pesares (is a vulture of grievous sorrows)." The final image of the *Soledad segunda* (and thus of the poem as Góngora left it) is that of Ascalaphus, who, after betraying Persephone to Pluto, was changed into a fearsome owl, "injuria de la luz, horror del día (bane of light, horror of day)," having deprived Ceres, the earth, of her "sweet daughter" and left "la estigia deidad con bella esposa (the Stygian god with a beautiful wife)."[68]

The shipwreck with which the *Soledades* began was thus reinforced at the "end" by this comment on a hunting scene whose savagery and pitiousness the poet chose particularly to emphasize. The violent springtime fertility symbolized by Jupiter's rape of Europa at that same beginning was then sealed by the wintry bleakness of the final lines of the second *Soledad*.[69] As a bitterly distant commentary was not, however,

[66]The best study of Erasmian *copia* and its literary consequences remains Cave's *Cornucopian Text*.
[67]Cervantes, *Don Quijote*, 2:1348–51; *Adventures*, pp. 937–40: II.lxxiv.
[68]Luis de Góngora y Argote, *Soledades*, ed. Dámaso Alonso (1927; rpt. Madrid, 1982), pp. 53, 100: I.509, II.975–79.
[69]John R. Beverley takes this "counterpoint" of a springtime "myth of ascension" (Jupiter and Europa) and an autumnal "myth of descension" (Pluto and Persephone), of the opening line's "Era del año la estación florida" and the last line's "y a la estigia deidad

how most of the original readers of the poem understood it. They took it much as Woolf read Sidney. "Oh diabolical poem!" exclaimed Francisco Cascales in 1634. "What do you think our poet was trying to do? I will tell you: destroy poetry. . . . And how? By turning things back to their first chaos; causing our thoughts not to be understood nor our words comprehended, by means of confusion and disorder."[70] Other contemporaries, it is true, sought to provide an allegorical reading that claimed to find behind surface *agudeza* a deep disillusion with the life of organized society, and ultimate faith in some solitary anchoretic life in the natural world. The implications of both views corresponded, of course, to what has already been traced here: a sense of society in decay, of a "world upside down," as Gracián later put it, in which the poetic text was impotent to intervene. Chaotic verbal profusion or disillusioned retreat was either way a counsel of practical despair.

The age's loss of textual authority had its political and social counterparts in unending religious dispute, in military confrontation through continual and increasingly bitter war and rebellion, in the economic scourge of rampant inflation, in discomforting uncertainties about hitherto familiar stabilities of rank and honor, obedience and duty. Sidney's *Arcadia*, Cervantes's novels, and Góngora's poems certainly reflected these sufferings and doubts, a wider despair with and in the world than a merely verbal or poetic emphasis might imply. For the sense of poetic distance obviously meant not a lack of implication of reality, but rather an absence of any possible effect on and within it. For *Arcadia*'s ultimate despair and lack of hope, in Sidney's own terms, lay in an inability to forge aspiration, no less than in the apparent practical futility of the aspirations it did at least *seek* to forge (a point much elaborated— again—by Cervantes). According to Greville, the aim had been "to turn the barren philosophy precepts into pregnant images of life," for the "enabling of free-born spirits to the greatest affairs of states."[71] As it stood at the last, however, the work remained an unfinished tissue of fantasy, a fairy tale of conceits reflecting an actuality in whose "dark webs" (Greville) the poet could not hope to intervene.

To be sure, when he started to revise his earlier text in 1582–84, Sidney sought to change his original rather lighthearted heroic pastoral into an epic taking seriously the political "tumult upon tumult arising" from the eclipse of political authority.[72] Arcadia could thus become the very image

con bella esposa," as supporting his argument that the *Soledades* are in fact complete and finished: *Aspects of Góngora's "Soledades,"* Purdue University Monographs in Romance Languages, vol. 1 (Amsterdam, 1980), pp. 111–12.

[70]Francisco Cascales, *Cartas filológicas* [1634], vol. 1 (Madrid, 1930), p. 220. Quoted by Beverley, *Aspects*, p. 11.

[71]Greville, "Dedication," pp. 10, 3.

[72]Sidney, *Arcadia*, p. 773. Henceforth references to *Arcadia* are indicated directly in my text and are taken from the edition given in note 2.

of disasters closer to home: in the Netherlands, in France, in both the southern and the northern Habsburg empires. Of these events Sidney and his circle were acutely aware. Greville could write that from 1677 on, Sidney was in close contact with William of Nassau, keeping "intelligence by words and letters, and in affairs of the highest nature that then passed current upon the stages of England, France, Germany, Italy, the Low Countries or Spain." He described a survey—a "fearful almanac"—of the European political situation purportedly undertaken by Sidney, which found everywhere an uneasy calm on the point of exploding, "an universal terror."[73] It may be that the fiction captured some of this: "For besides the universal case of Greece, deprived by this means of a principal pillar [Basilius's withdrawal and seclusion], [Euarchus] weighed and pitied the pitiful state of the Arcadian people who were in a worse case than if death had taken away their prince; for so yet their necessity would have placed someone to the helm. Now, a prince being and not doing like a prince, keeping and not exercising the place, they were in so much more evil case as they could not provide for their evil" (p. 791).

Some seventy years later Thomas Hobbes was to make the loss of such sovereignty a principal issue in the contractual theory of state expressed in final form in *Leviathan*. The matter was prominent in the polemics of the civil wars in France, from the arguments of such Protestant scholars and statesmen as François Hotman, Philippe du Plessis Mornay, and Hubert Languet (Sidney's patron, friend, and adviser) to those of Henri IV's more strictly political aides in the 1590s. Thus Michel Hurault wrote in the heat of real war against the Catholic Ligue:

> If at this moment you wanted to see the image of confusion and disorder, you would find it clearly painted in that party. To begin with, the duke of Mayenne calls himself *Lieutenant General of the Royal State and of the crown of France*. This is a great illusion: can there be a *Lieutenant*, if there is no head? And who is head if not the King? Yet the majority of this party doesn't want any king. *As to the State:* formerly one heard talk of the States of France, but never of the State: or if one heard it named it was when one said, "The King and his State." In that case the state was named in terms of obedience and not of command: and these madmen place it at the head.[74]

Hurault, exchancellor of Henri de Navarre, died in 1592, and this text must have been written around 1590–91 (we will be returning to it). Twenty years earlier similar questions of sovereignty had been raised,

---

[73]Greville, "Dedication," pp. 13, 51–52. For the entire survey, see pp. 48–64.
[74]Michel Hurault de l'Hôpital, *Second discours sur l'estat de France*, in *Quatre excellens discours sur l'estat present de la France . . .* (Paris, 1593), pp. 99–243. This citation, p. 146. The political questions raised here are discussed at length in my next chapter.

particularly by Jean Bodin and by the Protestant polemicists. Between the two, Sidney, witness of the Saint Bartholomew's Day massacre, friend of Languet and of William the Silent, joined his voice to the discussion of these doubts and uncertainties:

> This composition of conceits brought forth a dangerous tumult which yet would have been more dangerous, but that it had so many parts that nobody well knew against whom chiefly to oppose themselves. For some there were that cried to have the state altered and governed no more by a prince: marry, in the alteration, many would have the Lacedaemonian government of a few chosen senators [as Venice?]; others, the Athenian, where the people's voice held the chief authority [from Coke to Cromwell, such were to be heard in Sidney's own country]. . . . they that went nearest to the present case [as in a country that knew no government without a prince] were they that strove whom they should make, whereof a great number there were that would have the Princess Pamela presently to enjoy it [Elizabeth?]; some . . . inclining more to Philoclea [the threat of Mary, Queen of Scots?]; and there wanted not of them which wished Gynecia were delivered and made regent till Pamela were worthily married [as Catherine de Medicis in France?]. (P. 767)

The loyal but somewhat unyielding Councillor Philanax found himself opposed by the false Timautus (pp. 768–72), a man of "extreme ambition." The quarrel echoed those of court factions familiar to Sidney, whether in England, the Netherlands, or France, everywhere a potent ingredient of catastrophe. (Over all three loomed the shadow of the ambitious duke of Anjou, heir to the French crown since 1574, pretender to governorship in the Low Countries, as also to Elizabeth's hand: to Sidney's outspoken distress).[75] This "dangerous division of men's minds, the ruinous renting of all estates, had now brought Arcadia to feel the pangs of uttermost peril—such convulsions never coming but that the life of that government draws near his necessary period" (p. 783).

Timautus was defeated, albeit protected by Philanax (pp. 786–87). And if we might wish to see in this an echo of current strife, or even a preview of what was to come between the Guises and a new Bourbon king in France after 1589 (for where the basis of struggle is the same, we may expect like forms of activity), equally clearly the issues applied to Eliz-

---

[75]From 1575 until his death in 1584, Anjou's doings warranted constant international anxiety. He managed to involve Spain, England, France, Austria, divers German principalities as well as the Netherlands in his own interests. See Mack P. Holt, *The Duke of Anjou and the Politique Struggle during the Wars of Religion* (Cambridge, 1986); see, too, the remarkable volume by Frances A. Yates, *The Valois Tapestries*, Studies of the Warburg Institute, vol. 23 (London, 1959). Tradition notwithstanding, Sidney's 1579 letter to Elizabeth, arguing with some vehemence against the Anjou marriage, did not cause his departure from court or any breach with her. See Holt, *Duke of Anjou*, pp. 124–25, and Sir Philip Sidney, *Miscellaneous Prose*, ed. Katherine Duncan-Jones and Jan van Dorsten (Oxford, 1973), pp. 34–35.

abeth's authority in England. Zelmane, taken by all for a woman, put the matter in the very terms of those arguments:

An unused thing it is, and I think not heretofore seen, O Arcadians, that a woman should give public counsel to men, a stranger to the country people, and that lastly in such a presence, by a private person the regal throne should be possessed. But the strangeness of your action makes that used for virtue which your violent necessity imposeth. For certainly, a woman may well speak to such men who have forgotten all man-like government; a stranger may with reason instruct such subjects that neglect due points of subjection; and is it marvel this place is entered into by another, since your own prince, after thirty years' government, dare not show his face unto his faithful people? (P. 384)

Zelmane was Pyrocles disguised. Many would have liked to discover something similar about Elizabeth. Doubts and heated debate continued to be widely heard as to the wisdom, even the legitimacy, of a "private person" filling "the regal throne."[76] Publishing his *De constantia* in 1584 from the chief university of the land where Sidney was to die two years later, the Flemish scholar Justus Lipsius, star of Leyden, expressed the view that if in Britain "there have been continuall warres and slaughters, . . . in that now it resteth a while in peace, must be referred to the gouernment of a peaceable sex." In a political context, such a view was so rare as to be almost unique. Indeed, Lipsius would elsewhere counsel against female participation in rule.[77] Most thought a woman on the throne marked a serious inversion of the natural order, and few could forget the bloodletting in England under Mary, civil strife in France under Catherine de Medicis (fanned by the fervent Protestantism of Jeanne d'Albret, Queen of Navarre), or the outbreak of the Dutch Revolt under the governorship of Margaret of Parma.

The loyalty of Sidney and his circle was hardly in doubt, but the pages of

[76]See, e.g., Lisa Jardine, *Still Harping on Daughters: Women and Drama in the Age of Shakespeare* (Brighton and Totawa, N.J., 1983), pp. 169–98; and Constance Jordan, "Woman's Rule in Sixteenth-Century British Political Thought," *Renaissance Quarterly,* 40 (1987), 421–51. The standard works on the cult of Elizabeth are Yates, *Astraea* (esp. pp. 29–87), and Roy Strong, *The Cult of Elizabeth* (London, 1977). Philippa Berry has tried to bridge symbolic and political issues in *Of Chastity and Power: Elizabethan Literature and the Unmarried Queen* (London and New York, 1989). John N. King counters the static symbolism traced by Yates and Strong, in an essay showing how the queen's symbolic depiction changed with her aging and the developing political situation (Diana predominated only after 1680, for example), and how and for what political purposes the static image was fixed in the Jacobean years: "Queen Elizabeth I: Representations of the Virgin Queen," *Renaissance Quarterly,* 43, no. 1 (Spring 1990), 30–74.

[77]Recalling Livia's advice to Augustus to pardon Cinna (and see Chapter 4, below), Lipsius wrote: "Heare from a woman, no woman's counsell" (*Six Bookes of Politickes or Civil Doctrine* (London, 1594), p. 90. The previous citation is out of Justus Lipsius, *Two Bookes of Constancie,* written in Latine . . . , trans. Sir John Stradling, ed. Rudolf Kirk, with Clayton Morris Hall (New Brunswick, N.J., 1939), p. 199 (II.xxvi).

praise for the queen written after her death by Greville did not stop his claim that Sidney was given no high office by Elizabeth because the very exhorbitance of his prodigious talents "seemed too great for the cautious wisdoms of little monarchies to be safe in."[78] The threat of civil war in England was as real as its actuality in France and the Low Countries. Many perhaps were held back only by the seriously felt question, here put by Zelmane: "What could your enemies more wish unto you than to see your own estate with your own hands undermined?" (p. 385). In 1582–84 France (not a major power anyway) might well be distracted, but the Catholic Spanish Empire was ever an impending threat. The subversion of "the course of nature in making reason give place to sense, and man to woman" (p. 133), was but one sign of a general and universal undermining of polity: *Arcadia* was replete with the marks of inversion.

No solution to any of these enigmas seemed available. Pyrocles, for instance, was able to answer Musidorus's criticism of his transformation into a woman only with an entirely traditional and conservative claim: "I am not yet come to that degree of wisdom to think light of the sex of whom I have my life, since if I be anything . . . I was, to come to it, born of a woman and nursed of a woman. And certainly it is strange to see the unmanlike cruelty of mankind, who, not content with their tyrannous ambition to have brought the other's virtuous patience under them, like childish masters think their masterhood nothing without doing injury to them who . . . are framed of nature with the same parts of mind for the exercise of virtue as we are" (pp. 134–35). To praise women as mothers, and virtuous accordingly, tended if anything to reinforce doubts about the rule of a "private person" and the threat it left of some uprising by "the many-headed multitude whom inconstancy only doth guide to well-doing" (p. 387): not to speak of the menace of discontented feudal nobles, already rampant in France, stirring in England.

It might well be that Sidney's friend and client Edmund Spenser, echoing Ariosto's praise of Charles V (*Orlando furioso*, XV, 18), would hold out some hope of an Elizabethan settlement:

> Thenceforth eternall vnion shall be made
> Between the nations different afore,
> And sacred Peace shall louingly perswade
> The warlike mindes, to learne her goodly lore,
> And ciuile armes to exercise no more;
> Then shall a royall virgin raine, which shall
> Stretch her white rod ouer the *Belgicke* shore. . . .

But such hopes of dominion, indeed of Elizabeth as a healer of European disunity, themselves sank into despondency.[79] For finally the tale col-

---

[78]Greville, "Dedication," p. 24.
[79]Edmund Spenser, *The Faerie Queene*, in *Poetical Works*, ed. J. C. Smith and E. de Selincourt (1912; rpt. London, 1969), p. 158: Bk. III, Cant. iii, st. 49. On this, see Yates,

lapsed, unfinished. Spenser's moral treatise could no more resolve its nostalgic aspirations than could Sidney's ethico-political fiction. Small wonder that sometime during these very years was performed a play echoing just that collapse, devoid of any moral anchor and utterly pitiless in its savagery.

I mean *Titus Andronicus*, written and revised between 1591 and 1594. From the very outset the audience was cast into a Rome of which Titus could say to his son, Lucius, future emperor, that it was "but a wilderness of tigers" (III.1.53–54). Small distinction could be made among the "beastliness" of the "raving tiger" Tamora, her "hellhound" sons, her "inhuman dog" of a lover, the unfeeling self-interest of the emperor Saturninus, or the brutal inhumanity of Andronicus. The spectator was in a world where the wolves were out: Titus was instantly merciless to Tamora, at best injurious in agreeing to let Saturninus wed his daughter Lavinia when she and Bassianus were already betrothed, and murderous to his son Mutius. Lies, adultery, mutilation, murder, children eaten by parents, torture, and rape all might lead us to find Marcus Andronicus's question to Lucius after the final bloodbath overly mild: "Tell us what Sinon hath bewitched our ears, / Or who hath brought the fatal engine in / That gives our Troy, our Rome, the civil wound" (V.iii.84–86).

For this tale, too, was placed under the sign of Virgil. It recounted a bleak record of civil wound and uproar, a world justice has fled, a terrifying universe from whence all equity is gone: "Terras Astraea reliquit" (IV.iii.4–5). In this play the very possibility of its return was cast in the light of a cynical illusion, by means of the extraordinary scene in which Titus and his companions shot arrows at the heavens in hope of bringing Astraea/Virgo back to earth. Lucius, future emperor, was said to have hit her. But apart from the hunter's expectation that such a shot should be fatal, the announcement of his success was couched in a sexual innuendo surely undermining all hope: "O, well said, Lucius! / Good boy, in Virgo's lap" (IV.iii.64–65). Such cynicism seemed to blast any possibility at all of resolving disaster.[80] Only fifty years later, we will see, would new arguments be found.

The *Faerie Queene* petered out in the uncertainty of the Mutabilitie Cantos; *Titus Andronicus* recorded a world of unredeemed horror and despair. *Don Quijote* no doubt depicted a world of somewhat wistful individual hope where Quijote and Sancho were concerned, but otherwise of collective cynicism and manipulation at best, of barbarity at worst. Góngora created a private language of flight into a solitary pastoral, away from the violent decay of his perceived surroundings. *Arcadia*'s thrust was

---

Astraea, pp. 53–54. Yates also observes how widespread was the idea of Elizabeth as a kind of pan-European redemptress (ibid., pp. 118–20). I raise the issue of women in the political sphere, and then in literature, passim and discuss it in detail in Chapters 4, 7, and 9. It is central to the understanding of "literature."

[80]Yates has also commented on these aspects of *Titus Andronicus*, in *Astraea*, pp. 74–76.

toward the recovery of a merely nostalgic fantasy of feudal "equilibrium," requiring on the one hand a cowed people such as Arcadia's plaintive churls (told to "bide in patience," p. 708) and on the other a contract of faith between sovereign and nobility.[81] Sidney's worldly sympathies may have lain with the Protestant rebels of the Netherlands, but his ideal was a mythic Protestant feudalism whose political—if not religious—equivalent was in fact the French Ligue. Dutch revolt and French civil wars marked a completely different struggle, one between an old "feudal" concept of relations of force and a new concept of state and sovereign authority just starting to be found. It was emphatically not the poet Sidney who would find it. Like Virgil, he would not live long enough to sing the song of a new glory:

> O that a remnant of long life be mine,
> Giving me breath to celebrate your deeds:
> Orpheus would not vanquish me in song
> Nor Linus, though their parents stand by them,
> Calliope and beautiful Apollo.
> Even Pan, though Arcady should judge our contest,
> Pan would say Arcady judged him the loser.[82]

Sidney would have no such chance: sovereignty, right, ordered society, relations between women and men, the very claims of clear language were subject to endless catastrophe. The poet remained unable even to constitute any writerly authority. Jacqueline Miller, analyzing poems from Chaucer to Spenser, Sidney, and Herbert, could only conclude: "The sense of ending is always sober and irresolute. It is the sense that the word is fragile; that the maker's claims to autonomy are, in the end, insubstantial; that his reliance on other voices will prove misplaced; that his individual creations cannot endure, either by assimilating or by resisting the influence of the world outside them; that a writer's authorship and the authority of his text are never final, never unassailable, never absolute."[83]

Of all this, a play such as *Titus Andronicus* was the appalling image. And although the end of *Arcadia* may have proposed a happy married life for monarchs, it foretold unending further vicissitudes for its aristocrats. Sidney's argument would never get beyond that painful nostalgia. Boileau, Dryden, and their companions would one day urge the singing of new praises of power, content in the harmony of new political authority and legitimate rational writing. But then their order and the poets' place would

---

[81]Norbrook has analyzed the "Ister bank" eclogue of *Arcadia* in these terms in *Poetry and Politics*, p. 98.

[82]Virgil, Eclogue IV, ll. 53–59, trans. in Paul Alpers, *The Singer of the Eclogues: A Study of Virgilian Pastoral*, with a New Translation of the *Eclogues* (Berkeley, Los Angeles, and London, 1979), p. 31.

[83]Jacqueline T. Miller, *Poetic License: Authority and Authorship in Medieval and Renaissance Contexts* (New York and Oxford, 1986), p. 175.

be quite different. Sidney and his contemporaries had turned to Arcadia in vain:

> The last great age the Sybil's song foretold
> Rolls round: the centuries are born anew!
> The Maid returns, old Saturn's reign returns,
> Offspring of heaven, a hero's race descends.[84]

But England's own Astraea/Virgo proved too much a source of uncertainty. Justice had not returned to earth. The hesitant calm concluding *Arcadia* did not proclaim stability. It was a lull of exhaustion, asserting nothing other than the loss of a hopeful political nostalgia and, above all, here, the failure of writing itself. The story could be continued only if some other be found "to exercise his pen in that wherewith mine is already dulled" (p. 848). *Arcadia* incomplete and its poet's untoward death marked hope abashed, the "cloddy cumbers" not of a golden age recovered, but of an iron age prolonged.

[84]Virgil, Eclogue IV, ll. 4–7 (Alpers, *Singer*, p. 27).

Chapter 2

The Sense of an Ending

As from some stage or theatre, the knight
Saw play'd the tragedy of human state,
Saw death, blood, murder, wo and horror strange,
And the great acts of fortune, chance and change.
—Tasso, *Jerusalem Delivered*,
trans. Edward Fairfax, XX.73

The century between 1550 and 1650 was both in fact and in perception a time of dissolution and decay, of war and general disaster. From the Spanish peninsula to the Empire's central Europe, from the foot of Italy to the northern marches, the four horsemen rode with a vengeance across the land. Protestant uprising in the German countries; civil broil in France; revolt in the United Provinces, in Portugal, in Catalonia; war between England and Spain; interspersed with such additional discomforts as rampant inflation, famine, and plague; the outrageous barbarism of inquisitional punishment and ubiquitous witch hunting, all seemed to culminate after 1619 in the awful horrors—yet more generalized, were it conceivable—of the Thirty Years' War. To participants and observers at the time it could hardly but appear as though the millennium were indeed at hand. Rational analysis seemed helpless and desolately lost. Language was incompetent and vacuous, when not deliberately abused and deceitful. Spirit turned awry. Madness and unreason threatened all thought and action.

"These and greater changes," William Temple was to write at the end of the seventeenth century, "are made in the several countries of the world and courses of time, by the revolutions of empire, the devastations of armies, the cruelties of conquering, and the calamities of enslaved nations; by the violent inundations of water in some countries, and the cruel ravages of plagues in others."[1] Such remarks had been commonplace among writers a century earlier, and just as Temple found like considerations entirely in their place in "An Essay upon the Ancient and Modern Learning" (1690), so his forebears, too, had not hesitated to associate

---

[1] Sir William Temple, "An Essay Upon the Ancient and Modern Learning," in *Five Miscellaneous Essays by Sir William Temple*, ed. Samuel Holt Monk (Ann Arbor, Mich., 1963), p. 53.

linguistic decay and the loss of learning with the general dissolution of society and political order. As Montaigne famously put it:

> I have observed in Germany that Luther has left as many divisions and altercations over the uncertainty of his opinions, and more, as he raised about the Holy Scriptures. Our disputes are purely verbal. I ask what are "nature," "pleasure," "circle," "substitution." The question is one of words, and is answered in the same way. "A stone is a body." But if you pressed on: "And what is a body?"—"Substance."—"And what is sub-stance?" and so on, you would finally drive the respondent to the end of his lexicon. We exchange one word for another word, often more un-known. I know better what is man than I know what is animal, or moral, or rational. To satisfy one doubt, they give me three; it is the Hydra's head.[2]

This passage followed a long discussion of the many interpretations of laws given by legal theoreticians. It preceded an appeal to simplify these same laws and to eliminate the learned glosses that only increased "doubts and ignorance" (III.xiii.817, 1044) and caused "an irregular, per-petual motion, without model and without aid" (ibid., 818, 1045). Concep-tual obscurity and verbal convolution had made the very "command-ment" of the laws "confused and inconstant" (ibid., 821, 1050). A wide diversity of concern was brought together here: a question of right and law, one of religious opinion and thus of the civil wars, a question concerning language and its relationship to things and concepts, another about incon-stancy and change, and yet another on the subject and what it is capable of knowing. Montaigne's linguistic "Hydra's head" produced a whole mass of dilemmas of a quite different order. And through the same clichéd meta-phor, we will soon see, they were always linked with the disturbance of war and material disaster.

The fusion of linguistic failure and of actual catastrophe was repeated in another commonplace, used by Montaigne in the same 1588 edition of the *Essays* as that in which he wrote of his lexicon's futility. Now he wrote explicitly of the French civil wars, rating those who sought to "upset the state": "All sorts of new depravity gleefully draw, from this first and fertile source, examples and models to trouble our government. Men read in our very laws, made for the remedy of this first evil, an apprenticeship and excuse for all sorts of wicked enterprises; and we are experiencing what Thucydides says of the civil wars of his time, that men baptized public vices with new milder names to excuse them, adulterating and softening their true titles" (I.xxiii.87, 119). "Words," the Greek historian had writ-

---

[2]Michel de Montaigne, *Essays*, in *Complete Works*, trans. Donald Frame (Stanford, Calif., 1957), III.xiii.819, 1046. All future references quote this edition directly in my text. Roman numerals indicate book and essay number, arabic give page references first to the English translation, then to the French *Oeuvres complètes*, ed. Albert Thibaudet and Maurice Rat (Paris, 1962).

ten, "had to change their ordinary meaning and to take that which was now given them."[3] Little could he have foreseen how hackneyed his argument would become in political thought at the end of the French wars of religion. The association it made between linguistic and sociopolitical decay became a central tenet of writers who, like Montaigne, played considerable roles as much in public life as in what Pierre Mesnard has felicitously called the launching of political philosophy.[4]

In August 1570 Louis Le Roy signed at Saint-Germain-en-Laye the dedication to his *Exhortation aux François pour vivre en concorde, et iouir du bien de la Paix*. The text was dedicated to King Charles IX, who, at the same place and in the same month, had signed the pact known as the Peace of Saint Germain, putting an "end" to the third war of religion. In his work, Le Roy stressed that a single sovereign authority, embodied in the king's person, was essential to the continued existence of "all the Kingdom." He set the stability inevitably brought by such sovereignty against the total upheaval resulting from political sedition, the major consequence, he wrote, of the nobles' discontent.[5] The principal sign of such upheaval was that same verbal confusion written of by Thucydides, from whom Le Roy then quoted at great length.[6] And it is a matter of note that the dispersion of sovereignty was *always* linked with the inconstancy of anything like a rational individual (private) subject (as against the political—public—one) and with the failure of words. Indeed, it is simply not possible to discover anything *we* might think of as an autonomous subject.

When Stephen Greenblatt, for example, set out in quest of some autonomously "self-fashioned" subject in the Renaissance, he searched for something whose very concept was a presupposition of our own post-Cartesian thinking and acting. To admit, then, that he failed to find such a subject, because "fashioning oneself and being fashioned by cultural institutions—family, religion, state—were inseparably intertwined," is not at all

[3]Thucydides, *The Peloponnesian War*, trans. Richard Crawley, intro. John H. Finley, Jr. (New York, 1951), p. 189 (III.82–83). Cf. J. G. A. Pocock, *The Machiavellian Moment: Florentine Political Thought and the Atlantic Republican Tradition* (Princeton, 1975), pp. 94–95.

[4]Pierre Mesnard, *L'essor de la philosophie politique au xvie siècle*, 3d ed. (Paris, 1969). The role of philological debate in enlarging legal and political thought was early explored by Donald R. Kelley: *Foundations of Modern Historical Scholarship: Language, Law, and History in the French Renaissance* (New York and London, 1970), esp. pp. 53–85; "Legal Humanism and the Sense of History," *Studies in the Renaissance*, 13 (1966), 184–99; "Civil Science in the Renaissance: The Problem of Interpretation," in *The Languages of Political Theory in Early-Modern Europe*, ed. Anthony Pagden (Cambridge, 1987), pp. 57–78. The relation is now an axiom of historical and legal historiography; it always was in theology.

[5]Louis Le Roy, *Exhortation aux François pour vivre en concorde, et iouir du bien de la Paix* (Paris, 1570), pp. 2ro, 10ro. He could have culled these ideas from many places, however later argument may have credited them to Jean Bodin. They were a Gallican commonplace in pacification edicts and elsewhere. (I thank Donald Kelley for this reminder.)

[6]Le Roy, *Exhortation*, pp. 44vo–46vo.

the point.[7] The matter would rather be to understand what made possible, later, the construction of a subject that *did* so perceive itself and what kind of awareness of "being-in-the-world" preceded it.

The "post-Cartesian" subject could not, of course, see itself as a construct, for to do so would be to deny its self-understanding as autonomous (a circumstance that does not, however, make it any less of a social construct). Nonetheless, the fact that from Erasmus and More to Montaigne and Shakespeare people understood their nature as in some essential way imbricated in the social order did not imply they did so either: nor could they have envisaged such a social construct in a divinely made world. The point was that the very sense of "subjectivity" (we are constrained here by our vocabulary) was trammeled in instability and movement. Miller's analysis of several poets, mentioned at the end of the preceding chapter, is eloquent on this matter. The sense of being, we may say, could then be "fixed" only by situating it between some beneficent authority on the one hand and some alien antagonist on the other.

Catherine Belsey is quite right to observe that this played an important role in the agonistic definitions of women and men (and see Chapters 4 and 7 below). For political thinkers and actors at this time, the idea of unique monarchical sovereignty was virtually the only way conceivable to achieve social and political (and "personal") stability. The prince was precisely the kind of beneficent authority whose existence not only maintained the state itself, but defined the very nature of the political "subjects" who composed it. Not for nothing was the very meaning of "subject" confined to the nature of a political being.[8] This clarifies the significance of the king-centered poetry discussed in Chapter 1, as well as its constant risk of isolation: bereft of reference to authority, either it would collapse in on itself, perhaps pursuing a kind of verbal opulence, or it would seek new authority elsewhere—in Platonic idea or in the Divinity. Language, politics, and person formed a single composition, and collapse in one part meant dissolution in all.

The consequent signal importance of unique princely sovereignty was what Sidney had caught in his description of Euarchus's accession to the throne of Macedon:

He found his estate . . . so disjointed even in the noblest and strongest limbs of government that the name of a king was grown even odious to the

[7]Stephen Jay Greenblatt, *Renaissance Self-Fashioning: From More to Shakespeare* (Chicago and London, 1980), p. 256.

[8]Catherine Belsey, *The Subject of Tragedy: Identity and Difference in Renaissance Drama* (London, 1985), pp. 137–44. I have explored this notion of "subject" in "Montaigne and the Subject of Polity," in *Literary Theory/Renaissance Texts*, ed. Patricia Parker and David Quint (Baltimore and London, 1986), pp. 115–49. "Subject" did not have only a political meaning. It also had a theological sense of one owing obedience to a spiritual superior, and it had a meaning in logic (which, however, had nothing to do with human relations or being). It emphatically did not refer to anything in psychology or in some individualist philosophy. See, too, my *Discourse of Modernism*, pp. 58–72.

people. . . . Hence grew a very dissolution of all estates, while the great men (by the nature of ambition never satisfied) grew factious among themselves, and the underlings glad indeed to be underlings to them they hated least, to preserve them from such they hated most. Men of virtue suppressed . . . old men long nuzzled in corruption, scorning them that would seek reformation: young men very fault-finding but very faulty . . . merchandise abused, and so towns decayed for want of just and natural liberty: offices, even of judging souls, sold: public defenses neglected; and in sum . . . all awry, and (which wried it to the most wry course of all) wit abused rather to feign reason why it should be amiss than how it should be amended.[9]

Given that Sidney, militant Protestant and ardently idealistic defender of a chivalric nostalgia, was in many ways at loggerheads with a more pragmatic Elizabethan policy, such commentary was certainly aimed partly at what he and his friends saw as the flaws in that policy. But he was also in constant communication with friends on the Continent, most notably with his political "mentor" Languet, the Protestant polemicist close to William of Nassau in the Netherlands and deeply engaged in French struggles and debates—a central figure, indeed, in the polemics of the civil wars. Sidney was himself, of course, a major figure in the circle of his uncle, Robert Dudley, earl of Leicester, who unceasingly maintained the need for an aggressive united policy on the part of the Protestant powers. It was as a member of Leicester's small expeditionary force in the Low Countries that Sidney was to die at Zutphen in 1586. For him, as for the others, the English situation was of a piece with "the whole European scene" and needed "vigilant action abroad as well as at home."[10]

Corruption, decay, dissolution, faction, simony, neglect, and all kinds of abuse typified the entire European situation. And as for others, so for Sidney these multitudinous woes were not just political and social: "wit was abused," "reason amiss," and language adrift. Annabel Patterson rightly quotes the *Defence of Poesie* in this regard: "And not say, that *Poetrie* abuseth mans wit, but that mans wit abuseth *Poetrie*."[11] The loss of reason, the abuse of language and writing, and the dissolution of state were at one. Such was what Le Roy, Montaigne, and Sidney were all arguing. So, too, were more considerable political actors, for we must not believe the link was thought to be only a matter of insubstantial theory. The case of Henri de Navarre's chancellor, Michel Hurault, whom I mentioned earlier, was perhaps exemplary. His *Second discours sur l'estat de*

[9]Sidney, *Arcadia*, pp. 254–55.

[10]Norbrook, *Poetry and Politics*, p. 126. See, in general, pp. 91–108. For a useful quite detailed, but brief analysis of Elizabethan foreign policy issues and practice, see J. D. Ramsay, "The Foreign Policy of Elizabeth I," in *The Reign of Elizabeth I*, ed. Christopher Haigh (Basingstoke, 1984), pp. 147–68.

[11]Annabel Patterson, *Censorship and Interpretation: The Conditions of Writing and Reading in Early Modern England* (Madison, Wis., 1984), p. 36. She discusses the issues at some length, pp. 24–43.

France was written to denounce the ambitions and self-interest of the house of Lorraine (the Guises). According to him, they had provoked thirty years of war: "For religion was not yet at stake; they took it only for want of a better pretext."[12] After providing a brief history of the wars, he went on to denounce the specific example of struggle for interest which I quoted in the previous chapter: the duke of Mayenne *calling* himself Lieutenant General of the Royal State. The reference was to actual conditions and to concrete life: and it was, wrote Hurault, a matter of a complete verbal distortion of political realities.

In Hurault's view the Catholic Ligue had affirmed that the head of state was nothing other than the *guardian* ("lieutenant general") of a *state that has itself become sovereign.* It would, of course, be easy to find examples before this date of the phrase so criticized by Hurault: the "State of France." Hurault asserted, however, that the phrase had always signified the king's domain over which he was sovereign—an inalienable domain in some sense the "proper" characteristic of the king's immortal body. Such was the meaning of the doctrine of the king's two bodies.[13] If sovereignty was characteristic of the state itself (thus becoming an abstract concept, not personified by the king, which would eventually need the ascendancy of the doctrine of contract in order to fix and explain the relationship of the sovereign state to its individual members), then what counted would be the immortality of the state, so to speak, and not that of the mystical body of the king. The consequence, wrote Hurault, was very serious: the utter confusion of a state now without a language. Since there was no longer a sovereign prince, the officers of the exking did not know "how to pronounce. They dare not speak in the name of the King [i.e. Henri IV], they do not want to speak in the name of the people, and even less in that of Monsieur de Mayenne, for by the statutes of the Kingdom they can recognize no one but him who has absolute command" (*SD,* p. 147).

One was then up against a fundamental disorder, facing a "divided multitude of authorities" (ibid.). It was the birth of anarchy in the strictest sense of the term, for the loss of a single head could not but lead in the long run to an unending multiplication: the Hydra once again. And so Hurault complained of the creation of communes in the cities ("councils of certain persons of low degree in whose hands all authority has been placed"), writing that this "new democracy has undermined" the principal "Royal column," which was "justice": "Following the example of the capital city of Paris, all the other cities are doing the same thing; we have a Republic in every town" (*SD,* p. 148). Were events to continue to unfold in this manner, all the other cities, big and small, would do the same: "And thus by degrees there will eventually be no village in France that has not made itself into a

[12]Hurault, *Second discours,* p. 116. Future citations are signaled in my text by the letters *SD.*
[13]Ernst H. Kantorowicz, *The King's Two Bodies: A Study in Medieval Political Theology* (Princeton, 1957).

48 *The Meaning of Literature*

sovereign state" (*SD*, p. 149). It will be worth following a little further the perspectives being opened up by Hurault's commentaries, for not only was the debate central to the anxieties of the time, but we will see how its arguments link directly with those of the discussions providing the context for the later invention of literature.

Hurault had been arguing that the Ligue found itself in a contradictory position. On the one hand it assumed the total sovereignty of the state, while on the other it confronted a real splintering of this very same state, a disintegration of the country's local units into a bunch of tiny sovereignties. His argument turned on the essential idea that the state and its prince were inextricably linked. Royal sovereignty (inherent in the immortal and mystic body) formed the keystone of the state as a single unit: remove this stone (by denying the king or his unique authority), and the state disintegrated. Each part was driven into independence, and chaos ensued—whence the constant appeal of Montaigne to "natural and simple obedience," an obedience that had to come from "subjection" and not from "discretion" (I.xvii.51, 73). The twisting of that obedience was exactly what had led to the upside-down world of Sidney's *Arcadia.* For such submission was essential: "The ordinary discipline of a state that is in a healthy condition does not provide for those extraordinary accidents; it presupposes a body that holds together in its principal parts and function and a common consent to its observance and obedience" (I.xxiii.89, 121). In 1595 Montaigne added that "the law-abiding pace is a cold, deliberate and constrained one, and is not the kind that can hold up against a lawless and unbridled pace."

One of the principal merits of the Christian religion was its "precise recommendation of obedience to the magistrate and maintenance of the government" (I.xxiii.88, 119). To this statement from 1588 Montaigne added in 1595 that it seemed "very iniquitous to want to subject public and immutable institutions and observances to the instability of a private fancy (private reason has only a private jurisdiction), and to attempt against divine laws what no government would endure against civil laws. These last, although human reason has much more to do with them, are still supremely the judges of their judges; and the utmost ability serves at best to expound and extend their accepted use, not to turn it aside and innovate" (ibid., 88, 120). Divine laws, social laws, sovereignty of the "magistrate," together these form a network, a "coherent body" that must dissolve under the pressure of any usurpation of "mastery" (I.xvii.51, 73: addition of 1595). For the mayor of Bordeaux as for Hurault, the consequence of such usurpation was concretely visible on all sides: "The unity and contexture of this monarchy, this great structure, having been dislocated and dissolved" (ibid., 87, 118: addition of 1588). An arrogation of this kind was just what was feared in the case of Elizabeth and why the supposed "private" nature of women was so debated an issue with respect to female monarchs. Sidney's more precisely English anxieties were wholly a part of European polemic about sovereignty. They would be repeated again in the great quarrel about reason in women some sixty or seventy years later, as we will see in Chapter 4.

The doctrine of sovereign authority as it was found in Bodin's *Six livres de la république* (1576) provided the foundation for these various arguments. It lay at the base of every response given to the question posed most clearly by La Boétie regarding what he called "voluntary servitude": How could one explain the fact that millions of people obey one?[14] This question was asked both by the Huguenots after the Saint Bartholomew's Day massacre and by the Ligue after the murder of Henri III as a way of justifying sedition: a misuse and exchange of words duly lamented by Montaigne in a 1595 addition to the *Essays* (II.xii.323, 420). The ultimate response found a century later by Hobbes would be the same as Montaigne's: to give free reign to "private fantasy" already assumed that the state did not exist, that there was no legitimate order and hence no society, since, as Hobbes was to write in *Behemoth*, his story of the English civil wars, the latter depended on the former.[15] For the one as for the other, the response would thus be to emphasize the *volontaire*, rather than the *servitude*. Sovereign authority would lie for Hobbes (but not for Montaigne, since for him voluntary obedience had to do not at all with peoples' "rights" but only with their "duties") not in the prince as an individual but in the state as a collective enterprise *represented by* princely governance. It would be John Locke, in his *Treatise of Civil Government* (1689), who would confirm the idea that sovereignty belonged to the state, whatever forms of representation it might now take (thereby giving necessary theoretical support to the effects of the 1688 revolution, although he had written his work earlier).[16]

Toward the end of the sixteenth century people were for the most part far from any such solution, although the debates leading to it were well advanced.[17] When Le Roy, in 1575, sought an answer to the problem, he

[14]Étienne de La Boétie, *Discours de la servitude volontaire*, ed. Simone Goyard-Fabre (Paris, 1983), pp. 133, 179.

[15]Thomas Hobbes, *Behemoth: The History of the Causes of the Civil Wars of England . . .*, ed. Sir William Molesworth (1840; rpt. New York, 1969), pp. 5–7.

[16]On this question, see particularly Julian H. Franklin, *John Locke and the Theory of Sovereignty: Mixed Monarchy and the Right of Resistance in the Political Thought of the English Revolution* (Cambridge, 1978), pp. 87–126. Such views culminated in the paper arguments just before the trial of Charles I. They were of such a kind that Samuel Hartlib, the probable author of a pamphlet entitled *Rectifying Principles* (1648) expressing the army's views, could insist: "The State at large is King, and the King so-called is but its steward or Highest Officer" (quoted by C. V. Wedgwood, *The Trial of Charles I* [London, 1964], p. 88). This view remained doubtless a minority one even in England, at least until the Glorious Revolution and the publication of Locke's *Second Treatise*.

[17]Quentin Skinner has shown how the notion of the state evolved in the second half of the sixteenth century. He argues that its modern idea was virtually complete by the end. He does not mention Hurault, who, it seems to me, came nearest to seeing the state as an abstraction (although neo-Thomists like Luis de Molina and Francisco Suarez may have), nor does he discuss the issues as raised here: *The Foundations of Modern Histor-*

did so expectedly in terms of the mystic royal body: "It is not scorn for oneself, nor madness that so many thousands of men risk themselves for a single head, and that through the deaths of many is saved the life of one who is often old and feeble. Just as the whole body, which is greater and more visible, serves the soul, which remains unmixed in a hidden and mysterious place." Michel de l'Hôpital couched his answer in similarly sacred terms: "For what is the cause that so many thousands, of diverse lands, tongues, customs, qualities and conditions, so willingly submit to the rule, law and dominion of one? It is but justice, which requires that one gives to each his due, beginning first with God, our Creator . . . ; next proceeding to earthly princes, and, from rank to rank, to those set to govern, order, protect, and save us from oppression." Even so ardent a critic of monarchy as Philippe du Plessis-Mornay did not try to justify revolt on the part of "private individuals," who were, he wrote, "not to be regarded as the basic parts of a community." The state is a whole body, and only such as have a public role in it were authorized to action.[18] Sidney (doubtless also acquainted with Mornay, who worked closely with William of Nassau on the latter's justification of revolt against the Spanish crown) gave an altogether more cynical reply to the dilemma by remarking that what kept the hierarchical pyramid in order was simply people's joy to be underlings to those they hated least rather than most.

Hurault did seem to perceive a newer solution, although he disputed it and considered it impossible: "This is not all, for even when the capital cities of the provinces have chased out the King, killed all the nobles, conquered each their own province and bailiwick, they will still have to form some sort of government afterwards and some judiciary link will have to be found to hold them together" (*SD*, p. 149). This idea of a "judiciary link" (*lien de justice*) was interesting indeed. It signaled a "justice" very different from l'Hôpital's or that of the order proposed by Le Roy: the royal column Hurault had seen overturned. For what might such a "link" be if not a contract? Equally striking is the fact that Hurault described it as an abstraction. Further, he did not say "they will have to find" (the construction one would expect considering what preceded it), but "will have to be found." The phrase *qu'il se trouve* accentuated the

---

ical Thought, 2 vols. (Cambridge, 1978), passim and esp. 2:151–58, 349–58. A useful introduction to the longer development of the idea of sovereignty is F. H. Hinsley, *Sovereignty*, 2d ed. (Cambridge, 1986). For the relation between the wars of religion in France and English political thought, see J. H. M. Salmon, *The French Religious Wars in English Political Thought* (Oxford, 1959), as well as two older works: John Neville Figgis, *The Divine Right of Kings* (Cambridge, 1914); G. P. Gooch, *History of English Democratic Ideas in the Seventeenth Century* (London, 1898).

[18]Louis Le Roy, *De l'excellence du gouvernement royal . . .* (Paris, 1575), p. 6vo; Michel de l'Hôpital, *Oeuvres inédites*, ed. P. J. S. Dufey, 2 vols. (Paris, 1825–26), 1:28–29; Philippe du Plessis-Mornay, *Vindiciae contra tyrannos*, (extracts) in *Constitutionalism and Resistance in the Sixteenth Century: Three Treatises by Hotman, Beza, and Mornay*, trans. and ed. Julian H. Franklin (New York, 1969), pp. 152, 154–56.

abstract nature of the idea by implying that the link would, so to speak, find itself.[19]

The formula suggested that in Hurault's eyes the question was one not of a person or of a concrete alliance but of an abstract doctrine that would permit the return of an ordered civil structure. Equally "Hobbesian" may seem his idea that the lack of such a link led of necessity to evil, since malice is the chief characteristic of natural man en masse: "I do not believe they could ever agree on anything except doing evil; for good action is not to be found amid such confusion." He added that "the nature of man is evil [*meschant*]" (*SD*, p. 150). Confusion, disorder, malice, and finally death ("you won't last long this way" [*SD*, p. 151]) would inevitably follow the destruction of the "ruling lord's" sovereignty (*SD*, p. 151). I cannot but recall Hobbes's famous phrase from the beginning of *Leviathan* (1651), according to which in the state of nature "the life of man is solitary, poore, nasty, brutish, and short." Hurault, of course, had an immediate and celebrated precursor in Bodin, who had asked: What was more reasonable than to think "that force and violence had been the source and origin of republics"? And if reason did not lead us to such a belief, then all the historians would, who have shown "that the first men had no honor, and no greater virtue than to kill, massacre, steal, or enslave humans."[20]

This was why, according to Hobbes, voluntary surrender of the individual's power to a central authority was absolutely essential. Hurault made no other claim, although the basis for his solution was finally (and unsurprisingly) closer to arguments of his contemporaries. According to Hobbes, the fundamental natural right was the protection and conservation of one's own life. For a rational being, it followed that the basic natural law was the law of peace (*Leviathan*, I.14). For Hobbes, the "natural" consequence of this was the contract that founded civil society, a contract that emerged from a rational accord among individuals possessed

---

[19]In view of the importance I am ascribing to this passage, I give the French: "Ce n'est pas tout, car quand bien les villes capitales des Provinces auroient chassé le Roy, auroient tué tous les nobles, conquis chacune son ressort & son bailliage, il faut encores qu'entre elles, apres elles prennent quelque forme de gouuernement & qu'il se trouue vn lien de iustice qui les tiene ensemble." The Calvinist Johannes Althusius, in 1603 and 1614, also saw society as linked by an abstract *pactum*. He envisaged a society of corporate associations in which *individuals* had no political role at all, however they were protected by the social "symbiosis," as he called it. In *that* sense Althusius was perhaps closer to Montaigne, as well as to other Protestant thinkers who devalued entirely the role of the private individual. Althusius was a genuinely original thinker, who did not accept any idea of a traditional monarchy and explicitly rejected Bodin's arguments on the matter, for example. Contemporaneously with Hurault, Guillaume Du Vaír yearned for "une si ferme noeud de bienveillance et si estroit lien de justice (so solid a bond of goodwill and so close a judiciary link)": "Exhortation à la paix, adressée à ceux de la Ligue [1592–93]," in *Actions et traictez oratoires*, ed. René Radouant (Paris, 1911), p. 66.

[20]Thomas Hobbes, *Leviathan*, ed. C. B. Macpherson (Harmondsworth, 1968), p. 186; Jean Bodin, *Les six livres de la république [1576]*, ed. Christiane Frémont, Marie-Dominique Couzinet, and Henri Rochais, 6 vols. (Paris, 1986), 1:112–13 (I. vi).

each of the same free will and, at least until the moment they relinquish it freely and willingly, of their own complete power. For Hurault, exactly the same condition depended on an act of the king and the subject's recognition of the advantage of obedience: for the one, will would be linked to right; for the other, it was linked to duty. So Hurault transformed a call to peace directed at all combatants in the wars of religion into an affirmation of the king's sovereignty within his state. Let the king think of peace, he wrote, "for perhaps this is one of the great secrets of his state. Peace offers the advantage that subjects necessarily bring their will and assent into obedience to the Prince, otherwise there would be no peace. War and force cannot achieve this end. For true obedience relies upon free will and not force. When a king commands peoples who are voluntarily obedient, he possesses in himself alone the force of his scepter and needs no one else but himself" (*SD*, pp. 192–93).

He underscored the fact that the king would then have no need of the many kinds of officers, captains, nobles, and the rest to whom he otherwise "owed" the maintenance of his crown. He would furnish no element apt to produce the present confusion, no cause for the loss of sovereignty and the creation of chaos. On the political subject's part, will corresponded to duty, and such duty appeared as the sign of a fixed position within a social hierarchy (exactly what Basilius had transformed with respect to Dametas). Such difference in rank in no way affected the equality of subjects with regard to royal authority, provided only that sovereignty be absolute. This notion of mutual dependence and utility seems to contain something postfeudal, "protocontractual" (in the Hobbesian sense of the contract, a sense having little to do with the Huguenot contractual theory, which implied a kind of constitutive accord between two separate entities, people and prince, ratified by their mutual relation to God; although it is less clear whether neo-Thomist Catholic debate was as far from Hobbes).

For Bodin and Le Roy, l'Hôpital and Sidney, Montaigne and Hurault, it was duty that cemented this mutual relationship of utility and dependence. Speaking of the teacher's need to train a pupil to social obligation, Montaigne affirmed: "If his tutor is of my disposition, he will form his will to be a very loyal, very affectionate, and very courageous servant of his prince; but he will cool in him any desire to attach himself to that prince otherwise than by a sense of public duty" (I.xxvi.114, 154). The idea was no mere theoretical abstraction. It answered a real need for mediation between extremes, between the Huguenot party of Henri de Navarre and the Ligue, between William of Nassau and Philip II, between Protestantism and Catholicism (an opposition increasingly treated by commentators of the period as a hypocritical pretext), between the old feudal upper nobility and the new upper bourgeoisie (often ennobled), between a desire to maintain a fragmentation of centers of power—be they Protestant cities or the great old fiefs—and an ever stronger tendency toward the centralization of power and the consolidation of the state into a nation. The perfect symbol of this last tendency was to be the transformation of Henri de Navarre into Henri IV; his conversion for political reasons from Protestant to Catholic (which corresponded perfectly to Montaigne's oft-repeated idea that public duty required the suppression of "private fantasy"); his passage from the Béarn and Pau, his native city, to the Île de France and Paris, capital of the country.

The theoretical notion of duty had its active parallel in those thinkers, statesmen, highly placed functionaries, and lawyers known as *Politiques*. They acted as mediators not only between opposing parties, but between old and new conceptions of the state. The case of the man I have been quoting at such length was in many ways exemplary. Michel Hurault de l'Hôpital was grandson of the chancellor of France. Both men were well known to Montaigne. As concerns his relationship to the great chancellor (himself a friend of La Boétie long before Montaigne), we have the essayist's own testimony, as well as others'. As for the grandson, circumstances are sufficient indication. He was Henri de Navarre's chancellor. Among other tasks, he had undertaken missions to the Netherlands and Germany on Henri's behalf. His duties were such that he was obviously suspected of Calvinism, although no one could discover exactly to which church he belonged. We know that Montaigne, on missions for Henri, had to undergo similar irritations and nuisance: "I was belabored from every quarter; to the Ghibelline I was a Guelph, to the Guelph a Ghibelline" (III.xii.798, 1021). When Henri became king of France, Hurault was named governor of Guillebeuf. He died in 1592. Montaigne's relations with Henri de Navarre, his court, his diplomacy, and his political interventions are today well known (even if not in every detail), and we should not be surprised to find profound coincidences between his thought and Hurault's.

This situation is not just of anecdotal interest. At issue were discussions and struggles that led directly to the modern concept of the liberal state. In the meantime they betrayed a profound sense of anxiety and a tremulous fear that civilization was at an end. In this light we may look at the specific case considered by both Hurault and (though less explicitly) Montaigne: that of the duke of Mayenne, second son of François de Lorraine, duc de Guise, and brother of Henri de Guise. Following his brother's assassination in 1588 (on the order of Henri III), Mayenne sparked a revolt in Burgundy and Champagne, then entered Paris on February 15, 1589. In the capital he organized a local government, called the *Conseil général d'union*—the very pattern for the disintegration of sovereignty deplored by Montaigne and Hurault. During this entire period, or at least throughout the Estates of Blois in 1588, which ended with the assassination of Mayenne's brother, Montaigne was present—along with Pasquier, who mentioned the essayist in this context.[21]

---

[21]Estienne Pasquier, *Les lettres d'Estienne Pasquier . . .* , 2 vols. (Paris, 1619), 2:379: "We were, [Montaigne] and I, familiars and friends, thanks to a meeting of minds and a common culture. We were together in the city of Blois at the time of that famous

To show these personal connections is important, for one may describe all these personages—Pasquier, Hurault, Montaigne, Le Roy, l'Hôpital, even Sidney and Greville, and perhaps even Henri IV himself—in the words Max Horkheimer has used of Bodin: "The tendency to remain neutral in religious questions, and to subordinate religion to reasons of state, the recourse to a strong state which would be the guarantor of the security of commerce and exchange, corresponds to the conditions of existence of the *parvenue* bourgeoisie and its alliance with absolute monarchy."[22] Their first puzzle, also, was how to establish stability and certitude. When Le Roy spoke of sedition, of the dispersal of sovereignty and the confusion of language, he cited at length the passage from Thucydides in which the historian commented on the false use of language as both symptom and cause of the civil wars. For Le Roy, the sovereignty of the principal subject, the king himself, was on the one hand set against the disintegration of sovereignty among the nobles and in the city councils, but it was also opposed on the other to the uncertainty of a language that false usage was destroying—along with the social fabric.

For all these people, the idea of a union between language and the social realm was an a priori. Le Roy's own work enjoyed international renown. Already in the 1580s the Englishman Gabriel Harvey wrote that it would be difficult to find a scholar who had not open on his desk "Le Roy on Aristotle or the *Six Books* of Bodin."[23] In fact, they had merely made familiar an old commonplace. They quoted not only Thucydides, but Plato, Aristotle, and Xenophon. Just a year before the 1588 edition of the *Essays*, in which Montaigne first referred to these clichés, there appeared the *Discours politiques et militaires* of François de La Noüe, a more redoutable personage, it may be, than almost all those so far mentioned:

The wise historian Thucydides describes summarily how the Greeks governed themselves during civil discord. . . . As soon as an insolent remark was made somewhere, he says, everyone else found the nerve to say something worse, either in order to do something new or to show that they were more assiduous than the others, or more insolent and eager to avenge themselves: and all the evils which they committed they disguised with praiseworthy titles, calling temerity magnanimity; modesty pusillanimity; precipitate indignation virility and boldness; consultation and prudent deliberation pale tergiversation. In this way, whoever showed himself always furious was reputed a loyal friend; and whoever contradicted him was held suspect. . . . Today I ask if in similar actions we have not equaled the Greeks.[24]

---

assembly of the Three Estates in 1588, whose end brought about so many of France's misfortunes."

[22]Max Horkheimer, "Montaigne et la fonction du scepticisme," in *Théorie critique: Essais* (Paris, 1978), p. 276.

[23]Skinner, *Foundations*, 2:300.

[24]François de La Noüe, *Discours politiques et militaires* . . . (Basel, 1587), pp. 55–56.

La Nouë was a considerable figure. He was a famous soldier (known as "Iron Arm" [*Bras de fer*]) and one of the chief lieutenants of Gaspard de Coligny, himself murdered during the Saint Bartholomew slaughter. Although La Nouë was thus one of the Huguenot leaders, he nonetheless deserves a place alongside the other "mediators." It was to him that Charles IX turned to attempt a reconciliation after the massacre. Like Montaigne or Hurault, he was perceived at least potentially as a mediator, as a participant in the launching of a different kind of future. And like them he understood the confusion of language, of social relations, and of political life as one and the same problem.

The same could be said of the duc d'Anjou (Henri III's brother, fourth son of Henri II), who, complaining of foreign (i.e., Italian) influence at court, allied himself with the Protestant forces at Dreux on September 15, 1575. Not much later, and though only under enormous pressure of circumstance, William the Silent maneuvered to have him accepted as governor of the United Provinces (only his death from sickness put an end to that). Anjou (Alençon) could thus also be presented as such a mediator, one to whom the rabid Calvinist Innocent Gentillet could address his "Souhait pour la France" at the end of his *Anti-Machiavel* of 1576: "That he will extinguish the fires of our civil wars in the countryside and the cities: And like a French Hercules cut off the heads of this monster who still today shows itself sworn enemy to our laws."[25] A few years earlier, in his *Arraisonnement* of 1569, François de Belleforest had called these confusions "the tortuous hydra of rebellions."[26]

In his text of 1593, Hurault applied this same metaphor very precisely to the Ligue: "It is thus that we must consider generally the Party of the Ligue today, this monster having been formed of many members which, for having been ill-proportioned from the outset, have rendered it so terrifying that it is no wonder if it has been seen to have several heads, like a serpent engendered out of the earth's putrescence" (*SD*, p. 153). "I sent your grace," said the archbishop in Shakespeare's *2 Henry IV:*

> The parcels and particulars of our grief,
> The which hath been with scorn shoved from the court,
> Whereon this Hydra son of war is born,

[25]Innocent Gentillet, *Anti-Machiavel*, ed. C. Edward Rathé (Geneva, 1968), p. 635. (The poem is left out of d'Andrea and Stewart's otherwise preferable modern edition.) I may add that both La Nouë and Bodin (a *Politique* leader) belonged to Anjou's household. So, too, did Louis de Bueil, sieur de Racan, father of the recipient of Malherbe's derisive remark about poetry's uselessness. Like Bodin, but as a representative of the second not third estate, Racan had been an outspoken defender of the *Politique* view at the December 1576 meetings of the Estates. He was then chamberlain of Anjou's bedchamber: Holt, *Duke of Anjou*, pp. 80, 85–86 n. 65. On Anjou, see also Yates, *Valois Tapestries*.

[26]François de Belleforest, *Arraisonnement fort gentil et proffitable sur l'infelicite qui suyt ordinairement le bonheur des grans ...* (Paris, 1569), f. 68ro (misnumbered; in reality, f. 60ro).

> Whose dangerous eyes may well be charmed asleep
> With grant of our most just and right desires,
> And true obedience, of this madness cured,
> Stoop tamely to the foot of majesty.
>
> (IV.11 [c. 1597–98])

And we may recall that the archbishop's commentary (concerned with a rebellion, although of course he pretended otherwise) preceded a whole series of deceptions, traps, and even two apparent betrayals: that of John of Lancaster toward the rebels and that of Hal toward Falstaff and then his father, Henry IV, when he "removes" his crown.

The metaphor was thus applied, like Thucydides' argument, at once to the disintegration of the political sphere and the collapse of the linguistic order. Pasquier used it to describe a situation of most particular interest to us, because it concerned the actual case of the Guises: again it linked Montaigne and himself, Guise and Mayenne, the real situation in France and the metaphor about language and state. In a letter written to "Monsieur Airault Lieutenant Criminel d'Angers," Pasquier spoke of the assassination of the duc de Guise and of his brother the cardinal during the meeting of the States-General at Blois. This was how he explained the situation:

> You should know that the King was enraged by several matters which occurred to his disadvantage during our assembly, and which he thought were only due to the direction of these two Princes. He felt that the more flexible he showed himself toward our members, the more intractable they became toward him (such that it was truly a Hydra, one of whose heads cut off gave birth to seven others; so much so that three or four days before Monsieur de Guise had quarreled with him both about his status as Lieutenant General and about the town of Orleans [which was *ligueur*]). He thus decided [*il se delibere*] to have the two Princes done to death, considering that their death would also be that of all these new councils.[27]

The comparison here is of considerable significance, not simply because of the complexity of the elements mentioned before and which it brought together, but because it linked in detail the birth of political factionalism with the birth of too many words (*nouueaux Conseils, une dispute, il se delibere,* and so forth): not to mention that the estates of November and December 1588 were themselves a matter of debates and endless discussions. The use of the hydra metaphor thus coincided with the use made everywhere of the passage from Thucydides: subject, sovereignty, power, language, right, law, war, and peace were all so many concepts concealed within these various texts. But they were immediately tied to real activity in the world . . . by actors of major importance.

Robert Garnier, who eventually became *lieutenant criminel* of the

---

[27]Pasquier, *Lettres,* 2:21. The assassinations occurred on December 23–24, 1588.

Maine and made the egregious error of siding very late with the Ligue, was long before thought of as the major tragedian in France, one whom we can well consider the dramatist of the civil wars: six of his seven tragedies dealt specifically with civil war, the seventh was *Hippolyte*, the exemplary tragedy of family strife. In the first of these plays, *Porcie* (1568), Garnier used the same metaphor to refer to a political problem of just the kind treated by Hurault: one sovereign killed and replaced by three, they replaced by others, and all accompanied by their warring factions: "For it is a real Hydra proliferating in heads, / The more one cuts off, the more they reproduce." And Porcie adds: "We would need a Hercules, to be able to kill it, / Even supposing a Hercules' strength could suffice." Later in the same play Marc-Antoine would call himself just such a Hercules,[28] and not only did he boast of being about to carry war all through Asia (shades of Rabelais, foretaste of *Tamburlaine*), but his audience knew, of course, that he was the very embodiment of continuing civil war (Garnier was to publish a *Marc-Antoine* in 1578).

Tragedy throughout this period was the most self-conscious of genres, emphatic in its reference to Antiquity, in its educational role, in its creation of a new vernacular, in its religious and political commentary. Ostensibly about particular actions, the tragedies of George Buchanan and others were much more frequently about the incapacity of language to grasp, utter, or even enable such action. A play such as the anonymous *Tragédie du sac de Cabrières*, probably written between 1566 and 1568, was as much about the power and misuse of language as it was about the Catholic massacre of its title.[29] Gillian Jondorf and Margaret McGowan have shown the political allusions constant in this theater.[30] One may add that *Porcie* was a tragedy wholly "about" disorder, its results, its unceasingness. It was thus to be expected that the philosopher Arée, companion to Octave, should call for the destruction of contemporary humanity and the creation of a new people from Chaos. The gods, he cries, must "Destroy in anger this vicious world, / So as to engender anew another kind of humans / A hundred times better and more complete than we are."[31]

---

[28]Robert Garnier, *Porcie, tragédie*, in *Oeuvres complètes (Théâtre et poésies)*, ed. Lucien Pinvert, 2 vols. (Paris, 1923), 1:37, 55 (Acts II and III).

[29]On this, see Timothy J. Reiss, *Tragedy and Truth: Studies in the Development of a Renaissance and Neoclassical Discourse* (New Haven and London, 1980), esp. pp. 40–161; and "The Origin and Development of French Tragedy," in *A New History of French Literature*, ed. Denis Hollier (Cambridge, Mass., and London, 1989), pp. 205–9. For the play mentioned here: *La tragédie du sac de Cabrières*, ed. Fernand Benoît and J. Vianey (Marseille, 1927).

[30]Gillian Jondorf, *Robert Garnier and the Themes of Political Tragedy in the Sixteenth Century* (Cambridge, 1969); Margaret McGowan, "The Presence of Rome in Some Plays of Robert Garnier," in *Myth and Its Making in the French Theatre: Studies Presented to W. D. Howarth*, ed. E. Freeman, H. Mason, M. O'Regan, S. W. Taylor (Cambridge, 1988), pp. 12–29. Both reflect on these allusions as distant commentary rather than as "participation."

[31]Garnier, *Porcie*, 1:43 (Act II).

To be sure, Arée set this rebirth into a mixture of models: those of the metallic ages of pagan mythology as well as of the millennial urges of Christian eschatology. Yet the fact remained that when (and if) an end could be put simultaneously to the disturbance of state and the failure of language, when a tool could be found to solve both, then a new form of rationality, a new class of discourse or realm of meaning would indeed have been consolidated. If it is the case that humanity creates itself in its history, then indeed a new humanity might be implied: one characterized by such notions of will, intention, subjectivity, possession, and the rest as did not earlier exist. The modern meaning of literature could be born with them.

In Montaigne's eyes one could not separate language from reason, and both shared in the inconstancy proper to all things human: "'We reason rashly and inconsiderately,' says Timaeus in Plato, 'because, like ourselves, our reason has in it a very large element of chance'" (I.xlvii.209, 276). Montaigne said in fact that human reason, "ridiculous" and "risible" as it is, cannot guarantee the very language on which the sociopolitical order nevertheless depends. Sidney had said nothing else about the state of Euarchus's Macedonia. But neither could language guarantee reason, for language, too, takes part in this constant movement. Only the *law* (itself, however, prey to manifold interpretations) could hope to resist: "The commonwealths that kept themselves regulated and well governed, like the Cretan and the Lacedaemonian, made little account of orators" (I.li.222, 292). The debate over arms and letters, over political authority and polite learning, which was a principal theme of *Don Quijote*, related still to this same set of issues. And those Spanish readers who a little later criticized Góngora on the grounds that he was making a chaos of language had in mind, among other matters, the same grounding of political stability (which was not foreign to Malherbe's reform of poetic language at the French court).

In opposition to the law, speech (the use made of language) might "manipulate and agitate a crowd and a disorderly populace"; it could persuade "the herd" and "the ignorant" in a state where "things were in perpetual turmoil." In such a case, speech *could* offer itself as "a medicine," albeit a very dangerous one. For it appealed precisely to the constant oscillation of the private being and not to the loyalty and obedience of the public one. Either it sparked anarchy (Mayenne in Paris, for example) or it was of use only where anarchy already reigned, for instance in the Rome of the civil wars, "when all affairs were in the worst state and agitated by the storm of civil wars" (I.li.222, 293). So we return to the commonplace of Thucydides. Thus Montaigne affirmed that the best way to obstruct these pernicious developments was to secure the power of one man: "It is easier to safeguard him, by good education and advice, from the effects of that poison" (ibid.). This power "of a monarch" could in turn guarantee the "good government" of the state.

Nonetheless, the conditional remained the operative term here. For in actuality—that very actuality to which all referred, helplessly—this power seemed everywhere to have failed. During these years another of Sidney's acquaintance (and of all the others), the scholar-printer Henri Estienne, had been giving much thought to just these issues and their intermingling.[32] In 1562 he was writing that if words lost their meanings, however conventionally established, the whole processes of language and learning became nonsense, degenerating into madness: "Similar absurdity (indeed, even more) is found in certain other locutions, which nonetheless please many, and for no other reason than that they are spoken against all reason. And it is the case that if this idiotic (indeed, insane) desire for novelty continues to gain ground, overturning everything wherever it goes, I fear that in the end we will have to call head foot and foot head. Especially will this be so once such a desire has entered the heads of ignorant people, be they courtiers or others."[33]

Estienne linked this unreason directly to political conditions, asserting that bringing Machiavellian political practices into France had crucially sapped linguistic and therefore conceptual certainties.[34] Not by chance did he assign blame in the matter to those who frequented the Medici-controlled court (foreshadowing the later defiant secession of a central member of that court, the duc d'Anjou). A century later a successor court to that one was to be extolled as the source of all order and the most excellent use of language. In 1562 Estienne's upside-down world of "fantaisie," where people functioned "sottement," "à tort et à travers," where indeed the "fou" had taken over language (to use but a few of the terms employed elsewhere in the preface to his *Conformité*), corresponded precisely to the fear of political and social dissolution. In his 1566 *Apologie pour Hérodote*, he satirized much of this even more thoroughly.

In the *Conformité*, Estienne had been very clear about the sources of linguistic perfection. It consisted, first, in the proper ordering of the system within itself. In this aspect it was more than merely analogous with arithmetic or any other mathematical order: a matter of the internal coherence of a logical process. Second, perfection consisted in the quan-

---

[32]According to Buxton, Sidney met Estienne in Heidelberg in 1573, when all of them—Languet, Estienne, the printer Andreas Wechel—had fled Paris after the massacre of August 1572. Sidney apparently went on to Vienna in the company of Languet and Estienne: *Sir Philip Sidney*, p. 56.

[33]Henri Estienne, *Conformité du langage françois avec le grec [1562]*, ed. Léon Feugère (Paris, 1853), p. 27.

[34]Henri Estienne, *Apologie pour Hérodote, ou traité de la conformité des merveilles anciennes avec les modernes [1566]*, ed. P. Ristelhuber, 2 vols. (Paris, 1879); *Deux dialogues du nouveau langage françois italianizé et autrement desguizé, principalement entre les courtisans de ce temps [1578]*, ed. P. Ristelhuber, 2 vols. (Paris, 1885); *Discours merveilleux de la vie, actions & deportemens de Catherine de Medicis royne mere. Auquel sont recitez les moyens qu'elle a tenu pour vsurper le gouuernement du royaume de France, & ruiner lestat d'iceluy* (Geneva, 1575). This last text was probably written with Gentillet.

tity of clearly and separately defined words available in a language for naming things: its ability adequately to correspond to that to which it referred.[35] With the use of such a language, Estienne could write in the much later *Précellence* (1579), humans had the great advantage "above all other animals" of "expressing their conceptions to one another by means of language."[36] For Estienne, this claim was also political, put forward after his savage attack on Catherine de Medicis (1575, if it *was* his: only three years after the Saint Bartholomew's massacre) and after his scathing satire on the distortion of the French language (*Deux dialogues*).

The hope expressed was also, however, entirely forlorn. Only much later would political and social order come together with a linguistic and rational one to forge the new culture sought by Garnier's Arée: at least potentially bringing Astraea peacefully back to earth. For the present there seemed no way at all out of what Pasquier called somewhere in his *Recherches de la France*, "the chaos of our troubles," "the pêle-mêle chaos of all things." Much more typical, too, than Estienne's hope was Montaigne's remark: "In this confusion that we have been in for thirty years every Frenchman, whether as an individual or as a member of the community, sees himself at every moment on the verge of the total overthrow of his fortune" (III.xii.800, 1022–23). "Let us turn our eyes in all directions," he wrote elsewhere, "everything is crumbling about us; in all the great states that we know, whether in Christendom or elsewhere, take a look: you will find an evident threat of change and ruin" (III.ix.734, 938). And one of their contemporaries did so, giving an entire volume to the matter: *De la vicissitude ou variété des choses en l'univers* (1575).

Le Roy began this volume as an encomium of present-day achievements, in so many ways equal to those of the greatest cultures of other times and places. But little by little, signs of catastrophe increase, until by the tenth Book he found himself lamenting that no misfortune or vice was absent from his era, and we read a kind of paean to disaster:

> Everywhere commonwealths have been afflicted, transformed or ruined, everywhere religions troubled with heresies. Not only the whole of Europe, but the uttermost regions of Asia and Africa, the inhabitants of new-found countries and of the East and West Indies, innumerable in their multitude and scattered through infinite spaces, all have suffered long-drawn-out foreign and civil wars. From this has come everything's exces-

[35]Estienne, *Conformité*, pp. 19–25. By the mid-1570s feelings against Italians were more than just vehement. Henri III's chancellor, René de Birague, and such principal advisers as Albert de Gondi, comte de Retz, and Louis de Gonzaga, duc de Nevers, as well as major bankers supporting the court, were all accused of primary responsibility in the wars (quite apart from Catherine herself): Holt, *Duke of Anjou*, pp. 49–50. That the members of the house of Lorraine were also considered foreigners merely exacerbated the issue.

[36]Henri Estienne, *La précellence du langage françois [1579]*, ed. Edmond Huguet, pref. L. Petit de Julleville (Paris, 1896), p. 10.

sive price, with famines and frequent plagues. We must believe that God in his anger against mortals has sent these general and particular calamities to correct our vices, and to bring us to His greater knowledge and reverence. For there has never been greater malice in the world, more impiety, more betrayal. Devotion has been extinguished, simplicity and innocence scorned, there remains but a mere shadow of Justice. Everything is topsy-turvy, confused, nothing follows its allotted path.[37]

It was certainly not surprising that Le Roy devoted his eleventh Book to a comparative history of warfare and weaponry, leaving but few pages for the arts of peace. His conclusion was veritably an announcement of the millennium:

Already I foresee in my mind several nations bursting over Europe, alien in their form, color, customs, language, religion: they will burn our libraries and destroy everything beautiful they find in the countries they occupy: so as to abolish honor and virtue. I foresee ubiquitous civil and foreign war: factions and heresies will grow to blaspheme everything divine and human; famine and plague will threaten all mortals; the order of nature, the rule of the celestial motions, the equilibrium of the elements, all will collapse, bringing flood on the one hand, excessive heat on the other, and most violent earthquakes. The universe will near its end through one or other of these disorders, carrying with it the confusion of all things, and will reduce them to their original chaos.[38]

We have seen that Le Roy was by no means alone. In the very last years of the century Spenser, for example, was producing the last few fragments of his *Faerie Queene*, those we know as the "Mutabilitie Cantos." In the first of these, we read of Diana chased out of the pastoral world, like Astraea before her, and chased by a male Faunus who, unlike the Actaeon of myth, would not be punished for it.[39] In the second Canto, Mutabilitie would then seek to take over absolute rule of the world: to be denied only by the goddess Nature herself, announcing that "time shall come that all shall changed bee, / And from thenceforth, none no more change shall see."

[37]Louis Le Roy, *De la vicissitude ou variété des choses en l'univers . . .* , ed. Philippe Desan (Paris, 1988), p. 381.
[38]Ibid., pp. 426–27. The most influential discussion of general decay in human achievement was already half a century old: Juan Luis Vives' *De disciplinis*, studying in turn decay of arts, sciences, and moral philosophy, although his purpose was to show how such decay could be overcome. Renaissance pessimism and optimism seem coeval (see Chapter 1, note 15). In 1581 it culminated in the most celebrated skeptical tract of the time: Francisco Sanches's *Quod Nihil Scitur*. I have seen only the 1618 second edition, which includes a *De litteris pereuntibus libellus* of "Maturini Simonii ivrisconsulti," discussing the forms and causes of the decay of "letters" (in the wide sense of Polydore Vergil and Mylaeus) in cycles from the ancient Greeks down (see the Bibliography, Part 1, under Sanches and Simonius for full references).
[39]Berry has pointed this out in *Of Chastity and Power*, p. 164.

Still, this would be no golden age renewed on earth. The time in question was a sacred time altogether out of the social and political. It was Judgment Day itself: "Thence-forth all shall rest eternally / With Him that is the God of Sabbaoth hight: / O that great Sabbaoth God, graunt me that Sabbaoths sight."[40] This was no solution, but ultimate despair.

In 1584 Lipsius brought Le Roy's past and Spenser's future generalizations together with Hurault's more precise anxiety. Although his purpose here was not politically theoretical, he observed Hurault's very issue. "We Flemmings," he wrote, "are shaken to and fro with wars not onely forrein, but ciuill: And not such onely, but intestine dissentions euen within our own bowels. For there be not onelie parties among vs, but new parties of these same parties." And such schisms were exacerbated by "pestilence, tributes, rapines, slaughters: Also the vttermost extremitie of tyranny; And oppressions not of bodies onely, but also of mindes." Nor could one, he added, find anything very different elsewhere in Europe.[41] Since it was "a naturall propertie to all things created to fall into mutabilitie and alteration," this was no surprise. All human affairs, he added, echoing Le Roy, "thorough this conduit of wastings and calamities slyde to the marke of their desolation. Death and destruction is this mark: And the means to come thither are plague, wars and slaughters." Europe, "like a diseased bodie," seemed to feel "her great confusion nigh at hande." Indeed, the world as a whole had now "come to his dotage."[42] Charles Langius, Lipsius's antagonist in the *De constantia*, might well be angered by these complaints, but his reply that Europe and Flanders were not special cases and that things had been far worse elsewhere and in other times was hardly an inspiration to optimism.[43]

As in France, England, and the Netherlands, so in Spain political writers deplored "dissolving social bonds" as they "denounced the evils of the epoch."[44] Such laments characterized those writers of the first decades of the seventeenth century called *arbitristas*, many of them political and legal counselors as well as would-be economic pundits. In 1600 Martín González de Cellorigo accused his compatriots of wanting "to turn our country into a nation of enchanted people who live outside the natural order."[45] "Never," wrote Luis Valle de la Cerda in the same year, "has Spain as a whole been as ruined and as poor as it is now." Twenty-five years later

[40]Spenser, *Faerie Queene*, in *Poetical Works*, p. 407: Bk. VII, Canto vii, st. 59, and Canto viii, st. 2.
[41]Lipsius, *Two Bookes of Constancie*, p. 182 (II.xx).
[42]Ibid., pp. 106–7 (I.xv), 110 (I.xvi).
[43]Ibid., pp. 184–94 (II.xxi–xxiv).
[44]José Antonio Maravall, "From the Renaissance to the Baroque: The Diphasic Schema of a Social Crisis," trans. Terry Cochran, in *Literature among Discourses: The Spanish Golden Age*, ed. Wlad Godzich and Nicholas Spadaccini (Minneapolis, 1986), p. 22; see also his *Culture of the Baroque: Analysis of a Historical Structure*, trans. Terry Cochran (Minneapolis, 1986), pp. 25–53, 149–61.
[45]Quoted in Jean Canavaggio, *Cervantes*, trans. J. R. Jones (New York and London, 1990), p. 218.

the count of Gondomar wrote to Olivares that the ship of Spain was sinking: "Se va todo a fondo."[46] Such *arbitristas* as Cellorigo, Sancho de Moncada, and Fernández Navarrete justify Elliott's remark that early seventeenth-century Spain was "not only a time of crisis, but a time also of the awareness of crisis—of a bitter realization that things had gone wrong." Castile, he adds, "surrendered itself to an orgy of introspection."[47] The immediate causes were similar to those Lipsius perceived in the Low Countries: plague (notably in Castile in 1599–1600), the very rich bleeding the very poor, falling population, now exacerbated again by the expulsion of the Moriscos between 1609 and 1614 (a catastrophic decision repeating the 1492 expulsion of the Jews, and to be echoed by the French with respect to the Protestants in 1685).[48]

Spain was, we have amply seen, by no means alone. Fear and trembling, that is to say, were not at all limited to any one locality, however such localities might vary in detail and in time. In his "Proem" to "Of the Interpretation of Nature" (c. 1603), Francis Bacon answered Le Roy by saying that although he did not "apprehend any more barbarian invasions," he did expect "civil wars," which would be most widespread and would "portend for literature and the sciences a tempest not less fatal" than such invasions.[49] With so partial a response, the future chancellor echoed the general expression of anxious dismay. The vision of catastrophe was ubiquitous. It was as though all control and understanding had lost its footing. Above all, for the welfare of that holy idea of society we saw expressed in Le Roy or l'Hôpital, and which was shared alike by Sidney, Greville, and Spenser (or by Cervantes and Góngora, for that matter) the schism of the church, the loss of Rome as both secular and sacred center, had been disastrous.

By 1575 one cannot help but gather the impression from Le Roy that his appeal to an avenging God was extraneous to the reality in which he lived. A point of no return in the relations of political life and religious sentiment had been passed, one also marked by the catastrophic failure of Henri III's penitential Catholicism. The church that had borne as much if not more of the burden than secular authority for keeping society together

---

[46]Both citations are from John H. Elliott, "Self-Perception and Decline in Early Seventeenth-Century Spain," *Past and Present*, 74 (1977), 53, 41. Jean Vilar has written extensively on the *arbitristas* and is (was?) preparing a book on them. In book form only his important work on their literary satirizing has appeared to date: *Literatura y economía: La figura satírica del arbitrista en el Siglo de Oro*, trans. Francisco Bustelo G.ª del Real (Madrid, 1973).

[47]John H. Elliott, *Imperial Spain, 1469–1716* (1963; rpt. Harmondsworth, 1970), p. 300.

[48]On this, see John H. Elliott, "The Decline of Spain," *Past and Present*, 20 (1961), 52–75; his chapter entitled "The Spanish Peninsula, 1598–1648," in vol. 4 of *The New Cambridge Modern History* (1970); and his recent works on Olivares.

[49]Francis Bacon, Lord Verulam, "Proem" to "Of the Interpretation of Nature," in *The Works*, ed. James Spedding, Robert Leslie Ellis, and Douglas Denon Heath, 14 vols. (London, 1857–74), 10:86; for Latin original, see 3:519.

was no longer whole. One consequence was its own "secularization." The "Machiavellian" argument that religion should be thought of as a kind of social glue was by the end of the sixteenth century a political commonplace: small wonder that religious and political issues were inseparable in the French and Spanish wars, in the 1618 execution of Jan van Oldenbarneveldt in the Netherlands, in the Thirty Years' War, and still in the English Revolution of the 1640s.

The very fact of those wars was clear evidence that age and alteration of the social material, violent changes in economic organization and commercial exploitation, the vicissitudes of time, temper, and place, as Le Roy had put it, were weakening the glue. Post-Reformation societies had lost an age-old control of their populations and, as Christopher Hill has put it for England: "The Tudor poor law, the Protestant emphasis on the wickedness of the mass of mankind and the Hobbist war of every man against every man, all seemed to make sense in this society. So too did the Puritan stress on discipline and hard work for the good of the commonwealth, which saw England through the economic crisis of the sixteenth and seventeenth centuries, performing a social role similar to that of Marxist theories in the Soviet Union and China in our own day."[50]

Furthermore, the division of the Catholic church was not simply in two. It was a real splintering. The attempt to urge a single reformed (Calvinist) faith at the 1571 Synod of Emden had been momentarily successful. But when Maurice of Nassau called the Synod of Dort in 1618, it was rather to gain political victory over Oldenbarneveldt and Grotius, however that aim may have been concealed under the religious dispute between Arminians and Gomarists, the liberal backers of the Advocate and his aide against the fanatically intolerant Gomarists (counter-Remonstrants) used by the prince. The young Joost van den Vondel's scathingly satirical tragedy, *Palamedes oft vermoorde onnozelheid* (Palamedes or Murdered Innocence) underscored the political nature of these events. In the Palatinate, political and religious ambition led to the outbreak of what would be known as the Thirty Years' War. The failure of the two most important Protestant powers, the United Provinces and England, to come to Frederick's aid (the latter despite his being James I's son-in-law) only emphasized the general collapse. James himself turned to marriage negotiations with Spain; no more productively. In France, Richelieu was soon to busy himself wiping out Protestant strongholds. When the Habsburgs were finally "checked in Germany," as Hill again put it, "it was by Lutheran Sweden and Catholic France."[51]

[50]Christopher Hill, "The Protestant Nation," in *Collected Essays*, 3 vols. (Amherst, Mass., 1985–86), 2:22.
[51]Ibid., p. 32. On James I's ambivalence, see especially Frances A. Yates, *The Rosicrucian Enlightenment* (1972; rpt. St. Albans, 1975), passim; Geoffrey Parker, *The Thirty Years' War* (1984; rpt. London, 1987), pp. 59–60, 63–69; and especially Anton Gindely, *Geschichte des dreissigjährigen Krieges*, 4 vols. (Prague, 1869–80), 3:42–74.

No clearer sign could be had that religion was now in the service of state power and that it could no longer provide any monolithic comprehension of human existence or singular guide to human action: hence perhaps the nostalgic yearnings of La Boétie and Le Roy, of Sidney and Greville, of Spenser and the last Valois king of France. Rome—Virgil's, Barbarossa's, or Leo X's—was done. In 1617 Cervantes brought his much-belabored lovers, Persiles and Sigismunda, through prison, disguise, sexual mix-up, treachery and war, shipwreck and hunger, not to mention divers other desultory violences, to be finally married in Rome: capital of the Western world, as once was, and thus a purported bulwark against the various barbarities they have undergone. Yet this was now a Rome accurately characterized as "a morally corrupt world of sophisticated violence." Wealth and appearance "se cubren muchas faltas" (conceal many sins): even at the very center, the sword was out, black sorcery was familiar enough to be unremarkable, betrayal, bribery, vehement jealousy, and sexual pursuit were but a few among customary vices. Such was the view, even from Spain, eldest child of the church.[52]

In the meantime, as religious motivation and sentiment faded, the "practical" response lacked any secular justification beyond that of the merest survival or of greed, of a melancholic or cynical mockery:

> I hear new news every day, and those ordinary rumours of war, plagues, fires, inundations, thefts, murders, massacres, meteors, comets, spectrums, prodigies, apparitions, of towns taken, cities beseiged in France, Germany, Turkey, Persia, Poland, &c., daily musters and preparations, and such like, which these tempestuous times afford, battles fought, so many men slain, monomachies, shipwrecks, piracies, and sea-fights, peaces, leagues, stratagems, and fresh alarums. A vast confusion of vows, wishes, actions, edicts, petitions, lawsuits, pleas, laws, proclamations, complaints, grievances are daily brought to our ears. New books every day, pamphlets, currantoes, stories, whole catalogues of volumes of all sorts, new paradoxes, opinions, schisms, heresies, controversies in philosophy, religion, &c.[53]

So Robert Burton, writing as late as 1636.

In Bohemia during these same years, Johann Amos Komensky (Comenius) published *The Labyrinth of the World* (1631, but written in 1623) a reversed utopia, as Frances Yates puts it, "where everything is wrong. All

---

[52]Diana De Armas Wilson, "Cervantes's *Labors of Persiles:* 'Working (in) the In-Between,'" in *Literary Theory/Renaissance Texts,* ed. Patricia Parker and David Quint (Baltimore and London, 1986), p. 155; Cervantes, *Trabajos de Persiles y Sigismunda,* p. 281; *Trials of Persiles and Sigismunda,* p. 324: IV. vii. Although it appeared too late for me to use it here, see also Wilson, *Allegories of Love: Cervantes's "Persiles and Sigismunda"* (Princeton, 1991).

[53] Robert Burton, *The Anatomy of Melancholy,* intro. Holbrook Jackson, 3 vols. (1932; rpt. London and New York, 1968), 1:18.

the sciences of man lead to nothing, all his occupations are futile, all his knowledge is unsound." The domestic sphere was sour and violent; workers mistook their labors and fought constantly; professors battled over cobwebs and nonsense; religious sects propounded their rival fanaticisms; government was in chaos, concealing its true character behind a principle of *"ratio status,"* with which it protected itself "as with a shield against the thrusts of vulgar gossip"; military protection was in utter disarray. There was small wonder, but deep terror, in the stockpiling of so many weapons "that even many thousands of wagons would not suffice to remove the accumulation. There were all kinds of terrible weapons for piercing, hacking, slashing, stabbing, felling, chopping, severing, tearing, burning and, in a word, killing." These were but the symbols of ubiquitous horror and emptiness. "Oh, my sorrow!" exclaimed the narrator finally. "Shall I ever find satisfaction in this miserable world? For all things are full of futility and misery." Ultimately, the narrator was to turn away from worldly things toward a mysticism situating the divine within the individual heart. Concern for the polis was thus replaced by inner contemplation.[54]

In Spain the sense of catastrophe would predominate for many years. In 1651 Gracián was still describing a world of total disaster that might almost have been based on Comenius's: the rich got richer and the poor nothing, authority was in the hands of the unworthy and politics had fallen into "a chaos of *la razón de estado,"* wild beasts roamed the cities and whatever was decent of humanity had fled to the mountains, the sexes were inverted, the ignorant ruled and thought to teach the wise, justice was bought and sold, gold was anything that glittered, vows and promises meant the opposite of what they said, and words were belied by the deeds that followed. Reason yielded to bestial passion, wise order to willfully ignorant disorder. Truth, fidelity, loyalty, and merit were replaced by falsehood and cruelty, betrayal and ubiquitous evil (shades of old Thucydides!). "It seems to me," exclaimed Andrenio, one of the principal interlocutors of *El criticón,* "que está trabucado y que el tiempo anda al revés. Pregunto, señores, ¿es día o es noche?" Indeed, replied the wise Quirón, taking up the very words, all was indeed upside down and backward; men had made day night and night day.[55]

Just a few years earlier (1621) John Barclay had published his *Argenis,* like so many of these texts a mix of arcadia, utopia, and historical commentary. It upheld, but in the face of always imminent savagery, the hope

[54]Yates, *Rosicrucian Enlightenment,* p. 203; John Amos Comenius, *The Labyrinth of the World and the Paradise of the Heart,* trans. Matthew Spinka (Chicago, 1942), pp. 115, 83, 102. Comenius's own mysticism did not lead to a withdrawal from the world. He became the principal educational reformer of the European seventeenth century.

[55]Baltasar Gracián y Morales, *El criticón,* ed. P. Ismael Quiles (1943; rpt. Madrid, 1980), pp. 49–59. The book appeared in three parts, in 1651, 1653, and 1657.

of monarchy founded on some kind of social pact à la Hurault. Here, too, the very status of the literary text recounting such a pact remained a fundamentally perplexing issue. So, wrote Barclay, *Argenis* was not just idle fiction, but dealt as well with serious matters—although it was not history either. A reader, he hesitatingly wrote, "shall not erre, as well, that will haue it all to be a true relation of things really done, as he that takes it to be wholly fained."[56] Such an irony had, of course, been a structural principle of the second part of *Don Quijote,* as it was also, for example, of *El criticón.*

The reasons were many for stressing the ambivalence of writing, not least among them a tense relation to political authority: *that,* especially when such authority was itself only too unsure (as was the case in the 1620s), not so much of its legitimacy as of its policies. These tensions and uneasiness were of a piece with the more diffuse anxieties reflected in writing's ambivalence. They signaled a sense of collapse and uncertainty which was everywhere in the writing of the time. From Le Roy's vicissitude to Lipsius's mutability, from Montaigne's "perennial movement" and constant instability to Cervantes's deeply sympathetic irony, from Góngora's bitter fireworks to Burton's melancholy, from Sidney's nostalgia to *Andronicus's* flinty cynicism, from Comenius's despairing mysticism to Gracián's hopeless inversions, in one way or another everywhere was echoed the urgent debate about thought and method, originality and authority, political and personal "subject," social order and sovereignty, criticism and knowledge, history and fiction. Only about ten years before *Argenis* a fortunate London audience had watched a haunting response to all this: no resolution, to be sure, and something hesitant—the more particularly because it was held to take place "ten leagues beyond man's life" (II.i.251).

The tumultuous opening of *The Tempest* is familiar. Natural order upturned, water and earth scarcely distinguishable from one another, all elements jumbled: "The sky, it seems, would pour down striking pitch / But that the sea, mounting to th' welkin's check, / Dashes the fire out" (I.ii.3–5). As with the natural, so the human order has lost its balance: "What care these roarers for the name of king?" (I.i.16–17). Small wonder the play's opening scene closed with Gonzalo's plea for order: "Now would I give a thousand furlongs of sea for an acre of barren ground." The scene was the play—and perhaps the age—in a nutshell. The disorder in which Alonso, Sebastian, and the rest found themselves was the very image of the disorder Antonio had introduced into the state by his usurpation: a betrayal whose implications would be continued in his and Sebastian's plotting against Alonso and in the bitter burlesque of Caliban's revolt

[56]John Barclay, *His Argenis,* translated out of Latine into English . . . , with a Clauio annexed . . . , trans. Sir Robert Le Grys (London, 1628), pp. 131–32. Cf. Jean Jehasse, *Guez de Balzac et le génie romain, 1597–1654* (Saint-Etienne, 1977), pp. 35–40.

against Prospero, abetted by the drunken sailors. Only Prospero, Miranda, and soon the audience knew that Gonzalo's plea had already been answered. For the storm arranged by Prospero's ministers presaged the beginning of a return to order.

The "return" was not, of course, a return. Prospero would relinquish the arts studied in Milan and practiced on the island. He would have to think on government and death. Long before the island plot, he had seen the need for a transformation of order, acknowledging to Miranda that his neglect of worldly ends had provoked his brother's seizure of power. He envisaged the prospect of new order with small hope and less joy. It entailed a loss of the familiar for a gain at best dismal. The island had always been a kind of time out of political and social reality, which seemed a nostalgic vision: " 'Tis far off / And rather like a dream than an assurance / That my remembrance warrants" (I.ii.44–46). The old mage confirmed the sentiment: "What seest thou else / In the dark backward and abysm of time?" If a new order was to be established, it would be by passing through an older and more familiar one. On the island Prospero was a disturbing influence who manipulated its order to his own ends, alien to its familiars: Ariel and his spirits of fire and air; nobles and sailors of water; Caliban, and then Trinculo and Stephano, of earth. Prospero but played with this scheme. Departure from the island was a farewell to all that, a leap into the uncertainty of political conflict, at once nostalgically familiar and dauntingly new—and accordingly viewed by Prospero with reluctant dismay:

> We are such stuff
> As dreams are made on, and our little life
> Is rounded with a sleep. Sir, I am vexed.
> Bear with my weakness; my old brain is troubled.
> Be not disturbed with my infirmity.
>
> (IV.i.156–60)

A strangely subdued and Lear-like request to come from the superbly confident Prospero, one might think. But Prospero was lamenting an order where only he was fully competent, yet which he had to use to make room for the new. It would be up to Ferdinand and Miranda to carry forward a new legitimate order: on whose legitimacy Prospero sometimes insisted. The island's parodic nature was suitably summed up in Gonzalo's utopia: king and no king, production aplenty but no work, trading but no commerce, eating but no planting, and so on. Yet if the island's order was no longer possible, that did not mean anything better was at immediate hand. Miranda could marvel at the fallible and often downright suspect agents of the new order, but Prospero cut her short with one of the best-known, briefest, and perhaps most hopeless pieces of irony in all of Shakespeare:

> *Miranda:*   O, wonder!
> How many goodly creatures are there here!
> How beauteous mankind is! O brave new world
> That has such people in 't!
> *Prospero:*   'Tis new to thee.
>   (V.i.181–84)

Earlier sixteenth-century writers had based their researches on a profound sense that learning and letters *could* be rediscovered. In such circumstance we need not be surprised by assumptions that to shape a
"precellent" language and renew letters could recreate sociopolitical order, establishing what might even have an air of some utterly new At-
lantis, that brave new world whose prospect so overjoyed Miranda before
her father sought abruptly to disabuse her. Nor would contemporary spectators have missed the similarity of Prospero's case to that of the premier
sovereign of Europe, the emperor Rudolph II: himself withdrawn from
affairs of state into study of the occult and deposed by his coarse and
sinister brother Matthias (as king of Hungary in 1608, as emperor in 1612)
after years of strife.[57]

"These sorts of accidents," Temple went on in the text quoted at the
start of this chapter, "sometimes lay them so waste that, when they rise
again, 'tis from such low beginnings that they look like new-created
regions, or growing out of the original state of mankind and without any
records or remembrances beyond certain short periods of time." Like so
many of his predecessors, Temple was convinced that "knowledge and
ignorance, as well as civility and barbarism," the orders and disorders of
social and political culture, went hand in hand.[58] Literature, I argue, was
to provide one major new bond of reason and guarantee of civil order, a tie
of "justice" and common assent.

---

[57]Without question the best study of the emperor is R. J. W. Evans, *Rudolf II and His
World: A Study in Intellectual History, 1576–1612* (Oxford, 1973). The adjectives describing Matthias are taken from this work. See, too, the same author's *The Making of
the Habsburg Monarchy: An Interpretation* (Oxford, 1979).
[58] Temple, "Ancient and Modern Learning," in *Five Essays*, pp. 53, 39.

Chapter 3

The Invention of Literature

Orlando was unaccountably disappointed. She had thought of literature all those years (her seclusion, her rank, her sex must be her
excuse) as something wild as the wind, hot as fire, swift as lightning;
something errant, incalculable, abrupt, and behold, literature was an
elderly gentleman in a gray suit talking about duchesses.
　　　　　　　　　　　—Virginia Woolf, *Orlando: A Biography*

In January 1635, less than a year after he had taken France into the
Thirty Years' War (not yet so known, of course) on the side of the Protestant powers, the cardinal Richelieu obtained a charter founding the Académie Française. Until this time, began its *Lettres-patentes*, the state had
been preoccupied by "the civil wars with which it has been afflicted," and
government had had to concern itself with "agitations enflamed in its
provinces," with foreign war and general "confusion." Although these
matters were not entirely settled, the time had now come to add "sciences
and arts" to increasing social tranquility, the growth of commerce, the
settlement of military discipline, and the reform of finance and luxury
expenditure. The academy's express purpose was to make French the
"most perfect of the modern" languages, "not only elegant but even able to
treat all arts and all sciences."[1] The repair of language and letters would
echo that of society and state.
　　Richelieu gave the academy's members a double charge: they were to
compile a dictionary and to elaborate a normative and rational grammar of
the language. The one would establish the precise and—ideally—singular
meaning of words; the other would set forth the general and universal
order of reason in language. The first was to provide adequacy of reference,
permitting ensured communication and accuracy of knowledge. The second was to furnish the rational analytical tools able to make such knowledge usable for human activity. The Parlement did not actually register
this charter until 1637, the year in which the quarrel sparked by Georges
de Scudéry over Corneille's *Le Cid* provided the cardinal with the opportunity to add a third charge: that of formulating the norms of "bonnes

---

[1]Louis XIII, "Lettres patentes pour l'établissement de l'Académie française," in *Recueil général des anciennes lois françaises,* ed. MM. Jourdan, Decrusy, Isambert, 30 vols.
(Paris, 1822–33), 16:418–20.

lettres," of the literature corresponding to that "bon sens" whose universality René Descartes had most recently proclaimed.

In his "Observations," Scudéry had argued that *Le Cid* ignored Aristotelian requirements for a proper subject and plot, contravened the "principales règles" (especially that "vraisemblance" demanding that a play agree with *reasonable* audience expectation), flouted morality (Chimène, he wrote, acted like "une prostituée"), and misused language: incorrect construction, misuse of particular combinations of words, abuse of individual terms. *Le Cid* did not meet demands for rational presentation of action, for performance of a normative morality, and for proper use of language (both in syntactic correctness and semantic adequacy—order and reference). Although Jean Chapelain and his colleagues softened these criticisms somewhat, the "Sentiments de l'Académie Française sur la tragi-comédie du Cid," which they produced at Richelieu's request and with his oversight, reconfirmed the main demands (prior, they added, to producing their own "art poétique").[2]

Richelieu's charge had indeed assumed a capacity of language and mind both to analyze the order of the world and to understand (referentially) its material actuality. It emphasized the possibility of a transparent ("elegant") mediating language and a collective and distinct comprehensibility of concepts: those very ideals the futility of whose proposal some sixty years earlier Estienne had bleakly linked with social and political disaster. The communal nature of concepts implied (eventually, at least) that human nature was permanent and unchanging, wherever and whenever it was found, and that therefore ethical norms could be prescribed: as the *Lettres-patentes* said, "the sciences and the arts" should be established because they were "one of the principal instruments of Virtue." Soon, too, would be declared the unique value of individuals, along with an assertion of their rights, capacity for knowledge, and of the fact that since all such individuals were alike in these rights and capacities, all were equal: thus the very individuality in question would be a common collective nature.[3]

---

[2]Both texts are in Pierre Corneille, *Oeuvres*, ed. Charles Marty-Laveaux, 12 vols. (Paris, 1862), 12:441–501. The charge to the Académie that it produce a dictionary, a grammar, a rhetoric, and a poetic was in the twenty-fifth of its statutes. The Académie Française was not, of course, the first French academy, nor even the first to receive full government endorsement by letters patent, for Jean-Antoine du Baïf and Joachim Thibault de Courville set up an academy of poetry and music in 1570. Under Henri III, this generated the "Palace Academy," which became ever more religious as sociopolitical conditions deteriorated. See Yates, *French Academies*. The letters patent of the 1570 academy of poetry and music are readily available as an appendix to Yates's book: pp. 319–22.

[3]These are fundamental elements of that analytico-referential discourse analyzed elsewhere: Reiss, *Discourse of Modernism*, pp. 31–45, 354–85; *Uncertainty of Analysis*, pp. 4–7. I have explored at length the issue as it concerns language and meaning in Estienne, Peter Ramus, Charles de Bouvelles, and others in "The Idea of Meaning and Practice of Method in Pierre de La Ramée, Henri Estienne, and Others," in *Humanism in Crisis: The Decline of the French Renaissance*, ed. Philippe Desan (Ann Arbor, Mich., 1991), pp. 125–51.

The ambiguities raised by the necessity to articulate both a coherence (analytical) and a correspondence (referential) theory of truth and knowledge, an aesthetic and a utilitarian theory of language, a notion of permanent human law and variable human societies, of individual and collective rights and obligations, as well as the ultimately "masculine" nature of these dogmas, were all anxieties probed through the invention of literature, which, like the social contract itself, would bring order into the collective lives of individuals.

Not only, in the view of Richelieu and the Académie Française, had the language of bonnes lettres to provide verbal adequacy and accuracy of reference and a rational analytical tool, but it had to express an apprehension of right reason, reflect the expectations of ethical habit, and echo doctrines that did not question particular forms of political authority. It was not surprising that when Adrien Baillet recorded the three founding and profoundly emblematic dreams of Descartes's wonderful new science some sixty years later, they echoed Richelieu's instruments: two dreams of chaos were followed by a dream of a dictionary and a book of poetry, whose "order" and "economy" he knew perfectly. The one provided right language and the entirety, had thought Descartes, of objective science; the other gave philosophy and wisdom, the distinctions of truth and falsity.[4] In 1635–37 Richelieu was clear that the language and belles lettres of France were to be suitable tools serving a new kind of centralized national authority and bureaucratized monarchy (although he surely did not foresee clearly the nature of either).[5] Saying this, however, we must recognize that philosophical and ethical thought, political practice and critical claims were of a piece. The invention of literature was but one aspect of making anew a whole cultural environment.

By the late seventeenth century critics could argue exhaustively that the well-written literary text was one with the order of nature and at the same time commentary on, and part of, nature and society as the external

---

[4]Adrien Baillet, *La vie de Monsieur Des-Cartes*, 2 vols. (1691; rpt. Hildesheim and New York, 1972), 1:81–86. Descartes recorded the dreams for November 1619. Paul Arnold has argued that they may compose a philosophical fiction: *Histoire des Rose-Croix et les origines de la Franc-maçonnerie* (Paris, 1955), Appendix I, pp. 290ff. A review essay by Bernard Rochot, mocking much else, did not dispute this suggestion: "A propos des Rose-Croix, de Descartes et des rêves de 1619," *Revue de Synthèse*, (July–Sept. 1956), 351–61. Henri Gouhier accepted it at least in part: *Les premières pensées de Descartes: Contribution à l'histoire de l'anti-Renaissance* (Paris, 1958), pp. 32–58. As a fiction, the dreams offer still more support for the interpretation of the instauration traced here.

[5]The cardinal alone could approve members, "officers, statutes, and rules." For that reason among others, a certain reticence among the group from which the Académie was created had had to be overcome: a fact emphasizing the *political* nature of the foundation. A useful analysis of the Académie's beginnings is to be found in Claudette Delhez-Sarlet, "L'académie française du temps du Cardinal de Richelieu," *Marche Romane*, Cahiers de l'A. R. U. Liège, 29, nos. 1–2 (1979), 41–60; and see Yates, *French Academies*, pp. 292–97.

places of perception, reference, and all other human activities. At once the treasure house of knowledge as data, literature also provided the logic of a commonsense rationality that formed the necessary basis of such knowledge. The link was an important one between Cartesian "good sense" and those "good letters" whose use signaled the "honnête homme," the cultured gentleman wit, he of a certain education, of sufficient leisure to spend the time reading or going to plays, of sufficient wealth to be able to purchase such a supplement to necessity. Joseph Addison would capture this view rather nicely in his much later claim that the ideal of the literary man should be to bring "Philosophy out of Closets and Libraries, Schools and Colleges, to dwell in Clubs and Assemblies, at Tea-Tables and in Coffee-Houses."[6] Order and the reality of objects, analysis and reference— the nomothetic and experiential values of literature—would be set by the late seventeenth and early eighteenth centuries, along with its urbanity, its particular ethical and aesthetic values. They have furnished the terms of literary discussion ever since.

Nor should we think writers experienced such aims as an imposition. On the contrary, they were a principal blazon of honor, most especially the political. "By doing this," wrote Chapelain in the mid-1630s, "I contribute what is most important to society's well-being." Others felt the same. The writer, F. E. Sutcliffe noted, "was conscious of mobilizing goodwill, of forming public opinion, of functioning as people's guide."[7] The writer will soon be claiming a yet more constitutive role, one involving the very establishment of right reason and its expression, of moral norms, of ideals of correct taste, and of state legitimacy. I refer to these literary functions as the epistemological, ethical, aesthetic, and political. The last was quite clearly initially predominant. But it was wholly embroiled with the others.

A half-century later the first of the professional literary critics, John Dennis, had not the slightest doubt as to the relation between political power and literature. He never tired of reminding his readers that Richelieu, than whom "no man among [the French] has express'd so much Passion for the Drama," wrote plays "with that very Hand, which at the same time was laying the plan of the *French* universal Monarchy." Indeed, he wrote, without literature a nation's political greatness would disappear. Dennis argued the case for the Athenians and the Romans, asserting their political greatness to be founded on the invention of a theater and to have been lost with that same theater's decay and dissolution. Again, he alluded to his always favorite example: "Cardinal *Richelieu* was the Person,

[6]Joseph Addison, Richard Steele, and others, *The Spectator*, ed. Gregory Smith, intro. Peter Smithers, 4 vols. (1907; rpt. London and New York, 1979), 1:32: *Spectator*, no. 10 (March 12, 1711).

[7]F. E. Sutcliffe, *Politique et culture, 1560–1660* (Paris, 1973), p. 7. The Chapelain citation is from his *Lettres*, ed. P. Tamizey de Larroque, 2 vols. (Paris, 1880), 1:3–4.

who at the same Time laid the Foundation of the Greatness of their
Theatre, and their Empire; and 'tis a surprizing Thing to consider, That the
Spirit of Dramatic Poetry, leaving them just before the Beginning of the
last War, by *Molière* and *Corneille's* Death, and by *Racine's* Age, they have
since that Time, lost almost half their Conquests."[8]

Dennis constantly returned to this theme. Nor did he use it only to
insist on the association of literature and sociopolitical order. He situated
their mutual reformation with what he and others saw as historical precision, and he did so in terms of particular national political interests: "For,
first, the Cultivating of the Poetical Art, advanc'd their Genius's to such a
Height as was unknown to *France* before; And, secondly, the appearance of
those great Genius's, was very instrumental in spreading their Language
thro' all the Christian World; and in raising the Esteem of their Nation to
that degree, that it naturally prepar'd the Way for their Intrigues of State,
and facilitated the Execution of their vast Designs."[9] Small wonder that in
1712, after victories at Blenheim, Oudenarde, and Malplaquet (1704, 1708,
1709) and not long before the Treaty of Utrecht put an end to the wars
between the Protestant powers and France, Dennis would be proud to
assert that the French greatness had been "sapp'd and undermin'd and
overturn'd by a *British* Poetick Ministry."[10] So he confirmed the fundamental nature of the association in question—in which the warlike diction was evidently no accident, any more than was the notion that literature and reason, politics and morality were all born of the same sense of
chaos and urgency.

The context out of which literature was invented was thus wide. Its urge
came, not unexpectedly, as much from the argument of theory as from the
dismay of practice. That is the light in which one should consider, for
example, the implication of Bacon's argument placing "writing" and what
he called *experientia literata* at the very foundation of all right and legitimate knowledge (the terms were his), whether in the sphere of natural-
philosophical or of political thinking. Indeed, even when speaking of the
former case, the chancellor tended to draw his metaphors either from his
own experience in political and legal life or from written histories of such
experience—Machiavelli's *Discorsi* being a favorite source. For Bacon,
ordered writing was the basis of all and any right method. In turn, method
was the basis of legitimate knowledge of nature and stability and growth
in a healthy political society. Galileo said little else when speaking of the
required alliance between the language of mathematics and that of the
world. In his familiar letter to Marin Mersenne of November 20, 1629,

---

[8]John Dennis, "The Usefulness of the Stage, to the Happiness of Mankind, to Government, and to Religion. Occasioned by a Late Book, Written by Jeremy Collier, M.A.
(1698)," in *The Critical Works*, ed. Edward Niles Hooker, 2 vols. (Baltimore, 1939–43),
1:164, 167.

[9]John Dennis, "Advancement and Reformation of Modern Poetry (1701)," ibid., 1:203.

[10]John Dennis, "An Essay on the Genius and Writings of Shakespeare (1712)," ibid.,
2:3.

Descartes spoke of the possibility of discovering a natural and universal philosophical language whose basic words and the letters composing them repeated the natural order that thinking established among concepts. He wrote that such a language depended on ordering "all men's thoughts" according to "the true philosophy." Descartes was clearly referring here to what he would publish eight years later as his *Method*. For him, as for Bacon and Galileo, right language and right method were one and the same: both essential to human knowledge and action.[11]

We can go further. We need not be reminded that the context of Bacon's writing was that of his career as lawyer, politician, and statesman, concerned all his life with the stability of government and civil society. It is hardly a surprise to discover that Bacon's concern, like Bodin's in his earlier *Method* for understanding histories, was to seek a new logic (as he always called it) able to reveal the general law underlying all particular customs of peoples and transformations of states.[12] For his part, from the publication of his *Sidereus nuncius* (1610) until the end of his life, Galileo dramatically confronted the political dimension of his search for a new language and method. "Logic" and the order of language, power and political process, went hand in hand. And what of Descartes? Well, there too the question of power formed an integral component of his argument.

As he recorded it in the *Olympiques*, Descartes's illumination concerning a "marvellous science" occurred on November 10, 1619. In the *Discours de la méthode*, he told his readers that it was in Germany, on his return from the emperor Ferdinand's coronation to the army participating in the beginning of what the future would know as the Thirty Years' War. Such a context is of fundamental importance to the *Discours*, and the goals of an ostensibly "merely" philosophical method were further politicized by the use of an architectural metaphor:

[11]The reference to Descartes here is to *Oeuvres philosophiques*, ed. Ferdinand Alquié, 3 vols. (Paris, 1963–73), 1:230–31, indicated in future by the initials *OP*. All translations from Descartes are mine, as literal as possible. I beg the reader's indulgence for referring here and elsewhere to writings of my own, but the attempt to provide a specific theoretical context seems to require it. Descartes's letter has been discussed at some length, and the Bacon material at even greater, in *Discourse of Modernism*, pp. 279–83, 198–225. On Galileo, see "Espaces de la pensée discursive: Le cas Galilée et la science classique," *Revue de Synthèse*, 85–86 (1977), 5–47.

[12]Jean Bodin, *Methodus ad facilem historiarum cognitionem*, in *Oeuvres philosophiques*, ed. and trans. Pierre Mesnard (Paris, 1951), p. 109. From history, wrote Bodin, "we have brought together [*colligimus*] the laws of the ancients, scattered here and there, so that we might unite [*conjungamus*] them in this work. And in truth, the best part of universal law [*iuris universi pars optima*] lies hidden in history: and whatever is of great weight and importance for the best appraisal and evaluation of laws [*ad leges optimè dijudicandas*], customs of peoples, as well as beginnings, increase, condition, changes, and end of all commonwealths are derived from it [history]. This forms the chief subject of this method." In the field of law, such a claim was clearly analogous to what was sought by Estienne in that of language or by Hurault in that of political society: nothing could be brought to order until some organizing "authority" was available—such as the thinking subject of the *cogito*.

It is true that we do not see anyone throw to the ground all the houses in a city, with the sole intention of rebuilding them differently, and of making its streets more beautiful. But you certainly do see lots of people knocking down their own houses to rebuild them, and sometimes they are even forced to do so, if they are in danger of collapsing by themselves and if their foundations are not quite solid. In the light of that, I came to feel that it was doubtless unreasonable for a private individual to undertake to reform a State, by changing everything from the foundations up, and knocking it down to stand it up again; and to reform the body of the sciences, or the order established in the schools for teaching them.[13]

So, he claimed, he wished only to correct his own thinking, and not at all those "things that concern the public," even though they do reveal certain "imperfections." He assured his readers that any stable situation was better than change, even though, he had written just before, the best-ordered states were certainly those that had, from the outset, "maintained the constitutions of some prudent legislator."

This remark, in its turn, had followed on the assertion that a building constructed by a single architect was generally incomparably better-ordered than one put together pell-mell by many hands, an argument Descartes had immediately applied to the construction of entire cities, to the only true religion—founded by the God of the Old and New Testaments—and to the excellence of the Spartan constitution, supposedly "invented . . . by one man." We may perhaps be forgiven for doubting the limits Descartes claimed to be placing on the potential use of his new Method: all the more when we see him return at the beginning of the next section to his architectural image. By its means he was able to compare his "morale par provision" to a temporary dwelling, useful while erecting a new one, and he was able to attribute the superiority of the laws to be followed while doing so only to the fact that he was accustomed to them: for the Persians and the Chinese may well be just as "sensible" (*sensés*) as the Europeans.

Such relativity suggests another commonplace, one we have already seen implied by Bodin: the idea that it should be possible to find the elements of universal law, the fundamental nomothetical rules of all human societies. Hobbes so described his object at the beginning of the *De Cive:* "Not," he wrote, "to point which are the laws of any country, but to declare what the laws of all countries are."[14] This idea would find its

[13]Descartes, *Discours de la méthode, OP,* 1:581. The earlier reference to the *Olympiques* is to *OP,* 1:52. I have discussed these questions at much greater length in "Descartes, the Palatinate, and the Thirty Years' War: Political Theory and Political Practice," in *Baroque Topologies: Literature/History/Philosophy,* ed. Timothy Hampton, *Yale French Studies,* no. 80 (New Haven, Conn., 1991), pp. 108–45.

[14]Thomas Hobbes, *Philosophical Rudiments Concerning Government and Society,* in *The English Works,* ed. Sir William Molesworth, 11 vols. (London, 1839–45), 2:xxiii: "Preface to the Reader." Future references are indicated by the initials *EW.*

counterpart of fundamental importance to literary and aesthetic theory in the constant opposition drawn between the universal laws of poetry common to all times and in all places, and the matters specific to a precise cultural context: the first equated with the permanent laws of nature, the second with the actions of humans and the elements of nature insofar as they related to such actions (Descartes's distinction between the universal rationality of the *Method* and the relative nature of the laws to be obeyed according to the injunction of the *morale par provision* was therefore utterly typical).

In Hobbes as elsewhere, the achievement of such a goal was possible only on the assumption that all humanity was fundamentally alike, whenever and wherever it has been, is, or will be found, and that humans were alike chiefly in their voluntarism (willful rationalism), their fear of death and therefore mutual divisiveness, their desire for power, and their right to (self) possession. Like Descartes's common sense and universal reason, these assumptions formed the fundamental axioms of a right method. Bacon, too, in a text dating from 1608, formulated his method of right reason in terms of clearing the ground and laying the foundations for a new building. And he, too, was quite specific that he was talking as much of civil society as of science, that he was talking of "rules of argument," of the "first principles" of a logical method, of new "forms of proof and a fresh basis of discussion," of new ways of "understanding" and of reformed "minds," of language and discourse.[15]

Late sixteenth-century writers had viewed the improvement of language and the stabilizing of civil society as a single question. The tetrad of Bacon, Galileo, Hobbes, and Descartes likewise saw method, language, natural philosophy, and political order as forming a single tissue of problems. And it is no wonder, therefore, to find Descartes's anxiety expressed, in a series of letters to Marin Mersenne of January–March 1630 (before the surety of *Method*), in a discussion of the *indeterminability* of the beautiful—closing with a claim that *le beau* could be defined only in terms of the numbers who appreciated a given artwork. The new concept of poetic or literary representation was to become a focal point organizing the tissue of related problems. Perhaps that was what lay behind Denis Diderot's assertion a century later, that in situating "the *beautiful* within the perception of relationships, . . . you will have the history of its progress from the birth of the world right up till today." "The perception of relationships," he would then insist, "is therefore the foundation of the *beautiful*," while the ability so to perceive them would be "taste, in general."[16]

By the fourth decade of the seventeenth century, then, it would be

---

[15]Bacon, *Redargutio philosophiarum*, in *Works*, 3:557–58.
[16]Descartes, *OP*, e.g., 1:246, 251–52 (Alquié has omitted the passage in the January letter); Denis Diderot, "Recherches philosophiques sur l'origine et la nature du beau," in *Oeuvres esthétiques*, ed. Paul Vernière (Paris, 1965), p. 428. The last passage quoted is from a letter to Mlle de la Chaux, dated May 1751, cited by Vernière, ibid., p. 388.

assumed that the right use of language accompanied the methodical use of reason, that the stable ordering of political power was concomitant with the rational (and still divinely created) order of nature. Language, correctly used, corresponded through its grammar with the universal rational order of methodical common sense. Such common sense, the general reason of humankind, was found to be at the very least adequate to the order of nature (the *mathesis universalis*) and at best fully conversant with its equally rational processes. Dominique Bouhours would select his own tongue as alone having achieved this: "It alone in my opinion is able to paint well according to nature, and to express things exactly as they are." Thomas Sprat, with an equally nationalistic sense of excellence, chose rather to praise the Royal Society's improvement of language: "They have exacted from all their members a close, naked, natural way of speaking, positive expressions, clear senses, a native easiness, bringing all things as near the Mathematical plainness as they can, and preferring the language of Artizans, Countrymen, and Merchants, before that of Wits and Scholars."[17]

Such a view came close to Bouhours's requirement of linguistic "transparency": "Fine [*beau*] language resembles a pure, clean water without any taste." And another century on, Dr. Johnson would be able to generalize further the same conception in his discussion of John Dryden's precepts: tragedy, he said, provided us with a poetical order that achieved its rational legitimacy and correctness to the truth of things because that order corresponded to "the nature of things and the structure of the human mind."[18] In 1655 John Denham had already uttered the hope that his own poetry might achieve such a consummation. He did so in four revised lines of his poem "Cooper's Hill," which remained celebrated throughout the eighteenth century and into the nineteenth. In them he offered the Thames as a model:

> O could I flow like thee, and make thy stream
> My great example, as it is my theme!
> Though deep, yet clear, though gentle, yet not dull,
> Strong without rage, without ore-flowing full.
> (ll. 189–92)

The poem had first appeared in 1642 without these lines. Added in 1655, they signaled an ever more widespread view, well confirmed by the time

---

[17]Dominique Bouhours, *Les entretiens d'Ariste et d'Eugène* [1671], ed. Ferdinand Brunot (Paris, 1962), pp. 37, 34; Thomas Sprat, *The History of the Royal Society of London* [1667], in *Critical Essays of the Seventeenth Century*, ed. J. E. Spingarn, 3 vols. (1908; rpt. Oxford, 1957), 2:118. On "common sense" from Aristotle to the seventeenth century, see Summers, *Judgment of Sense*.

[18] Bouhours, *Entretiens*, p. 37; Samuel Johnson, "Dryden," in *Lives of the Poets: A Selection*, ed. J. P. Hardy (Oxford, 1971), p. 162.

Dryden, in the 1697 Dedication to the *Aeneid,* made them a "test of poetic insight."[19]

I have jumped ahead briefly, taking these later examples of Bouhours, Denham, Sprat, Diderot, and Johnson so as to indicate immediately the installation of a mode of conceptualization that would endure at least into the nineteenth century and, I argue, with some slight variation, into our own time. The axiomatic assumption of these coherences of discourse, mind, and nature was in place by the mid-seventeenth century. It meant that the syntax of a properly ordered language (its "precellence," as it had been termed, certainly since the late sixteenth century) automatically provided its users with an analysis of the order of reason *and* of the order of the material world: the coherence theory of truth. At the same time, ways were found to argue that grammatical predicates were precise representations of mental concepts, while these latter were at least adequate representations of material phenomena: the correspondence theory of truth.[20] These were the fundamental assumptions of analytico-referential discourse. The mediatory role of a stable language is quite apparent, and one is immediately drawn to ask what permits such faith in its coherence with method, in the accuracy of its mediatory role, and in its necessary stability and universality.

Like Descartes, Hobbes ascribed such faith at least partly to the certainty of Method—whose exemplar was geometry: "Whatever things they are in which this present age doth differ from the rude simpleness of antiquity, we must acknowledge to be a debt which we owe merely to geometry. . . . were the nature of human actions as distinctly known as the nature of *quantity* in geometrical figures . . . mankind should enjoy . . . an immortal peace." Or again: "Geometry therefore is demonstrable, for the lines and figures from which we reason are drawn and described by ourselves; and civil philosophy is demonstrable, because we make the commonwealth ourselves." The same might be taken as applying to matters of art, though it could not apply to the material world: "Because of natural bodies we know not the construction."[21] Giambattista Vico was later to express just the same sentiment (ascribing it to Bacon). Method here, then, referred simply to a knowledge of the mutual coherence of all matters. It does not, alone, appear to be enough.

For Hobbes also wrote, in the same place as the earlier of the two passages just quoted, that "wisdom, properly so called, is nothing else but this: *the perfect knowledge of the truth in all matters whatsoever. Which*

---

[19] Sir John Denham, *The Poetical Works,* ed. Theodore Howard Banks, 2d ed. (New Haven, Conn., 1969), p. 77. The last quotation is on p. 54.

[20] See Timothy J. Reiss, "The *concevoir* Motif in Descartes," in *La cohérence intérieure: Études sur la littérature française du xviie siècle, offertes à J.-D. Hubert,* ed. J. van Baelen and D. L. Rubin (Paris, 1977), pp. 203–22.

[21] Hobbes, *Rudiments,* in *EW,* 2:iv: "Epistle Dedicatory"; and *Six Lessons to the Savilian Professors of the Mathematics,* in *EW,* 7:184.

being derived from the registers and records of *things;* and that as it were through the conduit of certain definite appellations" cannot but be the consequence "of a well-balanced reason; which by the compendium of a word, we call philosophy." But such a view implied not simply the mutual coherence we have just seen. It also required some kind of correspondence: to know "the registers and records of things." Here Hobbes did not require any formal proof of such a possibility. He merely appealed to a practical evidence. After Copernicus, he wrote, "the doctrine of the motion of the earth being now received, and a difficult question thereupon arising concerning the descent of heavy bodies, Galileus in our time, striving with that difficulty, was the first that opened to us the gate of natural philosophy universal, which is the knowledge of the nature of *motion,* so that neither can the age of natural philosophy be reckoned higher than to him."[22]

I have already mentioned Galileo's requirement concerning the coincidence of the language of mathematics and that of nature. Hobbes's point was that Galileo's equations *really* provided an analysis of concrete material substances in motion, and that insofar as they *worked,* the figures composing them could therefore genuinely be said to correspond to the moving objects composing the natural event to which they refer. The combination of geometry and Galilean experimentalism thus provided a method coherent with the *order* of nature and the mind, and at the same time correspondent with concepts on the one hand and discrete objects in nature on the other. This was what Hobbes meant by asserting that "Civil Philosophy" was "no older . . . than my own book *De cive*" and by remarking that he was going to put "into a clear method the true foundations of natural philosophy."[23] When René Rapin wrote of Aristotle's *Poetics* as being the only necessary rule for forming wit *(esprit),* he was certainly thinking as much of this Hobbesian method as of the Cartesian, with which he is usually credited: "Indeed, properly speaking, his *Poetics* are only nature put into method, and good sense reduced to principles."[24] Such a statement corresponded quite precisely to Hobbes's Galilean experimentalism and geometrical method—which alone furnished its legitimacy. (We will later see how a notion of the internal logic of literature will become a cliché of critical argument.)

In addition to the arguments of the philosophers concerning the faith one might have in the mediatory role of a stable language and a certain method, the other principal argument, if we may call it such, seems to have been one of power. My choice of Hobbes was not entirely accidental. The linking of power, of accurate knowledge of nature through a methodi-

---

[22]Hobbes, *Rudiments,* in *EW,* 2:iii.
[23]Hobbes, *Elements of Philosophy. The First Section, Concerning Body,* in *EW,* 1:viii–ix.
[24]René Rapin, *Réflexions sur la poétique et sur les ouvrages des poëtes anciens et modernes,* in *Oeuvres,* 2 vols. (Amsterdam, 1709), 2:113.

cal representation that analyzed and imitated at the same time, of the ordering of a stable civil society, and of the idea of a steady "progress" and expansion within that stability strikes me as fundamentally Hobbesian in its impulse. If one adds Hobbes's concern with matters literary throughout his life, his almost emblematic role may be the more deeply understood. The use of some idea of power as a foundation for these divers relationships, most particularly as they concerned the domain of language and literature, rapidly came to dominate discussion.

In 1640 Hippolyte-Jules de La Mesnardière had already distinguished between those who could enjoy great tragedy and those who clearly could never hope to do so. The distinction was made in terms of order and disorder, and by means of that very metaphor we have seen so generally used to this end in the sixteenth century: now it was used to insist on something almost like a class distinction between the polite and the vulgar, the useful and the superfluous, the delightful and the indifferent. La Mesnardière was writing of great theater, notably tragedy: "Now, if we want to pass from the consideration of Utility to that of Delight, matters which are inseparable in the judgment of Philosophers, it is easy to infer that the vulgar masses [*multitude grossière*] cannot obtain any pleasure from a serious, solemn, chaste, and truly tragic discourse; and that this many-headed Monster can at best only understand the superficial ornaments of the Theatre." In his Preface to *Gondibert*, Sir William Davenant viewed literature's task as that of fortifying us against "what was anciently call'd a Monster, the Multitude": echoes, here, of Sidney's comments in *Arcadia*, as well as of so many others.[25]

Another ten years later, Antoine Arnauld and Claude Lancelot addressed their 1660 *Grammaire générale et raisonnée* to one whose education would permit him, they wrote, a "scientific" access to linguistic usage and reason, others achieving it only through "habit." In his *Nouvelle méthode* of 1656, a text on the "purity" of the French language, Claude Irson had already distinguished on just this ground between "l'homme raisonnable" and "le vulgaire," who functioned only "par hazard." In 1647 Claude Vaugelas, dedicating his *Remarques sur la langue française* to the chancellor Pierre Séguier, noted that the latter was the absolute master of language, as well as being the genuine "souverain Magistrat" who represented the will of the prince. This last comment was accurate enough, for the chancellor held the great seal and this was during the regency: so far as the administration of justice was concerned, Séguier was indeed supreme. (In addition, according to the censorship laws, prospective publications had to be vetted by the chancellor or garde des sceaux.) The point is that

---

[25]Hippolyte-Jules de La Mesnardière, *La poétique* (Paris, 1640), p. p; Sir William Davenant, "The Author's Preface to his much honor'd friend, M. Hobbes," in *Gondibert*, ed. David F. Gladish (Oxford, 1971), p. 12. Future references to this work are indicated directly in my text by the initials *PG*.

political authority over language and literature, marked by the controlling role granted to Richelieu in the original *Lettres-patentes*, had thus quickly become generalized. In 1668 Gérauld de Cordemoy dedicated his *Discours physique de la parole* to Louis XIV, by this time firmly on his throne, identifying right language with the king himself, who used it perfectly and from whom proceeded language in its precellence.[26]

Assertions of this kind reached their paroxysm with Bouhours, who merits quoting at some length on the matter:

> Our great Monarch occupies the first rank among these fortunate ge-
> niuses, and . . . there is no one in the Kingdom who knows French as he
> knows it. Those who receive the honor of approaching him are astounded
> by the clarity [*netteté*] and precision [*justesse*] with which he expresses
> himself. That free and easy manner [*cét air libre & facile*] of which we
> have spoken so much, enters all he says: all his terms are right and well
> chosen [*propres, & bien choisis*], although they are not at all affected
> [*point recherchez*]; all his expressions are simple and natural [*simples, &
> naturelles*]: but the turn he gives them is the most delicate and the
> noblest in the world. In his most intimate talk, there never escapes a word
> unworthy of him, or that is not marked by the majesty which accom-
> panies him everywhere. He always acts and speaks like a King, but like a
> wise and enlightened King, who on all occasions maintains the pro-
> prieties required in each matter. Not even the tone of his voice lacks
> dignity, and that indescribable majestic something that conveys respect
> and veneration. Because good sense is the rule he follows when he speaks,
> he never says anything but what is reasonable; he says nothing useless; he
> somehow says more things than words: that can be seen every day in
> those so judicious and precise answers he gives without pause to the
> Ambassadors of Princes and to his subjects. In short, he speaks so well
> that his manner of speaking [*langage*] can provide a true idea of the
> perfection of our language [*langue*]. Kings must learn from him how to
> rule; but peoples must learn from him how to speak.[27]

The use made by Richelieu of poets and poetry is familiar, the role of such as Guez de Balzac and Chapelain entirely unambiguous. But they were not simply political hacks, for literature was by now held to be the place where language was generally displayed at its finest and where these various strands of action and thought were all brought together. Literature, as we have already begun to see, was also responsible for bringing both language and power to their summit. In a word, the king (the final and

---

[26]For further discussion of these references, see Timothy J. Reiss, "Du système de la critique classique," *XVIIe Siècle*, 116 (1977), 8–9. The censorship matter is mentioned by Henri-Jean Martin, *Livre, pouvoirs et société à Paris au xviie siècle (1598–1701)*, 2 vols. (Geneva, 1969), 1:442–44. See, too, David T. Pottinger, *The French Book Trade in the Ancien Régime, 1500–1791* (Cambridge, Mass., 1958), esp. pp. 55–82.

[27]Bouhours, *Entretiens*, p. 92.

model subject of all discourse) was both the principal poet of his country and the unique sovereign, the ideal Cartesian self. He brought political and linguistic stability. Literary writers were rapidly and urgently becoming an essential foundation of this stability—and all it implied. Dennis, that altogether exemplary critic, captured this with clarity half a century later (1701): "it was towards the beginning of the last Century, that the *French*, a subtle and discerning Nation, began to be sensible of this [overwhelming importance of literature to the "illustration" of state and language], and upon it several of their extraordinary Men, both Poets and Philosophers, began to cultivate Criticism. . . . it naturally prepar'd the Way for their Intrigues of State, and facilitated the Execution of their vast Designs."[28]

Dennis's slightly aggressive perception of literary and political history suggests we should not be surprised to find that the implications of the Académie's founding had their contemporary courtly counterpart in England, although that country was then facing increasing political instability. When Ben Jonson died in August 1637, there was a scramble to find a new "poet laureate." Officially, there was no such post at the time, although Jonson had effectively fulfilled such a function. In the end it was William Davenant who emerged, with or without the title. The debate and indeed rather violent quarrels suggest the growing recognition of the literary person's political role (no money was yet involved) and close link to government authority.[29] Goldberg and others have advanced a convincing argument that in England during the rather earlier Jacobean era the proximate relationship between poetry and power had grown apace. Yet the fact that, then, its first representative was the king himself—absolute monarch and principal poet—was not unimportant.[30]

In a real way, authority over language and political order was initially vested in the *person* of the king and flowed from him. Pierre Corneille was later to express such a view in *Cinna* (1642), when Auguste asserted his mastery over both language and empire: "I am master of myself as of the Universe" (*Je suis maître de moi comme de l'Univers:* V.iii.1696). While some new relation of writing and power was being set in place, its specific nature had not yet developed, any more than had that of the political order in which it would soon be functioning. This particular configuration would not last long, appearing rather to be an intermediate step in a yet ongoing development. At first the monarch remained the center of all conceivable authority. Personified in the king, Hurault's tentative expression of abstract state sovereignty had not yet made its way: as it would

---

[28]Dennis, "Advancement and Reformation" in *Critical Works,* 1:203: "The Epistle Dedicatory."
[29]Broadus, *Laureateship,* pp. 40–58; Norbrook, *Poetry and Politics,* pp. 266–68.
[30]Goldberg, *James I,* pp. 17–28. Others have put forward similar arguments (see Chapter 1, note 55).

have, by the time Corneille's Titus could turn his predecessor's exclamation: "Master of the universe without being so of myself" (*Maître de l'Univers sans l'être de moi-même: Tite et Bérénice* [1670], II.i.407). The nature of writing, the nature and practice of state authority, and the relationship between them developed at once. Sovereign power eventually would no longer be vested in the single person of the monarch. Rather it would be spread through a kind of council or bureaucracy. Authority derived from the monarch, to be sure, but it was the more potent for being "multiple."

We might, therefore, expect that but a year after Bouhours's encomium, Dryden in England would voice exactly similar sentiments, albeit rather more subdued. The recent refinement in "conversation" in England, wrote the poet laureate in 1672, was due to the court "and, in it, particularly to the King, whose example gives a law to it." Fortunate, said Dryden somewhat ironically, in having acquired an acquaintance with "the most polished courts of Europe," Charles II had been able to reform both the "barbarism" and the "rebellion" of the nation to which he had returned. (The claim that such art overcame barbarism would also become a critical commonplace.) Poets, Dryden now remarked, should be those who could most benefit from the king's twofold "excellency," his bestowal of political stability and his gift of eloquence and the art that would inevitably follow.[31]

Here we find the precise response to the problem posed at the end of the sixteenth century and still discussed in sociopolitical terms. "There would be no society among men," asserted Bernard Lamy, "if they could not give one another perceptible signs for what they think and what they want." No doubt such a sentiment could be found expressed in Antiquity and almost everywhere in the Middle Ages. Now it was found in a context that Sprat can serve once again to confirm: "The purity of Speech and greatness of Empire have in all Countries still met together. The *Greeks* spoke best when they were in their glory of conquest. The *Romans* made those times the Standard of their Wit, when they subdu'd and gave Laws to the World."[32] On the one hand, then, the king, with his possession of and power over language, guided all other users in social action and in natural knowledge. Poets, the most exquisite users of language, learned from him. On the other hand, however, poets were the legislators, poets led the way to action and representation, and poets held the ultimate power because they showed the path, in spite of everything, to the right and proper use of language—which they controlled.

---

[31]John Dryden, "Defense of the Epilogue or, An Essay on the Dramatic Poetry of the Last Age," in *Selected Criticism*, ed. James Kinsley and George Parfitt (Oxford, 1970), pp. 129–30.

[32]Bernard Lamy, *La rhétorique ou l'art de parler*, 4th ed. (Paris, 1699), p. 1; Sprat, *History*, in Spingarn, *Critical Essays*, 2:112–13. That the language/society equation is a perennial commonplace has not prevented its repeated reworking.

The most startling and best-known expression of that view was Jean Racine's speech to the Académie for the reception of Thomas Corneille and Jean-Louis Bergeret in January 1685. Praising Pierre Corneille, whose seat his brother was taking, the dramatist equaled the poet to the king: not only, he said, should "the excellent poet and great general be placed on an equal footing," but "the same age which today prides itself on having brought forth Augustus, is no less proud of having produced Horace and Virgil."[33] Indeed, the writer was greater: not only did he create and preserve culture as the king created and preserved civil society, but he made the memory of both immortal. Could Racine have found a clearer way of placing Louis and Corneille on a par? To say nothing of Racine himself, now occupying the cultural place of his dead rival: for which of them was Horace and which Virgil? The king himself took the point with some humor. According to Racine, Louis said to him afterward: "Je vous louerois davantage, si vous ne me louiez pas tant (I would praise you more, if you didn't praise me so much.")[34] The wordplay on *louer/Louis* caught the matter with some exactness. The poet was indeed giving himself pride of place, for he it was who could grant it to kings (or, implicitly, withhold it). Others clearly saw the strength of Racine's claim. Bouhours remarked: "One could not exalt poetry more, nor emphasize more ingeniously the worth of poets."[35] Raymond Picard has noted how widespread was the idea that "warriors as it were create glory, but writers dispense it and assure its immortality."[36]

By 1685 the idea was a familiar one and considerably more complex and profound than the citation of Racine might suggest. As early as 1650 Davenant had addressed the Preface to *Gondibert*, his epic poem, "To his much honor'd friend, M. Hobbes." The text was quite remarkable, forging a constant equation between reason and political action, between great poetry and power, between the rousing of Machiavellian *virtù* ("Ambition" and "Vertue," as Davenant called it) and the constructing of "this new Building" that great poetry had to be. One immediately recalls the new

---

[33]Jean Racine, *Oeuvres complètes*, ed. Raymond Picard, 2 vols. (Paris, 1966), 2:346.
[34]Ibid., 2:281. Cf. Jean Racine, *Oeuvres*, ed. Paul Mesnard, new ed., 8 vols. (Paris, 1865–73), 5:124. On this, see Raymond Picard, *La carrière de Jean Racine* (Paris, 1961), pp. 376–83. I am not sure how it matters that Louis (or Racine) probably found his phrase in the popular memoirs of Queen Marguerite de Valois, who began her (ironic?) dedication to Brantôme: "Je louerois davantage votre oeuvre si elle ne me louoit tant, ne voulant qu'on attribue la louange que j'en ferois plutost à la *philaftie* qu'à la raison, et ainsi que l'on pense que, comme Themistocle, j'estime celuy dire le mieux qui me loue le plus (I would praise your work more if it did not praise me so much, for I would not want people to attribute my praise of it to self-love rather than reason, such that people would think, like Themistocles, that I consider that he who praises me most speaks best)": Marguerite de Valois, *Mémoires et autres écrits de Marguerite de Valois, la reine Margot*, ed. Yves Cazeux (Paris, 1976), p. 35. Published in 1628, these memoirs went through at least fifteen editions in the seventeenth century.
[35]Dominique Bouhours, *Pensées ingénieuses* (Paris, 1689), p. 296.
[36]Picard, *Carrière de Jean Racine*, p. 380.

building that both Bacon and Descartes (not to mention Hobbes himself) spoke of erecting, referring to the methodical ordering of reason and common sense. It was indeed in those very terms that Davenant began, for Hobbes was to help him as much, he wrote, by criticizing "the Method as by judging the Numbers and the matter." The aim of the Preface was to let Hobbes "pass through this new Building with more ease," his friend now having set out his method of construction, ordering of verse, and reasoning of matter (*PG*, p. 3).

Poetry, wrote Davenant, had to be aimed first at "Divines," chief among men, because it could help them carry out the task to which they were ordained: "To temper the rage of humane power by spirituall menaces, as by suddain and strange threatnings madnesse is frighted into Reason" (*PG*, p. 28). Not only did this look back again to an age of dismay and dissolution, to comments of such as Hurault and Bodin, Cellorigo and Moncada, Bacon and Comenius, but it was exactly akin to Hobbes's conception of the state of nature as being that condition of humankind where all gave free rein to their "perpetuall and restlesse desire for Power after power."[37] Hobbes, of course, put an end to it through the consent of the contract, not by poetry. Still, we may have reason to pause a moment if we think the two were unconnected.

In the *Rudiments*, Hobbes related how he sought the fundamental "material" of human relations, able to be considered equivalent to the axioms of geometry, permitting him, as we saw, to elaborate a civil philosophy whose demonstrative power and rational (logical) certainty would be equal to those of geometry: "When I applied my thoughts to the investigation of natural justice, I was presently advertised from the very word *justice*, (which signifies a steady will of giving every one his *own*), that my first enquiry was to be, from whence it proceeded that any man should call anything rather his *own*, than *another man's*. And when I found that this proceeded not from nature, but consent; (for what nature at first laid forth in common, men did afterwards distribute into several *impropriations*." For Hobbes, this "justice," confirming the agreed-on distribution of personal property and avoiding the otherwise inevitable "contention," marked the moment when "all quit that right they have to all things."[38] It was, that is to say, the moment of "Covenant" discussed in *Leviathan*. In the *Rudiments*, the founding axiom of that moment, the inception of stable civil society, was the concept of Justice. Poetry's purpose, wrote Davenant for his part, was to conduce "to plaine demonstrative justice" (*PG*, p. 9).

We find here, then, a nice twist on Virgil's poetic prophecy of Justitia's return to earth, a clear reply to the fruitless nostalgia of Sidney's *Arcadia*, to the stark cynicism of *Titus Andronicus*, and to Don Quijote's mortal

[37]Hobbes, *Leviathan*, p. 161: Part I, chap. 11.
[38]Hobbes, *Rudiments*, in *EW*, 2:vi, xvii.

refusal of fantasy. It had, we have seen, been prepared throughout the previous century. As early as its second decade Machiavelli had written that humans had solved the problem of evil and constant injury by "making laws and . . . assigning punishments to those who contravened them. The notion of justice thus came into being."[39] Justice here was not yet foundational, although by the end of the century a writer such as Hurault seemed to glimpse such a function. The important point, I think, is that when it did come to be so, it played the same role at once in the politico-legal sphere and in the literary. By the mid-seventeenth century, perhaps, Virgil's prophecy had found a new applicability. It is in that context that we may understand Dryden's casting of himself, like Racine, "as a new Virgil proclaiming a new Augustan age of peace and prosperity."[40]

The matter should be kept in mind. We will see how Davenant pursued the question, referring specifically, it would seem, to Sidney's failure. We will see, too, how the later concept of "poetical justice" will come to be thought fundamental both to the way in which poetry could be at once a revelation of the true order of things and a representation of particular local realities, and to the way in which it presented as permanently legitimate the ethical and political assumptions of a given cultural environment. Finally, we will see Boileau (the so-called legislator of Parnassus) adopt an identical view of the relation between literature and civil society.

After "Divines," Davenant continued, the next in importance to whom poetry had to be addressed were the "Leaders of Armys" (*PG*, p. 30). For generals were to be esteemed

> as the painfull Protectors, and enlargers of Empire; by whom it actively moves; and such active motion of Empire is as necessary as the motion of the Sea; where all things would putrifie, and infect one an other, if the Element were quiet; so it is with mens mindes on shore, when that Element of greatnesse and honor, *Empire*, stands still; of which the largenesse is likewise as needfull, as the vastness of the Sea; For God ordain'd not huge Empire as proportionable to the Bodies, but to the Mindes of Men; and the Mindes of Men are more monstrous, and require more space for agitation and the hunting of others, than the Bodies of Whales. (*PG*, pp. 30–31)

We perhaps need reminding at this point, should we read such sentences with some slight feeling of surprise, that this is the preface to a poem. Yet

[39]Niccolò Machiavelli, *The Discourses*, ed. Bernard Crick, trans. Leslie J. Walker, S.J., rev. Brian Richardson (1970; rpt. Harmondsworth, 1978), p. 107: I. 2. The original reads, "Donde venne la cognizione della giustizia": *Il principe e Discorsi sopra la prima deca di Tito Livio*, ed. Servio Bertelli, intro. Giuliano Procacci (1960; rpt. Milan, 1977), p. 131.

[40]George de F. Lord, " 'Absalom and Achitophel' and Dryden's Political Cosmos," in *John Dryden*, ed. Earl Miner (Athens, Ohio, 1972), p. 158.

here we are being presented with Leviathan before the event. Further, the notion that states were stable in their expansive movement, that they must situate their ability to subsist only in their capacity to grow, was a fundamental claim of Machiavellian statecraft and of Hobbesian thinking (which made the unceasing movement of human action the very motor of those needs leading to the civil covenant). Such was the context in which the leaders of armies had always been "oblig'd to Poets," both for the record of their deeds and because "their Counsels have bin made wise and their Courage warm by" poetry, as those of the "Grecian Captains" were by Homer (*PG*, p. 31; cf. p. 27): a matter that Racine, as we saw, was to point out in no uncertain terms to Louis XIV. Lack of attention paid to poets meant to "be content with a narrow space of Dominion; and narrow Dominion breeds evil, peevish, and vexatious mindes, and a nationall self-opinion" (*PG*, pp. 31–32). Finally, after the generals came the "*Statesmen and Makers of Lawes*," equally in need of poetry. None of these four categories of leaders should believe "they could perform their worke without [poetry]" (*PG*, p. 32).

Government, he went on, "resembles a Ship, where though *Divines, Leaders* of *Armys, Statesmen,* and *Judges,* are the trusted Pilots; yet it moves by the means of Windes, as uncertaine as the breath of Opinion." And how could it be otherwise, he asked, when those pilots were "often divided at the Helme?" (*PG*, p. 34). Then, after discussing such divisions at some length (*PG*, pp. 34–37), the would-be epic poet concluded: "Thus wee have first observ'd the Foure cheef aides of Government, (*Religion, Armes, Policy,* and *Law*) defectivly apply'd, and then wee have found them weake by an emulous warr amongst themselves: it follows next, wee should introduce to strengthen those principall aides (still making the People our direct object) some collaterall help; which I will safely presume to consist in Poesy" (*PG*, p. 37). For poetry, he said, "like contracted *Essences* seemes the utmost strength and activity of Nature" (*PG*, p. 40: a view echoed and re-echoed down the next two centuries). Poetry, literary writing, would therefore guide all other activities.

Davenant, not being an overly modest person, certainly considered himself ideally suited to fill such a role (as he put it to Hobbes, he wished to show not just the "Building" but the "Builder": *PG*, p. 20). Raised in court circles (starting as page to Sidney's friend, Fulke Greville), he had authored many successful plays between 1629 and the closing of the theaters, themselves holding, as Kevin Sharpe has observed, to a vision of society in decay.[41] He had become at least unofficial poet laureate on Ben Jonson's death in 1638 (Dryden would succeed him on his own death in 1668). The part in his own past, therefore, of Sidney's circle and of the great age of public theater in England was intimate. During the civil wars

---

[41]Kevin Sharpe, *Criticism and Compliment: The Politics of Literature in the England of Charles I* (Cambridge, 1987), pp. 54–103.

he was lieutenant general of the ordnance under the duke of Newcastle. He could well assert his knowledge of "Courts and Camps" (shades of Greville on Sidney, and of Cervantes's view of himself and of Garcilaso), as well as of poetry, to be entire—and by no means free of danger: in the very year of the Preface to *Gondibert*, while trying to lead a French colony to Virginia, his ship was taken by the English, and Davenant was himself imprisoned on the Isle of Wight (where Charles I had preceded him by a year and where the poet wrote the third book of *Gondibert*). In October 1650 he was arraigned in London, where legend suggests that only John Milton's intervention saved his life (a favor he was to repay after the Restoration, when Milton was threatened with exclusion from the benefit of the Act of Indemnity: a hazard that could have led to his trial and execution as a regicide).

However that may be, and whatever Davenant's opinion of the roles of poetry and poet as they related to himself, so exalted a view of the aim and capacities of poetry (and of literature, in a broad sense) was not restricted to exiled Cavaliers or to the age of the Frondes. In 1712 Dennis would speak, we saw, of poetry—in both a narrow and a broad sense—as "the most noble and exalted of all Arts," written and appreciated by "all the great Statesmen who have best succeeded in Affairs of Government." His roll call provided a list running from Moses to Maecenas, from Solon to Scipio and Caesar, from Lycurgus, Plato, and Aristotle to Machiavelli and Harrington, from Alexander to Tacitus and Richelieu (who, we saw again, "laid the Foundation of the *French* Greatness"). Two years earlier, commenting particularly on Shakespeare, Charles Gilden had written that poetic law was indeed superior to politic law, for in uttering universal reason, it enveloped all the rules of personal opinion and local political life: "The Laws of Legislators place all their Reason in their Will or the present Occurrences; but the Rules of Poetry advance nothing but what is accompanied with Reason, and drawn from the common Sentiments of Mankind; so that Men themselves, become the Rule and Measure of what these prescribe." General laws of humanity were borne in literature; in political life local rule was more immediate.[42]

A century later (1787) Jean-François Marmontel would repeat the same theme, commenting on "the political and moral objectives [*l'objet politique et moral*] of heroic poetry, and above all of tragedy" in Greek Antiquity, and taking note of "the lyric poet's role, or rather ministry, in councils, armies, the special games, and at royal courts . . . and in the same way . . . the orator's function at the parliamentary assembly: he was counsel, guide, and censor to the republic; he attacked, he protected the Chief

[42]Dennis, "Genius and Writings of Shakespeare," in *Critical Works*, 2:2–3; Charles Gilden, "An Essay on the Art, Rise and Progress of the Stage in Greece, Rome and England," in *The Works of Mr. William Shakespeare*, [ed. Nicholas Rowe (and Charles Gilden for vol. 7)], 7 vols. (London, 1710; rpt. New York, 1967), 7:xix.

men of State." In Marmontel's case one could perhaps argue that his view at least partly reflected the political unease that would bring on revolution only two years later. But Voltaire had also said that just this profound connection between the political and the literary was why "the first philosophers, the lawgivers, the founders of Republics, and historians, were all poets."[43]

For Dr. Johnson, too, "poetry and learning were the true measures of nobility and the best way for kings to ennoble themselves was by true patronage." The poet, said Imlac to Rasselas in Johnson's novel, "must write as the interpreter of nature and the legislator of mankind, and consider himself as presiding over the thoughts and manners of future generations, as a being superior to time and place."[44] We are familiar with P. B. Shelley's similar claim; yet he would go even further: "Poets are not only the authors of language and of music, of the dance, and architecture, and statuary, and painting; they are the institutors of laws, and the founders of civil society, and the inventors of the arts of life, and the teachers, who draw into a certain propinquity with the beautiful and the true, that partial apprehension of the agencies of the invisible world which is called religion."[45] By the late eighteenth and early nineteenth centuries, that is to say, the political claim would have become entirely overarching: so much so that it no longer appeared to be "political" at all.

This conception of the literary man was the creation of the seventeenth century. It was, we have been seeing, bound to a particular idea and function of state authority. Rapin had remarked rather mildly: "Poetry, being an Art, must be useful by the quality of its nature, and by the essentially subordinate position that all Art must maintain in relation to Politics [*la subordination essentielle, que tout Art doit avoir à la Politique*], whose general goal is the public good." He was not suggesting that literature was secondary to politics, however, simply that its purpose was political through and through. He agreed with Rymer (who in 1674 translated the very text in which this remark occurred), who wrote twenty years later that "in the days of *Aristophanes*, it was on all hands agreed, that the best *Poet* was he who had done the most to make men vertuous and serviceable to the Publick."[46] Much stronger had been the abbé

---

[43]Jean-François Marmontel, "Essai sur le goût," in *Eléments de littérature*, 3 vols. (Paris, 1865), 2:16; François-Marie Arouet de Voltaire, Préface to *Oedipe*, in *Oeuvres*, 40 vols. (Geneva, 1775), 2:23–24.

[44]Samuel Johnson, *The History of Rasselas, Prince of Abissinia*, ed. D. J. Enright (1976; rpt. Harmondsworth, 1988), p. 62. The preceding quotation is from Robert De-Maria, Jr., *Johnson's Dictionary and the Language of Learning* (Chapel Hill, N.C., and London, 1986), p. 214. On Johnson's "liberal" political ideology, see, too, Robert De-Maria, Jr., "The Politics of Johnson's *Dictionary*," *PMLA*, 104, no. 1 (Jan. 1989), 64–74.

[45]Percy Bysshe Shelley, "A Defense of Poetry," in *The Selected Poetry and Prose*, ed. Harold Bloom (1966; rpt. New York, 1978), p. 418.

[46]Rapin, *Réflexions*, 2:122; Thomas Rymer, *A Short View of Tragedy; Its Original Excellency, and Corruption. With Some Reflections on Shakespeare, and Other Practitioners for the Stage [1692]*, in *Critical Works*, p. 95.

d'Aubignac's earlier assertion that the dramatic author had to "teach such things as maintain public society, which serve to keep peoples in their duty."[47]

For the writer did not only embody a particular form of state authority. Through deep acquaintance with and practice of the rules of reason, the writer also showed the right form and function of universal order. The combination of the two was potent. The purpose of poetry, Davenant had argued, was to "conduce more to explicable vertue, to plaine demonstrative justice, and even to Honor" (*PG*, p. 9). That was why on the one hand the great poets of Antiquity were "Men whose intellectuals were of so great a making . . . as perhaps they will in worldly memory outlast even Makers of Laws and Founders of Empires" (*PG*, p. 5), and why on the other they should refer always to "the most effectual schools of Morality [which] are Courts and Camps" (*PG*, p. 12).

Here, then, Davenant appeared to be deliberately picking up on what his early patron Greville had proffered as both the hope and the failure of his friend Sidney, on the debate that Cervantes had made a major theme of *Don Quijote:* the effort to bring together the might of "camps" and the culture of "courts," the attempt to create an efficacious literary expression (which has its counterpart in France, I would suggest, in the *salon* "movement"). But the real significance of the point lies both in what Davenant meant by the term "court" and in the fact that he chose to couch his argument in terms of that *justice* of which I have already spoken. By "courts," he wrote, "I mean all abstracts of the multitude, either by King or Assemblies," and they were par excellence places of justice (*PG*, p. 12). Armies themselves, furthermore, should be thought judges: as the latter were "avengers of private men against private Robbers," so armies were "avengers of the publique against publique Invaders, either civill or forraign, and Invaders are Robbers." The parallel then continued with a comparison of siege armies to circuit judges (*PG*, p. 12).

Like armies and like judges, literature fortified us against the wolves: "If any man can yet doubt of the necessary use of Armys, let him study that which was anciently call'd a Monster, the Multitude (for Wolves are commonly harmlesse when they are met alone, but very uncivill in Heards)": memories here, perhaps, of La Mesnardière's quite similar remark about literature and the gross multitude. Unfortunately, not all people are like "those Lovers that were bred in *Arcadia.*" And if any should doubt this, let them only ask why "Cittys have been at the charge of defensive Walls and why Fortification hath been practis'd so long, till it is growne an Art" (*PG*, pp. 12–13). Such a remark could have been taken wholesale out of Hobbes, of course, who, at the beginning of the *Rudiments*, made just this com-

---

[47]François-Hédelin, abbé d'Aubignac, *Troisième dissertation concernant le poème dramatique en forme de remarques sur la tragédie de M. Corneille intitulée l'Oedipe* (Paris, 1663), p. 30.

parison of nations to wolves and individuals to tamed animals, and ended by asking why "we see all countries, though they be at peace with their neighbours, yet guarding their frontiers with armed men, their towns with walls and forts, and keeping constant watches."[48]

Justice as it appeared in Hobbes was essentially a way to create and keep a balance among wolfish men. Davenant stressed the fundamental relation between such a notion of justice and ethical property, between power politics and human nature, between a concept of an elite few and a common "Heard." He wrote:

> I may now beleeve I have usefully taken from Courts and Camps, the patterns of such as will be fit to be imitated by the most necessary Men; and the most necessary men are those who become principall by prerogative of blood (which is seldom unassisted with education) or by greatnes of minde, which in exact definition is Vertue. The common Crowd (of whom wee are hopelesse) wee desert; being rather to be corrected by lawes (where precept is accompany'd by punishment) then to be taught by Poesy. (*PG*, p. 13)

This was surely a direct reply to Sidney and Greville, and the attendant comment about lovers bred in Arcadia merely emphasized the fact. For Davenant, literature had explicitly become the ideal training ground for both court and camp. The fusion of the two was in part possible because sovereign and state, court life as it embodied the king's presence and civil society as it represented and bore out his active policy, had become one. That was so, whether it were the bureaucratic monarch and his state in France or, after 1688, parliament and king as the embodiment of a corporate sovereign state in England. In such contexts the glorification of sovereign (and of sovereignty), the illustration of the actions and policies of the state on the one hand and of those who executed them on the other were eminently useful and purposive, both politically and socially.

Literature, then, was at once a centrally serviceable social activity and an entertaining supplement. Quite different from the debates under Habsburg, Tudor, or Valois would be the serious claim made for literature by the worthy Lord Chesterfield, advising his son to read books "of rational amusement . . . as Horace, Boileau, Waller, La Bruyère, &c. This will be so much time saved, and by no means ill employed."[49] Such an ideal, simply assumed by the early eighteenth century, was created by these writers of the mid-seventeenth, chiefly reacting to a felt crisis in society and its discourses. Indeed, Chesterfield could well have been responding to a remark recorded in Izaak Walton's *Compleat Angler* of 1653 and repeated in subsequent editions, which deliberately *separated* leisure and general

[48]Hobbes, *Rudiments*, in *EW*, 2:ii, xv.
[49]Philip Dormer Stanhope, 4th Earl of Chesterfield, *Letters*, 2d ed., 4 vols. (London, 1774), 2:334–35.

letters (let alone anything called "literature"). Sir Henry Wotton, provost of Eton College, used to say, Walton wrote, that the best repose "after tedious study" was "Angling": " 'Twas an imployment for his idle time, which was not idly spent."[50] One could scarcely be further removed from the later ideal.

But Davenant's and others' resolution depended in a quite specific way on a certain concept of social utility and on a quite particular idea of the *political* order necessary to achieve it. For we should not forget that the polity to which both Davenant and Hobbes were referring in the passages I quoted before was that which enabled the former to speak of courts, by which he meant (so he said) the center of governmental authority, as "all abstracts of the multitude, either by King or Assemblies." He specified in this manner that he was speaking of Hobbes's sovereign authority to whom all have voluntarily ceded their own powers, so that it may protect their rights and freedoms. Hurault's abstract *lien de justice*, that is to say, had been found.

Such a view of the establishment of state and civil society is what I have referred to as "authoritarian liberalism." It went back no doubt to Antiquity, but its modern appearance was due especially to two conditions: the perception of a real European-wide political and social crisis throughout the sixteenth and into the seventeenth century, and a theoretical combination of concepts of state sovereignty and natural rights, whose details gradually evolved during the same period. Both Machiavelli and Bodin (among many others, we saw) had thought of civil society as forged from an earlier circumstance of violent conflict and as requiring a strong, centralized sovereign authority for its settlement. This view was shared, with variants and disagreements, by such as Francisco Vitoria and Francisco Suarez, Thomas Hooker and Bacon, Giovanni Botero and Hugo Grotius, Cardin Le Bret and Richelieu.

Although some—notably Grotius—did not see any preceding condition of violence, the idea had become so common that Lipsius, speaking of quite other matters, threw it in offhandedly: "After that men forsook their wild and savadge maner of liuing, and began to build houses and walled townes, to ioyne in societie, and to vse meanes offensiue and defensiue: Behold then a certaine communion necessarily began among them, and a social anticipation of diuers things." No pact was here (since "communion" followed humans' first social intercourse), but the idea of natural violence did bring Lipsius to foreshadow Hobbes's and Davenant's fortifications. Equally to the point, debate in the late sixteenth century, Protestant and Catholic, had already established so generous a view of sovereign authority as Davenant's later one: "I call prince," wrote Bernardo Davanzati in a text read before the Florentine Academy in 1588 but

---

[50]Izaak Walton, *The Compleat Angler*, ed. Bryan Loughrey (Harmondsworth, 1985), p. 35. Wotton died in 1639.

published only in 1638, "the organism governing the state, whether it be one or many persons, a few citizens or all."[51] Grotius, who on the whole seemed to view the sovereign as an individual, had nonetheless understood sovereign power in just this light. "The subject of a power," he had written, "is either common or special. Just as the body is a common, the eye a special subject of the power of sight, so the state, which we have defined above as a perfect association, is the common subject of sovereignty." But if ultimate sovereign power always resided in or reverted to that "perfect association," it was equally clear, thought Grotius, that "the special subject" of such power "is one or more persons, according to the laws and customs of each nation." (The "state" was not, however, the same as the "people," whose renunciation of power did not imply they could take it back at whim—an opinion entirely denied by Grotius.) The precise manner in which sovereign authority was embodied thus varied mightily. Even so original a thinker as Althusius, asserting that the "right of sovereignty does not belong to individual members, but to all members joined together and to the entire associated body of the realm," nonetheless spoke of their "power" as being diversely represented by one or several "administrators."[52]

Among these authors, many were at the same time developing a theory of individualist natural rights. The strands came together in Hobbes and in Locke. Hobbes's understanding of civil society as created by every individual's ceding of natural power to a single sovereign authority was constitutive. The authority was "liberal" because it was held to guarantee to all individuals (in theory) the continued enjoyment of such natural rights as did not absolutely impede those of others. Nor did it matter whether the sovereign was an individual (Hobbes), some collective embodiment of a "general will" (Locke, Montesquieu, Rousseau), or the state itself (Hegel). The underlying structure of relations of power was in each case the same: it assumed that individuals were somehow free but subordinate and subject to a collective control whose form maintained their liberties. When Davenant noted the functional identity of kings and assemblies, that was exactly what he had in mind (although it seems less probable that an earlier thinker such as Davanzati did so, for however collective his "prince," he could nonetheless be called, in an unresolved contradiction, "father of all the citizens"—an expression exactly applica-

[51]Lipsius, *Two Bookes of Constancie*, pp. 95–96 (I.xi); Bernardo Davanzati, *Leçon sur les monnaies [Lezione della monete]*, in *Écrits notables sur la monnaie: xvie siècle, Copernic à Davanzati*, ed. Jean-Yves Le Branchu, 2 vols. (Paris, 1934), 2:228. For similar views in Molina and Suarez—and the neo-Thomist debate on consent and rights more generally—see Skinner, *Foundations of Modern Political Thought*, 2:148–66.

[52]Hugo Grotius, *De jure belli ac pacis libri tres*, ed. and trans. Francis W. Kelsey, with Arthur E. R. Boak, Henry A. Sanders, Jesse S. Reeves, and Herbert F. Wright, intro. James Brown Scott, 2 vols. (Oxford and London, 1913–25), 2:102–3, 112–30; Johannes Althusius, *The Politics*, an abridged trans. of the 3d ed. of *Politica methodice digesta . . .*, trans. and ed. Frederick S. Carney (Boston, 1964), pp. 65–66.

ble to views held by the early Corneille and others, as we will see, and a commonplace maintained for years in political theoretical debate, although in France later than in England; as we might expect).[53]

At the end of the seventeenth century a prominent English statesman, the marquess of Halifax, summarized the matter in his "Anatomy of an Equivalent": "There can be no government without a Supreme Power; that power is not always in the same hands, it is in different shapes and dresses, but still, wherever it is lodged, it must be unlimited. . . . Where this Supreme Power is mixed, or divided, the shape only differeth, the argument is still the same." The ultimate purpose of such governmental authority, he insisted, was to take care of the "rights inherent in men's persons in their single capacities." That sovereignty, he had written in his slightly earlier "Character of a Trimmer," had to further "all kind of right which may remain in the body of the People," protect "the common good of mankind," and uphold those individual liberties which are "the foundation of all virtue," that liberty which, as he described it, "is the mistress of mankind," for which (for whom?) every man's "reasonable desire . . . ought not to be restrained."[54]

In our own century Jean-Paul Sartre, for instance, substantially echoed such a view. So, too, in the eighteenth century had Immanuel Kant, who conceived of individual and society as in a conflict brought under control only by social laws whose irresistible force ordered individual freedoms: in his view these laws were in fact embedded in the mind as the "categorical imperative" of social duty. In Freud's later psychoanalytical system the superego was to perform a similar role. I do not, of course, claim that the functions of all these were identical, but the phrase "authoritarian liberalism" enables one to see the structural similarities—if not identities (as the seventeenth century saw them)—between what might otherwise be thought of as quite different political systems. Maurice Merleau-Ponty's 1947 "defense" of Stalinism, offering a kind of limit case, may help reveal the underlying similarity of assumption. One could consider it "fundamentalist," for its argument rested (precisely) on the party's need to uphold the rights of the many to the detriment of those of a few, whose freedoms (it was claimed) would impede the rights of the majority absolutely.[55] In this regard one would do well to consider the implications of interpretations of Rousseau's political thought which take it from revolutionary liberalism to totalitarianism. The point is that analytico-referential political discourse and action (authoritarian liberalism) run, but control, that entire gamut.

---

[53]Davanzati, *Leçon*, p. 229.
[54]George Savile, Marquess of Halifax, *Complete Works*, ed. J. P. Kenyon (Harmondsworth, 1969), pp. 135, 59–62.
[55]Maurice Merleau-Ponty, *Humanism and Terror: An Essay on the Communist Problem*, trans. John O'Neill (Boston, 1969). The basis of these paragraphs is my *Uncertainty of Analysis*, pp. 199–200 n. 32.

Not only had the late seventeenth century clearly seen that inclusiveness, but it had established literature as its major cultural guarantor. For poetry, literature, was to teach those "patterns," wrote Davenant, that were "fit to be imitated by the most necessary men." Quite clearly, those most necessary men were those who by birth, education, virtue, and a proper sense of their own place and value (what the ancients had called, like Corneille, their "magnanimity") were alone fitted to lead the multitude, a group of people often berated with quite remarkable violence: "Although the populace," wrote Gabriel Naudé in 1639, "(by which word I mean the ordinary people in a crowd, the mob, the common dregs, rabble in any way of an inferior, servile, or mechanick condition), may be endowed with reason, it abuses it in a thousand ways and by its means becomes the stage on which orators, preachers, false prophets, charlatans, cheating politicians, rebels, seditionaries, the embittered, the superstitious and the ambitious, in short all who have some novel scheme, perform their savage and bloody tragedies."[56]

This always menacing violence of the restless and credulous crowd, easily assimilated, as we saw in both Hobbes and Davenant, to humans in the state of nature, was one area of fear that made the question of who would control so powerful a tranquilizing instrument as literature a matter of huge importance. This seething violence also recalled earlier terrors concerning the condition of society itself. Indeed, Naudé's savage diatribe ("Rabelaisian," I would say, were it not that it lacked the humor) occurred in the context of his discussion of the Saint Bartholomew's Day massacre. Only the most necessary men could bring that violence to order and fulfill what Davenant might call the utmost possibilities of human action, reason, and achievement, and finally satisfy their "reasonable desire" for "the mistress of mankind," liberty.

[56]Gabriel Naudé, *Considérations politiques sur les coups d'estat* (Sur la copie de Rome, 1667), pp. 235–36.

Chapter 4

Violence and the Humanity of Reason

And even if men in many ways rob women of their share of the greatest benefits, they are wrong to take pride in their usurpation and tyranny: inequality of physical, rather than intellectual power readily accounts for this theft and suffering. And physical strength is a virtue so inferior that beasts have as much more than men, as men do than women. . . . Besides, properly understood, the human animal is neither man nor woman, sexual difference is neither fundamental nor constitutive of different species. . . . What uniquely forms and distinguishes this Animal is only the rational soul.
—Marie de Gournay, *Egalité des hommes et des femmes*

The emphasis on these most necessary men immediately raises another issue of exceptional importance. For it is a fact that the problem of violence and individual rights had been linked throughout the first half of the seventeenth century with an argument about reason and gender that had anxiously sought to respond as well to issues of exclusion and dominance. These matters became more problematic as they were felt to become increasingly central. The debate was a fundamental one: over nothing less than the question of who would have the right to produce and control the literary culture in formation. And if the illiterate mob was excluded from literary culture at any level, who then could actually be its consumers and recipients? Or was it to be consumed only by those who simultaneously produced, turning on itself solipsistically, and so uselessly, as a dog chasing its own tail? The debates and exclusions were a matter of male/female confrontation even before the quarrel over gender became an integral part of the *consolidation* of literary culture, as we will see in Chapter 7. Once again the work of Pierre Corneille in France at the time of the founding of the Académie Française was central in these early debates (presumably, not by chance do we find these late 1630s writings fundamental to all aspects of literary development). No less significant was the part taken by Richelieu and others who at first glance might seem to have been strictly political theorists and actors.

It was certainly not irrelevant either that almost without exception, the first members of the Académie had learned their linguistic crafts, polished their letters, and explored their ideals of manners and of reason in the *salon* created by Catherine Vivonne de Rambouillet and in polite conver-

97

sation with her women friends. There, as elsewhere, the particular debate about the status and nature of women was entirely caught up on the one hand in the more general debate over human reason and on the other with the urgent discussions about the confused and unstable condition of the political and social order, everywhere subverted by uncertainty and violence. Both matters played an essential role in what finally happened with respect to the cultural status of women and their role in literature. Discussion passed through three principal moments.

First, the argument that there was only one kind of human reason, that it was quite unconnected with sexuality, and therefore equally powerful in both men and women, grew ever stronger. The high points in this aspect of the debate may be situated in the mid-sixteenth century, in the 1620s–40s (Marie de Gournay, Descartes, Jacques du Bosc, Corneille in France, the "Swetnam controversy" in England), and at the very end of the seventeenth century, with the Cartesians, François Poulain de la Barre in France (1670s), and Mary Astell in England (1690s).[1] To these we should doubtless add Gabrielle Suchon, although her 1693 treatise on morality, published at Lyon and describing women's more or less systematic exclusion from all the liberal benefits enjoyed by men, seems barely to have been known at the time (even less than Poulain's).

Second, in the mid-seventeenth century some sort of almost subterranean feeling seems to have grown that because of the specific way in which men had participated in the historical development of societies, reason in them was inseparable from violence. On the other hand, however, because women had historically been excluded from the making of society and culture, reason in them (not *female* reason, but simply Reason as acting in women) was free of that violence and could thus offer a solution to the dangerous decay of political and civil order. The future perhaps lay with women, even though the arguments and hints remained ambiguous and unclear. They were made the more problematic because of political philosophy's theoretical *exclusion* of women from active participation in political order. In France the major proponents of the idea that women might rationally resolve the problem of the violent decay of

[1]This assumption clearly lay behind Descartes's close intellectual relations with Princess Elisabeth of Bohemia (1642–1650) and Henry More's with Anne Finch, Viscountess Conway (1651–79). Descartes declared the importance of Elisabeth's contribution to the elaboration of his ideas in his dedication to the *Principes de la philosophie*, and the correspondence showed it to be fundamental to the *Passions de l'âme*. Conway's abilities were apparent in a manuscript of hers that circulated sufficiently for Leibniz to have read it and to say it was the catalyst for his own thinking. It has been published: *The Principles of the Most Ancient and Modern Philosophy*, ed. and trans. Peter Lopson (The Hague, Boston, and London, 1982). It reflected More's thinking in its derivation of the nature of Being from a concept of the nature of God. Like More, Conway was in many ways indebted to Descartes, but she was professedly anti-Cartesian in her account of the inseparability of mind and body, derived from Christian Platonic views (pp. 191–219).

societies, besides the implications of the *salon* movement and the preciosity accompanying it, were Corneille and Poulain de la Barre.[2] Third, at the end of the seventeenth century a distinction between men's and women's reason was asserted more "violently" (perhaps just because of the preceding debate). The hopes for political salvation through nonviolent reason in women were abandoned.[3] The idea that women's reason was of a different order was again reaffirmed: tranquil passion, calm emotion, depth of sentiment, nurturing instinct, and the rest now defined such nonviolent reason, in a return to a belief in traditionally asserted female attributes. But they had acquired a positive, rather than a negative, value. By such means women, possessing no responsibility at all for cultural or political production (indeed, long since theoretically excluded from them), could nonetheless be included at least in the first—as consumers, of course, or as producers of a subordinate culture.

The turning point in the debate was signaled by the *Querelle des femmes* at the end of the century in France, most particularly by those writings of Boileau, Perrault, La Bruyère, Fénelon, Mme de Maintenon, and others which I discuss in Chapter 7. The issue arose afresh as an integral part of the *Querelle des anciens et modernes* (in England, the "Battle of the Books"). The dominant culture thus found the way to *co-opt* the strong arguments about women's reason, leaving it as a "positive" characteristic but making it gender specific and thus able to be subordinated to what was then given as men's more powerful reason. This reason had to do, then, first with what was said about women and women's status and second with what that *saying* established as a result. Corneille's plays

[2]An opposition between men and women in terms of their relative violence had already been tied to talk about reason in the sixteenth century and was clearly connected at one level with arguments about the virtues of women's passivity.

[3]Contrary to what some have suggested, the arguments had indeed been political: in question had been general recovery of society and particular improvement of women's status by education, participation in government, equality under the law (especially in marriage), and so on. Both in England and France the debate did "suggest broad political goals," notwithstanding Hilda Smith's contrary claim (*Reason's Disciples: Seventeenth-Century English Feminists* [Urbana, Ill., 1982], p. 201). She asserts that the "lack" of such goals explained the failure of the arguments. Here and in Chapter 7 I argue that the dominant culture managed to negate the complex debate and recuperate liberating arguments so as to assert a subordinate status for women. Both the negation and the recuperation *mattered* just because of the debate's political implications and objectives. My argument complements those advanced by Joan DeJean, *Fictions of Sappho, 1546–1937* (Chicago and London, 1989), and Elaine Hobby, *Virtue of Necessity: English Women's Writing, 1649–88* (Ann Arbor, Mich., 1989). Both see a major change in attitude and condition in the 1660s and 1670s. Londa Schiebinger has shown how women in science followed a similar trajectory, from a relative freedom as scientists in the seventeenth century to deprivation of such a role during the eighteenth and reification as stylized objects of study: *Mind Has No Sex? Women in the Origins of Modern Science* (Cambridge, Mass., and London, 1989). Now see, too, Joan DeJean, *Tender Geographies: Women and the Origins of the Novel in France* (New York, 1991). I read this too late for other than an occasional reference.

of the late 1630s and early 1640s were especially important texts in this process, both for articulating the political optimism about women's rationality and for representing the contours of its failure.

The treatment of women's status by the dominant Judeo-Christian tradition is largely familiar: woman was responsible for the Fall, she was lubricious, in thrall to sexual passion, instinct, animality, and so on. Her virtues were the corresponding ones of passivity, modesty, chastity, patience, silence, temperance, and obedience: virtues for which women had not infrequently been idealized in some quarters (Lipsius was perhaps recalling them in his remark about Queen Elizabeth quoted in Chapter 1, whatever its political context). Some early writers seemed to imply that women were fully as rational as men: writings by Hildegard of Bingen, Hroswitha, and Julian of Norwich were exemplary (although no one ever took them up), and Marie de France urged such a claim in the prologue of her *Lais*. But as the examples suggest, as Marie indeed said, and as was frequently asserted well into the seventeenth century and even later, such reason came from God, whose handmaiden woman was.[4] The view did parallel certain arguments about reason as manifest in man as well, but in either case it was entirely different from asserting that women share with men a human and self-responsible rationality. Despite ambiguities and equivocations, writers mostly agreed on the inferiority, danger, and irrationality of women.

Before the mid-sixteenth century the only real proponent of a relatively unambiguous view that women, like men, possessed and could use an entirely human reason was Christine de Pisan at the beginning of the previous century. And hers then remained a lone voice.[5] At the end of the fifteenth century, with Cornelius Agrippa, some truly new arguments did begin to be advanced. In his *De nobilitate et praecellentia foeminei sexus* (written around 1509, published in 1529, translated into French in 1530 and into English in 1542), Agrippa advanced at least two arguments that appear quite novel. Linda Woodbridge has remarked of the first of these that "in his initial flat statement of the complete spiritual and intellectual equality of the sexes," Agrippa deployed a previously unused claim. In David Clapham's translation, *A Treatise of the Nobilitie and excellencye of woman kinde*, this opening read as follows: "The woman hathe the

[4]See Merry E. Wiesner, "Women's Defense of Their Public Roles," in *Women in the Middle Ages and the Renaissance: Literary and Historical Perspectives*, ed. Mary Beth Rose (Syracuse, N.Y., 1986), pp. 17–21. As exemplars of later views she mentions Rachel Speght and Anne Wheathill, both early seventeenth-century writers. For the most part such a characterization holds for the writers studied by Hobby in *Virtue of Necessity*.

[5]For a fine recent discussion of Christine de Pisan's achievement, see Susan Schiba-noff, "Taking the Gold out of Egypt: The Art of Reading as a Woman," in *Gender and Reading: Essays on Readers, Texts, and Contexts*, ed. Elizabeth A. Flynn and Patro-cinio P. Schweickart (Baltimore, 1986), pp. 83–106. It remains the case, nonetheless, that the oppositional tone of *The Book of the City of Ladies* was largely contradicted by the "handbook"-style *Treasure*.

same mynd that a man hath, that same reason and speche, she gothe to the same ende of blysfulnes . . . Betwene man and woman by substance of the soule, one hath no higher preemynence of nobylytye aboue the other, but both of them naturally haue equall libertie of dignitie and worthynesse."[6]

Actually, I think this particular argument was less original than Thomas Elyot's later purely secular argument. It was clear for Agrippa that mind and soul were, if not identical, at least coterminous, directing the human toward some eschatological fulfillment ("the same ende of blysfulnes"). That argument was evidently not at all unknown. If from nowhere else, it could come directly from Augustine—scarcely a vehement defender of women's equality. Indeed, Augustine's claim asserted male and female equality in the hereafter (in bliss, a place of entire asexuality), but complete inequality in the secular city, where male dominance was resolutely upheld: in that light, Agrippa's opening gambit would have been entirely paradoxical.

Where Agrippa was definitely more original (although the suggestion was at least implicit in Christine de Pisan, in Chaucer's *Wife of Bath*, and very soon in Marguerite de Navarre's *Heptaméron*) was in his argument that women were in a socially inferior position to men not because of any natural infirmity, but because of men's deployment of force: "And thus by these lawes, the women being subdewed as it were by force of armes, are constrained to giue place to men, and to obeye theyr subdewers, not by no naturall, no diuine necessitie or reason, but by custome, education, fortune, and a certayne Tyranicall occasion."[7] This purely secular conclusion belied the beginning and genuinely did deploy a new argument—new at least in its explicitness. It also prefigured the later association of arguments concerning secular reason and violence, according to which the natural equality of reason was undermined by a historically situated deployment of violence.

When Agrippa was writing, the issue was at once unreal and idealist: in that there could be no authentic political, legal, cultural, or social consequences for women (not that there would be in the seventeenth century either, but by then, at least momentarily, the *possibilities* seemed genuine). The issue could then appear, if not as simply a rhetorical one (as Woodbridge claims), at least as a separate and isolated one. Violence of men to women was not yet viewed as one aspect of a more generalized violence. Reason, too, was rather a theological or metaphysical issue than an epistemological or political one. Half a century later this was no longer quite so clear.

In 1545 Sir Thomas Elyot's fictional debate between a traditional misogynist, Caninius, and a supporter of women, Candidus, clearly gave the

---

[6]Linda Woodbridge, *Women and the English Renaissance: Literature and the Nature of Womankind, 1540–1620* (Urbana, Ill., and Chicago, 1984), p. 39.
[7]Quoted in ibid., p. 43.

advantage to the latter (not surprisingly, if Constance Jordan is right in her argument that the text was written as a defense of Catherine of Aragon).[8] It did so, revealingly, by enabling Candidus to argue that women's reason was better than men's because it was ineluctably tied up with virtues of tranquility and guardianship (this claim, of course, makes the most of traditional patience and passivity—but it adds reason to them). Reason as it functioned in women was thus directly opposed to what could be seen in men, where reason was inseparable from the violent activities characteristic of the hunter. "And so ye conclude," Candidus exulted, "that the power of reason is more in the prudente and diligent kepynge, than in the valiaunt or politike geating: And that Discretion, Election [Judgment], and Prudence, whiche is all and in everye part reason, doo excell strengthe, wytte, and hardinesse: And consequentely they, in whome be those vertues, in that that they have them, do excell in iuste extimacion them that be stronge, hardy, or politike in geattynge of any thynge."

We have agreed, adds Candidus, that prudence ("which in effect is nothing but reason") is thus better conceived as belonging to women more than men and especially that prudence "in kepyng" is more useful than "valiauntnesse in geattyng" (a distinction already made by Aristotle, as Pasquier would later point out). Further, because prudence is better than courage, and because prudence *is* reason, so women are "more excellent than men in reason" and generally speaking "woman . . . as it seemeth is more perfit than manne."[9] Because "naturall reason is in women as well as in men," Elyot concluded that women could hold the highest political and social positions with entire propriety: "Then have women also Discrecion, Election, & Prudence, which do make that wisedome, which pertaineth to governaunce. And perdy [he finally concluded this exchange], many artes and necessarie occupations haue ben inuented by women."

This claim was identical to that made just ten years later by François de Billon, who attempted to list all the inventions in question.[10] He also based his argument on the claim that God had given men and women "an identical and unique form of soul, such that between these souls there is no sexual difference." Women, he added, "share the same understanding as men, the same reason, identical speech." Everything men can create, he remarked a little later, women can too, and "where the intellect of the one can penetrate, so too can penetrate the other's intellect."[11] Yet the identity of divine soul never had meant rational equality in the sphere of public action, and when it came to the purpose of such intellect, argument fell

[8]Constance Jordan, "Feminism and the Humanists: The Case of Sir Thomas Elyot's *Defence of Good Women*," in *Rewriting the Renaissance: The Discourses of Sexual Difference in Early Modern Europe*, ed. Margaret W. Ferguson, Maureen Quilligan, and Nancy J. Vickers (Chicago and London, 1986), pp. 242–58.

[9]Elyot, *Defence of Good Women*, pp. Ciii^vo–Cv^ro.

[10]François de Billon, *Le fort inexpugnable de l'honneur du sexe femenin*, Paris, 1555, intro. M. A. Screech (Wakefield, New York, and The Hague, 1970), pp. 22vo–32vo.

[11]Ibid., pp. 1vo, 7ro.

away once again. Billon urged identity of soul, reason, and speech, for "the wise woman edifies and ornaments a household." He had perchance been reading *The Courtier*. It was, I think, in that spirit and no other that certain women participated in the Palace Academy during the mid-1580s. Pierre de Bourdeille (Brantôme) spoke of women's membership. A contemporary English writer specified "the Queen of Navarre, . . . the Countess of Retz, and another lady or two." It was the case that Agrippa d'Aubigné praised Madame de Retz and Madame de Lignerolles for their part in a discussion on moral and intellectual virtues.[12] But the pattern was clearly that of Castiglione and Lope, of Urbino and Alba de Tormes.

So Billon went on to applaud certain Italian cities (particularly Naples) for being less concerned with "interior decoration" than with "striving to keep the Women quite orderly [*bien en ordre*] and brilliantly lovely [*claire-ment luysantes*]—and rightly so: since wherever a beautiful Woman appears, everything is brightened [*clarifié*] by her presence."[13] Nothing was remotely ambivalent in such remarks. For Billon, as for so many others, however "equal" women's reason might be, it was to be *used* in a man's world. Whatever the claims made by men for women and reason, "the lady, shall we venture to say, turns out to be merely a wife." As Ruth Kelso went on later: "The assignment of woman to the domestic end [was thought] perfectly natural and necessary because of her function in bearing and nourishing children. Her more delicate frame and more gentle disposition specially fit her for this, as they unfit her to endure the strenous exercises and turmoil of public life."[14] Women may have been blessed with the same reason as men, we were to conclude from all this, but it was to be put to use in the private, not public, sphere.[15]

Agrippa, Elyot, and others were walking a fine but quite visible line. They viewed men's reason as tainted by the presence of a profoundly negative tare: the mark of violence (Billon was not among these). Rather than simply remove that tare, in favor of some kind of *morally* "neutral" reason (i.e., a reason not internally predetermined, but freely used to achieve certain *human* goals), they elected to *add* a set of values seen as

[12]Yates, *French Academies*, pp. 32–33. Of the maréchale de Retz, John Nothnagle remarks: "Claude-Catherine de Clermont-Dampierre (1545–1603) . . . was a learned lady celebrated by the poets for her 'salon de Dictynne,' which flourished about 1570 in her house in the Faubourg Saint-Honoré in Paris" (d'Aubigné, *His Life*, p. 147 n. 15).

[13]Billon, *Fort inexpugnable*, p. 1ᵛᵒ.

[14]Ruth Kelso, *Doctrine for the Lady of the Renaissance* (Urbana, Ill., 1956), pp. 1, 31. Although she argues that *some* women succeeded in escaping the constraints imposed in Tudor times, Pearl Hogrefe actually confirms this view: *Tudor Women: Commoners and Queens* (Ames, Iowa, 1975).

[15]Many authors upheld this view throughout the seventeenth century (see, e.g., writings in *Half-Humankind: Contexts and Texts of the Controversy about Women in England, 1540–1640*, ed. Katherine Usher Henderson and Barbara F. McManus [Urbana, Ill., 1985]); indeed, at the end of the eighteenth century Mary Wollstonecraft began her publishing career with such an argument; Anna Barbauld and Hannah More never desisted from it.

positive. But those positive values came perilously close to the now-familiar ones of nurturing warmth, instinctual and childlike appreciation of the good and the beautiful, and some sort of boundless protective and passive absorption of the potentially harmful. Thomas More could write that he saw no difference between man and woman: "For both of them beare name of a reasonable creature equally whose nature reason only doth distinguish from bruite beastes, and therefore I do not see why learning in like manner may not equally agree with both sexes, for by it, reason is cultivated."[16]

Nevertheless, he certainly suggested no more than did his daughter Margaret Roper, widely famed for her intellect and learning, that she should use them for anything other than to become a better wife—more chaste, more virtuous, better able to order the household and raise children wisely. Such celebrated writers on the subject as those friends of More, Desiderius Erasmus and Juan Luis Vives, argued no differently. With the possible exception of Agrippa, all remained unable to elaborate a concept of neutral and purely *human* reason. Such a failure, the inability of all these writers to succeed in freeing reason from sexual bonds, to overcome the implications of violence, prefigured the more drastic and permanent failure of the late seventeenth century.[17]

At the very end of the century Pasquier picked up once again on the

[16]The citation, from a letter written by More to one of his daughters' tutors, is in Mary Agnes Cannon, *The Education of Women in the Renaissance* (1916; rpt. Westport, Conn., 1981), p. 99. Jardine has argued that this education to self-restraint and the avoidance of idleness, far from being a means of liberation, was a mark of women's redundancy. Not intended to enable activity in the social sphere, it was merely to fill idle moments at home: *Still Harping on Daughters*, pp. 37–67.

[17]Elaine Beilin has suggested that most women writers of the sixteenth century reconfirmed traditional views in all essentials. Those whose work she explores, however, were mostly aristocratic or wealthy bourgeois wives and daughters who identified themselves as such (when they were not, furthermore, writing religious works): *Redeeming Eve: Women Writers of the English Renaissance* (Princeton and Guildford, 1987). Matters were both more complex and more ambivalent. Tilde Sankovitch has argued that some women did attempt to ally a claim to equality of reason with a rejection of masculine violence. She takes the cases of Madeleine (1520–87) and Catherine (1542–1587) Desroches: see "Inventing Authority of Origin: The Difficult Enterprise," in *Women in the Middle Ages and the Renaissance*, ed. Rose, pp. 227–43. Sankovitch views this effort as a failure. The same was true of the Swetnam dispute in England (1615–1620s), although Woodbridge has glossed *An Apologie for Women-Kinde*, published in 1605 by one "I. G.," with more optimism: "War . . . is fit for beasts; if women find intellectual combat more congenial, women are more fully human: to humanity's proper pursuits, physical prowess is irrelevant." This view, she avers, was central to the Jacobean idea of women (Woodbridge, *Women and the English Renaissance*, p. 75). The issue was actually, as she allows, less clear and hotly debated throughout the period (pp. 159–65). It was indeed wholly imbricated, in England at least, with a rather fearful debate about *women's* innate violence and aggressivity (pp. 184–219). Belsey writes usefully on this aspect: *Subject of Tragedy*, pp. 135–44. Still, the view that in some women (but only in women) reason was free of violence was expressed in France by Gournay, Corneille, and the *salon* movement and would culminate in Poulain de la Barre's 1673 *Égalité des deux sexes*. Then it was defeated.

distinction Elyot had made between "getting" and "keeping," saying that he agreed entirely with Aristotle's opinion in the third book of his *Politics*, where the philosopher asserted the husband's task to be to "acquerir," while the wife was to "conserver." But he then added that because "in this common household both contribute their part, it seems entirely reasonable that she [*celle*] who shares the work, should share the profit." Pasquier was responding to a question drawn from legal fact: whether it should be in "the husband's power to dispose as he wishes of all communal goods to the wife's detriment." His reply was that as both contribute equally (as appropriate to their sex), so both should benefit equally. But this has to do with the equity of a proper distributive justice, on the basis of an argument that the two contributions are equal and so should receive equal remuneration, as it were. Pasquier's argument, indeed, liberal as it was in one sense, served if anything to confirm the fundamental difference between men and women: as it simultaneously denied men the right, on such a basis, to exercise any sort of oppressive violence against women. Slightly more abstractly, Comenius was to express a not dissimilar view in 1623, when he wrote of a revolt by women ending so that "all things outwardly would remain in accord with the ancient customs and yet the domestic dominance of women would be strengthened not a little."[18]

In any case, such symbolic gains as any of this may have represented had to be set against a more murderous reality: the more or less European-wide witch craze, steadily growing and spreading throughout these years. By the late sixteenth century even such "liberal" thinkers as Bodin found themselves upholding all the preposterous sins of witches: their ability to kill at a distance, to maim and make ill with spells, to change the weather, to copulate with devils, participate in sabbaths, and so forth (all this in his *Démonomanie des sorciers* of 1580). Further, even the symbolic gains, the set of positive (if perilous) values attributed to women's reason, were only the more sympathetic side of a coin of which Machiavelli, for example, showed the uglier obverse. The point was of major importance, for along with the difficulties and equivocations involved in the argument from reason itself (where it concerned women), the very political thinking that responded to the apparent dissolution of European polity during this period seemed actually to exclude women from participating in the organization of that polity—Agrippa's, Elyot's, or Lipsius's tentative counter suggestions notwithstanding. In France the exclusion was vehemently explicit, embedded in the Salic Law. Otherwise, it was predicated principally on those supposedly positive values. The question is significant, for women's *theoretical* exclusion from the political arena was a singularly important factor in the conceptual failure to assert women's equality and freedoms. We will see later how that exclusion eventually helped

---

[18]Estienne Pasquier, *Les recherches de la France*, in *Oeuvres*, 1:412–14; Comenius, *Labyrinth of the World*, pp. 115–17.

reconfirm the claim that women's reason was particular to their sex (whereas men's would be "neutral") and how it became integrated in literary culture.

Machiavelli's *Prince* had long since written male/female violence into reason of state itself, describing how the masculine *virtù* essential to the efficient ruler of a new state had to learn to take female *Fortuna* by force, just as, he wrote, a spirited, violent young man had to learn to take a woman.[19] Such metaphors were far from innocent, and it is therefore hardly coincidental that a century later Machiavelli's view was taken up, metaphorically and literally (as to the exclusion of women) by a man who was not simply a theorist, as the Florentine was by the time he wrote, but who had the power to make his word law: I mean Armand-Jean du Plessis, cardinal-duc de Richelieu, chief minister to Louis XIII. In the *Political Testament* he wrote for the king in case of his own prior death, the minister constantly emphasized the need for princes to enjoy a *"mâle vertu."* The phrase was no more than indicative of a general subordination of women to men's power as it was expressed throughout this text, written (more properly, dictated) between 1632 and 1638.

For my purpose, the matter and dates are important, for it often appears, we will see, as if Corneille were responding directly to Richelieu on this issue. But before coming to that, I would first like to take a look at a text of possibly even greater significance: Cardin Le Bret's 1632 *De la souveraineté du Roy.* By the time he published this volume, Le Bret was an old man. Trained in the law, he had started his public career in the anxiously violent days of the beginning of Henri IV's reign. By 1632, a recognized expert in the monarchical constitution, he had for years been a member (with Richelieu) of the Royal Council, the king's principal and immediate advisory body. Although he was obviously without Richelieu's enormous power, it is clear enough that Le Bret's position and reputation meant his voice would be heard. More than that, however, with his *Souveraineté du Roy* Le Bret had written what became the "textbook" of the monarchy under Louis XIV. That his arguments coincided with the far briefer ones set out by Richelieu should hardly surprise us. Nonetheless, the vehemence of his discussion where it concerned women might appear somewhat gratuitous, linking reason of state, human reason, and men's aggressivity.

Since Le Bret's book was presented as a discussion of French constitutional law, he began by running through the legal foundations of the monarchy itself. He quickly got to the question of the Salic Law (whose application to the crown he explicitly recognized as an interpretation of

---

[19]Hannah Fenichel Pitkin has explored this question in *Fortune Is a Woman: Gender and Politics in the Thought of Niccolò Machiavelli* (Berkeley, Los Angeles, and London, 1984). In the age of Mary Tudor, Mary Queen of Scots, Catherine de Medicis, and above all Elizabeth, debates about women rulers were extensive. See Chapter 1, note 76, for reference to some discussions.

the law governing the inheritance of fiefs), writing that "women are unable to succeed to the Crown." Such a maxim, he then continued,

conforms to the law of nature, which, because it created woman imperfect, weak, and feeble, as much in body as in mind, placed her under man's power. To that end, nature enriched him with stronger judgment, firmer courage, and more robust physical strength. We can thus see that divine law wills woman to recognize and render obedience to her husband, as to her head [*chef*] and to her King. And not only does such law not give woman any authority in Empires and Kingdoms, but on the contrary we see in Isaiah chap. 3 that God threatens to give his enemies women as mistresses, as an insupportable curse.

That, he immediately went on, "is why the whole of Antiquity greatly disparaged the Lacedemonians for letting themselves be ruled by their women."[20]

It was not, I think, mere chance that led Descartes (after many others) to take precisely this example of Sparta as the epitome of the well-ordered state. He argued the case in the second part of the *Discours de la méthode,* asserting that the best and most stable polity was founded on a coherent set of laws promulgated by a single author, as Sparta's were by Lycurgus.[21] Unlike Le Bret and Richelieu, Descartes implicitly included women in all human rational organization, as he did in the entire argument about reason itself. For if rational mind is of a different order from body, and if sexuality is attached only to the latter, then clearly reason is neither male nor female, but simply human. The singular rational authority lawfully ordering Lacedemonia, Descartes proposed, was exactly analogous to reason's authority over body and the emotions (as he was to write in the 1649 *Passions de l'âme,* following Richelieu's similar statements in the *Testament*).[22] In neither case could distinctions be made for sex.

Descartes's argument made women epistemologically and politically equal to men. Although he certainly never made such a conclusion explicit himself, its logic was adopted not only by Poulain de la Barre in 1673, but already by Corneille from the 1637 *Le Cid* on: what role was played by

---

[20]Cardin Le Bret, *De la souveraineté du Roy* (Paris, 1632), pp. 31–32. It was certainly not chance that brought Le Bret so rapidly to Salic exclusions. Pierre Ronzeaud has shown how these had been a central issue in political/legal debate from the fourteenth century and then above all through the sixteenth and into the seventeenth centuries: "La femme au pouvoir ou le monde à l'envers," *XVIIe Siècle,* 108 (1975), 9–33, esp. 11–16. The series of "arguments" provided by Le Bret were all part of the tradition: "cette pesante accumulation d'arguments," as Ronzeaud puts it (p. 16).

[21]The *Discours de la méthode* was published in 1636, but it had been written over the preceding ten years, almost exactly contemporaneously therefore with Richelieu's *Testament* (this last being known, but not actually published until 1688).

[22]Unlike either Le Bret or Richelieu, Descartes was, of course, a powerless exile in the Netherlands—as was the Palatine royal family, with whose daughter Elisabeth he was to become such a close intellectual friend.

the Infante, Doña Urraque (often asserted to be dramatically wholly re-
dundant), if not the demonstration of nonviolent reason taming passion?
(The only character in the play to do so, male or female.) The point was
also recognized by means of the same Spartan metaphor by one of Kath-
erine Philips's friends, precisely with respect to her translations from
Corneille. In a liminary poem prefixed to "the divine Orinda" 's 1667
Works, praising her translation of Corneille's *Pompée,* this woman poet,
"Philo-Philippa," wrote:

> Train'd up to Arms, we Amazons have been,
> And Spartan virgins strong as Spartan Men:
> Breed Women but as Men, and they are these;
> While Sybarit Men are Women by their ease.[23]

(The continued use of this comparison, as we will see, offers something
of a benchmark with regard to changing attitudes toward the status of
women.)

Women, wrote Le Bret however, had to be excluded from the throne
because monarchs needed to be "warlike and belligerent" (*guerriers et
belliqueux*). Those reasons, like women's feebleness, divine law, and tradition's condemnation of the Spartans, were added to the Salic exclusion,
just because that law itself nominally rejected women not from accession
to the crown, but simply from "succession to fiefs," an objection, be it
noted, that Le Bret rejected as "specious," despite all these hedges. Perhaps
we should be wary of crying "sexism" too readily. While the Salic Law was
certainly used to facilitate such critical views, recent events showed how
the Law could be used less tendentiously as a bulwark against disorder. In
1593 Guillaume Du Vair had made a celebrated (and perilously risky)
parliamentary speech in its support, to counter the Catholic League's
maneuvers to marry the Spanish Infanta to a French prince and use her
"claim" to the French throne (she was the daughter of Elisabeth de Valois)
to justify the election of that prince as king. The arrangement was meant
to block Navarre, but it would also have given the Spanish a hugely
important role in internal French affairs at a time when Spain remained
the most feared European power. First printed in 1606, Du Vair's work was
republished in 1625.[24]

---

[23]Katherine [Fowler] Philips, *Poems by the Most Deservedly Admired Mrs Katherine
Philips, the Matchless Orinda,* to which is added, Monsieur Corneille's *Pompey* and
Horace, tragedies . . . (London, 1667), liminaries (unpaginated). This posthumous edition (Philips died of smallpox in 1664) was edited by a member of her circle calling
himself "Poliarche" (Sir Charles Cotterel).

[24]Guillaume Du Vair, "Suasion de l'arrest donné au parlement pour la manutention de
la loy salique," in *Actions et traictez,* pp. 110–44. To grasp the stakes fully, one needs
also to read Du Vair's "Exhortation à la paix" (ibid., pp. 63–109). The terror was that civil
war would be further provoked and continue interminably. The preceding citation is
from Le Bret, *Souveraineté,* p. 33.

In fact, as we will shortly see with respect to the Medici princesses, such arguments themselves easily became anti-women. But first, because it helps embed Corneille further in this debate, I note a metaphorical use of the Salic Law entirely parallel to Le Bret's argument. It is a use I have not elsewhere come across, and here must certainly be considered entirely sexist. It occurred once again in a liminary poem to the Philips collection just mentioned. The author of this poem was the Royalist Abraham Cowley, and his reference was wholly demeaning to women. He wrote, slightly sneeringly (and in traditional terms of container and contained), that Orinda had canceled "great Apollo's Salick Law . . . / Man may be Head, but Woman's now the Brain."[25]

In effect (if not in both their intentions), Cowley and Le Bret differed scarcely at all from Richelieu, writing (at least in the second case) virtually at the same moment. The prince's reason (of state), we saw, was presented as a "masculine virtue" that overcomes "passion," enabling clear and distinct human "Reason" to function.[26] Since passion, Richelieu asseverated, was the proper characteristic of women, it followed that even if *some* women rulers had been more or less temperate (was this "moderation" in deference to Marie de Medicis, whose son was, after all, Louis XIII?), the fact remained that

> few are of this nature, and one must confess that just as a woman undid the world, so nothing [!] is more capable of ruining States than this sex, when, setting its foot firmly upon those who govern them, it moves them at will and as a result badly. For the best thoughts of women are almost always bad, given that they are led by their passions, which normally take the place of reason in their minds. But reason is the one and only true moving force that must kindle and stimulate to action those who are in the service of public affairs.[27]

Such views simply echoed general opinion, and the kinds of tales that circulated about women rulers testified to such repressive attitudes.

I cannot forbear telling one such story, partly because it was perfectly typical, partly because it concerned Marie de Medicis's aunt, Catherine (with whom we are already quite well acquainted), and partly because it

---

[25]Such attitudes on the part of the men presenting Philip's poems posthumously were ubiquitous—encouraged maybe by the poet herself, who wrote in a letter prefixed to the collection that writing poetry was "unfit for my Sex" and who translated Sabine's "pour le sexe" (in the first speech of *Horace*) as "our weak Sex." In that light, it was hardly surprising that her editor, Cotterel, echoed Cowley in his sentiments: "Some of [her poems] would be no disgrace to the name of any Man that amongst us is most esteemed for his excellency in this kind, and there are none that may not pass with favour, when it is remembred that they fell hastily from the pen but of a Woman."

[26]Armand-Jean du Plessis, Cardinal-Duc de Richelieu, *Testament politique*, ed. Louis André (Paris, 1947), pp. 276, 327, 329.

[27]Ibid., p. 31.

occurred in the correspondence of one of the most learned women of her time, Anne Conway. In a letter of November 1651 her brother related a visit to Rouen Cathedral. There, wrote John Finch, he saw the rich vestments belonging to the chapter: "There was in one of them a Diamond in the Centre of a Circle of Pearle, the Diamond was valued at 200,000 li [pounds] but as the Keeper told me it was stolne by Queen Katherine Medicis when the Archbishop of Rouen married her, she then cutt that Diamond off from the Archbishop's back and putt a Topaz in the Roome of it." As we might expect of Anne Finch's brother, he treated the story with appropriate skepticism: "How it could be done in the face of the congregation I know not."[28] She would have had to be an ace at more than the womanly virtues of cutting and sewing, clearly.

As we saw in Chapter 2, Catherine de Medicis had been victim of criticism stemming from the accusation (at once popular and learned) that she and her courtiers had introduced Machiavellian politics into France— further ammunition for antiwomen arguments and cries about hypocrisy. Queen Catherine would indeed remain the principal stalking horse for such attacks for many a long year. Still, at the turn of the eighteenth century Pierre Bayle thought it useful to remark in his influential *Dictionnaire*, about a book against queens by Denis Lambin, that it was written "when *Catherine de Medicis* govern'd all. 'Tis no wonder such Thoughts came into his Head in those days; for that Queen's ill Conduct was enough to infuse them into those very people, who were least-possess'd [= least taken] with the Salick Law."[29] As queen regent, Catherine's position had been impossible: theoretically and practically weak, she was open to attack by all those who sought power for themselves (just as were to be her niece and Anne of Austria in later years). Estienne's assault had an easy mark: blaming a victim of aggression for all the resulting horrors of that aggression—initially made possible by her perceived weakness. And subsequent commentators could readily lay responsibility for catastrophe at the door of a woman whose sins could be multiplied to make her even more exemplary.

Spurious testimony of the sort recorded by Finch certainly facilitated (for example) Richelieu's condemnation of women as hypocrites, incapable of keeping secrets, and generally irrational. Like Le Bret's, his vocabulary was quite violent and justified the criticism made of men by Gournay in 1622 and 1625, in two short but important texts (notably the first): *De*

[28]*Conway Letters: The Correspondence of Anne, Viscountess Conway, Henry More, and Their Friends, 1642–1684*, ed. Marjorie Hope Nicolson (New Haven, Conn., and London, 1930), pp. 56–57.
[29]*An Historical and Critical Dictionary* by Monsieur Bayle, 4 vols. (London, 1710), 3:2404, col. a. The translation was of the 1701 edition but remains accurate for the French edition I have been able to consult: Pierre Bayle, *Dictionnaire historique et critique*, 3 vols. (Rotterdam, 1715), 3:86, col. a. Lambin is reputed to have died right after the Saint Bartholomew's massacre in grief at the horror and especially at the death of his friend Petrus Ramus. I do not know to which of Lambin's texts Bayle was referring.

l'égalité des hommes et des femmes and *Grief des dames*. Like Agrippa and Elyot, she urged that women possessed the same rational minds as men and were just as capable of occupying all public office, except that they had been placed in a subordinate position by male violence and were currently kept there by an oppression no less real for being more subtle in its application of force: techniques of mockery, arrogance, condescension, disdain, and general dismissal of women's view and interruption of their arguments.[30] Her plea was a strong one, even though it was to have no long-term effect (it could almost be read as a reply to self-fulfilling accusations made against such as Catherine de Medicis). Gournay herself suffered the familiar fate of Renaissance women writers in a masculine culture: scornful and often scurrilous mockery in her lifetime, silence and total neglect after her death (the same would be true for such later writers as Madeleine de Scudéry and Aphra Behn, Delarivière Manley and Eliza Heywood, despite the great popularity of their work during their lifetimes). Unsurprisingly, Gournay's argument was repeated in 1643 in an anonymous text, *La femme généreuse:* "Having made women slaves and prisoners, men have deprived them of knowledge, as the sole weapon and tool available to make war on men and elaborate their deliverance."[31]

An equally strong argument was propounded by Corneille's Norman compatriot Jacques de Bosc, just three years after *Cinna*, the principal of the five plays I look at here. The Franciscan du Bosc had already published two fairly standard treatises on woman's place as a good wife, but in his 1645 *Femme héroïque*, he applied to women a quite different set of qualities: "The principle of heroic virtue is not reason alone, but something better and stronger." It is, he wrote, "a divine instinct or motion [that] it is better to follow than reason itself." It was no longer the rational soul, however, but something more akin to that Will of which Descartes said that it alone in humans was equivalent in its action and force to the divine will. Applied to kingship, the idea allowed Guez de Balzac to remark in

---

[30]These texts were available in a book whose editorial material did nothing to remove the slurs on Gournay (Mario L. Schiff, *La fille d'alliance de Montaigne: Marie de Gournay* . . . [Paris, 1910], pp. 55–97). They are now to be found in Marie de Gournay, *Fragments d'un discours féminin*, ed. Elyane Dezon-Jones (Paris, 1988), pp. 111–33, which also contains three short autobiographical texts and three letters. Apart from these, her writings on poetry, language, and Montaigne's *Essais* have been published by Anne Uildriks, *Les idées littéraires de Mlle de Gournay* (Groningen, 1962), and her "novel" has been reprinted in facsimile: *Le proumenoir de Monsieur de Montaigne* [1594], intro. Patricia Francis Cholakian (Delmar, N.Y., 1985).

[31]*La femme généreuse qui monstre que son sexe est plus noble, meilleur politique, plus vaillant, plus sçavant, plus vertueux, et plus oeconome que celuy des hommes* (Paris, 1643), pp. 97–98. Quoted in Ian Maclean, *Woman Triumphant: Feminism in French Literature, 1610–1652* (Oxford, 1977), p. 54. These terms of 1643 were not altogether surprisingly recalled by Woolf, whose Orlando expresses just that aspect of men's oppression, "armoured with every weapon as they are, while they debar us even from a knowledge of the alphabet!" (*Orlando: A Biography* [1928; rpt. New York, 1946], p. 100).

1631 that "the Prince *can* do anything, but he wills only what he must" (*le Prince peut tout, mais il ne veut que ce qu'il doit*). In du Bosc's rendering of the idea, the Cornelian overtones were quite apparent, and so too was the assertion of its equality in women and men. There might be diversity of some kind, du Bosc allowed, but if so, "it is small and does not justify teaching different ethical standards and expectations to the two sexes."[32]

However ineffective such assertions may have been in the long term, for the present they reinforced the arguments of such as Descartes and Corneille against writers like Richelieu or Le Bret. The ineffectiveness would, of course, be real, and the practical and theoretical exclusion of women from power (and the education necessary for it) has been demonstrated through the eighteenth century and into our own age, in the French Revolution and its aftermath, for example, or out of the writings of such German thinkers as J. G. Fichte or G. W. F. Hegel.[33] Over the first half of the seventeenth century, however, writers developed a strong argument in favor of a single *human* rationality, whose power had never been able to reach full fruition in women because of men's original violence and continuing oppression, but which might yet answer the menace of total social and political dissolution. For clearly, the continuing violence of oppression could readily be seen as one example of the endemic violence everywhere threatening an end to known social life.

The questions now to be posed were *how* could that fruition be realized and to *what end?* The answers would be found in the general condition of violence and political decay that appeared endemic in Europe at this time and in the search for a solution to it. Just as literary culture responded (partly) by reordering and consolidating the very language whose decay was considered a major cause of civil dissolution, so a solution to violence and oppression against women, as a part of the more generalized savagery, seemed (momentarily) capable of settling issues involving the very existence of society.

---

[32]Jean-Louis Guez de Balzac, *Le Prince,* in *Oeuvres,* ed. L. Moreau, 2 vols. (Paris, 1854), 1:136. Jacques du Bosc, *La femme héroïque* (Paris, 1645), pp. 7, 74: this last cited in André Stegmann, *L'héroïsme cornélien: Genèse et signification,* 2 vols. (Paris, 1968), 2:271.
[33]See, e.g., Michelle Perrot, "Women, Power, and History: The Case of Nineteenth-Century France," and Siân Reynolds, "Marianne's Citizens? Women, the Republic, and Universal Suffrage in France," both in *Women, State, and Revolution: Essays on Power and Gender in Europe since 1789,* ed. Siân Reynolds (Amherst, Mass., 1987), pp. 53, 113, 119. At least one English writer in the 1630s did try to give women some real-life effectiveness, furnishing a compilation of laws enabling them to overcome their considerable legal disabilities. The (male) compiler asserted that it was high time women knew how they stood in law. For, he accused, while women had no say in the laws' constitution, no assent in their acceptance, and no control over their discharge, "yet they stand strictly tyed to mens establishments, little or nothing excused by ignorance." A woman was a rational individual and thus in law "a temporall person": *The Lawes Resolutions of Women's Rights: or, The Lawes Provision for Women . . .* (London, 1632), pp. 2, 4–5. The preface was signed "I. L.," the address "To the Reader," "T. E."

In the major plays of the period between 1637 and the mid-1640s, I would suggest that Corneille undertook an examination of certain political solutions to just these questions.[34] In *Le Cid*, for example, the questions took the following form: supposing we wish to establish a strong stable state, under conditions where it is violently threatened from outside its borders (France's situation in 1637, fighting against Spain and the Empire, eventually to establish both its frontiers and its European-wide power), then what must be the relation between the subject and political authority? What will be the obligations of the one toward the other? What will be the rights and duties of each? What consequences flow from what relation? In a period when the highest aristocracy was still demanding a real share in political power, and when these claims were seriously undermining the unity of a state only just being created as a "nation," such questions were most urgent.

A gulf lay between the claims of Don Diègue and Don Gomès and the attitude of Rodrigue. The former put the satisfaction (violent, almost by preference) of personal quarrels and private concerns before all else. Rodrigue recognized a duty to place the public interest first.[35] The ques-

---

[34]Divers works have been written on Corneille's female protagonists and some putative "feminism." They range from "essentialist" (Maria Tastevin, *Les héroïnes de Corneille* [Paris, 1924]) to "separatist" (Josephine A. Schmidt, *If There Are No More Heroes, There Are Heroines: A Feminist Critique of Corneille's Heroines, 1637–1643* [Lanham, Md., 1987]) and include debate about variety in failure (Mary Jo Muratore, *The Evolution of the Cornelian Heroine* [Potomac, Md., 1987]), aggression in ambivalent success (Harriet Allentuch, "Reflections on Women in the Theater of Corneille," *Kentucky Romance Quarterly*, 21, no. 1 [1974], 97–111), and the heroines' force and independence taken to reflect their young author's struggle with his erotic impulses (Constant Venesoen, *Corneille apprenti féministe, de "Mélite" au "Cid"* [Paris, 1986]). With the evident exception of the last idiosyncratic case, all tend to forget they are writing of a male author depicting women. Even Schmidt does so, oddly enough (at least until the very end of her study). These writers are in any case analyzing Corneille's plays, not discussing their place within broader cultural developments. Michel Prigent, in his *Le héros et l'état dans la tragédie de Pierre Corneille* (1986; rpt. Paris, 1988) has sought to do this, but for him the strong "feminine" women come to portray a "triumph of sensibility" (pp. 79–113). As we will see, I take this to be a serious misreading—along lines specified by such later critics as those whose views are traced in Chapter 7.

[35]Rodrigue and Chimène love one another and are expected to wed. Don Diègue, Rodrigue's father, quarrels with Don Gomès, Chimène's father, over their respective abilities to protect the kingdom of Castille against the Moors and others. The latter strikes the former, who, too old to defend himself, exhorts his son to uphold family honor. Gomès is killed in the resulting duel. Chimène wants vengeance. In the meantime, Rodrigue beats off a Moorish invasion and saves the kingdom, receiving the honorary title of "Le Cid" from the Moors' leader. Don Sanche, pretender to Chimène's hand, challenges Rodrigue and is defeated. The search for vengeance now threatening to become unending, the King, persuaded by his daughter the Infante (who has herself been in love with Rodrigue and fought off temptation to take advantage of the situation), orders all to desist, and marriage is projected for Rodrigue and Chimène sometime in the future. Rodrigue replaces his father and Gomès as principal defender of the kingdom. Prigent, *Le héros et l'état*, also views the issue as a matter of public/private opposition (p. 40).

tion was one of a complete transformation of aristocratic attitudes and behavior. Rodrigue's final submission to the King and to state authority marked the recognition of a political and social necessity clearly and closely bound to demands proceeding from the contemporary situation in France (and elsewhere). Dramatic changes were in progress: the slow creation of a nation, the centralization of political power, the defeudalization of the nobility, the attempt to unify the internal forces of the state (industrial, social, economic, military), the invention of a national culture, the development of France as a European power.

In *Horace* (1640) the same kind of experiment was taken rather further: if the individual owed everything to the state (as Rodrigue seemed to accept at the end of *Le Cid*), what would that imply as to personal and private relationships? How could interhuman relationships persist that did not depend on the state? And how could civil society remain stable and secure without such personal and private relationships (once the individual was being supposed to exist *before* the state and to reap personal benefits from its existence)? It is worthwhile considering how many times words like "inhuman," "brutal," and their derivations occur in this play (and others). Very often they do so in terms of an opposition between men and women:

> But when you can be weak without shame,
> To affect resolve outwardly is mere cowardice:
> We leave to men the use of such tricks,
> And wish to appear only as what we are.[36]

Many other exchanges suggested a similar opposition, but this rejoinder, fairly typical of the resolute and determined Sabine, asserted a viewpoint toward which Corneille himself seemed entirely sympathetic: "Far from dispraising the tears I see you weep, / I think I do very well to be able

[36] Pierre Corneille, *Horace*, in *Oeuvres complètes*, ed. George Couton, 3 vols. (Paris, 1980–87) (in vol. 1), III. v. 941–44. All references are to this edition, by act, scene, and line. Because Philips's translation of *Horace* is incomplete, these are my own and stay as close to the original as possible. Her four acts were completed by Sir John Denham, and the play was staged by the King's Company in 1669: Samuel Pepys recorded it in his diary on January 19, 1669/70 (see Introduction to Elizabeth Polwhele, *The Frolicks or The Lawyer Cheated (1671)*, ed. Judith Milhous and Robert D. Hume [Ithaca, N.Y., and London, 1977], p. 47). The play was published in 1678: as far as I know, there was no later edition. Here and elsewhere I give the original French only when it seems essential. *Horace* was Corneille's version of the fight between the Horatii and the Curiatii to decide the dominance of Rome or Alba. Horace's sister, Camille, was Curiace's fiancée, but Corneille exaggerated the kinship by making Horace's wife, Sabine, Curiace's sister. The play starts before the decision to resolve the conflict by using champions, and we hear the events leading up to it. After Horace has returned victorious, Camille excoriates him for killing Curiace. Outraged and accusing her of treason, Horace stabs her to death. Brought before the king, Tulle, Horace is defended by Sabine and his father and prosecuted by Valère, who loved Camille. Tulle decrees that Horace should live, but only as Rome's defender. Here, too, Prigent views the issue in *Horace* as one of installing a "new order" that is inimical to "the idea of a person" (*Le héros et l'état*, pp. 48, 137).

to restrain myself from doing likewise" (III.v.951–52), says old Horace, whose patriotic virtue was never in doubt and with whose views tradition tends to ally Corneille himself.

And what resulted from an argument according to which the individual (here, Horace) owed everything to the state? According to *Horace*—however it might be justified, regardless of its ambiguities, and whatever attitude one might take toward it—the consequence was entirely clear: *violence.* Indeed, it permeated *all* levels and kinds of human relationships: violence toward the "enemy" (who was scarcely such, we may recall), toward one's friends, toward one's closest relatives, toward oneself, and even (at least potentially) toward the very political authority that demanded this duty. Valère (who aspired to Camille's love) might indeed have been biased in arguing that Horace should be punished for having placed himself above the law and for threatening, therefore, society and political authority. But Tulle was not, when he asserted essentially the same thing: that he owed Horace his scepter and his throne; and when he then, by his pardon, placed Horace above the law (saying the state had a need of protection greater than its need to punish its putative protector). And where would this violence lead? . . . That was just what could not be answered: for the state could no longer control it. In fact, *Horace* showed how this particular political path led toward the destruction of the very order it sought to maintain.

The question *Horace* raised—as "brutally" and uncompromisingly as possible—concerned, then, the matter of violence, its consequences, its term, the possibility of its control, and its inevitable querying of the very power in whose service it was supposed to be. Hannah Arendt has written in this regard: "The chief reason warfare is still with us is neither a secret death wish of the human species, nor an irrepressible instinct of aggression, nor, finally and more plausibly, the serious economic and social dangers inherent in disarmament, but the simple fact that no substitute for this final arbiter in international affairs has yet appeared on the political scene. Was not Hobbes right when he said: 'Covenants, without the sword, are but words'?"[37]

In its conclusion *Horace* sank into an entirely pessimistic view of the inevitability of such violence. It was a violence setting Horace himself, as the King repeated, "above the laws" (V.iii.1754), simply because the King owed to Horace not only his continued rule in Rome, but indeed his "mastery" over two states (*Qui me fait aujourd'hui maître de deux Etats,* V.iii.1742). In such a case, the bearer of violence menaced the very existence of political authority and so of the state itself. The spectator might finally agree with Valère's assertion:

> In winning victory for Rome he has made it his slave,
> He has right of life and death over us,

---

[37]Hannah Arendt, *On Violence* (1969; rpt. New York, 1970), p. 5.

And our criminal lives can last
Only as long as he is pleased to extend his clemency.
(V.ii.1507–10)

This potential threat of violence was to become the basic justification of Horace's existence: "Live to serve the state," said the King (V.iii.1764). The balance forged in *Le Cid* had been lost. Violence now reigned as the necessary sign of an absolute duty toward the state: witness, for example, the otherwise absurdly inexplicable quarrel between Sabine and Camille, as to which one of them was the more harmed by war between Rome and Alba (III.iv). Violence was thus established, without exception, within all human relations. At the same time, such violence could only be, in some sense, *impossible*, for it inevitably tended toward the overthrow of the very political authority it was supposed to uphold.

Cinna (1642) proposed a quite different response and a kind of solution to the difficulty. The play began just where *Horace* concluded: in a permanently violent situation. That violence was not only generally political (Émilie was determined to keep alive the memory of the bloody civil wars—whose events weigh no less heavily on Auguste, until his final decision) but also personal. At that level it was expressed as an opposition between Emilie's blind and confused passion and the reason *eventually* embodied by the Emperor.[38] Emilie expressed her situation in the first scene of the play, as she explained her wish to avenge herself: "impatients désirs (passionate desires)," "Enfants impétueux de mon ressentiment / Que ma douleur séduite embrasse aveuglément (Impetuous offspring of my bitter animosity / That my spellbound grief blindly embraces)," which, she lamented, were inflicted on her in spite of herself; "haine (hatred)", "rage (fury, madness)," her "abandon (self-abandonment)" to "ardents transports (burning paroxysms)," her "fureur (rage,)" and so forth. Such words are important signs.

Indeed, no less than Le Bret in his *Souveraineté*, Richelieu, as we have seen implied, spoke constantly both in his *Mémoires* and in the *Testament* of the absolute need for anyone ruling a state to submerge everything beneath Reason. In the minister's view, knowledge, power, will, and political action (*savoir, pouvoir, vouloir,* and *faire*) together composed a set. "Passion," lack of control, put an end to that political reason and led inevitably to ruin. Émilie herself was not unaware of this composition,

---

[38] I deal with this opposition in more detail, with emphasis on the political/personal relation and the general situation in France, in "La voix royale: De la violence étatique ou, du privé à la souveraineté," in *Pierre Corneille: Ambiguïtés*, ed. Michel Bareau (Edmonton, 1988), pp. 41–54. Some parts of this chapter come from that text. In this play Émilie and Cinna (at her urging) plot to kill Auguste, who has recently become emperor, after the civil wars and myriad conspiracies. Cinna hesitates. Auguste considers abdicating but is persuaded by Cinna to remain (for otherwise he has no excuse to assassinate him). Émilie exhorts Cinna to hold strong and avenge her father's death. The plot is revealed to Auguste. Persuaded by Livie, his wife, he pardons the conspirators.

hesitating before the decision that tempted her. Would she be drawn on by passion or return to reason? "I feel this furious outburst grow cold" (I.i.270); or again, "My disordered spirit contradicts itself, / I want, and I don't want, I am carried away, I dare not, and my confused duty . . . " (I.i.121–24). Cinna, too, was drawn between reason and passion, between Auguste's strong state and the total disorder that would follow their conspiracy's success. Violence has indeed focused itself in the protagonists' very minds and spirits.

The two events Corneille used to elaborate the play, Augustus's accession to the empire and Cinna's conspiracy, were in actuality separated by some twenty-five years. Bringing them together enabled Corneille to put the reason of state/passion contradiction in the form of two opposing "voices."[39] One of these sought to maintain violence (marked in the play by terms of confusion, darkness, blindness, anger, madness, and so on), while the other wanted peace and tranquility: indicated by clarity of sight, brightness, visible display, reason. Violence and state dissolution were thus given not as part of a historical process, but as simultaneous with the possibility of "redemption." A concrete solution (in the play) to the permanent threat of violence was implied by the imposition of one of those voices on the other: *then* presented as a dismissal of the past by the establishment of a particular form of sovereignty.

In *Cinna*, the question thus became one of words, embodied by particular *speakers*, and it could then be resolved not through physical conflict, but by the imposition of one form of discourse (Auguste's). The question might then be one of conflict and clemency, but it was above all one of the relation among language, power, and a certain conception of reason (reason of state as well as rationality in general): together these composed a network of relations potentially able to resolve the problem of violence performed in *Horace*, and everywhere urgent in the contemporary political reality of France and of Europe as a whole. That in Corneille the matter should have taken the form of verbal conflict may seem obvious, since we are speaking of the theater. But it had a specific importance in the present context: the most important speaker is a woman. She intervenes at the very moment when Auguste himself, having discovered the conspiracy and treachery of Émilie and Cinna, can imagine no alternative to continuing the violence that has racked Rome for decades. He recalls the details of the ghastly civil wars (IV.ii.1130–41) and then wonders:

But what! Always blood, and always torture!
My cruelty tires, and cannot [ne peut] cease,
I want [je veux] to make myself [me faire] feared, and only [ne fais que]
   aggravate;

---

[39]Although Auguste says later on (IV.ii.1248) that he has ruled for twenty years already, this nowhere affects the play's action or debate.

Rome has, for my downfall, too fertile a Hydra.
One head cut off gives birth to a thousand more,
And the spilled blood of a thousand conspirators
Makes my life more accursèd, and not more secure.

(IV.iii.1162–68)

Auguste finds himself confronting a situation he cannot resolve in any way: one put in the precise terms used by so many to discuss the political and social disarray of a few decades earlier, as we saw in Chapter 2. But Livie now comes to the Emperor's aid, offering him what she calls "les conseils d'une femme (a woman's advice [IV.iii.1197])." She requests that he moderate his male "sévérité (harshness)," which has so far made "beaucoup de bruit (a lot of commotion)" but "sans produire aucun fruit (without any result)." He should learn to show clemency.

Georges Couton tells us that the formula was already used both in Dion Cassius's and in Seneca's history.[40] Indeed, Le Bret had himself referred to Livia and Augustus when speaking of princely clemency in general, saying that she "often" told the Emperor how "the monarch's true clemency was to punish public injuries and forgive those committed against himself."[41] These matters seem to me much less important (although we will see Corneille perhaps remembering Le Bret's comment) than that Sabine had played a similar role throughout *Horace*, that the Infante in *Le Cid* had demonstrated like concerns, and that Pauline will perform such a part in *Polyeucte*.

More significant still may be the tradition intimated earlier, and stressed by Ian Maclean. He has argued that the "role of advocacy ascribed to women" in the drama of this period (citing Claude Boyer's *Porcie romaine*, Jean Mairet's *Marc-Antoine*, and Corneille's *Polyeucte*) reflected "the commonplace about female clemency and *misericordia*" and the belief in "the physical inferiority of women, who, unable to act, are reduced to pleading."[42] Such advocacy, that is to say, was merely an aspect of the traditional role ascribed to women. But clearly, the use of the word "reduced" prejudges the case—as if the nonviolence of speech were automatically inferior to the violence of action: one might think of it as the "Rambo syndrome." Yet that very issue was central to the seventeenth-century dispute, as it should be in our own critical debate. The point, surely (there can be no other of much importance, as Bacon always observed), is that it *worked*.

Auguste may well reply: "You did indeed promise me a woman's advice: / You keep your word, and those are such, Madame" (IV.iii.1245–46). He nonetheless follows the advice given to him: her woman's language, as he puts it, the speech she has made available (*Vous me tenez parole*). The

40Corneille, *Oeuvres complètes*, 1:1616.
41Le Bret, *Souveraineté*, p. 583 (mispaginated for p. 563).
42Maclean, *Woman Triumphant*, p. 180.

several possible meanings of his phrase are not unimportant (whether or not "intended" by Corneille): not only "keep a promise," but *tenir parole* perhaps as in *tenir un discours* ("to hold forth [in speech]," "to speak publicly"), *tenir* as in "hold out" or "offer" but also as in "hold on to." Not only has Livie kept her promise, but she has also provided Auguste with a language. And her speech translates indeed into immediate action on Auguste's part, provoking an instant change in Émilie's language as well.

Émilie speaks in the following scene (with Livie) of her "joy" (IV. iv.1267), but she especially exults in her *désaveuglement* ("unblinding"), her lack of confusion, her clarity of vision: "My noble despair has not blinded me, / My entire *vertu* [here something like "magnanimous, energetic positive faculties"] quickens without being carried away [*sans s'émouvoir*], / And in spite of myself I see more than I want to see" (IV.iv.1374–76). Livie has enabled the imposition of the Emperor's voice: as much hers as his. And that it is an achievement of speech, rather than of his physical violence, is emphasized right away by the demand that the opposition remain *silent*. The Emperor requires of Cinna:

> Follow exactly the rule I am imposing upon you
> Without interrupting me, lend your ear to what I will say to you,
> Do not interrupt with a word or a cry,
> Hold your tongue prisoner, and if this utter silence. . . .
>
> (V.i.1426–29)

Indeed, Cinna himself gives something like a promise, the verbal performance of acceptance—"I will obey you, my lord"—which, even if sometimes hard to keep, nevertheless implies that a complete transformation has taken place.

Once again it is the women who announce this change. Not only was Livie wholly responsible for the act of clemency, but it will be the Empress who first of all reminds everyone of what makes sovereignty inviolable and who secondly relates the fruitful consequences in the peace and tranquility these two will create. The importance of the act of mercy to this end is already apparent. The inviolability will mean (in this case) an end to civil war. What Livie observes is the unbridgeable distance lying between the Prince and any private being (including the Prince's own). Corneille may have been recalling Le Bret's remark about Livia's advice to Augustus to punish public and reprieve private offense, but the matter was at this time, both in theory and in practice, something of a cliché— provided, of course, the right to sole sovereignty was recognized in the person occupying it.

Speaking of the death of Émilie's father, Livie asserts:

> His death, whose memory inflames your rage

Was Octave's crime, not the Emperor's.
All crimes of State committed for the Crown,
The Heavens forgive them us, once they have granted it. . . .
                                                        (V.i.1607–10)

Émilie herself confirms this aspect of Auguste's victory, emphasizing that "the Heavens have determined upon your glory," as she simultaneously notes that her own change of "heart" but reflects the transformation of state (V.iii.1720–24). What has occurred is more than an imposition of attitude or even of a particular state power. Individuals are, as it were, "absorbed" by a state the form of whose power is expressed through Livie. That state will become divinized, and its glory will be "ratified," by Auguste's apotheosis. So, after her call to clemency (making present stability possible in erasure of the past), her reminder of sovereignty's inviolability (making stability possible by present political conditions), it is Livie, once again, who expresses the future fruits of tranquility:

> Listen to what the gods tell you through me,
> And what is the immutable law of your destiny.
> After this action you have nothing to fear,
> The yoke will henceforth be borne without complaint,
> And the least subdued will abandon their plans,
> And consider all their glory lies in dying your subjects.
>   (V.iii.1755–60)

Auguste accepts the "augury," emphasizing once again how the imposition is one of *speech:* the act of clemency and its results, he concludes, must now be "published" abroad (the verb is *publier:* here, "to announce publicly by word of mouth or written broadsheet or poster," V.iii.1779–80).

So yet again recurred that prophecy of the golden age recorded first in Virgil's Fourth Bucolic as failed in Arcadia and repeated from Anchises' lips in *Aeneid* VI:

> This,
> this is the man you heard so often promised—
> Augustus Caesar, son of a god, who will
> renew a golden age in Latium,
> in fields where Saturn once was king. . . . [43]

This time the golden age of Augustan rule was, however, announced not by some sacred and inhuman Sybil, nor by a father in Hades. Rather did it come from the lips of an entirely reasonable Empress. Of course, past failures might foreshadow future ones, but the voice now expressing hope

[43]Virgil, *Aeneid,* trans. Alan Mandelbaum (New York, 1971), p. 158.

is surely not without its significance. In *Livie* came together, however briefly, both the record of history and the weight of symbol. The future failure was the more dramatic. As the Augustan transformation is announced, we need to note not only how profoundly it is marked by what has been throughout presented as the voice of Reason specifically manifest in *Livie* (Émilie's lust for violence being essentially "manly" or, as it is often named, "brutish"), but also how gradually a hint of something "other" has become present. To assert the possibility of a stable state, Corneille seemed forced to appeal increasingly to divine warranty: as though human powers and politics had no hold on themselves. Cinna and Émilie's failure was finally not theirs alone but that of Corneille's own solution: in a kind of impossible utopia—confirmed subsequently perhaps by *Polyeucte* (1643), whose hero's apotheosis implied his abandonment of all real political action, while the distant Emperor's intentions appeared to promise the continued violence of Christian persecution. Indeed, Polyeucte's move had its typological predecessor in Jesus' assertion of depoliticization: "My kingdom is not of this world" (deliberately dissociating his actions from the Jewish struggle for liberation from Roman dominion). Just as Auguste's political and linguistic mastery still echoed an older configuration destined to be superseded (see above, pp. 83–84), so Corneille himself seemed now increasingly tempted by an eschatalogical nostalgia of which Spenser's second Mutabilitie Canto has already given us a forlorn foretaste.

Violence and the permanence of war may well have been gathered up into some higher stability and calm, but at the price, it would appear, of an abdication of the human (in favor now not of the brutish, but of the divine). In Corneille's own theater that development may be followed, after *Polyeucte* through *La mort de Pompée* (1643–44), the absence of whose eponymous protagonist, however glorious his death, only underscored the ultimate failure of violence, and then to the divine story of *Théodore* (1645–46). This exploration ended with the abandoned violence of the plays written during the Frondes (1648–53).

In this failure one might perhaps see prefigured a more general one of the future French polity itself, where under Louis XIV and between Colbert and Le Tellier was played out this opposition between a (relatively pacific policy and a wholly aggressive, militaristic one. The culmination of the latter in the Revocation of the Edict of Nantes, the wars of the Augsburg League and those of the Spanish Succession led directly to the catastrophic last years of the Sun King's reign (in Chapters 5 and 6 I explore some of these matters in relation to Boileau, Fénelon, and literary culture in France and England). We may also see here the future failure to achieve any change in the *view* of women or in their real status (Chapter 7). Through *Polyeucte*, where Pauline played the strongest role, Corneille had gradually come to an understanding of Reason in women as able to bring about stability and nonviolence. But action was becoming progressively less political and indeed ever more marginal with respect to political authority.

The sequence culminated in *La mort de Pompée* (1643), and it was doubtless not chance that inspired Katherine Philips to translate that very play twenty or so years later.[44] Two women, one the embodiment of romantic love, the other the representative of moral virtue and courage, Cléopâtre and Cornélie, struggle through the play to hold a middle course between the violence of Ptolemaic Egypt and the ruin of Republican Rome. Photin, Ptolémée's amoral counselor, is characterized by Cléopâtre as wholly given up to "violence" (II.iii.602); Ptolémée himself constantly yields to "transports violents" (II.iv.711); while César, if he does not actually cede to such a "transport violent," resists it only because he smolders with a slower and deeper anger (IV.i.1080–82). For her part, Cléopâtre, hating her brother's advisers and scorning his lack of moral courage, nonetheless tries to save Ptolémée and bring peace between Egypt and Rome. Her failure is signaled by the praise she receives from Antoine (III.iii.946–52) and her accession to the throne at the play's end. Both foretell future wars.

Cornélie is both more complex and more indicative of Corneille's failure. Philo-Philippa's liminary poem to Philips's collection of poetry picked her out especially for praise: "In the French Rock Cornelia first did shine, / But shin'd not like her self till she was thine." The particular praise was apposite because alone of all those in the play Corneille invented her role. In his 1660 "Examen," the dramatist noted that he had followed Lucan closely, save in this one detail: "I have added only what concerns Cornelia, who appeared to offer herself inevitably, since according to historical truth she was in the same ship as her husband when he landed in Egypt. That is what made me pretend she was captured and brought before Caesar, even though history does not mention it."[45]

It would appear that she was introduced to play a quite special part: a reasoned middle path between Rome and its destruction, between Caesar and her debt to and love for Pompey, and all the time under the tension of her desire for vengeance. From the first, she plays the role of the "femme forte." When she is brought before César, her initial speech is one of defiance:

---

[44]The translation was performed. In his notice to the reader, the printer says that the translator added various songs "to lengthen the Play, and make it fitter for the Stage, when those that could not be resisted were resolved to have it acted" (*Pompey* [v], in Philips, *Poems*). Sir Edward Dering's epilogue to the play tells us the performance occurred in Ireland (p. 65), presumably at the behest of the countess of Cork, to whom it was dedicated [iii–v]. This 1663 Dublin performance was followed by a London one later that spring. In August it was parodied in Act V of Davenant's *The Play-house to be Let*. Gerard Langbaine wrote that he saw later peformances of this translation (see Milhous and Hume's Introduction to Polwhele, *Frolicks*, p. 47). All translations of *Pompée* are Philips's.

[45]Corneille, *Oeuvres complètes*, 1:1075.

> Caesar, that envious Fate which I can brave,
> Makes me thy Prisoner, but not thy Slave,
> Expect not then my Heart should ere afford
> To pay thee Hommage, or to call thee Lord.
>
> (III.iv.985–88)

But the defiance only provides a setting to reveal her moral rectitude, as she later warns César of Ptolémée's plot against his life (IV.iv). When César praises her virtue, she responds simply that the reason for the warning is that she wants vengeance for herself, however much she may regret it (she earlier exclaimed: "O Gods! how many Virtues must I hate!" III.iv.1072). Once he releases her as he has promised, "I shall make new business for thy Sword" (*je te chercherai partout des ennemis,* IV.iv.1379).

Caught between Pompée's death and César's virtues, between the destruction of Republican Rome and the possible creation of some new order, between her duty toward Rome (the need to punish Ptolémée) and her desire to avenge her loss, she struggles to reason her way toward balancing them. As she says to César:

> But as a Roman, though my Hate be such,
> I must confess, I thee esteem as much.
> Both these extreams Justice can well allow:
> This does my [your] Virtue, that my Duty show.
> My sense of Honour does the first command;
> Concern, the last, and they are both constrain'd.
>
> (V.iv.1725–30)

The equilibrium breaks down, however. She foretells a conflict that will last for three generations (IV.iv.1387: indeed, Gnaius and Sextus Pompey were to fight on against Caesar's Rome; Cinna was the great Pompey's grandson). She foretells how Roman youth will rise against Caesar himself, once he has flouted them by marrying Cleopatra (V.iv.1750–52). Unable to keep the balance of reason, maintained by Livie at the end of *Cinna*, Cornélie foresees a future of ongoing war and violence. The voice of mediating Reason has collapsed. In real life the way was prepared for the Frondes.[46]

The final failure of this sequence of plays implied that for Corneille, although violence (the specific violence of Reason in men) was no solution to any political dilemma at all, no other kind of solution was any longer

---

[46]In Philips's case it may be that the choice of this play reflected her own commentary on Charles II's vengeance over the regicides (paralleling Caesar's over Ptolemy and his counselors). There, too, the future would confirm that violence only begets violence: not this time in Charles II's death, but in the Popish Plot and the Exclusion Crisis of 1678–82, the Monmouth Rebellion of 1685, and James II's exile and the Glorious Revolution of 1688.

available. He had started, like Gournay and perhaps the women of the *salons*, to find some sort of response in Reason in women: Doña Urraque, Sabine, Livie. Such a view, like Descartes's and Du Bosc's, was directly opposed to Richelieu's idea of woman (the singular generic is deliberate) as "what" was most "capable de nuire aux Etats (able to ruin states)".[47] Richelieu exacerbated metaphorical arguments advanced by Machiavelli and others, translating them into literal requirements. The theoretical exclusion of women from political authority would eventually have its counterpart in their exclusion (as primary producers) from the dominant culture and a renewed emphasis on a specifically "female reason." But that is to get a bit ahead of my argument.

Not only Richelieu, but Le Bret explicitly asserted women's exclusion from political authority (following "long" Salic tradition—although in 1694 the Académie was doing more than a little ideological exaggerating when it claimed that law was "aussi ancienne que la monarchie").[48] In this case, it was almost as though Corneille had the author of *De la sou-veraineté du Roy* (a lawyer, like the dramatist himself) textually in mind. On one occasion, rejecting any idea that queens might share in their husbands' power and adopting like Richelieu the pejorative dominant Judeo-Christian tradition that women were irrational and passionate, Le Bret wrote: "It would be most dangerous if women of this rank had power equal to their husbands; the more so as their ambitious nature never allows them to rest until they have usurped the benefits of sovereign authority, and finally subdued their husbands beneath their sway."[49]

Le Bret was thinking maybe of Catherine and Marie de Medicis, but Corneille did not hesitate to turn this claim about women's "naturel ambitieux" against him. In *Le Cid*, speaking of Don Diègue and Don Gomès, Chimène exclaimed: "Cursèd ambition, frightful madness, / Under whose tyranny the most magnanimous suffer" (II.iii.457–58). Her and Rodrigue's fathers were, after all, both men. For Chimène, ambition was another form of male violence—as it was for Gournay and others. On the evidence of *Le Cid's* action, she could scarcely be faulted. But Le Bret then went on to provide some precise examples of such behavior. Here is one of the most important, with his subsequent comments:

Roman history says the same about Livia, who wishing to share equal authority with her husband, tore from the Senate's hands, Virgulania and Plancina, accused of capital crimes. . . .

Assuredly, their weakspiritedness does not let them remain within the bounds of moderation, once they see themselves raised to this high degree of honor. They immediately give way to insolence and vanity, and that

[47]Richelieu, *Testament*, p. 301. Cf. pp. 324, 370–71, and esp. 328–29.
[48]*Dictionnaire de l'Académie Françoise*, 2 vols. (Paris, 1694), 1:667.
[49]Le Bret, *Souveraineté*, p. 43.

gives them such presumption as to feel wounded unless they rule absolutely.[50]

It is hard not to see Corneille as making a deliberate attempt to answer
specific charges against women, brought by such as Richelieu and Le
Bret.[51] In that regard one cannot justifiably dismiss the significance of
these female protagonists of Cornelian tragedy, these "femmes fortes," as
the century called them ("femmes héroïques" in Du Bosc's phrase), on the
grounds that they were distinguished from the multitude of women and
thus a source for no generally applicable characterization or argument.
So Maclean, acknowledging the "importance of feminism and feminist
thought to [tragedy] and the intimate connections between the portrayal
of the dramatic heroine and that of the *femme forte*," closes with precisely
that dismissal: "In both cases, these figures are contrasted with the mass
of their own sex, and associated with male attributes and roles."[52] Quite
obviously, male protagonists of tragedy were also to be distinguished from
"the mass of their own sex."

Both were figures asserting idealized qualities, rarefied beyond the everyday. They may be taken as expressing an ideal both in respect to human
qualities and in respect to human relationships. And here what is important—enormously so, it seems to me—was the very specific contrast
created between *certain* female protagonists and *all* male ones. Women
in all the plays were indeed associated with male attributes and roles:
Chimène, Camille, Émilie. . . . We may add Médée, Cléopâtre (in *Rodogune*), and to some extent Cornélie—hence the failure, there, of Reason in
women. All the men participated in these attributes. The important point
surely is that some women played a very different role: that of reason in
the service of nonviolence and a peaceful solution to all political conflict
and to the inevitable tendency of society toward dissolution.

Reason in women, that is to say, had been clearly distinguished from
Reason in men. But it had *not* become a qualitatively *different* "reason" (as
it had once been and would be again) apt for "domestic" or "nurturing"
circumstance. Reason in women was no different from that in men (as
Gournay, Descartes, Du Bosc, and others had said): the essential variant
was its freedom from other, external constraints. The development of
society in history had ineluctably made men dependent on violence. This
was clear in the historically descriptive parts of political writings by
Machiavelli, Le Bret, and Richelieu (to take only some of those mentioned

---

[50]Ibid., pp. 43–44.
[51]Corneille was a practicing judge of the king's bench who could not have failed to
know Le Bret's works well, simply from professional obligation: quite apart from his
own broader interests and the fact that he had a more than passing acquaintance with all
those at the center of power. He would almost certainly have known Lipsius' work as
well (see above, Chapter 1, note 77).
[52]MacLean, *Woman Triumphant*, p. 193.

here) and in the theoretical argument of Bodin, Le Roy, Hurault, and Hobbes. It was evident, too, in the political situations forming both the fictive and the real background to Corneille's theater. Those historical constraints had borne on women externally as part of that violence and inevitably, too, in the way they had themselves, like men, internalized it (as victims rather than oppressors, as victims rather than agents). Because such violence was not a basic element in their *use* of reason, however, women could show that Reason itself was not *essentially* violent and so hope to create a society free of it. Such would be the culmination of the debate, before it collapsed in the 1670s.[53]

Furthermore, the issue of women's place in (literary) culture, as we see it through Corneille, for instance, seemed to parallel the more general form it took in the French and English seventeenth centuries. Carolyn Lougee comments that from about 1620 on, "feminist" thinking in France, very soon supported in some manner by the *salons* of Rambouillet and (a little later) Lambert, by writings like Gournay's *Égalité des hommes et des femmes*, François de Soucy's *Triomphe des dames* (1646), and such others as I have already glanced at, questioned certain traditional ethical presuppositions: "Alterations in social values," she writes, "made weak women into the representative of delicacy." Further, such changes became a fundamental attack against "the heroic ethic of masculinity" and devalued mere "physical force." She argues that masculine encomia of brute strength and violence began to yield before a new vision describing "the social mission of women in public positions as pacification."[54]

I have already responded (above) to claims such as this last, but I do not think the general proposition can be sustained. Such an argument was

---

[53]It may be worth observing here that exactly this argument was made in a time of violence much closer to us. During the First World War many argued that masculine violence led inevitably to women's subordination and could be stopped only by using the reason and experience of women, themselves untainted by a history of militaristic violence: see, e.g., Catherine Marshall, C. K. Ogden, and Mary Sargant Florence, *Militarism versus Feminism: Writings on Women and War*, ed. Margaret Kamester and Jo Vellacott (London, 1987). The same point was made, of course, in Virginia Woolf's 1938 *Three Guineas*. As for Corneille, he seemed to give up on this issue after *Pompée*. Of his subsequent female protagonists, some ended totally isolated, as Dircé in *Oedipe* or Bérénice in *Tite et Bérénice;* some committed suicide to escape oppression, as Cléopâtre (*Rodogune*), Marcelle (*Théodore*), or Sophonisbe (*Sophonisbe*), others coming close but finally submitting, as Arsinoé in *Nicomède;* some adopted queenly power with an authority and violence that at once equated them with male violence and confirmed Le Bret's and Richelieu's strictures, as Isabella in *Don Sanche*, Viriate in *Sertorius*, Pulchérie in the play of that name, Cléopâtre, Médée, or Edüige (*Pertharite*); some acquired power in spite of themselves, as Rodogune; while others simply resigned themselves to suffering and dominion or to joyless love—Camille in *Othon*, Honorie in *Attila*, Eurydice in *Suréna*, Hypsipyle in *Toison*, Aristie in *Sertorius*, Laodice in *Nicomède*, Plautine in *Othon*. Urraque, Sabine, Livie, and even Cornélie were clearly no longer possible.

[54]Carolyn Lougee, *"Le paradis des femmes": Women, Salons, and Social Stratification in Seventeenth-Century France* (Princeton, 1976), pp. 31–33.

certainly being made, as we have seen at some length, and a masculine ethic of reason-in-violence was indeed being challenged. Yet on the one hand, the challenge was not from "delicacy" or some version of "feminity" (let us but recall those strong-willed aristocratic women who rode out in 1650 to make the wars of the second Fronde). Rather was it from a strong-minded rationality of common sense to which violence was an *unreason*—and one customary among men. With equal certainty, on the other hand, this masculine ethic did not yield its place and was to return in force and with cultural effects due to last into the twentieth century.

Nonetheless, the dispute *was* put in these terms in the 1630s and 1640s, and I have tried to show how importantly Corneille participated in it. In this regard the choice of Livia was significant. We have just seen how Le Bret used her to make the pejorative argument (we saw earlier how he used her name—once—more generously). It is certainly the case that this personage was wholly given both by Seneca and by Cassius Dio—the one supplying a good part of Auguste's speech to Cinna (V.i: including the order that he not speak), the other recounting the entire conspiracy and giving Livia a speech of considerable length. Both quoted her as speaking of "woman's advice," Augustus merely thanking her for it.[55] The fact remains that Corneille *chose* to emphasize that aspect of the story, that it *did* stand as a reply to Le Bret, and that Livia would become (thanks to Corneille?) one of the major illustrations of female ability and power.

In his *Femme héroïque* of 1645, Du Bosc used her case as an example of wise prudence: "But if Livia advises Augustus to try the way of gentleness, she does not counsel him subsequently to trust Cinna too imprudently: what she advises is fine for stopping hatred, but not for being overconfident in his friendship."[56] In 1668 Marguerite Buffet was to write: "Livia, Augustus's wife who ruled with him. This great Emperor consulted her in all the most important business of the Empire. Tiberius her/his son [*son fils*] valued her counsel so highly that he preferred it to [that of] his closest associates concerning the public business of his state." Margaret Cavendish, duchess of Newcastle, wrote more or less contemporaneously that she gloried "more to be [Newcastle's] wife, than Livia to be Augustus's wife."[57] No doubt Du Bosc, Buffet, and Cavendish were all thinking of

---

[55]Lucius Annaeus Seneca, *De Clementia*, in *Moral Essays*, trans. and ed. John W. Basore, 3 vols. (London and New York, 1932), 1:380–87 (*De Clementia*, I. 9); Cassius Dio Cocceianus, *Dio's Roman History*, trans. and ed. Earnest Cary, 9 vols. (London and New York, 1914), 5:426–51 (Bk. 55, paras. 14–22).

[56]Du Bosc, *Femme héröique*, 2:474. Quoted by F. E. Sutcliffe, "Le pardon d'Auguste: Politique et morale dans *Cinna*," in *A Modern Miscellany*, presented to Eugène Vinaver . . . , ed. T. E. Lawrenson, F. E. Sutcliffe, and G. F. A. Gadoffre (Manchester and New York, 1969), p. 250. In a hugely successful work of 1621 (praised by Claude Favre de Vaugelas as a prime example of "le beau langage"), Nicolas Coëffeteau had used the same story quite neutrally, although he tended to praise Augustus for having risked accepting "le conseil d'une femme": *Histoire romaine . . .* (Paris, 1621), Pt. I. 124–26.

[57]Marguerite Buffet, "Traitté sur les eloges des illustres sçavantes, anciennes et mod-

Corneille's play. But that itself would be of more than passing interest for the study of "feminism" in this period. So far as I know, any such connection has passed unnoticed. Similarly, it may be no accident that Bayle included in his dictionary a long article on Urraca (i.e., Urraque), daughter of Alfonso VI of León and Castille, the real Cid's eleventh-century contemporary. She provided the opportunity for a long diatribe on the disorders endemic to female monarchy, proving, he wrote, that those states that had not adopted the Salic Law were open to all kinds of trouble and chaos, thanks to the lasciviousness and impudicity of queens.[58] Here, too, I would suggest that Corneille left his mark.

With respect to the broader questions raised by Corneille's plays (and others), it is scarcely unimportant that in 1673, in his *Égalité des deux sexes*, Poulain de la Barre was to maintain that violent male reason was necessary only at a certain stage in the evolution of societies. He provided a wholly Hobbesian story about the formation of civil society ("Freudian" too in that it told of a seizure of power by younger brothers from fathers or older brothers), in which male violence was inscribed from the outset: a violence, injustice, and tyranny that excluded women from all types of power, education, and freedom. Women were characterized from the start by "gentleness and humanity" and naturally abhorred "carnage and war." Reason played but a small part in this social formation, being essentially submissive to the authoritarian violence of men. At a later stage, however, a more civilized moment, women's "precision, discernment, and culture" would have to become dominant if society were to survive.[59]

In *The Unnatural Tragedie*, published in her 1662 *Playes*, Cavendish had already used terms drawn perhaps from Davenant (and Greville) to make Poulain's point:

> *Second Virgin:* . . . Good statesmen are bred in courts, camps and cities, and not in schools and closets, at bars and in pulpits; and women are bred in courts and cities, and only want the camp to give them the perfect state breeding.
>
> *Third Virgin:* Certainly, if we had that breeding, and did govern, we should govern the world better than it is.
>
> *Fourth Virgin:* Yes, for it cannot be governed worse than it is: for the

---

ernes," in *Nouvelles observations sur la langue françoise* . . . (Paris, 1668), p. 327; Margaret [Cavendish], Duchess of Newcastle, *Life of the Duke, Memoirs of Her Own Life, and Certain Sociable Letters,* ed. Ernest Rhys (London, Toronto, and New York, n.d.), p. 278.

[58]Bayle, *Dictionnaire,* 3:843, col. a–b.

[59]François Poulain de la Barre, *De l'égalité des deux sexes* (Paris, 1984), pp. 22–26, 37. The Cartesian and Hobbesian aspects of Poulain's work have yet to be studied, as too its relation with the later work of Mary Astell, whose arguments in *A Serious Proposal to the Ladies for the Advancement of Their True and Greatest Interest . . . ,* 4th ed. (London, 1701; rpt. New York, 1970) reveal many similarities, both verbal and conceptual. Part 1 of this work first appeared in 1694, part 2 in 1697.

whole world is together by the ears, all up in wars and blood, which shows there is a general defect in the rulers and governors thereof.[60]

The attempt and the need to pass from violence to tranquility, and its specific connection with an opposition between male and female, had been clearly elaborated in Corneille's theater between *Le Cid* and *La mort de Pompée*, before the equally clear failure of the plays written during the Frondes.[61] By this time, indeed, the opposition between an essentially masculine violence and the feminine as pacific reason had become something of a commonplace. The 1670 free translation (into English) of Agrippa's celebrated text may provide a last exemplary indication:

So had Women but the power of *making Laws*, and *writing Histories*, what Tragedies might they not justly have published of Mens unparalleled villany? Amongst whom are daily found so many *Murderers*, *Theeves*, *Ravishers*, *Forgers*, *Fierers of Cities*, and *Traytors*, who in the time of *Joshua* and King *David* [we may well recall here the association forged between Charles II and David by this date] *robb'd* in such vast multitudes, that they *march'd* in a posture of War, and made them Captains of their *padding Bands*, (a trick they have scarce forgot at this very day) whence so many *Prisons* became crowded, and so many *Gibbets* loaded with their Carkasses. Whereas on the contrary, to Women we owe the *invention* of all things usefull or beneficial to Mankind, which may either adorn and enlighten our dark *Minds*, or relieve and accommodate the necessities of our frail *bodies*.[62]

We need not, then, be very surprised to find a theatrical discussion echoing that of the *salons* and even of the later thought of someone like Poulain: opposing masculine violence to a new feminine voice of reason, of a reason that was, besides, fundamentally social and collective rather than individualist. At the same time, it was profoundly political. In Corneille, for instance, Doña Urraque, Sabine, Livie, and Cornélie were all preoccupied not just with personal concerns (though that, too), but with a legitimate order of civil society and the state. Such reason was publicly manifested among the *précieuses* of the *salons*, by a kind of physically ascetic worldly freedom that contrasted visibly with the traditional ideal of women's virtue as a "chastely" repressed behavior, itself supposedly required to counter irrational female sensuality.

Lougee spoke, we saw, of women coming to represent a sort of delicate,

---

[60]Margaret Cavendish, Duchess of Newcastle, *Playes* (London, 1662), p. 332. Cited in Hobby, *Virtue of Necessity*, p. 108.

[61]On these plays, see Georges Couton, *Corneille et la Fronde* (Clermont-Ferrand, 1951).

[62]Henry Cornelius Agrippa, *Female Pre-Eminence: Or, the Dignity and Excellency of That Sex, above the Male . . .* , in *The Feminist Controversy of the Renaissance*, intro. Diane Bornstein (Delmar, N.Y., 1980); p. 51.

pacific reason. At a first stage (and still, but with finality, in Poulain) this was clearly not particular to women, but was a common *human* reason typified by Descartes's arguments—whether or not his writings (as I doubt) were a direct or immediate source. People asserted that such universal reason was quite separate from a violence resulting from specific historical conditions and which therefore was not at all some essential or inevitable element attached to reason. They further argued that those same *historical* conditions meant that such untrammeled and pure reason was found only in (some) women, in no men. But it was not difficult to see how the premise of the debate—and thus any potential resolution—could be changed. One needed only to argue that violence was *not* the characteristic of a particular *historical* moment or process, but was, rather, endemic to the human condition. Then civil society itself, far from giving rise to violence, in fact overcame and prevented it. Such a claim would, of course, transform the terms of the debate. Right reason, justice, and contract, and above all those who ordered them, would once again find their legitimacy. There we return to Davenant and Hobbes, to the relations between politics and literature, and to the debates about their nature and about their control. We also discover the conditions of late Stuart England and the Sun King's France.

Chapter 5

Literature and Political Choice

A writer has no choice. Whether or not he is aware of it, his works reflect one or more aspects of the intense economic political, cultural and ideological struggles in a society. . . . What he or she cannot do is to remain neutral. Every writer is a writer in politics. The only question is what and whose politics?

—Ngugi Wa Thiong'o, *Writers in Politics*

The civil contract—some idea of "justice"—was presented as the rational answer to violence. So, too, we saw in Davenant, was poetry: at once resolving a presocial savagery and acting as a buttress against any continued temptation to barbarity after the covenanted establishment of order. To achieve this, poetry needed to teach those now familiar "necessary men" not only "patterns" (of mind and language, of concepts and the world), but the actual events and actions that complete them, filling out their coherent syntax as the correspondent variables of reference do a set of logical constants. The purpose of the "Heroick Poem," thus wrote Davenant, was "as in a perfect glass of Nature to give us a familiar and easie view of our selves" (*PG*, p. 3). Literature's chief aim was "to represent the Worlds true image often to our view" (*PG*, p. 4).

Literature had to provide the "truth operative, and by effects continually alive." That truth was "the Mistris of Poets, who hath not her existence in matter but in reason" (*PG*, pp. 10–11). Such truth was the poet's mistress much as for Halifax a little later liberty was the "mistress of mankind." Indeed, truth and liberty would go together like truth and beauty: abstracted general "rights" of humanity to be granted by social order, or justly seized if not. Poetry was a contemplation of "the general History of Nature," rather than a "selected Diary of Fortune" (*PG*, p. 4). Yet the detail of the diary remained of major importance. Without it, the rest lost its meaning. The poet, Rymer would write, must know all things, but must "by a particular Chymistry extract the essence of things."[1] As Dave-

---

[1] Thomas Rymer, "The Preface of the Translator" [to Rapin's *Reflections on Aristotle's Treatise of Poesie . . . (1674)*], in *Critical Works*, p. 7.

nant had written, the poet required "a full comprehension . . . and an ability to bring those comprehensions into action" (*PG*, p. 19). Literature taught the patterns from which the most powerful ("necessary" and "noble") could learn as well as the discrete events filling out those patterns. It showed the rationality of the natural order, coherent with mind and correctly ordered language, as it simultaneously reflected the elements concretizing that rational structure.

The model itself might no longer be seriously questionable, any more than one's participation in it or its constraining power. But where "things" and "actions" were in question, choices were evidently available. And they quickly offered a secondary "truth" to that of the rational model itself with its underlying and universally valid rules of order. The secondary truth lay on the plane of what Dryden called the "superstructure." It was the truth of a particular political stability, whose operative model was now that "authoritarian liberalism" described earlier, whatever its local variants. It could readily spread its coherence across all those more general areas of which I have been speaking: ethical, epistemological, political, and aesthetic.

Just so, in 1675 Boileau's discovery of right reason was quite deliberately related to a particular policy by the ninth Epistle's dedication to Colbert's eldest son, the marquis de Seignelay, minister of the navy. Boileau started by praising the father's pacific policies and French maritime expansion, adding that such praise depicted Louis XIV in very truth. The political encomium was directly tied to reason, truth, and beauty:

> Rien n'est beau que le Vrai. Le vrai seul est aimable.
> Il doit regner par tout, et mesme dans la fable:
> De toute fiction l'adroite fausseté
> Ne tend qu'à faire aux yeux briller la Verité.

> (Nothing is beautiful but truth. Only truth is lovely. Everywhere it must rule, and even in story [plot]: the clever [also "upright"?] falsehood of all fiction only aims to make truth shine before our eyes.)[2]

This identification of political, epistemological, and aesthetic criteria was basic in the previous year's *Art poétique*. "Bon sens" was the basis of all right poetry, which was necessarily subordinate "au joug de la Raison (to the yoke of Reason)." His first advice to all literary writers was thus: "Aimez donc la Raison. Que toûjours vos écrits / Empruntent d'elle seule et leur lustre et leur prix (So love Reason. May your writings always borrow from her alone their luster and their value)."[3]

---

[2]Nicolas Boileau-Despréaux, "Epître IX," in *Oeuvres complètes*, ed. Françoise Escal (Paris, 1966), p. 134.
[3]Ibid., p. 158: *Art poétique*, Chant I.

This identity of values had been a constant in Boileau's writing from the outset. His first Satire was a condemnation of corrupt financiers and of Nicolas Fouquet's regime at the very time he was being pursued by Colbert (Fouquet had been arrested in 1661, but the surintendent was finally condemned only in December 1664). The second Satire, addressed to and in praise of Molière, was printed in 1665, having been written probably between 1663 and 1665. It appeared during the fight over the comic playwright's *École des femmes*, the author being attacked by a particular group of writers and courtiers to whose importance I return. The first Epître (1668–70) celebrated the peace of Aix-la-Chapelle, the fourth dealt with the French crossing of the Rhine and divers victories obtained against the Dutch in July and August 1672 (an English poem sought to rebuff this Epître, just as twenty years later Matthew Prior would mock Boileau's "Ode sur la prise de Namur" when the English retook the town), and so on.

Many of these preoccupations came together in the ninth Satire (1667), a comprehensive self-defense and dismissal of all the objections raised against his previous writings. Indeed, when it was published in 1668, Boileau had accompanied it with his "Discours sur la satire," in which he asserted the right to speak at once of literary and of state affairs, arguing that it had been so for satirists in Antiquity and that such double concern was indeed a very duty, to be neither eluded nor criticized. On the one hand, he said, criticism of certain political figures was not to be confused with that of bad writers (as the *Ridicules* had done in his own case); on the other, such people did deserve to be held up to scorn—and he would not hesitate to do so.[4]

The ninth Satire itself, ironically setting out to criticize his own wit (his "Esprit") for having been too scornful of bad scribblers, suggested that a more worthwhile occupation would be to "chanter du Roi les augustes merveilles (sing of the king's exalted wonders)"; more worthwhile, that was, than to condemn such ludicrous writers as he then went on to exemplify. Yet, he suggested, the two were perhaps not so very different. For the responsible satirist, however others might criticize, could well "regler les droits, et l'estat d'Apollon." Of course "Apollo's State" was both Parnassus, the abode of poets, and the France of Louis XIV, Apollonian King of the Sun and of reason. Lest his reader mistook the double attribution, the poet went on to ironize at the expense of literary writings such as those of Chapelain and Charles Cotin and to savage under the pseudonym of Alidor, one Dalibert, a Parisian financier who had had to flee Paris during the Fouquet trials (to die in Rome in 1671 stripped of all his possessions).[5] The poet claimed the right, indeed the duty (as in the "Discours"), to discuss and regulate both matters of aesthetic taste and questions of political and social justice.

In a sense, the entire argument of the ninth Satire served to set up the

[4]Ibid., pp. 57–61: "Discours sur la satire."
[5]Ibid., pp. 53 (Satire IX), 922 n. 3.

celebrated conclusion in which the poet spoke again to his *Esprit*, mocking Cotin once more. His remark was at once aesthetic, political, and regulatory (although only after the *Art poétique* of 1674 would Boileau's word become authoritative). The import and repercussions of his argument were broad indeed. Like the writers who were his principal antagonists here, Chapelain and Cotin, Boileau was as concerned with political utility as he was with aesthetic propriety, and he accused them and their companions, too, of mixing literary and political affairs. All you need do, he wrote, was criticize their writing, and instantly you will have them on your neck:

> Vous les verrez bient-tost feconds en impostures,
> Amasser contre vous des volumes d'injures,
> Traiter en vos écrits chaque vers d'attentat,
> Et d'un mot innocent faire un crime d'État.
> Vous aurez beau vanter le Roy dans vos ouvrages,
> Et de ce nom sacré sanctifier vos pages.
> Qui méprise Cotin, n'estime point son Roi,
> Et n'a, selon Cotin, ni Dieu, ni foi, ni loi.[6]

In 1667 Boileau's sarcasm was itself far from innocent. The appearance the previous year of the first authorized edition of his *Satires* had provoked the group of writers officially approved by the court, through Colbert's factotum Chapelain, to cries of scandalized outrage. In particular, the abbé Cotin had accused Boileau of undermining the very foundations of religion and state. His ancestor in Antiquity, Juvenal, "gave offense neither to the emperor, nor to religion, nor to his gods." Not so Boileau and Molière—especially Boileau, in this instance. The poet was, he wrote in specific reference to the dithyrambic "Discours au Roy" of 1662–65, "a corruptor, and not a corrector of youth, for he degrades reason, and he abolishes respect toward his Monarch." Matters were in fact even worse, for

> what can be the effect of a young man's satire, except everywhere to erect altars to debauchery, by contempt of reason and justice, by profanation of the throne? In whatever fine phrases insolence and licentiousness are clothed, they are but to be feared the more for them! They glide all the more dangerously into the mind, just because they do so with all the graces of style. Lucianism is introduced by means of the purity of language; Arianism beneath the banner of eloquence. Innovators in France

[6]Ibid., p. 56: "You will instantly see them pour out fraudulent claims, / Pile up against you whole volumes of blame, / Treat every line of your writings as a criminal outrage, / And make a state crime of an innocent word. / In vain will you praise the King in your works, / And sanctify your pages with his sacred name. / Whoever scorns Cotin, has no respect for his King, / And has, so Cotin says, no God, no faith, no law."

and Germany would not have been listened to, had they not been eloquent.[7]

These writings all date from the period during which the chancellor Séguier was trying to satisfy the king's demand to obtain Fouquet's condemnation to death for treason.[8] At the same time, Molière had found himself under serious attack for the "scandal" of *Tartuffe* (performed in May 1664) and *Dom Juan* (played in February 1665). Both plays had to be taken off despite Louis XIV's patronage of the playwright. These were the plays, together with Boileau's poems, that Cotin accused of attacking both "religion" and "the state."[9] In such an atmosphere these charges could not be taken lightly. They were by no means harmless. One need only recall that as recently as September 1662, a young lawyer named Claude Le Petit, after having had his hand severed at the wrist, was burned at the stake in the Place de Grève for having written libertine and impious poems: as Claude Brossette, Boileau's editor in 1716, was at pains to emphasize.[10] In addition, although the issue was perhaps somewhat less menacing, the personal necessity for an author to receive official protection was ineluctable: whether physical (as Molière had discovered) or financial (even a *rentier* like Boileau needed the official recognition—and right to the pen—thus afforded). Further, Colbert and the king had not delayed in understanding the propagandistic possibilities of literary culture, its potential as a tool of political warfare which Richelieu had made manifest in the 1630s and to which we have already seen Dennis refer.

Boileau was no less aware of this than any other. To that end he had penned the encomiastic "Discours au Roy" (so criticized by Cotin) in praise of royal policy, certainly hoping to find his way in the footsteps of his brother Gilles onto the list of those pensioned by Colbert in the king's name. His mockery of Cotin did not then indifferently refer to the centralizing monarchical battle cry of "un Roi, une Foi, une loi," which had

[7]Abbé Charles Cotin, La "*Satyre des satyres*" et la "*Critique désintéressée sur les satyres du temps*," avec une notice par le bibliophile Jacob (1867, 1890; rpt. Geneva, 1969), pp. 17, 38, 42. These citations are all from the *Critique*. Both texts were originally published in 1666.

[8]Fouquet had been accused not only of financial depredations, but also of having built up a private navy, whose purpose was held to be seditious. Further, although the point was not raised in these terms, the château de Vaux that he had built for himself was far above the kind of housing suitable to a person of his station according to habitual sumptuary usage (see Norbert Elias, *The Court Society*, trans. Edmund Jephcott [New York, 1983], pp. 41–65). The king did not succeed in having Fouquet condemned to death but did obtain his banishment in perpetuity. Dissatisfied, Louis added a sentence of permanent imprisonment (despite Fouquet's many defenders: Jean de La Fontaine, Paul Pellisson, Madeleine de Scudéry, Marie de Sévigné, and others). See "Jugement par commissaires qui condamne le surintendant des finances Fouquet au bannissement perpétuel pour trahison et concussion," in *Recueil général*, 18:43–45.

[9]Cotin, *Critique désintéressée*, p. 12.

[10]Boileau, *Oeuvres*, p. 995 n. 30.

been since the Wars of Religion the rallying cry of Gallican monarchism. Most historians of Colbert and of his economic and political projects are convinced that his influence was the principal barrier against Catholic extremism and alone maintained some balance on behalf of the Protestants and others. The growing power of the *dévots* at court was a major threat to such a policy. Elisabeth Labrousse has characterized these people as "the direct heirs of the Ligue," who interpreted the old Gallican cry in terms of the most extreme Catholicism (destined to grow harsher over ensuing decades as Louis adopted an increasingly narrow piety).[11] It was they who were attacking both Molière and Boileau.

Even more dangerously, the group's views were largely shared by Colbert's special antagonists, the bellicose and intolerant Michel Le Tellier and his son the marquis de Louvois, respectively secretary and undersecretary of state for war. After the Fouquet affair had been settled, the next most urgent piece of business was the long-overdue reform of justice. This was finished in April 1667 with an edict destined to hold sway until the Revolution, the "Ordonnance civile touchant la réformation de la justice."[12] Once such internal concerns had been resolved, the king was free to turn his attention in other directions, guided now largely by the suasion of the Le Telliers. So, after the necessary colloquies and debates had prepared the way, August 1667 found Louis enjoying himself at the siege of Lille. But his advisory *conseil d'en haut* was fraught with dissension: Le Tellier and Marshal Turenne on one side, Colbert and Hugues de Lionne (foreign affairs) on another. Louvois was not in fact a council member, but Louis found his views especially congenial. This more than countered any hesitations in belligerency caused by the poor relations between Le Tellier and Turenne, due to the latter's Protestantism. Thus, after Lille's surrender, Louis was not long in Paris: by February 1668 he was in Franche-Comté following the Prince de Condé's invasion. Still, peace was concluded by May, with the signing of that Treaty of Aix-la-Chapelle celebrated by Boileau in his first Epître.[13] For a moment Colbert and Lionne seemed to be on top.

Boileau, like his friend Racine, was an enthusiastic supporter of Colbert's economic, commercial, and cultural policies. We may perhaps understand his use of the Gallican maxim as an effort to recapture the symbol for a less inflexible and harsh policy, one not unreminiscent of the sixteenth-century *Politiques*. At the same time, however, emphasizing inward-looking Gallican moderation, Boileau implicitly supported those

---

[11]Elisabeth Labrousse, *"Une foi, une loi, un roi?" Essai sur la révocation de l'Édit de Nantes* (Geneva and Paris, 1985), p. 73.

[12]The "Ordonnance" is available in the *Recueil général*, 18:103–80. I have elsewhere sought to show how Racine incorporated the debates about justice and the conclusions of the reform in *Les Plaideurs* (1668): "Racine and Political Thought: *Les Plaideurs* and Law," *Cahiers du Dix-Septième*, 1, no. 2 (Fall 1987), 1–19.

[13]See Paul Sonnino, *Louis XIV and the Origins of the Dutch War* (Cambridge 1988), pp. 9–28.

policies of self-sufficient stability pushed by Colbert and at best contradicted by the risky adventurism, whether religious or military, of his
opponents' policy of aggressive imperialism. During this period a real
battle was being fought over the very nature of government, whose leadership remained for some years after the beginning of Louis XIV's personal
rule in 1661 what one historian has called "conciliar." But as we have just
seen, the *conseil d'en haut*, for a while truly a deliberative body, was
increasingly riven with factional strife. By April 1672 Louis had begun the
Dutch War. During its first year, more or less by chance, the style of
government changed radically. As Carl Ekberg has put it, Colbert was
preoccupied with finances and building the new château at Versailles, the
elder Le Tellier was recovering from a stroke, so that only Louvois and the
marquis de Pomponne (minister for foreign affairs since Lionne's death)
accompanied the king on his campaign. The latter was, however, of small
importance: he was new and his views were strongly opposed to Louis's
often rather careless military provocation of the Empire. "During the
summer of 1673," writes Ekberg, "Louis XIV and Louvois ruled France."[14]

The provocations may well not have been simply haphazard, however.
Louis could not have failed to understand the July 1673 investment of
Trier (following the speedy capture of Maestricht in June) as such a provo-
cation. So, too, was his reduction of the Alsatian cities in August and
September of the same year, even though such towns as Colmar and
Sélestat had been ambivalently French since the signing of that part of the
Westphalian agreements (1648) known as the Treaty of Münster: their
feudal arrangements were both anachronistic and perilous to royal authority. In rejecting the diplomats' advice and pursuing that of Louvois, Louis
was following his own inclinations, to the detriment of the Dutch War and
with the risks attendant on his taunting of the Empire.[15] But the king may
well have had his eye on certain dynastic "interests." We know from his
Mémoires how much he coveted the Empire, feeling that the French
crown had been unjustly deprived of an age-old dynastic right.[16] Satisfac-

---

[14]Carl J. Ekberg, *The Failure of Louis XIV's Dutch War* (Chapel Hill, N.C., 1979), p. 9.
[15]Ibid., pp. 29–31, 36–37.
[16]Louis XIV, *Mémoires, suivi de Réflexions sur le métier de roi, Instructions au duc
d'Anjou, Projet de harangue*, ed. Jean Lognon (Paris, 1978). J. J. Winckelmann recorded
how this desire had been inscribed in pageantry from the outset of the reign: "*King Louis
XIV* at the age of 4, after the death of Louis XIII, was depicted on a medal sitting on a
shield which was held up in the air by France and Providence, with the inscription:
Ineunte regno. This refers to the custom of the old Franks, who put their new kings onto
a shield which was held aloft and then showed him to the people, who acknowledged
him as their lord by this solemn action" ("Attempt at an Allegory [1766]," trans. Susan
Powell, in his *Writings on Art*, ed. David Irwin [London, 1972], p. 151). The greatest of
the Franks was no doubt Charlemagne, originator of the French monarchy, of which the
imperial rights had been argued at length in Jacques de Cassan, *La recherche des droicts
du Roy, & de la couronne de la France sur les royaumes, duchez, comtez, villes & pais
occupez par les princes estrangers . . . ensemble de leurs droicts sur l'empire . . .* (Paris,
1634). As its title indicates, this volume sought to justify the French crown's claims to
various neighboring territories. Cassan's book was one of many: e.g., Henri de Rohan's

tion of *that* desire would depend on a clearly singular sovereignty and a militarily strong France. At the same time, the very first of the many wars it would inevitably involve "was destroying the finance minister's hopes for economic growth and reform." For Colbert and a few others (including Pomponne), ensured and stable growth had to be economic, commercial, industrial, and cultural, and it required a ruler strong but with a deep sense of the state's primacy (even over dynastic concern) and of his government's responsibility to the "entire French nation."[17]

The inclination to Empire, "Holy" and "Roman" as it was, was doubt-less no idle aspect of religious policy as well. The first *dragonnades* against the Protestants (May–November 1681 in Poitou) were after all authorized by Louvois.[18] It was, of course, Le Tellier, by then chancellor and garde des sceaux, who signed the Revocation of the Edict of Nantes in October 1685. Racine showed no little courage when, in a speech written by him and delivered by Colbert's second son before the king in August 1685, he besought Louis not to deal harshly with those who disagreed with the established church, but to use persuasion and negotiation (precisely the arguments used by Pomponne and others a dozen years earlier about the "Dutch" wars—with no greater success).[19] It was no mere coincidence that the Jean-Louis Bergeret welcomed with Thomas Corneille to the Académie in Racine's celebrated January 1685 encomium was premier *commis* to Charles Colbert de Croissy, younger brother of the "grand" Colbert and minister and secretary of state for foreign affairs from 1680 to 1696. During that very summer an immense *dragonnade* had started in Béarn, spread throughout Languedoc, and by September had moved well up the Rhône valley in the east and into the Aunis and Saintonge in the west. Fitful violence against Protestants and others (Racine's Jansenists among them) had been endemic since the 1650s; it was now reaching a savage peak to which the Revocation added impetus.[20]

De l'interest des princes et estats de la chrestienté, à M. le Cardinal Richelieu (Paris, 1638) or Pierre Dupuy's *Traitez touchant les droits du roy tres-chrestien sur plusieurs estats et seigneuries possedées par divers princes voisins . . .* (Paris, 1655). This volume had originally been undertaken by Dupuy and the royal historiographer, Théodore Godefroy, at Richelieu's express request. Between 1649 and 1667 Antoine Aubéry published two volumes specifically on this issue, and another on Richelieu, in which the dispute with Spain over Catalonia provided an excuse for similar claims (see the Bibliography, Part 1).

[17]Ekberg, *Failure*, pp. 174–76, 179.

[18]Labrousse, *Essai sur la révocation*, pp. 173–77.

[19]Racine, *Oeuvres complètes*, 2:351–55. Jean Orcibal has argued that like pleas for tolerant pluralism were advanced in *Esther* (1689) and *Athalie* (1691), the two plays Racine wrote for St. Cyr at Maintenon's request: *La genèse d'Esther et d'Athalie* (Paris, 1950). Racine and Boileau themselves maintained relations with both Port-Royal and the Jesuits. Indeed, the theological condemnation of Port-Royal never resulted in its receiving any less respect in intellectual and court circles, although Racine showed his courage again in his ever more active defense in the 1680s and 1690s of an increasingly beleaguered Port-Royal (Picard, *Carrière de Jean Racine*, pp. 447–68).

[20]Labrousse, *Essai sur la révocation*, pp. 192–95. The growth of proscriptions in the provinces has been explored at length, for example, by Paul Bert, *Histoire de la Révoca-*

Boileau's twelfth *Epître*, "L'amour de Dieu," written in 1696, was to be a plea against the grown theoretical and practical power of the Jesuits and of ultramontanism (drawing for that reason Jacques-Bénigne Bossuet's praise—even though Bossuet had been in favor of the Revocation—at least if we can judge from his funeral oration for Le Tellier, fulsome on that score: to the effect that all was calm, all had peaceably been brought back to the fold, and that this edict was the signal high point of his "glorious ministry").[21] Boileau's last satire (also a twelfth), against Jesuitical hypocrisy and laxness, was banned by the king himself, under pressure from his fanatical Jesuit confessor, another (unrelated) Michel Le Tellier—also responsible for the destruction of the Jansenist Port-Royal-des-Champs. The poem was published, posthumously and surreptitiously, in 1711. By then it represented the views of a group of "Colbertians," who would become leading counselors under the regency: a combination of high government officials, parlementarians, and *noblesse de robe*, who could succeed in making of the monarchy something akin to what Colbert and Pomponne had been seeking in the 1670s and 1680s.[22]

These matters were all closely linked. Literature, that is to say, was part of a political struggle for power. It was, I should judge, a contest vital to the future of France. The growing strength of the *dévots* at court and the military and religious aggressiveness of the Le Tellier party were pitted against the more generous views of Colbert and his colleagues. The *contrôleur-général's* preoccupation with Versailles in 1673 was singularly

---

tion de l'Édit de Nantes à Bordeaux et dans le Bordelais. *Diocèse de Bordeaux, 1653–1715* (1908; rpt. Geneva, 1977), and by Paul Jean Louis Gachon, *Quelques préliminaires de la Révocation de l'Édit de Nantes en Languedoc (1661–1685)* (Toulouse, 1899). See, too, Elisabeth Israels Perry, *From Theology to History: French Religious Controversy and the Revocation of the Edict of Nantes* (The Hague, 1973). Just as it was Colbert who had done so much to hold a line against anti-Protestant violence, so he had tried to prevent kindred savagery. Although he did not, as is so often claimed, put an abrupt stop to witch trials in France by abolishing the charge of *sorcellerie sabbatique* in 1672 (see, e.g., Hugh R. Trevor-Roper, *The European Witch Craze of the Sixteenth and Seventeenth Centuries and Other Essays* [New York, 1969], p. 167), he was responsible in the years 1670–72 for halting several witch trials. There was no national policy until 1682, when he did finally succeed (with Le Tellier, let it be said) in enacting a nationwide policy whose result *was* to put a stop to such trials. See Robert Mandrou, *Magistrats et sorciers en France au XVIIe siècle: Une analyse de psychologie historique* (Paris, 1980), pp. 464–66, 478–86.

[21]Jacques-Bénigne Bossuet, *Oeuvres*, ed. l'abbé Velat and Yvonne Champailler (Paris, 1961), p. 184. Things are never simple, and Bossuet was a great compromiser. He may, though, have been seeking to calm catastrophe. In 1686 the then abbé Fénelon was sent with Claude Fleury into the Aunis and Saintonge to proselatize Protestants in a rather more tranquil manner—as well as to report on the situation.

[22]These questions have been explored by Lionel Rothkrug, *Opposition to Louis XIV: The Political and Social Origins of the French Enlightenment* (Princeton, 1965). He suggests that the Enlightenment was "a direct outgrowth" of an aristocratic and merchant opposition to "the centralizing programs and economic philosophy of the King and his ministers" during these years (pp. 176–77). Matters were more ambivalent: the struggle took place inside the highest levels of government. The "opposition" was within the Royal Council itself.

telling: art of all kinds, he had said in 1664, was a principal glory of state, useful to its welfare and a chief area of its concern. Above all, he said, it should be a matter of *public* debate and achievement. It should indeed "pay hommage to the Grand Monarchy," but in turn "state sponsorship of the arts would render French talent the finest in the world, the envy of all other nations."[23] This would be a portion of the national treasure perhaps not much less valuable than that acquired through commercial and indus- trial endeavor. The Le Telliers were endangering the kind of stability on which such developments utterly depended. They were doing it by creat- ing a cluster of hostile nations abroad and alienating many of "those most necessary" at home.

In Colbert's view, Protestant industrialists and merchants were essen- tial to the success of his and Louis's mercantilist project.[24] The effort to build a satisfactory navy, he thought, would (and did) fail without them. Molière's run-in with the growing influence of the Catholic *dévots* and Boileau's confrontation were early instances of the strength of a move- ment that was to put France in a straitjacket for the next century and, one may argue, made some kind of violent revolution almost inevitable—a view captured to a nicety some hundred years later by Mary Wollstone- craft, as she commented on Louis XVI going to trial: "My fancy instantly brought Louis XIV before me, entering the capital with all his pomp, after one of the victories most flattering to his pride, only to see the sunshine of prosperity overshadowed by the sublime gloom of misery."[25]

The Revocation, signed just two years after Colbert's death in Septem- ber 1683, was a disastrous blow to what was left of his commercial and industrial policies, just as Louis's Dutch War had earlier been (although

---

[23]The first reference is to a text provided by André Félibien, recorded in *Letters, instructions et mémoires de Colbert*, ed. Pierre Clément, Vol. 5: *Fortifications, sci- ences, lettres, beaux-arts, bâtiments* (Paris, 1868), pp. 498–99. The other citations are from Andrew Trout, *Jean-Baptiste Colbert* (Boston, 1978), p. 179. The principal schol- arly works on Colbert and his economic, political, and cultural accomplishments re- main those of C. W. Cole and P. Clément indicated in my bibliography. I. Murat's *Colbert* (Paris, 1980) is extremely useful: see pp. 173–96 for his "politique des beaux- arts."

[24]The old claim that great numbers of Protestants (and Jews) were financiers—espe- cially venal ones—was certainly a canard, sign of rising bigotry. There were some, and others may have hidden their religious affiliation, but Catholics were far more numer- ous: see Julian Dent, *Crisis in Finance: Crown, Financiers, and Society in Seventeenth- Century France* (New York, 1973), pp. 118–19; and Daniel Dessert, *Argent, pouvoir et société au Grand Siècle* (Paris, 1984), who notes that just under 5 percent were Protes- tant (pp. 94–95). Among them, one shared the controller-generality with Colbert and Louis Le Tonnelier de Breteuil until 1665–66, doing the job alone from 1653 to 1661: he was particularly dishonest. See Dent, *Crisis in Finance*, p. 97; Guillaume Depping, "Un banquier protestant en France au xviie siècle: Barthélemy Herwarth, contrôleur général des finances (1607–1676)," *Revue Historique*, 10 (1879), 285–338; 11 (1879), 63–80; Claude Badalo-Dulong, *Banquier du roi: Barthélemy Hervart (1606–1667)* (Paris, 1951); Dessert, *Argent*, p. 605.

[25]Mary Wollstonecraft, "Letter to Joseph Johnson" [December 1792], in *A Wollstone- craft Anthology*, ed. Janet M. Todd (Bloomington, Ind., and London, 1977), p. 121.

then for financial rather than demographic reasons). The large-scale flight of Protestants deprived France of its strength in commerce and industry, while increasing that of its neighbors. It forced subsequent ministries to rely basically on agricultural production (which doubtless explains both the often-criticized views of such as Fénelon and the agrarian economic theories of the French eighteenth-century physiocrats). It deprived the nation of variety in production and forced a split even greater between city and country. At one blow, perhaps, it made impossible the kind of gradual and diverse transformation experienced in England.

Recent revisionist efforts have suggested that the Revocation was not quite so catastrophic or that it was only one factor in disaster.[26] The last is evidently a truism. But the first just will not do: we have ample information both of the economic consequences and of the personal horrors. Then the question really is, To what extent could these results have been foreseen? What I am suggesting in this chapter, of course, is that those engaged in these debates did in fact have a variously clear idea of both short- and long-term effects, and that their discussions therefore did suppose a quite precise practical political role for (e.g.) literature. The evidence surely lies in the twenty-year struggle of Colbert, Pomponne, Sébastien Le Prestre de Vauban, Pierre de Boisguillebert, and many others. It lies too in the growing barbarity supported by the *dévots* and the militarists. Apart from recorded physical violence, edicts, orders, and laws from the 1650s show how Protestants suffered a progressive deprivation of civil rights: from officeholding to midwifery, from participation in foreign trade to baptizing or even raising their own children. Only those who did so willfully could have failed to have a sense of what would result from a generalized policy of state oppression. And I think it is useful to look quickly at some of those consequences: the stakes were enormous and intimately bound to the case of the other country I have been discussing, England. As we will soon see again, literary culture was also caught closely up in them.

In 1900 Émile Levasseur wrote that the effects on industry were such that France "did not recover for the rest of the reign."[27] In fact, recovery took very much longer. Except for the royal manufacturies (established c. 1669), which benefited from special advantages and were by law directed by Catholics or foreign Protestants (officially unaffected by the Revocation), the consequences for unprotected small manufacturers and tradespeople were flagrant and dramatic. The repression affected artisans in all the industries Colbert was trying to build up: wool combers, carders, weavers, tailors, in textiles; tanners, glove makers, cobblers, in leather;

---

[26]See, e.g., Thomas J. Scheaper, *The Economy of France in the Second Half of the Reign of Louis XIV*, ICES Research Report/Cahier de Recherche du CIEE, no. 2 (Montreal, 1980). He provides many references to like-minded scholars.

[27]Émile Levasseur, *Histoire des classes ouvrières et de l'industrie en France avant 1789*, 2d ed., 2 vols. (Paris, 1900–1901), 2:344.

silk workers; various producers of luxury goods; and perhaps most important, manufacturers of sailcloth. Germain Martin has recorded that in Picardy, at Abbeville, 80 of 160 families left; 1,600 of 2,000 quit the Amiens district; 60 of 100, Doulens; 28 of 40, the Boulonnais. The Ardres, Calais, and Alençon regions lost close to 6,000. Such departures took time, for not only were they evidently complicated in the extreme, but punishment for such as were discovered before the event was barbarous. Still, Martin records, in Champagne the Reims *généralité* had 950 looms in 1698, down from 1,812 in 1686; the Réthel area had 37 woolcloth manufactures in 1698, down from 80 in 1686; in the town of Mézières and its surroundings 8 looms remained from the 109 in existence twelve years earlier. To a person, the Metz Protestants left for Brandenburg. Four hundred families from Sedan went to Leiden and the Amsterdam area.[28]

Not only textiles were affected, as this may so far have suggested. In the Angoumois, by 1698, only 16 paper mills remained from the 60 that had operated before 1686. In Tours, even before 1685, 3,000 Protestants had left, and by 1698 there remained 54 tanneries, 1,200 looms, 70 silk producers, 60 ribbon weavers, and 4,000 workers: in 1683 there had been 400 tanneries, 8,000 looms, 700 silk producers, 3,000 ribban weavers, and 40,000 workers. At Saint-Jean-d'Angély the leather industry, flourishing before 1685, was nonexistent ten years later; in Lyon 18,000 cloth looms dropped to 4,000. The effect on external commerce was no less disastrous. About 60,000 refugees went to England. Before 1685 that country had been purchasing 200,000 pounds sterling worth of cloth from France. By 1698 it could prohibit the importing of taffeta. According to a Neapolitan writer in 1730, the way to praise silk was to say it was of English manufacture: there had been none before. England had been purchasing an annual 5,000,000 pounds worth of sailcloth, until refugees started to manufacture it at Ipswich—French revenues fell to zero. At Exeter one Passarau, a skilled artisan from the Gobelins, taught the English the art of tapestry. Germany, the Netherlands, Denmark, and Switzerland all benefited equally or more.[29]

The modernization of the Great Elector's army was helped more than a little by the exodus of highly trained officers from France, and his Brandenburg foundries were entirely run by Protestant refugees.[30] The navy lost equally disastrously, for the Revocation "drove thousands of Protestant sailors out of the country." The Atlantic and Channel seacoasts were particularly Protestant and "provided some of the best sailors in the kingdom." Vauban estimated that by 1689 some eight to nine thousand had taken overseas service: that meant, of course, service with the enemies of France. Furthermore, the naval officer corps was disproportionately Prot-

[28]Germain Martin, *La grande industrie sous le règne de Louis XIV (plus particulièrement de 1660 à 1715)* (1899; rpt. New York, 1971), pp. 204–6.

[29]Ibid., pp. 206–11.

[30]Labrousse, *Essai sur la révocation*, p. 209.

estant, and those who did not or could not leave became a source of distrust, suspicion, espionage, and an ever-present threat of mutiny.[31] France lost twice over, that is to say. First, by the simple loss of those who fled—skilled workers and artisans in textiles, silk, leather, paper, and divers luxury goods; trained army officers and munitions experts; experienced seamen and naval officers; and second by the fact that these refugees were swiftly integrated into the industrial, commercial, and military forces of the Protestant powers: England, the German lands, the Netherlands, Scandinavia.

This transfer of the balance of power was observed by Basil Kennet in 1706 with irony no doubt, but with specific regard to the relation of art and empire and in the particular terms of mercantilist expansionism: with its assumption that a limited overall sum of wealth gave inevitable advantage to whoever could grab the largest slice, adding most to their own "treasure" (as Thomas Mun had long since called it). The remark was the more meaningful because it came after Blenheim, at the time of Ramillies, and was made in the "Preface to the Publisher" before Kennet's translation of Rapin's commentary on Aristotle's *Poetics* (earlier translated by Rymer). Not only was Kennet practicing his very preach, but the observation emphasized, therefore, the very role of literature: "While France aspires to be absolute in arts and empire, our nation, that so well disputes the double prize with its neighbours, has, at the same time, made use of their industry, to set bounds to their ambition, has studied their critics, to exceed their authors, and practised their martial discipline, to maintain advantage over them in courage and strength."[32]

Military affairs, industrial affairs, those of state, those of the arts—above all literary—here all find their place (shades of Davenant), and in the utmost mercantilist terms. Such crowing would find its perfectly natural continuation a century later in this remark from the English translator of A. W. Schlegel's *Lectures on Dramatic Art* (1815), writing of the "hostility" of the French to its publication: "In this country the work will no doubt meet with a very different reception. Here we have no want of scholars to appreciate the value of his views of the ancient drama; and it will be no disadvantage to him, in our eyes, that he has been unsparing in his attack on the literature of our enemies."[33]

Martin concluded his sorry history of disaster by observing with no little irony how Louvois, more than belatedly, had sought to forestall such hostility: on January 13, 1686, he succeeded in obtaining "a judgment

---

[31]Geoffrey Symcox, *The Crisis of French Sea Power, 1688–1697: From the "Guerre d'Escadre" to the "Guerre de course"* (The Hague, 1974), pp. 12–18, 29–30. See pp. 80–82, 89, 106, 160 for continuing fears of revolt.

[32]Quoted by Alexander F. B. Clark, *Boileau and the French Classical Critics in England (1660–1830)* (1925; rpt. New York, 1965), p. 235.

[33]August Wilhelm Schlegel, *Lectures on Dramatic Art and Literature*, trans. John Black, 2d ed., rev. A. J. W. Morrison (London, 1909), "Preface of the Translator."

permitting all foreign Protestant merchants to enter the Kingdom."[34] We may suppose they did not come in their thousands. The year 1685 was a disastrous turning point. Yet the Revocation was only the culmination of a development marked by strife between Colbert and Le Tellier, by conflict between those who supported the idea of an economically and politically expansionist France and those who clung to the idea of a nation whose leadership was put in moral, religious, and military terms. The extent of the consequences may have taken leaders by surprise, but there could have been no question at all that they would be serious, once repression became official government policy. Their beginnings had been seen years before.

I began this seeming excursus with Boileau's ninth Satire and its Gallican cry. I can now return to that period. For this political and social history may not simply be found in the literary text—as one of those four structural roles previously mentioned and as participating in their same goals. It was played out in literary culture more generally. Indeed, strictly at the level of practical political conception and bureaucratic action, Colbert's literary and cultural policies were parallel to and intimately linked with his commercial and economic ones. Nor would that link disappear with the fading of any specific policy, or the quarrels cease whatever the fate of any specific element or particular practice. Boileau's sarcasm at Cotin's (and Chapelain's) expense was not aimed against the politicizing of literature as such. It was intended on behalf of a certain concept of literary culture, a certain notion of state and society, a particular idea of rationality; against a specific policy, a particular court group, a certain literary clique.

In 1674, simultaneously with his *Art poétique*, his translation of Longinus, and Rapin's *Réflexions*, Boileau also published his comic epic, *Le lutrin*, maybe partly as a joke. But its uninhibited praise of Guillaume de Lamoignon, First President of the Paris Parlement and leader in a sober and erudite "parliamentary intellectualism" that contrasted sharply with certain court tendencies both of a mundane and a theological order, bore implications concerning at once the idea of state (Parlement being strongly in favor of peace and economic stability) and the concept of literature (Rapin was its "accredited" theorist). Further, when the English took Boileau's burlesque to their hearts as an attack on the established and increasingly extremist Catholic church, they were perhaps not so very far wrong. At least until Lamoignon's death in 1677, Boileau strove always to keep one foot in court and one in Parlement, so to speak, heeding no doubt his own advice to "study the court, and know the town, / The one and the other are always fruitful in models."[35]

Although he himself had yet to receive any signs of favor by the time of

[34]Martin, *Grande industrie*, p. 212.
[35]Boileau, *Oeuvres*, p. 178: *Art poétique*, Chant II.

the ninth Satire (and had voiced disapproval of Colbert's autocratic style and even more of Chapelain's control over the literary pursestrings at least since 1666), he knew that Molière had retained the king's largesse despite his conflicts with the *dévots:* his troupe having become "Comédiens du roi" in 1665. Boileau's own writing was aimed no less at asserting a legitimate "party line" than was that of his opponents. His success was evidenced by his placement at the king's behest on the list of pensioned writers in 1674 (although he apparently received nothing for two more years), his nomination to the post of royal historiographer in October 1677 with Racine (who had claimed his own aptitude for the position in his 1666 *Dédicace* of *Alexandre le grand* to the king), and his admission to the Académie in 1683, again under royal pressure.

The dispute, then, between Boileau and Chapelain (or Cotin) was never over the fact of the intimate relation between literature and policy, but was simply over which policy and whose control. None of these writers questioned that they who ranked as the accredited thinkers of the newly dominant order should be "active creators of its ideology" or instruments of its authority.[36] The serious issue at hand was simply that of who would have the right to dictate literary form and matter in relation to what specific policy and social and cultural concerns, and of who would have the right to judge appropriate literary production. That is why Bossuet, no less than Boileau, thundered as much about literature as about politics or theology. That is why Fénelon's *Télémaque* (so admired by a Voltaire and a d'Alembert) was both a political document and a literary "masterpiece" (said the sempiternal decision of the age). And we should remember that even if the two churchmen, Bossuet and Fénelon, opposed one another, both played as important a role as they held high ecclesiastical office under the aegis of the same sovereign authority.

The bishops were replaying the more overtly social, economic, and political battle being waged between the Colbert and the Le Tellier families, whose alternating occupation of the powerful posts of political power and patronage dominated the second half of the century. Yet they fought for the same spoils, beneath the ever watchful eye of a single authority. The squabble between the Ancients and the Moderns, between Boileau and Perrault or Fontenelle, was a matter of passing authority from one group of men in power to another—but always, always under the same sovereignty. Indeed, we can characterize this period as a series of minor struggles for power, concluding a century or more of radical transformation, on the verge of consolidating the victory of a particular discursive class (as I have elsewhere called it) and particular forms of analysis and action. I am suggesting that certain (discursive) facts, objectively present

[36]The citation is from Karl Marx as quoted by Karl Radek, "Contemporary World Literature and the Tasks of Proletarian Art," in *Problems of Soviet Literature: Reports and Speeches at the First Soviet Writers' Congress,* by A. Zhdanov, Maxim Gorky, N. Bukharin, K. Radek, and A. Stetsky, ed. H. G. Scott (New York, 1934), p. 75.

as the context for the foundation of the theory and practice of literature, both imply and did create certain constraints, providing the logical framework of what were then and are now "literature" and "literary criticism."

In 1672, on the death of the chancellor Séguier, until then Protector of the Académie, Colbert persuaded the king to provide its members with chambers in the Louvre. Six delegates were sent to the minister's residence to thank him for this favor. "Assuredly," said François Charpentier,[37] "the Alliance of Letters and of Arms is not new . . . but that a King should have loved Letters sufficiently to lodge an Academy in his own House; that is a matter that posterity will find only among the deeds of LOUIS LE GRAND." Further, he went on, the king "is not satisfied with granting us his all-powerful protection, he wishes to attach us as serving members of his household [*à titre de domestiques*]; he wants royal Majesty and *belles Lettres* to occupy the same Palace." This attachment was so far from being "a mere matter of chance" as to have occurred at the very moment "when this magnanimous Monarch is marching at the head of his armies to punish his ungrateful allies and restore their wealth to those Princes who have called him to their defense" (the reference was to the Dutch War!). To their mutual advantage, literature and power would be conjoined (as Kennet asserted with more precision some three decades later), the first to sing praise of the second and urge it on—and more, to create the context for its action. Colbert replied that such was exactly why the king had set the Académie in the Louvre, and he encouraged it to do all possible to "work for the glory of this great Prince."[38]

In 1674 Boileau concluded his *Art poétique* in these very terms, praising the victories of French arms against the Dutch in 1673 and in Franche-Comté in 1674 and exclaiming: "Auteurs, pour les chanter, redoubler vos transports, / Le sujet ne veut pas de vulgaires efforts (Authors, to sing them aloud, redouble your raptures. / The matter surpasses common endeavors.)" His own task would be: "Seconder vostre ardeur, échauffer vos esprits, / Et vous montrer de loin la couronne et le prix (To encourage your ardor, to excite your spirits, / And show you from afar the crown and the prize.)"[39] While Racine might assimilate himself, we saw, even to

---

[37]Charpentier would later figure importantly on the side of the moderns in the *Querelle*. As a protégé of Colbert, he had written the 1664 prospectus for the projected French East India Company. He had been a victim of Boileau's mockery in the *Discours au Roy*: Boileau, *Oeuvres*, pp. 864–65 n. 4.

[38]Institut de France, *Les registres de l'Académie Française, 1672–1793*, 3 vols. (Paris, 1895), 1:38–40.

[39]Boileau, *Oeuvres*, p. 185: *Art poétique*, Chant IV. Revealing the fundamental identity of interest, Boileau's major antagonist of the 1680s and 1690s, Charles Perrault, would emphasize precisely the same relation. Praise of military and political power framed encomia of arts and sciences in his poem "Le siècle de Louis le Grand." His *Parallèle des anciens et des modernes* began in like manner, as Perrault, setting his scene in the Versailles's gardens, started by speaking of "the King's absence, who had gone to visit Luxemburg and his most recent conquests" (*Parallèle des anciens et des modernes en ce qui regarde les arts et les sciences. Dialogues. Avec le poème du siècle*

Louis XIV, Boileau might perhaps play Colbert to him. Nor was the matter one of political action alone. Not for nothing did Boileau reject "de vulgaires efforts": he was concerned, once again, with those "most necessary men" who must make the state function and with the proper basis for political action.

The poem set out, just before the passage just quoted, the very foundation of all such action, repeating Davenant's assertion about literature's task of founding rational public society. Reason and right language once again performed the Hobbesian *Fiat* of *Leviathan:*

> Avant que la Raison s'expliquant par la voix,
> Eust instruit les Humains, eust enseigné des Loix:
> Tous les Hommes suivoient la grossière Nature,
> Dispersés dans les bois couroient à la pasture.
> La force tenoit lieu de droit et d'équité:
> Le meurtre s'exerçoit avec impunité.
> Mais de discours enfin l'harmonieuse adresse
> De ces sauvages moeurs adoucit la rudesse,
> Rassembla les Humains dans les forests épars
> Enferma les citez de murs et de remparts,
> De l'aspect du supplice effraya l'insolence,
> Et sous l'appui des loix mit la foible innocence,
> Cet ordre fut, dit-on, le fruit des premiers vers.[40]

This described with considerable exactness a Hobbesian contractual passage from a state of nature ("la grossière Nature") to that of civil society ("les citez"): those very walls of which Davenant and Hobbes had also spoken. In both of them, as here in Boileau, literature and rational justice ("law and equity") performed the same contract. And he managed to slip in a neat response to Cotin at the same time, in this "harmonious art of discourse," criticized by the abbé as the siren sound of evil. Now it was the foundational art of state. And here, too, the instruments were the pure poets, uncontaminated by "a sordid love of gain," who now acted under "an enlightened Prince," "a favorable Star." That is the foundation on which Boileau now immediately set his description of Louis's victories—

---

de Louis le Grand et une épistre en vers sur le genie, 2d ed., 4 vols [1692–97; rpt. Geneva, 1971], p. 16 [I. 1]). The "Siècle" was read to the Académie on January 22, 1687; the first volume of the *Parallèle* appeared in 1688.

[40]Ibid., p. 183: "Before Reason, expressing itself in speech, / Had instructed Humans, had taught them Laws: / All Men followed brutish Nature, / Dispersed in the woods ran after their fodder. / Force took the place of law and equity: / Murder was practiced with impunity. / But at last the harmonious art of discourse / Softened the brutality of savage habits, / Brought together humans scattered in the forests, / Enclosed cities with walls and ramparts, / Frightened insolent presumption with the severest punishment, / And set helpless innocence beneath the protection of the laws. / This order, it is said, was the fruit of the first poetry."

Maestricht and Besançon, Dole and Salins—and cried his encouragement to the littérateurs.

Nor need we think this was particular to a particular form of monarchy, even if one could imagine that there was in fact so great a difference between, for example, the British and the French. Many have observed how the French monarchy was tied both theoretically and practically to a form of "consensual" bureaucratic action: theoretically, because while the prince's right was held to be a function of divine authorization and genea-logical legitimacy, it was also held that such right depended at least to a degree on some implicit accord with the people composing the nation (a matter on which Colbert felt strongly and which provided the basis for Fénelon's end-of-the-century accusations against Louis); practically, be-cause there were always executive constraints on the king's action.[41] The English case was even clearer: and apart from its "constitutional" nature after the Glorious Revolution, it, too, saw "the growth of a powerful and efficient executive [which] was to prove, perhaps, more important in the development of political stability than the resolution of the arguments between Whig and Tory, or that crushing of the electorate which was a marked feature of politics between 1689 and 1729."[42] That powerful and efficient executive was quite exactly the necessary unique soverign authority discussed at the end of Chapter 3. In the cases of both France and England, practice and theory echoed one another to perfection.

I would further wish to argue that those debates between "Whig" and "Tory" were analogous to those we have been watching in France. Nor were they any less bound to literary culture. The alliance of literature and power was always emphasized, most frequently with direct reference to France and to the relations between the two countries. I have mentioned how in 1712 Dennis could refer to the politician and poet Richelieu as having been able to lay "the foundations of the *French* Greatness," pre-cisely because of this combination, just as, we saw him continue, that very greatness was to be "sapp'd and undermin'd and overturn'd by a *British* Poetick Ministry" (nor were the siege metaphors accidental, of course). Writing to Dryden in 1694 during those wars of the Augsburg League following the Revocation of the Edict of Nantes, the same author re-marked of Boileau that he provided the sole standard by which one must judge contemporary satirists, adding: "Though I can but hope that the Confederate forces will give chase to De Lorges and Luxemburgh [French

[41]See, e.g., Elias, *Court Society,* p. 3.
[42]J. H. Plumb, *The Origins of Political Stability in England, 1675–1725* (Boston, 1967), p. 13. Cf. pp. 100–28. Linda Colley has responded to Plumb's arguments (and those of others) with respect to the Hanoverian period, in *In Defiance of Oligarchy: The Tory Party, 1714–1760* (1982; rpt. Cambridge, 1985). My discussion is of an earlier time and in any case concerns less the specific details of authority than the nature of its practical cultural inception and its general theoretical foundations.

generals], I am very confident that Boileau and Racine will be forced to submit to you."[43]

These were by now commonplaces; from Davenant, writing to Hobbes an entire treatise on the matter, to Dryden, with *Annus Mirabilis* just ten years later; from Rapin, noting the necessary "subordination" of all art to political aims, as both having the public welfare as their fundamental, general goal, to Rymer, whom we saw remarking in 1692 (a further twenty years after Rapin's comment) that in ancient Greece, as for the moderns, "the best *Poet* was he who had done the most to make men vertuous and serviceable to the Publick."[44] As Kennet likewise made clear, literature was of a piece with political development and dispute, in analogous ways and to the same extent as any other human practice, whether military or commercial, industrial or epistemological, scientific or economic—to mention those most often placed in parallel by critics of the period.

Anne Finch Winchilsea put the case with considerably more humor as she besought her husband (sometime in 1691) to leave his desk, where he was tracking the progress of the Augsburg war, and accompany her into their gardens:

> Think not tho' lodg'd in Mons, or in Namur,
> You're from my dangerous attacks secure.
> No, Louis shall his falling Conquests fear,
> When by succeeding Courriers he shall hear
> Appollo, and the Muses, are drawn down,
> To storm each fort, and take in ev'ry Town.
> Vauban the Orphean Lyre, to mind shall call,
> That drew the stones to the old Theban Wall,
> And make no doubt, if itt against him play.
> They, from his works, will fly as fast away,
> Which to prevent, he shall to peace persuade,
> Of strong, confederate Syllables, affraid.[45]

Literature was a servant—indeed, an integral part—of political order and might, an instrument for the maintenance, after the creation, of a particular society and its values. In France the very ranks that were to be politically dominant in the eighteenth century, the *noblesse de robe* and the *parlementaires*, were those that had done most to foster literary culture. Jean-Marie Apostolidès has remarked of the artistic "intellectuels d'Etat"

---

[43]Dennis, "Genius and Writings of Shakespeare," in *Critical Works*, 2:3, for the first reference. The letter to Dryden, printed in *Letters Upon Several Occasions* (London, 1696), is quoted in Clark, *Boileau*, p. 9.

[44]Rapin, *Réflexions*, 2:122; Rymer, *Short View of Tragedy*, in *Critical Works*, p. 95.

[45]Anne Finch, Countess of Winchilsea, *Selected Poems*, ed. Katharine M. Rogers (New York, 1979), p. 39: "An Invitation to Dafnis," ll. 33–44.

that they worked in terms of "an equivalence between military function and that of the writer. Men of arms and men of letters [fought] on different fronts, but their task [was] similar."[46] Indeed, it is less than obvious from what we have seen that even the "fronts" were different.

Certainly Dryden did not think so when he wrote *Absalom and Achitophel* as a part of the battle between Whigs and Tories during the Popish Plot and the Exclusion Crisis of 1678–82. As in Boileau's case, Dryden's political activities were accompanied by a discussion of language, literature, and control of literary culture (*Mac Flecknoe*). And as in Boileau's case, the events in which Dryden was participating ended in real violence: in England with the Monmouth rebellion after Charles II's death and with the tensions that finally led to the Glorious Revolution and the landing of William of Orange in 1688–89. But as in France, little was new in such circumstance. The Restoration settlement had always been a cause of sharp division, fluctuating tension, and sporadic violence, kept under control only by draconian measures: most important, the so-called Clarendon Code of the 1660s and the Test Act of 1673.[47] Nor were England's relations with its neighbors at all conducive to tranquility. If Dryden could celebrate the wonders of Charles II's reign after the naval victories over the Dutch in 1666 (in *Annus mirabilis*), 1667 had brought the humiliation of the Dutch sailing into the Thames to destroy the English fleet at anchor and tow away its flagship.

The 1668 Triple Alliance of England, the Netherlands, and Sweden put a momentary end to the savage commercial competition being waged between the first two, in favor of a rather vague effort to contain France. In 1670 a treaty between England and France speedily altered the situation once again—to the anger and disgust of many English people, to whom an alliance of Protestant nations was infinitely more welcome than one with France. Had they known of the secret provisions of the Treaty of Dover of that year, by which Charles accepted money from Louis in return for a commitment to work to make Catholicism the state religion, Charles and

---

[46]Jean-Marie Apostolidès, *Le roi-machine: Spectacle et politique au temps de Louis XIV* (Paris, 1981), p. 121.

[47]The Clarendon Code included four principal measures: the Corporation Act of 1661, requiring magistrates and other officials to abjure any oath taken to the Solemn League and Covenant (a 1643 English/Scottish agreement to abolish "popery and prelacy" and, so it added, to maintain religious freedom) and to take the Anglican sacraments before they could hold office; the 1662 Act of Uniformity, which forced the clergy to use the Book of Common Prayer and forbade anyone not episcopally ordained from ministering; the Conventicle Act of 1664, imposing penalties on all who attended church services not of the Established Church; and the 1665 Five Miles Act, preventing clergy who had not subscribed to the Act of Uniformity from living within five miles of a town, borough, or parish whence they had been ejected. By this last act, nonconformist ministers had also to swear an oath to seek no change in the established order of church and state. The Test Act, aimed chiefly at Catholics, forbade anyone from holding office who could not produce an attestation of attendance at Church of England sacraments.

James would no doubt have had to join their sister again at the French court. Political, religious, commercial, and economic interests all seemed to divide the two countries. Not only Andrew Marvell (who printed a tract on the matter in 1677), but a majority of the English, that "Headstrong, Moody, Murmuring race," as Dryden gruffly called them, viewed relations between the two countries with considerably more than mere skepticism.[48]

By early autumn 1678 it was possible for word of a seemingly vague and quite absurd plan by Papists to murder Charles, and if necessary his brother the duke of York and son the duke of Monmouth, to grow rapidly into the hysteria and witch-hunting violence of the Popish Plot. Throughout 1679 and into 1680, on the basis of Titus Oates's false testimony, a series of trials and what can only be called judicial murders took place—to great popular satisfaction. That James might be murdered along with his brother was said to be because his affection for Charles was such that it would be perilous to leave him alive. For otherwise it was evidently illogical: York's resignation as Lord High Admiral following the Test Act of 1673 had made official what had until then simply been rumors of his Catholicism. Now, seven years later, the opposition and its leader the earl of Shaftesbury grasped the freshly roused anti-Catholic sentiment as an occasion to exclude James from accession to the throne.

Although the party was not generally agreed on who might succeed, if not York (for Monmouth, however much a Protestant hero, had against him the legal impediment of his illegitimacy, and Mary would mean William of Orange as well), it did manage to get such a Bill of Exclusion through the Commons in November 1680. It was rejected by the Lords, and Charles dissolved Parliament two months later. In hopes of obtaining a more favorable hearing, he announced a new Parliament away from Whiggish London, in Oxford, where at least the university supported him and where the population was both smaller and calmer. By March 1681, when this Oxford Parliament convened, once again with a strong Whig majority, the king would very soon no longer need the money he usually had to seek from the Commons. In the middle of that same month Louis XIV guaranteed funds for the next three years on the wholly welcome condition that Charles not summon Parliament. At the end of the month, after some halfhearted compromise attempts, Charles prorogued that body: it would not meet again before his death. Shaftesbury was arrested at the beginning of July, and although he was not found guilty by a (Whig)

---

[48]On Marvell, see Annabel M. Patterson, *Marvell and the Civic Crown* (Princeton, 1978), and the very useful commentary on *Absalom and Achitophel* in *The Works of John Dryden, vol. 2: Poems, 1681–1684,* ed. H. T. Swedenberg, Jr., and Vinton A. Dearing (Berkeley, Los Angeles, and London, 1972), esp. pp. 211–13. The Dryden reference is to the first part of the poem (l. 45). All quotations are from this edition, henceforth indicated in my text by the initials *AA*.

grand jury at the end of November, he fled into exile in the Netherlands in 1682 (with his political secretary and doctor, John Locke), dying there in January 1683.

In November 1681, about a week before Shaftesbury was brought to trial for high treason, Dryden printed the first part of *Absalom and Achitophel*, an attack on Shaftesbury, on Whig "revolutionary" pretensions, and on Monmouth's credulity and betrayal of his father. The poem is a literary and political masterpiece. In October 1682 he published *Mac Flecknoe* and in November the second part of *Absalom and Achitophel*. The sequence is important. For just as someone like Shaftesbury was a political foe, so Buckingham, Shadwell, and others were rivals with regard to his efforts to refine language and literature, in line with the exigencies being brought to bear on literary culture across the Channel. In Buckingham's case ("Zimri" in *Absalom*), Dryden could depict a person who was both a political and a literary enemy. Thomas Shadwell, bated in the second part of *Absalom* (along with Elkanah Settle) as unable to rise from nonsense and dullness, was dismissed in *Mac Flecknoe* as a writer who "never deviates into sense." "Confirmed in full stupidity" and "dullness," writing far from the court and indeed on the very fringes even of the town ("Close to the Walls which fair *Augusta* bind": yet another recollection of Virgil and, we will see, the idea of an incipient golden age), he was fit successor to the ex-Catholic priest Richard Flecknoe, whose reign over "all the Realms of *Non-Sense*" had been undisputed. Language and culture, its upset and renewal were also at issue in the seemingly more simply "political" poems, as was the entire history I have just recounted.

Shadwell, of course, was to replace Dryden as poet laureate when William was placed on the throne in 1689, just as Shaftesbury did at least survive the trial and attacks, even though he lost the Exclusion battle. But Dryden's setback was very far from permanent. As George McFadden has put it, "In a different age the latter's grandson [the third earl of Shaftesbury, author of the *Characteristics*] was a brilliant convert (though unacknowledging) to the urbane, witty mode and its social utility. The difference between the civility of 1681 and that of 1711 is one that Dryden did more than anyone else to create."[49]

That such a difference was indeed quite explicitly at stake is indicated by another, more literary, aspect of the poem. For *Mac Flecknoe* itself "descended" from Marvell's earlier *Flecknoe*, first published only one year earlier, in 1681 (although probably dating for the most part from many years before). Marvell had given Richard Flecknoe the "triple property" of "priest, poet, and musician" and compared him to the biblical priest-king "Melchisédek." He had lamented the "hideous verse" that succeeded only in provoking a "last distemper of the sober brain." He thus prepared the way for Dryden to make of Flecknoe and Shadwell the prophets, priests,

[49]George McFadden, *Dryden: The Public Writer, 1660–1685* (Princeton, 1978), p. 19.

and kings of Dullness. But at the beginning of his poem Marvell had also remarked that Flecknoe "derives himself from my Lord Brooke." Indeed, in 1671 the poetasting priest had published commendatory verses on Greville and in 1675 had linked him with Sidney as among "the prime wits and gallants of the time."[50]

Flecknoe's self-established relation with poets of the late sixteenth century added a further dimension to Dryden's satire, akin to Boileau's dismissal of the verbal devices of earlier poets or to the scorn poured on Marie de Gournay in the 1630s and 1640s for her defense of the verbal creativity of Ronsard, the Pléiade, and the later Philippe Desportes. Dryden, like Boileau, was attacking a particular genealogy of poetry, one that would emphasize the kind of verbal copiousness we saw urged by those earlier poets and still pursued into the middle of the seventeenth century by such as Góngora in Spain, with his multitudinous followers, and by Tesauro in Italy, almost contemporary with Boileau. A different use of the word was involved, for whose suppression Dryden and others were battling.

In *Absalom*, the new urbane mode lay not simply in the mere fact of the poem itself, with its sparklingly intellectual and often savage wit, but also in its depiction of the evil and the good uses of that "harmonious art of discourse" Boileau thought politically foundational. And in that opposition between Achitophel's persuasion of Absalom and David's of the restless people of "Jerusalem," Dryden was simultaneously very clear that he was speaking to a theoretical opposition between Hobbes and Locke (with William Russell and Algernon Sidney, "republicans" who would be executed after the 1683 Rye House Plot), between ideas of a one-time contract producing "a setled Throne" and a "resuming Cov'nant" subject to the people's continual approval and judgment: under which "Kings are onely Officers in trust" (*AA*, ll. 759–810). But as in Boileau's case, the argument was framed in the specific and practical details of recent history and in the increasingly familiar terms of a particular literary culture.

Absalom, of course, adjusted to modern England the biblical story of the evil Achitophel's persuasion of David's son to rebel against his father (though there was and is exiguous evidence that Shaftesbury had done anything of the kind in Monmouth's case). The association of Charles II with the exiled and returned David was evidently a familiar one.[51] The most recent editors of the poem have shown too how "Achitophel" had long since become a name for the archetypal evil counselor in many writings available to Dryden. He could, that is to say, rely on an immediate recognition of connotations on the part of his readers.[52] One previous text

---

[50]Andrew Marvell, "Flecknoe," in *The Complete Poems*, ed. Elizabeth Story Donno (1972; rpt. Harmondsworth, 1981), p. 28; and see notes, p. 224.

[51]See esp. Lord, "'Absalom and Achitophel,'" pp. 156–90, and Steven N. Zwicker, *Dryden's Political Poetry: The Typology of King and Nation* (Providence, R.I., 1972).

[52]Dryden, *Works*, 2:230–32.

not hitherto mentioned, however, seems of special significance in light of the theoretical and practical political interests Dryden expressed in the poem. This is Innocent Gentillet's *Discours contre Machiavel,* published in 1576 at the height of the post–Saint Bartholomew's Day wars in France and which was a discussion of maxims supposedly drawn from *The Prince,* by means of interpretive gloss and commentary. Gentillet was at once attacking the Machiavelli depicted by the most critical interpretations of his writings, and the French government, said to have entirely adopted the most pernicious doctrines found therein. The French wars and their stakes had been and remained matters of major concern to English political thinkers and actors.

At one point Gentillet discussed Machiavelli's supposed advice that to prevent princes from making peace with their enemies, some savage fraud might have to be invented or violence perpetrated. This, he wrote,

> was the exact counsel Achitophel gave Absalom, to make reconciliation with his father David impossible, and to create permanent division and confusion throughout his kingdom. For he advised Absalom to sleep with the very wives of David his father, which is the greatest and vilest injury he could do him: so that Absalom and his followers could never hope to make peace with David, and playing from desperation would do so with redoubled courage and seize the kingdom, because necessity and despair make men bold and valiant. But what was the result? Achitophel the author of this advice hanged himself and strangled, either from chagrin or fear of David's later punishment; while Absalom perished miserably soon afterward, because he heeded such evil counsel.[53]

For his part, Dryden expressed the hope that there might yet "be room left for a Composure" and remained willing to believe (in November 1681) that Shaftesbury should only "be Accus'd of a good natur'd Errour" (*AA*, p. 189).

Between 1576 and 1655 there were at least twenty Latin, French, and English editions of Gentillet's work (as well as three German and one Dutch). The book was thus an extremely well known one, and Dryden was more than likely to have had a copy in his hands. In 2 Samuel the advice recorded by Gentillet was indeed the first we see Achitophel giving. He was said actually to have hanged himself for a quite different reason: because Absalom and Israel *no longer* followed his counsel. That fact might have given Dryden his room for hope. The point, however, was the Machiavellian political theoretical context in which Gentillet inserted the tale: concerning the seizure of state authority, debates about sovereign rights and individuals' freedoms, arguments about the inception of new societies and the continuity of old ones. The line from Machiavelli to

---

[53]Innocent Gentillet, *Discours contre Machiavel,* ed. A. D'Andrea and P. D. Stewart (Florence, 1974), p. 245: IIIe partie, ii.

Hobbes and Locke was clear and straight, and passed directly through French civil-war polemics.

The Achitophel and Absalom story, however, enabled Dryden to make claims about the relation between theoretical absolutes and practical realities which were also of singular importance in an atmosphere of incipient revolt, such as did indeed reign in 1681. The Bible had hardly depicted David as the most pure-hearted of princes. His political behavior was autocratic, and other activities left more than a little to be morally desired. Absalom's revolt occurred shortly after the adulterous and murderous episode with Bath-Sheba and Uriah the Hittite. Absalom himself was David's son by Maacah, daughter of Talmai king of Geshur, and she had been kidnapped (and raped) during an attack that "left neither man nor woman alive."[54] Dryden's point in the poem would be that under *no* circumstances could revolt against a lawful monarch be sanctioned. The single most heinous and unforgivable sin against an anointed monarch was that of "ingratitude." Even more so when, as in the case of Dryden's "David," the king was further characterized by his "indulgence" and "mildness" (*AA*, ll. 31, 76).

Like David, Charles was also depicted as less than perfect. He appeared a king, as it were, almost in a state of nature, creating a multitudinous race of descendants, imparting "his vigorous warmth" alike "to Wives and Slaves," and scattering "his Maker's Image through the Land," prompted only by nature and denied by no law (*AA*, ll. 4–10). Dryden's somewhat humorous irony was well aimed here. But it also set the stage for the two most important aspects of his political discussion. First, the description prepared his way to present the proposed revolt as part of the eternal war inherent in the state of nature described in *Leviathan* (although it is more Lockean in that nature seems to have two moments: one of tranquility and one of war) and thus to depict the renewal of Charles's authority as a creation of civil society. At the same time, it left sufficient ambiguity for him to discuss the meaning of the contract within already existing civil society and the obligations of its members to constituted sovereign authority.

The most important piece of rhetoric was David's renewal of his authority, with which the poem concluded. The turning point, however, was the narrator's own discussion of forms of political contract at ll. 759–810, already mentioned. That followed a presentation of the events leading up to Achitophel's conspiracy from the time of David's restoration. Dryden presented them as a story of extremism, foolishness, and a lack of precisely the "common Sense" (*AA*, 134) that was as essential to political stability as *Mac Flecknoe* urged it to be to good letters. Such non-sense allowed the "Jews" to wish for the state of nature that Hobbes characterized as endemic until human reason brought about the Covenant. As one

[54] 1 Samuel 27.1. See, too, 2 Samuel 3.3.

might expect, such nature was both Edenic and bestial, both "Lockean" and "Hobbesian":

> These *Adam*-wits, too fortunately free,
> Began to dream they wanted libertie;
> And when no rule, no president was found
> Of men, by Laws less circumscrib'd and bound,
> They led their wild desires to Woods and Caves,
> And thought that all but Savages were Slaves.
>   (*AA*, ll. 51–56)

In *Behemoth*, Hobbes had also thought of the Interregnum as equivalent to his state of nature. The Restoration could then be seen as the *actual* establishment of the Contract and the *historical* advent of civil society. Under those conditions, Achitophel's rhetoric became part of the discussions leading up to it. At the same time, of course, because of the ambivalence established by Dryden, it was a rhetoric of revolt against established authority.[55]

This ambivalence was figured in the theme of a *false* Messiah: one who *could* be true were we really in a state of nature, but who is bound to be false in a circumstance of what was actually social and political decay and dissolution. Achitophel may proclaim Absalom a "second *Moses*" (*AA*, l. 234), just as Flecknoe saw himself playing John to Shadwell's Jesus ("sent before but to prepare thy way") and going on to anoint him with a "sacred Unction" that was in fact "a mighty Mug of potent Ale" (*Mac Flecknoe*, ll. 32, 118–21), but in both cases falseness and immorality were replacing right sovereignty, right reason, and right letters. Political authority and social stability were indeed being threatened (again) by "soothing Flattery," lying "Praise," "blind Ambition," and a Hobbesian "desire of power" after power: all too easily become "a Vitious Weed" (*AA*, ll. 303–5). Thucydidean misuse of language had yet again created the conditions of revolt: where "a whole Hydra more / Remains, of sprouting heads too long, to score" (*AA*, ll. 541–42).

Now perhaps we can see the full force of the Gentillet reference, for the many parallels between the events and arguments of the French and English civil wars (their very language and tropes, indeed) had not, we have seen, escaped contemporaries. Dryden himself was always especially fascinated by the parallel between the Catholic Ligue in France and the 1643 Solemn League and Covenant in Britain (see note 47), both marks of

---

[55]This ambiguity in Dryden has been nicely examined by Laura Brown, "The Ideology of Restoration Poetic Form: John Dryden," in *John Dryden*, ed. Harold Bloom (New York, 1987), pp. 101–19. She argues that while Dryden asserts an essentially conservative conviction (found in my analysis in the "Hobbesian" trope), it is undermined by the experienced contradictions of his age, the "blind" presence of more "liberal" exigencies (echoed in the Lockean trope).

fanatical intolerance organized against a legitimate monarch (he had made the connection as early as his *Astraea Redux* in 1660). Hobbes and many other political thinkers, while considering the contract, that *lien de justice*, to be a *theoretical* passage from the brute savagery of a natural state to the civility of ordered society, also understood it to signal a real passage in their own time from the uncontrolled violence of universal war to a new tranquility.

Dryden's ambivalence simply echoed an ambiguity always consciously present in political discussion. The smooth and lying speech of Zimri, Shimei, Corah, and others feeding the false passions of "deluded *Absalom*" (*AA*, l. 683) made a new era of dismay. Only then (but then inevitably) could the narrator intervene with a debate concerning the rights of peoples and of sovereign authority: which neither princes nor peoples could overturn, for to do so was to destroy the laws and therefore civil society itself. Likewise, if "the Pow'r for Property allowd, / Is mischeivously seated in the Crowd," then no one could any longer "be secure of private Right" (*AA*, ll. 777–79). Firm sovereign authority, once again, was essential to the securing of individuals' rights and freedoms.

And so the narrator, concluding his own debate, introduced on David's side the representatives of legitimate speech and right reason: Barzillai, Zadock, "sharp judging *Adriel* the Muses friend," "*Jotham* of piercing wit and pregnant thought," Hushai, and Amiel, who "Reason guided and . . . Passion coold" (*AA*, ll. 817–913). These were they whose good sense provided the support for the speech with which David put an end to revolt, reaffirming the need for established sovereign authority to maintain stability and individual liberties. Right reason, proper language, good letters ("the Muses friend") had at last overcome unreason, the language of passion, and the voice of nonsense. A new Virgilian renewal might be at hand:

> He said. Th'Almighty, nodding, gave consent;
> And Peals of Thunder shook the Firmament.
> Henceforth a Series of new time began,
> The mighty Years in long Procession ran:
> Once more the Godlike *David* was Restor'd,
> And willing Nations knew their Lawfull Lord.
> (*AA*, ll. 1026–31)

"Kings are," David had proclaimed, "the publick Pillars of the State" (*AA*, l. 953). Since they were the very embodiment of the Covenant establishing civil society, they were Justice itself.

For Claude de Seyssel at the beginning of the sixteenth century as for Gentillet at the end, such justice was one of the three "pillars" of the state (along with "*police*" embodied in princely authority, and religion). The French edict of 1667 reforming the law began: "Because justice is the most solid foundation of the continuity of states . . . " It was, of course, issued in the king's name, and symbolically at least this was his phrase. Rhetorical commonplace and political and legal cliché as it may have been, harking back beyond those just mentioned to Roman civil law and Greek political theory, by 1667 such a statement had obtained a quite specific inflection, the result of those discussions we have been following. The "pacts and covenants" by whose means Hobbes had argued that humans had rationally forged the great creature of statist civil society had started off as a theory of *justice;* of justice as the founding axiom of a scientific theory of ordered civil society and the rational organization of power, guaranteeing rights, setting obligations, and resolving freedoms. In both France and England the monarch embodied the authority derived from and continuingly inherent in the just contract. To a considerable extent, in both polities, princely authority was now a function of that contractual theory, however much older legitimations of monarchy might supplement it.

It was, I think, that perceived identity that allowed an author like Aphra Behn, in her 1684–87 *Love-Letters between a Nobleman and His Sister,* readily to transpose an English political story into "France" (as it similarly let Scudéry depict a French polity in its "Greek" and "Roman" models—a link not lost on her readers). In Behn's novel, a "true" tale of amorous and sexual betrayal by a partisan of Monmouth was equated with the political treason of Monmouth himself. Monmouth's own later sexual betrayal in turn had its analogy in his supporter's political infidelity. These analogies (found also, we may recall, in *Absalom and Achitophel*) were further complicated by the pretense that the Monmouth figure was the (late sixteenth-century) French Protestant leader Condé and that the king menaced by Caesario/Monmouth was not English, but French. In the spiritual and material decline of the two main protagonists, Philander and Sylvia, Behn portrayed the deep threat posed to social stability, political justice, and a familiar legal and economic hierarchical order. Their flouting of marriage vows, flaunting of adultery, and flourishing of sexual freedom was accompanied by a literal and metaphorical association with political and legal infidelity and betrayal. In all details Sylvia and Philander breached the accord of contract (and of specific contracts), as they denied all forms of authority: monarchical, familial, legal. The novel (and the Tory, Behn) showed this to be the very path of evil.

As in Dryden, the demonstration was caught up in the matter of writing itself: here, of a novel form derived from a distillation of the Scudérian romance. Part epistolary, part narrative, *Love-Letters* tightened up plot, removed extraneous detail, and created something like "psychologically real" characters, by the initial self-consciousness of protagonists constantly wondering whether their "pens" were capable of truly expressing what they wished. Only through that invention were politics and sentiment, reason and literature finally able to reestablish social stability. By the end Sylvia was an outcast prostitute, married to her pimp. Philander the turncoat reappeared at court, to be sure, but his true colors were known to "all good men" (as the final words of the novel had it). Nor was it accidental that the displacement from England to France preceded the fictional story of a passage from France to the Low Countries (where, of course, Shaftesbury and the English exiles—like Behn herself—all ended up in reality). *Love-Letters* very consciously displayed real historical instability, depicted as inseparably political and moral, as resulting from Whig betrayals. Part of the solution was through new literary device. *Love-Letters* was certainly that. There, too, the enforcement of contract was wholly coincident with the reestablishment of legitimate princely authority. Although more devoted to the personal than the political, Scudéry's novels had also shown that they could only with difficulty be separated— and recounted a similar trajectory.

From Davenant and Scudéry to Boileau, from Rapin to Dryden, from Marvell to Behn, the right reason, ethical action, and fine order realized in that authority was established, warranted, and authorized by *bonnes lettres*. Dryden had made the claim some twenty years before *Absalom and Achitophel*, when he announced that with the return of Charles II, like that of the biblical David, "times whiter Series is begun / Which in soft Centuries shall smoothly run."[56] He had moreover asserted this future in terms exactly similar to those with which he would conclude the first part of *Absalom and Achitophel:*

> Oh Happy Age! Oh times like those alone
> By Fate reserv'd for Great *Augustus* Throne!
> When the joint growth of Armes and Arts foreshew
> The World a Monarch, and that Monarch *You.*

Literature; the memory of Virgil; the reminder of Sidney's, Cervantes's, and Davenant's linkage of arms and arts, camps and courts; Boileau's future one of courts and town, all were here already in *Astraea Redux*, that hopeful encomium of a future stable polity.

[56]*Astraea Redux. A Poem On the Happy Restoration & Return Of His Sacred Majesty Charles the Second*, in *The Works of John Dryden, vol. 1: Poems, 1649–1680*, ed. Edward Niles Hooker, H. T. Swedenberg [and others] (Berkeley, Los Angeles, and London, 1961), pp. 30–31, ll. 292–93, 320–23.

Chapter 6

Politics and Reason,
Ethics and Aesthetics

Belles-lettres are the source of good taste, of good manners and of all good government.
—Anne Dacier, *Des causes de la corruption du goust*

Literary criticism is very often a treatise of ethics.
—Germaine de Staël, *De la littérature*

Literature was by now, as Rapin noted, "of all Arts the most perfect." It achieved both a coherence with the *order* of nature *and* a representation of the discrete phenomena constituting events in the world: "For the perfection of the other Arts is limited, that of Poetry is not at all: to succeed in it one must know almost everything."[1] Rounding out two centuries of debate, as we will see, Hegel would make just the same claim some one hundred fifty years later, arguing that because only poetic art (which included both theater and literature) could depict all aspects of human "action as in itself a total movement of action, reaction, and resolution of . . . struggle," an action whole in itself, showing both the discrete events that compose such action and the dialectical laws of its government by Idea, so literature was the greatest and most significant of the arts.[2]

For his part, Davenant had concluded that literature not only showed the universality of the rational order of things, but was also "the best Expositor of Nature (Nature being mysterious to such as use not to consider) [and] Nature is the best Interpreter of God" (*PG*, pp. 40–44). He wrote this, let us add, before an epic poem, *Gondibert*, which Sharpe has rightly described as "express[ing] an ethical, political and aesthetic philosophy," through its tale of a love story about the King of the Lombards.[3] Not to accept such an idea and use of literature (for the term "poetry" was by now almost always used in a wide sense) was therefore to "give a sentence

---

[1]Rapin, *Réflexions*, 2:117.
[2]G. W. F. Hegel, *Aesthetics: Lectures on Fine Art*, trans. T. M. Knox, 2 vols. (Oxford, 1974–75), 2:219. Hegel's *Aesthetics* is discussed in Chapter 10.
[3]Sharpe, *Criticism and Compliment*, p. 102.

against the Law of Nature: for Nature performes all things by correspondent aides and harmony" (*PG*, p. 41). Nature and Homer, one might say,
were the same many years before Alexander Pope thought further to
specify the fact. Literature, Davenant had argued, not only expounded
nature by providing a knowledge of events and phenomena, but also
functioned *like* nature. For "Nature (which is Gods first Law to Man,
though by Man least study'd)" and "Reason" were fundamentally one:
reason "is Nature, and made Art by Experience" (*PG*, p. 42). Perhaps, too,
there was a memory of Bacon's *experientia literata* in such a phrase.

On the one hand was an idea of literature as in a referential relationship with what was here called "nature": a concept that corresponded to
Thomas Sprat's praise of the Royal Society on the grounds that among
other things its achievements would be useful "in furnishing to wits and
writers an inexhaustible supply of images from nature and works of art."[4]
(This itself reflected an order of human endeavor giving the advantage to
literature.) On the other hand was an idea of literature that saw it not as a
representation of things, but as a methodical presentation of underlying
order: Johnson's equation of nature, mind, and literary discourse, or the
"identity of values" we saw in Boileau (above, pp. 132–33). These views
would be echoed by Hegel. As Jack Kaminsky has summarized Hegel's
position, the human spirit sought to achieve its full self-consciousness by
attaining a "knowledge of the rational structure that permeates the world;
that is, [it] tries to organize sensuous data in such a way that the presence
of the Idea is recognizable. Out of this endeavor arises Art."[5]

Earlier we saw Rapin assure us, in his commentary on Aristotle, that
when we speak "properly" of literature, we are speaking "only of nature
put into method, and good sense reduced to principles." The same applied
to the political sphere. In *Astraea Redux*, Dryden had noted (a touch
ironically) that Charles's absence had allowed his abilities to mature:

> ripen'd by digestive thought
> His future rule is into Method brought:
> As they who first Proportion understand
> With easie practice reach a Masters hand.[6]

Of course, Hobbes's whole intent had been to make of civil philosophy a
methodical science. Everyone echoed these symmetries. Dennis claimed
that "the Rules of Aristotle are nothing but Nature and Good Sense
reduc'd to a Method." Rapin spoke of the rules as reducing "nature to a

---

[4]Thomas Sprat as quoted in Richard Foster Jones, *Ancients and Moderns: A Study of
the Rise of the Scientific Movement in Seventeenth-Century England*, 2d ed. (St. Louis,
Mo., 1961), p. 233.
[5]Jack Kaminsky, *Hegel on Art: An Interpretation of Hegel's Aesthetics* (1962; rpt.
Albany, N.Y., 1970), p. 23.
[6]Rapin, *Réflexions*, 2:113; Dryden, *Astraea Redux*, p. 24, ll. 89–92.

method," but only "so as to follow it step by step." By these rules, he went on, "everything becomes just, proportionate, and natural, just because they are founded upon good sense and upon reason."[7]

There were many statements of this isomorphism. Complex and ambiguous in some ways though it may have been, it was gradually established as the principal analytical model for thinking about rational, natural, cultural, and ethical circumstance. Once the discursive dominance was consolidated, the model's ambiguity at least seemed to yield to clarity, if to no less complexity:

> There is nothing in Nature that is great and beautiful, without Rule and Order; and the more Rule and Order, and Harmony, we find in the Objects that strike our Senses, the more Worthy and Noble we esteem them. I humbly conceive, that it is the same in Art, and particularly in Poetry, which ought to be an exact Imitation of Nature. Now Nature, taken in a stricter Sense, is nothing but that Rule and Order, and Harmony, which we find in the visible Creation. The Universe owes its admirable Beauty, to the Proportion, Situation, and Dependence of its Parts. And the little World, which we call Man, owes not only its Health and Ease, and Pleasure, nay, the Continuance of its very Being, to the Regularity of the Mechanical Motion, but even the Strength too of its boasted Reason, and the piercing Force of those aspiring Thoughts, which are able to pass the Bounds that circumscribe the Universe. As Nature is Order and Rule, and Harmony in the visible World, so Reason is the very same throughout the invisible Creation. For Reason is Order, and the Result of Order. And nothing that is Irregular as far as it is Irregular, ever was, or ever can be either Natural or Reasonable. Whatever God created, he designed it Regular, and as the rest of the Creatures, cannot swerve in the least from the Eternal Laws pre-ordain'd for them, without becoming fearful or odious to us; so Man, whose Mind is a Law to itself, can never in the least transgress that Law, without lessening his Reason, and debasing his Nature.[8]

One would indeed then find oneself back in the brutish state of nature: a fact making contractual civil society itself *natural* and emphasizing the foundational role of literature as expressed in Davenant, Boileau, and Dryden.

More briefly, as she said, Mary Astell similarly expressed the homology of the natural, rational, and linguistic orders: "In short, as Thinking conformably to the Nature of Things is True Knowledge, so th'expressing our Thoughts in such a way, as most readily, and with the greatest Clearness and Life, excites in others the very same Idea that was in us, is the

7. John Dennis, *The Impartial Critick: Or Some Observations Upon a Late Book, Entituled, A Short View of Tragedy, Written by Mr. Rymer,* in *Critical works,* 1:39; Rapin, *Réflexions,* 2:126–27.

[8]Dennis, *"Advancement and Reformation,"* in *Critical Works,* 1:202.

best Eloquence."[9] In his often rather confused and contradictory manner, Charles Gilden added his own panegyric on this order of reason, social and natural law, and morality (again placing poetry, "eloquence," above other forms of writing): "All that pleases is according to the Rules, and all that disgusts or is insipid, wild, or extravagant contrary to them; for good Sense and right Reason are of all Countries. Human laws indeed which regard the State alter according to the Circumstances and Interests of the Men, for which they were made; but these are always the same, and ever support their Vigour, because they are the Laws of Nature, which always acts uniformly, revives them continually, and gives them a perpetual Existence."[10] Here, too, we find the equation of nature, political and moral order, beauty, and the best literature.

Davenant had long before echoed Hobbes's desire for a methodical treatment of matters human, asserting, as Rapin, Dennis, and many others were to do, that Aristotle simply labored "to make Poesy universally current by giving Lawes to the Science" (*PG*, p. 52). Hobbes's own aesthetic also aimed, as one would expect, at accommodating the poetic, the rational, and the natural. Rymer took the claim about as far as it could go: "The truth is, what Aristotle writes on this subject, are not the dictates of his own magisterial will, or dry deductions of his Metaphysicks: But the Poets were his Masters, and what was their practice, he reduced to principles. Nor would the *modern Poets* blindly resign to this practice of the *Ancients*, were not the Reasons convincing and clear as any demonstration in *Mathematicks*. 'Tis only needful that we understand them, for our consent to the truth of them."[11] The poet revealed that "essence of things" of which we earlier saw him speak (above, p. 131).

Dryden likewise argued that the fundamental rules of tragedy should always be copied from the ancients, for these were the rules of reason and nature: "Those things only excepted," he went on, "which religion, customs of countries, idioms of language, etc., have altered in the superstructures." It was these superstructures that provided what Dryden had earlier called "a just and lively image of human nature, representing its passions and humours, and the changes of fortune to which it is subject; for the delight and instruction of mankind."[12] Kaminsky's summary of Hegel's view is once again revealing here: "The artistic experience, Hegel will argue, however, is not divorced from its temporal and environmental setting. The Idea . . . is the force that permeates all living things and makes them evolve spiritually as well as physically. Each successive age

[9]Astell, *Serious Proposal*, p. 121. Part 2, from which this citation is taken, was first published in 1697.
[10]Gilden, "Essay," 7:xix.
[11]Rymer, "Preface," in *Critical Works*, pp. 2–3.
[12]John Dryden, *An Essay on Dramatic Poesy* (1668); "The Grounds of Criticism in Tragedy," in *Selected Criticism*, pp. 25, 165.

produces a little more consciousness of how the Idea manifests itself in spirit and in nature."[13] Hegel could have found his evolutionary view of art in that eighteenth-century arbiter of taste, the abbé Jean-Baptiste Du Bos, who wrote in 1719 that artists had not only progressed technologically in the use of pigment and color, but knew of a wider variety of nature, thanks to voyages of discovery and modern science. The lively image of which Dryden spoke was achieved both by knowledge of law and by widening apprehension of facts and local variety. Modern tragedy was superior to that of Antiquity because "natural causes are more known now." The order of tragedy could thus better "fulfill that law" fundamental both to thinking and to the world.[14] The idea provided the basis for Hegel's later evolutionary concept of Art and Spirit: a continuity, we will see in Chapter 10, fundamental to my argument about the meaning of literature.

So far I have been speaking mainly of the political and epistemological (analytical and referential) aspects of literature: although, quite clearly, these were themselves taken as large elements in the understanding of beauty. Astell, Boileau, Bouhours, Anne Dacier, Dennis, Gilden, Rapin, and Rymer, we have seen, were all unanimously clear on this point. But we must also see how these aspects were wholly imbricated with arguments about aesthetic pleasure and the ethical (so involved, indeed, that they cannot easily be kept apart).

What is by now absolutely clear is that a good deal of the "pleasure" of poetry (of literary and dramatic art, that is to say), a pleasure widely and universally claimed as essential to all significant literary activity throughout the neoclassical period, came precisely from this combination of law and superstructure, brought together and given focus (we have seen) by a particular idea of "justice." This very concept made the law/superstructure equation at once a social and political affair, stretched to literature and predicated of nature as well.

And pleasure was, one may say, as pleasure did. Judged through the actual experience of readers, spectators, or listeners, it was nonetheless taken to be determined by the lawful, nomothetic identity of nature, reason, and art. It was certainly the case, for example, that Jean de La Fontaine in 1668 appeared to insist on the idea that "in France, only what gives pleasure is given consideration; that is the great rule, and, so to

[13]Kaminsky, *Hegel on Art*, p. 29.
[14]Abbé Jean-Baptiste Du Bos, *Réflexions critiques sur la poësie et sur la peinture*, 7th ed., 3 vols. (1770; rpt. Geneva and Paris, 1982), 1:407–13; Dryden, *Essay*, p. 32. Jean de La Fontaine disagreed with Dryden's granting of superiority to the moderns, but he preferred the ancients for identical reasons: in the "Epître à Huet," he said he followed the ancients for their "idea, devices and laws." These provided "the art of pure nature" that corresponded to "the taste and good sense" common to "all people" and "all countries." His own century had not yet attained such literary proximity to nature and its rules (*Oeuvres diverses*, ed. Pierre Clarac [Paris, 1948], pp. 646–47 [ll. 21–57, 71–72]). Again: there may be dispute, but it was no longer over fundamentals. On those, all now agreed. The question was who best judged and applied them.

speak, the only one." So he wrote. But La Fontaine had just completed elaborating a distinction between the body and soul of literature, telling his readers that the first is "plot" (*fable*), while the second is moral teaching (*moralité*). He had observed that although the substance of the story as such (*fable*) might fluctuate and change, in no way could one dispense with the moral or change its burden: the first was, one may say, "superstructural," but the second was quite other. For *moralité* was bound up in all essential ways with the ethical laws of nature of which we will shortly see Dryden speak.[15]

No less was it caught up as well in the essentially political concept of the "morale par provision" of a Cartesianism whose establishment had meant that of a "morale coutumière": an ethics dependent on the "mathematical" assumptions of a new dominant ideology.[16] Corneille had made a similar argument. This idea of *moralité*, Dryden's "ethics," Rymer's or Davenant's "justice," was a fundamental ingredient of aesthetic pleasure. And such ethical order had, of course, to be matched by the legitimate ordering of society. Literature showed the way and then guaranteed the *value* of those orders.

An identical view was clearly that of an equally celebrated contemporary of the fabulist, all too often interpreted as having divorced the idea of pleasure from those nomothetic assumptions whose development I have been tracing. I mean Jean-Baptiste Molière. Apparently speaking for the comedian in his *Critique de l'École des femmes*, played before the king in June 1663, Dorante asked forcefully whether "the great rule of all rules is not that of pleasing?" Once again, the pleasure he had in mind was no simpleminded hedonist's orgiastic dream of anarchic delight. It relied on the assumption with which Descartes began the *Discours de la méthode*, to the effect that "good sense is the most widely shared capacity in the world." Dorante assumed the groundlings (*le parterre*) combined "common sense" with competent knowledge of the most necessary "rules" and of the "good way of judging" according to the ordinary discernment of the sensible theatergoer.

Like Descartes, Molière emphasized the universality of good sense and its accessibility to methodical reason. Nor did he (of course) confine the claim to the groundlings. Like so many of his contemporaries, as we saw in earlier chapters, he underscored the reliability of "the Court's judgment." For that place of privilege was composed of a cross-section of

---

[15]Jean de La Fontaine, *Fables choisies mises en vers*, ed. Ferdinand Gohin, 2 vols. (Paris, 1934), 1:12.

[16]Some of these implications of a new (post-Cartesian) conception of mathematics, an emphasis on problem solving rather than theorem proving (as the Greeks) and on constructivism and instrumentality, have been explored or suggested in David Rapport Lachterman, *The Ethics of Geometry: A Genealogy of Modernity* (New York and London, 1989). Both in this chapter and in Chapter 10, we will see the importance of this for aesthetic debate.

tasteful courtiers, of "gens savants," of people of "simple good sense" and that good "conversation" we already saw Dryden and others praise ("le commerce de tout le beau monde"): all of quite expert judgment. The rules themselves, concluded Dorante, proceeded from a "relaxed observation" and from general good sense. These were necessary, although not alone sufficient. They had to be allied with modern habit and taste and with contemporary awareness and sensibility: the exactly equivalent combination, in spectator and reader, to the law/superstructure combination in the artwork itself.[17]

Pleasure, then, was not to be confused with some sort of freewheeling intemperance. Rather it was a peculiarly nonchalant liaison (no less strict in its grounding for all that) between law and superstructure, soul and body, analysis and reference, and the rest. In a way it corresponded to the Hobbesian notion of "Fancy": as important, said Hobbes, to the philosopher as to the poet. Fancy was the ability to soar over the objective concepts developed in the mind by "Judgement" after that last had duly registered "by Letters," the "order, causes, uses, differences and resemblances" of "all the parts of Nature." Thereby Fancy "traced the wayes of true Philosophy" and "produced very marvellous effects to the benefit of mankind." Fancy, assuming the lawful coherence of reason—on which judgment depended to register the natural referents of (as) concepts—was the pleasing search into and through reason and thinking itself. Judgment relied on "truth" (corresponding in knowledge to the "Historicall"), Fancy relied on the "Resemblance of truth" (corresponding to "Poeticall Liberty"): "beyond the actuall workes of nature a Poet may now go; but beyond the conceaved possibility of nature never." Fancy was a sort of innate knowledge of lawfulness enabling a bounded playing with the objective realities of nature as recorded by "Experience" in "Memory" and transformed by "Judgement" into concepts.[18] Where judgment recorded nature and its order, fancy methodized it: the first gave the "is," the second produced an "ought."

Racine, too, admonished critics to believe that if they drew pleasure from any artwork it was because a knowledge of the rules was inborn (common sense methodiz'd, one might say): "I beg them to have a good enough opinion of themselves not to believe that a play that touches and gives them pleasure could be entirely against the rules. The main rule is to please and touch: all others are made only to achieve this first one." For pleasure presupposed laws, he wrote, without which there could be no enjoyment: the two were essentially linked. As his older rival had said eleven years earlier: "The poet's goal is to please according to the rules of

[17]Jean-Baptiste Poquelin de Molière, *La critique de l'École des femmes,* in *Théâtre complet,* ed. Robert Jouanny, 2 vols. (Paris, 1962), 1:494–95, 504–7.

[18]Thomas Hobbes, "The Answer of Mr. Hobbes to Sir Will. D'Avenant's Preface before Gondibert," in Davenant, *Gondibert,* pp. 49–51.

his art."[19] In the middle of the nineteenth century E. S. Dallas was to define "pleasure" in entirely analogous terms, as *"the harmonious and unconscious activity of the soul,"* a definition whose possibility he ascribed to a recognition of the "laws" governing such activity.[20]

By the time nineteenth-century writers adopted the idea, authors such as Du Bos had long since codified it into a fundamental claim of taste. "The first aim of poetry and painting," he wrote in 1719, "is to touch us. Poems and paintings are good only to the extent they move and possess us." Reason should intervene only to explain "the decision of feeling" or "what faults prevent pleasure." Yet he justified these claims in answer to an almost absurd question: "Does one use one's reason to know whether the stew is good or bad?" No, he says (like Molière and the others before him), we do not have to do so, for the "chef has made it according to the rules of his art." Matters are just the same in the case of artworks composed "to please by touching us." Because our "heart" is "organized" to grasp those rules by some innate understanding (thanks, again, to the measured identity of mind and world orders), so "a work in which the essential rules were violated could not please."[21] Pleasure came from the commonsensical ability to make the connection between the superstructural and universal, to see and enjoy how the rules of the one underlay the lawful variety of the other.

The political counterpart of this was the theoretical contrast between natural and positive law, between the rules of nature and those of societies. The universal *nomos* of the first underlay the variety of the second. This interplay was basic to political order after the late seventeenth century (echoed at a different level, perhaps, in the tense relation between individual and natural rights on the one hand and state and collective rights on the other—the foundational conflict of authoritarian individualism). The play was unbroken between natural law and political (social)

---

[19]Jean Racine, "Préface" to *Bérénice*, in *Oeuvres complètes*, pref. Pierre Clarac (Paris, 1962), p. 165; Pierre Corneille, "Discourse de la tragédie" (1660), in *Oeuvres complètes*, 3:171.

[20]Eneas Sweetland Dallas, *The Gay Science*, 2 vols. (1866; rpt. New York, 1968), 1:17–18. (Dallas was an interesting writer whose work merits analysis as a forerunner to certain of Freud's ideas—at least as they concern literature.)

[21]Du Bos, *Réflexions*, 2:339–47. "REASON," Sir Joshua Reynolds was to write of appreciating a painting, "without doubt, must ultimately determine every thing; at this minute it is required to inform us when that very reason is to give way to feeling": *Discourses on Art*, ed. Robert R. Wark (San Marino, Calif., 1959), p. 231: 13th Disc., Dec. 1786. Jean Starobinski argues that Du Bos in fact placed feeling before reason and that this represented a freeing of classical rigor: *L'invention de la liberté, 1700–1789* (Geneva, 1964), pp. 10–11, 39–53. Both claims are flawed. First, the public's wholly *reasonable* "sentiment" was possible because all essential rules were innate (in nature, mind and right language, or pictorial order)—the artist, however, had to know and use consciously what the rational public thus knew unconsciously. Second, such arguments predominated from the very beginnings of modern literature.

right, between the common permanent nature of humanity and the various fleeting societies ordering the individual's present existence, between—as many literary writers put it—the heart and the head, the permanence of sentiment and common reason and the impermanence of opinion and social reason (which had necessitated Descartes's *morale par provision*). These contrasts underlay the Glorious Revolution of 1688 no less than the French Revolution of 1789 still: "It was, Sieyès maintained, natural law that was old, and the errors of existing societies were new." Jacob Talmon showed that these views of Emmanuel Joseph Sieyès, chief spokesman for the "Revolutionary forces" at the outset, were to last throughout the nineteenth century: not surprisingly, since they continued much older claims.[22] In fact, they asserted that the fundamental laws of reason and nature ultimately founded and legitimated any and all local variants.

The late seventeenth century therefore saw the pleasurable and the useful as an essential association of ideas, neither paradoxical nor contradictory. They were united as the aesthetic manifestation of natural, political, rational, linguistic, and artistic stability. The association of fundamental rational law and cultural superstructures, of the permanent and ubiquitous stability of methodical reason and the transitory instability of local customary phenomena, was the double truth whose utterance was literature's privilege and whose perfect expression was the criterion of beauty and the only true source of aesthetic pleasure. That was what Rymer meant when he wrote that the authors of tragedy, "like good Painters must design their Images like the Life, but yet better and more beautiful than the life"; or Pope, writing that the rules of fine letters "Are *Nature* still, but *Nature Methodiz'd*"; or Hume, writing about "the original structures of the internal fabric"; or Joshua Reynolds, asserting (after Rymer?) that the painter's task was to depict the "Ideal Beauty" that is "above all singular forms, local customs, particularities, and details of every kind"; or Marmontel, stating that "art does not consist in going against nature, but in improving it, in embellishing it through imitation, in doing better than it, while doing the same as it," and more or less paraphrasing Dryden's contrast: "Nature has only one road, custom has a thousand twisted and broken pathways." Only thirty years after this last writer, Hegel's view remained very similar: "Art . . . is superior to nature. It tries to indicate the goals at which nature is aiming. In art man tries to succeed where nature often fails."[23]

---

[22]Jacob L. Talmon, *The Origins of Totalitarian Democracy* (1952; rpt. New York, 1960), pp. 25, 69.

[23]Thomas Rymer, *The Tragedies of the Last Age Consider'd and Examin'd by the Practice of the Ancients, and by the Common Sense of All Ages, in a Letter to Fleetwood Shepheard, Esq.*, in *Critical Works*, p. 32; Alexander Pope, *Essay on Criticism*, in *The Poems*, ed. John Butt (New Haven, Conn., 1963), p. 146 (I, l. 89); David Hume, "Of

Fundamentally, this had long since been the distinction made by Corneille in the "Au lecteur" to *Héraclius* (1647), when he asserted of the important concept of verisimilitude that it was "a condition necessary to the organization (*disposition*) and not to the choice of subject, nor to the incidents that are supported by the story." Indeed, the elements of a poem might be true, likely, or in line with opinion: they then followed, respectively, history, natural law, or public acceptance. The subject would be a matter of history, its incidents one either of what actually occurred or of what could be expected to have occurred. Verisimilitude, what Davenant called "likelihood" (*PG*, p. 2) and Rymer would refer to as a "general probability," related entirely to the laws of nature and of common sense: the *organization*, the order, of the matter. Provided probability held at the level of these laws—what Rymer called the "accuracy" of literature, and Henry Reynolds long before (around 1633) "the perfect and strait line" rather than the "oblique one"—the subject itself might, indeed almost had to, be unlikely (said Corneille): at least as concerned tragedy, which depicted human affairs and events taken to an extraordinary degree (as long as they did not overstep the logical—natural—limits of a situation, however extraordinary in itself).[24]

Corneille's argument was exactly the one Joseph Addison later used of John Milton. "The sentiments in an epic poem," he wrote, "are *just* when they are conformable to the characters" and to the situation. A good deal of Milton's greatness, Addison wrote of *Paradise Lost*, lay in his ability to achieve this justness for characters who "lie out of nature, and were to be formed purely by his own invention." Addison was not in the least praising originality (which would contradict his often repeated claim that true wit lay in saying well what was already known—shades of Astell). Quite the opposite: Milton's invention of "proper sentiments" and "apt circumstances" merited praise just because readers remained satisfied that they would be "proper" and "apt" were they *in* nature—they were thus taken *for* nature. Where he could not rely "upon tradition, history and observation," the conformity of Milton's "genius" ("good sense" raised several degrees) to the deepest laws of nature enabled the poet to set the extraordi-

---

the Standard of Taste," in *Of the Standard of Taste and Other Essays*, ed. John W. Lenz (Indianapolis and New York, 1965), p. 9; Reynolds, *Discourses*, p. 44: 3d Disc., Dec. 1770; Jean-François Marmontel, "Essai sur le goût," in *Éléments de littérature*, 3 vols. (Paris, 1865), 1:7, 18; Kaminsky, *Hegel on Art*, p. 31.
[24]Corneille, "Au lecteur" to *Héraclius* (1647), in *Oeuvres complètes*, 1:357; Rymer, *Tragedies of the Last Age*, in *Critical Works*, p. 23; Henry Reynolds, "Preface to *Mythomystes*," in Spingarn, ed., *Critical Essays*, 1:149; Corneille, "Discours de la tragédie," in *Oeuvres complètes*, 3:166–68. Terence Cave (and others) seem to accept at face value Corneille's remark that people might think all this a paradox. Not only was the duality *vraisemblance/invraisemblance* not paradoxical, in fact agreed wholly with theory. See Cave's fine essay, "Recognition and the Reader," in *Comparative Criticism: A Yearbook*, vol. 2, ed. E. S. Shaffer (Cambridge, 1980), pp. 58–62.

nary in the probable. *Paradise Lost* became the representative poem of humanity because it tapped the very roots of that universal moral order in which the rules of reason and those of nature conformed.[25] La Fontaine's body-soul distinction was a clear parallel to both Corneille's and Addison's argument.

"What there is in any Poem which is out of Nature, and contrary to *Verisimilitude* and *Probability*," concluded Gilden in 1710, "can never be *Beautiful*, but *Abominable*. For the Business of Poetry is to copy Nature truly, and observe *Probability* and *Verisimilitude* justly; and the Rules of Art are to shew us what Nature is, and how to distinguish its Lineaments from the unruly and preposterous Sallies and Flights of an irregular and uninstructed Fancy."[26] There was, then, a kind of tension between *making* sense (a matter of the coherence of law) and imaging the real, between *poiesis* and *mimesis*. As in the case of the epistemological difficulty confronted by Hobbes, this tension was resolved by an appeal to "justice," by an idea of society and then of nature as ethical, and by the technical term of "poetical justice." The phrase itself seems first to have been used by Rymer in 1677, but we have seen its implications already in Hobbes and Davenant, where the concept of justice as an equilibrium in nature and in human affairs provided the fundamental axiom for the elaboration of a methodical theory of civil society in the one and of an ethical poetry guiding society's business in the other.

For it may well be the case that "poetic justice undoubtedly came from France, and specifically from La Mesnardière," as Katherine Wheatley long ago insisted.[27] But it had been substantially transformed by the time it had been through the hands of Davenant and Hobbes. In 1640 La Mesnardière had made it a matter of poetry showing the reward of virtue, the punishment of vice: "The most just Tragedies are those where vicious actions have their right punishments, and virtues their rewards."[28] That was why "pity is infinitely sweeter, more human and pleasanter than terror and fear." We need suppose, he wrote even, that people were not necessarily so convinced "of God's justice" as to be willing to "believe anything rather than His injustice"; that they "do not absolve God of all sin." Part of poetry's task (especially dramatic poetry's) was therefore to

---

[25]Joseph Addison, *Critical Essays from the Spectator, with Four Essays by Richard Steele*, ed. Donald F. Bond (Oxford, 1970), pp. 70–71. A century later Germaine de Staël expressed a similar view of "true wit": which "is nothing other than the faculty of seeing clearly; common sense belongs more to wit than false ideas. The more good sense, the more wit; genius in good sense applied to new ideas. Genius increases the treasure of good sense; it wins victories for reason" (*De la littérature considérée dans ses rapports avec les institutions sociales*, ed. Paul van Tieghem, 2 vols. [Geneva and Paris, 1959], 1:22).

[26]Gilden, "Essay," p. viii.

[27]Katherine E. Wheatley, *Racine and English Classicism* (Austin, Tex., 1956), p. 250.

[28]La Mesnardière, *La poëtique*, p. 223.

reinforce the security of a just world order: created at least by human ethical norms, if not by divine justice.[29] One can readily see how this sort of argument would feed a notion of justice as enabling a passage from bestiality to civil order.

Once that had occurred, the idea of poetical justice became far more complex and profound than was suggested simply by the argument about the just reward of vice or virtue. By his phrase Rymer sought to indicate what he called a "general probability" of the literary text, such that it could be seen to adhere to the laws of nature and of common sense, and forge a balance between a representation of the potential chaos of events on the one hand and the expectation of law on the other: verisimilitude held that rational laws of mind corresponded to those of nature and social order, and the literary depiction of acts and events (however seemingly chaotic in the real world) should show them in agreement with order. Only then would literary writing be ethical and *just*. "Poesy," wrote Dryden, "must resemble natural truth, but it must *be* ethical. Indeed the poet dresses truth and adorns nature, but does not alter them."[30] Such ethical truth of the natural order, corresponding to reason and good sense and allowing the poet not simply to show but indeed to rely on the justice of the various phenomena to be represented (mostly of the "superstructure"), was precisely what "poetical justice" was all about. Soon it would be Leibniz's "all is for the best in the best of worlds possible," a claim about metaphysical necessity (if a rational God created the world, its order had to agree with and be determined by a rational logic) willfully misunderstood by Voltaire.

Some three decades after Rymer's use of the phrase, Addison wrote an essay in *The Spectator* mocking both the term and the concept. Dennis took up the cudgels immediately. He argued that the objection was quite *unreasonable:* "For as *Hobbes* has observ'd, that as often as Reason is against a Man, a Man will be against Reason; so often as the Rules are against an Author, an Author will be against the Rules." In this case the rules were those connoted by the phrase "poetical justice." Saying he was defending Aristotle as much as Rymer (which last would have been most odd), Dennis asked the author of the *Spectator* paper whether he could not see that the

doctrine of poetical Justice is not only founded in Reason and Nature, but is itself the Foundation of all Rules, and ev'n of Tragedy itself? For what Tragedy can there be without a Fable? or what Fable without a Moral? or what Moral without poetical Justice? What Moral, where the Good and

[29]Ibid., pp. 19, 171–72.
[30]John Dryden, "A Defense of an Essay of Dramatic Poesy" (1668), in *Selected Criticism*, p. 85. Some of these remarks and references are drawn from my *Tragedy and Truth*, pp. 6–9, where there is a parallel discussion.

the bad are confounded by Destiny, and perish alike promiscuously. Thus we see that this Doctrine of poetical Justice is more founded in Reason and Nature than all the rest of the poetical Rules together.

Poetical justice was, he concluded, the "fundamental rule."[31]

Such justice was therefore the essential link between the rational order of nature and the natural order of reason. It was likewise axiomatic in the well-ordered state, because such a society was necessarily ordered in accordance with the same common sense. Furthermore, the well-ordered state was precisely the state that most matched action to natural and lawful morality, justice. Once we know the difference between law and superstructure, between the one true path of nature and the thousand twisted pathways to which custom is heir, we can forge the truly moral, ethical state corresponding to a natural rational ethics. Indeed, though the nature in question may have been the material world observed and practiced on by humans, it shaded readily into the social and political world created by them.

That explains why Davenant wrote a political theoretical preface to a literary work and why Boileau ended his *Art poétique* with a similarly based argument. Hegel would accompany his *Aesthetics* with a *Philosophy of Right*. Dryden was both poet laureate and historiographer royal, as were Racine and Boileau in effect (France had no official laureateship). Dennis noted that his *Grounds of Criticism in Tragedy* (1704) was written expressly to be "instrumental to the reforming Her [Queen Anne's] People."[32] Anne Dacier and Germaine de Staël said the same a century apart (see the epigraphs to this chapter). For all these writers, as for Vico in 1725, the chief referent, the principal place of order, would eventually be not nature but society and human history—some understanding of nature simply providing the regulatory and experiential ground (ensured by the identity of its logical, rational structure and process). Reynolds was to say that "reiterated experience" provided the artist with "the idea of that central form," enabling him to reduce "the variety of nature to the abstract idea."[33] He merely confirmed a century-long debate. These claims also meant, of course, that *their* society was a universal standard; as Reynolds again put it: "taste" was addressed to the "organisation of the soul," its principles being invariable and depending on "an appeal to common sense deciding upon the common feelings of mankind."[34]

At the end of the third Part of his *Théodicée*, Leibniz told the story of how the high priest Théodore was sent by Jupiter to consult the goddess Pallas at her temple in Athens, that he might discover how a Sextus

[31]John Dennis, "To the Spectator, Upon His Paper on the 16th of April 1711" (1712), in *Critical Works*, 2:18–20.
[32]John Dennis, *The Grounds of Criticism in Tragedy* (1704), in *Critical Works*, 1:328.
[33]Reynolds, *Discourses*, pp. 46–47: 3d Disc., Dec. 1770.
[34]Ibid., p. 131: 7th Disc., Dec. 1776.

Tarquinius could be a part of the best possible of worlds. Pallas told him that God could have made any number of worlds. But as long as their conditions of possibility remained insufficiently determinate, they were simply ideas: just as in geometry, "when the conditions of a required point do not sufficiently determine it, and there is an infinite number of them, they all fall into what geometers call a locus, and this locus at least, which is often a line, will be determinate." This was like the succession of possible worlds, each of which, varying in the slightest degree, offered a different story of Tarquin and different consequences. Pallas then took Théodore through the various rooms of a pyramid-shaped palace, in each of which he saw a different life of Sextus (the first being one in which he became wealthy and respected by cultivating a garden—a world lying at the *bottom* of the pyramid). At the very top of the palace lay the finest world of all: "Because amongst an infinity of possible worlds, there is the best of all, else would God not have determined to create any." This was the "real true world" where one is "at the source of happiness," the world in which Tarquin's evil deeds were instrumental in establishing "a great empire which will give grand examples. But that is nothing in comparison with the worth of this whole world, at whose beauty you will marvel."[35]

This world of "grands exemples" both political and ethical, a world whose beauty was admirable, was thus gathered by Leibniz into a literary device, "une fiction" giving the reader, he concluded, that "knowledge of simple intelligence . . . wherein the origin of all things must ultimately be sought": common sense, beauty, political and moral order all came together *because* and under the aegis of the literary fiction (itself referring to an earlier one of Lorenzo Valla).[36] Once again, too, the exemplar was taken to be geometrical order.

Much later, more or less of the same generation as Sieyès and Marmontel, Anna Laetitia Barbauld caught this homology of the natural, social, and rational world perfectly, as well as the relation of the universal to the local. In one of her earliest and best-known published writings, "Against Inconstancy in Our Expectations" (1773), she wrote that the world was ruled by an essential equity, such that one could always expect to obtain what was properly worked for: "We shall find, in the moral government of the world, and the order of the intellectual system, laws as determinate fixed and invariable as any in Newton's Principia. The progress of vegetation is not more certain than the growth of habit; nor is the power of attraction more clearly proved than the force of affection or the influence of example." To these universalist claims, she added some local color, an extended metaphor of economic interest:

[35]Gottfried Wilhelm Leibniz, *Essais de Théodicée, sur la bonté de dieu, la liberté de l'homme, et l'origine du mal,* ed. J. Brunschwig (Paris, 1969), pp. 361–62. With certain changes, I have followed the English text in *Theodicy,* abridged, ed. Diogenes Allen (Indianapolis, 1966), pp. 173–75.

[36]*Théodicée,* p. 362; *Theodicy,* pp. 175–76.

If you refuse to pay the price, why expect the purchase? We should consider this world as a great mart of commerce, where fortune exposes to our view various commodities, riches, ease, tranquility, fame, integrity, knowledge. Every thing is marked at a settled price. Our time, our labour, our ingenuity, is so much ready money which we are to lay out to the best advantage. . . . Such is the force of well-regulated industry, that a steady and vigorous exertion of our faculties, directed to one end, will generally insure success.[37]

This economistic view was, of course, shared by writers from Mandeville to Adam Smith. But as a metaphor for ordered comprehension and action, it had long since been used (like geometry) by Descartes, aimed precisely at those whose understanding would create a new rational, instrumental knowledge of the world.

All alike concurred in affirming that literature was aimed at the rational elite, who alone led such a society. The poet and critic always addressed what Addison called the "politer part." And that "politer part" was really nothing but a generalizing of the prince's superiority or of that of government leaders more broadly (as the embodiment of sovereign authority): Davenant's prince and priest, general and poet. Such people as these, in whom reason and will ruled passions, were endowed, Yves-Marie André was to write toward the mid-eighteenth century, with "a natural royalty." In 1747 the celebrated Charles Batteux still adopted the idea in telling the Dauphin he embodied the very principles of a taste for the true and simple, appreciating fine nature: he knew the "single sovereign law."[38] This elite grasped all these relations with no strain, with correct nonchalance (surely akin to Castiglione's *sprezzatura*). The opening of Bouhours's most successful *Entretiens d'Ariste et d'Eugène* (1671) was emblematic in this regard, depicting the privileged site and entirely proper activity of the "honnête homme."

Eugène and Ariste stroll beside the sea. The "occasion" is appropriate, the spot is pleasant and delightful (*commode et fort agréable*), their walk is easy and comfortable (*la promenade aisée*). It is "the most beautiful time of year." They are near a "beautifully built fortress," in a nature that is simultaneously wild and humanized: amid unkempt dunes resembling

---

[37] Anna Laetitia [Aikin] Barbauld, *The Works*, with a Memoir by Lucy Aikin, 2 vols. (London, 1825), 2:184–85.

[38] Père Yves-Marie André, "Discours sur la liberté," in *Oeuvres philosophiques*, ed. Victor Cousin (1843; rpt. Geneva, 1969), pp. 224–35. The exact date of this text is unknown. It was read to the Caen Academy probably after 1741. The second reference is to abbé Charles Batteux, *Les beaux arts reduits a un même principe* (1747; rpt. New York 1970), pp. aij^ro–vo (Dedicace), iii (Avant-propos). This work's recall of earlier preoccupations was extremely close: "So, my Lord, while an august Father will cover himself with new glory, to force Europe to accept peace; you take joy in encouraging the Arts to celebrate his exploits, and to repeat them in durable monuments" (pp. aiij^ro). Subsequent history has endowed this praise of the future Louis XVI with a certain dark irony.

"an old ruined palace." The signs of power, both "camp" and "court," provide background to a methodized and (hence) beautiful nature and are intricate with the relaxed pleasure of good company (*ils furent fort aisés d'avoir occasion de jouïr un peu l'un de l'autre*): "That is where Ariste and Eugène had some time for those free and familiar conversations shared by well-bred people [*honnêtes gens*] when they are friends; and which do not fail to be witty, and even learned, although they do not concern themselves with wit, and study has no part in the matter."[39]

Bouhours's own text was itself to be taken as the very embodiment of such rational pleasure and liberal authority: literature as the site of an easy and clear knowledge, within ready reach of a well-bred public. It was now a treasure of social wisdom and insight. Its clarity and assurance were assumed sufficient to provide a knowledge so full, ready, and rational as to appear a matter of unstrained common sense. The *honnête homme* had only to gaze on nature for it to be reduced to reason. In fourteen lines Bouhours carefully emphasized the association of reason and vision, beauty and right judgment. His interlocutors "look attentively upon the sea," an "admirable spectacle" (the etymologies of both words referring to vision). Not to find it so, "one would have to be blind or stupid." It gives rise to "a most reasonable little reverie." "I admire the sea," says the one, who has made "a journey expressly to see it." "Seeing it," says the other, "I admired it." Indeed, he concludes, "I saw it . . . as if I had never seen it."[40] Literature, reason, clear-sightedness, and nonchalant good sense went together as did blindness, stupidity, and unreason. We would do well to recall here what we saw in Corneille and Richelieu: the association of reason and justice against passion and political catastrophe.

Such texts as Bouhours's *Entretiens* (or even Leibniz's *Théodicée*) asserted, confirmed, and embodied the new order of literature. In this instance it also presented ideal critics in their ideal environment. Ariste and Eugène stood in perfectly for the qualified readers who would understand that great literature owed its superiority to its twofold truth: to the fundamental and universal laws of all things (at once logical and ethical— "geometric" and "economic") and to the "superstructural" reality of particular societies. When literature achieved the proper expression of that double truth, it attained to beauty. The coupling of the two, beauty and truth, epistemological and aesthetic legitimacy, rapidly became an Enlightenment cliché.

In his ninth Epistle (1675), Boileau had written, in an avowedly political context as we saw, "Nothing is beautiful but truth. Only truth is lovely." In the 1701 preface to his works, the same poet linked inextricably such

[39]Bouhours, *Entretiens d'Ariste et d'Eugène*, pp. 5–6.
[40]Ibid., p. 6. For Descartes, in the *Passions de l'âme*, "admiration" was a unique passion, first mark of the mind's reaction to the world and origin of practical knowledge: Descartes, *Oeuvres philosophiques*, 3:1006–7 (Pt. II, arts. 70–71).

beauty and truth: "A thought is beautiful only as it is true."[41] Not much later Addison, discussing what constituted true wit, suggested tentatively (quoting Dryden with some unease) that it might not be so different from "good writing in general" (Astell's "Eloquence"), which, he remarked, would make Euclid the greatest wit of all. He went on to speak more confidently of Bouhours and Boileau: "Bouhours, whom I look upon to be the most penetrating of all the French critics, has taken pains to show that it is impossible for any thought to be beautiful which is not just, and has not its foundation in the nature of things: that the basis of all wit is truth; and that no thought can be valuable, of which good sense is not the groundwork. Boileau has endeavoured to inculcate the same notion in several parts of his writings, both in prose and verse."[42]

"Beauty is truth, truth beauty," John Keats was to muse a century later, uttering essentially the same sentiments. Nor was Hegel's view of aesthetic verity to be so very different. But Keats could easily have found his thought in Shaftesbury's affirmation that beauty and good were "one and the same." For the beauty and good in question, like Keats's or Addison's truth, referred to the natural ethical harmony that allowed Shaftesbury's Philocles to ally "Nature, reason, and humanity," and his Theocles to apostrophize: "O glorious nature! supremely fair and sovereignly good!" One thinks again of Leibniz or of de Staël later praising a similar universal harmony of nature, truth, moral virtue, and beauty: "Perfect virtue is the beautiful ideal of the intellectual world. The impression it produces upon us is related to the feeling anything sublime provokes in us, be it in the fine arts or in material nature." "The good and virtuous man alone," Reynolds had said, "can acquire this true or just relish even of works of art."[43]

De Staël and Reynolds could have taken their assertions from Shaftesbury: "What is beautiful is harmonious and proportionable; what is harmonious and proportionable is true; and what is at once both beautiful and true is, of consequence, agreeable and good." As Dryden, Bouhours, Boileau, Leibniz, Rymer, and Rapin agreed, the world was ethical in very essence. And Keats, too, could have found his equation almost verbatim in the writings of Achitophel's grandson: "The most natural beauty in the world is honesty and moral truth. For all beauty is truth. . . . In poetry, which is all fable, truth still is the perfection."[44] Perception of this com-

---

[41]Boileau, *Oeuvres complètes*, pp. 134, 3.
[42]Addison, *Critical Essays*, p. 19.
[43]Anthony Ashley Cooper, 3d Earl of Shaftesbury, *Characteristics of Men, Manners, Opinions, Times*, ed. John M. Robertson, 2 vols. (Indianapolis and New York, 1964), 2:37, 98; de Staël, *De la littérature*, 1:20; Reynolds, *Discourses*, p. 134: 7th Disc., Dec. 1776. It is the case that in *The Laws* (817 a–d), Plato spoke of comedy and tragedy in terms of *kalos*, meaning both "beautiful" and "good." But his political and philosophical context was utterly foreign to that of which I am speaking here. Certainly, no one had him in mind.
[44]Shaftesbury, *Characteristics*, 2:268–69; 1:94.

bination was the chief characteristic of a polite elite of wits, the *honnêtes gens* blessed with access to literary production, Davenant's most necessary men. Bouhours had presented their exemplars, and not much later, in his *Manière de bien penser*, he would show how one might hope to acquire something of their abilities. It is not at all surprising that in the middle of the following century Lord Chesterfield would twice recommend this work to his son, in terms themselves indicating the success of this nonchalantly rational literature: "I wish you would read this book again, at your leisure hours; for it will not only divert you, but likewise form your taste, and give you a just manner of thinking." Three years later he added: "I do not know any book that contributes more to form a true taste."[45]

For "taste" was the name given this perception, and it, too, shared the double truth. We already saw that when Molière, through Dorante, spoke of pleasure and the rules, he relied on precisely the spectator's sensitivity to the combination in question: whether the spectator was of the groundlings or of the court. A century later, confronting similar assumptions, Marmontel could thus admit that there were many different particular tastes, varying according to time, place, and culture, but they were only *correct* when joined with one basic norm: "Thus there is only one supreme judge, one judge alone from which, in matters of *taste* there is no appeal: and that is nature." Rational, ethical nature, of course.[46]

Somewhat earlier than this writing of the *encyclopédiste*, Hume said nothing else, when he added to the perception of "the original structure of the internal fabric" those "general observations, concerning what has been universally found to please in all countries and in all ages," and when he asserted that both the structural perception and the general observations were "drawn from established models, and from the observation of what pleases or displeases." The critic "acknowledged by universal sentiment to have a preference among others" was the one who could judge both by particular "experience" and by universal "models and principles." We recall Hobbes's combination of geometrical law and "Galilean" mathematical experimentalism—as they were found, for example, in Davenant and Rapin. Or we might remember the linking of the geometric and the economic. Judgment of truth and beauty took into account general rational law, "the different humors of particular men," and "the particular manners and opinions of our age and country."[47] Again, the foundation

[45] Philip Dormer Stanhope, 4th Earl of Chesterfield, *Letters to His Son and Others*, ed. E. K. Root (1929; rpt. London and Melbourne, 1984), pp. 28, 161 (letters of April 14, 1747, and Feb. 8, 1750).

[46] Marmontel, "Essai sur le goût," in *Éléments*, 1:3. "The real substance," wrote Reynolds, "of what goes under the name of taste, is fixed and established in the nature of things" (*Discourses*, p. 134: 7th Disc., Dec. 1776). For a good study of the *honnête homme*, see Domna C. Stanton, *The Aristocrat as Art: A Study of the "Honnête Homme" and the "Dandy" in Seventeenth- and Nineteenth-Century French Literature* (New York, 1980), esp. pp. 200–211, 217–24.

[47] Hume, "Standard of Taste," pp. 7, 9, 11–12, 18–19.

provided by Rapin and Dryden, Bouhours, Dennis, and all the others was clear enough—not to mention its apparent culmination fifty years after Hume in Hegel.

The Scottish philosopher, like the others, also insisted on the *necessary* quality of the ethical dimension in general law. Beauty, truth, and justice were one. The ability so to see them was essential to the true critic, who had to know that the laws governing their association provided the regularities of all moral human action (and thus, potentially, the *science* of such action): "With what pretense could we employ our *criticism* upon any poet or polite author, if we could not pronounce the conduct and sentiments of his actors either natural or unnatural to such characters, and in such circumstances? It seems almost impossible, therefore, to engage in science or action of any kind without acknowledging the doctrine of necessity, and this *inference* from motions to voluntary actions, from characters to conduct."[48] As so often, these last lines are reminiscent of Hobbes's argument relating to the founding *Fiat* of civil society, of the idea of a voluntary rational contract among previously agitated humans, a contract founded in some sort of natural justice and producing ethical social behavior.

Thirteen years before Hume's essay on taste, the Scottish poet Mark Akenside, principally influenced by Addison and Francis Hutcheson (of whom more in Chapter 10), brought many of these elements together in his celebrated poem of 1744, *The Pleasures of Imagination*. The world order was indeed benevolent, for God had "chosen,/ The best and finest of unnumbered worlds / That lay from everlasting in the store / Of his divine conceptions." The poet made the philosophical claim explicit in a footnote referring the reader to "the vision at the end of the *Théodicée* of *Leibnitz*."[49] An aspect of this ethically and rationally ordered world was embodied in the sublime powers of the human mind and its consequent ability to understand *and* embody those relations of which I have been speaking. This produced the familiar association of ideas and terms:

> Thus was BEAUTY sent from heaven,
> The lovely ministress of TRUTH and GOOD

[48]David Hume, *Enquiries Concerning Human Understanding and Concerning the Principles of Morals*, ed. L. A. Selby-Bigges, 2d ed. (Oxford, 1902), p. 90.

[49]Mark Akinside, M.D., *The Works . . . in Verse and Prose; with His Life*, a Fac Simile of His Hand-Writing, and an Essay on the First Poem, by Mrs. Barbauld, 2 vols. in 1 (New Brunswick, N.J., 1808), 1:44:II.334–37. Further references are indicated parenthetically in the text. (The author's name is now generally written Akenside, the spelling he adopted in his later years.) René Wellek seems to claim that Johann Jakob Bodmer was original in combining Leibnizian possible worlds with "Western theories of imagination" (*A History of Modern Criticism*, 1:147–48). Akenside's great Continental popularity may imply rather that the idea of an imaginative ability to grasp infinite possibility, to identify the best, and to tie such ability to pleasure and beauty was an association drawn from the Scottish poet. German culture drew its new terms from Britain and France, as we will have further occasion to note.

> In this dark world: for TRUTH and GOOD are one,
> And BEAUTY dwells in them, and they in her,
> With like participation.
>
> (I.372–76)

And as did everyone else, so Akenside linked them to justice, since such truth, "wisdom," and "reason" decked "the honoured paths of JUST and GOOD" (I. 546). Such truth and beauty, goodness and justice produced just that rectitude of taste of which Hume, Reynolds, de Staël, and so many others were to speak, taste that was thus innate, akin to methodized good sense:

> These internal powers
> Active, and strong, and feelingly alive
> To each fine impulse [;] a discerning sense
> Of decent and sublime, with quick disgust
> From things deformed, or disarrang'd, or gross
> In species. . . .
>
> (III.515–20)

Akenside represented a further development of the establishment enacted during the late seventeenth century. I have jumped ahead (again) only because I wish to emphasize that although there may be development and complication, no *essential* changes will now occur in these concepts and practices for at least two centuries. Of this we will see more in subsequent chapters. For now, let me just underscore how, already by the late seventeenth century, the combination of a concept of universal rational law and one of natural justice as the foundation both of that law and of all right action led to an idea of ethical necessity following the same kind of laws as direct physical or material causal relations (if not the very same ones). In the same way, and coming from *the very same set of arguments*, the aesthetic pleasure provoked by beauty in literature—and its "truthful" double relation to an "ethical" nature—was thus *essentially* rational (as such, it could at least initially be opposed to the "sublime," which was, rather, irrational).[50]

These matters were, further, just as predictable as the Laplacean uni-

---

[50]I would argue that the idea of the sublime, a naming of the *je ne sais quoi* (the "I-know-not-what," as Shaftesbury had it), inevitably accompanied the idea of rational beauty: the "system" excluded as irrational what it could not explain, while trying to keep it as an essential component of the literary. Hence both the naming and claims of its inexplicability. The creation of a science of aesthetics during the eighteenth century may be understood as an effort to explain the sublime—usually psychologically. A century later Hegel would define it as specific to those literary works in which free individuals were set in such critical situations as could show the spectator or reader the meaning of ideal action—or rather of action in the presence of Idea (Sophocles' *Antigone* being exemplary in Antiquity, Shakespeare's tragedies in the modern era).

verse. As early as the 1680s Bernard Le Bovier de Fontenelle (Corneille's nephew) had written: "Someone of considerable wit, simply taking account of human nature, would deduce all past and future history, although never having heard speak of any event."[51] Nor was he being ironic. The claim that the study of history provided the real facts and structure of human activities, with an assurance due at once to the assumed constancy of the human and its lawfulness (furnishing the facts just because it had access to the structure), was to underpin Friedrich August Wolf's founding of ancient historical and philological studies, and his and Wilhelm von Humboldt's Prussian educational reforms at the turn of the eighteenth century (I return to some of these matters in Chapter 10). Wolf himself was to claim of his "renewal" of Homeric studies: "All our research is historical and critical not of *things* to be hoped for but for *facts*. Art should be loved but history revered."[52] As German culture recovered, it adopted its discursive devices from France and England.

This view lasted at least through the nineteenth century: it underlay, for example, Leopold von Ranke's (1795–1886) celebrated remark that scientific historiography had to present history "wie es eigentlich gewesen," as it really was (whose culmination would, nonetheless, be some "universal" view of events). It was behind Auguste Comte's and John Stuart Mill's claims for a similarly scientific historiography (whatever their disagreement on detail).[53] Once his logic was out of the way, wrote Samuel Taylor Coleridge in 1803, he would "set seriously to work . . . in pushing forward [his] Studies, & [his] Investigations relative to the omne scibile of human Nature—*what* we *are*, & *how* we *become* what we are; so as to solve the two grand Problems, how, being acted upon, we shall act; how, acting, we shall be acted upon."[54] The idea can readily be traced from Daniel Defoe to Julien-Offray de La Mettrie, from Bernard Mandeville to Barbauld and de Staël. It inevitably accompanied the identification of reason, justice, ethical order, material process, and artistic beauty.

I began with civil wars and with Richelieu and Hobbes. I draw these arguments toward a close with Locke, philosopher of the Glorious Revolution and of Whig liberalism. Akenside, Hume, and Reynolds were to summon a taste able to sift the necessary laws of truth and beauty. A generation earlier, considering the intimate connection between the na-

---

[51]Bernard Le Bovier de Fontenelle, "Sur l'histoire," in *Textes choisis (1683–1701)*, ed. Maurice Roelens (Paris, 1966), pp. 216–17.

[52]Friedrich August Wolf, *Prolegomena ad Homerum*, 2d ed. (Halle, 1804), p. xxvi, quoted by Martin Bernal, *Black Athena: The Afroasiatic Roots of Classical Civilization, vol. 1: The Fabrication of Ancient Greece, 1785–1985* (New Brunswick, N.J., 1987), p. 286.

[53]See, e.g., Reiss, *Uncertainty of Analysis*, pp. 5–6. I am aware that this view of history had a tradition going back at least to Lucian. I am suggesting here that it had become part now of a discursive network whose dominance was marked by its ubiquity.

[54]Samuel Taylor Coleridge, letter to William Godwin, June 4, 1803, in *Collected Letters*, ed. Earl Leslie Griggs, 6 vols. (Oxford, 1956–71), 2:948–49.

ture of things and right reason (as well as correct writing), Addison called for the critic's acquaintance with the great poets of Antiquity and, perhaps recalling Euclid, his possession of a "clear and logical head." Just so, he remarked, again thinking maybe of an earlier writer (Rymer and his similar comment), "Aristotle, who was the best critic, was also one of the best logicians that ever appeared in the world." Logic, control of the right use of language, knowledge of nature and the affairs of humanity were the essence of the great critic as they were of the great writer of literature:

> Mr Locke's *Essay on Human Understanding* would be thought a very odd book for a man to make himself master of, who would get a reputation by critical writings; though at the same time it is very certain, that an author who has not learned the art of distinguishing between words and things, and of ranging his thoughts, and setting them in proper lights, whatever notions he may have, will lose himself in confusion and obscurity. I might further observe, that there is not a Greek or Latin critic who has not shown, even in the style of his criticisms, that he was a master of all the elegance and delicacy of his native tongue.

"The truth of it is," he added with obvious zest, "there is nothing more absurd, than for a man to set up for a critic, without a good insight into all the parts of learning." The true critic knew the standard of taste and the real beauties of a written work, as well as its coherence with natural rational law (its analytical or logical power) and the exactness of its correspondent image of superstructural phenomena (its referential adequacy): for he was possessed of "a relish for polite learning."[55] The completeness of such learning provided access to the double truth and to the pleasure derived from its perception.

We have come a long way indeed from the concern with the incapacities of poetry and rhetoric, the instability and dissolution of state, and the confusion of language from which I set out on these tortuous pathways. A fundamentally *political* preoccupation had by now led to the establishment of a new epistemology based on a concept of natural reason and methodical common sense. It had furnished an acceptable (if distinctly complex) claim for the objective referentiality of language, discourse, and thinking. It had produced the authoritarian liberal concepts of unique sovereignty and "possessive individualism," enabling a new idea of civil society to be forged. Within this conjuncture literature had been created, with a particular and privileged role of leadership to perform. Addison's linking of the author of the *Two Treatises of Government* to the ideal of the true critic was therefore fitting and not in the least fortuitous. The modern meaning of the word "literature" is not timeless: it is attached to a specific political order. (This does not, of course, mean that literary artworks themselves do not have characteristics, capacities, and qualities

[55]Addison, *Critical Essays*, pp. 81–82.

enabling them to outlast such attachment: my constant references, e.g., to Virgil have not been accidental.)

The deep embroiling of poetic/literary texts in political, philosophical, and ethical debate—as instrument *and* participant—was new. It was not new in action, for after all Chaucer and Dante, Boccaccio and Gower, Chrétien de Troyes and Christine de Pisan, not to mention so many others, all wrote texts that had to be read in terms of such preoccupations (to say nothing of those Greek and Latin writers who were already thought of or made into precursors within the same tradition: see Chapter 8). Such deep embroiling was new in kind. In that sense, if Brian Stock is right (in a different context) to remark that as of the tenth century a new relation arose between "oral and written traditions in medieval culture," such that, without complete supercession of the oral by the written, the former did nonetheless begin "to function within a universe of communications governed by texts,"[56] so we may say that the production of texts (certainly poetic and philosophical) began to function within a universe of political debate and conflict, a universe in which relations of power began, at any number of different levels, to play a predominant role in culture.

They had always done so, of course. But now they were subject to analysis, exploration, debate, and argument in a way and to a popular degree unprecedented. Conflict itself was theorized after the mid-sixteenth century—be it in polemic or less partisan discussion—more rapidly than ever before (and far more widely and diversely). Political action and theory became themselves an increasingly widespread and subtle tool of analysis at the same time. By the seventeenth century, it is probably true to say, no text could be free of some political implication for a reader. In almost all, the implication was no arbitrary reader's addition: the writer was no less a player in this new scheme of things. And as I have been suggesting, nowhere was this more the case than in the new texts of literature. Again: whether or not the written artwork—"poetry," or "literature"—has political implications, plays a political and social role, or refers quite specifically to such goals and objectives is not at all the point. It *always* does. The point at issue is its place in relation to actual political authority and the role it acquires in a real social and cultural process.

Sidney, to be sure, had spoken of Amphion's poetry as building Thebes, but emphasis throughout the *Apology* had been on poetry as the origin of learning, not of society. When Louis Le Roy expounded his philosophy of history in 1575, he viewed the civilizing arts as a matter of techniques discovered to overcome the growing weakness of humans in nature—the arts in the narrower modern sense were never so much as hinted at. Letters (as general learning) came after a time when physical need had been satisfied by technical invention. In his *Methodus*, Bodin, like others we saw, had simply scorned poets as quite useless. Nowhere in Aristotle,

[56]Stock, *Implications of Literacy*, p. 3.

their more or less common source, had the origins of civil society (for him an irrelevant question, except as it might concern society and family) been set in relation to letters, and Plato's view was as notorious then as now: so far from an element of foundation, letters were bound to perturb civil order. Lucretius, from whom Le Roy had perhaps borrowed his view of society as originating in a state of nature (or chaos), never spoke of letters at all.

In the *De inventione*, Cicero certainly gave reason and eloquence—especially the latter—the essential role in transforming wild beasts into social beings, as he put it. But this eloquence was very far from the literature of which the late seventeenth-century critics and authors were to speak, although Cicero's writing and views were an all-important element in the new instauration. Horace had spoken of the poet as sage and prophet, of Orpheus as the restrainer of savage natural man, of Amphion as the poetic builder of Thebes, and of ancient bards as civil legislators. (Actually, he called none poets, but referred to them as priests and prophets, further emphasizing that the familiar tales were but *told* of them: "dictus.") In Horace this reference was swift, the time of efficacity was thought long past, and his remarks were directed against shame lest poets blush at their uselessness. No doubt his chief assumptions about poetry—that it was a civilizing tool, both instructing and delighting, one that observed and taught "decorum"—were all found in the new view of literature. But they now corresponded to different epistemological exigencies and obtained a function of quite different significance in a particular political edifice.[57]

Of the late seventeenth century's most immediate predecessors, perhaps only George Puttenham came close to a *theoretical* expression of literature's purpose at all similar to the one then established.[58] Neoclassicism made the relations of which I have been speaking foundational. It did so, I have suggested, quite specifically in response to a question associating civil and linguistic decay, political and poetic improvement. Nor was it just a matter of original impulse. More importantly yet, literature became essential to the orderly continuation of society and a guarantor of fundamental values. The remarkable emphasis placed by Davenant and Hobbes, Boileau and Dryden, Fénelon and others on the direct link between letters and the origins of civil society, between justice and poetical justice, between social contract as a balancing of a natural order of universal rights and a social ordering of individual needs, duties, and obligations on the one hand, and literary verisimilitude as an equilibrium of universal common reason and order and the particular representation of discrete

[57]Marcus Tullius Cicero, *De Inventione [etc.]*, ed. and trans. H. M. Hubbell (1949; rpt. Cambridge, Mass., and London, 1968), pp. 6–7 (I. ii. 2–3); Quintus Horatius Flaccus, *Satires, Epistles, and Ars Poetica*, ed. and trans. H. Rushton Fairclough (1929; rpt. Cambridge, Mass., and London, 1978), pp. 482–83 (*De Arte Poetica*, ll. 391–407).

[58]Puttenham, *Arte of English Poesie*, esp. pp. 22–23.

events, objects, and sensibilities on the other, appeared something entirely new. These assumptions accompanied renewed certainties in the social and political world.

At the end of Chapter 2 I suggested how Shakespeare's *Tempest* engaged the sense of general political doubt and social ending. Sixty years later all this seemed to have changed. At the conclusion of Dryden's and Davenant's reworking of the play (1667), Prospero was able to cry joy at the burial of "all past crimes." The usurping Antonio, inexhaustibly sinister in Shakespeare, had been duly repentant from the very moment of the shipwreck. Prospero's new daughter Dorinda finally exclaimed over the beauty of mankind, while her future spouse, the noble savage Hippolito, repeated the earlier Miranda's "O brave new World that has such people in't!" Only this time Prospero no longer saw fit to comment on their innocence of the world. Hippolito was to be "Lord of a great People," with Dorinda to wife. Ferdinand would wed Miranda as before. Both couples would legitimately extend their dynasties in perfect harmony. Political order was at last quite restored. No threats remained to its future good form. All was indeed for the best in the most orderly of worlds.

This reworked *Tempest* came close to being an illustration of Hobbes's creation of the state. Brought to the island, the various victims of the storm were reduced to that condition of nature that preceded and necessitated the invention of a sovereign authority. The sailors all disputed with one another their right to power, Prospero informed Hippolito that men and women were natural enemies, Ferdinand and Hippolito argued the right to ownership of women as property: "She was mine first; you have no right to her." It was, in fact, this last debate whose conclusion resolved the play. Certainly Alonzo and Antonio now recognized their guilt from the start, and Gonzalo remarked how they had already made the penance of going to Portugal to kill "the Moors of Spain" for Christianity. But not before the first scene of the final act did a dispute between Prospero and Miranda (about his right to take another's life and be both judge and executioner) mark the beginning of that legitimacy to be consolidated in V.ii. That final scene was a celebration of legitimate order, one founded on Prospero's *right* to power and property, his right to control the distribution of that power and property, and others' acceptance of those rights. Nor was there now any question but that those others' evaluation of his right was the correct one: all recognized the justice of his distribution of those things. Leviathan had been created: in an *"Enchanted Island"* that was no doubt England itself.[59]

Much the same was true of another Shakespearean play to which I

[59]John Dryden [and Sir William Davenant], *The Tempest or the Enchanted Island* [1670], in *The Works of John Dryden, vol. 10: Plays—The Tempest, Tyrannick Love, An Evening's Love*, ed. Maximillian E. Novak and George Robert Guffey (Berkeley, Los Angeles, and London, 1970), pp. 1–103. My references are in turn to V.ii; II.iii; II.iv; IV.i (ll. 286–87); II.i (ll. 26–30). For a longer analysis of the Dryden and Davenant *Tempest* supporting these suggestions, see Katharine Eisaman Maus, "Arcadia Lost: Politics and

referred in Chapter 1. When he reworked *Titus Andronicus* in 1686, Edward Ravenscroft cut out the more perturbing madnesses—in particular, that of shooting arrows at the moon. And at the end, when Andronicus's son Lucius was proclaimed Emperor, the dramatist took care to emphasize both the legitimacy of such acclamation and how it would name a stable dynasty. As Rome was brought back to order, Lucius's son Junius addressed his "Father," lamenting his "poor dear Grandfather." The change was perhaps slight (although that of his name was not: from Shakespeare's "young Lucius"), but the ordered legitimation was thereby made the clearer. The change matched that of Dryden's and Davenant's *Tempest*, as it did those of such plays as *Antony and Cleopatra* (to *All for Love*) and *Troilus and Cressida*.[60]

For the eighteenth century, one new form of text in particular might almost be considered exemplary of these political and literary concerns. It was the modern epic, epitomized in Fénelon's *Télémaque*. In this text, indeed, the author came close to writing an entire novel on the theme of Colbert's ideal state and Dryden's hopeful encomia of political stability and cultural—even commercial—glory. The work was written for Louis XIV's grandson. It was published at a time (1699) when its author had been for some years criticizing the condition of his country in the strongest of terms. It related the travels of Odysseus's son in the company of "Mentor" (Minerva in disguise) around the Mediterranean, ostensibly in search of his father, but actually in search of the ideal society. Since the duc de Bourgogne's grandfather was Louis XIV, we may well agree with the latter in seeing the novel as a rather vehement criticism of his monarchy. The more particularly so as in a letter to the king of December 1693 Fénelon had long since written that in the wake of the Revocation and the subsequent wars, "the whole of France [was] nothing but a great infirmary, desolate and starving."[61]

When, therefore, Télémaque recounted his adverse judgment of Pygmalion, King of Tyre, there was no reason not to take it as a further criticism of Louis: "He is a man who has sought only to make himself happy; he thought he could achieve that through wealth and absolute power; he owns all he could wish; and yet he is miserable on account of his wealth and that very authority."[62] If Fénelon's depiction of the Phoeni-

---

Revision in the Restoration *Tempest*," in Mary Beth Rose, ed., *Renaissance Drama as Cultural History: Essays from "Renaissance Drama," 1977–1987* (Evanston, Ill., 1990), pp. 127–47.

[60]Edward Ravenscroft, *Titus Andronicus, or The Rape of Lavinia* (1687; rpt. London, 1969), p. 56 (V.i). On *Antony and Cleopatra, All for Love*, and the two *Troiluses*, see my *Tragedy and Truth*, pp. 204–18, 292–97.

[61]François Salignac de La Motte-Fénelon, *Correspondance*, ed. Jean Orcibal, ? vols. (Paris, 1972–), 2:277. Also in his *Oeuvres*, ed. Jacques Le Brun, ? vols. (Paris, 1983–), 1:547.

[62]François Salignac de La Motte-Fénelon, *Les aventures de Télémaque*, ed. Jeanne-Lydie Goré (Paris, 1987), p. 161. All future references to the novel are to this edition, cited directly in my text.

cians and of Tyre represented in part Louis XIV's France at the end of the seventeenth century, we can also take it as an oblique comment on the consequences of failing to follow Richelieu's political advice (and that of those who belonged within a not dissimilar tradition), of allowing power to become corrupting, of yielding to passion over reason, of accepting the advice of poor counselors. In his dialogue between Richelieu and Mazarin, Fénelon made explicit that the former represented the "true" against the latter's "false" political ideas.[63] He was closely allied with the Beauvillier family (whose duke was Colbert's son-in-law), and the reformer Claude Fleury, an important member of the Lamoignon circle, was an intimate friend and companion. By this time, in Fénelon's view, Louis and the religious and political advisers who now surrounded him were profoundly out of step with the rational, political, ethical, and literary environment: out of step in the serious sense that the nations' political and cultural realities no longer responded to their assumptions.

That was not to say, however, that matters were back where they stood in the first decades of the century. On the contrary, it was precisely the new certainties we have seen that enabled Fénelon's adverse judgment and permitted him the expressions of hope apparent in his many pedagogical texts, implicit in the advisory letters sent to the king (via Mme de Maintenon) and explicit in *Télémaque*, probably the most celebrated novel of the European eighteenth century. In Fénelon's view it was necessary somehow to bring back the earliest condition of a good civil society, the moment of contractual civil association following hard on the "savage and brutal life" of the state of nature (*Télémaque*, p. 146). Such a society, no doubt particularly aware of the proximity of natural warfare, would be quite different from Louvois's militaristic (and now desolated) France. Indeed, it would be suspiciously similar to Colbert's ideal. Once again, that is to say, differences were now all based on the same set of premises. The disputes were over who would occupy the place of authority, under the same sovereignty.

But first, for Fénelon in his novel, it mattered how that contractual civil association was to be established. For that, like Davenant and Boileau, or even Colbert himself (in 1664), he wrote that one had "to cultivate the Muses" (p. 145). To achieve "this beautiful order . . . , the love of arts and letters" was essential (p. 138). Indeed, in 1714 in the entirely nonfictional context of his *Lettre à l'Académie*, about what that body's objectives should be, Fénelon was to repeat Boileau in even more detail (often in his very words): "Besides, poetry gave the world its first laws. It softened brutal and savage men, brought them together out of the forests where they had been scattered and wandering, set them in political order, gave rule to their habits, formed families and nations, made them aware of the

---

[63]François Salignac de La Motte-Fénelon, *Dialogues des morts* [written between 1692 and 1695, published from 1700 on], in *Oeuvres*, 1:490–95.

blessings of society, recalled the use of reason, cultivated virtue, and invented the fine arts. It was poetry that raised stout spirits for war, and which calmed them for peace."[64] Established by such letters was just precisely the state admired by Mentor/Minerva when "she" and Télémaque arrived in Egypt: "The good organization of its cities; justice practiced in favor of the poor against the rich; good upbringing of children, who are accustomed to obedience, work, temperance, love of arts or letters; punctual attention to all religious rites; equity, desire of honor, loyalty toward men and fear toward gods, inspired by every father in his children. He did not tire of admiring this beautiful order" (p. 138).

The good king was father to his people. If there was one single constant in Fénelon's thinking, it was indeed this seeming cliché of a certain tradition in political philosophy. He was a father precisely to the extent that he maintained the established order: the power of the aristocracy—without "insolence," but also without "destroying their resolution, degrading nobility itself, confusing all ranks, making all favor venal."[65] Justice toward the poor, national frontiers maintained, religion established without intolerance, internal and external peace enabling internal wealth and international commerce—not to mention international peace—all these things were the objective of the wisely run state, whose monarch thought only of benefiting a population to whom he owed the establishment and maintenance of his authority. One thinks of Colbert's efforts at tax reform, his determination to permit all worship, his attempts to create a diversified industrialization of France, his encouragement of commerce.

One thinks as well of the *Projet de paix perpetuelle* published by Charles-Irénée Castel de Saint-Pierre in 1713, so admired by Jean-Jacques Rousseau half a century later in his *Émile*, as he simultaneously lauded *Télémaque*: such a polity as advanced in the *Projet*, he then wrote, might be possible if only one could find "fortunate Salente and wise Idoménée."[66] In 1712 Saint-Pierre submitted to his colleagues at the Académie the *avis* on its business that provoked, among others, Fénelon's "Lettre à l'Académie." This group of people—Fénelon, Fleury, Saint-Pierre, Vauban, Boisguillebert, Beauvillier, Chevreuse, the Colberts—admired later by Voltaire as much as by Rousseau, believed thoroughly in the possibility of ongoing improvement. They did not think there was any fundamental wrong—even less any catastrophic evil—in state and society. But there was any amount of need for correction of error and abuse. Such devia-

---

[64]François Salignac de La Motte-Fénelon, *Lettre à l'Académie*, ed. Maxime Roux (Paris, 1934), p. 33.

[65]Fénelon, *Dialogues des morts*, in *Oeuvres*, p. 493.

[66]Abbé Charles-Irénée Castel de Saint-Pierre, *Projet pour rendre la paix perpetuelle en Europe* [1713–17], ed. S. Goyard-Fabre (Paris, 1986); Jean-Jacques Rousseau, *Émile*, ed. Charles Wirz and Pierre Burgelin, in *Oeuvres complètes*, gen. eds. Bernard Gagnebin and Marcel Raymond, 4 vols. (Paris, 1959–69), 4:348–49.

tions, they thought, were clearly ascertainable just because there was now a standard of justice, reason, behavior, and taste. Like Davenant and Hobbes, Dryden, Halifax, or even Locke, they combined conservatism and Enlightenment: a quite traditional notion of rank could readily be assimilated to Davenant's "most necessary men." Le Bret's definition of sovereignty could easily make a place for contractual claims. Divinity could be seen in the sureness and clarity of self-possessed reason, as in the admired objects of its gaze. A natural and universal ethics underpinned the vagaries of local habit. Eternal and rational truths buttressed the feelings of taste, whose lawful regularity gladly made an important place for the "unreason" of the *je ne sais quoi*, the sublime.

Taste itself was precisely that accord of private and public, a cession of private desire and perception to public ethical order and probable general truth which matched the yielding of private power to public welfare depicted in the contract. There, civil association absorbed the individual into the collectivity, while yet guaranteeing individual freedoms. In the sphere of reason, taste and contract were matched by "concept": in which individual perception of natural order could be understood as a collective reality. Coherence in alliance with correspondence, analysis with reference, likewise gave "truth." Justice, we saw, whether political or poetical, functioned similarly. Literature now caught these general realities. And we may appropriately recall here Descartes's century-old doubts about determining *le beau*, as well as Diderot's 1750s claim that to do so required perceiving relations of just this sort (see Chapter 3, p. 77).

This equilibrium was why Voltaire, like Rousseau, later praised Fénelon with such elaborate enthusiasm. All the archbishop's works, he wrote, "proceed from a heart full of virtue, but his *Télémaque* inspires it." Fénelon, he added, was "unjustly blamed" for his activities, but above all, he had been harassed by Louis XIV—for even the most perfect times are not "free of misfortunes and crimes." "Ramsay," added Voltaire, "a pupil of the celebrated Archbishop, wrote these words to me: *if he had been born in England, he would have developed his genius, and fearlessly given wing to those principles of his of which no one knew.*"[67] Voltaire and others did not hesitate to emphasize the similarities between England and France. Saint-Pierre's "Polysynodie" was not very different from the practice of a constitutional monarchy and deliberative parliament. Fénelon was to have been president of a national council and member of the regency council under the duc d'Orléans, had he not died the year before Louis XIV. We should doubtless not be misled by all this into establishing identities of political action between England and France, but we have already seen much similarity in political process, and certainly the rational ideals taken to permit such action were the same. Just as Dryden's attitudes and tone were dominant less than a generation after his death, so Fénelon's

[67]François-Marie Arouet de Voltaire, *Le siècle de Louis XIV,* in *Oeuvres,* 18:183, 82.

once-suspect novel had become by 1717 "what its author wanted, the breviary of a prince *honnête homme.*"[68] A leveling of disturbed waters was occurring; a balance found. A particular form of constitutional, contractual authoritarian liberalism, kinder and gentler than Stuart or Bourbon claims, was becoming dominant.

Télémaque expressed a loyal opposition. It contrasted good and bad princes: not, be it understood, Louis XIV and some other, but Louis XIV as he naturally was and Louis XIV as he had been made by evil counselors (pp. 288–89), a view Fénelon had earlier expressed in his 1693 letter to the king. *Télémaque* opposed a future utopia to the current poor state of France, a centralized state where all suffered (not from its nature but again from those counselors) to a state both old and new, a state that would bring back "the golden age" of the first era of civil association, avoiding military expansionism and aiding universal trade and commerce (p. 149). Again, the golden age in question would be brought by the arts of Apollo (pp. 145–47). Further, the final image left by the novel was not that of Tyrian evils or Egyptian disasters, nor was it the utopia of *la Bétique,* where no one worked or owned property and where simplicity, equality, freedom, and virtue reigned (pp. 263–71). Fénelon left the reader with *Salente,* essentially a depiction of France renewed—under something like a constitutional monarchy, whose sovereign ruled according to the now-familiar order of justice, virtue, reason, and truth; where general law underlay and guaranteed particular local interest and custom; and whose good functioning was best compared to the arts (pp. 527–29). Work and rational knowledge would bring back an actual golden age: "May our descendants remember the gift we receive today and renew, from generation to generation, the peace of the golden age" (p. 517).

While Fénelon thus famously appealed to a Homeric model (at a time when the meaning of that model, as we will see in Chapter 8, was malleable in the extreme), only two years earlier Dryden in England had referred to a Virgilian one. If anything, he made the identification yet more precise in the Dedication to his translation of the *Aeneid.* Arguing how Virgil had recorded the passage from republic to empire, he spoke of Augustus as a usurper. Yet "though of a bad kind, [he] was the very best in it," comparing him, ironically and hopefully, to William III. A genealogy remarkably similar to that of Orange was ascribed to Aeneas, held to have usurped the line of Latinus, "descended from *Saturn.*" That prince had displayed "the proper Character of a King by Inheritance," which was to be "just and gracious" and "solicitous for the welfare of his People; always Consulting with his Senate to promote the common Good"—a claim scarcely appro-

---

[68]Goré, Introduction to *Télémaque,* p. 101. The abbé de Saint-Pierre's text mentioned is *Discours sur la polysynodie, où l'on démontre que la polysynodie, ou pluralité des conseils, est la forme de ministère la plus avantageuse pour un roi, & pour son royaume* (Amsterdam, 1719).

priate to the Stuarts, but certainly applicable to William and Mary. Dryden could then identify Sylla with Cromwell and so on, and praise Virgil for having granted Aeneas the next-best title to that of a hereditary monarch, "that of an Elective King."[69] None of this suggests that Dryden was "betraying" his Stuart attachment. It does imply that in making the best of a by-then (1697) clearly irrevocable change, Dryden was relying on the certainties of the contractual model: the new settlement could work, provided its beneficiaries adhered to the constraints of the justice and truth whose establishment we have been following.

To be sure, Latinus's Saturnine golden age could not return, but perhaps then something only slightly less glorious might. And it could do so as much as anything through the literary discussions between France and England: the former "as much better CONTRACTKS than the *English*, as they are worse Poets." But both were necessary, and from his discussion of the current political situation in England, Dryden passed directly into a discussion of critics, readers, and writers. He ended his long Dedication with a description (taken from Jean Regnault de Segrais, he said) of three levels of readers. At the lowest, where literary, political, religious, and economic standing were remarkably identified with one another, he placed the "Mobb-Readers": "They are but a sort of *French Hugonots*, or *Dutch Boors*, brought over in Herds, but not Naturaliz'd: who have not Land of two Pounds *per Annum* in *Parnassus*, and therefore are not priviledg'd to Poll." Next was "a middle sort of Readers (as we hold there is a middle state of Souls) such as have a further insight than the former; yet have not the capacity of judging right . . . who are not yet arriv'd so far as to discern the difference betwixt Fustian, or ostentatious Sentences, and the true sublime." Finally, there came those whom a Virgil chose to please—"the most Judicious: Souls of the highest Rank, and truest Understanding."[70]

Dryden could equally well have obtained this hierarchy of readers from Anne Le Fèvre Dacier, already well known as a translator of the classics. She spoke of it in her 1684 preface to Aristophanes. Her ordering corresponded precisely to that of Dryden. At the lowest level were readers diverted simply by narrative and incident. At the second were "cultivated audiences capable of developing taste" and of being guided at least by the judicious critic. But the truly superior readers were those "whose training and natural sensitivity make them able to understand and appreciate so difficult a poet as Aristophanes."[71] The question then was, Who were

[69]John Dryden, "Dedication to the Aeneis," in *The Works of John Dryden, vol. 5: Translations of Virgil*, ed. William Frost and Vinton A. Dearing (Berkeley, Los Angeles, and London, 1987), pp. 278–84.

[70]Ibid., pp. 287, 326–28. Zeynep Tenger has detailed the historical invention of the reader as critical category in literary theory: "Inventing the Reader and the Writer: Eighteenth-Century Literary Theory," Ph.D. diss., New York University, 1990.

[71]Fern Farnham, *Madame Dacier: Scholar and Humanist* (1976; rpt. Monterey, Calif., 1980), p. 114. This triple division of readership was destined to continue in eighteenth-century theory. André established three levels of understanding of beauty: "de génie,"

these readers? Who, once the "rabble" had been automatically excluded, might they be if not authors who would then end up writing merely for their own consumption? Were they simply, that is to say, those most necessary men we have already seen? How were they to be found? What was their task and their relation to the literary work and its writer? What readers best matched the imperfect, but at least to some degree perfectible, "golden age"? To a considerable extent it was this debate that "closed" the arguments we followed in Chapter 4. At the same time, it could not but be wholly imbricated with the debates that were settling the nature and role of literature more generally. That Dryden named Segrais rather than Le Fèvre was not an idle omission. The new literature needed a public. The conflicts over that issue occurred in intricate relation with these final quarrels about the nature of literature itself.

"de goût," and "de pur caprice." The first depended on knowledge of "essential beauty" and general principles, the second relied on "an enlightened sentiment of natural beauty," and the third was based "on nothing" and was to be accepted nowhere except maybe "on the comic stage." André exactly repeated Le Fèvre Dacier and Dryden: *Essai sur le beau*, in *Oeuvres philosophiques*, p. 20.

Chapter 7

Critical Quarrels and
the Argument of Gender

Men, by force rather than natural right, have usurped authority over women. . . . Women could say: How great is men's tyranny! They wish us to make no use whatever of our mind or our feelings. Is it not enough for them to command the motion of our heart, without taking over our intelligence as well? . . . Can women not say to men: what right have you to forbid our study of the sciences and fine arts? Those women who have applied themselves to them have surely succeeded both in the sublime and the pleasant? If the poetry of certain Ladies had the benefit of antiquity, you would grant it the same admiration as the works of the Ancients, to whom you do justice.
—Mme de Lambert, "Réflexions nouvelles sur les femmes"

The political institution of literature and the unique importance of the poet to state policy and the ordering of power, first most clearly put forward by Davenant, had within a generation become commonplaces. By 1674 Boileau not only put poetry in the particular service of the Sun King but asserted that literature, like the Hobbesian political contract, enabled the passage from the rude state of nature to the polite stage of civil society. In the same year, Jean Desmarets de Saint-Sorlin noted how artistic genius had deserted France's neighbors in favor of his own country—thus forestalling Dennis's later remarks. Just a year earlier the anonymous author of a comedy on the two Bérénice plays of Racine and Corneille remarked how France was now most "favored on Parnassus and everything coming thence is well-received; for this powerful kingdom . . . is presently the most celebrated seat of our empire."[1] Precisely analogous comments were simultaneously rife among most English writers. We have seen, too, how they were embedded in a whole series of complex arguments bearing on reason, on ethical claim, and on aesthetic demand.

Less common was any avowed recognition that at least in France, as I

[1]*Tite et Titus ou les Bérénices* (Utrecht, 1673), in G. Michaut, *La "Bérénice" de Racine* (Paris, 1907), p. 328. For Desmarets, see Hugh Gaston Hall, *Richelieu's Desmarets and the Century of Louis XIV* (Oxford, 1990).

192

wrote earlier, nearly all the original members of the Académie had acquired their interest in language, perfected their style, and examined
ideals of manners and reason in the *salon* of Catherine de Rambouillet and
in the gracious society of her women friends. One of the most assiduous of
participants had been that very Saint-Sorlin just mentioned, the Académie's first chancellor.

In the 1620s Marie de Gournay had excoriated male violence, lack of
couth, manipulation of women, unmannerliness, and general unreason.
Rambouillet's *salon* practiced the reason free of violence that Poulain de
La Barre would assert in his 1673 *Egalité des deux sexes* to be characteristic of women for specific historical reasons. But Poulain was only making
explicit what was already implicit in Gournay, in the *salons*, and, more
importantly for Poulain's eventual argument, in Descartes's assertions
separating reason and material substance: that reason in women, untainted by the violence with which the history of social development had
contaminated reason in men, would reestablish a stable political order. It
would do so through polite conversation and good letters. Among others,
Corneille had been an important participant in these debates, from which
it looked for some years as if women and men might emerge as equal
partners in cultural production (as we saw in Chapter 4). Indeed, more
than a century later the conservative Hannah More referred to just this
period with retrospective forboding:

> At the revival of letters in the sixteenth and the following century, the
> controversy about this equality was agitated with more warmth than
> wisdom; and the process was instituted and carried on, on the part of the
> female complainant, with that sort of acrimony which always raises a
> suspicion of the justice of any cause; for violence commonly implies
> doubt, and invective indicates weakness rather than strength. The nov-
> elty of that knowledge which was bursting out from the dawn of a long,
> dark night, kindled all the ardors of the female mind, and the ladies fought
> zealously for a portion of that renown which the reputation of learning
> was beginning to bestow.[2]

The cultural ferment of the first three-quarters of the century and some
of its later results have been explored in detail. We need now to look at the
twenty short years from 1674 to the mid-1690s. The debate about the
foundation and nature of literature was then brought to a close simultaneously with that concerning the relation of women to cultural production. The details and manner of that closure beat a track on which More

---

[2]Hannah More. *Strictures on the Modern System of Female Education; With a View
of the Principles and Conduct Prevalent among Women of Rank and Fortune*, in *The
Works*, 7 vols. (New York, 1835–47), 6:142–43. Catharine [Sawbridge] Macaulay made
similar assertions: *Letters on Education, with Observations on Religious and Metaphysical Subjects (1790)*, intro. Gina Luria (New York, 1974), p. 49.

(for example) would be a typical traveler. These years were marked both by the *Querelle des anciens et modernes* and by a renewed outbreak of the *Querelle des femmes*. In France, especially, the participants in both debates were the same. That is, of course, not surprising when we consider the small number of those who had the necessary financial wherewithal, leisure, literacy, and access to print. Nevertheless, the fact is surely important.

The establishment of literature and its social place and role required the constitution of a particular group "authorized in its domain," as Richelieu had once asserted the legitimacy of the prince authorized in his. Such establishment thus also demanded certain exclusions. Judith Drake spoke aptly in 1696 of her difficulty—nay, impossibility—of confronting "so great Wits as have strongly attacked" women: "Not that I can, or ought to yield, that we are by Nature less enabled for such an Enterprize, than Men are. . . . But because through the Usurpation of Men, and the Tyranny of Custom (here in *England* especially) there are at most but few, who are by Education, and acquir'd Wit, or Letters sufficiently quallified for such an Undertaking."[3] Women, she was by then arguing, had been deprived even of the means of self-defense. The practical result of the denial of reason and deprivation of letters would be a self-fulfilling prophecy: without the education made possible by Arthur's Fund (as Woolf would later put it in *Three Guineas*), reason was deprived of necessary lettered instruments.

In light of these matters, Davenant's "most necessary men" begin to appear considerably less innocuous. Indeed, they lead to an altogether broader pattern. When Boileau published the *Art poétique* in 1674, he was working at the same time (just a year after Poulain's *Egalité*) on a first version of his tenth Satire, that utterly violent diatribe against women. Although this poem seems to have been known privately, it was not widely circulated for some years and not actually published until 1694: at the height of the quarrels, which historians usually consider to have run from 1686 to the late 1690s. During 1673 and 1674 Boileau was also writing his "Dialogue des héros de roman" against Madeleine de Scudéry. This work *was* known at once, although again he did not publish it at the time, claiming, he wrote later with remarkable condescension, that he had not wanted to "donner ce chagrin à une Fille, qui aprés tout avoit beaucoup de mérite, et qui, s'il en faut croire tous ceux qui l'ont connuë, nonobstant la mauvaise Morale enseignée dans ses Romans, avoit encore plus de probité et d'honneur que d'esprit."[4] Adding insult of disdain to

---

[3][Judith Drake], *An Essay in Defence of the Female Sex . . .* (London, 1696; rpt. New York, 1970), p. 26.

[4]Boileau, *Oeuvres complètes*, p. 445: "cause this pain to a *Fille* [= unmarried woman, with divers connotations of immaturity and "girlishness"], who after all was very worthy, and who, if one can believe those who knew her, despite the evil Ethic taught in her Novels, had yet more probity and honor than wit." A decade later Scudéry gave as good as she got, answering with some scathing comment of her own: "I seem to see some contemptible fungus, believing its little shadow has eclipsed the sun in its im-

condescending injury, his final phrase not so subtly allowed Scudéry the familiar "womanly virtues" of uprightness and chastity, while denying her "manly" wit and reason.

At the same time, he confessed, however, to having had a foible for her *Cyrus* and *Clélie*, due entirely, he wrote, to his "extreme youth," when he thought them "masterpieces of our language." Since then, he added, "la Raison m'ayant ouvert les yeux, je reconnus la puerilité de ces Ouvrages [Reason having opened my eyes, I recognized the puerility of these writings]." Here the term *puerilité* certainly had its etymological sense of "immaturity" as well as that of "foolishness." One may recall young Dorothy Osborne's exclamation to Temple in 1653, when proposing to send him Gautier Costes de La Calprenède's multivolume *Cléopâtre*. She must be an "asse," she wrote, "to think [he] can be idle enough at London to reade Romances."[5] But such considerations did not stop her from sending him the successive volumes of Scudéry's novels as they read them throughout 1653 and 1654, echoing Boileau's youthful admiration (and in Temple's case provoking him to try his own hand at writing short romances).[6] Temple, too, would later see such sympathy as an aspect of youth's warmth, having eventually to yield its place to reason. In 1690, with his essay on "Ancient and Modern" learning, he would set in motion the English version of the quarrel.

In 1675, as we saw, Boileau explicitly linked the discovery of right reason to a particular policy by dedicating the ninth Epistle to Colbert's eldest son. Praise of his father's pacific policies and of commercial expansion was held "truthfully" to depict the king. That "Truth" led directly to reason, truth, and beauty in literature (see above, pp. 132–33). In the *Art poétique*, letters and state order likewise ran hand in hand. A major aspect

---

mense and brilliant journey, admired by the whole world." There may be, she admits, some use in defamers, for medicine can discover some utility even in "gnats, scorpions, basilisks, toads, and a thousand other harmful creatures" (Madeleine de Scudéry, "De la médisance" [1686], in *Choix de conversations*, ed. Phillip J. Wolfe [Ravenna, 1977], pp. 140–41).

[5]Dorothy Osborne, *Letters to Sir William Temple*, ed. Kenneth Parker (Harmondsworth, 1987), p. 57. The translator of La Calprenède's *Cassandre* in 1652 was Sir Charles Cotterell, Katherine Philips's friend and future editor. Annabel Patterson rightly remarks that such romances were not escapist (*pace* Osborne): "They became a medium of cultural reinforcement, an expression of esprit de corps for their preselected audience, selected both by their royalist sympathies and their literary alertness, their knowledge of what the French connection meant. The generic comments on romance in these works are themselves keys to a *kind of thinking*, as well as its medium" (*Censorship and Interpretation*, pp. 189–90). Most contemporaries made no mistake in the matter: see, e.g., Marie-Jeanne L'Héritier, "Lettre de Mademoiselle Lhéritier à Madame D. G. sur les contes de fées," in Charles Perrault, *Les contes de fées en prose et en vers*, ed. Charles Giraud, 2d ed. (Lyon, 1865), p. 291. We may suppose that Marguerite Buffet had these tales in mind in 1668, when, praising women's "learning abilities" and the "vivacity and excellence of their minds," she spoke of a "natural, agreeable . . . and unforced style" dependent on both art and natural talent (*Nouvelles observations*, pp. 9, 173–74).

[6]Sir William Temple, *The Early Essays and Romances . . .* , ed. G. C. Moore Smith (Oxford, 1930).

of their discussion was the signally important issue of audience, intimately bound, as we may suppose, with the consolidation of a literary culture. To that issue, I wish to show, the linked questions of women's relation to culture in general and the status of the woman writer in particular were fundamental. They were so no doubt because literature had adopted the "masculine" job of founding rational public society. Reason and right language, held in the literary work, performed the Hobbesian *Fiat* of *Leviathan*.

We saw how Dryden debated this question in *Absalom* and how toward the end of the *Art poétique* Boileau described quite precisely the Hobbesian contractual passage from state of nature to that of civil society, from the "forests," where "force," "murder," and general brutishness reigned, to protected "cities," where justice corrected wrongdoing and equitable law defended innocence. And for Boileau, in the passage immediately preceding, there is no question at all about who may be the best poet. It was he who did not seek "sordid gain," who was not "grasping after money," who was not degraded by "a vile love of gain," who did not "traffic in discourse and sell words." It was he who served an "enlightened prince," the now "favorable star." Traditionally, this diatribe has been thought aimed at Corneille, who, not benefiting like Boileau from inherited wealth, did indeed work for material gain and who, of course, achieved his celebrity under an earlier monarch.

It may be no accident that all the grand women writers of the French 1650s to 1680s, from Scudéry to Lafayette and Sévigné, from Deshoulières to Bernard and L'Héritier, were Cornelians; and if the analysis of Chapter 4 is correct, Boileau could well have had other disagreements in mind. This is the more likely in that one of his most frequent targets in the *Art poétique* was (yet again) Madeleine de Scudéry, who, apart from the sin of her sex, was also the most celebrated novelist of her day and among the most financially successful of authors. Her writing, Boileau claimed, went entirely against the grain of a politically foundational, ethical, rational, and fine literature. It is therefore not surprising that in his(?) 1655 (1642) *Femmes illustres*, Georges de Scudéry had taken just the opposite tack: good sales and liberal patrons would produce greater literature: wealth and beauty went together, and a poet at ease wrote better than one constantly worried about survival.[7] But the market did not appear to select by gender. Left alone, its effects might well be those intended by Corneille's or Gournay's earlier arguments, and implied by the English legal compilation of 1632, also mentioned before (Chapter 4, note 33). More deliberate exclusions seemed required.

In Davenant's Preface, poetry and justice had served to temper "the rage

[7]Georges [?] de Scudéry, *Les femmes illustres, ou les harangues heroïques, de Monsieur de Scudery, avec les veritables portraits de ces heroïnes, tirez des medailles antiques* (Paris, 1655), pp. 313–18. This was first published in 1642. DeJean writes that it was certainly by Madeleine de Scudéry (*Tender Geographies*, p. 229, n. 13).

of humane power . . . frighting it into reason." Such terms were very close to Hobbes's rational contract, tempering the "desire for power after power" characterizing humans in the state of nature, and to the argument of Boileau's poem. Literature was instrumental in establishing such order— fruit, as Rymer said in 1677, of "poetical justice." One of Dennis's rare agreements with Rymer concerned this doctrine: "founded in Reason and Nature" and "the Foundation of all Rules."[8] In Boileau's poem and later argument, Madeleine de Scudéry and other women writers and novelists came to serve as foils for such claims. Women, one supposed, could only inappropriately fulfill the right task of poets: which, among other matters, required that one sing praises of the military exploits of such princes as Louis XIV.

Now if one were inapt to participate in political life, we may imagine one was equally inapt to sing of it. Boileau's celebrated instruction in the art of writing correct, legitimate, and rational poetry—binding once again letters and political authority, just as Davenant had brought together poet and prince, general and rational legislator—thus implicitly excluded not only Scudéry, but all women. Ending the *Art poétique* with the very phrases in which Charpentier had thanked Colbert for persuading the king to place the Académie in the Louvre, Boileau again underscored the issue of who might be admitted to that citadel of power. Bernard de Fontenelle repeated them in a 1675 submission for the Académie's poetry prize, given that year for a eulogy of Louis XIV:

> Du héros pacifique et du héros guérrier,
> Qu'il accorde en lui seul des titres si contraires,
> C'est ce que n'ont point vu les siècles de nos pères;
> C'est de quoi nos destins, plus heureux et plus doux,
> Ne donneront jamais le spectacle qu'à nous.

We now see, he ended, "l'illustre accord des Muses et de Mars (the superb agreement of the Muses and of Mars)."[9] The poem did not take the prize, but its echoing of the cliché further emphasized the exclusivity of power and the election of those admitted to its proximity.

In one aspect of this cliché Boileau was at odds with both Fontenelle and Charpentier: their assertion that something quite new was at issue. Indeed, we will soon see that the "Moderns" were able to tie their rejection of the ancients quite exactly to a subordination of women. To achieve the same end, the "Ancients" had the less exacting job of simply repeating

---

[8]Dennis, "To the Spectator," in *Critical Works*, 2:18–20.
[9]Bernard Le Bovier de Fontenelle, "Poeme. Présenté pour le prix de l'Académie fran-çoise de 1675: La gloire des armes et des lettres sous Louis XIV," in *Oeuvres*, 8 vols. (Paris, 1790), 5:203, 205: "That he harmonizes in himself alone these contradictory titles / Of pacific hero and warlike hero, / Is a thing our fathers' ages did not see; / Is a spectacle which our destiny, more fortunate and sweet, / Will stage only for us."

familiar antique misogynies. Such different ways of realizing similar goals are already familiar to us, of course, and we have earlier seen how seemingly different views were now based on a single dominant set of assumptions and a more or less uniform version of authority. So claims about the nature of literature and the kind of its producers, even variants on a political constant or a historical hierarchy, as Fontenelle's verses implied, were no provocation to doubt. The association was no looser even when the precise form of political authority being encouraged was quite different.

In his 1672 *Essay Upon the Original and Nature of Government*, Temple spurned the Hobbesian contractual theory (also rejecting intemperate support of the ancients).[10] We may certainly link this political-theoretical hostility to his dismissal of Davenant, Hobbes's alter ego in matters aesthetic: "Are Sleyden's commentaries beyond those of Caesar? The flights of Boileau above those of Virgil? If all this must be allowed, I will yield *Gondibert* to have excelled Homer, as pretended; and the modern French poetry, all that of the ancients."[11] Temple denied the contract to give more authority to unique sovereignty. He felt that founding civil order on general agreement weakened it. Yet his admiration for wider participation and individual freedoms was amply indicated in his encomiastic 1673 volume on the United Provinces, as well as in briefer essays.[12] He may have emphasized authority, but his paternalistic sovereignty ruled over a state according due rights to individuals. Its ground, that is to say, remained that of what I have called "authoritarian liberalism." Similarly, his rejection of the moderns was on just the same grounds as others' praise: their insistence on rules he found *irrational* and unlovely; even at their best he thought them more preoccupied with form and pedantry than with ethical content or beauty; he blamed them for giving altogether too much place to individual decision. He was not, in fact, very far here from Boileau's criticism of Scudéry.

These terms were precisely the same as those of Saint-Evremond's rejection of the ancients. Once again they were perceived to have failed the test of fourfold instrumentality (may I call it?). Homer was flawed because "politics had not yet united men with the bonds of a rational society; it had not yet got them well formed for other people; morality had not yet moulded them for themselves. Good qualities were not sufficiently clearly distinguished from bad." Such political, rational, and ethical failures were inevitable, because "truth was not to the taste of the first ages; a useful lie, a happy falsehood, was in the interest of the fraudulent and to the pleasure of the credulous." The claim was not, then, surprising that

---

[10]Sir William Temple, *An Essay Upon the Original and Nature of Government* (1680), intro. Robert C. Steensma (Los Angeles, 1964).

[11]Temple, "Ancient and Modern Learning," in *Five Essays*, p. 62.

[12]Sir William Temple, *Observations Upon the United Provinces of the Netherlands*, ed. Sir George Clark (Oxford, 1972).

Homer also failed to capture true literary beauty in metaphor and sim-ile.[13] Fontenelle similarly showed his readers in 1683 a Homer argu-ing that he had inextricably mixed truth and falsity because the latter was in essential sympathy with the human mind. In 1688 Fontenelle re-peated Saint-Evremond's remarks on Homer's weaknesses (especially his "strange confusion of languages," which must have been "the language of the gods; it is at least quite certain it was not that of men"), simulta-neously praising Descartes's discovery of right reason.[14]

The issue here was no longer what literature should be, no longer its very nature or cultural role, but who should have control over it and how that cultural role should be deployed. Ultimately, all those engaged in these quarrels would agree on the identity of their interest, regardless of which party they had ostensibly represented. Matthew Prior caught the matter precisely in a 1704 verse "Letter" addressed to Boileau on the British victory at Blenheim: "Old Friend, old Foe, (for such we are / Alternate, as the Chance of Peace or War)."[15] The "wars" had always been both literary and political. The question thus became less that of who should be included than that of how to *exclude* those perceived as out-siders, of how to exclude such people without turning them into op-ponents. One begins to see clearly the significance of the exclusion of women: an action as much political as cultural.

We need not wonder, then, at the sight of Swift in the *Battle of the Books* repeating his patron's sarcastic putdown of Davenant while embroidering it most revealingly. He told how, to challenge Homer, Gondibert went out to do battle only "clad in heavy armour and mounted on a staid sober gelding, not so famed for his speed as his docility in kneeling whenever his rider would mount or alight." "Madman," exclaimed Swift of the confrontation with well-armored Homer, "who had never once seen the wearer, nor understood his strength!" Davenant's unthinking, insane rider was, of course, overthrown and trampled by the Greek epic poet, who went on to slay Denham and Wesley and destroy Perrault and Fontenelle "with the same blow dashing out both their brains."[16]

Are such satirical metaphors as important as I am implying? Well, yes,

---

[13]Charles de Saint-Evremond, "Sur les anciens," in *Oeuvres en prose,* ed. René Ter-nois, 4 vols. (Paris, 1962–69), 3:353–56.

[14]Bernard Le Bovier de Fontenelle, dialogue between Aesop and Homer, in *Nouveaux dialogues des morts* [1683], ed. Jean Dagen (Paris, 1971), pp. 142–44; "Digression sur les anciens et modernes," in *Oeuvres,* 5:299, 289–90. On reason, see the dialogue between "Le troisième faux Démétrius et Descartes," in *Nouveaux dialogues,* pp. 376–84.

[15]Matthew Prior, *Poems on Several Occasions* (1709; facs. rpt. Ilkley and London, 1973), p. 190. Robin Howells also implies this identity of underlying assumptions: see his "La religion des 'chefs' dans la querelle: Boileau, Perrault, Dacier, La Motte," in *D'un siècle à l'autre: Anciens et modernes. Xvie colloque (janvier 1986).* Ed. Louise Godard de Donville and Roger Duchêne (Marseille, 1987), pp. 53–62.

[16]Jonathan Swift, "A Full and True Account of the Battle Fought Last Friday between the Ancient and Modern Books in Saint James Library," in *A Tale of a Tub and Other Satires,* intro. Lewis Melville (London and New York, 1970), pp. 160–61.

of course. Swift's emasculated, passive horse cast down by Homer's manly violence was no mistake. Nor was its rider's folly accidentally matched with the "furious" but "shining" reason of the ancients. (Not too many years later, writing in defense of Homer, but as a woman, Le Fèvre Dacier would make an implicit criticism of such an association: "Only too often do we see this excessive force is accompanied by violence, injustice and fury, and looks upon reserve, modesty and reason as characteristic of the weak.")[17] In Boileau's *Art poétique*, many things ran counter to such reason, but principal among them were the weaknesses of a Cyrus turned into an Artamène or the disorder of gallicizing an ancient Clélie. Above all they embodied ethical flaws, those many "petitesses" of the "héros de Roman" (Chant III). Their problem was that their author, Scudéry, lacked (we saw) that reason discovered by the Parnassian legislator and essential to good letters as now set out in the *Art* and elsewhere. As a result, her heroes were as linguistically confused as Fontenelle had accused Homer of being (Boileau's Dialogue satirically dramatized *his* accusation), irrational and unethical in behavior, ugly in performance, and utterly unequal to the political authority of the ancient sovereigns whose successors they nominally were.

Scudéry was by no means the only author to become the butt of Boileau's sarcasm. But she was the only one to find herself taken to task at some length in at least two other texts, in a manner that made her an *object* of ridicule, rather than a potential interlocutor (as even Cotin had been, for example), depriving her of authorial reason and deriding her as a female body that did not meet customary norms of beauty.[18] In the tenth Satire, Clélie once again became emblematic of false and unethical behavior. In the Dialogue, Scudéry was mockingly given her own proud pen name of Sapho, "cette Precieuse renforcée (this arrant *précieuse*)," "laide (ugly)" and not so unlike some Cerberus who, according to her own description, would be just as beautiful. She is as well "la plus folle de toutes (the craziest of all)," "impertinente (irrelevant and boorish)," "ridicule," and prone to such false descriptions as those of which Saint-Evremond was to accuse the immature ancients: thus betraying, of course, the very purpose of "bonnes" and "belles lettres."[19]

Literature as the manifestation and purveyor of right reason, of certain norms of beauty, of vested ethical custom and particular political authority, clearly had to be in the safe hands of those to whom such prescription

---

[17] Anne Le Fèvre Dacier, *Des causes de la corruption du goust* (Paris, 1714), p. 2.

[18] He was not alone in such remarks, Scudéry herself noting her lack of beauty. In 1653 Osborne wrote: "She has an Exelent fancy sure, and a great deal of Witt, but I am sorry to tell it you, they say tis the most ilfavourd Creatur that ever was borne, and it is often soe, how seldome doe wee see a person Exelent in any thing but they have some great deffect with it that pulls them low enough to make them Equall with Other People, and there is Justice in't" (*Letters*, p. 128).

[19] Boileau, "Dialogue des héros de roman," in *Oeuvres*, pp. 470–74. An appraisal of many of these issues is found in DeJean, *Fictions of Sappho*.

could be entrusted. The only outsiders, legally, politically, economically, in the group as it existed in the 1670s were quite evidently such women as Scudéry. Hence the significance of the two simultaneous quarrels: as modern literature was invented, so its agents and its consumers were constructed. Reason in women had to be made into woman's reason. Women themselves had to be turned into consumers or, at best, second-class producers. Such were the objectives—and the stakes—of the quarrels.

One may well suppose, therefore, that the traditional antimarriage theme of Boileau's tenth Satire was (at least by the time of its publication) in part a disguise. Not only was the attack on women accompanied by an assault on Perrault and the moderns, but the satire itself was placed in its preface under the protection of "Homère, Horace, Virgile."[20] The establishment of literature and the argument of gender, that is to say, were now explicitly parallel. The buying and selling of women (analogous to the selling of literary productions he had criticized in the *Art poétique*), their or men's servitude, the unbalance of passion and reason typical of marriage, questions of lubricity, gallantry, preciosity, pedantry, avarice, malice or folly, and such familiar terms, all had their clear congener in the more apparently purely literary dispute. For just that reason, no doubt, most were met head-on by his modernist opponents: of whom the dramatist Jacques Pradon, the satirist Jean-François Regnard, and the essayist Bernard de Fontenelle were but a few among some tens of others who threw themselves into the fray after the publication of Boileau's satire.

Where Boileau spoke metaphorically of the husband's bondage (*ton joug*, p. 63), Regnard assaulted the entirely real legal servitude of the wife:

> You will not go, a slave in servitude to love,
> And place yourself for ever beneath a husband's yoke,
> Nor, content with the injustice of a servile custom,
> Sacrifice to him your wealth and your heart.

Where Boileau always spoke of women's culpability, Regnard responded:

> Women are always innocent victims,
> Whom the laws of interest, whom false precepts
> Abjectly sacrifice to false-hearted husbands.[21]

Where Boileau spoke of the divers sins of typical wives, Regnard retorted with the sins of equally typical husbands. Just so did Pradon and the others. But to one issue they all reacted rather differently.

---

[20]Boileau, "Satire X," in *Oeuvres*, pp. 62–80. All references are henceforth given in my text.
[21]Jean-François Regnard, "Satire contre les maris," in *Oeuvres complètes . . .* , ed. M. Garnier, new ed., 4 vols. (Paris, 1810), 4:438–49: these quotations, pp. 439, 440. See also his "Le Tombeau de M. Boileau Despréaux. Satire," in ibid., pp. 450–56.

Where Boileau remarked that in marriage women were *always* unreasonable, "extravagante[s]" (p. 72), more or less by definition, neither Regnard nor Perrault (nor anyone else) took up the question of reason, as such. What they discussed was the nature of the extravagance: as if women could be "reasonable" in their very lack of reason, a kind of tamed animal. *That*, of course, was what Boileau had found impossible. The debate, that is to say, began to make some idea of rational difference fundamental. That was why, in a 1692 addition to his *Caractères*, La Bruyère viewed women as children or as appreciated objects. They failed to achieve knowledge, he wrote, either because their intellectual makeup was simply insufficient, or because they were lazy-minded, because they were too concerned with their appearance, because their concentration span was too short, because their talent was for manual work, because they preferred to pay attention to their household, because they could not concentrate on serious matters, because their curiosity was for nonintellectual affairs, or because their tastes ran to matters other than mental ones.

Such claims had always lain in the background. During the first three-quarters of the seventeenth century there had seemed a genuine possibility that claims of rational equality might actually meet with some political and cultural success. The quarrels of the last quarter century resulted in the dismissal of such hopes. They were, at least, driven underground (perhaps, recent researches suggest, into the novel—authored largely by women in late seventeenth-century France: Scudéry, Marie-Catherine Desjardins [Mme de Villedieu], Marie-Jeanne L'Héritier de Villandon, Catherine Bernard, Henriette-Julie de Castelnau [Mme de Murat], Anne de La Roche-Guilhem, Marie-Catherine d'Aulnoy, Charlotte-Rose de La Force).

The dismissal took several forms. A first had to do with the nature of women's reason. A second concerned the proper role of women. A third related to expressions of cultural control. A fourth, and perhaps most complex, bore on women's relation *to* culture. All had to do with the consolidation of literature and the establishment of roles in respect to cultural production.

Throughout the first part of the century a strong claim had been made that reason in women and in men was identical, unconnected to physical form, and differing only as a consequence of history and local context. Certainly, even among some of those who appeared the strongest supporters of such a view, the claims remained ambivalent (although not in the work of a Gournay). Pierre Le Moyne's Cliton, in his *Peintures morales* (1640), had argued that women's reason was more "angelic" than men's since their temperament was less physical and mind was anyway not bound to sexuality. Cliton admitted the claim to be controversial and proceeded to reduce its extent: "The Angels . . . chose to inform Women of their Knowledge; because in the realms of Grace, of Nature, and of the Arts, all engendering principles communicate more readily with one another, and with more propensity toward beautiful Things."[22] A few years later the same author's *Gallerie des femmes fortes* set out to display models of encouragement for temperance and chastity, fidelity, restraint, and devotion, helping women bear "the shackles of marriage" and resist passion and temptation. For, as Le Moyne added in his preface, "Women's Virtue" was "one of the principal elements of political well-being." In women, he wrote, mind and reason could be just as strong, and women as capable of philosophy and rule as men . . . save only that they were better as subordinate rulers, and their philosophy was a passive one of withstanding life, rather than an active or even a forcefully contemplative one.[23]

On the death of Katherine Philips in 1664, Temple had written a poem in which he (perhaps) inadvertently (the more significantly for it, if so) indicated a similar distinction, saying the "divine Orinda" surpassed her contemporaries because she "more than Men conceiv'd and understood, / And more than Women knew how to be good." This assumption of difference was repeated nine years later about the Netherlands, where women have "a certain sort of Chastity [which is] hereditary and habitual among them, as Probity among the Men." There women were the ideal domestic helpmates—a view adopted by Judith Drake as showing how Dutch women were "in a state of more improvement" than others, "managing not only the Domestick Affairs of the Family," but conducting all its business and financial affairs "as well as their, or our Men can do."[24]

---

[22]Le Moyne, *Peintures morales*, pp. 204–6.

[23]Pierre Le Moyne, *La gallerie des femmes fortes* (Paris, 1647), pp. aaij[ro], 10–24, 250–62.

[24]Sir William Temple, "Upon M[rs.] Philipp's Death made at the Desire of My Lady Temple," in *Early Essays*, p. 181; *Observations Upon the United Provinces*, p. 89; Drake, *Essay*, p. 35. This reference to Dutch women seems to have become something of a commonplace. Bathsua Makin wrote: "Married Persons, by vertue of this Education, may be very useful to their Husbands in their Trades, as the Women are in Holland." More significantly, perhaps, she asserted that such education and the resulting *domestic* equality was the primary cause of Dutch economic and political success: "One great Reason why our Neighbours the *Dutch* have thriven to admiration, is the great care they take in the Education of their Women, from whence they are to be accounted more vertuous, and to be sure more useful than any Women in the World." After rehearsing the varieties of learning suitable to women, she concluded: "This seems to be the description of an honest, well-bred, ingenious, industrious Dutch-woman. I desire our Women (whose condition calls them to business) should have no other breeding, but what will enable them to do those things performed by this Woman" (Bathsua Makin, *An Essay to Revive the Antient Education of Gentlewomen (1673)* [facs. rpt. of London, 1673 ed.], intro. Paula L. Barbour, Augustan Reprint Society, no. 202 [Los Angeles, 1980], pp. 27, 28). Long before, Joseph Justus Scaliger had written of the Dutch to his friend Isaac Casaubon: "The country people, men and women, and almost all the servant girls can read and write" (Scaliger, *Autobiography* . . . , trans. and ed. George W. Robinson [Cambridge, Mass., 1927], p. 49: letter of 1605). In 1694 Aphra Behn spoke of the Netherlands as "a country of much freedom" for women (*Love-Letters between a Nobleman and His Sister*, intro. Maureen Duffy [Harmondsworth, 1987], p. 118). Simon Schama has noted how Dutch women's "freedom and informality," "artlessness" and "modesty," "honesty and truth," virtue and natural beauty were clichés among travelers of the period (*The Embarrassment of Riches: An Interpretation of Dutch Culture in the Golden Age*

Twenty years after his claim in that regard, at the zenith of the quarrels, Temple would make a grosser distinction, asserting the divinity of two "endowments of nature" or "improvements of art"—"heroic virtue and poetry"—over a possible third, prophecy, which itself was but a direct gift of God, "bestowed according to his pleasure, and upon subjects of the meanest capacity, upon women or children, or even things inanimate."[25]

That conceptual trajectory might be taken as emblematic of the entire period, which saw someone like Mary Astell eventually advising intelligent women to live in a separate environment, or Samuel Chappuzeau (who had met Gournay in the early 1640s) writing two plays in 1656 and 1661 of quite extraordinary bitterness about men's violent abuse of women and their reduction to "slavery."[26] By the end of the century the savage vehemence of Astell had become quite rare: "If *all Men are born Free*, how is it that all Women are born Slaves? As they must be, if the being subjected to the *inconstant, uncertain, unknown, arbitrary Will* of Men, be the *perfect Condition of Slavery*? And, if the Essence of Freedom consists, as our Masters say it does, in having a *standing Rule to live by*? And why is Slavery so much condemn'd and strove against in one Case, and so highly applauded, and held so necessary and so sacred in another?"[27]

Astell was not wholly alone. Drake had also lamented how Western women were treated as "cruelly" and as "tyrannically" as in the East, "where the Women, like our Negroes in our Western Plantations, are born slaves, and live Prisoners all their Lives."[28] In France, Gabrielle Suchon had just earlier published her *Traité de la morale et de la politique*, which discussed the philosophical issues of "liberty, knowledge and authority," making a titular point of the claim that "although persons of the female sex have been deprived of these, they have no less a natural capacity, which can make them participants." The majority of the separate chapters of her treatise concluded with an examination of the way in which women had been systematically barred from all the benefits enjoyed by men. In her preface, she wrote that her aim was to provide a buckler against "servile constraint, dumb ignorance, and base and degraded subjection," provoked, she argued in the treatise, by men's violent tyranny. Women, she wrote, were treated "like negative beings," forced by men to look on "their own country and their city as a tomb in which they are buried, and

---

[Berkeley, 1988], pp. 402–4). One wonders what was the role in this reputation of a single emblematic figure: the "tenth muse," Anna Maria Van Schurman; early in the century Anna and Tesselschade Visscher had been major figures in a circle that included Grotius, Constantijn Huygens (Descartes' future friend), and Vondel.

[25]Temple, "Of Heroic Virtue," in *Five Essays*, p. 98.

[26]Samuel Chappuzeau, *Le cercle des femmes et l'académie des femmes*, ed. Joan Crow (Exeter, 1983).

[27]Mary Astell, *Some Reflections Upon Marriage* with Additions, 4th ed. (London, 1730; rpt. New York, 1970), pp. 107–8.

[28]Drake, *Essay*, p. 39.

as the sepulcher which they are not allowed to leave." They were com-
pelled to respect and obey the very powers that crushed them.[29]

By and large, however, Astell, Drake, and Suchon were isolated cases
whose voices were readily silenced by those of the Boileaus and Temples,
the Perraults and Swifts, as Astell clearly foresaw: as males, only "their
Pen gives Worth to the most trifling Controversy."[30] Indeed, their vehemence perhaps signals the deep distress of hope extinguished. In 1674,
that already much-mentioned date, the Cartesian philosopher Nicolas
Malebranche showed just how far things had gone from his master's
implied argument. Women's brains were not strong enough, he wrote, for
the abstract truths of philosophy, and their imagination "has not enough
strength and breadth to plumb its depths." A few strong women might be
found, but their minds were mostly fit "to decide fashions, to judge language, to discern distinction and fine manners." An exactly similar argument had been made by Dominique Bouhours just three years earlier.[31]
The work of Anne Finch Conway, Henry More's close friend and correspondent, of which Leibniz later said that it had provided the impetus for
all his thought, sank into oblivion.[32] So, too, did Suchon's treatise. Wits
like Saint-Evremond, La Bruyère, Steele, or Addison came to agree with
the more abstract Malebranche. Women's cultural work was at best to
produce journals, letters—the novel (or, at great risk to reputation, an
occasional comedy).[33]

Few were arguing then that women were without reason. The point was
rather that women's different reason suited them to different tasks. The
argument was not new compared to those, say, of the sixteenth century, but the evaluation was now positive and the details more complex.
Women should not be excluded from culture, for such exclusion could put
them in a perilously oppositional case. So they would be included in
particular ways.

My second point concerns the first of such inclusive "proper" roles,

---

[29]Gabrielle Suchon, *Traité de la morale et de la politique, divisé en trois parties.
Scavoir la liberté, la science, et l'autorité. Ou l'on voit que les personnes du sexe pour
en être privées, ne laissent pas d'avoir une capacité naturelle, qui les peut rendre
participantes. Avec un petit traité de la faiblesse, de la legereté, & de l'inconstance,
qu'on leur attribue mal à propos,* Par G. S. Aristophile (Lyon, 1693). The first half of the
first part is now in a modern edition: *Traité de la morale et de la politique, 1693: La
liberté,* ed. Séverine Auffret (Paris, 1988). Auffret has given as well some extracts from
the "Préface générale." My quotations, respectively, pp. 221, 91.

[30]Astell, *Reflections,* p. 60.

[31]Nicolas Malebranche, *De la recherche de la vérité,* in *Oeuvres,* ed. Geneviève
Rodis-Lewis, avec Germain Malbreil (Paris, 1979), p. 201 (Livre II, 2e partie, ch. 1);
Dominique Bouhours, "Le bel esprit," in *Entretiens d'Ariste et d'Eugène,* pp. 136–38.

[32]Conway, *Principles.*

[33]It is true that the large number of women novelists in France was matched at the end
of the seventeenth and beginning of the eighteenth century by an equally considerable
number of popular women playwrights in England: Behn, Susannah Centlivre, Eliza
Heywood, Delarivier Manley, Mary Pix, Catherine Trotter.

which, according to Le Moyne, meant so much to public political felicity. It was, of course, the role of wife and mother, women as among those "principes qui engendrent," as we saw him put it. Perrault's reply to Boileau's satire was couched in just such terms. In his *Apologie des femmes*, he defended not so much women as their chastity and purity as wives and mothers, their ability to run a household, to look after husbands and raise children suitably (shades of those praises of Dutch women). And, like Boileau, he placed the issue in the literary context of the controversy pitting moderns against Antiquity.

"Conjugal amity," he wrote in the preface, agreed entirely with the "first laws of Nature and of Reason, which require a perfect union between those who marry: such wise, suitable and honorable laws." In his eyes, these claims were one with his opinions in favor of the moderns, whatever appearance might suggest to the contrary. Certain "women of high rank," he admitted, seemingly aware that he was wanting to impose values of a particular sort, political, aesthetic, and social, "will find these manners quite *bourgeoises*, and my opinion about them outdated [*antique*] for a defender of the Moderns; but whatever they may say, and however they may be sanctioned by use and fashion, it will always be more honorable for them to busy themselves with tasks suited to their sex and their rank, than to spend their lives in constant idleness."[34] In England even Astell wrote that women's education would enable them better to fulfill their maternal tasks.[35] It is not always easy to tell when Astell was being sarcastic, but her dismissal of husbands as by and large worthless and an unnecessary weight on the backs of wives accompanied the dismissal of the public world in favor of the private. As in the case of Perrault and others, that tended to a positive evaluation of women's familial role, or at least a negative—or despairing—one of any public function.

While less abusive, that is to say, even those who claimed to be defending women certainly did not assume their status was equal to that of men (clearly Astell's case here was altogether different). Fénelon, Françoise de Maintenon's friend, educational ally, and preceptor of her step-grandson (son of the Dauphin), echoed these views: in body and mind women were weaker than men, but by nature industrious, clean, good householders, and ideally suited to the private sphere: the only anxiety was too much idleness. Indeed, we may well wonder whether Fénelon's later choice of the name Salente for his practical utopia, his depiction of France renewed, was not itself partly determined—or at least suggested—by memories of the mass of arguments adduced for the subordination of women by means of the Salic Law. The dictionaries of the time furnished various etymologies for its name, but the most common was its derivation from the Salians, a Frankish people living around the Lower Rhine, in the region of

34Charles Perrault, *L'apologie des femmes* (Amsterdam, [1694]), p. 35.
35Astell, *Serious Proposal*, pp. 38, 129.

the river Sala (now the Yssel). The *Dictionnaire de Trévoux* added that it came from the land of "Sallandt"—a name whose French pronunciation was identical to that of Fénelon's utopia.[36]

Virtually echoing Fénelon (or he, her), the fictional Princesse de Clèves's mother advised that a woman's duty to herself and others was to prepare always for domestic life, to be wary of her own passions, and to take "great care to cling to what alone can make for a woman's happiness, which is to love and be loved by her husband." We may take the Princess's final self-isolation as both a criticism and a confirmation of oppression internalized. For her part, even Drake thought women particularly "furnish'd with Ingenuity and Prudence for the orderly management and distribution of [necessities of life], for the Relief and Comfort of a Family; and [to be] over and above enrich'd with a peculiar Tenderness and Care requisite to the Cherishing their poor helpless Off-spring."[37]

The very education organized by Maintenon and idealized by Fénelon was made the subject of the Académie's poetry prize in 1687: "Le soin que le Roi prend de l'éducation de la noblesse dans ses places et dans Saint-Cyr (the care the King takes for the nobility's education in his forts and in Saint-Cyr)." Its authors unknown to the jury (submissions were anonymous), it thoroughly incorporated the *Querelle*. The winning poem compared its author, however "timide," to Virgil, "le Pasteur de Mantoue," inspired by Apollo himself (here, of course, the Sun King). Like God, the king took care of training his soldiers and educating the innocent daughters of impoverished nobles: "Tel cét Etre infini dont Louis est l'image, / Par les sécrets ressorts d'un pouvoir absolu (Like the infinite Being of whom Louis is the image, / By the hidden springs of absolute power)." The poem added that Saint-Cyr had been created "par les soins pieux d'une illustre personne / Que le sort outragea, que la vertu couronne (by the devout concern of an illustrious individual, / Whom fate persecuted, whom virtue crowns)": Françoise de Maintenon, needless to say, whose own history had so much in common with that of the intended pupils, "jeunes plantes (young plants)," of her school. As it did also with the poem's author, Antoinette-Thérèse Deshoulières, whose competition with Virgil himself was expressed in her hopes that her "vers pourront des siens égaler la durée (poetry will equal the longevity of his)."[38]

No such praise of Maintenon was to be found in Fontenelle's submis-

[36]François de Salignac de La Motte-Fénelon, *De l'éducation des filles*, in *Oeuvres*, 1:91–93; *Dictionnaire universel françois et latin . . .* , 3 vols. (Trévoux, 1704), 3:507. (I have found no earlier dictionary giving this derivation, including Antoine Furetière's [1690] and that of the Académie Française [1694].)

[37]Marie-Madeleine de La Vergne de Lafayette, *La Princesse de Clèves*, ed. Émile Magne (Paris and Lille, 1950), p. 18; Drake, *Essay*, p. 37.

[38]Antoinette-Thérèse de la Fon de Boisguerin Deshoulières, "Ode de Mademoiselle Deshoulieres sur le soin . . . ," in *Poësies* de Madame Deshoulieres, 2 vols. (Paris, 1688), 1:216–21.

sion for the prize. And far from suggesting that a woman poet might compete with the sage of Mantua, his poetry belittled women's abilities and firmly circumscribed their place in life. Fulsome encomia were awarded to men's violent military training on the one hand and to the raising of a sheeplike "troupe nombreuse (numerous flock)" of women in the "asyle solitaire (solitary shelter)" of Saint-Cyr on the other. There moral training secured a combination of "ignorance," "beauté," and "innocence," so that whoever made his choice of a marriage partner from among them would be most fortunate, assured of possessing a "noble douceur (noble gentleness)" and "conduite fidelle (faithful conduct)." Any pupil not taken in marriage could anticipate a yet more estimable life vowed "toute entière à des devoirs plus purs (quite entirely to purer duties)." Although the nunnery could be an exemplary option, the major objective of such education ("training" seems the more appropriate term) was marriage. As orphans or daughters of impoverished noble families, they were not good financial "catches," however Maintenon might help; but the unusually copious domestic virtues acquired in the school redeemed such lack.

Elsewhere Fontenelle made no doubt that financial interest was one duty of a woman entering marriage—although he agreed wholly with the laws' claims that she could not keep such interest. In a fragmentary and undated text exploring an ideal "République," he wrote that women there "n'auront rien en mariage (will have nothing in marriage)." They would be the submissive property of men, who would have the right to choose marriage with any woman of their town. Refusing such a "proposal," a woman would have to wait at least a year before marrying unless some better person "wanted" her! He did allow women to initiate divorce, but then the same conditions would apply to a new marriage.[39] The moderns' objectifying of women was thus no wit less than that endorsed by the ancients.

Throughout the next century the poetry of the two Deshoulières—mother and daughter—was re-edited and widely read. Both were famous in their time. Antoinette Du Ligier de la Garde, the mother, was a member of the Arles Academy and of the Ricovrati in Padua (as was her daughter). As a woman, she could not be elected to the Académie Française, but her works received public readings there. Both women were pensioned by the king, Antoinette Deshoulières continuously from 1688 until she died in 1694 (receiving the large annual sum of 2,000 livres). Like Sévigné, she was a Cornelian. As her encomiastic poems show, she was politically a Colbertian: addressing verses to Colbert, Louis XIV, Montausier, Saint-

---

[39]Fontenelle, *Oeuvres*, 5:211–12, 447. Competitions for poetry and eloquence were held in odd years from 1671. That year the latter prize went to Madeleine de Scudéry. In 1691, 1693, and 1697 the poetry prize went to Catherine Bernard: Paul Pellisson-Fontanier and Pierre-Joseph d'Olivet, *Histoire de l'Académie Française*, ed. Ch.-L. Livet, 2 vols. (Paris, 1858), 2:15n. Submissions were always anonymous.

Aignan, Maintenon, and Vivonne. Her tragedy, *Genséric,* which premiered in January 1680, was exceptionally successful, with some forty performances.

She was, certainly, not alone in public favor. In 1689 Catherine Bernard's tragedy, *Laodamie,* ran for twenty performances in a row, and her *Brutus* for twenty-five in 1690–91: both were immense successes for the time. Anonymously (I suppose), the same author won the Académie's poetry prize three times (see note 39). In these same years L'Héritier, who published a "Triomphe" for Antoinette Deshoulières in 1694 and an "Apothéose" for Madeleine de Scudéry in 1702, was celebrated for her prose and verse writings (in 1732 she published a translation of Ovid's *Heroides*). Both were members of the Toulouse Académie des Jeux Floraux (where Bernard again won three first prizes, in 1696 and 1698 for odes, in 1697 for an eclogue). Both were elected to the Ricovrati. Nonetheless, despite these divers theatrical successes, despite the admiration heaped on their verses, despite the fact that women were elected to literary academies, despite even the prizes won by Antoinette-Thérèse Deshoulières and Bernard (was it indifferent in this era that Bernard may have been Corneille's niece and was certainly a close friend of Fontenelle, if not, then, his cousin, and that L'Héritier was Perrault's niece?), Fontenelle and his colleagues were winning the longer cultural war.[40]

L'Héritier might still write a hopeful fairy tale, whose heroine swept all before her, alike defeating evil male opponents and winning over good but nerveless and suggestible ones.[41] But Bernard's writing, like most of La Force's, was eloquent of frustration and defeat, communicating something close to despair. She wrote a series of short novels, *Les malheurs de l'amour* (1687), *Le comte d'Amboise* (1690), *Inès de Cordoue* (1696), whose vision was one of unremitting pessimism with respect to relations between women and men. *Malheurs* (*Éléonor d'Yvrée*) recounted a series of tricks by family and friends, justified by social claim, whose outcome

[40]I have also consulted an edition based on Mlle Deshoulières's own edition (1688–95) of this poetry, dating from the revolutionary years: *Oeuvres,* Nouvelle édition, dédiée au sexe amateur de la poësie agréable, 2 vols. (Paris, An VII [1798]). My information about their lives is from the "Éloge" prefixed to the first volume of this edition. For Bernard and L'Héritier, I have used general biographical dictionaries. For Bernard, see also the editor's introduction to Catherine Bernard, *Les malheurs de l'amour: Première nouvelle, Éléonor d'Yvrée,* pref. René Godenne (1687; facs. rpt. Geneva, 1979), pp. vii–viii. For L'Héritier, see the introductory "Lettre critique" by Charles Giraud to Perrault's *Contes de fées* (1865), pp. lxvi–lxix. On the gradual exclusion of women writers from the canon in the later eighteenth century, see Joan DeJean, "Classical Reeducation: Decanonizing the Feminine," in *The Politics of Tradition: Placing Women in French Literature,* ed. Joan DeJean and Nancy K. Miller, Yale French Studies, no. 75 (New Haven, Conn., 1988), pp. 26–39. The Ricovrati seem to have been particularly receptive to women writers: besides both Deshoulières, Bernard, and L'Héritier, members included d'Aulnoy, La Force, Anne Le Fèvre (Dacier), Scudéry, and Villedieu.

[41]Marie-Jeanne L'Héritier, "L'adroite princesse [ou les aventures de Finette]," in Perrault, *Contes de fées,* pp. 239–83.

was death, loneliness, and unhappy marriage. *Inès* told a story whose heroine retreated to a convent, her unfortunate lover dead. In this novel, two fairy tales likewise told disaster: one, "Le prince rosier," whose transformed prince successfully begged to be turned back into the rosebush that had originally won his now jealous and carping bride; the other, a "Riquet à la houppe" in which, unlike Perrault's version, the ill-favored hero became not a handsome prince but a cuckolded husband, the lover himself growing as ugly as Riquet. "In the end," concluded the author, "lovers become husbands."[42] Bernard, like Astell and Drake, told tales of failure and rejection.

Matching and "justifying" their removal of women to the private sphere once again, and their reduction to the possessed objects of husbands (I am, of course, speaking in all this only of a certain "class"), was the third mark of dismissal mentioned: seen in expressions of cultural control. It is found in La Bruyère's unsubtle equation of women with animals or inanimate objects: fish, ornamental guns, or racehorses. We have already seen him dismiss women as essentially immature *children*. He also made them into decorative *things*. In the 1692 edition of his *Caractères*, he wrote: "Women are to be judged solely from footwear to hairstyle, much as you take the measure of a fish from tail to head." "A learned woman," he mocked, "is looked upon like a beautiful weapon [*une belle arme*]: it/she is artistically tooled, admirably furbished, and most choicely worked; it is [*c'est*] a museum piece, shown to the curious, not for use, no good for war or the hunt, any more than is a showhorse, be it the best trained in the world." From "femme" to "elle" to "ce," the trajectory is clear enough. Such views are found, too, in Fontenelle's deeply offensive sexist joke in his dialogue between Sappho and Laura, in which Sappho, saying that men allow women only a passive "duty" of self-defense and give themselves a more satisfying aggressive role, complained how this was unfair because men followed their proclivities when they attacked whereas women had no such inclination to defend themselves.[43] This sort of thing is perfectly familiar and there is small point in adding more here; the more so because such expressions are perennial: from Juvenal's sixth satire to Ariosto's fifth, or Boileau's tenth, and down to more recent times (see below, e.g., note 77). They are of exiguous interest. (Expressions of control could, of course, go further: justly or unjustly, d'Aulnoy and La Force both spent time in exile or in prison; Behn, Manley, and others were subject to constant abuse.)

More subtle, more complicated, and ultimately more pernicious was the fourth mark of dismissal. It was indicated by way of two forms of

---

[42]Catherine Bernard, *Les malheurs de l'amour; Inès de Cordoue: Nouvelle espagnole*, préf. René Godenne (1696; facs. rpt. Geneva, 1979).

[43]Jean de La Bruyère, "Des femmes," in *Les caractères de Théophraste traduits du grec, avec les caractères ou les moeurs de ce siècle*, ed. Robert Garapon (Paris, 1962), pp. 113, 126–27 (secs. 5, 49); Fontenelle, *Dialogues*, p. 163 (1e. partie, sec. 2, dial. 2).

cultural subordination. The separate reason of women, making them instinctively suited to the nurturing and engendering family life (we saw), as it justified their relegation to the domestic sphere, was also taken to make them the ideal consumers of culture. This last had three stages. First, they were not recognized as proper producers. Even in her much earlier letters, Dorothy Osborne had adopted the commonplace supposition that Scudéry was not the author of her novels: "They say the Gentleman that writes this Romance has a Sister that lives with him as a Mayde and she furnishes him with all the little Stories that come between soe that hee only Contrives the main designe." And she was indeed adamantly against women actually writing for publication, saying of Margaret Cavendish, duchess of Newcastle: "Sure the poore woman is a little distracted, she could never be so rediculous else as to venture out writeing book's and in verse too. If I should not sleep this fortnight I shall not come to that."[44]

The canard that Scudéry was not the author of her novels was even repeated by her old and close friend Pellisson in his *Histoire de l'Académie Française*, and it was left in, despite the correction added by d'Olivet. For her part, Cavendish told of "the malice and aspersions of spightful tongues, which they cast upon my poor writings, some denying me to be the true Authoress of them."[45] Once it was discovered that the winning poem in the Académie's 1687 competition was by Mlle Deshoulières, an instant (and false) claim was asserted that her mother must have written it.[46] One could not have too many of these women writing. Boileau was not alone in dismissing stories and fairy tales written not only by Perrault, but above all by d'Aulnoy, L'Héritier, Bernard, and others. Indeed, mere disenfranchisement might not suffice. Perhaps women should be wholly barred from writing. Pierre Bayle worried what might occur "if women continued to study and to write books." One had to "fear they would turn from the novel to thinking [*du Roman au raisonnement*], and tumble head-first into religious libertinism."[47] He was speaking here of La Force,

---

[44]Osborne, *Letters*, pp. 128, 75.

[45]Cavendish, *Life of the Duke*, pp. 4–5; Pellisson and d'Olivet, *Histoire*, 1:306–7.

[46]Deshoulières, "Éloge," in *Oeuvres*, 1:xxxiii. (DeJean compounds the mistake by saying that only Scudéry and Mme Deshoulières received such prizes [*Fictions of Sappho*, p. 114]. The latter *did* receive the prize in 1671, and DeJean has corrected herself in the admirable appendix to *Tender Geographies*.) It is the case that in 1673 Bathsua Makin argued both that women excelled in poetry and that this ability implied an excellence in all other realms of learning: "For, besides natural Endowments, there is required a general and universal improvement in all kinds of Learning. A good Poet, must know things Divine, things Natural, things Moral, things Historical, and things Artificial, together with the several terms belonging to all Faculties, to which they must allude. Good Poets must be universal Scholars, able to use a pleasing Phrase, and to express themselves with moving Eloquence" (*An Essay*, p. 16). She continued to insist, however, that even such learning did no more than improve women's activity and freedom in the domestic sphere.

[47]Pierre Bayle, *Oeuvres diverses*, 4 vols. (The Hague and Rotterdam, 1727–31), 4:735. Quoted by Ingrid Fröberg, *Une "histoire secrète" à matière nordique: "Gustave Vasa,*

whom the king did indeed exile from Paris for blasphemy, but he was, of course, lumping all women writers together.

Second, unable to produce, women would become the special audience for such instructive narratives as Fontenelle's *Entretiens sur la pluralité des mondes*, written, he said in his preface, for women to read as easily as the *Princesse de Clèves*, even though its matter was slightly more difficult. (It was perhaps not surprising, however, that by the time of Perrault's 1696 *Hommes illustres*, women had disappeared altogether from the text.)[48] Their kind of reason was quite capable of learning, although less able to produce *new* learning. So, in the English *Athenian Mercury* of 1691, as answer to the question whether women were able to learn, the reply was: "On the whole since they have as noble souls as well, a finer genius [= sensibility], and generally quicker apprehension [= instinct], we see no reason why women should not be learned, as well as Madam Philips, Van Schurman and others have formerly been." Elizabeth Elstob in 1709 justified her work in Anglo-Saxon on the grounds that it kept her from idleness without interfering with her household duties—small wonder if she recommended Fénelon's *Education* to her readers; but she also expressed her profound gratitude to William Wotton, Temple's old opponent in the Battle of the Books, for all the encouragement given her.[49]

Astell justified a "learned Education" much as Elstob had done.[50] But she was also, as far as I know, the only person to remark that such concentration on learning abilities and achievement was little more than a distraction from the major point: which had rather to do with the nature of reason itself. Descartes had long since shown, and by no means "to the general Liking of the Men of Letters," that "Sense is a Portion that God Himself has been pleased to distribute to both Sexes with an impartial Hand." Men did not like it, for Descartes's method was, she wrote, "so natural and easy as to debase Truth to common Understandings, showing

histoire de Suède" (1697), *roman attribué à Charlotte-Rose de Caumont La Force (vers 1650–1724)*, Acta Universitatis Upsaliensis: Studia Romanica Upsaliensia, 31 (Uppsala, 1981), p. 11.

48Bernard Le Bovier de Fontenelle, *Entretiens sur la pluralité des mondes*, 4th ed. (Paris, 1698); Charles Perrault, *Les hommes illustres qui ont paru en France pendant le xviie siècle*, 3d ed., 2 vols. in 1 (Paris, 1701).

49*The Athenian Mercury*, no. 18 (1691). Quoted in Florence M. Smith, *Mary Astell* (1916; rpt. New York, 1966), p. 46; Elizabeth Elstob, "Preface" to *An English-Saxon Homily*, in *First Feminists: British Women Writers, 1578–1799*, ed. Moira Ferguson (Bloomington, Ind., and Old Westbury, N.Y., 1985), pp. 241, 243. As a mark of the closeness of English and French debate, it may be worth observing that Du Bos specifically chose to note the less acerbic nature of the English quarrel in his comment that in Wotton and Orrery's dispute, the first, mainly agreeing with Fontenelle, argued that while the moderns were superior to the ancients in most arts and sciences, they were inferior in poetry and eloquence: *Réflexions*, 1:148–49. We saw how Temple also curbed vehemence of argument. On relations in this respect among Temple, Swift, Wotton, and Bentley, see Joseph M. Levine, *Humanism and History: Origins of Modern English Historiography* (Ithaca, N.Y., and London, 1987), pp. 155–77.

50Astell, *Serious Proposal*, p. 37.

too plainly, that Learning and true Knowledge are two very different Things."[51] It was almost as though Astell were responding directly to Fontenelle's partly contrary claim: that Descartes brought to reasoning not just new rigor, but greater difficulty. The ancients and more recent precursors had been often confused, vague, and unserious. Nor had anyone seen much wrong with such a state of affairs. Those centuries had been the childhood of humanity, their heedlessness a confirmation of immaturity. Before Descartes, claimed Fontenelle, reasoning had been easier, not harder.[52] Distinguishing learning from "true knowledge," Astell countered that clear reasoning and the discovery of truth did not require greater difficulty—simply a better method. Descartes had supplied one, and through it the right use of common good sense was now readily available to all.

Not surprisingly, Astell's protest went unheeded. On the whole, the *Athenian Mercury*'s allowance of equality of rational soul made for *difference* of active reason. This created the third stage. Not only could women *learn* from such as Fontenelle, but they could judge more immediately of art, of all those products of less instantly practical concern. It was not chance that accused the writing of ancients and women alike of immaturity. And this, too, would become a way of distinguishing between women's and men's reason: according to Giambattista Vico in the early eighteenth century, for example, men's rational minds developed; women's did not. What was simply a stage of development in men was fixed nature in women. Men in Homer's heroic age were "like children in the weakness of their minds, like women in the vigor of their imaginations, and like violent youths in the turbulence of their passions."[53] Anne Le Fèvre implied a similar view (although she did not suggest it as a way to distinguish between women and men). Immaturity, passion, imaginative vigor were thus again brought together: but men grew out of them, women did not. Fontenelle's became the dominant view. And what role would it then play, one may wonder, in Kant's claim that "enlightenment" was social maturity?

There was no harm in women becoming learned, for that did not depend on a claim that reason was unsexed. But common participation in all areas of sociopolitical life obviously did, and moreover would be a legitimate result if such assertions were accepted. Nor did they depend on a Cartesian claim, for just as specific political variants did not change the argument in the case of literature, neither did philosophical—more precisely, epistemological—ones in the case of women's status. Drake had made the same argument on Lockean principles: if it is the case that "all Souls are equal, and alike, and that consequently there is no such distinction, as

[51]Astell, *Reflections*, pp. 111–12.
[52]Fontenelle, "Digression," in *Oeuvres*, 5:289–90. See also p. 199 above and note 14.
[53]Giambattista Vico, *The New Science*, rev. trans. of the 3d ed. (1744) Thomas Goddard Bergin and Max Harold Fisch (Ithaca, N.Y., 1968), p. 304 (para. 787).

Male and Female Souls; that there are no innate *Idea's*, but that all the Notions we have, are deriv'd from the Senses, either immediately, or by Reflection," and because the sources of sensation are alike in women and men, again no such distinction was possible.[54] That argument, too, was ignored. For the many reasons already seen, difference was now crucial. No woman must claim equality with Virgil, upholder and creator of Augustan power and a poetic tradition of empire.

The fact was that women had become not only special, potentially learned, consumers of such texts as those of Fontenelle. They also became ideal consumers of aesthetic works. "Whatever is a matter of taste," Malebranche had continued in the passage I quoted before, "is their province." Four years earlier, in his 1670 *Comparaison*, Desmarets had already made a rather slighting appeal to women's critical abilities—although he certainly thought of it as laudatory. On the basis of his book's information, he wrote: "Even women who by their gifts of mind and body provoke the finest passions, the strongest and most exquisite thoughts, will better judge the passionate feelings in poetry, than the most erudite scholars of the university: with their lively imagination, they will know more readily what best touches the mind."[55]

The same tone was caught by English male commentators. In his 1686 preface to Saint-Evremond's *Miscellanea*, Ferrand Spence supported such a view at some length: "Yet, let men say what they will, there is *such* a thing as *Good sense*, in the *General* Notion whereof everyone does *agree* as *much* as in the *Idea* of a *Triangle*. I have *frequently* met with it in the *Pit* among the *Women*, who have *judged* with that *undebauch'd upright-ness* and Integrity, that I could hardly find any *Imperfection*, left by *tra-duction* in their *Souls:* Their minds enjoy'd their *Native Purity*, were *unsophisticated* and *free* from all the *Illusions* of *Prejudice*, or *Interest*."[56] Just six years later Rymer was putting the case with greater condescension. Women, to be sure, were the exemplary judges of the rectitude of plot in tragedy: "Rarely have I known the *Women-judges* mistake in these points, when they have the patience to think, and (left to their own heads) they decide with their own sense." But he emphasized that women had this capacity just because of their lack of learning and ignorance of critical "Subtilties." For the English critic, such tasteful instinct was possible only because, he said of the female lead in *Rollo*, in women "reason is said to be more feeble, so the Passions are suppos'd to be the more violent and

---

[54]Drake, *Essay*, p. 32. The question about learned women is perhaps most nearly related to the matter of their role in science. On this, see Labalme's collection cited in note 60, but above all Schiebinger, *Mind Has No Sex?*

[55]Jean Desmarets de Saint-Sorlin, *Comparaison de la langue et de la poësie françoise, avec la grecque et la latine* (1670; rpt. Geneva, 1972), pp. aiijro–vo.

[56]Ferrand Spence, preface to Charles de Saint-Evremond, *Miscellanea* (London, 1686), sigs. A7vo–A8ro: quoted by the editor in Rymer, *Critical Works*, p. 198. In 1680 Spence had published his translation of Catherine Bernard's *Fédéric de Sicile* of the same year: *The Female Prince, or Federick of Sicily* (London, 1680).

precipitate." So while a woman "might be presum'd not so well to understand" the finer details and obligations of rational morality, she could nonetheless be a fine critic of sentiment.[57]

In his celebrated *Parallèle,* whose first part appeared in 1688, the year of Rymer's comment, Perrault insisted that such was women's role. When his "president" rejected feminine judgment as arbiter of taste, Perrault's surrogate, the abbé, instantly jumped in. Whether women's taste should be absolute he could not say, but "it at least gives our cause great likelihood. We know the exactness of their discernment for fine and delicate things. The feeling they have for what is clear, lively, natural and of common sense [*le bon sens*]; and their immediate distaste at the sight of anything obscure, dull, strained and involved." Women would no doubt not be the only arbiters of taste, but they would be principal.[58] Their good sense was natural, their feel for the beautiful and fine immediate, instinctive, and artless. As Marie-Anne de Lambert, raised to seventeenth-century ideas (1647–1733), would say: "Accuracy of taste judges what is called charm, sentiment, seemliness, delicacy, or very flower of wit."[59]

The connection of such arguments to the nurturing and engendering ideals already noted appears obvious enough. The scholar Elstob soon confirmed it, justifying her work on Anglo-Saxon with the claim: "The language we speak is our Mother-Tongue; And who so proper to play the Critiks in this as the Females."[60] Behn captured this sense of an innate feminine ability to work through emotion, as well as its supposed unfamiliarity to the masculine mind, when she described Oroonoko's surprising acquistion of it: "He admir'd by what strange Inspiration he came to talk of things so soft, and so passionate, who never knew Love, nor was us'd to the Conversation of Women . . . some new, and, till then, unknown Power instructed his Heart and Tongue."[61]

The novel, indeed, could become the privileged genre for the expression and communication of such ideals. Initially not considered a part of "high" culture (or only sporadically so: *Télémaque* being certainly excep-

[57]Rymer, *Tragedies of the Last Age,* in *Critical Works,* pp. 18, 37.

[58]Perrault, *Parallèle des anciens et des modernes,* 1:30–31, 37–38. R. J. Howells has published a fine analysis of this work: "Dialogue and Speakers in the 'Parallèle des anciens et des modernes,'" *Modern Language Review,* 78, no. 4 (1983), pp. 793–803.

[59]Marie-Anne Thérèse de Marguenat, marquise de Lambert, "Réflexions nouvelles sur les femmes," appendix in Marie-Josée Fassiotto, *Madame de Lambert (1647–1733) ou le féminisme moral* (New York, Berne, and Frankfurt a/M., 1984), pp. 123–44. This quotation, p. 128.

[60]Elizabeth Elstob, *The Rudiments of Grammar for the English-Saxon Tongue* (1715). Quoted by Natalie Zemon Davis, "Gender and Genre: Women as Historical Writers, 1400–1820," in *Beyond Their Sex: Learned Women of the European Past,* ed. Patricia H. Labalme (New York and London, 1980), p. 182 n. 43. The complete text is available as *An Apology for the Study of Northern Antiquities (1715)* [facs. rpt. of the "Preface," pp. i–xxxv of *The Rudiments*], intro. Charles Peake, Augustan Reprint Society, no. 61 (Los Angeles, 1956).

[61]Aphra Behn, *Oroonoko, or the Royal Slave,* ed. Lore Metzger (New York and London, 1973), p. 10.

tional), it was available as a kind of "empty field," as a space on the margins of the dominant culture available for "occupation" by those excluded from the production of that culture.[62] Josephine Donovan writes that "this attitude kept male writers of the educated elite from appropriating the novel as 'theirs.' This meant that even though critically disparaged, it was nevertheless a genre which women and other cultural outsiders (less well-educated men) were free to use."[63] There is no irony or paradox in this. For it is in the very nature of cultural dominance to allow such an empty space: readily functioning as a safety valve, as an area of permitted activity, marginalized yet providing a field in which revolt (for example) would be unthinkable—because seemingly unnecessary. One might call it, with some mild mockery of certain contemporary argument, a space of authorized carnival.[64]

Pierre-Daniel Huet had long since hit this to perfection. Like Fontenelle and Chesterfield later, he wrote in 1669 that reading novels was an especially ready way to acquire knowledge, for imagination was a readier instrument than judgment, with its "laborious operations": "Knowledge which attracts and charms [the soul] most is that which it acquires easily and where imagination works almost alone, on matters similar to those ordinarily striking our senses, and especially if this knowledge rouse our passions, which are the prime movers of all desires, actions, and pleasures of life. That is what novels do." That, he said, was why passionate, imaginative, naturally sensitive people were novel readers. "Like children and untrained people," they are struck particularly by the "fictions themselves." In his day, he concluded, France had become the great producer of novels, unequaled by any: due, no doubt, "to the great freedom in which men live . . . with women." It was not surprising, therefore, that women were in fact the principal readers "de cette lecture si délicieuse" and had produced their greatest author, Madeleine de Scudéry, who, by the time of Huet's treatise, had taken to writing such shorter novels (than *Clélie* and *Cyrus*) as *Célinte* (1661), *Mathilde d'Aguilar* (1667), and *Celanire* (1669).[65]

---

[62]Catharine R. Stimpson, "Female Insubordination and the Text," in *Women in Culture and Politics: A Century of Change,* ed. Judith Friedlander, Blanche Wiesen Cook, Alice Kessler-Harris, Carroll Smith-Rosenberg (Bloomington, Ind., 1986), p. 166.

[63]Josephine Donovan, "The Silence Is Broken," in *Women and Language in Literature and Society,* ed. Sally McConnell-Ginet, Ruth Borker, Nelly Furman (New York, 1980), pp. 209–10.

[64]See my *Uncertainty of Analysis,* pp. 135–52.

[65]Pierre-Daniel Huet, *Lettre-traité sur l'origine des romans . . .* suivie de *La lecture des vieux romans par Jean Chapelain,* ed. Fabienne Gégou (Paris, 1971), pp. 132, 139; Madeleine de Scudéry, *Célinte, nouvelle première,* ed. Alain Niderst (Paris, 1979). In his 1667 *Bibliothèque françoise* (1st ed. 1664), Charles Sorel praised *Célinte* as "a serious and most beautiful novel, believed to be from the pen of one of the most excellent women [*filles*] ever to have written, and that is Mademoiselle de Scudery" (p. 180). In his later work, *De la connoissance des bons livres, ou examen de plusieurs auteurs* (Amsterdam, 1672), Sorel first made a slashing attack on contemporary novels (pp. 113–59) and then a much shorter—and distinctly qualified—defense (pp. 159–76), whose conclusion was that novels needed to be approached with considerable care and hesitation.

A century later Barbauld would still present just the same arguments. And indeed, these late seventeenth-century disputes had more or less sealed *all* the terms for at least two centuries. She wrote that novels were received with "universal applause" because they were easy to understand. Writers of other kinds of texts had to have a narrower audience because they required trained knowledge and reasoning: "Few can reason, but all can feel; and many who cannot enter into an argument, may yet listen to a tale." Further, the "romance" writer "has even an advantage over those who endeavour to amuse by play of fancy; who, from the fortuitous collision of dissimilar ideas, produce the scintillations of wit." For novelists dealt with "common life," with "events to which all are liable," treating "passions which all have felt." Above all, they "please the imagination and interest the heart." In a slightly later letter to her brother (1774), we learn that women must be the most immediate such readers, for men are naturally cold, "haughty," and not yet "sensible to all the delicacies of sentiment"—only passion can lead them to this. Women, however, "are naturally inclined not only to love, but to all the soft and gentle affections; all the tender and kind sympathies of nature."[66]

With that, I think, we may mark the end of these debates. Ideal consumers of high culture, admitted producers of subordinate cultural artifacts (short novels, fairy tales, letters), women now had their role essentially set for a long time to come. However much it might still be subject to occasional debate, Richard Steele's remarks in *The Tatler* of 1710 captured a new consensus—and its very tone—to perfection: "I am sure, I do not mean it an injury to women, when I say there is a sort of sex in souls. I am tender of offending them, and know it is hard not to do it on this subject; but I must go on to say, that the soul of a man and that of a woman are made very unlike, according to the employments for which they are designed. The ladies will please to observe, I say, our minds have different, not superior qualities to theirs. The virtues have respectively a masculine and a feminine cast."[67] Such views would remain standard at least through the Enlightenment, expressed by liberal and conservative thinkers alike. Among the former, Condorcet's views are quite familiar. One of the latter, Justus Möser of Osnabrück, also wrote in the early 1780s, to the poet and novelist Sophie von La Roche: "It is not a bad trade to have received a bit more heart than brain [as a woman]. The former contains the sum of all total impressions which nature or the things themselves have made in us. The latter, on the other hand, contains nothing more than we can think or express."[68] At the start of the next century Hannah More's ideal wife, Lucilla, must never be the source of any original or witty phrase, of any

---

[66]Barbauld, *Works*, 2:171–75, 3–4.

[67]Sir Richard Steele, *The Tatler*, ed. George A. Aitken, 4 vols. (London, 1898), 3:304 (no. 172, May 16, 1710).

[68]Quoted in Jonathan B. Knudsen, *Justus Möser and the German Enlightenment* (Cambridge, 1986), p. 162.

"things to be quoted," for while she is a "nice judge of the genius of others," she is not at all "a genius herself."[69]

Judges of good sense and right reason, swiftly disgusted by anything of doubtful morality, immediately and instinctively apprized of the beautiful, women had become the ideal subordinate subjects of the authority of the now more-or-less stable liberal state (in both the political and psychological sense of the word "subject"). Now excluded from high cultural production, they had been permitted a presence as its audience. Unable and unsuited to engage in forceful origination of cultural products, women were nonetheless the ideal consumers of these products: at once within and outside the dominant cultural group. That situation made women essential to the group's activities and products (of which they were "allowed" to create "subordinate" ones) and guaranteed its dominance. The simultaneous debates about the nature of literature and the status of women were thus essential to the establishment of what we still think of as literature and to one aspect of a set of sociocultural power relations that also still remains, by and large, in place.

The grand project of general human Reason had been defeated. There were now a man's reason and a woman's reason, qualitatively different. Each was certainly a reason rather than an unreason. Yet that simply made the distinction the more invidious. Women were included, but as second-class citizens. Consumers of the dominant masculine literary culture, they could nonetheless have their little corner to themselves. When English women started to produce large quantities of writing after the lapse of the Licensing Act in 1695, it was principally chapbooks and diaries, letters, and novels aimed, we see, specifically at women: a whole "subculture" of literary production. Women were not excluded from literary culture (a dangerous proposition), but the point was that men dictated "the criteria of achievement."[70] When Wollstonecraft dared argue a century later that women did share the same rationality as men, that therefore they should have equal rights of productive access to the dominant culture (up to a point, anyway), she swiftly drew down on herself the savage wrath of such as Horace Walpole, Hannah More, and Richard Polwhele. She was by no means an isolated voice (Mary Ann Radcliffe was a particularly strong one), but she was herself caught in many of the difficulties caused by an internalization of this "separate but equal" doctrine. Women (as audience) were now "safely" excluded from culture in just the same way as they were disenfranchised by the law.

The difference between male and female reason given credence in the late seventeenth century by such as Boileau and Perrault, La Bruyère and Swift, Malebranche and Spence was quickly and entirely consecrated. The novel was held to deal especially with the sentiments and affections

---

[69]Hannah More, *Coelebs in Search of a Wife*, in *Works*, 2:79–80.
[70]Pat Rogers, *The Augustan Vision* (London, 1978), p. 98.

because such affairs were supposed to be particularly suited to female instinctual reason.[71] *That* was a way of recuperating and subduing Reason in women by making it qualitatively different from, and inferior to, Reason in men. In various forms of writing, there was during the eighteenth century an "increased female participation in literary culture," but it was clearly held to be subordinate and secondary. Throughout these years we find an ever-increasing "use of literature to maintain a restrictive status quo."[72]

In Chapter 4 I mentioned how the example of Sparta became something of a constant motif with regard to the equality of men and women. We may therefore with some interest see how that case was turned toward the subordination I have been tracing. In Descartes and others, Spartan rule was used with entire approbation. Even when (in 1647) Le Moyne found Lycurgus reprehensible for having abandoned Spartan women "to public and authorized disorder, to freedoms founded upon exception and built into custom," he was soon answered by Suchon, quoting a legendary Spartan woman who, asked what she knew, replied: "I know nothing but how to be free." Suchon glossed this by adding that it allowed "us to see that women yield nothing to men in strength and generosity of mind— even though their freedom is always flouted."[73] Throughout the period we have been examining, Lacedemonian polity was held to have treated men and women alike (this being adjudged a good or a bad thing according to varying opinion). By and large, interest was in "the Spartan heroines."[74]

By 1790 Catharine Macaulay had changed this rather considerably: "Bodily strength was the chief object of Spartan discipline. Their cares on the subject began with the birth of their offspring; and instead of entailing the curse of feebleness on their women for the sake of augmenting their personal beauty, they endeavoured to improve their natural strength, in order to render them proper nurses for a race of heroes."[75] From a training to entire equality to one of ideal maternity, it would clearly be but a short step to complete futility. In 1868 (and so nearly contemporaneously with the texts mentioned in note 77), the Belgian doctor Hyack Kuborn wrote in a report on women miners commissioned by his government (telling us

[71]Georges May, *Le dilemme du roman au xviiie siècle: Étude sur les rapports du roman et de la critique (1715–1761)* (New Haven, 1963), pp. 204–45.

[72]Kathryn Shevelow, "Fathers and Daughters: Women as Readers of *The Tatler*," in *Gender and Reading: Essays on Readers, Texts, and Contexts,* ed. Elizabeth A. Flynn and Patrocinio P. Schweickart (Baltimore, 1986), pp. 121–22. See also Jean E. Hunter, "The Eighteenth-Century Englishwoman: According to the Gentleman's Magazine," in *Women in the Eighteenth Century and Other Essays,* ed. Paul Fritz and Richard Morton (Toronto, 1976), pp. 73–88. Great "sympathy" was shown to women in the *Gentleman's Magazine,* says Hunter, but that, of course, was precisely how the subordination succeeded.

[73]Le Moyne, *Gallerie,* p. aaij^ro; Suchon, *Traité,* p. 66.

[74]Elizabeth Rawson, *The Spartan Tradition in European Thought* (Oxford, 1969), pp. 202–9.

[75]Macaulay, *Letters,* pp. 24–25.

a lot about the possible practical results of the developments explored here): "However it may be, the andromaniacal daughters of Lacedemonia wrestling on Mount Taygetus never achieved the equanimity, robustness and powerful energy of the Spartan men."[76]

All this is to say, as I have been increasingly suggesting by references to eighteenth-century authors who generally adopted the assumptions elaborated in some detail by the late seventeenth century, that by and large these underlying assumptions would no longer change in any essential way for at least two or more centuries. Developments there would be, but attitudes and claims would remain virtually the same.[77] One other example is telling on this score: the apparently changed views on Dutch women. By the late 1770s, when Diderot compiled his *Voyage en Hollande* from various sources, he replaced praise of Dutch women's literacy, modesty, learning, and managerial skills with a more ordinary misogyny. Dutch women, the *encyclopédiste* was concerned to note, were so ugly that one had no desire "to verify the reputation of their bosom and to get to know their other charms." Such schoolboy salaciousness was altogether in place in a work devoted wholly to men's activities, where women served the police as decoys and husbands and families as objects of exchange or settings for the display of wealth.[78] In Diderot's report, they had become *too* economical and *obsessively* clean.[79]

[76]Hyack Kuborn, report to the Belgian government, 1868, pp. 8–9. Kuborn's main source was the ideologue Pierre-Jean-Georges Cabanis. Mine is Patricia J. Hilden, "Women in Coal Mines: Belgium's *hiercheuses*, 1890–1914," unpublished lecture, 1986–87. See, too, her *Social History of Belgium: Women, Work and Politics, 1830–1914* (Oxford, forthcoming), esp. chap. 5.

[77]In the mid-nineteenth century, for example, Charles Darwin produced a curious and quite offensive imitation of La Bruyère. In a footnote whose Latinity is, as far as I know, unique, he presented a case "proving" that male apes distinguish and are attracted to women: "Mares e diversis generibus Quadrumanorum sine dubio dignoscunt feminas humanas a maribus. Primum, credo, odoratu, postea aspectu. . . . Illustrissimus Cuvier etiam narrat multa de hâc re, quâ ut opinor, nihil turpius potest indicari inter omnia hominibus et Quadrumanis communia (The males of various kinds of primates without question distinguish human females from males. First, I think, by smell, then by sight. . . . The celebrated Cuvier has also said much about this, than which nothing worse can be shown among all those things common to humans and primates). That Darwin put his note in Latin, and that it clearly equated primate and human females as biologically determined objects of male sexual appetite, suggests strongly that the note and its language refer not so subliminally to the old principle commonly expressed as "mulier propter uterum id est quod est (because of her uterus, that is what a woman is)" (whose neuter grammar itself marks an objectification): Darwin, *The Descent of Man*, in *The Origin of Species by Means of Natural Selection . . .* and *The Descent of Man and Selection in Relation to Sex* (New York, n.d.), p. 397n. Sociobiological claims are not, it would appear, very new. But a few years later Havelock Ellis, that supposed supporter of suffrage and much else besides, wrote that "nature has made women more like children, in order that they may better understand and care for children" (quoted in Ruth Brandon, *The New Women and the Old Men: Love, Sex, and the Woman Question* [London, 1990], p. 104). La Bruyère, Boileau, and the rest cast a long shadow.

[78]Denis Diderot, *Voyage en Hollande*, ed. Yves Benot (Paris, 1982), pp. 38, 75–77, 83, 91–92.

[79]Ibid., p. 91.

Just a decade earlier James Boswell had likewise spent some time in Holland. When he chose to speak of women, it concerned whom he should "have" as a wife (a woman who could at least "read and talk" and "entertain your friends"), his many flirtations, and whether he could persuade a female friend to "have the goodness to" sew up the crotch of his breeches. He found it fitting to dwell at length on the humor of this last proposition.[80] His views and attitude, that is to say, differed hardly a jot from Diderot's. Indeed, responding to a friend's epistolary commendation of Catherine Macaulay's just-published history of James and Charles I (recalling Samuel Johnson's derision of her "republicanism"), he linked scorn for her with rejection of any favorable tradition regarding Dutch women:

> Men must not still in politics give law;
> No, Kate Macaulay too her pen must draw,
> That odious *thing*, a monarch, to revile,
> And drawl of freedom till ev'n Johnson smile.
> Like a Dutch *vrouw* all shapeless, pale, and fat,
> That hugs and slabbers her ungainly brat,
> Our Cath'rine sits sublime o'er steaming tea
> And takes her dear Republic on her knee;
> Sings it all songs that ever yet were sung,
> And licks it fondly with her length of tongue.[81]

This doggerel exactly fit the post-Boileau tradition. Misogyny was integral to the issue of cultural participation. Boswell ridiculed the Bluestockings' literary and philosophical claims as idle gossip ("sublime o'er steaming tea"), derided their literary abilities as so much babytalk ("sings it all songs"), and dismissed Macaulay's own title to being a historian, rejecting above all her right to participate in political debate. His view was certainly strengthened by the fact that her history was written explicitly against Hume's Tory history of the same period and that her strongly expressed Whig views challenged Johnson's and Boswell's allegiances. Politics, reason, literature, and the status of women remained fixed in a kind of grotesquely rigid dance. Its references seemed drawn from a commonly developed stock, and its meanings barely appeared to change.

In a play begun during the Glorious Revolution, finished in the early years of Queen Anne's reign, and finally performed with many cuts only under George I, Thomas Southerne summed up many of these issues. *The Spartan Dame* put on stage an ambitious Cleombrotus (William of Orange) and a loyal Spartan, Celona (Mary), daughter of King Leonidas. The

---

[80]James Boswell, *Boswell in Holland, 1763–1764,* Including his Correspondence with Belle de Zuylen (Zélide), ed. Frederick A. Pottle (New York, London, and Toronto, 1952), pp. 24, 29, 59–60.

[81]Ibid., pp. 77–79. In a note, Pottle gratuitously remarks that Macaulay "was the object of a good deal of ridicule, not all unjustified." Plus ça change. . . .

former wants to depose Leonidas. Like Corneille's Livie, Celona claims the right as his wife to persuade him against revolt, not to replace a hereditary monarch by an "elected" one.[82] In this play, however, the plea is unsuccessful. Leonidas is deposed and Cleombrotus duly declared king. Now, says a citizen, everyone will be equal, as in the days of Lycurgus, who "was a wise Man, and lov'd the People. In his Days we were all equal." Maybe we were, chimes in another, but "those were Times indeed." Now all are "rascals," matters are sadly decayed, Lycurgus's golden age is gone (I.i.304–11). Torn between her husband and father, Celona laments that she cannot plead the former's case, "a Theme for *Athenian* song [tragedy]" and one that "fits the Virtue of a *Spartan* Wife" (II.i.215–16)—a constantly repeated motif: with her "*Spartan* spirit," she says, she will leave Cleombrotus and mourn Leonidas. Obedient to her husband and loyal to her father, she will be "a *Spartan* daughter" and "a *Spartan* wife" (III.iv.27–29). *Cinna* has been reversed.

In the meantime, Cleombrotus has had enough of Celona and lusts after her sister Thelamia, chastely married to honest Eurytion, whom he now plans to kill. He does this and rapes Thelamia. Leonidas eventually comes back and succeeds in having Cleombrotus killed. The multitudinous voices of the masses are stilled; revolt, murder, rape, and faction come to an end. Leonidas, one of those "*Spartan* Kings / Deriv'd from the rich Blood of *Hercules*" (I.i.105–6), has at last cut off the hydra's head, as so many years before Garnier's Marc-Antoine had hoped to do (see above, p. 57).

The play thus marked the nostalgic memory of a Spartan golden age by recalling a far closer and more actual violent history: that of sixteenth- and seventeenth-century rebellions and wars, to be sure, but also of more recent battles, such as those for which Boileau could seek an author to write a new *Aeneid*, recounting the approach of a new Hercules to the banks of a trembling Rhine; or the yet closer horror of the 1685 Revocation, when Racine, in his speech written for the abbé Colbert before the event, spoke of reducing a "hydra," and Fontenelle, after it, wrote of faith having "tamed the hundred-headed hydra."[83]

Like Antoinette Deshoulières a little later, Scudéry might well be granted (in 1683) a royal *pension* of 2,000 livres.[84] But in vain would she turn Boileau's own image against him: "Were I fated . . . to be an exterminator of vices, as fabled Hercules was of monsters, I would start with defamation [*médisance*]," for, she wrote, "no vice is so contrary to char-

[82]Thomas Southerne, *The Spartan Dame,* in *The Works,* ed. Robert Jordan and Harold Love, 2 vols. (Oxford, 1988), 2:273–351. This citation: I.i.101–5.

[83]Boileau, "Art poétique," in *Oeuvres complètes,* p. 185 (Chant IV). Racine's text was referred to above. The Fontenelle reference is from *Économistes-financiers du xviiie siècle,* ed. Eugène Daire, vol. 1 (Paris, 1843), p. 3 n. 2.

[84]Alain Niderst, *Madeleine de Scudéry, Paul Pellisson et leur monde* (Paris, 1976), p. 509.

ity" in the religious sphere and none "so cowardly and dangerous" in the purely human.[85] For her part, Antoinette-Thérèse Deshoulières would compete equally vainly with Virgil. Southerne, Boileau, and Fontenelle, all male, simply took the Virgilian, Herculean clichés for granted. Southerne further took for granted the brave but feminine woman, who knew her place as wife and daughter, and the recreation of a stable polity under a legitimate monarch. In his dedication to the duke of Argyle and Greenwich, even court and camp returned. All these things were by now clichés: but that was precisely what gave them strength in this eminently political play. The maintenance of the polity depended on the right use of these various terms: literature's task was to observe the rectitude of norms whose force was that all agreed with them. It was not indifferent that Sparta became, here, their bond. The violence of forced subordination (long since expounded by such as Gournay, and more recently by Poulain, Suchon, Drake, and Astell) was made quite clear in this play. If the horrors of witch hunts had once been one way to make sure outsiders did not encroach on the realm of power, whether in the church's efforts to hang on to it (of which the *Malleus maleficarum* was sufficient evidence) or in a new bourgeoisie's efforts to obtain it (as Bodin's 1580 *Démonomanie des sorciers* had suggested), clearly as physical violence died, so oppression could no longer take so unambiguous a shape. Colbert's final abolition of witch trials in 1682 was exactly contemporary with the intellectuals' establishment of other kinds of subordination and exclusion.[86]

In this dramatic establishment women as subordinate audience had a very clear part. Leonidas's three daughters played wholly emblematic roles. Thelamia poisoned herself after being raped by Cleombrotus. Celona withdrew to a nunnery. Luckily for their father, a third daughter, Euphemia, remained to give him support in his old age—although he "had forgot [her] in the Crowd / Of busy Fate" (V.i.232–33: shades of La Bruyère—indeed, she had not previously appeared). Restored to his crown, with a last daughter to look after him (as Cordelia was to care for Lear in Tate's more popular Restoration version of that play), paternally to take care of his people's freedoms, he could look forward to a new "posterity of happy Times" (as Celona put it). With her sister "happily" dead (V.i.190), herself in a convent, and Euphemia playing the role of dutiful daughter, Celona now announced "the Promise of the Year," suggesting that "a golden harvest rises to [their] Hopes" (V.i.245–46):

> So shall her gentle Influence cheer Mankind,
> And ripen this into an Age of Gold.
> *Saturnian* Days may then again return,
> And e'en *Celona*'s Griefs forget to mourn.
>
> (V.i.250–51)

[85]Scudéry, "Médisance," in *Choix de conversations*, p. 142.
[86]See Chapter 5, note 20, above.

This was a profoundly subdued golden age, akin to that of Dryden or Fénelon (who had remarked, at the end of *Télémaque*, that all the hero then needed was to find his father and to "obtain a wife worthy of the golden age"). Its "winners" and "losers," victors and vanquished, were clear. We have come a long way from Sidney's *Arcadia* or even Livie's hope for a new golden age. Yet there was a consolidated polity, a sense of rational strength, a claim of ethical norm, and an organized literary culture. The producers and organizers of all four were established. So, too, were its appropriate consumers.

It is no accident that within a generation, Alexander Gottlieb Baumgarten would write a thesis whose eventual culmination (in 1750) would be the establishment of a new science of Aesthetics. In his 1735 "Reflections on Poetry" (*Meditationes philosophicae de nonnullis ad poema pertinentibus*), he set out the basis for such a science as would describe the kind of perfection proper to the "lower" faculty of perception and sensation, as Logic sought (he said) to describe the "higher" faculty of thought (reason). Baumgarten had doubtless taken his cue from Du Bos's 1719 *Réflexions*. "The soul," wrote the abbé, "has its needs as does the body; and one of man's greatest needs is that the mind be busied." There were two ways of doing this: "Either the soul gives itself up to the impressions made on it [*elle*, of course] by external objects; and we call this feeling [*sentir*]: or it [*elle*] busies itself with speculating on useful or curious matters; and we call this reasoning and thinking [*réfléchir & méditer*]." The first, he wrote, was entirely inferior to the difficult second and simply responded to the need to satisfy our passions: "for people [*les hommes*] generally suffer yet more from living without passions, than passions make them suffer."[87]

It was not Du Bos, of course, who had made the distinction, as we have quite sufficiently seen. He merely codified it at the very outset of what became an enormously influential text. Baumgarten then sought to make a science of the "lower" faculty that found its ideal fulfillment in women (said common accord), best critics and appreciators of beauty, arbiters of loveliness and fine taste, most percipient of that *je ne sais quoi* that would become the Sublime of eighteenth-century philosophical aesthetics. The entire process could thus be universalized. To be sure, Baumgarten did not say as much, but the division between Logic and Aesthetic was exactly that traced out by those distinctions we have been examining between the male reason productive of cultural artifacts and the female reason that judged and consumed them. Neither Boswell nor Diderot, and certainly not Hume or Burke or Kant, would be saying or implying anything at all

---

[87]Alexander Gottlieb Baumgarten, *Reflections on Poetry/Meditationes philosophicae de nonnullis ad poema pertinentibus*, trans. and ed. Karl Aschenbrenner and William B. Holther (Berkeley and Los Angeles, 1954). Du Bos, *Réflexions*, 1:6–7, 12. Baumgarten's thesis led directly to its expansion in the same author's *Aesthetica* (Frankfurt a/d. Oder, 1750; rpt. Hidlesheim and New York, 1970).

different. Not surprisingly, such women as Macaulay or La Roche, as Barbauld or More, found themselves at least accepting, and not seldom propounding, a like view.

As that internalization itself suggests, the establishment of aesthetics as "science," and indeed of cultural order more generally, inevitably depended on a universalization and a fixing of criteria and matter taken to surpass any parochial case. It was necessary to exceed the local. People had to fit Dryden's "superstructure" into a universal scheme. Readers and producers could not be only locally important. Literary science and cultural order needed, depended on, generalization. Its apostles had thus to forge and to establish a tradition.

Chapter 8

Inventing the Tradition

By ancient Writings Knowledge is convey'd
Of famous Arts the best Foundation laid;
By these the Cause of Liberty remains,
Are Nations free'd from Arbitrary Chains,
From Errors still our Church is purified,
The State maintain'd, with Justice on its Side.
                    —Daniel Defoe, *A Vindication of the Press*

From the beginning of this work, I have been arguing that during the second half of the sixteenth century and the first third of the seventeenth there developed both a real and a felt series of disjunctions: within a social order riven by violence, certainly, but also of society from the divine, of knowledge from the world, of poetic and rhetorical practice from political and cultural needs. I claimed that this development was common to central and southern Europe as well as to north and west. In the particular case of poetics, I tried to show that sixteenth-century debate was characterized by a consensus on its *distance* from reality, however defined, and by a growing sense of the poet's authority.[1] I then sought to

[1]The phrase "however defined" is essential: what is held to be real evidently engages a whole network of concepts. The central medieval concept of *fabula*, for example, defining fictive writing as a speculative integument to be pierced or stripped for access to some inner divine meaning, assumes the reality of such meaning. To post-sixteenth-century writers, such a relationship marked a distance from the real. It could not conceivably do so for medieval thinkers, for whom the divine was wholly immanent. For them, *fabula* was the way to a wisdom having to do not with the physical or the social, but with hidden truths of the divine order as they were "immanent in the universe" (Peter Dronke, *Fabula: Explorations into the Uses of Myth in Medieval Platonism*, Mittellateinische Studien und Texte, 9 [Leiden and Cologne, 1974], pp. 6–7, 32, and passim). On this, see also A. J. Minnis and A. B. Scott, with David Wallace, eds., *Medieval Literary Theory and Criticism, c. 1110–c. 1375: The Commentary Tradition* (Oxford: 1988), esp. pp. 119–22. One need only measure the difference between such *fabula* and Descartes's *fable* (true, not speculative; objectively verifiable in nature; a rational, systematic, logical order whose coherence, even identity, with the natural world was ultimately taken as demonstrable) to realize that "distance" is not always the same thing. In Chapter 1, I suggested that the passage from the immanent to the transcendent itself signaled a distancing not evident in texts alone: as who should think it would be (except maybe literary critics)? I should also note that I am not speaking here of the historians' "general crisis" (of which this would be a simplistic version). On this, see in my bibliography (part 2), not so much Rabb, as the essays in the three collections

show the complex elaboration of "literature" both as a reply to that sense of disjunction and as a main element in the formation, consolidation, and order of something like a new social compact, itself dependent, among other things, on new forms of authority.

Such authority, of course, would be much less effective were it understood as the result of a development of parochial interests and concerns. Its validity had to be universal and ubiquitous. Indeed, as we saw, the arguments made about human nature, taste, truth, literary art, and the rest assumed such universality and ubiquity. Similarly, literature needed to conceal its particular elaboration and its local habitation. Besides, as I hope to have made clear, the disjunctions were by no means entire. However radical the development may have been, it *was* a development and not some kind of rupture—as my many references to Virgil should have implied. If Frederick Garber is right that the surface wholeness of pastoral, for example, *always* masks a subterranean sense of loss, retreat, and failure, the presence of those effects in Theocritus and Virgil would have been the very reason why that poetic (and rhetorical) mode would be taken up again in a time and a place of desperate unease.[2] Such texts certainly survived partly by practical accident of transmission, but once there, they could be appropriately used for any suitable purpose.

A "literature" claiming universality, asserting the thinking it embodied to be that of general human reason, its moral values to be good for all humanity everywhere and always, the political order it helped sustain to be the wisest and most legitimate so far achieved in the way of human progress, its standard of taste to be as valid for the Chinese as for the Jivaro, for the Greek as for the modern European, had necessarily to demonstrate that it was a natural outcome of artistic development—of the same fundamental kind wherever it may be found. Hence the importance of being able to use certain surviving texts (whose kind is largely fortuitous: classical scholars have estimated that 90 percent of the texts of Graeco-Latin antiquity have not survived). It must, that is to say, invent its tradition and create a canon of which it is the natural and proper successor and descendant. Late seventeenth-century writers were fully aware of this need. They set out to fill it.

This chapter examines the naming of that tradition (as "literature") and its semantic enrichment (notably through the use made of *Télémaque*). It goes on to explore two of the principal cases in the establishment of a canon, two that became genuinely foundational. The first is the Homeric

---

by Aston, Hilton, and Parker and Smith (chiefly on political and economic matters). For later debate and developments, see Aston and Philpin (mostly economic and demographic issues). My remarks here concern rather how people expressed feelings and reactions.

[2] Frederick Garber, "Pastoral Spaces," *Texas Studies in Literature and Language*, 30 (1988), 431–60. That such pastoral poetry *was* taken up again was, of course, because of, according to the present argument, local sociopolitical needs.

epics (*Télémaque's* connection with these is no accident), and the second is the Shakespearean corpus. I do not discuss here the case of Virgil, although it has been and will be mentioned. This absence is not because the "invention" of a modern Virgilian tradition could not be demonstrated equally well. Indeed, in all its complexity, Frank Kermode long since addressed that issue in reply to T. S. Eliot.[3] Further to discuss the Virgilian corpus would stretch this chapter unnecessarily, since the cases of Homer and Shakespeare seem convincing enough. But nor do I wish the constant mention of Virgil to imply that his poems somehow escaped the invention of tradition. I hope instead that they will lend a needed ambiguity: that invention is always accompanied by, and making use of, forms of continuity. A tradition would doubtless function improperly if it could not use precisely that ambivalence.

Eric Hobsbawm has written that cultural traditions may be deliberately and quickly developed and instituted or may rather establish themselves slowly in a "less easily traceable manner." Even so, their development occurs "within a brief and dateable period." He provides a variety of examples of swiftly established traditions, from Britain's Royal Christmas broadcast to the rituals of the Boy Scout movement, from the construction of Nazi symbolism to the wearing of wigs by lawyers in England. Others in the collection these remarks introduce analyze slower establishments: of Scots Highland culture in the eighteenth century, of a Welsh past more recently, of supposedly age-old British monarchical ceremonial in the nineteenth century, and so on. One can easily see how varied and multiple, how broad and narrow such traditions may be. All have in common that they are demonstrably datable inventions. Hobsbawm adds: "They seem to belong to three overlapping types: a) those establishing or symbolizing social cohesion or the membership of groups, real or artificial communities, b) those establishing or legitimizing institutions, status or relations of authority, and c) those whose main purpose was socialization, the inculcation of beliefs, value systems and conventions of behaviour."[4]

Certainly, if one understands society as an accumulation of "discourses" (different types of signifying practices), then to the extent their inception is visible, cultures invent a tradition for each and every discursive sphere. Most discourse no doubt develops so slowly as better to fit the designation of custom than that of tradition. Some, however, are so speedily developed and enveloped in ritual forms as to fit Hobsbawm's suggested definition rather closely: Galilean science was probably one such. The invention of literature, I want to show, was a particularly striking modern case. At its

---

[3]John Frank Kermode, *The Classic* (London, 1975). Nor do I discuss the case of *Paradise Lost*, comparable in some ways to that of Shakespeare. On this, see, e.g., Leslie E. Moore, *Beautiful Sublime: The Making of "Paradise Lost," 1701–1734* (Stanford, Calif., 1990).

[4]Eric Hobsbawm, "Introduction: Inventing Traditions," in Hobsbawm and Terence Ranger, eds., *The Invention of Tradition* (Cambridge, 1983), pp. 1, 9.

datable outset in late seventeenth-century France and England, literature clearly satisfied all Hobsbawm's criteria. It symbolized membership in a particular educated and leisured group in close—indeed, essential—contact with ruling authority, whose institutions it partly legitimized and guaranteed. We have already seen how it fulfilled both these criteria, as well as the third. By now there can surely be no doubt that its purpose was avowedly "the inculcation of beliefs, value systems and conventions of behaviour." Since literature also led slowly to expanding literacy, it can certainly be said to have sought to socialize: in the terms and at the service of now recognized forms of authority.[5]

Nevertheless, however clear the nature of that invention might be, it had as yet no clear name. For, first, we must distinguish the "literary" from such (earlier) categories as those of the "poetical" or the "rhetorical." The modern concept of literature was born simultaneously with a professional and semiprofessional criticism: Bouhours, Rymer, Rapin, Boileau, Dryden, Dacier, Dennis, Addison, and all those others we have seen. Even a Grub Street hack like Charles Gilden would now be able to make his (precarious) living in large part from his writing of "literary" criticism: editions of letters and essays, accounts of the English poets, an edition of Buckingham's *Essay on Poetry,* editions of Aphra Behn, commentaries of Shakespeare, a biography of Wycherley, a *Complete Art of Poetry,* and probably best known of all, a scathing attack on *Robinson Crusoe.* None of this was at all possible until something was called, and practiced as, literature.

The changes in the meaning of the very word are thus not just instructive. They are essential. For Cicero and Tacitus, *literatura* merely meant writing or the alphabet. Quintilian used the word to refer to what we would call grammar or philology. By the time of the early church fathers it signified rather a general erudition (in Tertullian, for example, in the second century). This meaning lasted throughout the European Middle Ages and into the Renaissance, at which time the term gradually came to mean less general learning than a broad knowledge of a particular area of learning (as in such modern usage as "the scientific" or "the sociological" *literature*). As we saw in Chapter 1 (e.g., Polydore Vergil and Mylaeus), the term long kept all three senses. By the mid-eighteenth century the word had acquired a wholly new dimension of meaning. To Johnson, it meant "polite" or "humane" culture, involving making what *we* call "works of

---

[5]Lest there be confusion on this matter, let me add again that I do not at all intend this enumeration to be pejorative. I take it as a fact that these establishments occur. Their value lies in their enabling or disabling consequences. It seems to me unquestionable that for at least two centuries the former far outweighed the latter. Nor, I insist, do inventions of tradition imply cultural relativism. The very fact that they can and do make repetitive use of artifacts drawn from a variety of other traditions suggests that the accessibility of such artifacts to the wealth of meanings and implications that thereby accrue to them is itself a human value beyond any particular tradition.

literature": works having formal beauty and emotional effect, as the *OED* has it. But the *OED* itself called on Johnson's 1755 *Dictionary* for its definition. There its editors found *belles lettres* defined as "polite literature," *polite* defined as "elegant of manners," and *literature* as "learning; skill in letters." These definitions had a circularity to which Johnson put a stop by quoting Addison's *Freeholder*, no. 377 (1716): "When men of learning are acted by a knowledge of the world, they give a reputation to *literature*, and convince the world of its usefulness." This combination of knowledge and urbanity formed, as we have by now sufficiently seen, the very crux of the matter, and elegant "usefulness" was essential.

Lionel Gossman has remarked, respecting an analysis of the role played by literature in nineteenth-century education, that although "it would be tedious to quote dictionary definitions," they bore out Matthew Arnold's view that the broader senses of the term retained important currency even so late.[6] That is certainly so, but my point concerns its new meaning—and it cannot be stressed sufficiently strongly that it was *entirely* new. Here definitions are not cause for tedium, because they reflect a major transformation. Indeed, they come close to demonstrating the invention itself. For at the beginning of the seventeenth century the term often had no separate semantic place at all. In Jean Nicot's important 1606 *Thresor de la langue francoyse*, neither literature nor letters (in the later sense of belles lettres) occurred, although *poësie* and *poëte* were both to be found. In Junius's *Nomenclator* of the same year, the term *literatura* was absent, but one could find *literatus* and *literator:* not as separate entries, but respectively under *gramaticus* and *gramatistes* (the last a degenerate *literatus*, like poetaster to poet). In Henry Cockeram's 1623 *Dictionarie*, *literate* and *literature* were defined with admirable brevity, as learned and learning. One could give innumerable identical examples from John Bullokar, Robert Cawdrey, and others.

In the first part of the century, that is to say—and precisely as we would expect—literature retained only its earlier meanings. By the end of the century a dramatic change had occurred. It did so precisely contemporaneously with the quarrels explored in my previous chapter. In the first edition of his *Dictionnaire* (1680), Pierre Richelet had already introduced major elaborations. In the 1690 edition, *literature* was (1) "la science des belles lettres," (2) "honnêtes connoissances" (where "honnête" connoted the "honnêtes gens," the wits), and (3) "Doctrine. Erudition." It could also mean, he wrote, "tout le corps des gens de lettres (the whole body of people of letters)"—only figuratively, he hastened to add. This set of definitions is profoundly interesting: they provide the old meaning, but now entirely inflected by the new. The third was the old alone, but the second, though still broad, added the important qualifier "honnêtes"—the very word

[6]Lionel Gossman, "Literature and Education," *New Literary History*, 13, no. 2 (Winter 1982), 342.

Johnson would later translate as "polite," but translated earlier, as we will see in a moment, as "humane" (the word reproduced in the *OED*).

More should be said of Richelet, however. His first definition, "la science des belles lettres," requires analysis, for "belles lettres" itself was defined as follows: "C'est la connoissance des Orateurs, des Poëtes & des Historiens." That was a narrow definition. It was narrower even than may at first appear. For the eventual consensus of the debates of the period about historiography was that historical writing was a telling of events for a fundamentally moral purpose: it could even be argued that fictional events, provided they were "probable" (*vraisemblable*), might often be more usefully recounted than real ones. For its part, oratory had long since taken an analogous route. Increasingly, "poetry" was assimilating to itself a sense broad enough to include both: finely ordered fictional works providing a polite knowledge of probable realities according to a rational and ethical consensus (usually still in verse). Already entirely different from Nicot, when the assimilation was complete, *that* meaning of "poetry" would take the name "literature."

Richelet was Englished in 1688 by Guy Miege in his *Great French Dictionary*. Although he nowhere acknowledged having done so, Miege simply gave the French author's definitions with their English equivalent. Under the entry "Lettres," we find: "Les Belles Lettres, *cd*. la Connoissance des Orateurs, des Poëtes, & des Historiens, Literature, Learning, humane Learning." This definition embodied in its very form that gradual narrowing of meanings indicated by Richelet. Miege already made that assimilation of belles lettres to literature to be spelled out in the *Dictionnaire de l'Académie Française* of 1718 (although not in the 1694 edition), whose article on "littérature" ended with the phrase, "ce mot regarde proprement les belles lettres (this word properly concerns belles lettres)." The sentence became standard in later editions of that dictionary, as it did, too, in those of Furetière after 1727.

All of this, however pedantic, is important. It becomes yet more so when we begin to broaden our horizons and take in terms that for us belong in the same paradigm. Throughout most of the seventeenth century, for example, *novel* or *nouvel(le)* meant either "new" or, as a noun, "the 168 volumes of the Civil-Law added to the Codex by the Emperor Justinian." Only later did it come to mean "certain small romances." *Romance* itself, once it could be found at all, was a "feigned story"; *roman*, likewise. Until Richelet and Furetière. Richelet gave the following definition: "Nowadays the novel [*le Roman*] is a fiction involving some amorous adventure, written in prose with wit [*avec esprit*] and according to the rules of the epic poem, for the reader's pleasure and instruction."

This was a revealing definition, for the literary status of the *roman* was still theoretically very much in doubt. Yet more instructive is the fact that its definition as fiction coincided with what Richelet said that poetry had come to mean. In the entry defining "poëte," he wrote: "A word coming

from the Greek, and properly meaning *he who makes* [*celui qui fait*]";
now, however, it had come especially to mean "he who invents, pretends
[*celui qui feint*]." This dictionary assimilation of the novel to the literary
and to poetry in a rather narrow sense was of considerable theoretical
importance. Identical considerations were to be found in Furetière in
1690, and he, unlike Richelet, had very definite normative and prescrip-
tive goals. For that reason, it is worth looking at some length at his
definition of *roman*.

Once, he wrote, it meant the most serious of histories. For they were
written in "Roman," the polite language of princely courts. Now, however,
"it only means those fictional books [*livres fabuleux*] containing stories of
love and chivalry, invented to amuse and busy the idle." Still, he continued, "our Moderns have made polite and instructive *novels* [*Romans*],
such as d'Urfé's *Astrée*, Mademoiselle de Scudéry's *Cyrus* and *Clélie*,
Gomberville's *Polexandre*, La Calprenède's *Cléopâtre*, etc." Such a listing,
after his earlier dismissal, reads almost as an attempt to avoid censure. It
especially does so when he then went on to assimilate such novels to the
earlier serious and polite form meant, he said, by the word *roman*: "Fictional poems [*les poëmes fabuleux*] are also to be ranked as *novels*, such as
the *Aeneid* and the *Iliad*. The *Roman* de la Rose is a *roman* in verse.
Ariosto's *Orlando* is a *roman*. In a word, all these fictional [*fabuleuses*] or
rather improbable [*peu vraisemblables*] stories are considered *romans*."
Where Richelet assimilated the novel "up" to the epic, Furetière preferred
rather to assimilate the epic "up" to the novel.

By the time of the *Encyclopédie*, *Télémaque* had become the exemplary
support of this view: a "beau poëme sans vers," as the Chevalier de Jau-
court wrote there in 1765. But he was only copying the earlier 1721 edition
of the *Dictionnaire de Trévoux*, which called it a "poëme en prose" and
added that "it contains nothing able to harm morality, nothing but what
can provide considerable instruction." Indeed, Du Bos had written in his
germinal *Réflexions* (1719), "if the poetry of the style of the novel *Télémaque* had been dull, few people would have finished reading the work, even
though it would have profited them no less. Our praise of a poem thus
depends upon our pleasure in reading it." The argument of this sentence
simply took for granted an assimilation of prose and poetry, while its
structure straightforwardly equated novel and poem.[7] Before Du Bos nothing published had taken *this* identification quite so for granted, however
admired Fénelon's novel had been.

Two things were happening. One was that the nature of the perfect
literary text was gradually being defined (here by means of *Télémaque*—a
matter to which I return). The other was that "poetry" and "poet" were
slowly obtaining a far wider definition. Certainly, the cases just given are
later than the 1680s and even more distant from Davenant and what I
suggested before as his broad use of the words. Once we no longer confine

[7]Du Bos, *Réflexions*, p. 304.

ourselves to dictionaries, however (as my citation from Du Bos suggests), we indeed find this widening occurring earlier. (The 1721 *Trévoux* credited Bouhours with having long since invented the term "littéraire.") This is of the first importance for my argument, for if one can show literature and poetry to be synonymous, what was said about the one clearly applied to the other as well. The very fact that "literature" now meant not just "belles lettres" but also "poetry" in some wide sense was itself indicative of a major change.

The assimilation of novel to epic (*some* novels) was made quite early. The importance of this cannot be overstressed, because in all discussions of poetry, epic was—and continued to be—treated, with tragedy, as the highest form of literary art. By 1701 even Boileau, seeking accommodation with Perrault, could write in praise of modernity—especially of "those prose poems we call *novels*, and of which we have in France examples unable to be esteemed too highly."[8] He certainly had in mind the recently published *Télémaque*, rather than any reappraisal of Scudéry and others. Indeed, at least one writer held against Fénelon himself that he had "learned the secret of crafting fine novels" from La Force and Murat without acknowledgment.[9] It may well be that the abbé Pierre-Valentin Faydit, who made this accusation, was one who deliberately went out of his way to offend establishment figures, but the fact remained that the assimilation of certain novels to poetry and epic required their removal from female authorship.

Such eulogies as Boileau's concealed the very existence—let alone the important role—of women novelists. For better or worse, only novels by male authors could be thought poetry. Already in 1678 Primo Visconti was on record as remarking how the seigneurs d'Urfé were ashamed of their grandfather's having written "le poëme de l'Astrée."[10] L'Héritier, it is true, remarked in the mid-1690s that novels had been brought to their perfection by "l'illustre mademoiselle de Scudéry," writing works that posterity would agree were "véritables poëmes en prose, mais d'une prose aussi éloquente que polie (true poems in prose, and a prose as eloquent as it was polite)."[11] Her voice was a lonely one. It would be echoed by none of the male literary arbiters.

---

[8]Nicolas Boileau-Despréaux, *Lettre à M. Perrault,* in *Oeuvres complètes,* p. 572.
[9]Pierre-Valentin Faydit, *La Télémacomanie ou la censure et critique du roman intitulé, les Aventures de Télémaque fils d'Ulysse* ("Eleuterople," 1700), p. 42: quoted by Fröberg, "Histoire secrète," p. 7. The *Biographie Universelle* called Faydit's work "disgusting satire," noting that he attacked Bossuet's sermons in the same text. Faydit's refusal to discriminate between the two churchmen (see above, Chapter 5, for their disagreements beneath a single, now unique establishment), to take them as other than the embodiment of a single authority, and his apparent protest against the increasingly thorough occultation of women's cultural role seem an apt confirmation of arguments so far advanced.
[10]Primo Visconti, *Mémoires su la cour de Louis XIV (1673–1681),* trans. J. Lemoine (Paris, 1909), quoted by Picard, *Carrière de Jean Racine,* pp. 64–65.
[11]L'Héritier, "Lettre," in Perrault, *Contes de fées,* p. 291.

In the third volume of his *Parallèle* (written in the early 1690s), in the dialogue concerned, precisely, with poetry, Perrault had his chevalier note that if novels could be equated with epic poems, then the arguments of the modernist abbé would gain emphasis and support. The abbé, Perrault's voice, replied: "Since plays written in prose are no less dramatic poems than plays written in verse, why should fictional [*fabuleuses*] stories told in prose not be poems as much as those told in verse. . . . Verses are but an ornament of poetry, very important to be sure, but they are not in the least its essence. Everyone knows what the poet replied to him who asked how he was getting along with his play: It's done, he said, I have only to compose its verses."[12]

The representative of the ancients did not choose to dispute the remark. Indeed, we have already seen these claims accepted by Boileau himself, so-called legislator of Parnassus. For Perrault, verse was reduced to mere ornament, just as poetic artifacts had been with respect to language by Du Bellay in his *Deffense et illustration*. The "essence" of the literary text was something else. To discover elements of this view, we need not await L'Héritier in 1696, Perrault in 1692, or Visconti in 1678. Georges Couton, speaking of Richelieu and the group of *cinq auteurs* who wrote plays collectively, has remarked that versification was the very last point of a play, the story line being the place of true poetic invention. The rest was merely a matter of professional know-how: "In the seventeenth-century, it was thought that once the canvas was fixed, a play was practically completed; only the verses remained to be written, just a small matter. The idea is common; it can be found, for example, in Corneille's *Discours*" of 1660. So, says Couton, "versification is entrusted to professional authors, technicians; I would almost say hacks."[13] By 1692 Perrault was, of course, taking the assumption wholly for granted, since he based his argument about novels on it.

I do not think one can make too much of this. For if verse was just an ornament, then what was the "essence" of "poetry"? If the highest form of poetry could itself be assimilated to a new form of writing called the "novel," then what was *specific* to poetry? If the novel was defined as a story at once *poli* and *instructif*, how did it differ from the nature of literature more generally: as humane letters, storehouse or treasury of polite knowledge? In 1765 it was precisely with regard to the novel that the *Encyclopédie* was to give the following exemplary definition—of a literary form that it was hard put to define, but in which we can certainly recognize the novel:

Prose poem. (Belles lettres). A kind of work where we find the fiction and style of poetry, and which are therefore true *poems*, excepting only

---

[12]Perrault, *Parallèle*, p. 234 (III.148–49).
[13]Corneille, *Oeuvres complètes*, ed. Couton, 1:1408.

rhythm and rhyme. It is a particularly successful invention [*une invention fort heureuse*]. To prose poetry we owe several works full of events at once probable and extraordinary [shades of Corneille], as of simultaneously wise and practical precepts. These might never have seen the light of day, had their authors had to subject their genius to rhyme and rhythm. The laudable author of *Télémaque* would never have given us that delightfully bewitching work if he had had to write it in verse. There are beautiful *poems* without verse, as there are beautiful paintings without the richest coloring.

As I have said, *Télémaque* was now the perfect model of the novel and of literary purpose and practice more generally. It gave a clear answer to the set of questions just put: above all to that concerning the essence of literature. I have already indicated how its appearance persuaded Boileau to modify his views. The same poet was reported by Addison to have told him that *Télémaque* gave a better idea of Homer than any translation.[14] By 1710 the English essayist was reviewing the novel in the *Tatler*, as the "beautiful romance published not many years since by the Archbishop of Cambray," that "great and learned author." "The story of Telemachus," he wrote, "is formed altogether in the spirit of Homer, and will give an unlearned reader a notion of that great poet's manner of writing, more than any translation of him can possibly do." The reminiscences of so many writers on literature as the storehouse of knowledge readily available, "delightful," and "admirable" are evident.[15]

A sort of paroxysm was achieved just a few years later in a text the more revealing for its being ostensibly but the official approbation for the novel's 1717 edition. Because it was thus presented as a "disinterested" justification for publishing the text (although the censor's approbation was normally noncommittal), and because it summarized to perfection the claims of literature, it needs to be quoted at length:

[*Télémaque*] deserved not only to be printed, but indeed to be translated into all the languages spoken or understood by peoples who aspire to happiness. This epic poem, although in prose, means our nation has no cause in this respect to envy the Greeks or the Romans. The story it elaborates in no way ends just by tickling our curiosity and flattering our pride. The tales, descriptions, coherence, and graces of its discourse amaze the imagination without leading it into false paths. Its longest reflections and dialogues seem always too short to our minds, which they enlighten no less than delight. Among so many different human characteristics found there, none fails to engrave on the reader's heart a horror of vice or love of virtue. The mysteries of the healthiest and surest policy are

[14]Joseph Addison, *The Letters*, ed. Walter Graham (Oxford, 1941), p. 24.
[15]Joseph Addison, *Tatler*, no. 156 (April 8, 1710). in *The Works . . .* , ed. George Washington Greene, 5 vols. (New York, 1853), 3:523–28.

unveiled; passions are seen to be but a burden, as shameful as it is disastrous; duties reveal only attraction, making them as agreeable as they are easy. Through Télémaque himself we learn to become inviolably attached to religion, in good as well as in bad fortune; to love one's father and one's country; to be a king, a citizen, a friend, and even a slave, if fortune wills. Through Mentor we soon become just, human, patient, sincere, discreet and unassuming. He never speaks but he pleases, engages, moves, and persuades us. We feel only admiration when we hear him. Nor do we admire him without feeling that we like him even more. Happy the nation for whom this work will one day fashion a Télémaque or a Mentor![16]

We will not, then, be surprised that Henry Fielding chose to place *Joseph Andrews* under the sign of *Télémaque* in 1742 (picking up again on the notion of the prose epic in the preface to his sister's *David Simple* two years later); that Rousseau made his Sophie in love with its eponymous hero, depicted in Émile himself; or that Hannah More, at the beginning of her novel *Coelebs in Search of a Wife*, equated Sophie's captivation by Télémaque with her hero's devotion to "Milton's Eve."[17] It was perhaps no accident that Addison had consecrated both *Télémaque* and *Paradise Lost* in his magazines. Both, but especially the novel—as the quite extraordinary approbation shows—were signal representatives of literature, now something quite new. Literature had acquired new meaning, a formerly unheard-of social function. It was, in fact (I hope previous chapters have shown), organized differently. On the one hand, it now had its place in a different set of cultural parameters. On the other, the internal elements and structures controlling its functioning were not the same as those of earlier poetry or rhetoric.

These considerations bring us directly to the question of how older texts become adjusted (or do not) to such a new set of parameters; of how older texts are reinvented; or, in the terms of the new invention of literature, of what makes a classic. If we think, as many do, that literary texts reflect some basic "truth" of what it is to be human, some fundamental tenet of meaningful life (however many subsidiary meanings may accrue), one may see Literature as only peripherally inflected by history. In its essence, it will remain unchanging, although the tastes, styles of thought, and

[16]Fénelon, *Aventures de Télémaque*, p. 101. Fénelon's company in respect of censorial approbation was rare. An illustrious predecessor was Cervantes, extravagantly praised in the censor Márques Torres's *aprobación* for the Second Part of *Don Quijote* (the author, here, not the work): Canavaggio, *Cervantes*, pp. 300–301.

[17]Henry Fielding, *The History of the Adventures of Joseph Andrews and of His Friend Mr. Abraham Adams . . .* , intro. Howard Mumford Jones (1939; rpt. New York, 1950), p. xxxii; Henry Fielding, "Preface," to Sarah Fielding, *The Adventures of David Simple . . .* , ed. Malcolm Kelsall (Oxford and New York, 1987), p. 6; Jean-Jacques Rousseau, *Émile*, ed. Charles Wirz and Pierre Burgelin, in *Oeuvres complètes*, 4:761–63, 769, 775–77, 826, 849 (not really "Sophie," wrote Rousseau, but someone so alike as to be virtually identical); More, *Coelebs*, in *Works*, 2:9.

customs into which divers eras insert any particular text may surround it with a sort of dust of ages, an accumulated detritus of time. This is a standard view, one that comes to us from Dryden, Fontenelle, Rymer, and Perrault. According to it, the literary text is our connection with humanity of all ages and places, and all literature performs fundamentally the same function. This has the advantage of common sense. For how can one consider a given text—one and the same more or less unchanging artifact, after all—to be subject to serious change? And were it to change, how (and why) could it even remain available to people of various times and places?

In fact, there is nothing very complicated about such matters. One need first only follow the process of change. A fish, we may say, is not a bird, but a paleontologist may be able to construct the process by which the one "became" the other. A dollar is not a penny, but an economic historian may be able to show how one has come to have the value of the other. One may perhaps object that such reconstructions demand, precisely, sets of constants that have not changed: some common property of bone structure, some universal determinant of monetary value. No doubt this is the case, but such "constants" are themselves identifiable only because we know, or can discover, their intermediate states, because, that is to say, we understand them as *changing*, self-transforming processes. In the case of the literary classic, what changes is not, of course, the text (as a concrete object), but everything about its environment. Since a text, once produced, exists for its recipient as, and only as, a complex meaning, as such it does indeed change. One may say—as already proposed—that the "classic" is just that text able to change as a set of meanings, to be adapted—as meaning-ful—within a new sociocultural environment, to accrue new layers of sense.

A grasp of such commonplaces was quite usual among the authors we have been examining. When Du Bos, Reynolds, or Marmontel (after Rymer and others) asserted the artist's task to be one of depicting some central essence or ideal, their view was not *opposed* to that of such as Diderot or Buffon, with their idea of infinite diversity and flux. It was the other face: the one signaled process, the other enabled its grasping. Process did not contradict stable perfection. It was a part of it. Infinite variety was not chaotic disorder, but variation on a principled theme. Nature was both lawful ideal and dynamic "energy in process, a source never tired of producing."[18] But this was not release from order. Rather did it match Dryden's balancing of law and superstructure, Rymer's of general rule and local variety. A century later than these two, Reynolds caught the matter to perfection:

If what has been advanced is true, that beside this beauty or truth, which is formed on the uniform, eternal and immutable laws of nature, and

---

[18]I disagree here with Starobinski's claim that these views are contradictory: *Invention de la liberté*, pp. 117–18, 145.

which of necessity can be but *one;* that beside this one immutable verity there are likewise what we have called apparent or secondary truths, proceeding from local and temporary prejudices, fancies, or accidental connexions of ideas; if it appears that these last have still their foundation, however slender, in the original fabrick of our minds; it follows that all these truths or beauties deserve and require the attention of the artist, in proportion to their stability or duration, or as their influence is more or less extensive.[19]

The task of the work of art was then to capture stable rule and dynamic process, ideal meaning and infinite variety. Individual diversity would be caught in and by the whole of which it was but a type: the political and the aesthetic met once again. The great work could be examined down to its revelation of the universal, as it simultaneously lent itself to endless variety of local purport, allusion, and interpretation.

At the inception of our new literature, one of the things critics, authors, and adapters set out to do was to provide such texts. I take the cases of Homer and Shakespeare partly because so many late seventeenth-century commentators equate them with one another, partly because of *Télémaque,* and partly because they have subsequently become so vital to our tradition. That vitality was by no means so certain to the Renaissance, although little more than a century later, by the time of Pope's "Preface to Homer's *Iliad*" (1715), the unequivocally encomiastic sentence with which the poet began his commentary would be typical: "HOMER is universally allow'd to have had the greatest Invention of any Writer whatever."[20] It took much debate to reach that point.

Speaking of the development in the modern appreciation of Homer, Kirsti Simonsuuri comments that "Homer shows us perhaps that the definition of a good poet should be more concerned with the diversity of responses a poet can evoke than with the quality of the verse. Everyone can read his own myths in Homer."[21] Indeed: although we might well question her assumption of dissonance between diversity of response and quality of verse. In any case, the thrust of her claim clearly agrees with what was just said, with eighteenth-century accord, and with what the gradual acceptance of the Homeric epics indicates. We do not strain the concept of criticism too much, I think, when we add that one of *its* principal roles is to educe those myths (taking the word in a broad sense) that best fit the moment; those being "best" that, as Victoria Lady Welby put it, provide "starting-points for the acquisition of fresh knowledge, new truth."[22] In the present case these would be the elements that most

[19]Reynolds, *Discourses on Art,* p. 141: 7th Disc., Dec. 1776.

[20]Alexander Pope, *The Iliad of Homer,* ed. Maynard Mack [et al.] in *The Poems,* gen. ed. John Butt, 10 vols. (London and New Haven, Conn., 1954–67), 7:3.

[21]Kirsti Simonsuuri, *Homer's Original Genius: Eighteenth-Century Notions of the Early Greek Epic (1688–1798)* (Cambridge, 1979), p. 3.

[22]Victoria Lady Welby, *What Is Meaning? Studies in the Development of Significance* (London, 1903), facs. rpt., intro. Gerrit Mannoury, pref. Achim Eschbach (Amsterdam,

usefully fit the definition and practice of literature, as it in turn found its place in the sociocultural environment. As the instances of Boileau's and Saint-Evremond's use of Homer began to suggest, the more adaptable an artwork—so to speak—the more traditions it can be a part of: the cases of Homer and Shakespeare are exemplary.

One could say of the story of the so-called Homeric question (which is not really singular) that it is a tale of inventing traditions. Such has been the case from the claim about the "Peisistratid recension" (the idea that the poems as the later Greeks had them resulted from a sixth-century editing and compiling of several earlier poems), to the analyses of third-century Alexandrian critics, who produced the earliest statement of the poems' anomalies, to the folk-historical realism of the European eighteenth century and the allegorizing of the nineteenth, and then down to contemporary assertion that the poems are a fundamentally true, though distorted, oral storage of a culture's memory of its past. To eighteenth-century British travelers like Robert Wood, who rediscovered the actual geography of the poems, the *Odyssey* embodied their own dearest image of themselves as individual seekers after truth, beauty, and virtue.[23] To nineteenth-century German philologists, the epics gave voice to their own most immediate concerns. They delighted in them as the treasure house of a perennial Aryan civilization whose historical existence was thereby proven.

For my purpose, this tradition has a more particular importance, marking an invention of moment for our culture more broadly: that of literature itself. So far I have left a gap in the Homeric story. I did not accidentally jump from the Alexandrians to the eighteenth century. Into that gap the European Renaissance inserted its own special wedge. Once Roman culture took over from the Greek, during the first centuries B.C. and A.D., Virgil replaced Homer as a cultural model. The Latin poet lent himself to Christianizing exegesis as Homer did not. Throughout the Middle Ages each European vernacular strove to follow Virgil and find some Trojan hero to originate its national establishment. Even so, Virgil in no way escaped a movement of adaptation and change: "His historical survival has always depended on processes of accommodation, on centuries of apologetic and exegetical effort. To make him speak in a manner acceptable to times later than and different from his own it was necessary to treat him either as divinely inspired, or as having wrapped his knowledge in a poetic integument that only subtle interpretation could remove."[24] The

---

1983), p. 150. On Welby's own arguments in this direction, see my "Significs: The Analysis of Meaning as Critique of Modernist Culture," in *Essays in Significs*, ed. H. Walter Schmitz (Amsterdam, 1990), pp. 63–82.

[23]Robert Wood, *An Essay on the Original Genius of Homer, with a Comparative View of the Antient and Present State of the Troade*, ed. J. Bryant (London, 1775 [first version published in 1767]).

[24]Kermode, *The Classic*, p. 38. On the significance of such "poetic integument," see note 1 to this chapter.

growing secularization of culture in the sixteenth century and the rediscovery of texts from Greek antiquity rapidly led to discussion of a new place for the Homeric epics.

Indeed, there are two remarkable aspects about the "return" of Homer into Western European culture. One is that speed of occurrence. The other is the fact that in Italy and Spain, France and the Netherlands, England and Germany, despite the different moments when the retrieval occurred and the apparent variety of their respective cultures, by the mid-eighteenth century the view scholars held of the Homeric poems was essentially uniform. This latter aspect justifies the claim that we are dealing with a single sociocultural environment. Both aspects lead one to infer, as this chapter proposes, that the retrieval was part of a wider cultural transformation, a more general invention.

Many medieval manuscripts of Homer remain extant, testifying to the poems' afterlife among the learned. They date chiefly from the twelfth century, owing existence to the Eastern Empire of Constantinople, and from the late fifteenth, when they form a kind of commentary on that city's fall (as did the Renaissance more generally). Even then Homer was more a sort of cultural myth than a lively presence. Sir John Myres recounted the great efforts to which Petrarch went to acquire a copy of the *Iliad*, even though, he concluded somewhat wryly, he "could not read it because he did not know Greek." The first printed text dates from 1488 and was soon followed by the Aldine editions of 1504 and 1517. They still, however, "exercised a far less profound influence on the Renaissance of the fifteenth and sixteenth centuries, than we should perhaps have been prepared to expect."[25] All commentators concur in this judgment. Indeed, Noémi Hepp argues that actual knowledge of Homer in fact *decreased* in France at least during the first half of the seventeenth century, if the number of editions is evidence.[26] Simonsuuri adds that Homer was probably poorly known in the original, for little effort was made to improve the Greek text: "The line-by-line version thrown together by Leonzio Pilato in 1369 survived without much change until the Cambridge edition of 1689." The epics were read with the help of fifteenth-century Latin interlinear or prose translations.[27] This implies that Homer long remained something of a distant (and incomprehensible) glory rather than a living source of inspiration. The epics were a kind of empty receptacle ready to be filled with the riches of critical debate.

On the Continent, although ambivalence was extreme, Homer was essentially a source of dismay. Scholars were well aware of the unique esteem in which he was held by Antiquity, and at least one simply repeated it: "Without question, Homer has won first place among all poets

[25]Sir John L. Myres, *Homer and His Critics*, ed. Dorothea Gray (London, 1958), pp. 37–38.

[26]Noémi Hepp, *Homère en France au xviie siècle* (Paris, 1968), pp. 11–31.

[27]Simonsuuri, *Homer's Original Genius*, pp. 10–11.

of every nation and all ages that have ever been." So Le Roy, who continued his imprecise encomium for some pages.[28] But specialists were at a loss to explain that esteem. J.-C. Scaliger, whose *Poetices Libri Septem* (1561) was the most influential critical work of its age and for years to come, condemned Homer unequivocally. He scorned the poet for his too ordinary realism, his almost blasphemous treatment of the gods, his lack of *decorum* and *gravitas*, his failure to depict in either epic any unifying hero, and his portrayal only of unsavory and brutal characters. Furthermore, Scaliger complained, whereas Virgil told the great story of Rome's founding and later enduring empire (a view of the classic re-echoed by T. S. Eliot and F. R. Leavis in our own time), Homer recounted a perfectly trivial conflict and did so with no "sense of organized dramatic development."[29]

This view predominated on the Continent until the end of the seventeenth century. In 1664 the abbé d'Aubignac still attacked the epics for their vicious morality, bad taste, poor style, and confusion of plot, concluding there was no such individual author as Homer in any case.[30] Saint-Evremond uttered identical views. Later yet, the many references to Homer in Bayle's *Dictionary* were (and remained in subsequent editions) unrelievedly disdainful. By those later years, however, matters were on the verge of changing, and a Claude Fleury could soon turn an interpretation of these very elements into proof of Homer's expression of the universal laws of literature and the human mind. Earlier, some explained Antiquity's awe for the vacuity blasted by Scaliger by taking it for allegory. Jean Dorat called Homer the "divine allegorist." A Dutch student interpreted Ulysses' sleep as "symbolizing death and the arrival in the heavenly country." D'Aubigné defended his use of "tableaux célestes" in the fifth book of the *Tragiques* by appealing not just to Virgil and Tasso, but also to Homer.[31]

Others remained noncommittal, taking the reputation for granted and without comment. In the Preface to his *Franciade* (1573), Ronsard wrote that he wished to become the "Homère françois." The phrase was ambiguous as far as Homer's glory was concerned. On the one hand, it marked Virgil's untouchability: Ronsard could not be so arrogant as to rival the Roman poet. On the other, it did signal Homer's reputation as the poet of the beginnings of Greek language and poetry, just as Ronsard and his Pléiade companions sought to be of the French. In his *Pantagruel* of 1537, Rabelais had already called Homer the "paragon de tous les philologes

---

[28]Le Roy, *De la vicissitude*, pp. 207–8.

[29]Simonsuuri, *Homer's Original Genius*, p. 12.

[30]Abbé François-Hédelin d'Aubignac, *Conjectures académiques ou dissertation sur l'Iliade*, ed. V. Magnien (Paris, 1925). The text was written and known about 1664, although first published many years later.

[31]The first two are recorded by Yates, *French Academies*, p. 14. For the third, see Théodore-Agrippa d'Aubigné, *Les tragiques*, ed. Jacques Bailbé (Paris, 1968), p. 39: d'Aubigné started writing these in 1577; the *Aux lecteurs* to which I refer was published in 1616.

(the exemplar of all word lovers)." Scaliger's eventually more famous son turned to Homer for just this reason: learning Greek by reading him before turning to other Greek poets. Heinsius said he was so intent on these language studies that he failed even to hear the noises of the Saint Bartholomew massacre outside his Paris window.[32] "Homer" was often pronounced with such a sense and always with some ambivalence.

In England the story was very different, although not entirely until George Chapman's celebrated translation. Of this, the first part was published in 1598, the whole appearing almost twenty years later, while between the two ever fuller editions succeeded each other. As one might expect, Chapman was unable to praise Homer highly enough: "Of all bookes extant in all kinds, Homer is the first and best," he asserted in his general Preface to the Reader.[33] He viewed poetry as the chief instrument for praising God and thus as the principal achievement of humanity. Homer became the illustrator of "all Arts." These claims repeated the common sixteenth-century view of poetry as I explored it in Chapter 1. In that context Chapman remarked how Alexander correctly considered Homer "so divine a creature," spoke of "his Angel's tongue," "the kingly flight of his high Muse," and so forth. He, too, saw allegory: "Nothing can be imagined more full of soule and humaine extraction: for what is here prefigurde [on Achilles's shield] by our miraculous Artist but the universall world?" Homer was now far above Virgil, who wrote with "a courtly, laborious, and altogether imitatorie spirit." Homer's "poems were writ from a free furie, an absolute & full soule." They showed "not onely all learning, government, and wisedome being deduc't as from a bottomlesse fountaine from him, but all wit, elegancie, disposition, and iudgement."[34]

He positively exploded with indignation when faced with the obtuseness and effrontery of the Continent and its translators' inability to provide any adequate rendering of the Greek, whether into Latin, Italian, or French. Dedicating his translation of *Achilles' Shield* in 1598, he burst into a veritable paroxysm of anger and contempt:

> But thou, soule-blind Scalliger, that never hadst any thing but place, time and termes to paint thy proficiencie in learning, nor ever writest any thing of thine owne impotent braine but onely impalsied diminution of Homer (which I may sweare was the absolute inspiration of thine owne ridicu-

[32]Joseph Justus Scaliger, *Autobiography*, pp. 31, 76. Equally noncommittal, though clearly laudatory, was an exchange of letters between Quevedo and Lipsius in 1604–5. The first wrote of his desire to defend Homer in Spanish against Scaliger's "iniurias." Lipsius encouraged him, writing that he could "do nothing more worthy, or more pleasing to the learned than to treat this matter": *Epistolario de Justo Lipsio y los Españoles (1577–1606)*, ed. Alejandro Ramírez (Madrid, 1966), pp. 400, 412. Lipsius recalled his own praise of Homer in the *Manuductio ad philosophicam stoïcam*.

[33]George Chapman, *Chapman's Homer: The Iliad, The Odyssey, and the Lesser Homerica*, ed. Allardyce Nicoll, 2d ed., 2 vols. (Princeton, 1967), 1:14.

[34]Ibid., 1:3–6, 543–44.

lous Genius) never didst thou more palpably damn thy drossy spirit in al
thy all-countries-exploded filcheries, which are so grossly illiterate that
no man will vouchsafe their refutation, than in thy sencelesse reprehen-
sions of Homer, whose spirit flew as much above thy groveling capacities
as heaven moves above Barathrum.[35]

Although at the very beginning of his now familiar Preface, Davenant
upheld Homer as an eminent standard for reference but not for following,
by and large English views adhered closely to Chapman's. Temple, kinder
to Virgil than his predecessor, yet claimed Homer as "the vastest, the
sublimest, and the most wonderful genius," the one in whom "the poetical fire was more raging."[36] That general agreement may well explain why
English commentators debated the quality of translations rather than the
virtues of the original. Pope thus rejected Chapman, not only for his "loose
and rambling" paraphrase, his "frequent Interpolations," his seemingly
deliberate errors ("one might think he deviated on purpose"), his "strong
Affectation of extracting new Meanings out of his Author," and his "Neg-
ligence," but also for his bombastic "Fustian" and his "arrogant Turn."[37]
Chapman thus lay condemned for having *lost* that very simplicity and
realism for which, on the Continent, writers from Scaliger to d'Aubignac,
Saint-Evremond, and Bayle criticized Homer. Hobbes found himself criticized by Pope for similar reasons, although from divergent technique. He
generally kept close to the sense, however unforgivable his carelessness,
wrote Pope, but too often omitted many "Particulars and Circumstances,"
among them "the most beautiful."[38] Hobbes, Pope was saying, had left out
too much of the *realistic* detail that accounted for Homer's simple beauty.

All this, of course, is already showing how Homer is being reinvented
toward new purpose. Chapman had replied to Scaliger's criticism by insisting on Homer's "daring fiery spirit," a view echoed by Temple, and the
only aspect of Chapman's version praised by Pope (although he interpreted
the term rather differently). Chapman then embodied the kind of primitive originality one might expect an Augustan to bless in a contemporary
of Shakespeare, especially in the translator of that poet who occupied in
Greek culture the same position as the dramatist would be held to take in
the English. His fire, however, showed up in the *ornament* of which Du
Bellay once spoke, whose absence Scaliger criticized, and which the era,
we saw, viewed as the essential aspect of poetry. By Pope's time Scaliger's
criticisms would have been turned around. We can follow this process
with utmost clarity in a late seventeenth-century text by Fleury.

This work was published only in 1728 (and again in 1731, revealingly
under Pope's name), but it was written in 1665. Fleury began by taking on

---

[35]Ibid., 1:545.
[36]Sir William Temple, "Of Poetry [1692]," in *Five Essays*, p. 181.
[37]Pope, *Iliad*, ed. Mack, in *Poems*, 7:21.
[38]Ibid., pp. 21–22.

the terms made temporarily customary by J.-C. Scaliger. He agreed that
when one first read Homer, he "seems ridiculous": because of the "freedom he affects in composing his verse," a style "entirely simple and
rough," and certain "peculiarities in the way of life of those he describes,
who seem to us ignoble and churlish to the utmost degree." We find, he
wrote, a complete absence of "what we are used to value in our poetry:
gracious axiom, subtle allusion, epigram, delicate feeling, extravagant
magnanimity." This being so, Fleury asked, how could one explain the fact
that Homer "has been praised by all Antiquity above any other writer
known to us, and that his works have been almost as respected by the
Greeks as the Bible is by us?"[39]

On the one hand, he wrote, one could not accuse the ancients of lacking
in intelligence. But nor could one deny the lack of pleasure experienced on
an initial reading of the epics. The most reasonable reaction, therefore,
was to suppose "that the ancients had a taste quite different from ours"
(p. 138). At this point he quoted from Jean-François Sarasin to the effect
that different peoples had difficulty understanding one another because of
the diversity of "life," "customs," and the rest (Dryden's future "superstructure").[40] Sarasin himself was here referring specifically to Homer,
and the idea was to become a commonplace: in Saint-Evremond, Fontenelle, Perrault, and Dryden, a distinction was to be made between
changing custom and event, with their echo in literary trope and design,
and universal law of human functioning, with its reflection in the necessary perennial rules of literature. The Homeric question was coming to
echo a more general issue.

Fleury went so far as to admit this mutual incomprehensibility, noting
that "Homer is no longer *un livre d'usage* [a familiar work]" (p. 139). The
phrase "un livre d'usage" had the dual meaning that the poem was no
longer *being read* and was no longer *useful.* The statement *could* imply
that one should accept Antiquity's view without trying to understand it.
But Fleury wanted, rather, to comprehend the matter. So, he said, he
decided to read the poem quickly, seeking only the plot and the disposition
of story (the celebrated distinction between "story" and "plot" frequently
credited to twentieth-century Formalists was a seventeenth-century commonplace, often divided into "action" and "plot" or even, as we saw in La
Fontaine, into "body" and "soul"). Doing this, Fleury remarked, what one
found was "un grand dessein fort bien proportionné et fort bien conduit (a
grand design, very well proportioned and very well managed)." It contained, he went on, "small matter, but well conducted; a very simple
action, that is to say, but depicted [*peinte*] very exactly, ordered most
adroitly, and accompanied by every circumstance able to make it more
beautiful: and it is all explained with marvellous clarity" (pp. 139–40).

[39]Noémi Hepp, ed., *Deux amis d'Homère au xviie siècle: Textes inédits de Paul
Pellisson et de Claude Fleury* (Paris, 1970), pp. 137–38. References are henceforth given
directly in my text.
[40]Jean-François Sarasin, *Les oeuvres de Monsieur Sarasin,* 2 vols. (Paris, 1683), 2:36.

Fleury was suggesting a way of reading Homer that adjusted the epics to a new aesthetic and a new idea of literature. One need but examine his terms. The *Iliad* was *well proportioned* as to its action (the commonsensical story being told). It was simple and methodical, exactly and correctly representational (*peinte*), *vraisemblable*, clear, and distinct (*fort exactement, fort adroitement, une netteté merveilleuse*). The critic insisted that the episodic events (*touttes les circonstances*) were needed by the action and its embellishment and that therefore the epic did not deviate from the necessary singularity and unity of such action. The *Iliad*, furthermore, clearly revealed its "fondement de vérité (foundation of truth [p. 144])." Additionally, it did for its reader what all literature should ideally do: provoke empathy. The reader "sees passions *expressed so naturally that he feels them simultaneously*" (p. 143: Fleury's emphasis).[41] In short, he wrote, the *Iliad* "must give all the pleasure given by novels and histories, which is always to see something new and always have one's expectations aroused by it." The idea that reasoned suspense was essential to a literary (or dramatic) work was also new.

The *Iliad* was praised for its "simplicité," its "netteté," and because "I have formed so distinct an idea of what he describes that I seem to see" everything Homer set down (p. 152). He thus concluded that almost everything found displeasing in Homer came only from the difference "of customs and language," matters of which moderns were unsuitable judges because they inevitably saw them through the spectacles of their own bias of local custom and national language (p. 157). Homer, however, correctly set down and followed the fundamental rules, while the text remained useful as a genuine storehouse of knowledge: "We further find there what the Ancients had no need to learn, for they knew it from other sources: infinite details, that is to say, about the way people lived in his time— things most useful for our literal understanding of the Bible" (p. 157).

Homer thus fulfilled with nary a flaw all the principal demands of the new literature. He had, one may say, been reinvented in its image. This did not mean the dispute was over: far from it. Certainly, when Hobbes prefaced the full version of his translation of the two epics in 1676, he virtually repeated many of Fleury's arguments (although he certainly had not read him).[42] But six years before, Desmarets accused Homer of having no subject, and Chapelain had earlier gone so far as to belittle Homer in

[41] The achievement of such empathy—or "identification"—was a principal aim of the dramatists and writers of the age, an important aspect of the new way in which literature was to achieve its goals and play its role. See, e.g., my *Toward Dramatic Illusion: Theatrical Technique and Meaning from Hardy to "Horace"* (New Haven, Conn., and London, 1971), esp. pp. 141–46, 150–52.

[42] Hobbes, *English Works*, 10:iii–x. The same view was defended at greater length by René Le Bossu in a celebrated text of 1675, englished as a *Treatise of the Epick Poem.* . . . Le Bossu argued that Homer thoroughly embodied both reason and ethical and political rectitude: *Treatise of the Epick Poem . . . , [with] an Essay upon Satyr by Mons. D'Acier; and a Treatise upon Pastoral by Mons. Fontanelle [sic].* 2d ed. . . . , 2 vols. (London, 1719), pp. 1–2, 34–50.

comparison to the medieval *Lancelot,* calling him "entirely common and boorish," although he did find some good to say.[43] By the last decades of the century the question came to be that of distinguishing between universal law and customary superstructure. That enabled the moderns to reject what they saw as the naiveties, the confusions, the theological errors of Homer, while yet concluding, as did Saint-Evremond (despite the vehement criticism we saw earlier): "No one has more admiration than I for the Ancients' works. I admire the design, economy, elevation of mind, breadth of knowledge. But the change in religion, government, customs, manners, has made so great a change in the world, that we need something like a new art in order to enter properly into the taste and spirit [*génie*] of our own age."[44]

The theme was common among the moderns. Nor did the ancients deny the distinction; they simply concluded that one should seek to understand superstructural differences, not reject them. When the Homeric quarrel culminated in the second decade of the eighteenth century, its broader elements (those that were not a matter of scholarly dispute over meanings, nor a question of style and exactness of translation) were still by and large the same. The central figure was Anne Le Fèvre Dacier, whose defense of Homer (when it was not of her interpretation or of her translation) was essentially a more elaborate version of Fleury's.[45] All concurred, basically, in a statement such as that made earlier by Saint-Evremond that literature should reflect the current idea humans have of themselves: we may be in the hands of God or subject to general laws at some profound level, but we are, he said, "in our own hands to deliberate and to act."[46] That willful self-possessive individual belonged within a new superstructural environment.

This was not at all to deny the existence of "certain eternal rules," but otherwise "everything has changed: the gods, nature, politics, customs, taste, manners."[47] Le Fèvre could then maintain that Homer's greatness was to have elaborated the first and grandest lawful literary text, setting

---

[43]Desmarets, *Comparaison de la langue,* pp. 37–39; Jean Chapelain, *La lecture des vieux romans [1647],* in Huet, *Lettre-traité sur l'origine des romans,* p. 172.

[44]Charles de Saint-Evremond, "Sur les anciens," in *Oeuvres en prose,* 3:348.

[45]Anne Lefèvre Dacier, *Causes de la corruption du goust; Homère défendu contre l'apologie du R. P. Hardouin. Ou suite des causes de la corruption du goust* (1716; rpt. Geneva, 1971). Her main rival was Antoine de La Motte, but many others joined the fray. For the most part their titles are self-explanatory: Jean Boivin, *Apologie d'Homère et bouclier d'Achille* (Paris, 1715); abbé Jean-François Pons, *Lettre à Madame Dacier sur son livre des causes de la corruption du goust* (Paris, 1715); Jean Terrasson, *Dissertation critique sur l'Iliade d'Homère, où à l'occasion de ce poëme on cherche les règles d'une poëtique fondée sur la raison, & sur les exemples des anciens & des modernes,* 2 vols. (Paris, 1715–16); Etienne Fourmont, *Examen pacifique de la querelle de Madame Dacier et de Monsieur de La Motte sur Homère,* 2 vols. (Paris, 1716). The expense of paper, one can see, was considerable, but the dispute was soon over. Then began the task of finding who Homer was and what his place in his culture.

[46]Saint-Evremond, "Sur les anciens," pp. 349–50.

[47]Ibid., pp. 357–58.

forth the common and universal rules of human existence and behavior, at the same time as he depicted the specific details of the life and manners of the ancient Greeks. Such claims led directly to Vico's assertions that the poems were "civil histories of ancient Greek customs, . . . two great treasure houses of the natural law of the gentes of Greece," while they also presented fundamental law: "class concepts or universals."[48] One need hardly emphasize again how such statements repeated the claims we saw (in Chapters 5 and 6) gradually established on behalf of literature more generally.

What was true of Homer was no less so of Shakespeare. As Gotthold Lessing could write in 1766 that "Homer was the best model of all," so in 1769 Elizabeth Montagu could end her immensely successful *Essay on the Writings and Genius of Shakespear* with the fear that she had fallen short of a "genius . . . so extensive and profound."[49] A century earlier such an expression would have struck people as bordering the absurd. The case would barely have echoed even the ambivalence of the Homeric debate. Yet by 1766–69 Lessing was writing: "What has been said of Homer, that it would be easier to deprive Hercules of his club, than him of a verse, can be as truly said of Shakespeare." Montagu contended: "All our critics allow Shakespear to be an original. Mr. Pope confesses him to be more so than Homer himself." The word "original" here bore quite special weight. As she wrote at the beginning of her essay, "Homer's works alone were sufficient to teach the Greek poets how to write, and their audience how to judge." He had originated a culture in that perfect poetry avouched by Lessing. After a barbaric, "coarse," "gross and ignorant" age in England (to use Montagu's language), Shakespeare had played the same part: indeed, "in delineating characters he must be allowed very far to surpass all dramatic writers, and even Homer himself."[50] Shakespeare's work, like Homer's, had played the political-contractual role attributed to literature by Boileau and Dryden. Nor was the appeal to Pope's authority any less loaded than the comparison with Homer.

That particular coupling had become a commonplace of English crit-

[48]Vico, *The New Science*, pp. 65 (para. 20), 74 (para. 49). Catherine Labio has examined Homer's place in Vico's hermeneutics and his understanding of human history in "Enlightenment and the Epistemology of Origins," Ph.D. diss., New York University, 1991, chap. 2 (she analyzes chiefly Vico's Book Three).

[49]Gotthold Ephraim Lessing, *Laocoön: An Essay on the Limits of Painting and Poetry,* trans. and ed. Edward Allen McCormick (1962; rpt. Baltimore and London, 1984), p. 104; Elizabeth [Robinson] Montagu, *An Essay on the Writings and Genius of Shakespear, Compared with the Greek and French Dramatic Poets. With Some Remarks Upon the Misrepresentations of Mons. de Voltaire,* 5th ed., corr., to which are added *Three Dialogues of the Dead* (London, 1785), p. 284.

[50]Gotthold Ephraim Lessing, *Hamburg Dramaturgy,* trans. Helen Zimmern (New York, 1962), p. 173 (the essays were published separately in 1766, collectively in 1769); Montagu, *Essay,* pp. 281, 18–19. How the Homeric epics were worked and developed into the German tradition has been examined by Thomas Bleicher, *Homer in der deutschen Literatur (1450–1740): Zur Rezeption der Antike und zur Poetologie der Neuzeit* (Stuttgart, 1972).

icism from the late seventeenth century. With its elaborate set of relationships, Dryden's familiar comparison of Shakespeare and Jonson was a kind
of model: "If I would compare him [Jonson] with Shakespeare, I must
acknowledge him the more correct poet, but Shakespeare the greater wit.
Shakespeare was the Homer, or father of our dramatic poets; Jonson was
the Virgil, the pattern of elaborate writing; I admire him, but I love
Shakespeare."[51] In an essay of 1712, Dennis added: "One may say of
[Shakespeare] as they did of *Homer*, that he had none to imitate, and is
himself inimitable."[52] Remarks of this sort may be thought rather unfair
to such as Christopher Marlowe and other contemporaries of Shakespeare.
The point was not to compare playwrights. It was to equate Shakespeare
with Homer both with respect to wit, genius, originality, and invention,
and as a candidate for adaptation in the same way to a new cultural
environment.

Indeed, Pope's Preface to Shakespeare's *Works* (1725) left an impression
that the dramatist's legacy was even in detail little different from that of
Homer. By this time the major issue of Homeric study was that of authorship. Pope's Preface suggested that the dispute over single or multiple
authorship applied no less to Shakespeare than it did to Homer.[53] Pope
related how he could work from no acceptable copy, that he had to correct
the manifold errors due to interference of players, pirates, editors, printers,
and other authors. The absence of any creditable version implied the
irreparable loss of any original and, as a direct result, an unavoidable need
to "invent" them. After all this meddling, where could one hope to discover the real authentic Shakespeare? And where would such "correction"
come to a halt? (The question is as apt for modern scholars working with
essentially the same texts as Pope.) What was one to make of the fact that
Elizabethan and Jacobean playwrights habitually wrote works together?
Or of the generally recognized fact that plays were considerably worked on
in rehearsal—that they genuinely were in some senses collective projects?

Pope might wish, as he wrote, to reject some plays as only in part by
Shakespeare, but that desire worked equally well in reverse. Custom
admitted the possibility of multiple authorship of plays (as of the Homeric
epics) without embarrassment or disapprobation. Only slowly did it become necessary to ascribe them to a single author and to maintain an
authorized canon (as also occurred in Homer's case): as a new Shakespeare,
one may almost say, was invented. However Pope might want to argue that
his Shakespeare was the original and real one, the habit of collaboration

---

[51]John Dryden, *The Works*, ed. Walter Scott, 18 vols. (London, 1808), 15:354.

[52]Dennis, "Genius and Writings of Shakespear," in *Critical Works*, 2:4.

[53]"The Homer that we hold in our hands now," Friedrich August Wolf would write in
1795, "is not the one who flourished in the mouths of the Greeks of his own day, but one
variously altered, interpolated, corrected, and emended from the times of Solon down to
those of the Alexandrians": *Prolegomena to Homer, 1795*, trans. and ed. Anthony
Grafton, Glenn W. Most, and James E. G. Zetzel (Princeton, 1985), p. 209 (chap. xlix).

continued. During the age of Davenant and Dryden, of Nahum Tate, Lewis Theobald (*Richard II* in 1719), and Ravenscroft no one was the slightest troubled by alterations to the plays. On the contrary, Tate wrote of *King Lear*, such collaborative effort was essential: "I found the whole to answer your account of it," he wrote to Thomas Boteler, "a heap of jewels, unstrung and unpolished, yet so dazzling in their disorder that I soon perceived I had seized a treasure. 'Twas my good fortune to light on one expedient to rectify what was wanting in the regularity and probability of the tale."[54]

Through the first half of the seventeenth century Shakespeare was diversely praised, albeit without detail or depth and in a way that quickly became a repetition of clichés. The man, more than the plays, was commonly called "sweet" and "gentle," a model representative of the theater of his time, but appreciated, as Jonson put it, well "this side idolatry." This initial approval gave way to a growing tension between a view emphasizing his natural genius and one condemning his utter disregard of rules: "The tension could only be resolved by changing the poet rather than the taste of the age." It led to that array of adaptations to contemporary taste of which Brian Vickers remarks that "there is no comparable instance of the work of a major artist being altered in such sweeping fashion in order to conform to the aesthetic demand or expectation of a new age."[55] Well, maybe Homer (not least by the diversity of translation). We should note that the adaptation continued as the plays were translated for German and French publics.

As important as the diluted praise of the early period was Shakespeare's frequent absence from enumeration. By the subsequent tradition, of course, this could be seen only as a failure of taste. Richard Foster Jones thus criticizes George Hakewill's influential *Apologie of the Power and Providence of God in the Government of the World*, which had already gone through three editions between 1627 and 1635. In the wake of Bacon and William Gilbert, Hakewill hoped to sweep away the widespread notion of the world's progressive decay and to assert the superiority of the moderns over Antiquity. Jones's lament stems from the book's small reference to literary and aesthetic matters (surely reflecting the minor and extraneous role then still played by literature) and above all its slighting of the Bard. Hakewill lauded the "inventive parts" of Sidney's *Arcadia*, writings of Ariosto and Tasso, Guillaume Du Bartas and Spenser, George Buchanan and Ronsard (via Scaliger's comments on them) as equaling the finest of the ancients, but made no mention whatever of Shakespeare.

[54]Nahum Tate, *The History of King Lear [1681]*, ed. James Black (1975; rpt. London, 1976), p. 1. The notorious "expedient" was a love between Cordelia and Edgar that enabled a final rescue of Lear and a marriage ensuring the continuity and stability of a kingdom governed by a wholly English pair.

[55]Brian Vickers, ed., *Shakespeare: The Critical Heritage*, 6 vols. (London and Boston, 1974–81), 1:5–6.

Jones, beneficiary of later tradition, avers that to advance *Arcadia* "against the poetry of the ancients" just "ten years after Shakespeare's death" was "a sad commentary on the state of poetic appreciation in that day."[56] It was nothing of the sort. Shakespeare's preeminence was not yet a part of a tradition, and his growth to that status also required that of what we think of as literature, its judgments becoming part of the atmosphere we breathe.

Nothing was unusual in Thomas Cartwright's 1647 encomium in the Folio of Beaumont and Fletcher (incomparably more widely performed than Shakespeare in the early years of the Restoration): "*Shakespeare* to thee was dull." He stood accused of

> Old fashion'd wit, which walkt from town to town
> In turn'd hose, which our fathers call'd the Clown,
> Whose wit our nice times would obsceanness call,
> And which made Bawdry pass for Comicall;
> Nature was all his Art, thy veine was free
> As his, but without his scurility.

Twenty years later the prologue to James Shirley's *Love Tricks* pronounced like criticism: what "the World call'd Wit in *Shakespeare*'s age, / Is laught at, as improper for our Stage." Vickers sums up the Restoration period's commentary in terms of the ubiquity and density of "the general disapproval of this irregular, unlearned dramatist, who violated every critical principle."[57]

By the 1690s Shakespeare was something of an embarrassment. Rymer was not untypical. In a single text, he could approve of the "inimitable Shakespeare" while yet asserting:

> Many, peradventure, of the Tragical Scenes in *Shakespear*, cry'd up for the *Action*, might do yet better without words: Words are a sort of heavy baggage, that were better out of the way, at the push of Action; especially in his *bombast* Circumstance [we recall Pope on Chapman's Homer], where the Words and Action are seldom akin, generally are inconsistent, at cross purposes, embarrass or destroy each other; yet to those who take not the words distinctly, there may be something in the buz and sound, that like a drone to a Bagpipe may serve to set of the Action.[58]

His chapter on *Othello* became notorious. After uttering his profound scorn for the play's plot and the absurd moral to be drawn from it, for its

[56]Jones, *Ancients and Moderns*, p. 29.

[57]Vickers, *Shakespeare*, 1:3, 2:7.

[58]Rymer, *Short View of Tragedy*, pp. 93, 86. I have argued that such dissonances characterized a dramatic experience now largely unfamiliar to us (except in cases of experiment): *Toward Dramatic Illusion*, pp. 13–137. On Shakespeare from this point of view, see my *Tragedy and Truth*, pp. 165–69.

treatment of "*Characters* or Manners . . . not less unnatural and improper, than the Fable was improbable and absurd," for "Thoughts" that simply failed to meet any minimal critical standard, Rymer came to the question of "expression": "In the *Neighing* of a Horse, or in the *growling* of a Mastiff, there is a meaning, there is as lively expression, and, I may say, more humanity, than many times in the Tragical flights of *Shakespear.*"[59] The abuse reminds one of Chapman's virulence over Scaliger's treatment of Homer, and one wonders whether Swift may not have found here an idea for his Houyhnhnms. Rymer had yet harsher comments to make of Shakespeare's understanding of "nature": "There is not a Monky but understands Nature better; not a Pug in *Barbary* that has not a truer taste of things."[60]

To be sure, Rymer was roundly criticized for such views even in his own day, let alone by later writers. In a phrase that may recall the idea that Homer was the Greeks' "Bible," Dryden wrote to Dennis accusing Rymer of "blaspheming Shakespeare." Yet he and others found themselves obliged to admit that Rymer was right (except for the "nature" issue): "Let us therefore," Dryden had written in 1672, "admire the beauties and the heights of Shakespeare, without falling after him into a carelessness, and, as I may call it, a lethargy of thought, for whole scenes together."[61] What other critics disliked in Rymer was less his judgment than his refusal to allow the redeeming grace of genius and natural wit. "I am far from approving his manner of treating our Poet," Gilden wrote in 1710, "tho' Mr. *Dryden* owns, that all, or most of the Faults he has found, are Just." Indeed, Dryden's criticism of Rymer and refusal to let the latter's evidence alter an uncritical admiration of the dramatist was, Gilden went on, "a greater Proof of the Folly and abandon'd Taste of the Town, than of any Imperfections of the Critic."[62]

No one, in fact, could give a satisfactory response to Rymer, although many tried, including Dryden, Dennis, and Gilden themselves. One finds them repeating his criticisms, although less abusively. The reason why they could not provide a satisfying reply was, of course, that they were all accepting the same premises concerning the ordering and function of tragedy in particular and of literature in general, concerning the necessity of law and the fact of a fundamentally ethical world and society. Shakespeare and Fletcher, Dryden contended in a line recalling Saint-Evremond and Fleury on Homer, "have written to the genius of the age and nation in which they lived." So, he added, had the Greeks. That was what Gilden meant by asserting that Shakespeare's "errors . . . expos'd the ignorance of the Age he liv'd in."[63] Like Fleury with the understanding of Homer,

---

[59]Rymer, *Short View of Tragedy*, pp. 134–36.
[60]Ibid., p. 136
[61]John Dryden, "Defence of the Epilogue [c. 1672]," in *Selected Criticism*, p. 130.
[62]Gilden, "Essay," 7:iv.
[63]Dryden, "Heads of an Answer to Rymer [1677]," in *Selected Criticism*, p. 145; Gilden, "Essay," p. iv.

Dryden's own practice of rewriting such plays as *Antony and Cleopatra,* *The Tempest,* or *Troilus and Cressida* clearly argued for another new age, with a new art to match it. These efforts had to overcome the frequent nonsense, the carelessness and lethargy of which he spoke. But they, of course, did so by using the entirely valid models provided by Shakespeare to furnish their ordered structure.

In 1747 Lord Chesterfield could still write that "if Shakespeare's genius had been cultivated, those beauties, which we so justly admire in him, would have been undisguised by those extravagances and that nonsense with which they are frequently accompanied." Twenty years later Montagu admitted "his many and great faults," analyzing a large number of them as sins against sense. Indeed, in our own century Woolf has repeated Rymer's own argument as to the dissonance of words and action: "The later plays of Shakespeare, where there is more of poetry than of action, are better read than seen, better understood by leaving out the actual body than by having the body, with all its associations and movements, visible to the eye."[64] The value given to this dissonance by Montagu and then Woolf was, however, quite different from Chesterfield's grant. He still really hankered after an earlier age, regretting what he saw as its lost grace. They saw in this disheveled genius evidence of a surpassing grandeur, proof of a generosity of effect equal only to nature's own . . . or Homer's. Such nature embodied, we saw, the idea of universal rule: the word "nature" had itself so varied a sense as to be meaningless, said Gilden, unless tempered by a concept of law.[65] The juncture was echoed in the models provided by Shakespeare. Planted inevitably on it, and on them, were the superstructural varieties whose unfamiliarity Chapelain and Dryden, Fleury and Gilden, Rymer and Saint-Evremond understood as non-sense and sought to adjust to the new "genius of the age."

The assimilation of Homer and Shakespeare to an identical role in the invention of the same literary tradition was especially apparent in Pope, some of whose remarks on Shakespeare we have already seen. And Pope it was who made clearest the role they both played in that invention:

> Be *Homer's* works your *Study* and *Delight,*
> Read them by Day, and meditate by Night;
> Thence form your Judgment, thence your Maxims bring,
> And trace the Muses *upward,* to their *Spring.*
> Still with *It self compar'd,* his *Text* peruse;
> And let your *Comment* be the *Mantuan Muse.*
>   When first young *Maro* in his boundless Mind
>   A Work t'outlast Immortal *Rome* design'd,

---

[64]Chesterfield, *Letters to His Son and Others,* p. 52 (letter of April 1, 1748); Montagu, *Essay,* p. 19; Virginia Woolf, "On Not Knowing Greek," in *The Common Reader, First Series* (1925; rpt. New York, 1953), p. 30.
[65]Gilden, "Essay," p. ix.

Perhaps he seem'd *above* the Critick's Law,
And but from *Nature's Fountains* scorn'd to draw:
But when t'examine ev'ry Part he came,
Nature and *Homer* were, he found, the *same.*

The familiar lines from the 1709 *Essay on Criticism* (I.124–35) were noteworthy. Not only did they deny the commonplace separation of Homer and Virgil (as in the passage where Dryden related Shakespeare and Jonson to Homer and Virgil, which Pope might well have had in mind), but they identified the Homer of Fleury's rule, clarity, simplicity, and reason with nature itself.

Pope presented Homer as the great original, a natural power unto himself. Yet Shakespeare, Pope wrote in his preface to the dramatist's work (as Montagu was to remind her readers), was even more "an Original" than Homer: "He is not so much an Imitator, as an Instrument, of Nature."[66] Pope was not, of course, the first to make the claim. As early as 1664 Margaret Cavendish certainly had some such idea in mind when she called Shakespeare "a natural orator, as well as a natural poet," whose "subtil observation" and "deep apprehension" enabled him to "transform himself" into those he staged (especially women) and to identify the true processes of nature.[67] Excepting Rymer, all the later seventeenth-century critics opined likewise. By Montagu's time the characterization was no longer debatable. In his *Liberal Opinions* of 1777, Courtney Melmoth recorded a dialogue in which a stranger told the narrator he had read but two books besides the Bible: " 'The volume of Nature, and the volume of Shakespear.' 'Why Shakespear?' 'Because *one* is a commentary upon the *other.* Shakespear was born to illustrate Nature.' " In the early nineteenth-century A. W. Schlegel likened him to "an Alpine *avalanche*" that would "continue to gather strength at every moment of its progress." With Calderón, Shakespeare was, he said, the only dramatic poet "entitled to be called great."[68] The key question, as Pope had it, was that of original instrumentality.

What qualified such inventors as Homer and Shakespeare was that "Fire" Pope had been willing to grant even to Chapman:

This *Fire* is discern'd in *Virgil*, but discern'd as through a Glass, reflected from *Homer*, more shining than fierce, but every where equal and constant: In *Lucan* and *Statius*, it bursts out in sudden, short, and interrupted Flashes: In *Milton*, it glows like a Furnace kept up to an uncommon ardor

---

[66]Alexander Pope, *Selected Poetry and Prose,* ed. William K. Wimsatt, 2d ed. (New York, 1972), p. 173.

[67]Cavendish, *Life of the Duke,* pp. 284–87.

[68]Courtney Melmoth, *Liberal Opinions,* vol. 5 (London, 1777), given as an appendix in Joyce M. S. Tompkins, *The Popular Novel in England, 1770–1800* (1961; rpt. Westport, Conn., 1976), pp. 370–74; Schlegel, *Lectures,* pp. 345, 342.

> by the Force of Art: In *Shakespear*, it strikes before we are aware, like an
> accidental Fire from Heaven: But in *Homer*, and in him onely, it burns
> every where clearly, and every where irresistibly.[69]

The possible reminiscence of *The Merchant of Venice* emphasized how
exceptional was Shakespeare's presence in this enumeration, a playwright
among epic poets, but an inventor like the others in their various kind.
And since inventions—of literature, of tradition—are here the object of
discussion, it is, I think, incumbent on me at least to glance at how this
idea itself was understood: the more so as the issues of invention, difference, and change underlie my final chapters.

Pope continued the passage just quoted, with the words: "This strong
and ruling Faculty was like a powerful Star, which, in the Violence of its
Course, drew all things within its Vortex." The Cartesian image is of
special interest, because this fiery inventiveness was perhaps not merely
the source, but the very essence, of the sublime—all too often presented as
the irrational in art. Here, on the contrary, Pope made it into an aspect of
reason, its center point, as it were. In itself it might be largely inexplicable,
because it was at the very source of what was understood as the rational,
although aesthetic science would be founded on the effort to explain the
sublime as a part of reason (as we will see in Chapter 10 and as was already
suggested at the end of the last chapter). Indeed, in Hegel, it would no
longer remain just one aspect of great art or of fine reason: it would be the
only aspect specific to such art, its principal character. That development
was rooted in the debates we have been following.

For Pope, invention had already become the spring of a new rational
knowledge, of which Homer (or Shakespeare) was the epitome. He ended
the paragraph we have been following:

> It seem'd not enough to have taken in the whole Circle of Arts, and the
> whole Compass of Nature to supply his maxims and reflection; all the
> inward Passions and Affections of Mankind to furnish his Characters, and
> all the outward forms and Images of Things for his Descriptions: but
> wanting yet an ampler Sphere to expatiate in, he open'd a new and bound-
> less Walk for his Imagination, and created a World for himself in the
> Invention of *Fable*. That which Aristotle calls the *Soul of Poetry*, was first
> breath'd into it by *Homer*.

Yet at the same time he contained a "pure and noble Simplicity" found "no
where in such Perfection as in the *Scripture* and our Author."[70] Pope thus
summed up the strain and the development that "began" with Fleury, was
continued by the late seventeenth-century critics, and culminated in Le
Fèvre Dacier's work of 1714. That was just the year before Pope published
his Preface, to whose formulations her writing was so important.

---

[69]Pope, *Iliad*, ed. Mack, in *Poems*, 7:5.
[70]Ibid., 7:5, 18.

The reinvention of Homer and Shakespeare was thus inseparably bound up with the invention of literature, the creation of a tradition, and the development of ideas of invention and originality themselves. Simonsuuri has noted that these critical notions of "fire" and "invention" were drawn from classical Antiquity. The first derived from the concept of *furor poeticus*, of poetic inspiration as original invention in a sense not unfamiliar to us (although because its source was beyond the poet, in the sacred, it was also not what we would think of as *invention* at all). The second, *inventio*, was altogether more prosaic, meaning simply the sifting out of material appropriate to an argument from a more or less familiar stock. By the late seventeenth century matters were changing: "In neoclassical criticism the notion of 'fire' had come to be dissociated from the idea of poetic inspiration and had been reduced to mean merely an elevated, impassioned style. *Inventio*, on the other hand, was traditionally the finding of material and had nothing to do with originality." But this term had also been undergoing a shift in meaning since the sixteenth century, one that would conclude in the eighteenth.[71]

The word "fire" was then once again available to Pope to indicate something close to poetic creativity, the source of the profundity that underlay writing whose passionate elevation was genuine, not just an effect of style. Then, too, a place was left for "invention" to be used in a sense nearer to the modern. It had come close, writes Simonsuuri, "to the sense in which imagination was used by the Romantics in the nineteenth century."[72] Fire was the practical capacity of mind that made original invention possible. To be sure, invention was still associated with the idea of sorting material out of available knowledge (with the idea of tropes in rhetoric), but increasingly, it had to do with a deeper capacity to know. So Pope urged in his *Iliad* preface: "It is the Invention that in different degrees distinguishes all great Genius's: The utmost Stretch of human Study, Learning, and Industry, which master every thing besides, can never attain to this. It furnishes Art with all her Materials, and without it Judgment itself can at best but *steal wisely*."[73]

Invention was thus already akin to what Kant would refer to in the Third *Critique* as the "suprasensible substrat" of all knowing—indeed, to what Hegel would speak of as the universal Idea embodied in all great art in concrete form, itself then available as a separate object of knowledge. That embodiment, precisely, was the special achievement of the great artist. Through the debate about Homer and Shakespeare, Pope had already concluded that the artistic genius was a person able to act in a way

---

[71]Simonsuuri, *Homer's Original Genius*, pp. 60–61; Grahame Castor, *Pléiade Poetics: A Study in Sixteenth-Century Thought and Terminology* (Cambridge, 1964), esp. pp. 86–136, 168–83. For the Renaissance, see above all David Quint, *Origin and Originality in Renaissance Literature: Versions of the Source* (New Haven, Conn., and London, 1983).

[72]Simonsuuri, *Homer's Original Genius*, p. 61.

[73]Pope, *Iliad*, ed. Mack, in *Poems*, 7:3.

similar to what such later argument suggested. In his view judgment enabled the tempering of fire's high flights, giving lesser mortals access to invention's results. Only so was Homer's sublimity available to the ordinary reader. Having made something with no prior existence, the poet made a gift of it to others. People could already read such a view in Boileau's 1674 translation of Longinus's *Sublime*, whose major exemplum of the sublime, the *fiat lux* of Genesis, would remain as central to Hegel's *Aesthetics* as it was to Hobbes for the presentation of *Leviathan*.

Together invention and judgment produced a more equanimous and "reasonable" work. And surely we may find here the germ of that distinction between the sublime and the beautiful so important for eighteenth-century aesthetics. Judgment, aided by invention in something close to its older sense—an ability wisely to select elements from not unfamiliar realities—could so organize them in a fine and clear language (or equivalent other medium) as to provide those well-ordered relations in which beauty could be recognized. As Homer's irresistible fire, invention took judgment to the limit of sense, forcing the reader, the listener, or the spectator to strain reason to the utmost. Such "sublimity" required a century of debate before it could at last be held firmly within reason: as that immensity of effect that brings reason to the simultaneous apprehension of its limits and its infinite capacities.

But the distinction was forged in the earlier debates. And as Pope had done by reference to Homer, so did Rymer in commenting on Shakespeare: "But *Fancy*, I think, in Poetry, is like *Faith* in Religion; it makes far discoveries, and soars above reason, but never clashes, or runs against it. *Fancy* leaps, and frisks, and away she's gone; whilst *reason* rattles the chains, and follows after. *Reason* must consent and ratify what-ever by *fancy* is attempted in its absence; or else 'tis all null and void in law."[74] The evident source of this passage lay in the arguments Hobbes advanced about "Fancy," "Reason," and "Judgment," whose relation to French debate I suggested before (see pp. 166–67). After the inquiries of Addison, Pope, and others, their claims became habitual. "By genius," wrote Fielding in 1749, "I would understand that power, or rather those powers of the mind, which are capable of penetrating into all things within our reach and knowledge, and of distinguishing their essential differences. These are no other than invention and judgment." After seeming to deny that invention was "a creative faculty" rather than just "discovery, or finding out," he then explained how it was "a quick and sagacious penetration into the true essence of all the objects of our contemplation." Homer was naturally among those instanced.[75] By the time of Lessing's *Laocoön* or of Montagu's *Essay*, Homer and Shakespeare had become undisputed masters of

---

[74]Rymer, *Tragedies of the Last Age*, in *Critical Works*, p. 20.
[75]Henry Fielding, *The History of Tom Jones. A Foundling* (New York, 1964), pp. 338–39 (Book IX, chap. i).

the tradition, no longer its creation but its origin. Indeed, they had become exemplary for understanding inventive originality itself. To the nineteenth century the question was closed: Homer and the tradition were not invented, they were a part of the unchanging legacy of humankind.

John Keats could thus tell of his acquisition of the tradition not as historically determined, but as part of an unbroken Graeco-Roman heritage of civilized humanity:

> Much have I travelled in the realms of gold,
>   And many goodly states and kingdoms seen;
>   Round many western islands have I been
> Which bards in fealty to Apollo hold.
> Oft of one wide expanse had I been told
>   That deep-browed Homer ruled as his demesne;

until at last, he said, he had been privileged to taste the power at first hand: "Yet never did I breath its pure serene / Till I heard Chapman speak out loud and bold": that Chapman whose fulminations we saw against Scaliger for his very failure to understand Homer's "wide expanse."[76] Apart from the fact that Keats was after all referring to a translation, it is clear that such "pure serene," such immediate experience was itself enabled only by the tradition of which it was now a part. Homer was the *"artless"* communicator of that *"Virtue"* without which "there can be no *true Poetry"*; he was the exponent of *"Nature,"* whence he "took his Plan"; he had "painted *Places, Persons, Animals,* and *Seasons,* with their proper *Marks* and Qualities."[77] That very artlessness was what enabled the immediate communication of nature and its effects, the exposition of universal value and behavior.

Shortly after Keats's poem (1816), Hegel was confirming Homer's preeminence in discussing how ideal art (shades of Reynolds and others) had to avoid too much detail: "Things of this sort may of course be adopted as topics of artistic representation in poetry, and in this connection it is granted that Homer, for example, has the greatest conformity to nature." At the same time, the "soul of his poetry," as Pope had put it, was also the soul of nature, its ideal forms: "Yet he too, despite all *enargeia,* all clarity for our vision, has to restrict himself to mentioning such things only in general terms."[78] Homer was now the standard by whom all others were to be measured. What even Homer could not permit himself was viewed as an absolute restriction on art: but, of course, the poetry that did not embody the ideal in those concrete forms it used was not art at all, let

[76]John Keats, "On First Looking into Chapman's Homer," in *The Complete Poems,* ed. John Barnard, 3d ed. (Harmondsworth, 1988), p. 72.

[77]Thomas Blackwell, *An Enquiry into the Life and Writings of Homer* (1736; rpt. Hildesheim and New York, 1976), pp. 24, 58, 325.

[78]Hegel, *Aesthetics,* 1:166.

alone great art. Since Homer was great art, he inevitably fulfilled its demands; and because the Homeric epics date even from the prehistory of Greece, those demands could not be more recent or more local than that.[79]

We may turn to a later poem of Keats's to obtain the full flavor of Homer as the very epitome of the artist:

> So wast thou blind!—but then the veil was rent,
>   For Jove uncurtained Heaven to let thee live,
> And Neptune made for thee a spumy tent,
>   And Pan made sing for thee his forest-hive;
> Ay, on the shores of darkness there is light,
>   And precipices show untrodden green;
> There is a budding morrow in midnight;
>   There is a triple sight in blindness keen;
> Such seeing hadst thou, as it once befell
> To Dian, Queen of Earth, and Heaven, and Hell.[80]

"The poems of Homer and his contemporaries," wrote Shelley, "were the delight of infant Greece; they were the elements of that social system which is the column upon which all succeeding civilization has reposed."[81]

The storied Homer of Antiquity, of whom it can properly be said that for the Greeks he was the equivalent of what the Bible was to be for the Christian West—not a religious icon but the principal source of culture— had thus been recreated for the Great Tradition of modernism. Invented in a different image, along with Shakespeare, he was adapted not so much to the thundering voice of fiery Chapman as to the more measured prosody of Hobbes and Dryden, of Le Fèvre Dacier, Pope, and William Cowper (1791). This was what Hegel called, perhaps after Blackwell's "artlessness," *keine Manier:* "To have no manner has from time immemorial [*von jeher*] been the one grand manner, and in this sense alone are Homer, Sophocles, Raphael, Shakespeare, to be called 'original.' "[82] In our own time Woolf has rightly taken this kind of statement apart:

> But again (the question comes back and back), Are we reading Greek as it was written when we say this? When we read these few words cut on a tombstone, a stanza in a chorus, the end or the opening of a dialogue of

[79]A recent (Marxist) thinker's comments on Homer reveals the durability of such claims, even when the writer is trying to replace idealist with materialist aesthetics: "And yet Homer retains an attraction, an extraordinary freshness (at least in the most 'beautiful' fragments)": Henri Lefebvre, *Contribution à l'esthétique* (Paris, 1953). The parenthesis says more than Lefebvre intends.

[80]Keats, "To Homer" [1818], in *Complete Poems*, p. 255.

[81]Shelley, "Defense of Poetry," in *Selected Poetry and Prose*, p. 423.

[82]Hegel, *Aesthetics*, 1:298; *Asthetik*, ed. Friedrich Bassenge, intro. Georg Lukács, 2 vols. (Berlin and Weimar, 1965), 1:291.

Plato's, a fragment of Sappho, when we bruise our minds upon some
tremendous metaphor in the *Agamemnon* instead of stripping the branch
of its flowers instantly as we do in reading *Lear*—are we not reading
wrongly? losing our sharp sight in the haze of associations? reading into
Greek poetry not what they have but what we lack?[83]

To argue that Homer (or Shakespeare) was part of a tradition's invention
in this way is not in the least to assert either that the power of the *Iliad* and
the *Odyssey* is a matter of subjective or simply relativist judgment—
however collective—or that artworks, taste, and aesthetic judgment in
general are wholly (or merely) questions of local decision. It is, however, to
maintain that the ways power is understood, value ascribed, and meaning
developed do depend as much on context and local environment as on the
presence (not seldom accidental) of the work itself.[84] That is why there
may be such debate, anxious or assured, about certain works, at certain
times, in certain places. When Juan López de Vicuña published Góngora's
poetry in 1627 as the *Obras en versos del Homero español*, perhaps un-
wittingly he emphasized this condition.[85] We earlier saw how diversely
belabored was Góngora's poetry when it appeared: was it mere chaotic
nonsense? or was it profound allegorical commentary? Was it radical,
conservative, or just vacuous pretension? None of that was clarified in the
address "al Letor," in which Vicuña called Góngora "nuestro Poeta, pri-
mero en el mundo." In that, he was genuinely "el Homero español": such
primacy could mean "best," "original," or merely first in time and so
excusable as to his faults.

For at least two centuries the dispute around Homer was no less vehement: not simply a battle over the nature of the author and the kind of
poetic work (questions still contested in our own time), but—more important—a battle as to whether the poems were worth bothering about at all.
Were the Homeric epics the kind of *summa* ancient Greek culture had

---

[83]Woolf, "On Not Knowing Greek," in *Common Reader*, p. 36.

[84]Does one need to answer the tired claim that only the "great works" survive? "It has
been estimated," writes Dana Ferrin Sutton, "that approximately ninety percent of
ancient literature has disappeared" (*The Lost Sophocles* [Lanham, Md., 1984], p. x). E. J.
Kenney speaks of "sheer hazard" as "the most potent force at work" in the survival of
works from the Golden and Silver Ages of Rome (ed., *The Cambridge History of
Classical Literature, vol. 2: Latin Literature* [Cambridge, 1982], p. 23). Cf. John Frank
Kermode, *Forms of Attention* (Chicago and London, 1985), p. 73. Nor is the issue just
one of actual physical survival. A suitably receptive state of public mind is needed for
works to be published and diffused. An author must probably belong to a group acceptable to those who hold the multifold reins of diffusion, if her or his work is to be seen. An
appropriate form of writing is generally necessary. And so forth. On these matters
Michel Foucault has been eloquent: *L'ordre du discours* (Paris, 1971). Not by chance in
the sixteenth and early seventeenth centuries had Le Roy, Sanches, Simonius, and
others discussed just this loss and decay of "letters."

[85]Luis de Góngora y Argote, *Obras en versos del Homero español, que recogió Juan
López de Vicuña (edición facsímil)*, ed. Dámaso Alonso (Madrid, 1963).

taken them to be? the many-layered vision of human and divine interaction foundational of a culture that provided Virgil and subsequent writers of epic with their appropriate model? Or were they so much repetitive and empty clichéd gossip, a compilation of childish folklore, a mishmash of mythical error, written in a language unworthy of serious attention? Were Chapman, Hobbes, Le Fèvre Dacier, and Pope right? Or Scaliger, Saint-Evremond, and Perrault?

That the epics could be simultaneously *all* of these things is part of the power of the artwork—not a "wager" on transcendence or "real presence," as George Steiner has asserted, so much as a presentation of that multi-plicitous power of mind that the later eighteenth century understood to be suscitated by and within the sublime.[86] That simultaneous diversity was one reason why the epics survived to be read: they could mean so much to so many (a necessary but not sufficient condition for survival, which also depends, as we know from the vast store of lost artworks, on the endless accidents of history: see note 84). But it should be no surprise that local, "superstructural," understanding could not alone deal with the chaos of such endless variety and needed the coherence of a tradition corresponding to its idea of the human and its capacities. To have found Homer in a mess of unknown cultural reference, with Greek newly learned (small awareness of dialect and none of temporal layering) and amid a growing welter of creative translation, was like meeting the raw experience of nature that Galileo and Bacon called unusable. Only make experience "literate," however, extract some unifying language, and then something could be done with it.

Homer and nature were one, therefore, in another way: both came initially as a cluttered and incomprehensible chaos. That recognized, nature could be reduced to usable order, while Homer could be adjusted, "invented" to confirm the way that order, its practices, and its values were envisaged: to guarantee a new cultural tradition. Late seventeenth-century England had discovered a figure in its own immediate past able to be equated in many ways with Homer. It was certainly no accident that caused Wollstonecraft a century later to identify the rereading of Shakespeare and the interpretation of political history. Spurning Edmund Burke's claim that the established church was the traditional guardian of English liberties, she exclaimed that his overweening, overwealthy, and not popularly established church had nothing to do with a constitution protective of "the liberties of the community." He was ignoring the now stable achievements of a constitutional history in the same way as "some of the laborious commentators of Shakespeare" ignored equally widely agreed interpretation: "You have affixed a meaning to laws that chance, or,

[86]George Steiner, *Real Presences* (Chicago, 1989). On the sublime in this context, see below, Chapter 10.

to speak more philosophically, the interested views of men, settled, not dreaming of your ingenious elucidation."[87]

Wollstonecraft captured both the link between politics and literature and the fact that each had required instauring. We have amply seen how the idea that literature was at once development, evidence, and guarantor of civil stability had become a quite standard topos and a central claim. Like many others, Pope had understood literature in the age of Dryden in just such terms:

> We conquered France, but felt our Captive's charms;
> Her Arts victorious triumphed o'er our Arms;
> Britain to soft refinement less a foe,
> Wit grew polite, and Numbers learned to flow.
> Waller was smooth; but Dryden taught to join
> The varying verse, the full resounding line,
> The long majestic March, and Energy divine,
> Though still some traces of our rustic vein
> And splayfoot verse remained, and will remain.
> Late, very late, correctness grew our care,
> When the tired Nation breathed from civil war.[88]

Not by chance, perhaps, was Wollstonecraft to make the connection between proper reading of Shakespeare and right understanding of the English constitution when criticizing Burke's *Reflections on the Revolution in France*. And Burke, in the passage that was the butt of the cited onslaught, was upholding an established church whose composition was entirely male.

In the context of Wollstonecraft's thought, that was clearly not accidental. But it was far from indifferent in a broader context as well. To the verses just quoted, Pope added a note at his mention of Waller, observing that he was above all thinking of the poet's translation "about this time with the Earl of Dorset, Mr. Godolphin, and others" of Corneille's *Mort de Pompée*, exemplary of the work produced by "the more correct French poets." We saw that this drama had already been successfully translated by Katherine Philips. Pope ignored the fact. The growth of correct literature as integral part and even patron of civil stability had been typically illustrated by a metaphor of conquest (Boileau and Dennis, Charpentier and Prior, Fontenelle and Pope all wrote in the vein, as Swift did satirically of Homer himself). The trope also depicted masculine dominance of the feminine: a conquered France relinquishing to victorious Britain her

---

[87]Mary Wollstonecraft, *A Vindication of the Rights of Men (1790)*, intro. Eleanor Louise Nicholes (Gainesville, Fla., 1960), p. 93.

[88]Pope, "The First Epistle of the Second Book of Horace Imitated," in *Poems*, pp. 644–45 (ll. 263–73).

captive charms (and catch the ambiguity of Pope's "Arms"), or Waller's smooth Cornelia yielding to Dryden's majestic march and divine energy. It was not inevitable that literature should become an essentially masculine product, as we saw through mid-seventeenth-century debate. It did, however, become so—and here, too, the choices of Homer and Shakespeare played their part in fixing particular cultural norms. It is in terms of this specific aspect of the instauration that my next chapter explores the degree to which its dominance was or was not flexible and adaptable. The chapter following examines the later development and sealing of correctness, legitimacy, sublimity, and perhaps literature itself.

Chapter 9

Revolution in Bounds

I know not how the Men will resent it to have their enclosure broken down, and Women invited to taste of the Tree of knowledge they have so long unjustly *Monopoliz'd.*
—Mary Astell, *A Serious Proposal*

Do not forget however, that the Muse was not given to add refinements to idleness, but for the highest and most invaluable purposes. Act up to the magnitude of your destiny.
—William Godwin, *Caleb Williams*

Once in place, the view of women's reason argued by such as Fontenelle and Perrault was subject to little change. The avowedly Cartesian arguments advanced by Mary Astell in Part 2 of *A Serious Proposal* (1697) urged woman to charity and piety, improving her status as wife and mother and revalorizing the private sphere in general. She argued a case for the purpose of women's education that differed little not only from the contemporary views of Fénelon or Maintenon, Makin or Hannah Wooley, but also from those later advanced by Condorcet in 1791–92, or by Hannah More, Barbauld, and Stéphanie Ducrest de Genlis in the same period. Perrault's ideas on women's place in the home were entirely similar to those encouraged by James Fordyce in the 1760s and by Dr. John Gregory a decade later. La Bruyère's scorn of women's reason was echoed by that of the ideologue Pierre-Jean-Georges Cabanis. Although many voices were raised throughout the eighteenth century in favor of educational opportunity for women, the very idea of Enlightened reason aggressively excluded what it claimed as female, relegating it to a domain of sensibility, instinctual receptivity, nurturing protectiveness, and childlike fancy. For women, said the sympathetic Condorcet in 1790, "are superior to men as to the soft and domestic virtues . . . [they] are not guided by men's reason, it is true, but they are by their own."[1]

How different was this from what earlier writers had asserted to be in

---

[1]Antoine-Nicolas Caritat, marquis de Condorcet, "Sur l'admission des femmes au droit de la cité," in *Oeuvres,* ed. A. Condorcet O'Connor and M. F. Arago, 10 vols. (Paris, 1847–49), 10:124–25.

fact beneficial to women? In 1739, for instance, the anonymous author of *The Ladies Library*, acknowledging that the restriction of women to family life was unfair and marked a double standard, yet contended that "this *Injustice*" was balanced: "If in this the *Sex* lies under any *Disadvantage*, it is more than recompensed by having the *Honour* of *Families* in their keeping." "That providential economy," added Hannah More years later, "which has clearly determined that women were born to share with men the duties of private life, has as clearly demonstrated that they were not born to divide with them in the public administration."[2] The constant claim we saw earlier to the effect that women's reason must not impede domesticity and its values remained the refrain throughout the century.

Outside their proper sphere women were objects and playthings for men. Woolf in *Orlando* caught the consensus nicely by citing in turn Addison and Chesterfield. The one had written in *The Spectator:* "I consider woman as a beautiful romantic animal, that may be adorned with furs and feathers, pearls and diamonds, ores and silk." This was La Bruyère's gun, horse, or fish. The other had notoriously written: "Women are but children of a larger growth."[3] Chesterfield, too, it was who wrote to his half-grown godson: "I tell you very sincerely, that I never thought a woman good company for a man tête-à-tête, unless for one purpose," a comment one may equate with Lord Kames's similarly brutal remark: "What is love, for example, but a pleasant emotion raised by a sight or idea of a beloved female, joined with the desire of enjoyment."[4] My point in mentioning such remarks is not to highlight their oppressive brutality. Rather I wish to observe how they occurred in contexts where they were seemingly quite irrelevant to the subject at hand. Chesterfield was discussing polite manners, Kames was writing of art and literature (like the author of *The Ladies Library*). Exclusion from the public sphere meant, without further thought, some exclusion from the literary, and the cultural more generally.

It is important to insist again, however, that women were not wholly excluded from that dominant culture. To have done so might have created

---

[2]*The Ladies Library. Written by a Lady*, 3 vols., 5th ed. (London, 1739), 2:73, quoted in Mary Poovey, *The Proper Lady and the Woman Writer* (Chicago and London, 1984), p. 8; Hannah More, in *Moral Sketches of Prevailing Opinions and Manners*, quoted in Janet Todd, *The Sign of Angellica: Women, Writing, and Fiction, 1660–1800* (London, 1989), p. 225.

[3]Woolf, *Orlando*, pp. 134, 136.

[4]The Chesterfield letter is quoted in Rogers, *Augustan Vision*, p. 89. The second remark is from Henry Home, Lord Kames, *Elements of Criticism* (London, 1824), p. 27. A far more positive (and rarer) view was put forward by Pierre-Nicolas Lenglet-Dufresnoy, arguing the power and authority of women, and that if he ever could form a government, for example, he would make sure "royal authority was always in women's hands alone." So far, only novels could show this; it was high time for history to do so. Here, too, the case was situated in a literary discussion: *De l'usage des romans où l'on fait voir leur utilité et leurs différents caractères . . .* , 2 vols. (1734; rpt. Geneva, 1970), 1:83–84, 96, 115.

a group as fearsome as the poor of nineteenth-century industrial cities—
London's outcasts or Paris's dangerous classes. Rather, women were incorporated as second-class participants. As such they could be controlled and
dominated. In 1777 More described women's necessarily subsidiary role in
the culture of Enlightened reason:

> Women have generally quicker perceptions; men have juster sentiments.
> Women consider how things may be prettily said; men, how they may be
> properly said. In women (young ones at least), speaking accompanies
> and sometimes precedes reflection; in men, reflection is the antecedent.
> Women speak to shine or to please; men, to convince or confute. Women
> admire what is brilliant; men what is solid. Women prefer an extempo-
> raneous sally of wit, or a sparkling effusion of fancy, before the most
> accurate reasoning, or the most laborious investigation of facts. In literary
> composition, women are pleased with point, turn, antithesis; men, with
> observation, and a just deduction of effects from causes. Women are fond
> of incident, men, of argument. . . .
>   In short, it appears that the mind in each sex has some natural kind of
> bias, which constitutes a distinction of character, and that the happiness
> of both depends, in a great measure, on the preservation and observance of
> this distinction.[5]

More's estimate disagreed only slightly with La Bruyère's or Chesterfield's opinion that women were either children or ornamental objects
existing for men's titillation. So prevalent did this strain remain that one
is not surprised to see Richard Polwhele use the very remarks just quoted
from More to footnote his violently antifeminist poem *The Unsex'd
Females*, written in 1799 in reaction to the Wollstonecraft of Godwin's
Memoirs.[6] From the late seventeenth century until well into our own,
some more or less extreme version of this view was standard in law as in
literature, in social reality as in the cultural discourse that apprehended it.

More's view of woman's mind as incapable of sustained attention, ornamental rather than logical, superficial not deep, anecdotal not analytic,
suitable for the invention of fanciful fictions but unable to philosophize or
think clearly, was the exact counterpart of La Bruyère's opinion. A century
later such views received their satirical comeuppance:

> It is sometimes stated that as several women of genius in modern times
> have sought to find expression for their creative powers in the art of
> fiction, there must be some inherent connection in the human brain

[5]Hannah More, *Essays on Various Subjects Principally Designed for Young Ladies*, in
Works, 2:335–36.
[6]Richard Polwhele, *The Unsex'd Females. A Poem*, and Mary Ann Radcliffe, *The
Female Advocate. Or, an Attempt to Recover the Rights of Women from Male Usurpation* [facs. eds.], intro. Gina Luria (New York and London, 1974), Polwhele facs., pp. 36–
37n.

between the ovarian sex function and the art of fiction. The fact is, that modern fiction being merely a description of human life in any of its phases, and being the only art that can be exercised without special training or special appliances, and produced in the moments stolen from the multifarious, brain-destroying occupations which fill the average woman's life, they have been driven to find this outlet for their powers as the only one presenting itself.[7]

Between the strong demands on behalf of women and reason characteristic of the first half of the seventeenth century and the understanding that human nature is largely the creation of social action and the result of particular socializing practices which characterizes the twentieth, lie three centuries throughout which every effort was made in the dominant discourse to depict women as naturally subordinate to men. For they lacked, it was said, the very qualities essential to the dominance of a culture, in which they might therefore participate but which they could never hope to direct or lead.

The young Wollstonecraft began by more or less echoing such familiar views. They were apparent both in her 1787 *Thoughts on the Education of Daughters* and her 1789 anthology *The Female Reader*. In this last she drew as many extracts from such writers as Dr. Gregory and his like as she did from less conservative sources, while the views laid out in its preface would have been familiar from More's pen. A woman must learn to speak, to read, and to think well, but not "to obtrude her person or talents on the public." She did not cling long to these opinions. Indeed, in the phrase qualifying the one just quoted, she hinted something of what was to come. A woman was not to obtrude only "when necessity does not justify her and spur her on." Could a growing sense of women's exclusion from culture and social activity provide such necessity? The deceptively mild statement with which she ended her preface implied it might: "As we are created accountable creatures we must run the race ourselves."[8] Already, too, this overt acceptance but implicit rejection of women's cultural subordination provided a foretaste of her eventually unsuccessful struggle to solve these complex issues and an explanation of the violently abusive reaction to Godwin's 1798 *Memoirs*.

The incorporation of women within culture in a subsidiary position but from whence various demands could be urged, the seemingly conditional acceptance of such subordination, and the growing demand that men justify their domination and aggression were processes that explain, I think, both why Wollstonecraft's contentions could be perceived as menacing and why they stayed nonetheless limited. She did not see herself as a member of a totally deprived class seeking to be included in the fold (she

[7]Olive Schreiner, *Women and Labour* [1911], pref. Jane Graves (London, 1978), p. 158.
[8]Mary Wollstonecraft, ed., *The Female Reader* (1789), intro. Moira Ferguson (Delmar, N.J., 1980), pp. v, xv.

was not *pace* Simone de Beauvoir, some "Other"). Rather was she trying to readjust the order of beneficiaries, as it were, in the dominant order. For this very reason, she had no difficulty seeing other groups as candidates for exclusion. We need not be surprised, but we should be armed against taking her for something she was not. Zillah Eisenstein has warned against this.[9] But it deserves more attention: not to belittle Wollstonecraft's achievement, whose grandeur needs no presumptuous auxiliary at this late date, but rather to contribute to a general understanding of how a dominant discourse can absorb dissenting voices and recuperate apparent subversion. We need to know why such strong voices as those of Mary Wollstonecraft and her contemporaries Catherine Macaulay, Mary Hays, and Mary Ann Radcliffe (not to mention Olympe de Gouges, Manon Roland, and others in Paris), writing during the revolutionary years at the turn of the eighteenth century, achieved little or no effect.[10]

Two explanations offer themselves. At one level, ineffectiveness was bound to the seemingly trivial and obvious fact that such alternative ways of understanding as the materialist social explanation just quoted from Olive Schreiner (or any others) were unavailable to Wollstonecraft and her contemporaries: which is not to say they would be better, simply profoundly other. As I try to show in this chapter, that constraint meant being forced to adhere to the norms of the very reason whose oppressive dominance was the object of attack. The result was a discomfiture that Wollstonecraft certainly felt deeply. At another level, blockage had no doubt to do with the very nature of the "revolutionary years" themselves. Ambivalence was endemic, vehement disagreement was habitual, the role of Enlightened thinking unclear.[11] That is the issue to which I turn first, so as to provide something of the historical context within which the debates remained embedded.

On July 14, 1789, the Bastille fell to an angry Parisian crowd. The event

[9]Zillah Eisenstein, *The Radical Future of Liberal Feminism* (New York and London, 1981).

[10]Contrary to what Frances Ferguson wrote in her response to the original version of what is now this chapter, none of this is to suggest Wollstonecraft's arguments went "unheard": "Wollstonecraft Our Contemporary," in *Gender and Theory: Dialogues on Feminist Criticism*, ed. Linda Kauffman (Oxford, 1989), p. 52. What follows both assumes and says they certainly were heard. How otherwise could one explain the violent reactions? And why would one bother to write about her? What this chapter tries to answer is why her writings had no *effect*, why they changed nothing—despite the hearing . . . or because of it. For it may be, we will see, that the familiarity of her terms ultimately removed any real threat from them and made her increasingly aware of their limitations.

[11]The bicentennial outpouring of reevaluations of what the French Revolution was and what it "meant" provides evidence of this: from conservative plaint that it was a setback to progressive developments already at work, to reaffirmation of its radically transformative achievement, to almost any variant in between. I am not competent to enter that debate. My simple point here is twofold: that the 1790s saw no less a medley of debate and ambivalence and that all sides perceived the Revolution as a violently profound test of Enlightened thought.

was hardly of major military importance in the Revolution. Although its fall could be heralded as the sign that Louis XVI had lost his capital, it was not until 1880 that July 14 was decreed the national holiday of the French Republic. It is perhaps not irrelevant that this occurred just nine years before the erection of the Eiffel Tower (begun in 1887, completed for the 1889 Exposition) was equally symbolically to confirm the republic's burgeoning prosperity founded on the back of a repressive industrialization, nor that the awful depression of 1880 might have made so positive a symbol essential. The Bastille's fall may well symbolize less the democratization of the French state than it does the bourgeoisie's creation of the conditions for industrialization and its own wealth.

Such ambiguity was widespread in contemporary evaluation. "Oh wond'rous power of words," as William Wordsworth exclaimed in 1805, "how sweet they are / According to the meaning which they bring."[12] For factual ambivalence has little enough to do with the symbolic clarity ascribed to such events, and one may well agree with those historians who have argued that the Revolution did not rupture European history, however much it changed the direction of France. It doubtless remade both in the sense that more people were enabled to participate in the benefits of Whiggish history and to see some of the issues under a particularly fiery light. It surely quite altered the form of political discourse in France, providing it (exactly) with a *symbolic* moment of break and new departure. France was catching up with England, eventually even creating a constitutional monarch. But by no means was everyone to participate in expanding access to the benefits of industrialization and political debate. For women, especially, no Bastille, symbolic or otherwise, was to fall.

For Wollstonecraft, however, the Bastille had early become a personal and political symbol. As early as October 30, 1786, on her arrival as governess at the Kingsboroughs' castle in Mitchelstown, Ireland, she had written to her sister, Everina: "I entered the great gates with the same kind of feeling as I should have if I was going into the Bastile." On November 19, 1789, she complained to her friend and protégé George Blood that he had not written: "You were not shut up in the Bastile."[13] For Wollstonecraft, the image perfectly depicted women's bondage. In the posthumously published *Maria,* her eponymous heroine explained how "marriage had bastilled me for life," and how, once a man had left his wife, he was free but for the small allowance whose payment was "thought sufficient to secure his reputation from taint," whereas a woman who left her husband was "despised and shunned." "Such is the respect," she added, "paid to the master-

[12]William Wordsworth, *The Prelude, or Growth of a Poet's Mind (Text of 1805),* ed. Ernest de Selincourt, new ed. Stephen Gill (1970; rpt. London, 1975), p. 108: Part VII.121–22.

[13]Mary Wollstonecraft, *Collected Letters,* ed. Ralph M. Wardle (Ithaca, N.Y., and London, 1979), pp. 120, 185.

key of property!"[14] The Bastille readily symbolized this combination of bondage and deprivation, and Maria's lament could be taken as a commentary as well on the tale of Jemima, who had earlier related how misery and dispossession led her "from absolute necessity" down the path from publicly approved morality to her position as keeper of the "poor wretches" now confined in the insane asylum.[15] Interestingly, this tale was a nearly exact fictional depiction of the conditions Radcliffe condemned in *The Female Advocate*. Such confinement was also emblematic of the failure to discover how to change the actual status of women. These problems were indeed clearly tied, for Wollstonecraft, to the hope of the Revolution.

Just as women's position did not change, and as feminist voices fell silent in the snare of Enlightened reason's dominance, so too the Revolution in France confirmed reason's hold on the social order. European history did not suddenly make some qualitative leap into difference. One important Romantic's reaction may be helpful in understanding this, especially because he took up some of the very issues on which Wollstonecraft focused. In a text much abused by critics, Wordsworth did exclaim: "Bliss was it in that dawn to be alive. / But to be young was very heaven!"[16] In the *Prelude*, he apostrophized:

> Oh! most beloved Friend, a glorious time
> A happy time that was; triumphant looks
> Were then the common language of all eyes:
> As if awak'd from sleep, the Nations hail'd
> Their great expectancy. . . .
>
> (*Prelude*, VI.681–85)

Some critics have read these lines as an outpouring of ardent revolutionary fervor, expressing the successful rejection of a yoke of oppression by the only truly revolutionary literary movement in our tradition (Romanti-

[14]Mary Wollstonecraft, *Maria or The Wrongs of Woman*, intro. Moira Ferguson (New York and London, 1975), pp. 103, 106. Margaret Kirkham has argued that in Jane Austen's *Mansfield Park* rather veiled references to the Bastille evince a feminism similar to Wollstonecraft's: who would be its source. In that novel, Kirkham writes, "Maria [Bertram] sees Sotherton as 'a dismal old prison,' and, as she sends Rushworth off to fetch the key for the iron gate through which she wishes to pass with Crawford, quotes Sterne's starling which, imprisoned in the Bastille, sang, 'I can't get out, I can't get out'": *Jane Austen, Feminism, and Fiction* (1983; rpt. New York, 1986), p. 37. The first comment was Rushworth's, in fact, not Maria Bertram's: Jane Austen, *The Complete Novels* (New York, n.d.), pp. 500, 529. Victor Brombert has observed that in French writing the Bastille was a literary cliché from André Chénier on (1762–94—his poetry was published only in 1819): above all it meant, as Michelet put it, "a prison of thought": *The Romantic Prison: The French Tradition* (Princeton, 1978), pp. 30–45.

[15]Wollstonecraft, *Maria*, p. 55. Jemima's tale occupies pp. 52–69 in this edition.

[16]William Wordsworth, "The French Revolution as it appeared to enthusiasts at its commencement" (1804), quoted from *Selected Poetry*, ed. Mark Van Doren (New York, 1956).

cism), which, at least for a time, succeeded where political revolution "failed." It was a revolution destined to be crushed by unwonted government censorship (as though such censorship had not always been endemic—like the repression that some of these "revolutionaries" certainly suffered: Joseph Priestley, for example, at the hands of a church-and-king mob in 1791: but earlier examples are legion). As we will see, such a view strikes me as untenable: in the many ways and for the many reasons implicit and explicit in this book. These verses surely did glory in a hope, but it was equally surely a hope past. In this writing, moreover, that nostalgia did not imply a reckoning with change or any suggestion of its possibility. The Revolution's failure, for example, to release women from servitude found an echo in this same poem.

Wordsworth gave voice to the prevailing ideology of women's place in the cautionary tale of "Mary of Buttermere," "the Maiden" "in her cottage Inn," who overwhelmed the poet with "delight" and "admiration of her modest mien, / And carriage, mark'd by unexampled grace," a lady of "discretion," "just opinion," "female modesty," "patience," and the rest. Above all, she merited approbation because "her new-born Infant, fearless as a lamb" now "sleeps in earth." This she praiseworthily managed despite "betrayal" by " 'a bold bad Man.' " And now "happy are they both / Mother and Child!" (*Prelude*, VII.321–60). The poet thus commented on a celebrated case of a country woman betrayed by an adulterer after she had come to the city. His tone was one of pity, but his imaginary recreation of her recovery of grace could not avoid characterizing her in the long-familiar and normative terms of feminine perfection. That Wordsworth went on from Mary's story to depict a small boy's innocence surrounded by dissolute town dwellers, and to lament the shame of a "Woman . . . abandon'd," emphasized the clear link made between woman, innocence, childishness, modesty, patience, and the victim's role (although we will see that the poet did not at all suggest that the moral abandonment of the last case was other than chosen: an issue whose relation to "woman's nature" as revealed in Mary posed difficulties for Wollstonecraft as well). The poet's attitude toward this may be variously interpreted, of course, but the terms and associations selected are clear.[17]

Mary of Buttermere and the others were victims of the city (to be pitied or condemned), as the Revolution and Enlightenment were considered its product. In that light the poet's praise of Mary (whose Christian name is as relevant as her "lamb"-like child) relates directly to Romanticism's ideal-

---

[17]In the essay mentioned earlier, Frances Ferguson vehemently criticized my interpretation of Wordsworth ("Wollstonecraft Our Contemporary," pp. 54–57). Her censure seems to me based mostly on a misreading, and I have therefore sought to clarify my analysis. At the same time, while quarreling with her reading, I have adopted some of the points she raised, and I thank her for the exchange. See, too, her *Wordsworth: Language as Counter-Spirit* (New Haven, Conn., and London, 1977).

ization of nature: "The Spirit of Nature was upon me here; / The Spirit of Beauty and enduring life / Was present as a habit" (*Prelude*, VII.736–38). Shades of Shaftesbury, one might say: but after the Revolution, as it was carefully placed by the poet, such a phrase looked back from, or at least to one side of, what was now viewed as harmful to a degree. Mary with her lamb of God, the innocent boy, the doubtless redeemable prostitute do not accidentally recall the gospels. This was the Wordsworth who, in the same year as he wrote the first version of *The Prelude*, related in *The Recluse* how

> On Man, on Nature, and on Human Life,
> Musing in solitude, I oft perceive
> Fair trains of imagery before me rise,
> Accompanied by feelings of delight
> Pure, or with no unpleasing sadness mixed. . . .
>
> (754–58)

Here we find the same nostalgia for a lost wholeness with Nature, with the Divine presence of some untrammeled absolute Justice (happy Mary with her dead child in her pauper's cottage), as Oliver Goldsmith urged years earlier in *The Traveller* and *The Deserted Village*, two other poems often co-opted by left-wing critics with small sense of history (Goldsmith might be damning enclosures, but he was elegizing an agrarian past with its alleged oneness of people and land, not inviting a proletarian future). Wordsworth's later addition to *The Prelude* of fulsome praise for Burke ("Genius of Burke! forgive the pen seduced / By specious wonders" [VII.512ff.]) surprises only those who forget the latter's own revolutionary ambivalence and ignore what (in the poem) came soon after the disagreeably sentimental passage about Mary of Buttermere.[18]

On his journey to Cambridge the poet encountered a prostitute. Perhaps he simply met (as well?) an emancipated woman, for he wrote not only of "public vice" but also of the speaking of "blasphemy." What really happened is evidently both undiscoverable and irrelevant. The point is that as he related his thoughts about the encounter, the distinction became impossible:

[18]On Wordsworth and sentiment, see Janet Todd, *Sensibility: An Introduction* (London and New York, 1986), pp. 62–63, 140, 143. It is here "disagreeable" just because it enabled the poet to ignore the real life and hardships of the person whose experience he nonetheless so used. Ferguson (see previous note) asserts that he was reclaiming on the victim's behalf the self-possession of which she had been deprived by city melodrama and "theatrical appropriation" for others' ends and "desires." But the "pity" expressed through sentimentality can only strike one as spurious and is in any case no less appropriative. Roger Sales views Wordsworth's nostalgic pastoral much as I do: *English Literature in History: 1780–1830, Pastoral and Politics* (London, 1983). As the title suggests, he examines a broader spectrum than the present chapter: on Wordsworth, see pp. 52–69.

> It was but little more than three short years
> Before the season which I speak of now
> When first, a Traveller from our pastoral hills,
> Southward two hundred miles I had advanced,
> And for the first time in my life did hear
> The voice of Woman utter blasphemy;
> Saw Woman as she is to open shame
> Abandon'd and the pride of public vice.
> Full surely from the bottom of my heart
> I shuddered; but the pain was almost lost,
> Absorb'd and buried in the immensity
> Of the effect: a barrier seemed at once
> Thrown in, that from humanity divorced
> The Human Form, splitting the race of Man
> In twain, yet leaving the same outward shape.
> Distress of mind ensued upon this sight
> And ardent meditation. . . .
>
> *(Prelude, VII.412–29)*

Despite the confusion provoked by the discovery that the human form itself was no guarantee of moral rectitude, the poet did manage to overcome his horror:

> Afterwards
> A milder sadness on such spectacles
> Attended; thought, commiseration, grief
> For the individual, and the overthrow
> Of her soul's beauty

—a final phrase belonging to the same sentimental strain as before.

That it is hard to know whether Wordsworth was speaking of prostitution or simply of emancipation is not surprising: at least once Wollstonecraft confronts us with the same difficulty. The conflation was typical of contemporary opinion (perhaps more so in France than in England) that often made small distinction between the authority and self-possession meant by the second and an unconfined sexuality of which the first was the extreme embodiment. Polwhele's 1799 poem was merely a belated and vulgar version of such views. On the one hand, he lamented the new woman's "imperious mien," "dismissal of the heart," and claim to "mental energy"; on the other, he deplored her lack of "decorum," her surrender to "Passion's fire," and (with a salaciousness reminiscent of Diderot and Boswell, Chesterfield and Kames) her readiness to expose "in full view, the meretricious breast."[19] Less vulgar, Wordsworth's poem echoed such views and could do so precisely because the sensibility that ignored Mary's

---

[19]Polwhele, *Unsex'd Females*, pp. 7, 13, 15.

life also ignored the social realities behind the prostitutes (discussed at length by Radcliffe). Understanding depended on the tropes of a familiar discourse.

This can readily be seen in other poems, whose supposedly revolutionary context serves further to clarify the issue. Take, for example, the romanticized cottage spinners of the poem "Nuns Fret Not": "Maids at the wheel . . . / Sit blithe and happy." When we consider that women spinners earned only an eighth as much as their male counterparts, that hand-loom weavers worked between fourteen and sixteen hours a day, that the poet dismissed the idea of women operating power machines, we realize the poetry was not the artless embodiment praised by Blackwell and Hegel.[20] Such views shed new light on Mary of Buttermere, as they also bring us to understand that the idealization of the women in their cottages close to Nature was a way of concealing the harsh realities forcing the Jemimas and the women spoken of by Radcliffe into a life of prostitution and crime. The landscapes of Thomas Gainsborough, John Constable, and others depicted country life in the same way, either losing their workers in the woods and fields or sentimentalizing their affections and homes.[21] In such paintings the husband (if present) might be depicted finishing some work, but the wife would be touchingly keeping the hearth. Woman close to nature, nurturing and protective, was also a counter to the Enlightenment prescription of rational, logical man.[22] Woll-

[20]I owe these last remarks to an unpublished paper by Claire Collins. Reality behind the Wordsworthian glow was bleak. Dorothy George observed that well into the eighteenth century at least half the (5.5 million) population of England and Wales was "dependent in varying degrees on the charity of the nation," while a large proportion of the remainder, as much as 15 percent of the total population (small farmers) lived virtually at subsistence level. Only by the second half of the century did this really begin to change, at first as various improvements in city life trickled out to the countryside. Health and life expectation seemingly improved "between 1780 and 1815." As this was a time when "the first onslaught of industrialization" and a "great war" were dramatically destabilizing matters, George wondered how such improvement could be explained at all and further how it could "be reconciled with the poverty and distress of which we hear on all sides." Her answer was categorical: "Bad as things were they had been worse before." Tolerance for such conditions was waning, but the level and extent of suffering remained appalling: M. Dorothy George, *England in Transition: Life and Work in the Eighteenth Century* (1931; rpt. Harmondsworth, 1969), pp. 11, 72–73. See, too, her *London Life in the Eighteenth Century* (London, 1925).

[21]John Barrell, *The Dark Side of the Landscape: The Rural Poor in English Painting, 1730–1840* (Cambridge, 1980); Ann Bermingham, *Landscape and Ideology: The English Rustic Tradition, 1740–1860* (Berkeley and Los Angeles, 1986). Barrell has explored the ideas behind this art in his *Political Theory of Painting from Reynolds to Hazlitt: "The Body of the Public"* (New Haven, Conn., and London, 1986).

[22]The frontispiece to the 1847 New York edition of Hannah More's *Strictures on Education* (*Works*, vol. 6) captured these relations quite beautifully. It showed a well-kept cottage (finely thatched, of course) in front of which a group of well-dressed ladies, perhaps accompanied by a black servant, is visiting with a country woman who continues her spinning in the doorway. She is surrounded by children and happily playing animals. Behind the cottage is a peaceful dovecot, before it a busy beehive. The whole scene is overlooked from behind and above by a great castle, standing on the horizon against the light sky. The engraving is almost a parody of the earlier landscape painting.

stonecraft took on Rousseau over his expression of the relationship between men and women in *Émile* in just these terms.

These views, like Burke's *Reflections* (1789) and the opposition expressed in texts such as Wollstonecraft's 1790 *Vindication of the Rights of
Men* or Tom Paine's *Rights of Man* of the same year, were all reactions to
the Revolution and, perhaps more particularly in the English context
(though not in Paine's case), to fears that another revolution might occur
north of the Channel. All, I am arguing, were caught up in the same
singular process of Enlightenment of which the Revolution itself was one
very physical manifestation. And just as women were ultimately excluded
from the benefits of the Revolution, so they were cast as the embodiment
of anti-Enlightenment ideology. That, I think, finally prevented the argument of a truly revolutionary case: for a change in the dominant order
itself. (The permanent existence and "value" of oppositional discourses is
not at issue here, but their effect is.) To argue against the casting meant to
argue for Enlightenment, using its terms to justify an extension of equality without regard (at least) to gender. To accept the casting was to accept
exclusion. Wollstonecraft asserted women's right to catch up with men, in
the same way as Paine argued that the enfranchisement of the dispos-
sessed, whether colonials, the poor, or the aged, had to catch up with that
of the proprietors—as we saw Maria exclaim in *The Wrongs of Women*. It
was always a matter of the right to participate in the system, not the need
to change it.

The English provoker of fears that the revolutionary "plague" (as Burke
called it) might spread across the Channel was Dr. Richard Price. This
proximate instigator of Burke's diatribe against the French Revolution was
also Wollstonecraft's close friend and supporter. The foundations of his
arguments were no more startling or new than were hers and are typical
enough of an era running from the late seventeenth century almost to the
present. Indeed, it was to commemorate the Glorious Revolution that
Price preached his "Discourse on the Love of Our Country" in the Old
Jewry on November 4, 1789. The sermon and pamphlet that followed
caused a considerable furor. Price set out to show, on the basis of an
argument from onto- to phylogenesis, that love of country inevitably led
to love of one's neighbor—and thence to a sort of individualistic love of
the world, of humankind. One may be reminded of little so much as
Defoe's assertion something over half a century old: "The World, I say, is
nothing to us, but as it is more or less to our Relish: All Reflection is
carry'd Home, and our Dear-self is, in one Respect, the End of Living."[23] In
Price's words:

> With this view, I must desire you to recollect that we are so constituted
> that our affections are more drawn to some among mankind than to

[23]Daniel Defoe, *Serious Reflections During the Life and Surprising Adventures of
Robinson Crusoe: With His Vision of the Angelick World, Written by Himself* (London,
1720), p. 2.

others, in proportion to their degree of nearness to us, and our power of being useful to them. It is obvious, that this is a circumstance in the constitution of our natures which proves the wisdom and goodness of our Maker; for had our affections been determined alike to all our fellow-creatures, human life would have been a scene of embarrassment and distraction. Our regards, according to the order of nature, *begin with ourselves; and every man is charged with the care of himself.* Next come our families, and benefactors, and friends; and after them, our country. We can do little for the interests of mankind at large. To this interest, however, all other interests are subordinate. *The noblest principle in our nature is the regard to general justice,* and that good-will which embraces all the world.[24]

This was surely that very justice that had figured so importantly in prior writings of the tradition. We saw Hobbes writing in the *Philosophical Rudiments* (1651) how the concept of justice had provided him with the fundamental axiom enabling a scientific study of civil society and an understanding of the passage out of the state of nature: it was the foundation of the political contract. In his 1650 preface to *Gondibert*, Davenant had used the same concept to explain a wholly parallel argument regarding the *poetic* establishment of society. A quarter of a century later Rymer had used "poetical justice" to denote that alliance—even identity—among the political, ethical, rational, and aesthetic orders which was the underlying claim of literature.

It may be Burke who brought this concept of justice to its rhetorical peak. Finishing his series of speeches in the impeachment proceedings against Warren Hastings in the 1790s, the Honorable Member first reminded the Lords of their precarious situation (thinking here of the French contagion) and then expatiated in his best preacherly manner:

There is one thing, and one thing only, which defies all mutation,—that which existed before the world, and will survive the fabric of the world itself: I mean justice,—that justice which, emanating from the Divinity, has a place in the breast of every one of us, given us for our guide with regard to ourselves and with regard to others, and which will stand after this globe is burned to ashes, our advocate and accuser before the great Judge, when He comes to call upon us for the tenor of a well-spent life.[25]

The apocalyptic tone, the notion of justice as the divine ethical guiding principle of the world, echoed not only Price but a whole century of thought and action: such justice was as common to Leibniz's idea of a rightly ordered world as it was to Mandeville's assertion that the service of

[24]Richard Price, *A Discourse on the Love of Our Country,* delivered on November 4, 1789, at the Meeting-House in the Old Jewry, to the Society for Commemorating the Revolution in Great Britain (London and Boston, 1790), p. 12: my italics.
[25]Edmund Burke, *Works,* rev. ed., 12 vols. (Boston, 1867), 12:395–96.

private interest was morally useful to the whole of civil society, and indeed as it was to Rousseau's elaboration of the relation between the individual and the general will. It was still to be found in Hegel's 1821 *Philosophy of Right*. From the late seventeenth century until the libertarian claims of our own day, it has been the main ethical justification for the articulation of "collective" social action on individual interest. It was, one might say, the absolute ethical idea behind the contract, the foundation of what I have called authoritarian liberalism. Most recently, John Rawls's *Theory of Justice* (1971) springs readily to mind.

In his 1795 "Thoughts and Details on Scarcity," Wollstonecraft's adversary Burke thus typically asserted that we should feel only gratitude toward "the benign and wise Disposer of all things, who obliges men, whether they will or not, in pursuing their own selfish interests, to connect the general good with their own individual success."[26] This view was held as much by Price as by Defoe, as much by Mandeville as by Wollstonecraft's friend and eventual husband, William Godwin, whose *Enquiry Concerning Political Justice* (1793) argued at great length in favor of a civil association founded entirely on the total freedom of every individual. In her Scandinavian letters (1796), Wollstonecraft likewise remarked that growth of mind and stimulation of human industry required that the faculties "be sharpened by the only thing that can exercise them, self-interest."[27]

So it should hardly surprise us if Wollstonecraft adopted these principles and ascribed them to women. Indeed, she could borrow almost verbatim from Price: "Speaking of women at large, their first duty is to themselves as rational creatures, and the next, in point of importance, as citizens, is that, which includes so many, of a mother."[28] What is interesting in such a claim, however, is the way in which citizenship (for women) has been narrowed to, or better perhaps, equated with, motherhood. When Samuel Richardson, for example, placed similar arguments in a (fictional) woman's mouth, he did not appear to make such a limitation. Analyzing *Clarissa*, Christopher Hill records an affirmation of just this relation of self to world. He quotes Clarissa's explanation of her behavior to Miss Howe, as arising "principally from what offers to my own heart, respecting, as I may say, its own rectitude, its own judgement of the *fit* and the *unfit*; as I would without study answer *for* myself *to* myself, in the *first* place; to *him* [Lovelace] and to the *world*, in the *second* only. Principles that *are* in my mind; that I *found* there; implanted, no doubt, by the first gracious Planter: which therefore *impel* me, as I may say, to act up to

[26]Ibid., 5:141.

[27]Mary Wollstonecraft, *Letters Written During a Short Residence in Sweden, Norway, and Denmark*, ed. Carol H. Poston (Lincoln, Neb., 1976), p. 48. Henceforth cited in the text as *Letters*.

[28]Mary Wollstonecraft, *A Vindication of the Rights of Woman*, ed. Miriam Brody Kramnick (Harmondsworth, 1975), p. 257. Henceforth cited in the text as *VRW*.

them . . . let others act as they will by *me.*"[29] (Of course, this was before all her disasters.)

Writing as a woman, using the means of the dominant discourse at the same time as querying some of its most oppressive aspects, Wollstone-craft's situation was at once more ambiguous, more complicated, and more conflicted than the masculine one that Richardson could give *his* heroine. Wollstonecraft was partly under the blinding sway of an ideology imposing marriage and motherhood as a woman's duty, and her difficulty was to put those citizenship "duties" in terms that would not deny that equality of reason and social function. The only terms available for such assertion were the Enlightened ones Price and others offered: "Reason," she wrote, "is . . . the single power of improvement; or, more properly speaking, of discerning truth. Every individual is in this respect a world in itself" (*VRW,* p. 142). Thence she linked the expansion outward from self, to family, to nation, to the idea of progress and the development of the rational understanding: "The grand actions of the heart, particularly the enlarged humanity which extends to the whole human race, depend more on the understanding, I believe, than is generally imagined." Thus, while the underdeveloped Norwegians had got only as far as the ability to con-sider their families, progress would augment their reason's capacity: "Which I conceive will always be the case, till politics, becoming a subject of discussion, enlarges the heart by opening the understanding" (*Letters,* pp. 63n, 64).

Quite clearly here we can see precisely the same conceptual scheme as in Defoe or Price, Burke or Godwin: the idea of the uniqueness of the individual is the primitive statement, so to speak, out of which all subse-quent statements may be elaborated—in this case creating an idea of society in every way customary. And if I put the matter in these idealist and disembodied terms, the reasons are deliberate. Arguing her case in this way forced Wollstonecraft to make motherhood the primary function of women as social beings, as "citizens," despite her own actual and stated experience of the subordinate status this *inevitably* imposed on women: for within this conceptual scheme by now women's reason had been equated with the nurturing and the instinctual, with some rather vague notion of "wholeness" with the natural world. Not seldom such subor-dination took the form of a moral and intellectual brutalizing of the mind, when it did not lead to actual physical brutality. Placing the statement of individuality first, Wollstonecraft found the distinguishing *human* char-acteristic to be the familiar one of reason, and the distinguishing *female* characteristic that of childbirth.

[29]Christopher Hill, "Clarissa Harlowe and Her Times," in *Puritanism and Revolu-tion: Studies in Interpretation of the English Revolution of the Seventeenth Century* (1958; rpt. New York, 1964), pp. 391–92. The reference is to Samuel Richardson, *Cla-rissa or the History of a Young Lady,* ed. Angus Ross (Harmondsworth, 1985), p. 596 (Letter 185).

The sentence about motherhood quoted from *A Vindication of the Rights of Woman* repeated a concern of the 1787 *Thoughts on the Education of Daughters:* "A woman may fit herself to be the companion and friend of a man of sense, and yet know how to take care of his family." The use of the adjective "his" was clearly not anodyne: "To prepare a woman to fulfil the important duties of a wife and mother, are certainly the objects that should be in view during the early period of life."[30] Even when she much later (in *VRW*) raised the family to a kind of ideal form—where woman and man were equal—the home arrangement would remain the woman's primary function: and that must remove her from the public sphere in which *social* reason more clearly operated. So far Hannah More could have agreed. In *VRW* Wollstonecraft insisted on something like the need for *social* differences even as she argued an absence of natural ones, although failing to show why such difference was necessary: "Women, I allow, may have different duties to fulfil; but they are *human* duties, and the principles that should regulate the discharge of them, I sturdily maintain, must be the same" (*VRW*, p. 139).

Wollstonecraft was from the first aware of this contradiction and remarked at the very outset of her educational writing on the necessary imperfection of rational educational projects: "To be able to follow Mr. Locke's system (and this may be said of almost all treatises on education) the parents must have subdued their own passions, which is not often the case to any considerable degree" (*Thoughts*, pp. 11–12). All divorce of theory and practice, of discourse and action, as we saw in Wordsworth's case, produced flawed judgments. The moral and conceptual dilemmas into which the contradiction led were clearer yet when Wollstonecraft commented at the end of the work on the dangers facing the "young innocent girl when she first enters into [the] gay scenes" of public places, in tones akin to those later used by Wordsworth in *The Prelude:* "She would often be lost in delight," she wrote, "if she was not checked by observing the behaviour of a class of females who attend those places." "What a painful train of reflections do then arise in the mind, and convictions of the vice and folly of the world are prematurely forced on it. It is no longer a paradise, for innocence is not there; the taint of vice poisons every enjoyment, and affectation, though despised, is very contagious" (*Thoughts*, pp. 158–59).

As in the poet's case, precision is lacking here. It is not clear whether she was speaking of prostitutes or of those idle wealthy women whom she despised and constantly castigated. Perhaps she had both in mind and

---

[30]Mary Wollstonecraft, *Thoughts on the Education of Daughters: With Reflections on Female Conduct, in the Important Duties of Life* (1787; rpt. Clifton, N.J., 1972), pp. 56, 58. Henceforth cited in the text as *Thoughts*. My comments, here and elsewhere, on Wollstonecraft's ideal of the rational married woman perhaps require the qualifications of Kathryn Kirkpatrick, "A Contextual Reading of Maria Edgeworth's *Castle Rackrent* and *Belinda*," Ph.D. diss., Emory University, 1990, esp. chap. 4.

wished to equate them. Yet what does seem clear is that her remark cried out for an elaboration examining the social conditions that forced women into such situations. That consideration would have mined her own theoretical language and required her to reappraise the divide between theory and practice which she already recognized. To be sure, critics and biographers of Wollstonecraft often dismiss *Thoughts* as a rather conservative early work, in which she was simply testing some ideas, many of which she would later discard. Yet on this issue ambivalence remained.

The 1792 *VRW* seemed at first to moderate her earlier disapprobation, as she described the perils faced by "those unfortunate females who are broken off from society," frequently through no fault of their own: "Asylums and Magdalens," she went on, "are not the proper remedies for these abuses. It is justice, not charity, that is wanting in the world!" In her view, such situations were caused by an education that trained women to remain subordinate to men:

> Losing thus every spur, and having no other means of support, prostitution becomes her only refuge, and the character is quickly depraved by circumstances over which the poor wretch has little power. . . . Necessity never makes prostitution the business of men's lives; though numberless are the women who are thus rendered systematically vicious. This, however, arises in a great degree from the state of idleness in which women are educated, who are always taught to look up to man for a maintenance, and to consider their persons as the proper return for his exertions to support them. (*VRW*, p. 165)

Here she clearly equated idleness with prostitution (whether in marriage or on the streets). The passage can be viewed as a commentary on the equation only suggested in *Thoughts* and as an explanation of the scorn she heaped on such women as Lady Kingsborough, her mistress when she worked as a governess in Ireland. At the same time, of course, it repeated all those earlier strictures we saw (in Chapter 7) concerning the perils of idleness in women. In just the same way as they, it proffered education to sagacious domesticity as the solution.

Nor did she sustain so sympathetic a handling of the question. As far as I am aware, the passage just quoted is unique in Wollstonecraft's writing. More readily, she adopted the earlier tone:

> The shameless behaviour of the prostitutes, who infest the streets of this metropolis, raising alternate emotions of pity and disgust, may serve to illustrate this remark [that bashfulness is not modesty but only ignorance]. They trample on virgin bashfulness with a sort of bravado, and glorifying in their shame, become more audaciously lewd than men, however depraved, to whom this sexual quality has not been gratuitously granted, ever appear to be. But these poor ignorant wretches never had any modesty to lose, when they consigned themselves to infamy; for modesty

is a virtue, not a quality. No, they were only bashful, shamefaced in-
nocents; and losing their innocence, their shamefacedness was rudely
brushed off: a virtue would have left some vestiges in the mind, had it
been sacrificed to passion, to make us respect the grand ruin. (*VRW*, p. 228)

Not only did she now hold these women responsible for their own
situation—logically enough, given the primacy of the individual ("they
consigned themselves to infamy")—but she appeared to view women,
unlike men, as having a "sexual quality gratuitously granted." She thus
repeated one of the eighteenth century's more unsavory commonplaces
about women—later reaffirmed by Wordsworth (also in the context of
anxiety about the city, an issue that will return). No longer did Wollstonecraft so much as hint at her suggestion of male responsibility. This is a
long way even from Lady Mary Wortley Montagu's earlier battle cry:
"Begin then Ladies, by paying those Authors with Scorn and Contempt,
who, with a Sneer of affected Admiration, would throw you below the
Dignity of the human Species."[31] Wollstonecraft's confusion on the issue
was not shared by all her contemporaries who addressed these questions.
A brief discussion of the ideas of her less-known peer, Mary Ann Radcliffe,
suggests that other commentators were untroubled by the popular condemnation of prostitution, finding on this issue at least a way behind the
bonds of theory by turning its terms against its self-proclaimed proprietors.

In *The Female Advocate* (1799), Radcliffe elected to stress the dominant
discourse's own claim to plead for equality of opportunity for the down-
trodden, by assuming inequality was not innate (women's domestic versus
men's political reason) but produced. Most especially, she put the case for
women who had been forced into prostitution by poverty, by orphan- or
widowhood, or by the lack of access to work endemic to the condition
of middle-class feminine "gentility" (a case frequently adumbrated by
Wollstonecraft). With derisive irony Radcliffe contended that men, who
claimed to be more powerful than women, should therefore protect them
just as (and because) they asserted the right to: "I contend not with the
Lords of the creation for any other privilege than that protection which
they themselves avow to be the real rights of women."[32] She did not query
the dominance of men, but urged they had then to do their utmost to help
those they called the weaker sex: "As women seem formed by nature to
seek protection from man, why, in the name of justice, refuse the boon?"

[31]Lady Mary Wortley Montagu, *The Nonsense of Common-Sense, 1737–1738*, ed.
Robert Halsband (Evanston, Ill., 1947), p. 28.
[32]Radcliffe, *Female Advocate*, p. 398 (see note 6 for full reference). Henceforth cited in
the text as *FA*. The prostitution issue was serious: "In 1812, a letter to the *Examiner*
estimated that there were in London 50,000 'public prostitutes' (*Examiner*, 5 January
1812) and Shelley himself in the notes on *Queen Mab* says that a tenth of the female
population of London were prostitutes": Paul Foot, *Red Shelley* (London, 1980), p. 99.

(*FA*, p. 404: the contrast between the particular, "women," and the general, "man," itself seems infused with a certain mockery, reversing the usual individualization). All who refused support should "appear and give cause, why they are entitled to oppress these poor women, in order to enjoy indolence and ease" (*FA*, p. 468). Her sarcasm could become ferocious as she argued that they who asserted a right to dominance had to take responsibility with it. Biting irony accented the thought that both were unjustifiable: "Nor is there the smallest danger, when once the business is commenced, that the deep penetration and humanity of the guardians of the common weal will ever be baffled in so laudable a pursuit" (*FA*, p. 467). Fifty years earlier Eliza Heywood had criticized men for refusing to carry out their self-imposed superiority and duty: "How highly ungenerous is it then to give [women] a wrong turn, and then despise us for it." "Men," Wortley Montagu had laughed, "that have not Sense enough to shew any Superiority in their Arguments, hope to be yielded to by a Faith that, as they are Men, all the Reason that has been allotted to human Kind, has fallen to their Share."[33]

As in Wollstonecraft's case, no doubt, this attack on the dominant ideology and rhetoric did not go beyond the demand that women have access to the same advantages and benefits. Radcliffe did not propose any different order of activity or discourse (even supposing that to be possible). The ironic demand for men's protection in fact amounted to a demand for access to the advantages of privileges men enjoyed: "Then is it not highly worthy the attention of men, men who profess moral virtue and the strictest sense of *honours* to consider in what mode to redress those grievances! For women were ultimately designed for something better, though they have so long fared otherwise" (*FA*, p. 409). The value system remained that of Enlightened rationalism. "In the name of reason, justice, and truth" (*FA*, p. 463) was a constant refrain, offering a familiar view of human reason, whose claimed equality but actual partiality received suitable attention from Radcliffe: "As it is not expected a female can have much knowledge in judicature [due to improper education], I go upon the grounds of common sense and reason, and not activated by any other motive than a wish to see happiness prevail" (*FA*, p. 465).

In Radcliffe's work, ridicule of the propriety of male domination made for an argument akin to our contemporary notion of gender: that much of what we see as sexual difference is socially produced. At one point, for example, she accused men of robbing women even of the jobs that were rightly theirs, contending that men so deprived women of the last poor barriers between them and destitution: "For can it be termed either manly, honourable, or humane, to oppress industry and helpless innocence, and

---

[33]Eliza Heywood, *The Female Spectator: Being Selections from Mrs. Eliza Heywood's Periodical (1744–1746)*, ed. Mary Priestley, intro. J. B. Priestley (London, 1929), p. 56; Wortley Montagu, *Nonsense*, p. 27.

place them under the absolute necessity of sacrificing their virtue, their happiness, and everything they hold dear, at the shrine of the avaricious, *and* (for the sake of distinction) *effeminate tradesmen?*" (*FA*, p. 426: Radcliffe's emphasis). The term "effeminate," as the parenthesis showed, was intended both in a literal sense (taking women's jobs, men were "becoming" female) and in a rather different way: such jobs, the last resort of women, were so designated in a masculine system. This thought provoked a further sarcasm, a "joke," as she called it: "Suppose no lady would suffer herself to be served, in the shops of these effeminate traders, by any of the short-clothed gentry, would it not be a means of compelling all those who chuse to carry on the tragi-comic farce, to effect the business under the disguise of gown and petticoat?" (*FA*, p. 428). And then what would happen to job distinctions? (I am reminded of Cynthia Ozick's joke about sexual difference being marked by a choice between wearing two long cloth tubes or one short one, or Woolf's remark that if the male and female Orlandos had dressed alike, they might have thought alike.)[34]

Her idea that the status of the sexes was socially specific did not prevent Radcliffe from viewing her own society as otherwise superior. She could not understand how efforts were made "by the humane friends of liberty" on behalf of "the poor slaves," when nothing was done for members of their own society. The slave, after all, was less human than a member of rational society (*FA*, p. 469). The idea that the greater maturity of such rational society placed it ahead of others was, of course, perfectly in line with a familiar Kantian view of what was Enlightenment, and within this better society, Radcliffe argued, British women should take their proper full place:

> The slave is little acquainted with the severe pangs a virtuous mind labours under, when driven to the extreme necessity of forfeiting their virtue for bread. The slave cannot feel pain at the loss of reputation, a term of which he never heard, and much less knows the meaning. What are the untutored, wild imaginations of a slave, when put in the balance with the distressing sensations of a British female who has received a refined, if not a classical, education, and is capable of the finest feelings the human heart is susceptible of? A slave, through want of education, has little more refinement than cattle in the field. (*FA*, p. 469: *Oroonoko* was long forgotten.)

Doubtless she could argue that because "the poor unfortunate women of our nation" were themselves laboring "under the very worst kind of slavery" (*FA*, p. 470), even though they lived in an Enlightened society, their

---

[34]The issue of men taking over traditional women's jobs was especially bitter. The frontispiece of a 1793 work on midwifery depicted a human figure half in feminine, half in masculine dress. This "man-midwife" was titled a monstrous beast "unknown to Buffon." Throughout the eighteenth century, Schiebinger notes, men gradually took over any amount of such women's work: *Mind Has No Sex?* esp. pp. 102–18 (picture, p. 109).

full participation in its dominant discourse would *reasonably* precede that of "the African." His lack of refinement was due to ignorance and "want of education," no less than a British woman's inaptitude to participate in certain kinds of mature discussion was said to be. But she dwelt in a more refined and rational society. Clearly, Radcliffe was not questioning the legitimacy of the dominant discourse. Rather, she addressed, as so many had a century earlier, the matter of who "owned" it. Her concern was, in fact, with everyone's gradually maturing accession to the one *right* form of discourse: rational, just, true, commonsensical. What *was* unusual was Radcliffe's ferocious argument that men's claim to equality depended on the assertion of women's (and others') *in*equality. Showing how gender difference was wholly a matter of discourse, she had also shown how ideas of natural difference were used to justify an equality not of reason, as Enlightened thought alleged, but of the right to occupy naturally apt social roles.

In some of these areas I think it fair to say she went beyond her better-known contemporary. Wollstonecraft's arguments, however, also concerned access to the privileges enjoyed by (some) men in a society whose organization presupposed inequality for all, male or female. That was certainly why she did not pursue the issue of prostitution into the thickets of social and political conditions; why she was unconcerned, for example, with matters of class; and why she made no bones about maintaining the received understanding of self, subject, individual, and relations between many such selves, subjects, and individuals. *Thoughts* may have been the slightly conservative work of a beginner, but the assumptions underlying the book never really changed. And just as her arguments about the *nature* of "woman" (her title, after all) were caught in a familiar mesh, so too were those about reason and social or ethical place: even though in this regard matters did become more complicated. Indeed, it was here particularly that the glass finally became opaque, a blank screen to the apprehension of change.

The distinctly un-Lockean statement about the nature of the Subject with which she began *Thoughts* remained the basis of both *Vindications* as of her two novels: "It is, in my opinion, a well-proved fact, that principles of truth are innate. Without reasoning we assent to many truths; we feel their force, and artful sophistry can only blunt those feelings which nature has implanted in us as instinctive guards to virtue." By nature, mind is endowed with a "beautiful simplicity" (*Thoughts*, pp. 13–14). In the *Vindication of the Rights of Men*, she similarly asked: "What is truth? A few fundamental truths meet the first enquiry of reason, and appear as clear to an unwarped mind, as that air and bread are necessary to enable the body to fulfil its vital functions."[35] Truth, natural reason, simplicity, beauty—and motherhood for women. One is reminded not only of Des-

---

[35]Wollstonecraft, *Vindication of the Rights of Men*, p. 37. Henceforth cited in the text as *VRM*.

cartes (barring the last point), but of our literary and moral tradition flowing with nary a break from Boileau, Dryden, or Fénelon, through Shaftesbury, Addison, Akenside, Hume, and so many others, down to Keats, Shelley, and beyond. Nature, Truth, Beauty, and Justice furnished the metaphysical dwelling place of the Enlightened individual: "Henry," it was said of the worthy object of Mary's affections in Wollstonecraft's novel, "was a man of learning; he had also studied mankind, and knew many of the intricacies of the human heart, from having felt the infirmities of his own. His taste was just, as it had a standard—Nature, which he observed with a critical eye. Mary could not help thinking that in his company her mind expanded, as he always went below the surface. She increased the stock of her ideas, and her taste was improved."[36] The self and the feeling heart, a standard in individual judgment and in nature (the last viewed "critically," that is to say, in its methodiz'd beauty), the justice of an organizing taste, masculine guidance, and so forth . . . all are here.

This is not to criticize Wollstonecraft, I repeat, it is to test the limits of discursive change. Indeed, one can argue that women, Wollstonecraft no less than others, must occupy a place wholly equal to men's before hoping to be able to take on any more general project of changing society and its concept. If so, such an objective would be the only one appropriate—and wholly so.[37] Further, the real question may be whether lacking any such more general project of transformation, *any* change in practical status of *any* individual within society is possible. Such things do not alter separately, of course, and Wollstonecraft and her circle legitimately thought the American and French revolutions *did* herald such general transformation. History has shown *us* that to a large extent their belief would have to be moderated, although in the long run these events surely did alter the forms of political participation and kind of participant. Reading their texts in the light of subsequent history can show us *why* the persistence of prerevolutionary patterns of thought inevitably meant they *would* be wrong: such patterns comprised their way of thinking as well as that of everyone else.

Of course, if all qualities were already always determined by nature, then change would be incomprehensible. And it is certainly the case that

---

[36]Mary Wollstonecraft, *Mary. A Fiction*, ed. Janet Todd (New York, 1977), p. 47.

[37]It is well known that when she wrote *The Second Sex* and for many years after, de Beauvoir believed the transformation of society to be the most urgent project, on the grounds it would bring women's full emancipation with it. Only after 1968 did the failures of Western Marxism convince her that complete social change was certainly distant, if not quite utopian, whereas women's equality was a realizable goal. Her earlier view had absolutely no historical support. Among other things, Patricia J. Hilden has shown how women's participation (during the Second International) in workers' politics seeking to change society as a whole ended up not only in their *not* achieving equality, but in their being used by parliamentary parties that increasingly ignored women's concerns: *Women Workers and Socialist Politics in France, 1880–1914: A Regional Study* (Oxford, 1986).

in addition to her conviction that some qualities were innate (marking not only Truth, but also her and his Humanity), Wollstonecraft argued that people were products of a sociocultural environment. In some way she applied this even to motherhood, for speaking of breastfeeding and the "maternal feeling," she was of the "opinion, that maternal tenderness arises quite as much from habit as instinct" (*Thoughts*, p. 4).[38] Like the inconclusive discussion of prostitution, this "quite as much" begs pursuit, for it evidently leads to the issue of biological determinism. In point of fact, one logical terms of Lockean sensationalism would directly resolve such hesitation (as Judith Drake had earlier implied: see above, pp. 213–14). If one assumed human reason common to the whole species (without further precision), as Locke did (after Descartes, Malebranche, and the rest), if one then postulated this rationality was a female as much as a male quality, as Wollstonecraft did, and if one further supposed reason activated only from the exterior through the senses and that it was the unique principle of all human action, *as* human, it followed that all such action was always the result of external conditions in everybody's case. To take it as "male" or "female" was secondary to its being rational and human. Further, such a distinction would itself be possible only by virtue of some external stimulus. No innate nature could determine any action.

The Humean conclusion could be avoided only by positing the existence of some kind of "governor" (what in French is called a *"patron,"* thus allowing a wholly suitable wordplay—recalling "his" family), taking the form, for example, of innate truths and instinct. What Wollstonecraft had half cast out the front door returned by the back: the biological determinism, for example, present in the maternal instinct. On the one hand she wrote: "I here throw down my gauntlet, and deny the existence of sexual virtues, not excepting modesty. For man and woman, truth, if I understand the meaning of the word, must be the same." On the other she immediately went far (we saw before) toward taking up her gauntlet again: "Women, I allow, may have different duties to fulfil; but they are *human* duites, and the principles that should regulate the discharge of them, I sturdily maintain, must be the same" (*VRW*, p. 139). Human, rational duties they might be, but they were also and equally female duties as opposed to male. *Access* to the dominant order might be achieved by women, via the principles of reason, truth, and justice, but their participation would always and inevitably be different. And where might that not lead? Schiebinger has observed how eighteenth-century liberal thought had adapted itself to just this proposition, justifying "the denial of civil rights to women" by appealing to "proof of natural inequalities," which

---

[38]This, too, may be understood as a "Cartesian" notion. For Descartes, virtue as a habit and social intercourse as customary were ideas going virtually without saying. One finds them in Gournay as well, who also seemed to make a distinction equivalent to that of sex and gender.

underlay any claim of natural rights.[39] Radcliffe had seen through this. It is not altogether clear that Wollstonecraft had done likewise (nor what difference it could have made had she done so).

Once that has been said, we must also recognize that this apparent logical flaw permitted Wollstonecraft to protest that oppressing women distorted and brutalized their right to the *same* place in the sun enjoyed by men—a right due them as equal partners in the species called "human." As she wrote in *Maria,* her aim was to expose "the misery and oppression, peculiar to women, that arise out of the partial laws and customs of society," and especially out of marriage. In a letter used by Godwin to preface this posthumously published novel (1798), she observed:

> For my part, I cannot suppose any situation more distressing, than for a woman of sensibility, with an improving mind, to be bound to such a man as I have described for life; obliged to renounce all the harmonizing affections, and to avoid cultivating her taste, lest her perception of grace and refinement of sentiment, should sharpen to agony the pangs of disappointment. . . . These appear to me (matrimonial despotism of heart and conduct) to be the Peculiar Wrongs of Woman, because they degrade the mind.[40]

This was very far from the irony of the "Advertisement" preceding her earlier *Mary:* "In an artless tale, without episodes, the mind of a woman, who has thinking powers is displayed. The female organs have been thought too weak for this arduous employment; and experience seems to justify the assertion. Without arguing physically about *possibilities*—in a fiction, such a being may be allowed to exist."[41] Particularly, as Blackwell might have said, in an artless one, which after all uttered the profoundest truths.

The story related in *Mary* was indeed an animadversion against the kind of marriage into which the fictional heroine had entered with Charles and from which death alone could release her, but it was not at all a questioning of the institution of matrimony itself or of the fundamental duty (and instinct) of maternity (one need but look at the kind of relation the heroine desired with the invalid Henry). Mary may finally have been obliged to cut herself off from both social and family life and to take refuge in herself, looking to death as a welcome relief, but that was the consequence of a bad, forced marriage, not of the institution (whose improve-

[39]Londa Schiebinger, "Skeletons in the Closet: The First Illustrations of the Female Skeleton in Eighteenth-Century Anatomy," *Representations,* 14 (Spring 1986), 43.

[40]"Author's Preface" to *The Wrongs of Woman: or, Maria. A Fragment,* in Mary Wollstonecraft, *Mary, A Fiction* and *The Wrongs of Woman,* ed. Gary Kelly (London, 1976), pp. 73–74.

[41]*Mary,* ed. Todd, p. 4.

ment Wollstonecraft sometimes urged). Again: the dominant order was not wrong, it simply did not always function as it should.[42]

When the French Revolution broke out a year after the publication of *Mary*, the potential for some general transformation existed in Wollstonecraft's mind (in Hannah More's and Catharine Macaulay's as well, we saw at the beginning of Chapter 7). By the time of *Maria*, ten years later, little had changed, save the darkening of Wollstonecraft's vision. By then, we will see, it was almost as if she had come to feel that no alternatives were available. Indeed, thinking about transforming the order had become as impossible as the transformation itself. She may have become more fiery, more "emancipated" even, but her inability to push beyond conventional assumptions meant that in fact she differed little from those other women "who had been forming public opinion during the crucial years in which liberal views were gaining ground." They included such as Anna Barbauld and Hannah More, of whom Erna Reiss justly commented that they "accepted the old conventional idea of womanhood." So they "were quite content to sink the personality of woman entirely in that of man, to accept as her mission in life that she should not be complementary but ancillary to him."[43] Again, the terms of the discussion proffered their constant subtle snare.

In 1790 Wollstonecraft took on Burke, defending the French Revolution by opposing the bright flame of "liberty, civil and religious," and the idea of the "social compact" seemingly consummated in France, to "the demon of property" still passionately defended on her own side of the Channel (*VRM*, pp. 7–8). The first two were the fundamental social marks of a free, rational, human individual. The third was her scornful characterization of the system Burke was trying to protect from contagion:

> I perceive, from the whole tenor of your Reflections, that you have a mortal antipathy to reason; but, if there is anything like argument, or first principles, in your wild declamations, behold the result:—that we are to reverence the rust of antiquity, and term the unnatural customs, which ignorance and mistaken self-interest has consolidated, the sage fruit of experience: nay, that, if we do discover some errors, our *feelings* should lead us to excuse, with blind love, or unprincipled filial affection, the venerable vestiges of ancient days. These are gothic notions of beauty—

[42]Elsewhere I have argued that Swift's tale of the Houyhnhnms (even so early in the establishment) also represented a need for such correction: *Discourse of Modernism* pp. 328–50.

[43]Erna Reiss, *Rights and Duties of Englishwomen: A Study in Law and Public Opinion* (Manchester, 1934), pp. 3–4. Reiss was surely right as far as Barbauld's views of women and their education were concerned, but otherwise her political views were almost diametrically opposed to More's. Born and bred in Dissent, she was an ardent supporter of the Revolution in France and felt that Britain could well benefit from some of the ideas it embodied.

the ivy is beautiful, but, when it insidiously destroys the trunk from which it receives support, who would not grub it up? (*VRM*, pp. 9–10)

Burke's attempt to maintain a system in distortion was thus dismissed as passionate and irrational—in sum, "unmanly." The tables were neatly turned.[44] In Wollstonecraft's view a human truth—a tree trunk—underlay custom; paralleling, if you will, the innate truths underlying perceived sensation. It allowed correction, not transformation. What Wollstonecraft did not acknowledge, however, was that the choice of truths characterized and particularized a sociocultural environment, composing its reality. Not surprisingly, her views were those of her time, and they included certain claims about women's condition that she did not (could not?) set out to change.

Wollstonecraft's grubbed-up ivy thus differed little from Crusoe's rejection of the paternal yoke, done to *repeat* his father's mercantile success *for himself*. Unlike Wollstonecraft's Burke, Crusoe did not suffer from unprincipled filial affection. Modern Western society, like that of Swift's Yahoos, had degenerated from an original accord with liberty and contract. The ivy's removal restored that pristine association. Although such repetition appeared to give Wollstonecraft some assurance of human stability, one begins to see in such an argument the dangers of a nostalgia to which she would eventually abandon her thought. like Lafayette's Princesse de Clèves, she sought women's access to that restored social compact on a basis of full equality. However, she overlooked or ignored the fact that it was a *particular* compact: the one Hobbes had shaped from his earlier notion of "justice." Attacking Burke's "love of church," she would not bother, she said, to detail his argument and invective, aiming only at the "foundation": "On the natural principles of justice I build my plea for disseminating the property artfully said to be appropriated for religious purposes, but, in reality, to support idle tyrants, amongst the society whose ancestors were cheated or forced into illegal grants" (*VRM*, p. 125).

These natural principles of justice, we have amply seen, were what linked the individual with the community. They also permitted the articulation of human reason with the laws of nature, the verisimilitude of literature with the truth of the world, the moral imperatives of individual sensibility with the ethical rules placed in nature by divinity. (Radcliffe had, of course, picked up and run with this last assumption.) These principles marked mature reason, order, and judgment and were the very signs of that human maturity that, for Kant ("What Is Enlightenment?"), were the essential characteristics of progress. In respect to its treatment of such principles, it could be argued that a novel such as *Jacques le fataliste* was one of a kind (in France): for it queried in its own terms the dominance of that very lawful Reason of which the novel was one idealized manifesta-

[44]I owe this remark to Kathryn Kirkpatrick.

tion. That could be done meaningfully only once. In the English tradition it was achieved by Diderot's model, *Tristram Shandy,* the novel Viktor Shklovsky characterized as the most typical of all, just because it bared the rational principles of novelistic composition.[45]

Wollstonecraft took the relation between the political and the aesthetic just this seriously. That was why, I think, her argument about *Shandy* was rather different: not that her view was other, perhaps, but that such baring was not necessarily a good thing (hence, too, her difference with Radcliffe). To her, *Shandy* represented the immaturity of rampant childish fancy, opposed to judgment (as Huet had opposed *passion* to *entendement* in his writing on the novel more than a century before, and as so many others had contrasted the feminine apprehension of emotion to the masculine understanding of lawful reason). *That,* not its self-examination, was rather the reason why it could not be repeated (at least in its own language):

> Though it may be allowed that one man has by nature more fancy than another, in each individual there is a spring-tide when fancy should govern and amalgamate materials for the understanding; and a graver period, when those materials should be employed by the judgment. For example, I am inclined to have a better opinion of the heart of an *old* man, who speaks of Sterne as his favorite author, than of his understanding. There are times and seasons for all things: and moralists appear to me to err, when they would confound the gaiety of youth with the seriousness of age; for the virtues of age look not only more imposing, but more natural, when they appear rather rigid. (*VRM,* p. 141)

Burke and all he stood for and favored belonged to that passionate spring-tide. The times were now beyond it, his opponent argued. Political and social maturity demanded the restoration of the original compact in all its pristine rationality and justice.

Again, we see these same terms: judgment, reason, seriousness, rigidity, justice, truth, and so on. If, in light of this, one counts the number of times Wollstonecraft used the adjective "manly," it is soon clear that it was neither a device linked to the pseudonymity of the first edition of *A Vindication of the Rights of Men* nor simply an irony. It marked a particular mode of thought and evidence that even a revolutionary argument cannot escape from the constraint of its environment, save under conditions in which the *whole* environment is in doubt. If we may judge from the deeper despair of *Maria* (written during the time of her personally happy relations with Godwin), Wollstonecraft herself was quite aware of this constraint. The underlying argument of the first *Vindication* was that

[45]Viktor Shklovsky, "Sterne's *Tristram Shandy:* Stylistic Commentary," in *Russian Formalist Criticism: Four Essays,* trans. and ed. Lee T. Lemon and Marion J. Reis (Lincoln, Neb., and London, 1965), pp. 25–57. Originally published as "Art as Technique" (1917).

because matters had been done in some way since time long past was not only *not* a reason for so continuing them, as Burke claimed, but might itself mark the need for more abrupt change. Burke had been so absurd as to suggest the French should look to illustrious ancestors rather than present frailties. This might, she scornfully wrote, be good advice for a young painter, "but, in settling a constitution that involved the happiness of millions, that stretch beyond the computation of science, it was, perhaps, necessary for the Assembly to have a higher model in view than the *imagined* virtues of their forefathers; and wise to deduce their respect for themselves from the only legitimate source, respect for justice" (*VRM*, pp. 99–100). And, of course, common reason and innate truths . . . whose trouble was that they signaled a contextual constraint whose difference from Burke's mischief was not altogether clear.

Wollstonecraft herself dismissed Burke on grounds of anachronism. For that same reason, we could not now base a revolutionary appeal on a call to universal justice. She could do so—but precisely because the concept was long and deeply embedded in the dominant discourse. Its use as argument to urge women's access to men's privilege was thus at once understood and perceived as a threat (making her that "hyena in petticoats" abused by Horace Walpole). By that same token its revolutionary impact was limited. The very concept of universal justice was tied up in concepts of property and possession, self-interest and public contract, individualism and equality, which underlay the very *in*equalities Wollstonecraft was querying. One wonders what she might have made of the conservative turn taken later in life by Godwin: perhaps simply that it was the inevitable result of the kind of despair of ineffectiveness expressed in *Maria*—that or suicide (as intimated there).

For Wollstonecraft, the alternative became not something new (now found impossible of discovery), but Wordsworth's and Goldsmith's nostalgic yearning for old nature. The allure had glimmered from the start in her uncertainty over the unnatural power of the metropolis, her fears of city immorality. Nostalgia had always accompanied the appeal of revolution: "This sight I have seen;—the cow that supported the children grazed near the hut, and the cheerful poultry were fed by the chubby babes, who breathed a bracing air, far from the diseases and the vices of cities. Domination blasts all these prospects" (*VRM*, pp. 148–49). "Cheerful poultry"? Was this now the "Nature and reason" that in Burke's "system are all to give place to authority" (*VRM*, p. 157)? Well, no, of course not. But the nostalgic impulse once again made clear the contradiction inevitable in a revolutionary project that could be elaborated only from within the dominant system, but that found itself quite isolated, in the sense that its search for transformation was denied by a surrounding stability whose founding principles were the same.

As before, Wollstonecraft was quite clear that this *was* a nostalgia. In a short piece first published in the *Monthly Magazine* of April 1797 and reprinted by Godwin the next year in the *Posthumous Works*, she explored the question of "Poetry and Our Relish for the Beauties of Nature." Remarking that contemporary taste for nature seemed derived rather from poetry than from direct observation, she continued: "I was led to endeavour, in one of my solitary rambles, to trace the cause, and likewise to enquire why the poetry written in the infancy of society, is most natural: which, strictly speaking (for *natural* is a very indefinite expression) is merely to say, that it is the transcript of immediate sensations, in all their native wildness and simplicity, when fancy, awakened by the sight of interesting objects, was most actively at work."[46] This was to echo James Macpherson's claims for Ossian and the by-now common eighteenth-century view of Homer, not to mention Friedrich Schiller's contrast between the naive and the sentimental published in 1795–96. The argument was a familiar one. As early as 1759 Johnson's Imlac was asserting, "It is commonly observed that the early writers are in possession of nature, and their followers of art: that the first excel in strength and invention, and the latter in elegance and refinement."[47] The tension between invention and judgment settled in the disputes we followed in the last chapter thus found itself picked up in the general dialectic of nature and reason, of artless and artful, of nostalgia and progress.

Wollstonecraft herself had already approached the issue in *A Vindication of the Rights of Men*, in which she had discussed (we saw) the relation of fancy to immaturity, associating both with beauty and nature. Now in 1797 she wrote that the poet who could recapture "the image of his mind, when he was actually alone, conversing with himself, and marking the impression nature had made on his own heart," was then able to speak to us "the language of truth and nature with resistless energy." "In a more advanced state of civilization," she continued, "a poet is rather the creature of art, than of nature." Fancy had by then become "shrivelled by rules." Such later writers were no longer "the first observers of nature, the true poets." And this change in poetry accompanied a corresponding evolution in nonpoets. "Most people" would turn to poetry rather than to nature because they lack "a lively imagination," and because "the poet contracts the prospect, and, selecting the most picturesque part in his *camera*, the judgment is directed" (*PBN*, pp. 171–74).

While Wollstonecraft's age had replaced fancy by judgment, poetry was also preferred to direct observation of the world, because people would rather accept a traditional taste before exploring fresh vistas. *Mary*'s Henry was an exception to the norm only because he fulfilled the directness necessary to *true* Enlightenment. As she had angrily written ten years earlier: "I am sick of hearing of the sublimity of Milton, the elegance and

---

[46]Mary Wollstonecraft, "Poetry and Our Relish for the Beauties of Nature," in *Wollstonecraft Anthology*, p. 171. Henceforth cited in the text as *PBN*.
[47]Johnson, *History of Rasselas*, p. 60.

harmony of Pope, and the original, untaught genius of Shakespeare. These cursory remarks are made by some who know nothing of nature, and could not enter into the spirit of these authors, or understand them" (*Thoughts*, pp. 52–53). Twenty years before, Elizabeth Montagu had similarly written that Shakespeare copied "nature, as he found it, in the busy walks of human life, he drew from an original, with which the Literati are seldom well acquainted." She too noted the lack of original inquiry, speaking of "these connoisseurs, whose acquaintance with mankind is formed in the library, not in the street, the camp, or village."[48] Just as such poets had no authentic successors, so their modern critics merely echoed an ersatz and hollow judgment culled from custom.

The nostalgic impulse was, then, deliberately chosen—presented both as belonging to a more excellent past and as necessary to the transformation of modern culture and society: "In the present state of society, the understanding must bring back the feelings to nature, or the sensibility must have such native strength, as rather to be whetted than destroyed by the strong exercises of passion" (*PBN*, p. 174). The argument could readily be compared to that advanced by William Morris a century later. The two took it equally seriously. Sadly for Wollstonecraft's prescriptions for women's equal rights, it inclined her to natural and biological determinism. There was, she wrote in 1796, nothing social at all about maternal feelings, as she had discovered through her baby daughter: "You know that as a female I am particularly attached to her—I feel more than a mother's fondness and anxiety" (*Letters*, p. 55).

This nostalgic response was tantamount, it would seem, to an expression of genuine and deep despair. Yielding to it in 1797, she turned away from the very impulse that produced her most celebrated work, the *Vindication of the Rights of Woman*. There the nature metaphor stood quite exactly for what had to be *refused*, whereas reason and judgment were auspicious signs. Nature—an unhealthy nature, to be sure—was a sterility to be overcome only by reason:

> The conduct and manners of women, in fact, evidently prove that their minds are not in a healthy state; for, like the flowers which are planted in too rich a soil, strength and usefulness are sacrificed to beauty; and the flaunting leaves, after having pleased a fastidious eye, fade, disregarded on the stalk, long before the season when they ought to have arrived at

[48]Montagu, *Essay on the Writings and Genius of Shakespear*, p. 17. On the publication of his *Essay on the Application of Natural History in Poetry*, Barbauld wrote humorously to her brother, Dr. John Aikin: "I hope your Essay will bring down our poets from their garrets to wander about the fields and hunt squirrels. I am clearly of your opinion, that the only chance we have for novelty is by a more accurate observation of the works of Nature, though I think I should not have confined the track quite so much as you have done to the animal creation, because sooner exhausted than the vegetable": *Works*, 2:15–16.

maturity. One cause of this barren blooming I attribute to a false system of education, gathered from the books written on this subject by men who, considering females rather as women than as human creatures, have been more anxious to make them alluring mistresses than affectionate wives and rational mothers; and the understanding of the sex has been so bubbled by this specious homage, that the civilized women of the present century, with a few exceptions, are only anxious to inspire love, when they ought to cherish a nobler ambition, and by their abilities and virtues exact respect. (*VRW*, p. 79)

It may be said that this bad nature was produced by a false education just as poetry produced a restrained and controlled nature in the later text. Maybe so. But the point is that in the second *Vindication*, Wollstonecraft assumed that fine nature and human reason were on the same side, together creating a perfect, or at least perfectible, humanity. The difference between the good and the bad nature was the same as that between the strong tree trunk and the suffocating ivy of the first *Vindication*. And just as the latter reflected something "unmanly," so reliance on the former confirmed a typically "manly" Enlightenment. Elsewhere she tied just this alliance of reason and nature (apparent in the character of Henry) to the concept of civilization as a progress to maturity: those who have "traced [the] progress" of civilization, she declared, would know that it uses reason to enable "us to retain the primitive delicacy of our sensations." Here the ability to enjoy the sort of sensuous experience known to the first poets was joined with a notion of advanced reason in a way directly opposed to the slightly later writing looked at a moment ago. Now, "in that state of society in which the judgment and taste are not called forth, and formed by the cultivation of the arts and sciences, little of that delicacy of feeling and thinking is to be found characterized by the word sentiment" (*Letters*, pp. 20–21). This view of a rational nature courses through the letters from Scandinavia, and the Kantian tone of the following passage, for example, is unmistakable (albeit expressed in rather Burkean terms): "Nature is the nurse of sentiment,—the true source of taste; yet what misery, as well as rapture, is produced by a quick perception of the beautiful and sublime, when it is exercised in observing animated nature, when every beauteous feeling and emotion excites responsive sympathy, and the harmonized soul sinks into melancholy, or rises to extasy, just as the chords are touched, like the solemn aeolian harp agitated by the changing wind" (*Letters*, p. 58).

The possible loss of this alliance was the very reason for the anxiety expressed about her daughter. Her care came from reflection "on the dependent and oppressed state of her sex," which meant that she might be "forced to sacrifice her heart to her principles, or principles to her heart." As a mother she promised to "cultivate sensibility, and cherish delicacy of sentiment" in her daughter, in constant fear lest her simultaneous unfolding of "her mind" provoke inward conflict between sensibility to nature and the principles of reason, making her "unfit for the world she is to inhabit" (*Letters*, p. 55). Such strife would be inward but created by the abusive masculine order of things. We can readily see from such remarks how Wollstonecraft could envisage the right inclusion of women in the social order as feeding the very process of Enlightenment: "The world requires, I see, the hand of man to perfect it; and as this task naturally unfolds the faculties he exercises, it is physically impossible that he should have remained in Rousseau's golden age of stupidity" (*Letters*, p. 87).

The word "physically" was important here. It denoted not simply the thought that the evolution *was* actually a physical one, but the idea that improvement depended also on changing labor conditions and economic relations of production (*Letters*, p. 87). She always understood these as linear growth toward maturity. This was as typical of Enlightened reason as the nature/reason bond itself. Such thought could not function as a revolutionary ax. That inability seemed to lead Wollstonecraft to conceive a nature opposed to reason: to make it some healing balm for the withered soul of modern humanity. In the second *Vindication*, reason was supposed to repair the "faded" leaves of a false nature by providing proper nourishment. Five years later in the *Monthly Magazine* essay, nature would heal a fancy reason had "shrivelled": false reason, perhaps, but the point was that none other was now available.

Right reason would mean that women would be treated no longer "as a kind of subordinate beings," but as "part of the human species," endowed as much as men with "improvable reason" (*VRW*, p. 80). If good sense was the common distinction of humanity, as Descartes had it, then by definition women shared it. The theory allowed no exceptions . . . in theory. But that is a little like the case of general equality: only one kind of individual was "equal," and a wider inequality was essential to the idea's very maintenance. Reliance on such ideas was a source of all contradiction. In a sense this is revealed by the way Wollstonecraft spoke of the improvement in question, writing of the "exclamations against masculine women," even as she "corrected" herself: "If it be against the imitation of manly virtues, or, more properly speaking, the attainment of those talents and virtues, the exercise of which ennobles the human character, and which raises females in the scale of animal being, when they are comprehensively termed mankind, all those who view them with a philosophic eye must, I should think, wish with me, that they may every day grow more and more masculine" (*VRW*, p. 80).

Such contradiction remained concealed, of course. The discourse to which she sought access for women stated no premise of exclusion. It denied it. Access was not merely possible, it was supposed attainable. Contradictory the terms may have been, but they were the only ones available. Wollstonecraft would have been entirely pleased by the praise offered by John Adams after reading her *French Revolution* of 1794: that she was "a Lady of a masculine masterly understanding." Indeed, he was only echoing the beginning of her own preface to that work: "The revolution in France exhibits a scene, in the political world, not less novel and interesting than the contrast between the narrow opinions of superstition, and the enlightened sentiments of masculine and improved philosophy."[49]

When she rejected "sickly delicacy" in favor of "simple unadorned truth," and "false sentiment" for "natural emotions," seeking an education to prepare "a rational and immortal being for a nobler field of action" (*VRW*, p. 82), she was choosing the traditional female/male sets of oppositions. They were again the only available terms. But that her use of them was immediately perceived as a real threat at once to male privilege and to the place allotted women by such privilege was clear from the reaction of people like Walpole and More, who added their epithets of "hyena" and "serpent" to the vituperation that grew the warmer after her death. In every way it was reminiscent of the scorn heaped some one hundred fifty years earlier on the head of another woman writer, Marie de Gournay, by a male literary group and its aristocratic women supporters. At the beginning of the eighteenth century Eliza Heywood had more than once remarked on "that tide of raillery which all of my sex, unless they are very excellent, indeed, must expect when once they change the needle for the quill."[50]

Wollstonecraft made her appeal to that coercive male privilege itself: "I presume that *rational* men will excuse me for endeavouring to persuade [women] to become more masculine and respectable." And in any case, she added reassuringly, real difference "in bodily strength must render them in some degree dependent on men in the various relations of life" (*VRW*, p. 83). She returned to determinism, going indeed even further: "Let it not be concluded that I wish to invert the order of things. I have already granted that, from the constitution of their bodies, men seem designed by Providence to attain a greater degree of virtue. I speak collectively of the whole sex; but I see not the shadow of a reason to conclude that their virtues should differ in respect to their nature" (*VRW*, p. 109). This concession (which there is no reason to believe ironic) was enormous. Not only did it assume society as it was to be on the right path to the wisest constitution, but it allowed the measure of actual inequality already

---

[49]Mary Wollstonecraft, *An Historical and Moral View of the Origin and Progress of the French Revolution and the Effect It Has Produced in Europe (1794)*, intro. Janet M. Todd (Delmar, N.J., 1975), p. v. Adams's praise is quoted by Todd in her introduction, p. 14.

[50]Dedication to *The Fair Captive* (1721), quoted by Joyce M. Horner, *The English Women Novelists and Their Connection with the Feminist Movement (1688–1797)*, Smith College Studies in Modern Languages, vol. 11, nos. 1–3 (Northampton, Mass., 1929–30), p. 22.

claimed by men—merely suggesting it was too great, not that it was wrong. That was why she added that the adjustment should not be all one-sided: "Let men become more chaste and modest" (*VRW*, p. 84). How far these terms were ingrained can be seen in what was but a throwaway line: "Sometimes virtue and its shadow are at variance. We should never, per-haps, have heard of Lucretia, had she died to preserve her chastity, instead of her reputation" (*VRW*, p. 245). The remark exemplified the internalizing of oppression Wollstonecraft elsewhere insistently castigated. (In the po-litical sphere she argued, for example, that the Terror was a temporary failure due to the French having lived so long under tyranny: internaliza-tion produced a violence that had its counterpart in male/female rela-tions.)

The demand was always for equality of treatment and place as they allegedly could (and did) exist in a society based on the right universal premises. As she wrote in her dedication to Talleyrand:

> Contending for the rights of woman, my main argument is built on this simple principle, that if she be not prepared by education to become the companion of man, she will stop the progress of knowledge and virtue; for truth must be common to all, or it will be inefficacious with respect to its influence in general practice. And how can woman be expected to co-operate unless she knows why she ought to be virtuous? unless freedom strengthens her reason till she comprehends her duty, and sees in what manner it is connected with her real good. If children are to be educated to understand the true principle of patriotism, their mother must be a pa-triot [think of etymology here]; and the love of mankind, from which an orderly train of virtues spring, can only be produced by considering the moral and civil interest of mankind; but the education and situation of woman at present shuts her out from such investigations. (*VRW*, pp. 86–87)

The argument was concerned with correcting a flaw "subversive of morality" in society as it is, not with changing it (*VRW*, p. 87). Wollstone-craft insisted she simply wished to extend to the excluded half of human-ity the rights and benefits already enjoyed by men, often used to tyrannical ends. She sought to deploy in women's favor "the very arguments which [men] use to justify . . . oppression," to deploy them, unlike men's usage, "to promote their happiness." For, she asked: "Who made man the exclu-sive judge, if woman partake with him of the gift of reason?" (*VRW*, p. 87). As it was, women "may be convenient slaves, but slavery will have its constant effect, degrading the master and the abject dependent" (*VRW*, p. 88). She saw how men had managed to cause women to internalize their oppression: "Still the regal homage which they receive is so intoxicating, that until the manners of the times are changed, and formed on more reasonable principles, it may be impossible to convince them that the illegitimate power which they obtain by degrading themselves is a curse, and that they must return to nature and equality if they wish to secure the placid satisfaction that unsophisticated affections impart" (*VRW*, p. 103).

To avoid this result, education had to make sure girls never "be allowed to imbibe the pernicious doctrine that a defect can, by any chemical process of reasoning, become an excellence" (*VRW*, p. 126). Such had been the consequence of "the language of men, and the fear of departing from a supposed sexual character has made even women of superior sense adopt the same sentiments" (*VRW*, p. 143). "Considering the length of time that women have been dependent," she retorted to Rousseau, "is it surprising that some of them hunger in chains, and fawn like the spaniel? 'These dogs,' observes a naturalist, 'at first kept their ears erect; but custom has superseded nature, and a token of fear is become a beauty' " (*VRW*, p. 179). "Indignantly," she cried, "have I heard women argue in the same track as men, and adopt the sentiments that brutalize them, with all the pertinacity of ignorance" (*VRW*, p. 202).

The basic principles of humanity for Wollstonecraft were reason, virtue, and knowledge, the second two flowing from the right exercise of the first. These look extraordinarily like the three Kantian *Critiques*, of pure reason, practical reason, and judgment. The equation between Enlightenment and maturity was also Kantian. The three principles comprised her "rights and duties of man" (*VRW*, p. 91). She argued that all reasonable people recognized that the best society and wisest "constitution is founded on the nature of man" (*VRW*, p. 92) and asserted that they agreed by and large on what that nature was. But she thought that as society had been misshapen by piecemeal growth, much change was needed to align it with its own ideal. Present society deviated from truth and distorted human nature, not because it was wrong in essence, but because it had erred: just as the Europeans of Gulliver's fourth voyage, and even more the Yahoos, had strayed from the right path shown by the Houyhnhnms. The right remedy was not radical change, but a more orderly version of the same. The 1792 *Vindication* made the point in denying Rousseau's arguments about the state of nature as perfection: "Rousseau exerts himself to prove that all *was* right originally: a crowd of authors that all *is* now right: and I, that all will *be* right" (*VRW*, p. 95).

Progress followed an orderly path toward legitimacy and perfection. The issue concerned not a directional change, but decisions as to where humanity was currently placed on the path and how far it could continue on it. The founding principles themselves indicated, she said, that within society any power based wholly on command and obedience, on mastership and subjection—from that of an absolute monarch to that operating within an army, a navy, or a church—was a threat to a civil order founded on rational equality. As society "becomes more enlightened," it "should be very careful not to establish bodies of men who must necessarily be made foolish or vicious by the very constitution of their profession" (*VRW*, p. 98). It was, she concluded, "the pestiferous purple which renders the progress of civilisation a curse, and warps the understanding" (*VRW*, p. 99). Such relations of power utterly contradicted the theoretical principles of Enlightenment. The argument may have seemed revolutionary in the context of its time, but it was simply a logical application of the principles on which modern sociopolitical pacts claimed to rest. She always therefore emphasized equality, not power: " 'Educate women like men,' says Rousseau, 'and the more they resemble our sex the less power they will have over us.' This is the very point I aim at. I do not wish them to have power over men; but over themselves." Or again: "It is not empire,—but equality, that [women] contend for" (*VRW*, pp. 154, 204).

That actual social order did correspond in her eyes to these principles is suggested by her simultaneous argument that proper education to inculcate sound principles was essentially social: "Men and women must be educated, in a great degree, by the opinions and manners of the society they live in" (*VRW*, p. 102). Unless these somehow corresponded to the ideal sought, such a statement would be nonsensical. Although in practice these principles were imperfect and ultimately required that "society be differently constituted," nonetheless they were not so far distant from the right social order that humans might not, through them, "become virtuous by the exercise of its own reason" in addition to theirs (*VRW*, pp. 102–3). However presently imperfect, it was inevitable that Enlightened society would go in the right direction. The different constitution was thus a melioration, not a new instauration, and its local habitation was an order just for all humanity and echoed in the original three principles: "Surely there can be but one rule of right, if morality has an eternal foundation, and whoever sacrifices virtue, strictly so called, to present convenience, or whose *duty* it is to act in such a manner, lives only for the passing day, and cannot be an accountable creature" (*VRW*, p. 120).

The eternal rule of right reason, virtue, and knowledge was a source of all progress, when humanity heeded it and not those desires that opposed it. Then, "as sound politics diffuse liberty, mankind, including woman, will become more wise and virtuous" (*VRW*, p. 122). The belief was just as explicit in her work on the French Revolution, an event she thought (no less after the Terror than before) "the natural consequence of intellectual improvement, gradually proceeding to perfection in the advancement of communities, from a state of barbarism to that of polished society, till now arrived at the point when sincerity of principles seems to be hastening the overthrow of the tremendous empire of superstition and hypocrisy, erected upon the ruins of gothic brutality and ignorance."[51] Political revolution was entirely parallel to the sexual, and education for women as for

[51]Wollstonecraft, *French Revolution*, pp. vii–viii.

men had to be "the first step to form a being advancing gradually towards perfection" (*VRW*, pp. 142–43). The later trouble was that nothing seemed to have changed or be changing. On the contrary, old deviations appeared to return or be strengthened. Like many of her contemporaries, Wollstonecraft grew increasingly pessimistic.

Torn between the snare of the discursive order she first sought to escape and a nostalgic return to some vague kind of "wholeness" with nature, she bodied forth the problems, some of the traps, and some of the traces of resolution to be confronted in the political sphere by future women thinkers and in the aesthetic by current and future artists and critics. Ultimately, as Mary Poovey has observed, she was unable to escape the tyranny of the premises she had to use: "In doing this her voice hesitates and finally falters into silence." Wollstonecraft concluded by placing some hope in "feminine" ideals of sensibility, nurture, naturalness, and so on, but she was always aware how much those ideals depended on familiar liberal values and how she was caught in contradiction and conflict: "She cannot relinquish the individualistic values tied up with the sentimental structure itself." Like many others, she was unable to "abandon the ideal of 'true sensibility,' even after she had recognized that the romantic expectations endemic to such sensibility were agents of the very institutions she was trying to criticize."[52] She never completely accepted the retreat into some kind of asocial nature, nor was she able to see any order but that of possessive individualism and authoritarian liberalism. In the fragment she left of *Maria*, unable to choose between ending with her heroine's suicide or with a forlorn prospect of hope, Wollstonecraft fairly summed up her recognition of the snares she had spent her life trying to avoid and the meshes from which she was finally unable to disentangle herself.

These entanglements were obviously not unique to Wollstonecraft. As France became embroiled in foreign wars, as England grew increasingly fearful of the Revolution's course, critical of the Terror, and then began hostilities, and as the German lands, having evolved rather similarly, suffered actual invasion, the sureties of social reason and ethical nature began to waver. The Revolution, to be sure, was itself still cast as the fulfillment of the nature/reason bond, and many of its festivals were joyfully widespread celebrations of mature reason in an agrarian or pastoral setting. But for others, especially those who perceived revolution and war as a destruction of the social fabric, matters were not so clear. The beauties of rational nature seemed to have betrayed those who adhered to their claim.

Meanwhile, a parallel set of debates had sought to deal with the very elements of nature and art that appeared somehow beyond reason and rational treatment. They sought to describe and understand what became

[52]Poovey, *Proper Lady*, p. 108.

known as the sublime. Variously tied to most of the issues discussed so far, this debate eventually seemed to respond at least in part to a now enigmatic Enlightenment. For if nothing else, it seemed to make a place in reason for what questioned the limits of reason, to allow for some underlying natural naivety in the maturer artifice of aesthetic production. This debate began, of course, long before, in the late seventeenth century. It became perhaps the essential eighteenth-century discussion of literature and art. It drew to a close long after, simultaneously bringing to a sort of ending the discussion of what we now know as literature.

Chapter 10

Sublimity and the Ends of Art

Indeed there are no Characters which are so seldom seen in their highest perfection, as a great Poet, Lawgiver, and Statesman; as correcting the Morals, reforming the Laws, or regulating the Government of a Nation, are Works which as they demand the highest Talents, require but very few persons.

—Henry Fielding, *The True Patriot*, no. 8

Whoever would assert an equality of genius and elegance between Ogilby and Milton, or Bunyan and Addison, would be thought to defend no less an extravagance, than if he had maintained a mole-hill to be as high as Teneriffe, or a pond as extensive as the ocean. Though there may be found persons, who give the preference to the former authors; no one pays attention to such taste; and we pronounce, without scruple, the sentiments of these pretended critics to be absurd and ridiculous.

—David Hume, "Of the Standard of Taste"

Wollstonecraft, Schiller, Montagu, and many others felt there had been a sad falling-off in the literature of their age, as poets like William Collins and Thomas Gray had emphasized before them. The natural had yielded to the artificial, the naive to the sentimental, the truly beautiful to the merely pretty. The general decay of the times found its echo in the rottenness of literary art. Barbauld might joke that it was high time for poets to come down from their garrets to chase a few squirrels and take in the vegetation, but Schiller regarded with gloom an era in which the absence of genuine poetry accompanied general social breakdown. Only a few years later Hegel was telling his Berlin students: "We may well hope that art will always rise higher and come to perfection, but the form of art has ceased to be the supreme need of the spirit."[1]

---

[1]Hegel, *Aesthetics*, trans. Knox, 1:103. In the original: "Man kann wohl hoffen, dass die Kunst immer mehr steigen und sich vollenden werde, aber ihre Form hat aufgehört, das höchste Bedürfnis des Geistes zu sein," *Asthetik*, 1:110: the "perfection" of the English was already an "end" in the German. Henceforth these two sources are cited in the text respectively as *K* and *H*. Dino Formaggio has traced the future of the idea of art's end in *La "morte dell'arte" e l'estetica* (Bologna, 1983). He views Schiller as its forerunner (pp. 59–63) but adds: "Si rivela qui come il tema della morte dell'arte esca dalla

301

In Hegel's eyes, of course, art had played such a role only for the Greeks, during what he called the "classical" stage of art's development. The aim of the *Ästhetik* was not simply to establish the essence of fine art and its role in the growth of the human mind and the process of human history, but to trace its historical rise and fall as an *active* and *meaningful* participant in that development. Hegel's final view is well known: his own age marked the end of art's dialectical usefulness. Romantic comedy was both its last satisfactory exemplar and the ambiguous embodiment of "the dissolution of art altogether." It showed the separation of the Absolute from "the characters and aims of the real world" and thus its sublation (*Aufhebung*) "of everything not correspondent with it" (*K*, 1:1236; *H*, 2:585–86). "Considered in its highest creation," Hegel had said at the outset of the lectures, art "is and remains for us a thing of the past" (*K*, 1:11). The profound goal of all art, Hegel argued, was to present to sensuous contemplation the Absolute in the particular and its sensuous unity, to act "as the first reconciling middle term between pure thought and what is merely external, sensuous, and transient, between nature and finite reality and the infinite freedom of conceptual thinking" (*K*, 1:8). Or again: "Art is the middle term between purely objective indigent existence and purely inner ideas. It furnishes us with the things themselves, but out of the inner life of the mind" (*K*, 1:163). Quite evidently, when art came to embody the separation of those elements, as Hegel insisted it did in his own time, it marked its own final limit and the end of its efficacious activity.

In such statements we can readily identify both the methodized idea that neoclassical theory argued art revealed out of nature (whether it be Jean-Pierre de Crousaz's "Idée générale" of 1715 or Reynolds's "abstract idea" of 1770) and the concept of the sublime in art as what makes the mind suddenly and simultaneously aware of its miserable limitations and its infinite abilities.[2] These were but two aspects of a text that, however

---

grande *querelle des anciens et des modernes* sei-settecentesca, nella quale dispute il saggio schilleriano può esser fatto, per un certo verso, rientrare senza difficoltà (one sees how the theme of the death of art issues from the great seventeenth- to eighteenth-century *querelle des anciens et des modernes*, and in a certain way Schiller's study may without difficulty be brought into that dispute)" (p. 60). This chapter argues that not only this idea, but most others as well, developed directly from these earlier discussions, in a line quite unbroken.

[2] Jean-Pierre de Crousaz, *Traité du beau. Où l'on montre en quoi consiste ce que l'on nomme ainsi . . .* (Amsterdam, 1715; facs. rpt. Geneva, 1970), "Avertissement"; Reynolds, *Discourses on Art*, p. 47: 3d Disc., Dec. 1770. In 1738 Crousaz published a commentary on Pope's *Essay on Man*. Englished by Elizabeth Carter in 1739, it provoked a reply, and a counter by Crousaz, whose English translation (1742) was reportedly (Boswell) by Samuel Johnson. The event gives a nice example of mid-eighteenth-century French-English literary relations. Crousaz was chiefly a mathematician. His essay on beauty was thoroughly Cartesian, both in its ordering and its claims (as were many others: it may be that Descartes's principal influence at this time was in the realm of aesthetics).

exceptional, was also the very *type* of Romantic theories of art. This chapter tries to show how Hegel's *Aesthetics* was the final elaboration of a thinking about art whose beginnings were not Platonic or Aristotelian, but rather European seventeenth-century. His view of art, and that of the Romantics more generally, was *essentially* inflected by arguments whose origin and whose tradition were those I have been tracing, whatever he may assert to the contrary. Further than that: they were in many ways the end point of that tradition.

He made of Oedipus, for example, the exemplary figure of the heroic age. But Hegel's heroic age looked markedly like the state of nature that Hobbes used to legitimize the contractual association of the liberal state. Hegel, that is to say, was speaking rather of Renaissance and neoclassical tragedy than of Greek. His Oedipus showed "all the individualistic and unshakable unity of the hero whose acts, says Hegel, are a concrete man- ifestation of the concept of self—a concept quite foreign to the Greeks." This kind of argument picked up exactly on, say, André Dacier's *criticism*, which found these late tragedies to be "necessarily defective as being too much occupied with individuals rather than universal man."[3] All this raises many questions. I treat most of them in what follows, although the assumption of isomorphism between the different discourses (as between the political and literary just indicated, for instance) I take to have re- ceived sufficient attention. To some degree it underlies the arguments of this chapter. Generally speaking, these are divided into two parts. The first discusses the extent and nature of continuity in the new tradition of literature, from the mid-seventeenth century at least until the mid- nineteenth. The second argues that Hegel's *Aesthetics* was discussing not literature through the ages, but that of his own tradition: which he thereby universalized.

Since the seventeenth–eighteenth centuries a division betweel litera- ture and life has been more or less presupposed. In the Introduction to the *Ästhetik*, Hegel, after criticizing the French eighteenth-century aestheti- cians for having thus made art merely ancillary to other human activities (*K*, 1:7), summed up some of the consequences for art theory. First, art was but an imitation of nature (*K*, 1:41–46). Second, it existed to awaken universal human passions, bringing them into consciousness and so creat- ing a greater "receptivity for all phenomena" (*K*, 1:46). Third, art served "to mitigate the ferocity of desires" (*K*, 1:48), to teach moral rectitude and improvement. Each of these three views assumed some sort of separation from reality, understood as the external world of objects and events.

In the first case art produced an appearance of these events and objects. In the second it made humans more aware of them and of their own

---

[3]These few sentences (and the first citation) are from my *Tragedy and Truth*, p. 288. The Dacier remark is a paraphrase by Fern Farnham, *Madame Dacier: Scholar and Humanist* (1976; rpt. Monterey, Calif., 1980), p. 128.

passions and emotions as providing access to them. In the third it taught correct behavior in the world. These were, in fact, those functions to which I referred, respectively, as epistemological, aesthetic, and moral. Art itself, Hegel added, was then inevitably treated as a static object instead of as a self-developmental process. He criticized writers such as Kames, Batteux, and Karl Wilhelm Ramler because "what they take as their subject matter is derived from our perception as something really *there*" (*als ein Vorhandenes: K,* 1:16; *H,* 1:27). That was to say, these thinkers dealt with art just as they claimed art itself dealt with *its* content. They thought of it, he wrote, as an ersatz of the world, a poor or a "bad" appearance of a "real world" whose accidental and fleeting chaos itself was "bad" (*schlecht* was the word Hegel used: *K,* 1:9; *H,* 1:20). Such thinking, failing to consider its own self-production, became an alienated thought about an alienated object.

Hegel then argued that although the three consequences just summarized might all be, as it were, secondary effects of fine art, they could not be its primary aim. For "it is precisely the *freedom* of production and configurations [*Gestaltungen*] that we enjoy in the beauty of art" (*K,* 1:5; *H,* 1:17); in "its freedom alone is fine art truly art" (*K,* 1:7).[4] Its aim was not just to *express* objects and events, passions and emotions, thoughts and concepts, but to *perform* the self-development of concepts (of mind itself). Mind would then apprehend them and itself in and through them, both in themselves and in their alienation, in the process of their reification in and *as* the world.[5] For art itself first carried out that alienation or estrangement of the concept, "shifting" it, as Knox translates the thought, onto the grounds of sense (*eine Entfremdung zum Sinnlichen: K,* 1:12; *H,* 1:24), but it did so in such a way that Concept, mind, understood, grasped itself in that objectified, sensuous Other (*sich in seinem Anderen zu begreifen*) and in doing so "reverts to itself" in a more complete totality (*und so zu sich zurückfürt*). Concept, through the work of art, showed itself "the universal which maintains itself in its particularizations, overreaches itself and its opposite, and so it is also the power and activity of cancelling again the estrangement in which it gets involved" (*K,* 1:12–13). The German original needs citing: its terminology forces us to recognize the

---

[4]The idea of freedom in connection with the *Ästhetik* is treated at length in András Horn, *Kunst und Freiheit: Eine kritische Interpretation der Hegelschen Ästhetik* (The Hague, 1969).

[5]This view of the knowable world as mind-created was, of course, central to Hegel's thought: "It is precisely this whole sphere of the empirical inner and outer world which is not the world of genuine actuality; on the contrary, we must call it, in a stricter sense than we call art, a pure appearance and a harsher deception. Only beyond the immediacy of feeling and external objects is genuine actuality to be found. For the truly actual [*wirklich*] is only that which has being in and for itself, the substance of nature and spirit, which indeed gives itself presence and existence, but in this existence remains in and for itself and only so is truly actual. It is precisely the dominion of these universal powers which art emphasizes and reveals. The empirical, real world has its essence, no doubt, but it appears to us only in the form of accidents" (*K,* 1:8–9; *H,* 1:20).

central role of art in the phenomenology of spirit, the self-development of mind: "Denn der Begriff ist das Allgemeine, das in seinen Besonderungen sich erhält, über sich und sein Anderes übergreift und so die Entfremdung, zu der er fortgeht, ebenso wieder aufzuheben die Macht und Tätigkeit ist" (*H*, 1:24).

I return to these matters shortly, and I have mentioned them now only to show briefly what view Hegel thought he was opposing to those of the thinkers he criticized. For inasmuch as he asserted his arguments to be in opposition to current philosophy and theory of art, we need to ask whether his criticisms were correct and well aimed, or indeed whether his lectures were not rather their extension. If they were but an extension (however complex) of "neoclassical" aesthetic theory, then the consequences for our own understanding of art and its cultural role are considerable.

It is surely the case that much eighteenth-century theory did lend itself to Hegel's criticism. One of the most celebrated and productive texts on the matter produced in the century, Burke's *Enquiry*, in its emphasis on the argument that all knowledge "depends upon experience and observation" and in its tendency to make little or no distinction between the beautiful and the sublime in art and in nature, appeared to confirm Hegel's view—with a vengeance, one might almost say when reading a Burkean attempt to be all-inclusive in his description of the work of art: "As many of the works of imagination are not confined to the representation of sensible objects, nor to efforts upon the passions, but extend themselves to the manners, the characters, the actions, and designs of men, their relations, their virtues and vices, they come within the province of the judgment, which is improved by attention and by the habit of reasoning."[6] Hegel would be quite right to object that these elements were merely different objects of representation. Burke himself insisted on the matter, specifying that one should not seek "the rule of the arts in the wrong place," that is, among the arts themselves (Montagu's or Wollstonecraft's future criticism), but should rather use some other standard. That "true standard of the arts," he said, "is in every man's power." It was nothing other than "an easy observation of the most common, sometimes of the meanest things in nature" (Wood's comments, exactly, on Homer's advantage—not to mention many others' on Shakespeare, from Montagu's sobriety to Barbauld's humor). This, Burke concluded, "will give the truest lights, where the greatest sagacity and industry that slights such observation, must leave us in the dark, or what is worse, amuse and mislead us by false lights." Poets themselves have been misled because "they have been rather imitators of one another than of nature."[7]

[6]Edmund Burke, *A Philosophical Enquiry into the Origin of Our Ideas of the Sublime and Beautiful*, 2d ed., with an Introductory Discourse Concerning Taste, and Several Other Additions (London, 1759), pp. 20, 29. The introductory essay on taste was added for the 1759 edition and did not appear in the first edition of 1757.
[7]Ibid., pp. 91–92.

One could only with difficulty, we might think, discover a more precise vindication of Hegel's criticism. And if we look at the work of a certainly more influential thinker than Burke, one often named by Hegel, we would seem to find further confirmation. It would lie in what the abbé Batteux made of his requirement for a single principle enabling the comprehension and production of any work of art: the idea of representation. Representation cut through the disorder of the world and reduced multiplicity to order, on the basis of a proven, scientific model: "Rules have multiplied because of observation of written Works; they must be simplified, by reducing these observations to common principles. *Let us imitate real physicists, who accumulate experiments, and then base a system upon them*, reducing them to principles." Actually, only one principle was in question. From it, all others could be deduced: "A single sovereign law, which, once well understood, would be the basis, the summation, and the explanation of all others."[8]

One is reminded of Rymer's remark in the 1674 Preface to his translation of Rapin's *Aristotle*, that modern poets would not follow the "*Ancients'*" practice, reduced by Aristotle to clear principles, "were not the Reasons convincing and clear as any demonstration in *Mathematicks*. 'Tis only needful that we understand them, for our consent to the truth of them." We saw how Leibniz and others adopted just such a view. By 1741 père André had made this into a "géométrie naturelle (natural geometry)," underpinning the very "art du Créateur (Creator's art)" that modeled the "beau géometrique (geometrical beauty)" we enjoy in nature.[9] Adam Smith elaborated on the view in his Glasgow lectures during these same years, asserting that the best "systematic" method for writing and reading followed the guidance of "Didactick" eloquence: "In the manner of Sir Isaac Newton [in which] we lay down certain principles known or proved in the beginning from whence we account for the severall Phenomena, connecting all together by the same Chain." This "Newtonian method" was appropriate in all fields, "whether of Moralls or Natural philosophy, etc." It actually came from "the Cartesian Philosophy (for Des-Cartes was in reality the first who attempted this method)."[10] Crousaz (see note 2), André, Du Bos, Batteux, all those French critics condemned by Hegel provided Smith's evidence.

These were also the years when the German lands began to catch up after a century of suffering and cultural loss, created mostly by the traumas of the Thirty Years' War.[11] In 1742 Johann Elias Schlegel used just

---

[8]Batteux, *Beaux arts*, pp. i–ii, iii.

[9]Rymer, "Preface," in *Critical Works*, p. 3; André, *Essai sur le beau* [1741], in *Oeuvres philosophiques*, pp. 5–8.

[10]Adam Smith, *Lectures on Rhetoric and Belles Lettres*, ed. J. C. Bryce, gen. ed. A. S. Skinner (1983; rpt. Indianapolis, 1985), pp. 145–46.

[11]Ideas about the development of vernacular languages and literatures explored throughout the sixteenth century (see Chapter 1) were echoed in the German lands by

these terms to explain taste: "When I observe order, I have a sense of pleasure; and so, when I observe a similarity of imitation to original [through geometric proportion], I react in the same way." Clarity and distinctness, he added, were equally necessary. How, he asked, could poetic images "be clear" if they were not "vivid to our imagination"? Twenty years later Lessing repeated these sentiments in a paraphrase of Rymer: "I do not however hesitate to acknowledge (even if I should therefore be laughed to scorn in these enlightened times) that I consider the work [Aristotle's *Poetics*] as infallible as the Elements of Euclid. Its foundations are clear and definite, only certainly not as comprehensible and therefore more exposed to misconstruction."[12] Such writers appeared to confirm Hegel's contention that his predecessors of the eighteenth century reduced art to an alienated object, able to be treated as science was asserted to treat a real world of objects and events. It was a static imitation of a nature fixed in law. So far, so good. Nothing seems to contradict Hegel's account or the subsequently common and still predominant idea that the Romantics forged a new instauration.

We need to recall, however, that Burke's argument was far from typical. Indeed, in many ways he was fighting the widely known and accepted theories advanced by such as Francis Hutcheson (in a text that saw four editions in thirteen years: 1725, 1726, 1729, and 1738), John Baillie, and Alexander Gerard, who sprang to Hutcheson's defense in 1759, the very year of Burke's second edition. We should note that Batteux's, Schlegel's, and Lessing's works were far from unambiguous. Perhaps above all, we must remember that Hutcheson and Gerard deeply influenced Kant's thinking on the matter, which was itself in many ways a reply to Burke. Kant was, of course (after Schiller), the thinker whom Hegel believed had come closest to truth in aesthetic thought, even if he needed Schiller's correction. The latter had at last managed to break "through the Kantian

---

the early seventeenth. Most famous were the Weimar "Fruchtbringende Gesellschaft" (Fruitbearing Society) founded in 1617, and Martin Opitz's 1624 *Buch von der deutschen Poeterey* (Book of German Poetry). Literary achievement was thin: Jakob Bidermann's *Cenodoxus* of 1602, the midcentury drama of the Silesians Andreas Gryphius and Daniel Caspar von Lohenstein, the former's lyric poetry. Hans Jacob Christoffel von Grimmelshausen's exceptional *Simplizissimus* of 1669 embodied the sense of waste. (A disciple was the novelist Johann Beer.) Rudolf Vierhaus talks of "collapse" and "delayed development," of "stagnation" and "exhaustion." Only in the early 1700s did cultural matters start quickening: *Germany in the Age of Absolutism*, trans. Jonathan B. Knudsen (Cambridge, 1988), esp. pp. 4–8 and 68–75. See also W. H. Bruford, *Germany in the Eighteenth Century: The Social Background of the Literary Revival* (1935; rpt. Cambridge, 1968); Alan Menhennet, *Order and Freedom: Literature and Society in Germany from 1720 to 1805* (New York, 1973); and Henri Brunschwig, *Enlightenment and Romanticism in Eighteenth-Century Prussia*, trans. F. Jellinek (Chicago, 1974).

[12] Johann Elias Schlegel, *On Imitation and Other Essays*, trans. and ed. Edward Allen McCormick (Indianapolis, 1965), pp. 25–33 (paras. 15 and 18); Gotthold Ephraim Lessing, *Hamburgische Dramaturgie*, ed. Karl Eibl, in *Werke*, gen. ed. Herbert G. Göpfert, 8 vols. (Munich, 1970–79), 4:699–700; *Hamburg Dramaturgy*, trans. Zimmern, p. 263.

subjectivity and abstraction of thinking" correctly to understand "as the principle and essence of art . . . [the] *unity* of universal and particular, freedom and necessity, spirit and nature" which would finally reconcile self and world—a reference especially to the letters *On the Aesthetic Education of Man*, whose purpose was to turn such education to the construction of a truly free political state (simultaneously doing away with any further need for art: *K*, 1:61–62). That is a line of debate we need now to trace.

The late seventeenth century was still a period of some development in its ideas of *meaning*. It was an age struggling toward an understanding of how human discursive artifacts could, in any way at all, be meaningful, could produce the interaction we call understanding and communication. With his habitual sonority, Johnson caught the thought nicely, saying of Dryden: "He delighted to tread upon the brink of meaning, where light and darkness begin to mingle, to approach the precipice of absurdity, and hover over the abyss of unideal vacancy."[13] Science was certainly already considered a means to grasp the reality of nature both in its particular details and in its lawfulness. Rymer, Batteux, and the others had that in mind. But scientists were equally ready to recognize that instruments were at once productive and selective of the details whose observation they made possible, and that laws were—and could only be—probable. Science was still Johannes Kepler acclaiming its "voluptas," the delight in knowledge of a divine plan as joyous play with possible orders. He opposed this conception to the calculative utility of Galileo's science. Galileo himself insisted that an object seen through an instrument was not the same as the object seen without it, or that in changing the instrument (as altering the length of a telescope) the object itself was changed. Grasping reality was a most indirect process.

Science was Descartes in the *Monde* asserting the reality of a world he had built up, he wrote, out of a *fable*. It was Bacon remarking that a new scientific method would elaborate "a new world of facts." It was Newton still who, long after the *Principia* and the *Opticks*, spent his old age in those theological and alchemical speculations with which he had also begun.[14] When Bacon observed that the only real evidence for the reliability of scientific knowledge lay in its ability to produce predictable and verifiable events in the world, he asserted that the truth of such knowledge was not absolute, but wholly pragmatic. It let one do things in the world, intervene in the chaos of real events. Meaning was, one might almost say, as meaning did. Scientific truth was the mind's self-production in the world. . . .

No one in the late seventeenth century, and even less in the Enlighten-

---

[13]Johnson, "Dryden," in *Lives of the Poets*, p. 194.

[14]On this, see Betty Jo Teeter Dobbs, *The Foundations of Newton's Alchemy or "The Hunting of the Greene Lyon"* (Cambridge, 1975). The other examples are taken from my *Discourse of Modernism*.

ment, doubtless, would have gone quite that far. Yet it is the case that in the 1647 French translation of the *Principia philosophiae* (1644), Descartes had approved the addition of an important little phrase to his earlier statement that hypotheses were as useful as secure truth. Like truth, hypotheses could be used "en mesme façon pour disposer les causes naturelles à produire les effets qu'on désirera (in the same way to organize natural causes to produce the effects one wants)." If natural phenomena were practically unlimited, as Hans Blumenberg notes, then the technical interplay of any hypothesis with "natural causes" could be expected to produce the phenomena sought: that is, "new facts." Such a statement led straight to the mathematician Jean Le Rond d'Alembert (admiring Descartes as the heroic innovator of the modern age), who, under the entry "Découverte" in the *Encyclopédie,* came close to suggesting that material truth was at least in part mind-created. After contrasting several disciplines, he concluded by saying: "In Physics, on the contrary, because [facts] are outside us, more sagacity is usually needed [than in Metaphysics] to discover them; and sometimes, indeed, by combining bodies in a new way, we can create, so to speak, entirely new facts; such, for example, are several experiments in electricity, in chemistry, and so on."[15]

More usually, however, pragmatic effect became mechanical absolute, and Laplace would eventually be able to claim science's inherent capacity to predict any event whatever in the universe, much as Hegel admired Cuvier's ability to build a picture of an entire animal species (and by extension, the whole animal realm) from a "single bone" (*K*, 1:127–28). As Fontenelle to history or soon Coleridge to morality, so Marmontel applied the idea to poetry: "A poem is a machine in which everything must be combined to produce a mutually coherent movement."[16]

The way I have described the issue may indicate just how complex the matter became, however, once even the commonsense certainty of objective reality was removed. Already only ambivalently reliable in scientific knowledge itself, such certainty was found by most even more elusive once one was away from discourses apparently dealing directly with that reality (see, e.g., Lessing's strictures on the comprehensibility of Aristotle's *Poetics*). The urge to scientific order furnished an ideal epistemo-

---

[15]Descartes, *Oeuvres philosophiques*, 3:247 (*Principes de la philosophie*, III. para. 44); Jean Le Rond d'Alembert, "Découverte," in *Encyclopédie, ou dictionnaire raisonné des sciences, des arts et des métiers*, ed. Denis Diderot and Jean Le Rond d'Alembert, 36 vols. (Berne and Lausanne, 1779–82), 10:446. I owe the Descartes reference to Blumenberg, *Legitimacy of the Modern Age*, p. 208.

[16]"Invention," in *Encyclopédie*, ed. Diderot and d'Alembert, 18:968. For Fontenelle and Coleridge, see above p. 180. Some expected even greater utopian achievement from such a mechanism: "Whoever understands these things," wrote Henry Lloyd, a Welsh soldier of fortune (1720–83), "is in a position to initiate military operations with mathematical precision and to keep on waging war without ever being under the necessity of striking a blow" (cited by Michael Howard, *Clausewitz* [Oxford and New York, 1983], p. 13). Howard writes that the belief was common to all military theorists.

logical model most difficult to attain. When late seventeenth-century writers spoke, as Rapin, Rymer, and others frequently did, of applying scientific or mathematical principles to literary understanding, we should avoid the anachronism of believing they were writing in the light of an unambiguously realist interpretation of "Newtonian mechanism." To be sure, they sought some kind of certainty. They sought laws. They sought recurrent events and forms. By and large they did not find them in any simple illusionistic idea of representation—what Hegel scornfully called a *Nachahmung.*

Art was considered to provide access to nature or, rather, to an external world whether natural or social. Yet at the same time, art made manifest those laws of mind and nature enabling such a relationship at all. Writers like Dryden and Dennis, Bouhours and Boileau urged that literature simultaneously reproduced the world in some sense *and* actually showed how that reproduction was possible. In its very grammar and syntax (assuming the "correct" use of language that defined it), literature embodied the lawful processes of the reasoning mind and of an ordered world. It could not but show how its "images" of that world were trammeled in the way it produced them. Furthermore, within the best writing lay a small ghost: the indescribable *je ne sais quoi*, potent mark of the sublime.

Some later writers did tend to emphasize the lawfulness at the expense of the trammeling and the indescribable. Art could then become a kind of "science" of the represented world, whether, as we saw in Burke, its objects were from nature, society, the mind, the emotions, or whatever. That would provide a knowledge of what Hegel was to call self-alienated concepts, the estranged objects-of-the-world. Even then matters were unclear. In Burke, taste, the beautiful, the sublime, and the network of aesthetic concepts into which they fitted were attempts to understand how this could function, yet how it *differed* from a more precise, mechanistic science. Something such may be said of Batteux, of Lessing, or of Pope in a passage like the following familiar verses:

> First follow Nature, and your Judgment frame
> By her just Standard, which is still the same:
> *Unerring Nature*, still divinely bright,
> One *clear, unchang'd*, and *Universal* Light,
> Life, Force, and Beauty, must to all impart,
> At once the *Source*, and *End*, and *Test* of Art.

The Lockean origins of this are no doubt as evident as its consequences in Burke, and though they were not belied by what followed, they were most assuredly made more complicated:

> Those RULES of old *discover'd*, not *devis'd*,
> Are *Nature* still, but *Nature Methodiz'd*;

> *Nature,* like *Liberty,* is but restrain'd
> By the same Laws which first *herself* ordain'd.[17]

The rules were certainly in nature, but they had first to be discovered. It went without saying that they could be discovered only through the mind's work in and on the world: producing something akin to Bacon's pragmatic meaning of truth. When Pope likened methodized nature to liberty, as lawfully ordered by its own internal necessity, he was perhaps not so very far as it might seem from Hegelian *Freiheit* as the lawful self-development of Concept (not to mention the free and equal, limited but uninhibiting movement of the enlightened self-aware beings composing the well-ordered state of Schiller's *Letters*). Further, the manifestation in art of purified nature was at least prognostic of the Hegelian universal Concept manifested in true art. The human body portrayed in classical sculpture was "the existence and natural shape of the spirit," wrote Hegel, adding that it had to be idealized, for "in this way the shape is purified in order to express in itself a content adequate to itself" (*K,* 1:78). "Poetry should continually emphasize the energetic, the essential, the significant, and the essential expressiveness is precisely the Ideal and not what is merely at hand," he asserted a little later (*K,* 1:167). The thought, not at all dissimilar to so much of what we saw in Chapter 6, was constantly and lengthily emphasized:

Art has the function of grasping and displaying existence, in its appearance, as *true,* i.e. in its suitability to the content which is adequate to itself, the content which is both implicit and explicit. . . . Now since art brings back into this harmony with its true Concept what is contaminated in other existents by chance and externality, it casts aside everything in appearance which does not correspond with the Concept and only by this purification does it produce the Ideal. . . . For it is throughout necessary for the Ideal that the outer form should explicitly correspond with the soul. (*K,* 1:155)

Certainly, for the many who remained ambivalent on the matter, there were others who seemed less so. For Batteux, Hegel's bugbear, the sign of artistic genius was just precisely the ability to discover in nature the universal rules. The genius had "to make a choice among the most beautiful parts of Nature, so as to form an exquisite whole . . . more perfect than Nature itself, yet without ceasing to be natural." Invention in the arts was that ability to find in perfection what anyone could find in nature in less perfect form: in genius, creation and observation were the same. The laws of art were first of all those of nature: "The Arts do not at all create their rules: they are independent of caprice, and invariably traced in Nature's

[17]Alexander Pope, *An Essay on Criticism,* in *Poems,* p. 146:I.ll.68–73, 88–91.

example."[18] From Du Bos and André to Burke and Reynolds, such accounts were common. Yet even here the issue was open to doubt:

> With respect to this principle, we must conclude that if the Arts are imitators of Nature, it must be a sensible [*sage*] and enlightened imitation. It does not copy in a servile way. Choosing its objects and aspects with care, it presents them with all the perfection of which they are capable. In a word, an imitation in which one sees Nature not as it is in itself, but as it can be, and as we can perceive it by means of the mind [*telle qu'elle peut être, & qu'on peut la concevoir par l'esprit*].[19]

Once Batteux had introduced the term *concevoir* as the final determinant of literary "imitation," he could no longer maintain natural objects to be the sole determining factor. The eighteenth-century theorists struggled with the demand that the external world be somehow the regulator of human discursive systems, art among them. That was what Hegel criticized. He seemed not to notice the apparent fact that they very often yielded before the difficulty of that struggle and came close to asserting art to be mind seizing reality to produce itself into it, manifesting simply the power of its own self-ordering processes.

Comparing beauty in art to mathematical beauty (a comparison whose ambivalence we have already seen), Francis Hutcheson argued in 1725, perhaps for the first time (although Addison certainly came close in discussing Milton), that beauty had to do with the way in which art brought the mind to contemplate its own powers—in its capacity to contain not only an indeterminate quantity of particulars, but infinity itself: "For in one theorem [or work of art] we may find included, with the most exact agreement, an infinite multitude of particular truths, nay, often a multitude of infinites, so that although the necessity of forming abstract ideas and universal theorems arises perhaps from the limitation of our minds which cannot admit an infinite multitude of singular ideas or judgements at once, yet this power gives us an evidence of the largeness of the human capacity above our imagination." Beauty, for Hutcheson, arose from the "unity of an infinity of objects," from our ability to "reduce" such multiplicity to a "general canon," and from the accompanying contemplation of the mind's ability to do this.[20]

In 1747 John Baillie went even further, writing of the sublime as arising from "that *Exultation* and *Pride* which the Mind ever feels from the *Consciousness* of its own *Vastness*." Certainly, he said, it was an "*Object*" that so "dispose[d] the Mind to this *Enlargement* of itself, and [gave] her a lofty *Conception* of her own *Powers*." He thus seemed to agree with Batteux and even Burke that the mind merely reacted to externals, preced-

[18]Batteux, *Beaux arts*, pp. 8, 11, 13.
[19]Ibid., pp. 24–25.
[20]Francis Hutcheson, *An Inquiry Concerning Beauty, Order, Harmony, Design*, ed. Peter Kivy (The Hague, 1973), pp. 48–49.

ing its awareness of itself. But now we have a new turn: Batteux's *conception* was not simply the mind's conception of nature in its own way: it was also the mind's conception of itself. Then let us watch how Baillie proceeded from here, going on to discuss the soul's relation to the object *present* to it in sublime art:

> The *Soul* naturally supposes herself present to all *Objects* she perceives, and has higher or lower Conceptions of her own *Excellency*, as this Extensiveness of her being is more or less *limited*. An Universal Presence is one of the sublime *Attributes* of the *Deity;* then how much greater an Existence must the Soul imagine herself, when contemplating the *Heavens* she takes in the mighty *Orbs* of the *Planets*, and is present to a *Universe*, than when shrunk into the narrow Space of a *Room*, and how much nearer advancing to the *Perfections* of the *Universal Presence.*

"I could be bounded in a nutshell and count myself a king of infinite space," Hamlet had exclaimed some one hundred fifty years before, "were it not," he had added, "that I have bad dreams" (*Hamlet*, II.ii.258–60). Those dreams had now dispersed, and for Baillie, in the circumstance just quoted, "the Mind runs out into *Infinity*, continually *creating* as it were from the *Pattern.*"[21]

We are far from Burke's more prosaic approach, although Baillie was not here speaking of the sublime in art. What matters is his thought of how mind related to object—by being "present." In 1759 Gerard sought to tie these ideas to a more down-to-earth concept of imitation. Like Baillie, he saw mind as expanding, as it were, into being "present" in the object of contemplation and so rejoicing in its "lofty conception of its own capacity." But, he went on, in the fine arts "the sublime is attained chiefly by the artist's exciting *ideas* of sublime objects; and in such as are mimical, this quality is attained chiefly owing to our being led by the exactness of the imitation to form ideas and conceive images of sublime originals."[22]

Even here, Gerard made an exception for literature. There sublimity could be created by the way language related objects: "An advantage peculiar to the arts which imitate by language; for the rest can attain the sublime, only by copying such objects as are themselves possessed of that quality." Indeed, to the extent the sublime came from the artist's capacity with words, the work of art enabled one to enjoy both this self-contemplation and the contemplation of the mind's powers in others as well—as Gerard added in the 1780 edition.[23] This advantage given to literature found an echo in Hegel's argument that poetry, particularly its manifestation in theater, was the highest artistic form. The very ideas that

[21]John Baillie, *An Essay on the Sublime (1747)*, ed. Samuel Holt Monk, Augustan Reprint Society, no. 43 (Los Angeles, 1953), pp. 4, 6, 9.

[22]Alexander Gerard, *An Essay on Taste (1759), Together with Observations Concerning the Imitative Nature of Poetry*, Facsimile of the 3d ed. (1780), ed. Walter J. Hipple, Jr. (Gainesville, Fla., 1963), pp. 12, 20–21.

[23]Ibid., pp. 26–28.

the laws of mind and those of nature were isomorphic and that language could—in its very order—offer an analysis of the world and nature have come to enable this claim that the mind is in some way made "present" to itself in literary art's simultaneous depiction of the "world."

Gerard's ambiguous effort to adjust Hutcheson to Burke perhaps lets us see how far Hegel's criticism of his predecessors was applicable. It was mostly inappropriate. We seem to be dealing with two irreconcilable views. In Pope and Batteux both remained present. In Hutcheson and Baillie the idea of perfection clearly inclined toward the artistic goal of the mind's presence in or to the object and its resulting awareness of its own powers, its capacity to bring the contemplated object "back," so to speak, into the mind as a universal that only the human mind or the Divinity was able to comprehend. And how similar was the form of expression glimpsed in these two thinkers to what we find in Hegel:

> The external shape, like the spirit which fashions an existence for itself there, must be freed from every accident of external determinacy, from every dependence on nature, and from morbidity; it must be withdrawn from all finitude, everything transient, all preoccupation with what is purely sensuous; its determinacy, closely allied with the determinate spiritual character of the god [in the case discussed], must be purified and elevated into a free harmony with the universal forms of the human shape. Only flawless externality, from which every trait of weakness and relativity has been obliterated and every tiny spot of capricious particularity extinguished, corresponds to the spiritual inwardness which is to immerse itself in it and therein attain an embodiment. (*K*, 1:483)

In 1744 Akenside wrote:

> Call now to mind what high capacious powers
> Lie folded up in man, how far beyond
> The praise of mortals, may the eternal growth
> Of nature, to perfection half divine,
> Expand the blooming soul?

More later picked up the passage at the beginning of her didactic novel *Coelebs:*

> MIND, MIND alone, bear witness, earth and heaven!
> The living fountains in itself contains
> Of BEAUTEOUS and SUBLIME: here hand in hand,
> Sit paramount the Graces; here enthroned,
> Coelestial VENUS, with divinest airs,
> Invites the soul to never fading joy.[24]

---

[24]Mark Akinside, M.D., *The Pleasures of the Imagination,* in *The Works,* 1:22–25 (I. 222–26; 481–86); More, *Coelebs,* 2:43. Barbauld remarked that Akenside's poem was

In the very years when Akenside was at work (1742–44), Edward Young observed how human greatness lay in the ability to hold in mind a vision of divine infinity, despite a conjunct awareness of the mortal world as but a "Fantastic chase of shadows hunting shades," a site of "inhumanities," "wretched farce," and "miseries."[25] Bodmer's association of imaginative power and Leibnizian possible worlds (see Chapter 6, note 49) was surely connected with these explorations.

As far as I know, Hegel never mentioned any of those to whom I have just referred, except only Batteux and the last. One predecessor whom he *did* mention, however, was Lessing. In this case it might appear that his criticism was well taken. First of all, for Lessing, poetry and painting, both admitted in a much broader sense as "the plastic arts in general" on the one hand and as "the other arts in which imitation is progressive [*deren Nachahmung fortschreitend ist*]" on the other, were those "bildenden Künsten" that "the wise Greek" confined "to the imitation [*Nachahmung*] of beautiful bodies only."[26] Even though, wrote Lessing, "art has been given a far wider scope in modern times," its *Nachahmung* extending over all visible nature, yet "truth and expression are its first law," any disinterested imitation of beauty being sacrificed to "higher purposes [*höhern Absichten*]." It was the case that the pictorial artist had to choose to represent a moment within an action that would allow the spectator the greatest play of imagination, but that was simply to permit a more effective and affecting imitation. It was likewise the case that for the poet "the whole infinite realm of perfection lies open for his imitation [*das ganze unermessliche Reich der Vollkommenheit seiner Nachahmung offen steht*]," and mere physical beauty was "one of the least significant means" of engaging a reader's interest. Nor was the poet restricted as to choice of action.[27]

Nonetheless, whatever the writer chose to show, and whether an object

---

based on "Addison's Essays on the same subject" (*Works*, p. xiii). The poet himself indicated Shaftesbury and Hutcheson ("The Design," pp. 2–3).

[25]Edward Young, *The Complaint, or Night Thoughts*, vol. 1 of *The Poetical Works of Edward Young*, 2 vols. (London, n.d. [1834?]), pp. 184–85, 189. Some elements of this sublime were a part even of popular discourse before Hegel was writing. When Thomas Barnes wanted to praise Edmund Kean's Shakespearean performances, he wrote that while the actor "excited admiration for himself, [he] made also his admirers glow with a warmth of conscious superiority, because they were able to appreciate such an exalted degree of excellence": quoted from the *Examiner* of February 27, 1814 (p. 139) in Jonathan Bate, *Shakespearean Constitutions: Politics, Theatre, Criticism, 1730–1830* (Oxford, 1989), p. 39.

[26]Gotthold Ephraim Lessing, *Laokoon: Oder über die Grenzen der Malerei und Poesie*, ed. Albert von Schirnding, in *Werke*, 6:11, 16–17. I have used two English translations, but often neither is sufficiently accurate for my purpose: *Laocoön: An Essay on the Limits of Painting and Poetry*, trans. McCormick, here pp. 6, 12; and *Laocoön: An Essay upon the Limits of Painting and Poetry*, trans. Ellen Frothingham (New York, 1969), here pp. xi, 8.

[27]*Laokoon*, pp. 25–26, 28–29; McCormick trans., pp. 19–20, 23; Frothingham trans., pp. 16–17, 20–21.

was imitated directly or through some previously made model of it (what Wollstonecraft and others were to view as a sign of complete degeneracy), the distinction seemed to be only between kinds of imitation (*Nachahmungen*), however considerable their apparent difference: "In the first sort of imitation [direct] the poet is original, in the other he is a copyist. The first is part of the general imitation that constitutes the essence of his art, and he works as a genius, whether his subject be from other arts or from nature. But the second utterly debases his dignity. Instead of the thing itself, he imitates its imitations, and gives us lifeless reflections of the lineaments of another's genius, for original strokes of his own."[28]

As if this emphasis on imitation were not enough, Lessing sinned, too, in another direction, for imitation had as its final goal moral teaching. He thus wrote of the drama that in its "moral [world] everything must retain its natural course, because the theater is to be the school of the moral world." He went yet further, contending that "the Highest dignity of drama" was to be regarded and used "as supplementary to the laws." It was to correct all matters that were either too trivial for the law to bother with or so "abnormal in themselves, and . . . unfathomable in their consequences" as to escape altogether the domain of law.[29]

Yet even in Lessing one finds details leading to Hegel's subtler treatment. Indeed, the very distinction made in *Laocoön* between painting and poetry, or rather (since his exemplary case was the statue of Laocoön, and little painting survives from Antiquity save in fragment or verbal description—although Lessing mentioned the paintings preserved at Herculaneum, of which he had recently read in an essay by Johann Joachim Winckelmann) between poetry and sculpture:

> The gods and spiritual beings, as the artist represents [*vorstellet*] them, are not precisely those whom the poet needs [*nicht völlig eben-dieselben, welche der Dichter braucht*]. To the artist they are personified abstractions which must always retain the same characteristic if they are to be recognized. To the poet, however, they are real, acting beings who, beyond their general character, also have other qualities and feelings which, as occasion requires, may take precedence over the former.[30]

[28]McCormick trans., p. 45; Frothingham trans., p. 49–50; *Laokoon*, p. 58: "Bei der ersten Nachahmung ist der Dichter Original, bei der andern ist er Kopist. Jene ist ein Teil der allgemeinen Nachahmung, welche das Wesen seiner Kunst ausmacht, und er arbeitet als Genie, sein Vorwurf mag ein Werk anderer Künste, oder der Natur sein. Diese hingegen setzt ihn gänzlich von seiner Würde herab; anstatt der Dinge selbst ahmet er ihre Nachahmungen nach, und gibt uns kalte Erinnerungen von Zügen eines fremden Genies, für ursprüngliche Züge seines eigenen."

[29]Lessing, *Hamburgische Dramaturgie*, pp. 239, 263; *Hamburg Dramaturgy*, pp. 8, 20. Just a few years later Reynolds wrote of depiction of ideals in art, that "if it does not lead directly to purity of manners, obviates at least their greatest depravation, by disentangling the mind from appetite, and conducting the thoughts through successive stages of excellence, till that contemplation of universal rectitude and harmony which began by Taste, may, as it is exalted and refined, conclude in Virtue" (*Discourses*, p. 171: 9th Disc., Oct. 1780).

[30]*Laokoon*, pp. 70–71; McCormick trans., p. 52; Frothingham trans., p. 58. The reference to Herculaneum occurs at the end of chap. 19.

Certainly, the principle underlying the difference remained illusionistic imitation. What mattered was the spectator's or reader's *recognition* of a familiar object of beauty (in Lessing's view the fundamental requirement for ancient artists). But sculpture's calm embodiment of abstraction as a universal ("Venus is to the sculptor nothing but love"), as the "soul" fully expressed and embodied in the concrete work of art (an idea found in Winckelmann), as opposed to poetry's moving enactment of individual deeds and works, qualities and feelings, came very close to Hegel's argument. The poet, wrote Lessing, depicted an individual (Venus, in his example) in what Hegel would call its free-moving subjectivity, with both negative and positive traits. While Lessing emphasized this was possible because the poet had ways to make the individual recognizable that the sculptor did not, he nonetheless made a distinction, there, between different representations of modes of individual being which corresponded in many ways to the distinction Hegel would draw between classical and romantic art.[31] This is not to deny the chasm between Lessing and Hegel. Like Gerard, Lessing emphasized the imitative nature of art, and where the Scot referred to such as Hutcheson and Baillie for the general concept of the "object's" *presence* to the mind, of the mind's embodiment in the "object," and of the consequent exultation of mind in its contemplation of its own powers, so Lessing followed Winckelmann in seeing art as the concrete expression of some "soul," of the very essence of a universally comprehensible idea.

If I have looked at Lessing at slightly more length here than other writers on these matters, that is because Hegel never mentions him without implicit or explicit stern criticism, especially of the *Laocoön* (*K*, 2:769), which he appeared to dismiss, along with others, as the work of a "bookworm": perhaps a remark aimed at Lessing's own similar comment in the Preface to *Laocoön* about Baumgarten's *Aesthetica* ("indebted to Gesner's dictionary for a large portion of its examples"), to which Hegel also made slighting reference at the very outset of his lectures.[32] Lessing's and others' "preoccupation with . . . matters of psychological importance" was owing to their inability to grasp the import of "Winckelmann's enthusiasm and genuine artistic sense" (*K*, 2:769).

Apart from Goethe and Schiller, Winckelmann was the only one of his modern predecessors whom Hegel regarded with almost unalloyed approval. He had "opened up a new sense for considering art; he rescued it from ways of regarding it as serving common ends or merely imitating nature, and has powerfully encouraged the discovery of the Idea in works of art and the history of art" (*K*, 1:63). In Hegel's view, then, Winckelmann represented Lessing's very opposite. He had recalled and made important again for the modern age "the opposition of Ideal and nature" (*K*, 1:160).[33]

---

[31]*Laokoon*, p. 71 for the discussion of Venus, pp. 12–13 for the acknowledgment of debt to Winckelmann (first chapter).

[32]*Laokoon*, p. 11 (end of Preface).

[33]Cf. *K*, 1:19, 171–72; 2:723 and passim.

Here we may well wonder whether Hegel was not picking out precisely those earlier conceptions he took Winckelmann to be avoiding (or failing to see them in others). If any thought was central to Winckelmann's writings, it was that both "poetic spirit" in the artist and "good taste" in the recipient of an artwork were as much a matter of rule as of nature. Like the "poetic spirit," wrote the art historian, taste was "a gift from heaven; but it develops just as little spontaneously as that does, and would remain empty and dead without any rules or instruction."[34]

In a later passage from the same text, Winckelmann did indeed come close to asserting what Hegel thought he saw: the discovery of Idea in the work of art. Yet it was clearly a development out of the interplay of rule and nature: "Our consideration [of artworks] should commence with the effects of the intellect as the most worthy part of beauty, and from there proceed to the execution."[35] That intellect providing the innermost soul of the work was found in critics and thinkers throughout the tradition. Hegel and his contemporaries wanted some sort of clear break, so he read the new into Winckelmann as something not before seen in him. He had, Hegel wrote, made available "for the spirit a new organ and totally new modes of treatment" of artworks and the idea of art; yet the fact remained that "on the theory and philosophical knowledge of art his view has had less influence" (*K*, 1:63). Hegel did cite one example of putative influence, the work of his own contemporary, Carl Friedrich von Rumohr, but he criticized it as the work of one who had utterly misunderstood Winckelmann's and now others' concept of Idea. As a result, wrote Hegel, von Rumohr argued that the artist had above all to study the forms of nature, even though that artist might then find there an awakening of ideas— vague and imprecise as von Rumohr's notion of these might be. Art, Hegel said scornfully, was reduced to nothing but imitation.[36]

In Hegel's view von Rumohr's discussion was deeply ambiguous and wholly flawed. Not so that of another writer, whom Hegel thought signaled a break with the past: Johann Wolfgang von Goethe. He had come near to "solving the riddle" (*K*, 1:19). For Hegel, Goethe was always an exceptional case, and it thus appears that with the possible exception of Kant, whom he simultaneously criticized and approved, with the certain exception of Schiller, Winckelmann was the only one of his predecessors whom Hegel claimed had helped blaze a trail in the right direction. Hegel thus contended that Winckelmann was not part of the tradition either. On the contrary, his abnormal "insight into the ideals of the Greeks" (*K*, 1:63) enabled him to *reintroduce* "a recognition and a study of these master-

---

[34]Johann Joachim Winckelmann, "Essay on the Beautiful in Art," trans. Susan Powell, in *Writings on Art*, p. 89. The translation is from Winckelmann's *Abhandlung von der Fähigkeit der Empfindung des Schönen in der Kunst, und dem Unterrichte in Derselben* (Dresden, 1763).
[35]Winckelmann, "Essay," p. 102.
[36]See, e.g., *K*, 1:106–7, 161, 171–72.

pieces of art" (*K*, 1:161) which had been lost for the modern West. Even among those with the requisite knowledge (among whom, few as they were, Hegel surely allowed Lessing his place), his cast of mind made Winckelmann exceptional: "Amongst those with this knowledge and with an insight into Greek art and a burning love of it, it is Winckelmann above all who with the enthusiasm of his reproductive insight no less than with intelligence and sound judgement put an end to vague chatter about the ideal of Greek beauty by characterizing individually and with precision the forms of the parts of Greek statuary—the sole undertaking that was instructive" (*K*, 2:723).[37]

Winckelmann, then, was able to escape the distortions, inaccuracies, and untruths of recent tradition. The obvious implication was that Hegel, too, could avoid the transience, the solipsism, the provincial and even ethnocentric nature—indeed, the plain falsehood—of modern aesthetic theory. He would instead follow Winckelmann's exceptional trail toward an understanding of the eternal in art, a comprehension of art valid for all times and places. But if anything made Winckelmann exceptional, it would appear to have lain in his diversion of conceptions applied specifically to the sublime (in Hutcheson, Baillie, Gerard, and even Addison and Burke) to the function of all art as a whole. His place lay therefore in the mainstream of Enlightenment aesthetic thought. And the same may be said of Hegel, who also took ideas previously ascribed only to the special case of the sublime and forged from them a general theory of art. As Paul de Man remarked of the difference between Hegel and his predecessors (although the present argument differs rather): "The sublime for Hegel *is* the absolutely beautiful." And he added that to current theories, deriving directly from the Enlightenment in this matter, "nothing sounds less sublime . . . than the sublime in Hegel."[38]

Such a remark cannot but bring us straightaway to the thinker whose "recognition of the absoluteness of reason itself," Hegel averred, "has occasioned philosophy's turning point in modern times," even if his thinking must finally be pronounced "inadequate" (*K*, 1:56). At least in this realm, Kant seems a direct, although more sophisticated, inheritor of Scottish views: which is hardly surprising, given the signal importance Kant himself ascribed to Hume as his awakener from "dogmatic slumber."

Although he divided the sublime into two kinds, the mathematical and the dynamic, Kant provided a single explanation for them: the sentiment provoked in the mind by a sudden combination of pleasure and displeasure. The latter arose from the evocation of an infinite or an awful power so great that imagination could not grasp it or feared that the mind's own

---

[37]Cf. *K*, 2:727, where Hegel wrote that he would follow Winckelmann for this very reason; and see *K*, 2:733–63, 781–83, 787, where he did so.

[38]Paul de Man, "Hegel on the Sublime," in *Displacement: Derrida and After*, ed. Mark Krupnick (Bloomington, Ind., 1983), p. 144.

powers would be overwhelmed by it. The former arose in the first place from the fact that while the sensible faculties appeared unable to produce the infinite except as ever greater wholes, our reason could do so, and thus showed itself greater than sensibility, and the dominant faculty (so much for Burke's precedence of sensation: Kant was picking up on Du Bos's and Baumgarten's distinction of reason and sensation, replacing them in their "correct" order of hierarchy). In the second place pleasure arose from the fact that not only did one *not* actually fear the awful power of the unimaginably excessive (as a result of reason's self-consciousness), but one became aware of a "supersensible faculty" of mind "having dominion over our sensible faculties." The sublime object, whether in nature or in art, was thus that which provided us with the idea of a "supersensible reality" that "we cannot *know* but only *think* nature as its presentation"[39]

This seems to place us squarely between Hutcheson and Baillie, with their concept of the mind's self-contemplation in art (and in nature), and Hegel's universal Concept, which, having concretized itself in the work of art, then—or thus—reverted to a "higher totality where it maintains itself in its opposite, posits the natural as ideal, and expresses itself in and on the natural" (*K*, 1:432). Hegel's *Aesthetics* begins to look more and more like the outcome and a generalization of Enlightenment thinking about the artistic sublime.

At first glimpse, the Kantian argument just briefly rehearsed appeared to remove reason from any absolute position: for the sublime caused one only to *feel* the superiority of reason, not to *know* it. Such an interpretation would be to confuse understanding and reason. The point was that the disinterested (a priori, universal) judgment of the sublime allowed reason to think, correctly and no matter how indeterminately, supersensible reality. The indeterminacy had to do with the *way* in which the sublime forged the harmony of the cognitive faculties—imagination and understanding—essential to all and any cognition, and with the fact, obscurely put, that the sublime, as every judgment of taste, was based in "the concept of the general ground of the subjective purposiveness of nature for the faculty of judgment," a universal though indeterminate concept whose own "determining ground lies perhaps in the concept of that which may be regarded as the supersensible substrate of humanity."[40] Both the beautiful and the sublime allowed us to glimpse this supersensible, which was in fact the transcendental substrate of *all* judgment. Contrary to Burke's sensationalist views of the sublime (and the beautiful), Kant identified the sublime as what made mind aware of its noumenal "self." That awareness of the supersensible led straight to Schiller and to Hegel.

[39]See Donald W. Crawford, *Kant's Aesthetic Theory* (Madison, Wis., 1974), pp. 135–37. The last passage quoted is from Immanuel Kant, *Critique of Judgment*, trans. J. H. Bernard (New York, 1951), p. 105.

[40]Kant, *Critique of Judgment*, p. 185. On this, see Crawford, *Kant's Aesthetic Theory*, pp. 65, 75–78.

Not only, then, was the power of reason (as a faculty, not as the knowledge of things: understanding) made present to us in the aesthetic judgment, but the very basis of all cognition was at least indicated. The ability to know, explored in the first *Critique,* and the capacity to act morally, examined in the second, were both thus in a sense grounded in the aesthetic judgment, allowing as it did an awareness of the supersensible grounds of all judgment. Here, too, I agree with de Man's assertion that "in Kant, the articulation of the First Critique with the Third, of the schemata of theoretical reason with those of practical reason, has to occur by way of the aesthetic, successful or not. Aesthetic philosophy is critical philosophy to the second degree, the critique of the critiques." Even though the author's polemical enthusiasm for his argument appears to have led him to invert the order of the Critiques of Practical Reason and of Judgment, he is surely correct in referring to the last as examining "the inescapable burden of any linkage between discourse and action."[41]

In arguing that Kant never fully succeeded in avoiding solipsism (what he called "the Kantian subjectivity and abstraction of thinking"), Hegel affirmed that his predecessor was in fact unsuccessful in forging the necessary linkage. Yet for Hegel, too, just as art mediated between the inner and the outer, between thinking and the real world, so likewise it came between practical activity in the world and the process of pure thought, philosophy. This may now appear to us not only as a further projection of the Kantian argument, as Hegel certainly acknowledged. It was more than that, the further continuation of a long and complex eighteenth-century debate about art. *That* he denied most strenuously.[42]

So what? one may be inclined to respond. For no thinking can be in a vacuum, and no thinker denies a debt to predecessors. To do so may reveal an anxiety of influence, but little more. Well, the issue is more important than that. Those thinkers prior to Hegel whose work has been mentioned all claimed to be writing not merely of *their* art and of *their* literature, but of the literature of all times and places. Hegel argued that they were not, but had been diverted from this essential task of the philosophy of art by distortions in the art and art theory of their times, by which their taste had been formed and to which alone they responded. By jumping backward

---

[41]De Man, "Hegel on the Sublime," p. 140.

[42]"Our Imagination loves to be filled with an Object," Addison had written, "or to grasp at any thing that is too big for its Capacity. We are flung into a pleasing Astonishment at such unbounded Views, and feel a delightful Stilness and Amazement in the Soul at the Apprehension of them" (*Spectator,* no. 412, Monday, June 23, 1712): Addison, Steele, and others, *Spectator,* 3:279. Hegel's denial could almost be taken to indicate that he was tracing a passage in his own thinking identical to the one he saw in general aesthetic theory. In the last part of the 1817 *Encyclopedia* (well before the aesthetic lectures, therefore), he had insisted that art was but an imitation, a *Nachahmung*—the view he later dismissed with contempt: see *Hegel's Philosophy of Mind,* trans. William Wallace, together with the *Zusätze* in Boumann's text, trans. A. V. Miller, foreword J. N. Findlay (Oxford, 1971), sec. 538.

over them, so to speak, Hegel contended that he could avoid those local distortions and speak *in fact* of the art of humanity as a whole.

While I believe his conclusions were largely correct (although for reasons different from his), I also believe *they* applied only to the art of a specific time and place—and that they could not but do so. For art is always culturally and historically specific. It is a discourse caught in a particular environment. We should not speak of art as always and everywhere the same, although one given environment will almost always acclimatize earlier forms of art to its own ends, will reinvent it. Until now I have been suggesting how Hegel fit into a quite specific theoretical tradition within the philosophy of art in general, of literature more particularly. Within it, his work was a comprehensible, if remarkable, extension and in many ways an end. The second part of my discussion argues that he was also talking about the art of that tradition, either as it was in fact produced contemporaneously or as the tradition reinvented it. Here we will see that *literature* remained definable much in those terms we saw instituted in the late seventeenth and early eighteenth centuries.

We know that Hegel viewed art historically as having passed through three phases: the symbolic, the classical, and the romantic. The first manifested an effort to grasp the universal *as* universal in the external world. It was most clearly embodied in architecture. The second marked a moment when the individual became self-conscious and able to grasp and produce that self-awareness in the form of concrete particulars it produced in the world, but which it could then reincorporate as its opposite in a higher self-consciousness. This moment marked the highest achievement in art, when mind and world were able to be integrated. In this classical phase "art has reached its own essential nature by bringing the Idea, as spiritual individuality, directly into harmony with its bodily reality in such a perfect way that external existence now for the first time no longer preserves any independence in contrast with the meaning which it is to express, while conversely the inner [meaning], in its shape worked out for our vision, shows there only itself and in it is related to itself affirmatively" (*K*, 1:301). The art corresponding best to this phase was sculpture, that sculpture so well presented by Winckelmann.[43]

Romantic art showed the beginning of a passage to a new disequilibrium, for the self-awareness of spirit began to overwhelm its own self-concretization in the concrete particular. So where the symbolic accentuated the presence of self-produced Concept in the world, where the classical struck a perfect balance in a concretization that folded back into

[43]One may wonder how much Shelley, writing in 1821, might have been echoing views found in Schiller and soon to be offered by Hegel. Concluding an argument giving the very widest powers to the poet and extension to the idea of the poem, he wrote that it "is the very image of life expressed in its eternal truth": "Defense of Poetry," in *Selected Poetry and Prose*, p. 422. The claim is less vague if we understand "image" in terms of the concrete and "eternal truth" in those of mental concept. If such a reading is not illegitimate, it brings the statement well within the purview of German argument.

the self-conscious mind, the romantic phase tended to internalize objects to make them products wholly of mind. Its art sought to comprehend "spirit which is free in its own eyes." This could only tend toward a new dissolution of outer and inner and thus to a "separation of content and form." It meant that although such art could be said to transcend the "perfect unity of inner meaning and external shape" (*K*, 1:301–2), that very transcendence made it no longer perfect art, requiring its replacement by philosophy, as the discourse pertaining to the grasp of pure thinking. Further, the *separation* was what Hegel had been criticizing in the division of life and art in the eighteenth century, in the alienation of art and its theory and criticism, and in the dominant notions of representation and imitation.

In his letters on *Aesthetic Education*, Schiller had made a very similar commentary on a spiritual opposition whose consequences he saw as politically and socially catastrophic in his own time:

> In its striving after inalienable possessions in the realm of ideas, the spirit of speculation could do no other than become a stranger to the world of sense, and lose sight of matter for the sake of form. The practical spirit, by contrast, enclosed within a monotonous sphere of material objects, and within this uniformity still further confined by formulas, was bound to find the idea of an unconditioned Whole receding from sight, and to become just as impoverished as its own poor sphere of activity. If the former was tempted to model the actual world on a world conceivable by the mind, and to exalt the subjective conditions of its own perceptual and conceptual faculty into laws constitutive of the existence of things, the latter plunged into the opposite extreme of judging all experience, and of wanting to make the rules of its own occupation apply indiscriminately to all others. The one was bound to become the victim of empty subtilties, the other of narrow pedantry; for the former stood too high to discern the particular, the latter too low to survey the Whole. But the damaging effects of the turn which mind thus took were not confined to knowledge and production; it affected feeling and action no less.[44]

This sense of a time of decay, when the burden of external things had overborne human capacity to adapt to their demands, when mind was retreating entirely into its separated self or when activity became a frenetic concealing of its own futility, was widespread at the time. Yet it was far indeed from the despair endemic two centuries before. The sense was rather of a degeneracy than of a final dissolution. And degeneracy was capable of repair. Moreover, the earlier debates had provided an instrument, and they were many who considered that the realm of aesthetics could supply a solution in the political and social spheres.

Barbauld, Montagu, and Wollstonecraft all sought the melioration of

---

[44]Friedrich Schiller, *On the Aesthetic Education of Man, in a Series of Letters*, ed. and trans. Elizabeth M. Wilkinson and L. A. Willoughby (1967; rpt. Oxford, 1985), pp. 37–39.

poetry. In 1799 Coleridge wrote to Wordsworth suggesting he write a poem answering the general anti-intellectualism on the one hand and the sensed fragmentation of self on the other: "I wish you could write a poem, in blank verse, addressed to those, who, in consequence of the complete failure of the French Revolution, have thrown up all hopes of the amelioration of mankind, and are sinking into an almost epicurean selfishness, disguising the same under the soft titles of domestic attachment and contempt for visionary *philosophes.*" Twenty years later Shelley would similarly write that "the cultivation of poetry is never more to be desired than at periods when, from an excess of the selfish and calculating principle, the accumulation of the materials of external life exceeds the quantity of the power of assimilating them to the inner laws of human nature."[45] The purpose of Schiller's 1795 *Aesthetic Education* was wholly to show how this degenerate condition could be overcome.

Hegel himself was to argue that before this separation degenerated on the world stage as indicated by Schiller, its Idea was embodied in romantic forms of art: painting, music, and poetry. Within the historical schema developed by Hegel for the modes of art (symbolic, classical, and romantic), we know too that the forms of art could and did exist synchronically, such that architecture, for example, the epitome of the symbolic, itself passed through the three stages. But the point I wish to make is that Hegel's aesthetic system, like Schiller's and the less systematic proposals of such as Coleridge, Shelley, or Wordsworth, was an analysis of and a response to the felt degeneracy of the times.

Symbolic art, Hegel contended, was constantly tempted toward dissolution. In grasping the universal by means of figures drawn from the outer world, it inevitably had to strive against the very multiplicity of external objects and events. Indeed, for Hegel, the massive flaw in most Oriental art (typical of the symbolic) was precisely due to that urge to chaos and tendency toward mystery and incomprehensibility. The view was not at all without precedent. James Thomson had constructed a major theme of *The Seasons* from it. In the rewritten *Summer* of 1744, his narrator flew an exotic path around the world. After passing through "the wonders of the torrid zone," by the tempests and the treasures, the wealth, the decadent profusion, and the softening balm of African and oriental climes, he concluded that all this was bootless.

> Ill-fated race! the softening arts of peace,
> Whate'er the humanizing Muses teach,
> The godlike wisdom of the tempered breast,
> Progressive truth, the patient force of thought,
> Investigation calm whose silent powers
> Command the world, the light that leads to Heaven,
> Kind equal rule, the government of laws,

[45]Coleridge, *Collected Letters*, 1:527; Shelley, "Defense of Poetry," p. 442.

And all-protecting freedom which alone
Sustains the name and dignity of man—
These are not theirs.

This recounts an opposition between the civic culture of the West—
especially as represented in Greece and Rome and what were now taken to
be their successors—and the "rage," the "horrid fire," of Africa or the
Orient, however mighty its effect, that matched Hegel's later view.[46]
Classical art, the art of Greece and Rome, was art in its perfection *as* art.
How Hegel described its inception in the passage from the symbolic may
thus be thought important. His argument is wholly fascinating.

First, it coincided with the moment Hegel himself qualified as sublime,
a concept he used only in relation to the symbolic. Hegel's *Erhabene* had
seemingly little to do with the now traditional idea of the sublime. For
Hegel, the sublime occurred when the thinking mind (or feeling mind,
since it could not yet be said to *think*) first sensed the presence of Oneness,
of the Divinity in things and in itself. But the very moment when consciousness caught a sense of unity was also that of definitive disunion and
separation: for mind simultaneously caught a sense of itself as such.[47]
One begins to understand why symbolic art was always—at least—on the
edge of chaos. Denis Hollier implies a similar view, when discussing the
difficulty Hegel confronted when he posited architecture as the first form
of art (remembering he spoke of the sublime *only* in connection with
symbolic art). Because the first buildings, cabins or temples, had non-
aesthetic aims, Hegel was pushed to intimate that architecture was actually preartistic. In the end, he used the Tower of Babel to illustrate symbolic art at its best, on the grounds that its aim and content were the
expression of human community as Universal.[48] Problematically, it was
also the image of total dispersion—as Hegel observed (*K*, 2:638–39). The

---

[46]James Thomson, *The Seasons and The Castle of Indolence*, ed. James Sambrook
(1972; rpt. Oxford, 1984), pp. 54–62 (ll. 632, 874–84, 897). The same opinion was behind
Collins's 1743 "Epistle to Hanmer" (on a Shakespeare edition) and Gray's "Progress of
Poesy" (1752–54). For what it is worth, such views about Oriental—specifically, Egyptian—art had long been current. "All their discourses are figurative," said Huet in 1669;
"they communicate by allegories; their theology, their philosophy, and chiefly their
politics and morality are all enveloped beneath fables and parables. Egyptian hiero-
glyphs show us how mysterious was this nation; almost everything was disguised in
their land and they had made art of their habit of expressing themselves in images":
Huet, *Lettre-traité*, pp. 52–53. He added later that "our Hurons and Iroquois speak only
in symbols and images" (p. 128). In 1736 Blackwell wrote of the Egyptians in like terms:
that their knowledge and learning were "wholly *fabulous* and *allegorical*." "Never was
there," he added, "a People so addicted to *Metaphor* and *Allusion*." Homer acquired this
ability from them, he said: Blackwell, *Enquiry*, pp. 102, 169. That Hegel took up such
views may reveal an aspect of that ideological "discovery" of the Greek origins of Europe
of which Martin Bernal has written. More to the point here, I think, is that these
"Egyptians" were, we will see, a surrogate.
[47]Cf. De Man, "Hegel on the Sublime," pp. 143–49.
[48]Denis Hollier, *La prise de la Concorde: Essais sur Georges Bataille* (Paris, 1974),
pp. 21–22. Schiller had earlier noted a difficulty precisely analogous to Hegel's: "As long

sublime, marking the symbolic inception of art, was only a threshold, immediate passage to something else: the invention of classical sculpture and (for Hegel) the rational state.

For, second, Hegel situated the inception of classical art in what he called the "Heroic Age," that time of the Homeric heroes and—with some disregard for actual chronology—of the great efflorescence of Athenian culture. Yet while his prime examples were indeed the sculpture and theater of Antiquity, the way he described this heroic age was revealing in the extreme. He began by opposing it to a later stage in wholly political terms. The heroic age was marked by the development of the individual, conscious of self *as* individual (simultaneously, therefore, with the symbolic sublime). Hegel opposed this to a later stage when the individual realized himself (the gender inflection is not accidental) in the universality of "the fully developed State," of "the State proper," that is, "in the life of the *State* when political life comes into appearance according to the essential nature of the State" (*K*, 1:182). But this was the rational State as Hegel had explored it in *The Philosophy of Right*, a State corresponding, rather, to the romantic moment of art—if, indeed, it did not follow it.

Be that as it may (and the question will return), Hegel now wrote of the earlier stage: "But when there is no State the security of life and property depends entirely on the personal strength and valour of each individual who has to provide for his own existence and the preservation of what belongs and is due to him. Such a state of affairs is the one we are accustomed to ascribe to the *Heroic Age*" (*K*, 1:185). This quasi-definition was identical to the way Hobbes had described the state of nature. Indeed, the similarity extends into the very detail of Hegel's description: "Thus, for example, the Greek heroes [as opposed to Roman ones] appear in a pre-legal era, or become themselves the founders of States, so that right and order, law and morals, proceed from them and are actualized as their own

---

as man, in that first physical state, is merely a passive recipient of the world of sense, i.e., does no more than feel, he is still completely One with that world; and just because he is himself nothing but world, there exists for him as yet no world. Only when, at the aesthetic stage, he puts it outside himself, or contemplates it, does his personality differentiate itself from it, and a world becomes manifest to him because he has ceased to be One with it." This was when humans distanced themselves, Schiller went on, from the world and made objects into "a true and inalienable possession," when "time itself, the eternally moving, stands still," when, for the first time, "there is reflected against a background of transience an image of the infinite, namely form." How close this description was to Hegel's symbolic sublime is entirely apparent—even more so when we attend to Schiller's footnote: "I remind my readers once again that, necessary as it is to distinguish these two periods in theory, in practice they more or less merge one into the other" (*Aesthetic Education*, p. 183). Small wonder if Hegel thought Schiller his most immediate predecessor. Not to mention his colleague. "Symbolism," wrote Goethe in one of his *Maximen* (749), "transforms phenomenon into idea [*Idee*], idea into image, but in such a way that the idea remains forever powerful and unattainable within the image, and, even if expressed in every language, would still remain inexpressible": quoted by Peter Dronke, *Fabula: Explorations into the Uses of Myth in Medieval Platonism*, Mittellateinische Studien und Texte, 9 (Leiden and Cologne, 1974), p. 121.

individual work which remains linked with them" (*K*, 1:185). Speaking of tragedy much later in the lectures, Hegel repeated this:

> The general background of a tragic action is provided in a tragedy, as it was in epic [and sculpture], by that world-situation which I have previously called the "heroic" age. In that age the universal ethical powers have not been explicitly fixed as either the law of the land or as moral precepts and duties. Consequently, only in heroic times can these powers enter in original freshness as the gods who either oppose one another in their own activities or appear themselves as the living heart of free individuals. (*K*, 1:1208)

The Greek heroes, that was to say, embodied the fundamental nature of fine art itself, for they alone actualized in the world their own self-conscious development of self. Later individualism, caught up in the rationally organized state, was no doubt more fully realized but less liable to produce what Hegel called "true art." In its self-realization in the world such individualism had exceeded art's capacity to further its development, already concretized in the existence of the state. Art marked an earlier moment of development: romantic art, as the accompaniment of the later stage, could be called more conscious but less art. The Greek heroes before Rome, or the knights of medieval feudalism and chivalry before the nation-state (*K*, 1:186), were "the ideal artistic figures" (*K* 1:189).

That was why "Shakespeare, for example, has drawn much material for his tragedies out of chronicles or old romances which tell of a state of affairs not yet unfolded into a completely established organization but where the life of the individual in his decision and achievement is still predominant and remains the determining factor" (*K*, 1:190). Hence, too, art's preferred choice of "the class of Princes": "because of the perfect freedom of will and production which is realized in the idea of royalty" (*K*, 1:191–92). That was what explained some of Shakespeare's choices, said Hegel, when he did *not* select princes as heroes: "True, Shakespeare's characters do not all belong to the princely class and remain partly on historical and no longer on mythical ground, but they are therefore transferred to the times of the civil wars in which the bonds of law and order are relaxed or broken, and therefore they acquire again the required independence and self-reliance" (*K*, 1:192).

In the light of these descriptions, it was most significant that the choice instance of the Hegelian sublime, like that of the Longinian, was the originating *fiat lux* of Genesis (*K*, 1:373–74). Hobbes, of course, used the trope to mark the inception of the first form of the state and civil society out of the state of nature. Indeed, he equated the two moments with some precision: "The *Pacts* and *Covenants*, by which the parts of this Body Politique were at first made, set together, and united, resemble that *Fiat*, or the *Let us make man*, pronounced by God in the Creation."[49] The point

---

[49]Hobbes, *Leviathan*, pp. 81–82.

is that Hobbes's description of the passage from the individualistic chaos of the state of nature to the ordered, contractual, authoritarian liberal state did not only mark a stage in the historical development of political theory. It could readily be understood to describe an actual historical transformation: from the chaos of civil war to the stability of Restoration (or even the Protectorate, for that matter), which many indeed saw as a contract between prince and people. Hobbes himself implied this in his later *Behemoth*, that analysis of the causes and progress of the civil wars.

Both the Hobbesian and the Lockean descriptions corresponded to a quite precise establishment. But such was the case even if one wished to conceive of the passage from nature to civil society as taking a longer time, say some two centuries. They could equally well be taken to describe a passage through the French religious wars, through the uncertainties of the early seventeenth century, the Frondes, and consolidation under Louis XIV. These were political descriptions that could be, and indeed were, made only of a historically precise sociopolitical development, and none other. It surely was not mere accident that Hegel took Shakespeare as the last exemplar of classical art (even then showing signs of dissolution). Nor was it a trifle if, like Davenant and Boileau, Hegel conceived the work of fine literary art as *making* the passage in question.

Certain texts by Goethe and Schiller, Hegel thought, also appeared to have about them something of the classical. The case was less clear, for how could he see with precision such a passage in his own time? And yet a strong point could be made that late eighteenth-century Germany—especially its arts—was in a condition of flux not unlike the heroic age of Hegel's description and Hobbes's instauration. In 1766 Lessing, decrying the failure of the theatrical experiment in Hamburg, could exclaim: "Out on the good-natured idea to procure for the Germans a national theatre, when we Germans are not yet a nation! I do not speak of our political constitution, but only of our social character."[50] It was to this state of confusion that Schiller addressed himself in the *Aesthetic Education* and to which the educational reforms of Humboldt and Wolf (mentioned in Chapter 6) sought to respond.

By the 1820s, and even more by 1835, when Hegel's lectures on aesthetics were published, such a sense of disarray was well on the way to being dispelled. The fire of the French invasions and the nervous élan of Young Germany, as well as educational reform, were starting to make a nation both in political fact and in public sentiment. The Prussian Customs Union of 1834, uniting north Germany with divers states of the south, could be counted a first step toward unification of the Reich, although that finally occurred only under Bismarck in 1871. Even in Hegel's lifetime Prussia at least had achieved the statehood that other Western nations had attained one hundred fifty to two hundred fifty years

[50]Lessing, *Hamburgische Dramaturgie*, p. 698; *Hamburg Dramaturgy*, p. 262.

earlier. Hegel's sense that something of the sort was happening may well explain his conception of the roles of such as Goethe and Schiller. Such a sense of present division yielding to a balanced establishment, of a fractured society directed toward a stable civil association, was rather troublingly caught by A. W. Schlegel in 1809: "In the mental dominion of thought and poetry, inaccessible to worldly power, the Germans, who are separated in so many ways from each other, still feel their unity: and in this feeling, whose interpreter the writer and orator must be, amidst our clouded prospects we may still cherish the elevated presage of the great and immortal calling of our people, who from time immemorial have remained unmixed in their present habitations."[51] Again, literature would manage the passage.

Classical art, then, in Hegel's definition, corresponded to the moment of inception of our modernity, the moment when a willful subjectivity first became central to philosophy and the concept of the state. Recent work has sufficiently demonstrated that Hegel's concept of the self-developing subject was an idea wholly foreign to any moment of early Greek thought. It was, however, a concept gradually taking ever stronger shape from the European sixteenth century on. Classical art, for Hegel, was lost forever to us in that moment of the conceptual development of the self, lost just as soon as it further realized itself in the rational nation-state. But that moment was not Greek. It was modern.[52]

That was why, Hegel wrote in a phrase picking up on Schiller's analysis, "in relation to the state of affairs in the world of today, with its civilized, legal, moral, and political conditions, we see that nowadays the scope for ideal configurations [*ideale Gestaltungen*] is only of a very limited kind" (*K*, 1:193; *H*, 1:192). The term Hegel used here—*Gestaltung*—was the one he used (we saw at the beginning of this chapter) when telling how individual self-consciousness in classical art was "shaped forward" (*fortgestaltet*) into reality and advanced "to immediate unity and correspondence with that reality." There it formed "an ideal configuration [*Gestaltung*] of reality destined to embody and reveal the Idea" (*K*, 1:73–74; *H*, 1:80–81). As an exact concept, that is, it was identified with the classical moment. In Hegel's modernity it was lost—but only, and that is the point, only in a still recent past.

The comparison of art formation and political development is not in the least forced, therefore: the equation of heroic age with state of nature, or

[51]A. W. Schlegel, "Introduction," in *Lectures*, p. 6.
[52]My *Discourse of Modernism* (chap. 2) makes this argument at some length, and see also my *Uncertainty of Analysis*, esp. pp. 159–60 n. 16. For Greek Antiquity, see above all Albrecht Dihle, *The Theory of Will in Classical Antiquity* (Berkeley, Los Angeles, and London, 1982); the second two volumes of Michel Foucault, *Histoire de la sexualité* (Paris, 1984); and a fascinating essay by Nicole Loraux on *Antigone*, in which an analysis of the many occurrences of the prefix *auto-* shows, seemingly paradoxically, a dissolution of anything like a self: "La main d'Antigone," *Métis: Revue d'anthropologie du monde grec ancien*, 1, no. 2 (1986), 165–96.

rather with the passage to an original form of state, or that of romantic art with a later stage in the development of the "rational State." The comparison corresponded to the way Hegel himself argued, and the equation seems more than just implicit there. For him, the development of consciousness and that of the sociopolitical order were inextricably and obviously interwoven. So they had been for Schiller: "If man is ever to solve that problem of politics in practice he will have to approach it through the problem of the aesthetic, because it is only through Beauty that man makes his way to Freedom." Shades of Reynolds. And so they had been for de Staël, for whom literature would bring people "little by little out of the most horrifying [affreux] period of the public mind, egoism of the state of nature combined with the active multiplicity of social interests, corruption without manners, brutality without honesty, civilization without enlightenment, ignorance without enthusiasm."[53] In this thought literature and politics could no more be separated than they had been earlier. But the thought was also an extension of the *same.*

This was further specified by Hegel himself when he praised Goethe's *Götz von Berlichingen* precisely for its demonstration of the "contact and collision between the medieval heroic age and the legality of modern life" (K, 1:196). Here we can identify an example of the possibility that still remained under specifically German conditions of showing the passage from the classical to the romantic. Even so, it was barely successful. Like Schiller's *Wallenstein,* Hegel declared, the play showed the inevitable failure of the heroic individual. They were both attempts in literature "to win back again within the circumstances existing in modern times the lost independence of the [heroic] figures" (K, 1:195). But they did not simply *show* failure. They failed in themselves as art (for *Wallenstein,* see, e.g., K, 2:1224, 1230; for *Götz,* 2:1228, 1231–32), because they showed merely an individual confronting that very order in which participation would bring greater self-realization. We see "the mere downfall of individuals" (K, 2:1232) who have been "shipwrecked on a power confronting them which they had deliberately defied in pursuit of their own private ends" (K, 2:1230). The power was precisely the rational community representing a yet higher rationality. The plays chose to put in action heroes who were doing just the opposite of what Schiller, de Staël, Coleridge, and so many others were arguing was necessary to repair the times.

Now Hegel specifically excluded as characters in "real art" those whose actions and decisions rested "on purely private interest and personal character, on thirst for power, lust, honour, or other passions, the right of which can be rooted only in an individual's private inclination and personality" (K, 2:1212–13). Once again, we find ourselves in the fragmented

[53]Schiller, *Aesthetic Education,* p. 9; de Staël, *De la littérature,* 1:26. Cf. the following: "Progress in literature, that is to say the perfecting of the art of thought and expression, is necessary for the establishment and conservation of freedom" (1:30). Her pages were full of such remarks.

experience of Schiller's practical spirit of modern times. Hegel saw this as the essence of contemporary drama. He was indeed particularly scathing in this respect, accusing dramatists of "contempt for the public" and utter disregard for the community: "The German author insists on expressing himself according to his private personality and not making his works agreeable to hearers or spectators." Every writer's great desire was "to display his originality." "Everyone," he concluded with disdain, "pronounces judgement out of his own head, and approves or condemns just as the accident of his personal views, feelings, or caprices dictate." This matched the failures of German criticism, which, he accused, since "Tieck and the brothers Schlegel," had become entirely self-centered, fragmented, and anarchic (*K*, 2:1175).

Lessing had earlier advanced an identical criticism: "We have now, Heaven be praised, a generation of critics whose highest criticism consists in making all criticism suspicious. They vociferate: 'Genius! Genius! Genius overcomes all rules! What genius produces is rules!' Thus they flatter genius; I fancy in order that they too may be held geniuses." He himself hoped that his own work had helped put an end to that tendency "to pronounce it generally as pedantry to prescribe to genius what it must do or leave alone." "We were," he wrote, "on the point of wantonly throwing away the experience of all past times and rather demanding from the poet that each one should discover art anew."[54] At a similar moment in English literary development, Gilden, Dennis, and others had made identical complaints.

Hegel's view was that matters had become worse rather than better. Indeed, for the needs of his historical interpretation of the development of spirit, the final degeneration he noted in his own day was entirely necessary. He could then hope to show how spirit must pass beyond it to a state of a higher rationality. The drama corresponding to that moment failed, therefore, because it performed a denial of the spirit's process of self-development: of which the fully realized State was itself a further development from the heroic age and a more complete realization of the Ideal in its political and moral actualization. Romantic art was thus a dissolution of true art and the beauty proper to it.

Of the five types of art themselves, considered synchronically within the three diachronic modes or stages, the highest type, Hegel opined, was drama: "Because drama has been developed into the most perfect totality of content and form, it must be regarded as the highest state of poetry and art generally. . . . speech alone is the element worthy of the expression of spirit; and of the particular kinds of the arts of speech dramatic poetry is the one which unites the objectivity of epic with the subjective character

---

[54]Lessing, *Hamburgische Dramaturgie*, pp. 673, 700–701; *Hamburg Dramaturgy*, pp. 253, 264. In his *Lectures*, A. W. Schlegel also spoke of the "moral decline of taste in our time," of the "almost incurable vulgarity of our theatre," and of the "chaotic anarchy" of German literature and its writers (pp. 525–27).

of lyric" (*K*, 2:1158). It went almost without saying that its highest manifestation was the Greek (despite an earlier claim that drama, generally,
corresponded most nearly to the romantic moment).

Greek tragedy showed the result of individual self-development coming
into collision with the universal "harmony of the substance of the ethical
order," eventually calling forth a further human development and a new
political process (*K*, 2:1230). But then, true fine art was no more. For "in
the truly beautiful" art, wrote Hegel—and the accompanying demonstration of romantic drama's failure was the more powerful just because what
was in question here was especially the theater—"each side of the opposition which the conflicts disclose must still bear the stamp of the Ideal on
themselves and therefore may not lack rationality and justification. These
interests are the essential needs of the human heart, the inherently necessary aims of action, justified and rational in themselves, and precisely
therefore the universal, eternal, powers of spiritual existence" (*K*, 1:220).

That was exactly the opposite of his manner of speaking about contemporary drama. What Hegel asserted even of most of Schiller's and Goethe's
theater, as showing "den blossen Untergang der Individualen," who simply pursued "ihren besonderen Zweck" (*H*, 2:581, 580), clearly suggested
that it was no longer "ein wahrhaft Schönen (a genuine beauty)" (*H*, 1:216).
The present state of art in itself revealed its inaptitude to actual human
self-development. The view matched Hegel's scornful rejection in the
Phenomenology of the so-called "beautiful spirit" of popular Romanticism (an idea still much relied on). Hegel asserted that this marked a
refusal of that very *Bildung* essential to human motion and development:
the reimmersion of the self in culture and community. This "beautiful
spirit" was "self-consciousness withdrawn into its innermost being, for
which all externality as such has vanished—withdrawn into the contemplation of the 'I' = 'I', in which this 'I' is the whole of essentiality and
existence." So refined a consciousness, he added, was reduced to utmost
poverty of being. Indeed, collapsing in on itself in utter separation from all
else, it was "disordered to the point of madness."[55] So much for the
Wertherian *Weltschmertz:* which was, of course, the individualistic counterpart to the general decay of society and values Hegel was claiming to
record.

In the *Philosophy of Right*, he criticized the *Sturm und Drang* theater as
a whole for similar reasons: that it showed only specific modern interests
and private aims, thus departing entirely from the Ideal of culture and
community. In the same place, Hegel observed that that drama also often
erred from morality as well—which true art could not.[56] And of course,

[55]Georg Wilhelm Friedrich Hegel, *Phenomenology of Spirit*, trans. A. V. Miller, with
an Analysis of the Text and Foreword by J. N. Findlay (1977; rpt. Oxford, 1979), pp. 398–
99, 407.
[56]Georg Wilhelm Friedrich Hegel, *Philosophy of Right*, trans. T. M. Knox (1952; rpt.
Oxford, 1967), p. 85: Pt. II, para. 126.

the highest rational State was also a moral order. His principal counter-example was Sophocles' *Antigone,* which concretely embodied the collision of two universal concepts: those of family and State. That confrontation was just what made the play unique. In the same way, there were a few modern exceptions to the usual degeneracy: Goethe's *Iphigenia in Tauris* was one (*K,* 1:229–30). That play showed the reconciliation of its principal protagonist with the ideal society of Schiller's *Letters,* in an optimistic union beyond the individualism of the classical moment. It was a very rare epitome of romantic theater. The exceptional nature of such a case, thought Hegel, was itself evidence of a final dissolution of art.

For that, of course, was what he was now considering. But art had not gone from the Greeks (or before) to some indefinite time in the future, in some cyclical repetition of the three modes. Rather had it gone from an early modern period of which Shakespeare (and perhaps Dante) was the exemplar, to a present moment of which Hegel himself was the epitome. For, "while on the one hand we give the highest position to art, it is on the other hand just as necessary to remember that neither in content nor in form is art the highest and absolute mode of bringing to our minds the true interests of the spirit" (*K,* 1:9). Not only was art *not* "the highest form of spirit," but on the contrary it "acquires its real ratification only in philosophy" (*erhält in der Wissenschaft erst ihre echte Bewährung: K,* 1:13; *H,* 1:24). He did not tire of repeating the matter: art was "not the highest way of apprehending the spiritually concrete. The higher way, in contrast to representation by means of the sensuously concrete, is thinking, which in a relative sense is indeed abstract, but it must be concrete, not one-sided, if it is to be true and rational" (*K,* 1:71–72). So finally: "Art still has a limit in itself and therefore passes over into higher forms of consciousness. This limitation determines, after all, the position which we are accustomed to assign to art in our contemporary life. For us art counts no longer as the highest mode in which truth fashions an existence for itself" (*K,* 1:102–3).

This brings us back from a generalizing conception of art to what was taken as a statement of historical fact: the role of art in contemporary life. The final historic art form, said Hegel, was comic drama. In depicting the individual returning into itself, it showed a deep and ineluctable contradiction between individual interests and wider universal absolutes. Thus "Aristophanes presents to us the absolute contradiction between (a) the true essence of religion and political and ethical life, and (b) the subjective attitude of citizens and individuals who should give actuality to that essence." So, he ended, was "implicit one of the greatest symptoms of Greek corruption" (*K,* 2:1222). But modern conditions revealed an even deeper corruption.

First, modern tragedy itself decayed into the portrayal of self-interest alone, with its outcome in the indifferent consequence "of unfortunate circumstances and external accidents" (*K,* 2:1231). In this way the decay of the ultimate artistic genre, theater, matched the dissolution of the final, romantic mode of fine art. Second, that same tragedy was no longer specific. It could equally well be comedy: "A happy denouement [to such plays] has at least as much justification as an unhappy one" (K, 2:1232). Hence had come into existence a new contemporary form of drama, *Schauspiele und Dramen*, midway between tragedy and comedy—an almost bastard genre, whose interest was narrow and merely moralistic (K, 2:582). This was pretty much dismissed by Hegel as quite lacking in seriousness and any deep meaning (K, 2:1232–33). In like manner, comedy was reduced to a malicious enjoyment of discomfiture (K, 2:1233–34). The joyful reconciliation Hegel saw in Aristophanic comedy was quite lacking in anything since—again, with the sole exception of Shakespeare (K, 2:1236).

Classical art alone, therefore, was able to find some form of representation (the word *Darstellung* was always at the tip of Hegel's pen in this connection) beyond some mere illusion of imitation—that bad *Nachahmung* he scorned. Classical art achieved a representation (or *presentation*) of the self-producing Idea in and through the concrete particular, its estranged opposite, which, as produced out of that object, Idea was able to sublate into a higher totality where the opposite—Other—was brought back into a more fully realized self-contemplation. Although the language is more complicated, the idea of the concrete image forcing the mind into profound awareness of its own powers was quite familiar. For Hegel, that moment of achievement was short-lived. It was preceded by a phase when the external served to embody, not fully consciously, universal Idea (the symbolic) and was followed by a later time when "art falls to pieces, on the one hand, into the imitation of external objectivity in all its contingent shapes; on the other hand, however, into the liberation of subjectivity, in accordance with its inner contingency, in humour" (K, 1:608).

The fragmented scattering of persons, objects, and events was a profound alienation of the world from the mind; the turning inward of the subject was an equally drastic estrangement of mind from world. Thus was the contemporary situation deplored by Schiller in the *Aesthetic Education*. He followed earlier argument in presenting art—especially literary art—as the remedy, forging anew the passage from conflict and degeneracy to stability and progress. From the Hegelian analysis rather different arguments result. For Hegel, art no longer represented a world, the concrete self-contemplating universal. It now played out the mind's operations on itself, in a world from which it was entirely alienated. That was the end of art, and great comedy could mark it by performing the actual process of producing the reified illusions of that alienation, making them visible as such: in opposition to the organic life of State and community. Aristophanes and Shakespeare had achieved that. But when comedy did not so succeed, it decayed into something else entirely: the merely moralistic drama of which, for Hegel, August von Kotzebue was exemplary. That failure of the art form that completed the historical series marked the end of art's socially useful existence.

Art could go no further and had to yield to another discourse, to a philosophy that itself could not merely *show* the process of self-conscious thinking, but had somehow to make use of it in the recreation of community: Hegel's life project, of course, and a repetition in a different key of what we saw in England and France in the seventeenth century. Art itself—especially, for all of these writers, *literary* art—could then be seen as marking a particular phase in history, one in which it served a particular set of purposes. In showing how Hegel himself continued the aesthetic thought of his predecessors from the mid-seventeenth century to Schiller (or Wollstonecraft, de Staël, Coleridge, Shelley, and so many others), and how he spoke in fact about the writing of the modern age (or of the art reinvented in its own image), I have sought to show when that particular historical moment was. Although it is not finished, either.

Hegel, needless to say, did not, or could not, admit so much. One may say he first plunged into oblivion his memory of a speculative and critical tradition only so as to reconstruct it. And possibly, too, finally to bury it in the deep earth—or accumulated dust—of its own arguments and assumptions about the relations of mind and thought, of passion and emotion, of art and nature. The modern history of literary theory started with a thinking about the identity of mind and nature as shown in literary texts, *before* it proceeded to debates dependent on theories based on their radical separation: so that it became (among other things) the aim of art at once to reveal, to work on, and to overcome that separation. Hegel recuperated the first moment by showing that in "true art" such a separation never existed. His description of the passage from the sublime of the symbolic to the decay of the romantic was a description of that particular history. Thus it enshrined that history in a past, hoping to replace it (so he thought) with something quite different.

Art—literature—was a mode of knowing that had now sublated itself into another form of knowing (philosophy). It had done so just because the efficacy with which literature had endowed itself at the outset was now (thought the age) exhausted. Some thought it could be, as it were, restarted. Hence the urgings of Schiller and Coleridge, de Staël and Shelley. Others, like Wollstonecraft, did not. But poetry was not all. For Hegel, art came to show consciousness knowing more than it knew it knew—or could know: the Kantian sublime. Philosophy would be consciousness knowing what it knows. That passage was why the ultimate art form, comedy, said Hegel, made its own *making* visible. Doing so, it wrote *finis* to art: it had served its historical purpose. So he concluded:

> We ended with the romantic art of emotion and deep feeling where absolute subjective personality moves free in itself and in the spiritual world. Satisfied in itself, it no longer unites itself with anything objective and particularized and it brings the negative side of this dissolution into consciousness in the humour of comedy. Yet on this peak comedy leads at the same time to the dissolution of art altogether. All art aims at the

identity, produced by the spirit, in which eternal things, God, and absolute truth are revealed in real appearance and shape to our contemplation,
to our hearts and minds. But if comedy presents this unity only as its self-
destruction because the Absolute, which wants to realize itself, sees its
self-actualization destroyed by interests that have now become explicitly
free in the real world and directed only on what is accidental and subjective, then the presence and agency of the Absolute no longer appears
positively unified with the characters and aims of the real world but
asserts itself only in the negative form of cancelling [*aufhebt*] everything
not correspondent with it, and subjective personality alone shows itself
self-confident and self-assured at the same time in this dissolution. (*K*,
2:1236; *H*, 2:586)

Such was the condition in Germany and France, to mention the two
contemporary cases most often alluded to by Hegel (excepting—always—
Shakespeare). It was as though the deep laws of literature which for the
seventeenth-century writers had been coincident with the general rules of
world and mind (call them unity, Idea, absolute, or whatever) had ceded
before the superstructural events, customs, and habits of locality and
province, those "accidental" and "subjective interests" of the real world.

We seem to have come a long way from the concern with the instability
of the State and with the concomitant confusion of language with which
we began. A fundamentally political anxiety led to the establishment of an
epistemology based on concepts of natural reason and methodical common sense; it produced an acceptable (if complex) claim for the objective
referentiality of language, of discourse, of thinking; and it produced the
socioeconomic concept of possessive individualism, enabling the forging
of a new idea of civil society. Within this conjuncture, literature was
created, with a quite particular set of claims and a privileged role of
leadership to perform. Addison's linking of the author of the *Two Treatises on Government* to the idea of the true critic of such literature caught
the relationship nicely, marking it as not in the least fortuitous. The
modern meaning of the term and function of "literature" is not timeless: it
was attached to a particular sociocultural environment and political order,
whose ideology it could readily express.

What was forged in the late seventeenth century remained largely un-
bent and surely unbroken well into the nineteenth century. By and large,
perhaps, it still remains ours. Like the much earlier concept of the rational
idea underlying all things (from Rymer and Leibniz to Burke, Reynolds,
and beyond), Hegel's concept of Idea was offered as the underlying rational
law of all phenomenal events, as well as the binding Absolute of mind:
that Idea, and the sublation of any separation of mind and world, individual and community, was what fine literature achieved. But only during a
specifiable stage of human development. For when humanity became
sufficiently developed, then Art itself would be replaced by Philosophy,
telling formally what Art could only show performatively, and so, one

might say, "as in a glass, darkly." Like St. Paul, Hegel offered his Philosophy as a passage to clarity and ultimately whole knowledge: of Idea, the underlying unity of State, as it was of Reason and of Nature—indeed, uniting all three. That was just the task his predecessors had given literature. For him, literature, as the highest form of Art, was the penultimate stage in achieving such knowledge.

When Marx erased the Hegelian Idea, replacing its epistemological function with that of the concrete relations of economic production—as the actual, objective infrastructure, he qualitatively altered the relation of Dryden's, Hume's, or Hegel's law to what the former had already called the superstructure. For the law was no longer a fixed model, rule, or static rational idea. It was an ongoing and self-transforming process. That could not but change the idea of what literature was all about. It has not yet done so. We still emphasize either the nomothetic, lawful value of the literary text (nowadays understood as its self-realizing rhetorical impulse) or the moral, didactic, or conceptual significance of the literary artifact: the only difference being that now we tend to see them, as Hegel asserted, as opposed rather than complementary processes. If it has not exactly cracked from side to side (as the critical wilderness sometimes suggests), the glass has most certainly darkened.

Epilogue

If Hegel was right, then literature—and the other arts—were no longer socially and conceptually *useful* in the way they *had* been for the preceding era. They had reached the end of the particular role they had been playing in a human development. Why, then, have they continued to exist? The novel especially, one might exclaim, was alive and well—certainly in the period following Hegel's analysis. Yet might it also be understood as a fading continuation of the woeful tale of fragmented individuals' struggles to maintain a self ever more menaced either by its own dissolution in its self-estrangement from the world or by the external pressure of a fragmented and alienated reality. The genre itself would fall into a (debased) lineage of the Hegelian epic—if we followed Lukács's analysis of the novel, which itself could then be read as an attempt to extend the Hegelian project further into a period that, over its duration, saw the slow downfall of art continue.

Hegel himself, who scorned to treat the novel, might have echoed Shelley's view: "There is this difference between a story and a poem, that a story is a catalogue of detached facts, which have no other connection than time, place, circumstance, cause and effect; the other is the creation of actions according to the unchangeable forms of human nature, as existing in the mind of the Creator, which is itself the image of all other minds."[1] Such a view, disdaining story as not literature (a disdain perhaps also implied by the earlier and later theoretical exigency to distinguish story from plot), would help explain Charles Baudelaire's unknowing but seemingly precise imitation of Davenant: "Only three decent [*respectables*] beings exist: the priest, the warrior, the poet." Unlike Davenant's

---

[1]Shelley, "Defense of Poetry," in *Selected Poetry and Prose*, p. 422.

338

claim, of course, to emphasize "poet" in the mid-nineteenth century was to restrict the field of literary activity. Small wonder, therefore, if Baudelaire added in the following aphorism, that these beings were found in the only legitimate sort of state: that ruled by a single authority, the prince.[2] Like the English poet's, Baudelaire's claim might be understood as a conservative reaction to perceived fragmentation, a means to confine disorder.

Both Shelley's godlike poet and Baudelaire's authoritative actor were, for Hegel, long gone. Story, the novel, might then be seen as the post-comedic artform, writing fragmentation into its very procedures (a view unable to have been held under the earlier epic justification of a novel like *Télémaque*, but not far from Boileau's criticism of Scudéry's incoherence and confusion). Indeed, if we follow not only a writer such as Lukács, but even one like Lionel Trilling, then Hegel's conclusion was confirmed precisely in their reading of modern literature since the end of the nineteenth century, in which they saw a final fragmentation of the subject and dispersion of community. Lukács saw modernism's elevation of individual subjectivity against society as fundamentally pernicious, while Trilling praised it as the strong affirmation of modern individualism. But whatever the political spectrum covered, the analyses of literature entailed in these opinions were essentially similar.

For Hegel, this would represent the ultimate dissolution, a final denial of the universal—unless that universal were simply the willful diversity of the particular: an oxymoron and a consummation of his analysis that Hegel would certainly most devoutly have rejected. Nonetheless, in line with what was just suggested of the novel, we might then view certain literary forms as taking Hegel's purely subjective personality to its logical conclusion. From this perspective, a writer such as Samuel Beckett reveals a final breakdown, as the subject is at last despairingly and utterly separated from that Absolute with which it was once literature's role to show its unity. Others—Francis Ponge, Alain Robbe-Grillet?—utter the same despair through the loss of identity in the fragmented world of objects. The so-called minimalist writing characteristic of much contemporary North American literature would be further evidence of such despairing vacuity.

In this view, art has sunk into the decay Hegel observed one hundred fifty years before. It has removed itself from the actual history of community and human self-development, on which its effect can then be only pernicious. Thinkers such as Schiller and Hegel yet retained the optimistic view of human progress urged on them by the traditions of the European Enlightenment, however much they may have complicated the concept. But now art no longer has to do "with the liberation of the spirit from the content and forms of finitude, with the presence and liberation of the

---

[2]Charles Baudelaire, *Oeuvres complètes*, ed. Claude Pichois, 2 vols. (Paris, 1975–76), 1:684. For the story/plot, body/soul comment, see, e.g., above, pp. 165–70, 244.

Absolute in what is apparent and visible, with an unfolding of truth which is not exhausted in natural history but revealed in world history" (*K*, 2:1236). On the contrary, art shows that the spirit is incapable of such self-liberation. Hegel might well see confirmation of this in the fact that the favorite mode of absurdist nihilism—if that is not too strong a term to apply to such as Beckett and Peter Handke (and I mean it in a technical sense)—is the comic: but a strangely altered, unrejoicing, and grim comic; a grimace, rather, at the world and a mockery of self without identity.

The argument has been suggesting, however, that Hegel could be right only in a particular way. He knew as we all do that it is difficult, if not impossible, to find a human society devoid of some activity and creation able to be called "art" and even of something like "literature": whether oral or written, using the medium of natural language. With respect to this last issue, he claimed that written works were historically the most developed types of art, such that their presence or absence would indicate relative degrees of social progress. In that, he was a true son of the Enlightenment, inheritor of common eighteenth-century ideas about literary progress. Indeed, his argument said that literature would progress out of use. If it still existed in our culture, that was because human development within that culture had reached only a certain point. He sought to show the role literature (and all art) played in the development of society and consciousness up to that point—then reached—beyond which it could no more serve any purpose—indeed, beyond which it became positively counterproductive.

That view relied on a particular ethnocentricity: the idea that what would later be called the "Great Tradition" was what literature was all about: from Shakespeare to the European Romantics (and some beyond), including Homer, the fifth- and fourth-century Athenians, and some selected Romans, chiefly from the first century and a half of Empire. The very idea of something like literary "progress" itself implied that literary forms in different times and places were and are actually different, in their context, however much they may be able to "move" among such different times and places. Hegel could turn *Antigone* into a tragedy relaying modern ideas of subject and universal, just as the debate about Homer had adjusted the *Odyssey* and the *Iliad* to contemporary conceptions of what literature was and did, and as James Macpherson's *Ossian* and its immense European reception had made a Homeric past for the North in many ways essential to Romanticism's self-understanding as the embodiment of naive originality and immediacy.[3] None of that meant that litera-

---

[3] At the time, the Ossianic poems were indeed seen as such a making, and many saw nothing wrong with Macpherson's "recomposition" of the pretended epic. After all, they said, the history of the Homeric epics was as complicated and dubious. And what, in any case, was the role of their translators? See Fiona J. Stafford, *The Sublime Savage: A Study of James Macpherson and the Poems of Ossian* (Edinburgh, 1988). She urges the now received wisdom that the poems were part translation, part invention. For more on the

ture was made of texts having the same fundamental meaning for everyone in all times and places. It meant that they were at hand to attain
meanings and functions.

These texts do not, then, have the same meaning or serve the same
purpose always and everywhere. On the contrary, they are always in a
complex relation of reciprocal determination with the sociocultural environment as a whole. Unlike Hegel, I could assert not that the forms of
literary art are forever finished, but simply that the purposes they served
within a particular historical environment are. I therefore sought to show
just how Hegel was willy-nilly addressing a particular art and a particular
environment. The *Aesthetics* was not a perennial overview, but an element of a specific set of limited arguments and activities which (in spite of
him) still continues fundamentally to inform our own notion of literature.[4] Setting Hegel within his environment, I have tried further to grasp
that literature's character.

Its death was not in Hegel's eyes some sort of abstract idea to be suffered
or enacted. It was a statement at once of historical and conceptual fact.
Israel Knox saw with dismay that "Hegel does not seem to be shedding any
tears of lamentation. He is speaking of the death of art in no metaphorical
sense but in a definite historical and cultural sense."[5] Indeed, and that was
just why there was no cause for tears: its end was taken to mark cultural
advance, an increase and a broadening of human capacities. We need not
go along with that notion of progress to find Hegel's arguments useful.
Literary art may well on occasion shine forth in glory. But it can do so only
as an active process within human social and cultural development. That
does not necessarily mean it disappears: simply that it no longer merits
privilege—perhaps, too, that we need to understand what function some
new, yet unrecognized, form is serving.

Walter Benjamin observed this long ago, noting that by the mid-
nineteenth century the traditional value of the artwork had seemed to
start changing: "The work of art becomes a creation with entirely new

---

question, see, in the second part of my bibliography, Dunn, Haywood, Saunders, Smart,
and Van Tieghem. The term "naive" implies not that Romantic writers thought themselves to be returning to any pristine source, but that they sought to work from a "deeper
humanity" behind, yet through and within, the artifice of contemporary culture.

[4] I had intended to go on to two further arguments. Length and perhaps present
coherence forbid. One would show the many ways in which the concepts of Soviet
realism (I avoid "socialist," as suggesting a nonexistent monolith) and the activities of
Soviet cultural organisms (esp. the Writers' Union) repeated the earlier Western European inception of literature. A few hints of this are in my "Société, discours, littérature,"
pp. 173–76. The other would show how all contemporary Western criticisms, despite
differing claims, remain under the detailed sway of literature as explored here. A very
early and rather incoherent version of such an argument appeared some years ago: "The
Environment of Literature and the Imperatives of Criticism: The End of a Discipline,"
Europa, 4, no. 1 (1981), 29–64.

[5] Israel Knox, *The Aesthetic Theories of Kant, Hegel, and Schopenhauer* (New York,
1936), p. 101.

functions, among which the one we are conscious of, the artistic function, later may be recognized as incidental."[6] To bewail such changes is then a false and sentimental nostalgia: worse, it may be a turning away from something else. Art is material for the discursive expression of self and social making. When another material supersedes it, that would not seem to require lament. It will happen, too, that such new forms will supersede the very claims and concepts, activities and wishes borne in such older forms (even though they must inevitably derive from them).

Like Knox, Erich Kahler views with alarm a questioning of "traditional" forms of art, again seen as an art corresponding everywhere and always to some perennial human nature. Adopting a familiar individualist view of "artistic creativity," he asserts that "in our days, for the first time, such an artistic effort toward the achievement of a new comprehensive form seems lacking." Art, he thinks, would always have been characterized by some kind of "comprehensive" expression of a common human spirit. Nowadays, he writes, "the processes of analytic disjunction prevail over the creative ones, or, to be more correct, they have come to coincide with the creative ones so that, in the main, creation results in disjunction," in what he calls more generally "the disintegration of form." Hegel had said little else some one hundred fifty years earlier. And the reason for the degeneracy is the pernicious "influence of science and technology," marks, we may suppose, of the Hegelian and Schillerian fragmentation in specialization. The contemporary idea of the bottomlessness of the unconscious and the resulting fact that "the unconscious is unleashed as sheer raw material" thus find themselves combined with the other fact that the form of art (in literature, painting, and music) gives way to "the display of material objects as such, or better, of fragments of objects, of objects as fragments, of our overcrowded and disrupted world." Together these lead "to a formalism, a skeletal form in which all vital substance has faded away. A ghostly consciousness is confronted with itself."[7]

Kahler, author of *The Inward Turn of Narrative*, a study precisely of the modern literary installation of subjectivity, is here expressing, in the rather wistfully Hegelian terms of his diatribe, the end of literature—whether we call it Hegelian or Cartesian is no matter. Kahler fears "the elimination of human sentiment, of human significance, and of the sensitively registered part of happenings" that makes them "humanly incomplete." This, he cries, leads us toward the very disintegration of language itself; we come at last to a "triumph of incoherence." Shades perhaps of Thucydides and innumerable sixteenth-century commentators; of Karl Krauss, too, who at the beginning of our century argued "that it is in the hollowing-out of language that we can see the disintegration, and even the

[6]Walter Benjamin, "The Work of Art in the Age of Mechanical Reproduction," in *Illuminations*, ed. Hannah Arendt, trans. Harry Zohn (New York, 1969), p. 225.
[7]Erich Kahler, *The Disintegration of Form in the Arts* (New York, 1968), pp. 27–49.

disappearance, of the concept and existence of the autonomous individual, of the personality in its classical sense."[8] The whole process, writes Kahler finally, is leading away from the "awareness of coherence," toward the "deliberate, and that means, the conscious destruction of consciousness." Such a view sets aside any thought that consciousness itself (as Krauss implied) was the product of a particular kind of coherence, not just the reverse. For Kahler, all we have is "the outspoken attempt to *produce incoherence.*" Written in 1967, this movement was said to find its satanic prophets at that time in Timothy Leary, Marshall McLuhan, and Claude Lévi-Strauss, not to mention commercial television with its "orgies of idiocy."[9]

I am not meaning to take a straw man or to make fun at Kahler's expense (or my own, for those who do not question his assumptions). On the contrary, the issues are of the very greatest seriousness. Kahler's views of what is happening are far from isolated, and we are well aware of the debate continuing into the present decade, now involving all levels of the art world, of academia, and of government. But it is no accident that Kahler expresses in Hegelian terms a lament for an art whose complex parameters were firmly established in the European seventeenth and eighteenth centuries. Shulamith Firestone has made an analysis very similar to Kahler's. For her, of course, modern art's "gnawing on its own vitals," its "negation of reality," and so on, were signs of the dissolution of a masculine culture, signs therefore of a literature whose values "we shall not miss. . . . We shall no longer need it."[10] In the service of particular political goals, the Hegelian nature of these remarks and hopes is no less evident than it is of Kahler's. The analysis of art's role and nature is the same as Hegel's (and as that of more recent commentators): that is just why she views its disappearance and replacement as a cause for hope. As in the contrast between Lukács and Trilling, the underlying analysis and assumptions remain the same. Like Lukács (however different her debate), Firestone views these marks of decay as signs of a changing sociocultural environment whose transformation can only be for the better.

Just because Hegel's arguments may be seen as already marking a limit point of *that* art and literature (still and also ours), those arguments and that limit provoke some grave problems. For if, as I have argued, the *Aesthetics* is a natural continuation of Enlightenment views of art and an examination of the particular art historical moment corresponding to it, the matter becomes the more urgent to the very extent these views remain. For we are dealing no longer with Hegel alone, understood as an exceptional case, but with the summation of the entire line of modern

---

[8]Quoted in Leo Lowenthal, *Literature, Popular Culture, and Society* (Englewood Cliffs, N.J., 1961), p. 7.
[9]Kahler, *Disintegration,* pp. 49, 95–101.
[10]Shulamith Firestone, *The Dialectic of Sex* (New York, 1970), pp. 208–9, 215.

aesthetic thought and the art to which it referred and from which it drew sustenance. Then, as Geoffrey Hartman has said in terms strikingly similar to Kahler's (though he would certainly situate himself quite differently): "Something is needed to set a bottom for inwardness, to limit an endless and corrosive self-concern."[11] Perhaps it is just the point that that bottom can no longer be found either in or through art—or at least, not art functioning in the same way or with the same purpose. Perhaps again, the bottoming-out of subjectivity is no longer a concern. Its very thought is simply the nether end of a discursive and conceptual practice whose inception was the self-imposition of that subject. All this, if Hegel was speaking not of all and any art (whatever he asserts to the contrary), but of the art specific to the sociocultural environment of which that concept of subjectivity was a principal element.

In these terms, if Hegel was right, literature continues to exist only on the basis of a profound cultural inertia and, more seriously, as a *resistance* to any Hegelian (or other) self-development of mind, culture, and society. For finally, it matters little whether Hegel was "right" or not in aesthetic terms (whatever that might mean). What matters is that he was *historically* right: literature was set in place in the European seventeenth century, and it did perform specific functions in a particular sociocultural environment. Hegel was already discussing the end of a role whose lingering decay Kahler deplores as he simultaneously seeks to kindle it back into flame . . . as do his more recent, and more widely heard, successors.

Nor was Hegel alone even in his own time. Wollstonecraft earlier made fun of *Shandy*'s appeal to un- or immature reason. In 1820 Thomas Love Peacock called poetry "gewgaws and rattles for the grown babies of the age."[12] Hilary Putnam has recalled "Bentham's challenging judgment that 'prejudice aside, the game of pushpin is of equal value with the arts and sciences of music and poetry.' *Prejudice aside, pushpin is as good as poetry.*" I am not sure what Kahler would say of this, save perhaps to remark on the inevitable philistinism of utilitarians—although we might recall that Bentham did not originate the thought. We long since saw the French poet François de Malherbe make the identical point *before* the modern inception of literature to note poetry's futility in his time. Putnam himself concluded, "What makes this so shocking to the modern reader is how deeply it conflicts with our current cultural values. The arts have been exalted by us to a place much higher than any they occupied in Plato's day or in the middle ages."[13] Not by us, unless we think of all those earlier writers as our community: by three hundred years of debate.

---

[11]Geoffrey H. Hartman, *The Fate of Reading and Other Essays* (Chicago and London, 1975), p. 314.

[12]Thomas Love Peacock, "The Four Ages of Poetry," quoted by Murray Krieger, *Words about Words about Words: Theory, Criticism, and the Literary Text* (Baltimore and London, 1988), p. 28.

[13]Hilary Putnam, *Reason, Truth, and History* (Cambridge, 1981), p. 151

As he approached the study of Hegel's *Aesthetics*, de Man remarked on "the alacrity with which one rushes, as by instinct, to the defense of aesthetic values" and thus on the likely incompatibility of "the aesthetic dimensions of literature with whatever it is that its theoretical investigation discloses."[14] His aim, in the text referred to here, was in some way to set Hegel right. He was not very successful, because he sought to do it through a deconstruction of Hegel's text from within—an attempt convincingly undone, I think, by a later commentator.[15] Yet he seems right in maintaining, like Putnam, that "part of what he has to say is something that we cannot or will not hear because it upsets what we take for granted, the unassailable *value* of the aesthetic."[16] The problem is that the aesthetic was never some separate attribute, tied only to emotion, a judgment of taste, or some separate logic of sense. It was bound to the epistemological, political, and ethical underpinnings of a whole cultural environment.

With a pretty irony, Italo Calvino summed up the ideas and action of literature in the establishment we have followed, as a universal treasure house of human mind and sensibility: "Of all this, writing warns like the oracle and purifies like the tragedy. So it is nothing to make a problem of. Writing, in short, has a subsoil which belongs to the species, or at least to civilization, or at least to certain income brackets."[17] Calvino's narrator writes as if literature were still a familiar commentary on culture and society. But in a tavern of crossed destinies the mute traveler chooses his tale at random from a pack of signs whose permutations are finite, whose meanings are limitless. Sense is lost in the mere pursuit of permutation. Literature is no longer revelation, but an outpouring of signs whose babble may be interpreted at will—if muteness is not an absolute impediment. Here is literature at the end of its tether, made by a solitary "sedentary person" playing with the signs of a society from which she or he is ever separated. In these signs are contained the tales of our Great Tradition, Faust and Parsifal, Oedipus, Roland, Helen, St. George, and Midas—all and forever, down to Shakespeare and a simultaneous telling of *Macbeth*, *Hamlet*, and *Lear*. Macbeth's final lament would become ours and literature's: to "wish the syntax o' *The World* were now undone, that the playing cards were shuffled, the folios' pages, the mirror-shards of the disaster."[18]

The literary text confirms theoretical analysis—indeed, plays with it. And if Calvino echoed the dissolution of language, Beckett may have

---

[14]Paul de Man, "Sign and Symbol in Hegel's *Aesthetics*," *Critical Inquiry*, 8, no. 4 (Summer 1982), 762.

[15]Raymond Geuss, "A Response to Paul de Man," *Critical Inquiry*, 10, no. 2 (Dec. 1983), 375–82; De Man's "Reply to Raymond Geuss," ibid., pp. 383–90.

[16]De Man, "Sign and Symbol," p. 766.

[17]Italo Calvino, *The Castle of Crossed Destinies*, trans. William Weaver (1977; rpt. New York and London, 1979), pp. 103–4.

[18]Ibid., pp. 99, 120.

echoed that of subjective identity, lost in the bottomless well of language: "I must go on; I can't go on; I must go on; I must say words as long as there are words, I must say them until they find me, until they say me—heavy burden, heavy sin; I must go on; maybe it's been done already; maybe they've already said me; maybe they've already borne me to the threshold of my story; I'd be surprised if it opened." But as Foucault quoted these words from *Molloy* at the start of his *Ordre du discours*, they became an accepting—even joyous—affirmation of a speaker's place in discursive formations, of "identity" not as the unbrokenly teleological imposition of individual intention, but rather as the constant making of a site in a sociocultural environment, whose motion and complexity are guided by positive discursive practices open to such making.[19] Language is not bottomless. It is one of the expressive media through which these practices compose reality: of which a particular practical notion of literature, for instance, was a part. That would be the other side of the Hegelian coin: the dissolution of the subject and the decay of the language it controlled may have already produced a new practice of the person in community.

Some kinds of fictive writing, having fallen on those shards of disaster finally depicted by the multiple dissolutions of "postmodernism," have already perhaps taken us elsewhere. No longer is the representation or denial of the expectations of literature central to them: from Bertolt Brecht's effort to make his audience know its ability to forge history, to that of writers whose work reminds its readers or spectators of a past so as to change their relation to a present (Zora Neale Hurston or Kazuo Ishiguro, Primo Levi or Milan Kundera), of those who make a new cultural place in marvelous realism or magical realism, or of those whose presentation of difference has as at least one of its effects to deny any singular cohesion of interest (Buchi Emecheta or Ngugi wa Thiong'o, Edward Kamau Brathwaite or Bessie Head, Ama Ata Aidoo or Alice Walker).

It does not matter whether the interest and the place are those of Nadine Gordimer or Gabriel García Marquez, of Fay Weldon or Carlos Fuentes. The point lies in their otherness. It does not matter whether remembering the past denotes avoidance of catastrophe, as it often does in writings from within the formative places of Enlightenment (in Günter Grass or Christa Wolf—who has proven only too prophetic a Cassandra), or a gift of difference (Chinua Achebe's *Anthills of the Savannah* offers its Western readers, at least, a place and a past largely unknown).[20] "Something re-

---

[19]"The Discourse on Language," trans. Rupert Sawyer, printed as an appendix to Michel Foucault, *The Archaeology of Knowledge*, trans. A. M. Sheridan Smith (New York, 1976), p. 215.

[20]The Cassandra reference is to what Grass calls Wolf's "execution" by media and government voices in the process of German reunification. Such repression is an act by those who believe only a specific kind of individual producer (or reader) qualifies as exemplary of *mind*, German, American, or any other. Thus to put "Western art über alles" is the real closing of mind, and the need for it belies all claims that history is at an "end": Günter Grass, "The Business Blitzkrieg," *Weekend Guardian* (Oct. 20–21, 1990),

mains to be said that has not yet been put into words," Grass remarks; "an old story wants to be told altogether differently."[21] What matters in these writings and others is their hold on a "knowledge" of otherness that keeps a kind of familiarity in the unfamiliar. Yet they speak to and for a community, avoiding both endless iteration of self or language and any fall into self-regarding nostalgia. We have left usual bearings of time, local habitation, and customary interest—strange echo of a three-centuries-old upheaval. This, too, may explain the present popularity of historical writing and the volume of critical and theoretical debate. A known environment and the literature that was an integral part of it have lost their sway, and criticism its old familiar object.

Even if Hegel were wrong, therefore, we would need a new aesthetic of like dimensions, one yet to be elaborated (which is not to say no one has attempted it). For the *Ästhetik* threw down a gauntlet that anyone concerned in our time with the role of literature, and the arts more generally, is obliged to take up. If it is interpreted in some such way as suggested, however, I think he was right. What we then need is less an aesthetics than a totalizing concept of how societies become meaningful to themselves; of how that becoming is the sum of activities through which societies are always in movement and yet coherent to themselves at any given moment and place. Artworks are there just one set of functions among many, whose meanings, actions, and functions change with the entire environment.

---

p. 6. A longer discussion of the political and economic context and self-servingness of Wolf's victimization is Christine Schoefer's "Germany Rewrites History: The Attack on Christa Wolf," *The Nation*, 250, no. 3 (Oct. 22, 1990), 446–49. A recent work on the literary, political, and gender stakes of the Cassandra myth, from the Greeks to culmination in Wolf, now shows uncanny prescience: Pascale-Anne Brault, "Prophetess Doomed: Cassandra and the Representation of Truth," Ph.D. diss., New York University, 1990.

[21]Günter Grass, "Writing after Auschwitz," in *Two States–One Nation?* trans. Krishna Winston and A. S. Wensinger (London, 1990), p. 123.

Bibliography

Primary Sources

Académie Françoise. *Dictionnaire de l'.* . . . 2 vols. Paris, 1694.
——. *Nouveau dictionnaire de l'.* . . . 2 vols. Paris, 1718.
——. *Dictionnaire de l'.* . . . 4th ed. 2 vols. Paris, 1762.
——. *Dictionnaire de l'.* . . . 5th ed. 2 vols. Paris, 1798.
Achilles Tatius. [*Clitophon and Leucippe*]. Trans. S. Gaselee. London and New York, 1917.
Addison, Joseph. *The Works.* . . . Ed. George Washington Greene. 5 vols. New York, 1853.
——. *Critical Essays from the Spectator, with Four Essays by Richard Steele.* Ed. Donald F. Bond. Oxford, 1970.
——. *The Letters.* Ed. Walter Graham. Oxford, 1941.
Addison, Joseph, Richard Steele, and Others. *The Spectator.* Ed. Gregory Smith. Intro. Peter Smithers. 4 vols. 1907; rpt. London and New York, 1979.
Agrippa, Henry Cornelius. *Female Pre-Eminence: Or, the Dignity and Excellency of That Sex, above the Male.* . . . Done into English, with Additional Advantages, by H[enry] C[lare]. London, 1670. In *The Feminist Controversy of the Renaissance.* Ed. Diane Bornstein. Delmar, N.Y. 1980.
Akinside, Mark, M.D. *The Works . . . in Verse and Prose,* with His Life, a Fac Simile of His Hand-Writing, and An Essay on the First Poem, by Mrs. Barbauld. 2 vols. in 1. New Brunswick, N.J., 1808.
Althusius, Johannes. *The Politics.* An abridged trans. of the 3d edition of *Politica methodice digesta.* . . . Trans. and ed. Frederick S. Carney. Boston, 1964.
André, père Yves-Marie. *Oeuvres philosophiques.* Ed. Victor Cousin. 1843; rpt. Geneva, 1969.
Ariosto, Ludovico. *Orlando furioso.* Trans. William Stewart Rose. Ed. Stewart A. Baker and A. Bartlett Giamatti. Indianapolis and New York, 1968.
——. *The Satires of Ludovico Ariosto: A Renaissance Autobiography.* Trans. and ed. Peter Desa Wiggins. Athens, Ohio, 1976.
Arnauld, Antoine, and Claude Lancelot. *Grammaire générale et raisonnée.* . . . Pref. Michel Foucault. Paris, 1969.

349

Arnauld, Antoine, and Pierre Nicole. *La logique ou l'art de penser.* Ed. Louis Marin. Paris, 1970.
Astell, Mary. *A Serious Proposal to the Ladies for the Advancement of Their True and Greatest Interest. . . .* 4th ed. London, 1701; rpt. New York, 1970.
——. *Some Reflections Upon Marriage* with Additions. 4th ed. London, 1730; rpt. New York, 1970.
Aubéry, Antoine. *De la preeminence de nos roys, et de leur preseance sur l'empereur et le roy d'Espagne. . . .* Paris, 1649.
——. *Des justes prétensions du roy sur l'Empire.* Suivant la copie imprimée à Paris [Leiden], n.d.
——. *L'histoire du Cardinal Duc de Richelieu. . . .* Paris, 1660.
Aubignac, abbé François-Hédelin, d'. *Conjectures académiques ou dissertation sur l'Iliade.* Ed. V. Magnien. Paris, 1925.
——. *Troisième dissertation concernant le poeme dramatique en forme de remarques sur la tragédie de M. Corneille intitulée l'Oedipe.* Paris, 1663.
Aubigné, Théodore-Agrippa d'. *His Life, to His Children: Sa vie à ses enfants.* Trans. and ed. John Nothnagle. Lincoln, Neb., and London, 1989.
——. *Les tragiques.* Ed. Jacques Bailbé. Paris, 1968.
Austen, Jane. *The Complete Novels.* New York, n.d.
Bacon, Francis, Lord Verulam. *The Works.* Ed. James Spedding, Robert Leslie Ellis, and Douglas Denon Heath. 14 vols. London, 1857–74.
Bailey, Nathan. *An Universal Etymological Dictionary. . . .* London, 1721.
——. *An Universal Etymological English Dictionary. . . .* 24th ed. Enlarged and cor. Edward Harwood. London, 1782.
Baillet, Adrien. *La vie de Monsieur Des-Cartes.* 2 vols. 1691; rpt. Hildesheim and New York, 1972.
Baillie, John, *An Essay on the Sublime (1747).* Ed. Samuel Holt Monk. Augustan Reprint Society, no. 43. Los Angeles, 1953.
Baldwin, William [and others]. *The Mirror for Magistrates.* Ed. Lily B. Campbell. Cambridge, 1938.
Balzac, Jean-Louis Guez de. *Oeuvres.* Ed. L. Moreau. 2 vols. Paris, 1854.
Barbauld, Anna Laetitia [Aikin]. *The Works.* With a Memoir by Lucy Aikin. 2 vols. London, 1825.
Barclay, John. *His Argenis.* Translated out of Latine into English. . . . With a Clauio annexed. . . . Trans. Sir Robert Le Grys. London, 1628.
Batteux, abbé Charles. *Les beaux arts reduits a un même principe.* Paris, 1747; rpt. New York, 1970.
Baudelaire, Charles. *Oeuvres complètes.* Ed. Claude Pichois. 2 vols. Paris, 1975–76.
Baumgarten, Alexander Gottlieb. *Aesthetica.* Frankfurt a/d. Oder, 1750; rpt. Hildesheim and New York, 1970.
——. *Reflections on Poetry/Meditationes philosophicae de nonnullis ad poema pertinentibus [1735].* Trans. and ed. Karl Aschenbrenner and William B. Holther. Berkeley and Los Angeles, 1954.
Bayle, Pierre. *Dictionnaire historique et critique.* 3 vols. Rotterdam, 1715.
——. *An Historical and Critical Dictionary.* 4 vols. London, 1710.
Behn, Aphra. *Love-Letters between a Nobleman and His Sister.* Intro. Maureen Duffy. Harmondsworth, 1987.
——. *Oroonoko, or the Royal Slave.* Ed. Lore Metzger. New York and London, 1973.
Belleforest, François de. *Arraisonnement fort gentil et proffitable sur l'infelicite qui suyt ordinairement le bonheur des grans. . . .* Paris, 1569.

Bembo, Pietro. *Prose della volgar lingua.* In his *Prose e rime.* Ed. Carlo Dionisotti. 1960; rpt. Turin, 1966, pp. 73–309.

Bernard, Catherine. *Inès de Cordoue: Nouvelle espagnole.* Pref. René Godenne. 1696; facs. rpt. Geneva, 1979.

———. *Les malheurs de l'amour: Première nouvelle, Éléonor d'Yvrée.* Pref. René Godenne. 1687; facs. rpt. Geneva, 1979.

Billon, François de. *Le fort inexpugnable de l'honneur du sexe femenin.* Paris, 1555. Intro. M. A. Screech. Wakefield, New York, and The Hague, 1970.

Blackwell, Thomas. *An Enquiry into the Life and Writings of Homer.* 1736; rpt. Hildesheim and New York, 1976.

Boccaccio, Giovanni. *On Poetry: Being the Preface and the Fourteenth and Fifteenth Books of Boccaccio's "Genealogia Deorum Gentilium."* Trans. and ed. Charles G. Osgood. 1930; rpt. Indianapolis, 1956.

———. *Vita di Dante.* In *The Earliest Lives of Dante.* Trans. and ed. J. R. Smith. Yale Studies in English, 10. New York, 1901.

Bodin, Jean. *De la démonomanie des sorciers.* Paris, 1580.

———. *Methodus ad facilem historiarum cognitionem.* In *Oeuvres philosophiques.* Ed. and trans. Pierre Mesnard. Paris, 1951, pp. 107–473.

———. *Les six livres de la république [1576].* Ed. Christiane Frémont, Marie-Dominique Couzinet, and Henri Rochais. 6 vols. Paris, 1986.

Boileau-Despréaux, Nicolas. *Oeuvres complètes.* Ed. Françoise Escal. Paris, 1966.

Boivin, Jean. *Apologie d'Homère, et bouclier d'Achille.* Paris, 1715.

Bossuet, Jacques-Bénigne. *Oeuvres.* Ed. abbé Velat and Yvonne Champailler. Paris, 1961.

Boswell, James. *Boswell in Holland, 1763–1764.* Including His Correspondence with Belle de Zuylen (Zélide). Ed. Frederick A. Pottle. New York, London, and Toronto, 1952.

Bouhours, père Dominique. *Les entretiens d'Ariste et d'Eugène [1671].* Ed. Ferdinand Brunot. Paris, 1962.

———. *Pensées ingénieuses.* Paris, 1689.

Bryskett, Lodowick. *A Discourse of Civill Life [1606].* Ed. Thomas E. Wright. Northridge, Calif., 1970.

Buffet, Marguerite. *Nouvelles observations sur la langue françoise. . . . Avec les éloges des illustres sçavantes, tant anciennes que modernes. . . .* Paris, 1668.

Bullokar, John. *An English Expositor: Teaching the Interpretation of the Hardest Words Used in Our Language. . . .* London, 1616.

Burke, Edmund. *Works.* Rev. ed. 12 vols. Boston, 1867.

———. *A Philosophical Enquiry into the Origin of Our Ideas of the Sublime and Beautiful.* 2d ed. With an Introductory Discourse Concerning Taste, and Several Other Additions. London, 1759.

Burton, Robert. *The Anatomy of Melancholy.* Intro. Holbrook Jackson. 3 vols. 1932; rpt. London and New York, 1968.

Campion, Thomas. *The Works: Complete Songs, Masques, and Treatises with a Selection of the Latin Verse.* Ed. Walter R. Davis. London, 1969.

Cassan, Jacques de. *La recherche des droicts du Roy, & de la couronne de la France sur les royaumes, duchez, comtez, villes, & pais occupez par les princes estrangers . . . ensemble de leurs droicts sur l'empire. . . .* Paris, 1634.

Cassius Dio Cocceianus. *Dio's Roman History.* Ed. and trans. Earnest Cary. 9 vols. London and New York, 1914.

Castiglione, Baldesar. *The Book of the Courtier.* Trans. George Bull. Harmondsworth, 1967.

Cavendish, Margaret, Duchess of Newcastle. *Life of the Duke, Memoirs of Her Own Life, and Certain Sociable Letters.* Ed. Ernest Rhys. London, Toronto, and New York, n.d.

Cawdrey, Robert. *A Table Alphabeticall, Conteyning and Teaching the True Writing, and Understanding of Hard Usuall English Words. . . .* London, 1604.

——. *A Table Alphabeticall. . . .* 3d ed. London, 1613.

Cervantes Saavedra, Miguel de. *The Adventures of Don Quixote.* Trans. J. M. Cohen. 1950; rpt. Harmondsworth, 1970.

——. *Don Quijote de la Mancha.* Ed. Angel Basanta. 2 vols. Barcelona, 1985.

——. *La Galatea.* Ed. Juan Bautista Avalle-Arce. Madrid, 1987.

——. *Los trabajos de Persiles y Sigismunda.* 1952; rpt. Madrid, 1980.

——. *The Trials of Persiles and Sigismunda: A Northern Story.* Trans. Celia Richmond Weller and Clark A. Colahan. Berkeley, Los Angeles, and London, 1989.

Chapelain, Jean. *Lettres.* Ed. Philippe Tamizey de Larroque. 2 vols. Paris, 1880.

——. See also Huet, Pierre-Daniel.

Chapman, George. *Chapman's Homer: The Iliad, The Odyssey and the Lesser Homerica.* Ed. Allardyce Nicoll. 2d ed. 2 vols. Princeton, 1967.

Chappuzeau, Samuel. *Le cercle des femmes et l'académie des femmes.* Ed. Joan Crow. Exeter, 1983.

Chesterfield, Philip Dormer Stanhope, 4th Earl of. *Letters.* 2d ed. 4 vols. London, 1774.

——. *Letters to His Son and Others.* Ed. E. K. Root. 1929; rpt. London and Melbourne, 1984.

Christine de Pisan. *The Book of the City of Ladies.* Trans. Earl Jeffrey Richards. Foreword Marina Warner. 1982; rpt. London, 1983.

——. *Le livre des fais et bonnes moeurs du sage roy Charles V.* Ed. Suzanne Solente. Paris, 1936.

——. *The Treasure of the City of Ladies, or The Book of the Three Virtues.* Trans. and intro. Sarah Lawson. Harmondsworth, 1985.

Cicero, Marcus Tullius. *De Inventione [etc.].* Ed. and trans. H. M. Hubbell. 1949; rpt. Cambridge, Mass., and London, 1968.

Cockeram, Henry. *The English Dictionarie: or, an Interpreter of Hard English Words.* London, 1623.

——. *The English Dictionarie. . . .* 7th ed. London, 1642.

Coëffeteau, Nicolas. *Histoire romaine. . . .* Paris, 1621.

Colbert, Jean-Baptiste. *Lettres, instructions et mémoires.* Ed. Pierre Clément. 8 vols. Paris, 1861–82.

Coleridge, Samuel Taylor. *Collected Letters.* Ed. Earl Leslie Griggs. 6 vols. Oxford, 1956–71.

Collins, William. See Gray, Thomas, and William Collins.

Comenius, John Amos [Johann Amos Komensky]. *The Labyrinth of the World and the Paradise of the Heart.* Trans. Matthew Spinka. Chicago, 1942.

Condorcet, Antoine-Nicolas Caritat, marquis de. *Oeuvres.* Ed. A. Condorcet O'Connor and M. F. Arago. 10 vols. Paris, 1847–49.

Conway, Anne [Finch]. *Conway Letters: The Correspondence of Anne, Viscountess Conway, Henry More, and Their Friends, 1642–1684.* Ed. Marjorie Hope Nicolson. New Haven, Conn., and London, 1930.

——. *The Principles of the Most Ancient and Modern Philosophy.* Ed. and trans. Peter Lopson. The Hague, Boston, and London, 1982.

Cordemoy, Gerauld de. *Oeuvres philosophiques.* Ed. Pierre Clair et François Girbal. Paris, 1968.

Corneille, Pierre. *Oeuvres.* Ed. Charles Marty-Laveaux. 12 vols. Paris, 1862.

——. *Oeuvres complètes.* Ed. Georges Couton. 3 vols. Paris, 1980–87.

Cotin, abbé Charles. *La "Satyre des satyres" et la "Critique désintéressée sur les satyres du temps."* Avec une notice par le bibliophile Jacob. 1867, 1890; rpt. Geneva, 1969.

Crousaz, Jean-Pierre de. *Traité du beau. Où l'on montre en quoi consiste ce que l'on nomme ainsi, par des exemples tirés de la plupart des arts et des sciences.* Amsterdam, 1715; facs. rpt. Geneva, 1970.

Dacier, Anne Le Fèvre. *Des causes de la corruption du goust.* Paris, 1714.

——. *Homère défendu contre l'apologie du R. P. Hardouin. Ou suite des causes de la corruption du goust.* 1716; rpt. Geneva, 1971.

Daire, Eugène, ed. *Économistes-financiers du xviiie siècle,* vol. 1. Paris, 1843.

Dallas, Eneas Sweetland. *The Gay Science.* 2 vols. 1866; rpt. New York, 1968.

——. *Poetics: An Essay on Poetry.* 1852; rpt. New York, 1968.

Darwin, Charles. *The Origin of Species by Means of Natural Selection . . . and The Descent of Man and Selection in Relation to Sex.* New York, n.d.

Davanzati, Bernardo. *Leçon sur les monnaies [Lezione della monete].* In *Écrits notables sur la monnaie: xvie siècle, Copernic à Davanzati.* Ed. Jean-Yves Le Branchu. 2 vols. Paris, 1934, 2:217–42.

Davenant, Sir William. *Gondibert.* Ed. David F. Gladish. Oxford, 1971.

Defoe, Daniel. *Serious Reflections During the Life and Surprising Adventures of Robinson Crusoe: With His Vision of the Angelick World, Written by Himself.* London, 1720.

——. *A Vindication of the Press.* Intro. Otho Clinton Williams. Augustan Reprint Society, no. 29. Los Angeles, 1951.

Denham, Sir John. *The Poetical Works.* Ed. Theodore Howard Banks. 2d ed. New Haven, Conn., 1969.

Dennis, John. *The Critical Works.* Ed. Edward Niles Hooker. 2 vols. Baltimore, 1939–43.

Descartes, René. *Oeuvres philosophiques.* Ed. Ferdinand Alquié. 3 vols. Paris, 1963–73.

Deshoulières, Antoinette du Ligier de La Garde. *Oeuvres.* 2 vols. Paris, An VII [1798].

——. *Poësies* de Madame Deshoulieres. 2 vols. Paris, 1688–95.

Deshoulières, Antoinette-Thérèse de la Fon de Boisguerin. "Ode de Mademoiselle Deshoulieres sur le soin que le Roi prend. . . . " In *Poësies* de Madame Deshoulieres. Paris, 1688, 1:216–21.

Desmarets de Saint-Sorlin, Jean. *Comparaison de la langue et de la poësie françoise, avec la grecque et la latine.* 1670; rpt. Geneva, 1972.

Diderot, Denis. *Oeuvres esthétiques.* Ed. Paul Vernière. Paris, 1965.

——. *Voyage en Hollande.* Ed. Yves Benot. Paris, 1982.

Diderot, Denis, and Jean Le Rond d'Alembert, eds. *Encyclopédie, ou dictionnaire raisonné des sciences, des arts et des metiers. . . .* 35 vols. Paris, 1751–80.

——. *Encyclopédie, ou dictionnaire raisonné des sciences, des arts et des métiers.* 36 vols. Berne and Lausanne, 1779–82.

[Drake, Judith.] *An Essay in Defense of the Female Sex. . . .* London, 1696; rpt. New York, 1970.

Drayton, Michael. *Poly-Olbion.* In *The Works.* Ed. J. William Hebel. Vol. 4. Oxford, 1961.

Dryden, John. *The Works.* Gen. eds. Edward Niles Hooker and H. T. Sweden-berg, Jr. ? vols. Berkeley, Los Angeles, and London, 1956–.
——. *The Works.* Ed. Walter Scott. 18 vols. London, 1808.
——. *Selected Criticism.* Ed. James Kinsley and George Parfitt. Oxford, 1970.
Du Bellay, Joachim. *La deffense et illustration de la langue françoyse.* Ed. Henri Chamard. 4th ed. Paris, 1970.
Du Bos, abbé Jean-Baptiste. *Réflexions critiques sur la poësie et sur la pein-ture.* 7th ed. 3 vols. 1770; rpt. Geneva and Paris, 1982.
Dupuy, Pierre [and Théodore Godefroy]. *Traitez touchant les droits du roy tres-chrestien sur plusieurs estats et seigneuries possedées par divers princes voisins. . . .* Paris, 1655.
Du Vair, Guillaume. *Actions et traictez oratoires.* Ed. René Radouant. Paris, 1911.
Elstob, Elizabeth. *An Apology for the Study of Northern Antiquities (1715).* Intro. Charles Peake. Augustan Reprint Society, no. 61. Los Angeles, 1956.
——. "Preface" to *An English-Saxon Homily.* In *First Feminists: British Women Writers, 1578–1799.* Ed. Moira Ferguson. Bloomington, Ind., and Old Westbury, N.Y., 1985.
Elyot, Sir Thomas. *The Defence of Good Women.* In *The Feminist Controversy of the Renaissance.* Ed. Diane Bornstein. Delmar, N.Y., 1980.
Estienne, Henri. *Apologie pour Hérodote, ou traité de la conformité des merveilles anciennes avec les modernes [1566].* Ed. P. Ristelhuber. 2 vols. Paris, 1879.
——. *Conformité du langage françois avec le grec [1562].* Ed. Léon Feugère. Paris, 1853.
——. *Deux dialogues du nouveau langage françois italianizé et autrement desguizé. . . .* Ed. P. Ristelhuber. 2 vols. Paris, 1885.
——. *Discours merveilleux de la vie, actions & deportemens de Catherine de Medicis. . . .* Geneva, 1575.
——. *La précellence du langage françois [1579].* Ed. Edmond Huguet. Pref. L. Petit de Julleville. Paris, 1896.
Fabri, Pierre. *Le grand et vrai art de pleine rhétorique.* Ed. A. Héron. 3 vols. in 1. 1889–90; rpt. Geneva, 1969.
Fénelon, François Salignac de La Motte-. *Oeuvres.* Ed. Jacques Le Brun. ? vols. Paris, 1983–.
——. *Oeuvres complètes.* 10 vols. Paris, Lille, and Besançon, 1848–52.
——. *Les aventures de Télémaque.* Ed. Jeanne-Lydie Goré. Paris, 1987.
——. *Correspondance.* Ed. Jean Orcibal. ? vols. Paris, 1972–.
——. *Lettre à l'Académie.* Ed. Maxime Roux. Paris, 1934.
Fielding, Henry. *The History of the Adventures of Joseph Andrews and of His Friend Mr. Abraham Adams. . . .* Intro. Howard Mumford Jones. 1939; rpt. New York, 1950.
——. *The History of Tom Jones. A Foundling.* New York, 1964.
——. "Preface." In Sarah Fielding, *The Adventures of David Simple. . . .* Ed. Malcolm Kelsall. Oxford and New York, 1987.
Finch, Anne [Kingsmill], Countess of Winchilsea. *Selected Poems.* Ed. Katharine M. Rogers. New York, 1979.
Fleury, Claude. See Hepp, Noémi, ed.
Fontenelle, Bernard Le Bovier de. *Oeuvres.* 8 vols. Paris, 1790.
——. *Entretiens sur la pluralité des mondes.* 4th ed. Paris, 1698.
——. *Nouveaux dialogues des morts [1683].* Ed. Jean Dagen. Paris, 1971.
——. *Textes choisis (1683–1701).* Ed. Maurice Roelens. Paris, 1966.

Fourmont, Etienne. *Examen pacifique de la querelle de Madame Dacier et de Monsieur de La Motte sur Homère.* 2 vols. Paris, 1716.

Franklin, Julian H., trans. and ed. *Constitutionalism and Resistance in the Sixteenth Century: Three Treatises by Hotman, Beza, and Mornay.* New York, 1969.

Furetière, Antoine. *Dictionnaire universel.* . . . 3 vols. The Hague, 1690.

———. *Dictionnaire universel.* . . . Rev. Basnage de Beauval and Brutel de la Rivière. 4 vols. The Hague, 1727.

Garcilaso de la Vega. *Poesías completas.* Ed. Germán Bleiberg. 1980; rpt. Madrid, 1987.

———. *Garcilaso de la Vega y sus comentaristas. Obras completas del poeta, acompañadas de los textos íntegros de los comentarios de El Brocense, Fernando de Herrera, Tamayo de Vargas y Azara.* Ed. Antonio Gallego Morell. 2d ed. Madrid, 1972.

Garnier, Robert. *Oeuvres complètes (Théâtre et poésies).* Ed. Lucien Pinvert. 2 vols. Paris, 1923.

Gentillet, Innocent. *Anti-Machiavel [1576].* Ed. C. Edward Rathé. Geneva, 1968.

———. *Discours contre Machiavel.* Ed. A. D'Andrea and P. D. Stewart. Florence, 1974.

Gerard, Alexander. *An Essay on Taste (1759), Together with Observations Concerning the Imitative Nature of Poetry.* Facsimile of the 3d ed. (1780). Ed. Walter J. Hipple, Jr. Gainesville, Fla., 1963.

Gilden, Charles. "An Essay on the Art, Rise and Progress of the Stage in Greece, Rome and England." In *The Works of Mr. William Shakespeare.* [Ed. Nicholas Rowe (Gilden for vol. 7).] 7 vols. London, 1710; rpt. New York, 1967. [Vol. 7 has the poetry and was actually quite separate from Rowe's six volumes, although it was presented as a continuation.]

Godwin, William. *Enquiry Concerning Political Justice and Its Influence on Modern Morals and Happiness.* Ed. Isaac Kramnick. Harmondsworth, 1976.

———. *Things as They Are or The Adventures of Caleb Williams.* Ed. Maurice Hindle. 1987; rpt. Harmondsworth, 1988.

Góngora y Argote, Luis. *Obras en verso del Homero español que recogió Juan López de Vicuña (edición facsímil).* Ed. Dámaso Alonso. Madrid, 1963.

———. *Soledades.* Ed. Dámaso Alonso. 1927; rpt. Madrid, 1982.

Gournay, Marie le Jars de. *Fragments d'un discours féminin.* Ed. Elyane Dezon-Jones. Paris, 1988.

———. *Le proumenoir de Monsieur de Montaigne (1594).* Intro. Patricia Francis Cholakian. Delmar, N.Y., 1985.

———. See also Schiff, Mario L., and Uildriks, Anne (in Part 2).

Gower, John. *The English Works.* Ed. G. C. Macaulay. 2 vols. London, 1900.

Gracián y Morales, Baltasar. *Agudeza y arte de ingenio.* Madrid, 1942.

———. *El criticón.* Ed. P. Ismael Quiles. 1943; rpt. Madrid, 1980.

Gray, Thomas, and William Collins. *Poetical Works.* Ed. Roger Lonsdale. Oxford, 1977.

Greville, Fulke, 1st Baron Brooke. *The Prose Works.* Ed. John Gouws. Oxford, 1986.

———. *The Works in Verse and Prose Complete.* Ed. A. B. Grosart. 4 vols. 1870; rpt. New York, 1966.

Grotius, Hugo. *De jure belli ac pacis libri tres/The Law of War and Peace.* Ed. and trans. Francis W. Kelsey, with Arthur E. R. Boak, Henry A. Sanders, Jesse S. Reeves, and Herbert F. Wright. 2 vols. Oxford and London, 1913–25.

Guarini, Battista. *Il pastor fido/Le berger fidelle*. Trans. D. T. Paris, 1672.
Halifax, George Savile, Marquess of. *Complete Works*. Ed. J. P. Kenyon. Harmondsworth, 1969.
Hegel, Georg Wilhelm Friedrich. *Aesthetics: Lectures on Fine Art*. Trans. T. M. Knox. 2 vols. Oxford, 1974–75.
——. *Ästhetik*. Ed. Friedrich Bassenge. Intro. Georg Lukács. 2 vols. Berlin and Weimar, 1965.
——. *Phenomenology of Spirit*. Trans. A. V. Miller. With an Analysis of the Text and Foreword by J. N. Findlay. 1977; rpt. Oxford, 1979.
——. *Philosophy of Mind*. Trans. William Wallace. Together with the *Zusätze* in Boumann's text. Trans. A. V. Miller. Foreword J. N. Findlay. Oxford, 1971.
——. *Philosophy of Right*. Trans. T. M. Knox. 1952; rpt. Oxford, 1967.
Heliodorus. *Les Ethiopiques (Théagène et Chariclée)*. Ed. R. M. Rattenbury and T. W. Lumb. Trans. J. Maillon. Paris, 1935–43.
Henderson, Katherine Usher, and Barbara F. McManus, eds. *Half-Humankind: Contexts and Texts of the Controversy about Women in England, 1540–1640*. Urbana, Ill., 1985.
Hepp, Noémi, ed. *Deux amis d'Homère au xviie siècle: Textes inédits de Paul Pellisson et de Claude Fleury*. Paris, 1970.
Heywood, Eliza. *The Female Spectator: Being Selections from Mrs. Eliza Heywood's Periodical (1744–1746)*. Ed. Mary Priestley. Intro. J. B. Priestley. London, 1929.
Hobbes, Thomas. *The English Works*. Ed. Sir William Molesworth. 11 vols. London, 1839–45.
——. *Behemoth: The History of the Causes of the Civil Wars of England. . . .* Ed. William Molesworth. 1840; rpt. New York, 1969.
——. *Leviathan*. Ed. C. B. Macpherson. Harmondsworth, 1968.
Hôpital, Michel de l'. *Oeuvres inédites*. Ed. P. J. S. Dufey. 2 vols. Paris, 1825–26.
Horatius Flaccus, Quintus. *Satires, Epistles, and Ars Poetica*. Ed. and trans. H. Rushton Fairclough. 1929; rpt. Cambridge, Mass., and London, 1978.
Huet, Pierre-Daniel. *Lettre-traité sur l'origine des romans . . .* suivie de *La lecture des vieux romans par Jean Chapelain*. Ed. Fabienne Gégou. Paris, 1971.
Hume, David. *Enquiries Concerning Human Understanding and Concerning the Principles of Morals*. Ed. L. A. Selby-Bigges. 2d ed. Oxford, 1902.
——. *Of the Standard of Taste and Other Essays*. Ed. John W. Lenz. Indianapolis and New York, 1965.
Hurault de l'Hôpital, Michel. *Quatre excellens discours sur l'estat present de la France. . . .* Paris, 1593.
Hutcheson, Francis. *An Inquiry Concerning Beauty, Order, Harmony, Design*. Ed. Peter Kivy. The Hague, 1973.
Institut de France. *Les registres de l'Académie Française, 1672–1793*. 3 vols. Paris, 1895.
Irson, Claude. *Nouvelle méthode pour apprendre facilement les principes de la pureté de la langue française*. 2d ed. Paris, 1662.
Johnson, Dr. Samuel. *A Dictionary of the English Language. . . .* 2 vols. London, 1775.
——. *The History of Rasselas, Prince of Abissinia*. Ed. D. J. Enright. 1976; rpt. Harmondsworth, 1988.
——. *Lives of the Poets: A Selection*. Ed. J. P. Hardy. Oxford, 1971.
[Junius, Adrianus]. *Nomenclator octilinguis omnium rerum propria nomina continens*. Rev. Hermannus Germbergius. Paris, 1606.

Juvenalis, D. Junius. [*Satires.*] In *Juvenal and Persius.* Ed. and trans. G. G. Ramsay. Revised. 1940; rpt. London and Cambridge, Mass., 1961.

Kames, Henry Home, Lord. *Elements of Criticism.* London, 1824.

Kant, Immanuel. *Critique of Judgment.* Trans. J. H. Bernard. New York, 1951.

Keats, John. *The Complete Poems.* Ed. John Barnard. 3d ed. Harmondsworth, 1988.

La Boétie, Étienne de. *Discours de la servitude volontaire.* Ed. Simone Goyard-Fabre. Paris, 1983.

La Bruyère, Jean de. *Les caractères de Théophraste traduits du grec, avec les caractères ou les moeurs de ce siècle.* Ed. Robert Garapon. Paris, 1962.

Lafayette, Marie-Madeleine de La Vergne de. *La Princesse de Clèves.* Ed. Émile Magne. Paris and Lille, 1950.

La Fontaine, Jean de. *Fables choisies mises en vers.* Ed. Ferdinand Gohin. 2 vols. Paris, 1934.

——. *Oeuvres diverses,* ed. Pierre Clarac. Paris, 1948.

Lambert, Marie-Anne-Thérèse de Marguenat, marquise de. "Réflexions nouvelles sur les femmes." In Marie-Josée Fassiotto, *Madame de Lambert (1647–1733) ou le féminisme moral.* New York, Berne, and Frankfurt a/M, 1984, pp. 123–44.

La Mesnardière, Hippolyte-Jules de. *La poétique.* Paris, 1640.

Lamy, Bernard. *La rhétorique ou l'art de parler.* 4th ed. Paris, 1699.

La Noüe, François de. *Discours politiques et militaires.* . . . Basel, 1587.

The Lawes Resolutions of Women's Rights: Or, The Lawes Provision for Women. . . . London, 1632.

Le Bossu, père René. *Treatise of the Epick Poem.* . . . , [*with*] *an Essay upon Satyr by Mons. D'Acier; and a Treatise upon Pastoral by Mons. Fontanelle* [*sic*]. 2d ed. . . . 2 vols. London, 1719.

Le Bret, Cardin. *De la souveraineté du Roy.* Paris, 1632.

Leibniz, Gottfried Wilhelm. *Essais de Théodicée, sur la bonté de dieu, la liberté de l'homme, et l'origine du mal.* Ed. J. Brunschwig. Paris, 1969.

——. *Theodicy.* Abridged. Ed. Diogenes Allen. Indianapolis, 1966.

Le Moyne, Pierre. *La gallerie des femmes fortes.* Paris, 1647.

——. *Les peintures morales, où les passions sont representees par Tableaux, par Characteres, & par Questions nouuelles & curieuses.* Paris, 1640.

Lenglet-Dufresnoy, Pierre-Nicolas. *De l'usage des romans où l'on fait voir leur utilité et leurs différents caractères.* . . . 2 vols. 1734; rpt. Geneva, 1970.

Le Roy, Louis. *De la vicissitude ou variété des choses en l'univers [1575].* . . . Ed. Philippe Desan. Paris, 1988.

——. *De l'excellence du gouuernement royal.* . . . Paris, 1575.

——. *Exhortation aux François pour vivre en concorde, et iouir du bien de la Paix.* Paris, 1570.

——. *Les politiques d'Aristote, esquelles est montree la science de gouuerner le genre humain en toutes especes d'estats publics.* . . . Paris, 1568.

Lessing, Gotthold Ephraim. *Hamburg Dramaturgy.* Trans. Helen Zimmern. Intro. Victor Lange. New York, 1962.

——. *Hamburgische Dramaturgie.* Ed. Karl Eibl. In *Werke.* Gen. ed. Herbert G. Göpfert. 8 vols. Munich, 1970–79. Vol. 4, pp. 229–707.

——. *Laocoön: An Essay on the Limits of Painting and Poetry.* Trans. and ed. Edward Allen McCormick. 1962; rpt. Baltimore and London, 1984.

——. *Laocoön: An Essay upon the Limits of Painting and Poetry.* Trans. Ellen Frothingham. New York, 1969.

——. *Laokoon: Oder über die Grenzen der Malerei und Poesie.* Ed. Albert von Schirnding. In *Werke.* Vol. 6, pp. 7–187.

L'Héritier de Villandon, Marie-Jeanne. "L'adroite princesse [ou les aventures de Finette]." In *Les contes de fées en prose et en vers* de Charles Perrault. Ed. Charles Giraud. 2d ed. Lyon, 1865, pp. 233–83.

——. "Lettre de Mademoiselle Lhéritier à Madame D. G. sur les contes de fées." In ibid., pp. 285–300.

Lipsius, Justus. *Epistolario de Justo Lipsio y los Españoles (1577–1606)*. Ed. Alejandro Ramírez. Madrid, 1966.

——. *Sixe Bookes of Politickes or Civil Doctrine*. London, 1594.

——. *Two Bookes of Constancie*. Written in Latine. . . . Trans. Sir John Stradling. Ed. Rudolf Kirk, with Clayton Morris Hall. New Brunswick, N.J., 1939.

Longus. *Daphnis and Chloe*. Trans. George Thornley [1657]. Rev. and aug. J. M. Edmonds. With *The Love Romances of Parthenius and Other Fragments*. Trans. S. Gaselee. London and New York, 1924.

Louis XIV. *Mémoires, suivi de Réflexions sur le métier de roi, Instructions au duc d'Anjou, Projet de harangue*. Ed. Jean Lognon. Paris, 1978.

Lydgate, John. *Siege of Thebes*. Ed. Axel Erdmann. *Part 1: The Text*. London, 1911.

Lyly, John. *Euphues: The Anatomy of Wit*. In *The Descent of Euphues: Three Elizabethan Romance Stories—Euphues, Pandosto, Piers Plainness*. Ed. James Winny. Cambridge, 1957, pp. 1–66.

Macaulay, Catherine [Sawbridge]. *Letters on Education, with Observations on Religious and Metaphysical Subjects (1790)*. Intro. Gina Luria. New York, 1974.

Machiavelli, Niccolò. *The Discourses*. Ed. Bernard Crick. Trans. Leslie J. Walker, S.J. Rev. Brian Richardson. 1970; rpt. Harmondsworth, 1978.

——. *Il principe e Discorsi sopra la prima deca di Tito Livio*. Ed. Sergio Bertelli. Intro. Giuliano Procacci. 1960; rpt. Milan, 1977.

Makin, Bathsua. *An Essay to Revive the Antient Education of Gentlewomen (1673)*. [Facs. rpt. of London, 1673, ed.] Intro. Paula L. Barbour. Augustan Reprint Society, no. 202. Los Angeles, 1980.

Malebranche, Nicolas. *De la recherche de la vérité*. In *Oeuvres*, ed. Geneviève Rodis-Lewis, avec Germain Malbreil. Paris, 1979.

Malherbe, François. *Oeuvres poétiques*. Ed. Marcel Simon. Paris, 1972.

Marmontel, Jean-François. *Éléments de littérature*. 3 vols. Paris, 1865.

Marvell, Andrew. *The Complete Poems*. Ed. Elizabeth Story Donno. 1972; rpt. Harmondsworth, 1981.

Miege, Guy. *The Great French Dictionary*. . . . London, 1688.

Minnis, Alastair J., and A. B. Scott, with David Wallace, eds. *Medieval Literary Theory and Criticism, c. 1100–c. 1375: The Commentary Tradition*. Oxford, 1988.

Molière, Jean-Baptiste Poquelin, called. *Théâtre complet*. Ed. Robert Jouanny. 2 vols. Paris, 1962.

Montagu, Elizabeth [Robinson]. *An Essay on the Writings and Genius of Shakespear, Compared with the Greek and French Dramatic Poets. With Some Remarks Upon the Misrepresentations of Mons. de Voltaire*. 5th ed., corr. To which are added *Three Dialogues of the Dead*. London, 1785.

Montagu, Lady Mary Wortley. *The Nonsense of Common-Sense, 1737–1738*. Ed. Robert Halsband. Evanston, Ill., 1947.

Montaigne, Michel de. *Oeuvres complètes*. Ed. Albert Thibaudet and Maurice Rat. Paris, 1962.

——. *Complete Works: Essays, Travel Journal, Letters*. Trans. Donald M. Frame. Stanford, Calif., 1957.

Montemayor, Jorge de. *Los siete libros de la Diana.* Ed. Francisco López Estrada. 1954; rpt. Madrid, 1970.

More, Hannah. *The Works.* 7 vols. New York, 1835–47.

Mylaeus, Christophorus [Christophe Milieu]. *De scribenda universitatis rerum historia libri quinque.* Basel, 1551.

Naudé, Gabriel. *Considérations politiques sur les coups d'estat.* Sur la copie de Rome, 1667.

Nicot, Jean. *Thresor de la langue françoyse, tant ancienne que moderne. . . .* Rev. & augmenté. . . . Paris, 1606.

Osborne, Dorothy. *Letters to Sir William Temple.* Ed. Kenneth Parker. Harmondsworth, 1987.

Pasquier, Estienne. *Les oeuvres.* 2 vols. 1723; rpt. Geneva, 1971.

——. *Les lettres d'Estienne Pasquier Conseiller & Avocat general du Roy a Paris. Contenans plusieurs belles matieres & discours sur les affaires d'estat en France, & touchant les guerres ciuiles.* 2 vols. Paris, 1619.

——. *Les recherches de la France.* Reveuës & augmentees d'vn Liure. . . . Paris, 1607.

Pellisson-Fontanier, Paul, et abbé Pierre-Joseph d'Olivet. *Histoire de l'Académie Française.* Ed. Charles-L. Livet. 2 vols. Paris, 1858.

Perrault, Charles. *L'apologie des femmes.* Amsterdam, [1694].

——. *Les hommes illustres qui ont paru en France pendant le xviie siècle.* 3d ed. 2 vols. in 1. Paris, 1701.

——. *Parallèle des anciens et des modernes en ce qui regarde les arts et les sciences. Dialogues. Avec le poème du siècle de Louis le Grand, et une epistre en vers sur le genie.* 2d ed. 4 vols. in 1. 1692–97; rpt. Geneva, 1971.

——. See also L'Héritier de Villandon, Marie-Jeanne.

Philips, Katherine [Fowler]. *Poems by the Most Deservedly Admired Mrs Katherine Philips, the Matchless Orinda.* To which is added, Monsieur Corneille's *Pompey* and *Horace*, tragedies. . . . London, 1667.

Phillips, Edward. *The New World of English Words: Or, a General Dictionary. . . .* London, 1658.

——. *The New World of Words: or, Universal English Dictionary.* 6th ed. by J. K. London, 1706.

——. *The New World of Words: or, Universal English Dictionary.* 7th ed. Rev. corr. and impr. by J. K. London, 1720.

Plato. *The Sophist and The Statesman.* Trans. and intro. A. E. Taylor. Ed. Raymond Klibansky and Elizabeth Anscombe. London, 1961.

Poems on Affairs of State. Ed. George de F. Lord [et al]. 7 vols. New Haven, Conn., and London, 1963–75.

Polwhele, Elizabeth. *The Frolicks or the Lawyer Cheated (1671).* Ed. Judith Milhous and Robert D. Hume. Ithaca, N.Y., and London, 1977.

Polwhele, Richard. *The Unsex'd Females. A Poem,* and Mary Ann Radcliffe, *The Female Advocate. Or, an Attempt to Recover the Rights of Women from Male Usurpation.* [Facs. eds.] Intro. Gina Luria. New York and London, 1974.

Pons, abbé Jean-François. *Lettre à Madame Dacier sur son livre des causes de la corruption du goust.* Paris, 1715.

Pope, Alexander. *The Poems.* Ed. John Butt. New Haven, Conn., 1963.

——. *The Iliad of Homer.* Ed. Maynard Mack. In *The Poems.* Gen. ed. John Butt. 10 vols. London and New Haven, 1954–67. Vol. 7.

——. *Selected Poetry and Prose.* Ed. William K. Wimsatt. 2d ed. New York, 1972.

Poulain de la Barre, François. De l'égalité des deux sexes. Paris, 1984.

Price, Richard. A Discourse on the Love of Our Country, delivered on 4 November 1789, at the Meeting-House in the Old Jewry, to the Society for Commemorating the Revolution in Great Britain. London and Boston, 1790.

Prior, Matthew. Poems on Several Occasions. 1709; facs. rpt. Ilkley and London, 1973.

Puttenham, George. The Arte of English Poesie, 1589. Ed. Edward Arber. London, 1869.

Racine, Jean. Oeuvres. Ed. Paul Mesnard. New ed. 8 vols. Paris, 1865–73.

——. Oeuvres complètes. Pref. Pierre Clarac. Paris, 1962.

——. Oeuvres complètes. Ed. Raymond Picard. 2 vols. Paris, 1966.

Radcliffe, Mary Ann. The Female Advocate. See Polwhele, Richard.

Rapin, le père René. Oeuvres. 2 vols. Amsterdam, 1709.

——. Reflections on Aristotle's Treatise of Poesie.... By R. Rapin. [Trans. Thomas Rymer.] London, 1674.

Ravenscroft, Edward. Titus Andronicus, or The Rape of Lavinia. 1687; rpt. London, 1969.

Recueil général des anciennes lois françaises.... Ed. MM. [Athanase-Jean-Léger] Jourdan, [Alphonse-Honoré Taillandier et] Decrusy, and [François-André] Isambert. 30 vols. Paris, 1822–33.

Regnard, Jean-François. Oeuvres complètes.... Ed. M. Garnier. New ed. 4 vols. Paris, 1810.

Reynolds, Sir Joshua. Discourses on Art. Ed. Robert R. Wark. San Marino, Calif., 1959.

Richardson, Samuel. Clarissa or the History of a Young Lady. Ed. Angus Ross. Harmondsworth, 1985.

Richelet, Pierre. Dictionnaire françois.... New ed. 2 vols. Geneva, 1690.

——. Le nouveau dictionnaire françois.... New ed. 2 vols. Lyon, 1719.

——. Dictionnaire de la langue françoise, ancienne et moderne. New ed. 3 vols. Lyon, 1759.

Richelieu, Armand-Jean du Plessis, cardinal-duc de. Mémoires. In Nouvelle collection des mémoires pour servir à l'histoire de France.... Ed. Michaud and Poujoulat. Vols. 7–9. Paris, 1837–38.

——. Testament politique. Ed. Louis André. Paris, 1947.

Rohan, Henri, duc de. De l'interest des princes et estats de la chrestienté, à M. le Cardinal Richelieu. Paris, 1638.

Rousseau, Jean-Jacques. Oeuvres complètes. Gen. eds. Bernard Gagnebin and Marcel Raymond. 4 vols. Paris, 1959–69.

——. Émile. Trans. Barbara Foxley. Intro. André Boutet de Monval. 1911; rpt. London and New York, 1961.

Rymer, Thomas. The Critical Works. Ed. Curt A. Zimansky. New Haven, Conn., 1956.

Saint-Evremond, Charles de. Oeuvres en prose. Ed. René Ternois. 4 vols. Paris, 1962–69.

Saint-Pierre, abbé Charles-Irénée Castel de. Discours sur la polysynodie, où l'on démontre que la polysynodie, ou pluralité des conseils, est la forme de ministère la plus avantageuse pour un roi, & pour son royaume. Amsterdam, 1719.

——. Projet pour rendre la paix perpétuelle en Europe. Ed. Simone Goyard-Fabre. Paris, 1986.

Sanches, Francisco. *De multum nobili & prima vniuersali scientia Quod Nihil Scitur: Deque literarum pereuntivm agone, eiusque causis, libelli singulares duo.* . . . Frankfurt, 1618.

Sannazaro, Jacopo. *Arcadia and Piscatorial Eclogues.* Trans. and intro. Ralph Nash. Detroit, 1966.

Sarasin, Jean-François. *Les oeuvres de Monsieur Sarasin.* 2 vols. Paris, 1683.

Scaliger, Joseph Justus. *Autobiography,* with Autobiographical Selections from His Letters, His Testament, and the Funeral Orations by Daniel Heinsius and Dominicus Baudius. Trans. and ed. George W. Robinson. Cambridge, Mass., 1927.

Scaliger, Julius Caesar. *Poetices libri septem.* . . . 2d ed. N.p., 1581.

Schiller, Friedrich von. *Naive and Sentimental Poetry and On the Sublime.* Trans. and ed. Julius A. Elias. New York, 1966.

———. *On the Aesthetic Education of Man, in a Series of Letters.* Ed. and trans. Elizabeth M. Wilkinson and L. A. Willoughby. 1967; rpt. Oxford, 1985.

Schlegel, August Wilhelm. *Lectures on Dramatic Art and Literature.* Trans. John Black. 2d ed. Rev. A. J. W. Morrison. London, 1909.

Schlegel, Johann Elias. *On Imitation and Other Essays.* Trans. and ed. Edward Allen McCormick. Indianapolis, 1965.

Scudéry, Georges de. See Scudéry, Madeleine de.

Scudéry, Madeleine de. *Célinte: Nouvelle première.* Ed. Alain Niderst. Paris, 1979.

———. *Choix de conversations.* Ed. Phillip J. Wolfe. Ravenna, 1977.

———. *Les femmes illustres, ou les harangues heroïques, de Monsieur de Scudery, avec les veritables portraits de ces heroïnes, tirez des medailles antiques.* Paris, 1655. [Credited to Georges de Scudéry.]

Seneca, Lucius Annaeus. *De clementia.* In *Moral Essays.* Ed. and trans. John W. Basore. 3 vols. London and New York, 1932, 1:356–447.

Shaftesbury, Anthony Ashley Cooper, 3d Earl of. *Characteristics of Men, Manners, Opinions, Times.* Ed. John M. Robertson, 2 vols. Indianapolis and New York, 1964.

Shakespeare, William. *The Complete Works.* Gen. ed. Alfred Harbage. 1969; rpt. New York, 1977.

Shelley, Percy Bysshe. *The Selected Poetry and Prose.* Ed. Harold Bloom. 1966; rpt. New York, 1978.

Sidney, Sir Philip. *Miscellaneous Prose.* Ed. Katherine Duncan-Jones and Jan van Dorsten. Oxford, 1973.

———. *The Prose Works,* Ed. Albert Feuillerat. 4 vols. 1912; rpt. Cambridge, 1968–70.

———. *The Countess of Pembroke's Arcadia (The Old Arcadia).* Ed. Jean Robertson. 2 vols. Oxford, 1973.

———. *The Countess of Pembroke's Arcadia.* Ed. Maurice Evans. 1977; rpt. Harmondsworth, 1987.

Simonius, Maturinus. *De litteris pereuntibus libellus.* In Sanches [above], pp. 140–89.

Smith, Adam. *Lectures on Rhetoric and Belles Lettres.* Ed. J. C. Bryce. Gen. ed. A. S. Skinner. 1983; rpt. Indianapolis, 1985.

Smith, G. Gregory, ed. *Elizabethan Critical Essays.* 2 vols. 1904; rpt. Oxford, 1937.

Sorel, Charles. *La bibliothèque françoise.* 2d ed. rev. Paris, 1667.

———. *De la connoissance des bons livres, ou examen de plusieurs auteurs.* Amsterdam, 1672.

Southerne, Thomas. *The Works.* Ed. Robert Jordan and Harold Love. 2 vols. Oxford, 1988.

Spenser, Edmund. *Poetical Works.* Ed. J. C. Smith and E. de Selincourt. 1912; rpt. London, 1969.

Spingarn, J. E., ed. *Critical Essays of the Seventeenth Century.* 3 vols. 1908; rpt. Oxford, 1957.

Staël, Germaine Necker, baronne de. *De la littérature considérée dans ses rapports avec les institutions sociales.* Ed. Paul van Tieghem. 2 vols. Geneva and Paris, 1959.

Steele, Sir Richard. *The Tatler.* Ed. George A. Aitken. 4 vols. London, 1898.

Suchon, Gabrielle. *Traité de la morale et de la politique, 1693: La liberté.* Ed. Séverine Auffret. Paris, 1988.

Swift, Jonathan. *A Tale of a Tub and Other Satires.* Intro. Lewis Melville. London and New York, 1970.

Tasso, Torquato. *L'Aminta/L'Aminte.* Trans. D. T. Paris, 1666.

———. *Jerusalem Delivered.* Trans. Edward Fairfax [1600]. Intro. John Charles Nelson. New York, n.d.

Tate, Nahum. *The History of King Lear [1681].* Ed. James Black. 1975; rpt. London, 1976.

Temple, Sir William. *The Early Essays and Romances. . . .* Ed. G. C. Moore Smith. Oxford, 1930.

———. *An Essay Upon the Original and Nature of Government (1680).* Intro. Robert C. Steensma. Augustan Reprint Society, no. 109. Los Angeles, 1964.

———. *Five Miscellaneous Essays.* Ed. Samuel Holt Monk. Ann Arbor, Mich., 1963.

———. *Observations Upon the United Provinces of the Netherlands.* Ed. Sir George Clark. Oxford, 1972.

Terrasson, Jean. *Dissertation critique sur l'Iliade d'Homère, où à l'occasion de ce poëme on cherche les règles d'une poëtique fondée sur la raison, & sur les exemples des anciens & des modernes.* 2 vols. Paris, 1715–16.

Tesauro, Emanuale. *Il cannocchiale aristotelico.* Ed. August Buck. Bad Homburg, 1968.

Thomson, James. *The Seasons and The Castle of Indolence.* Ed. James Sambrook. 1972; rpt. Oxford, 1984.

Thucydides. *The Peloponnesian War.* Trans. Richard Crawley. Intro. John H. Finley, Jr. New York, 1951.

Tite et Titus ou les Bérénices (Utrecht, 1673). In G. Michaut, *La "Bérénice" de Racine.* Paris, 1907, pp. 305–53.

La tragédie du sac de Cabrières. Ed. Fernand Benoît and J. Vianey. Marseille, 1927.

["Trévoux, Dictionnaire de"]. *Dictionnaire universel françois et latin. . . .* 3 vols. Trévoux, 1704.

———. *Dictionnaire universel françois et latin.* 5 vols. Paris, 1721.

Urfé, Honoré d'. *L'Astrée.* Ed. Hugues Vaganay. 5 vols. Lyon, 1925.

Valdés, Juan de. *Diálogo de la lengua.* Ed. Juan M. de Lope Blanch. Madrid, 1976.

Valois, Marguerite de. *Mémoires et autres écrits de Marguerite de Valois, la reine Margot.* Ed. Yves Cazeux. Paris, 1976.

Vaugelas, Claude Favre de. *Remarques sur la langue française.* Paris, 1647.

Vega Carpio, Lope Félix de. *Arcadia.* Ed. Edwin S. Morby. Madrid, 1975.

——. *Jerusalén conquistada, epopeya trágica.* Ed. Joaquin de Entrambasaguas. 3 vols. Madrid, 1951–54.

Vergilius, Polydorus. *De rerum inventoribus libri octo.* . . . Basel, 1532.

Vickers, Brian, ed. *Shakespeare: The Critical Heritage.* 6 vols. London and Boston, 1974–81.

Vico, Giambattista. *The New Science.* Rev. trans. of 3d ed. (1744) Thomas Goddard Bergin and Max Harold Fisch. Ithaca, N.Y., 1968.

Vida, Marco Girolamo. *The De arte poetica.* Trans. with commentary, and with the text of c. 1517. Ed. Ralph G. Williams. New York, 1976.

Virgil [Publius Vergilius Maro]. *Aeneid.* Trans. Alan Mandelbaum. New York, 1971.

——. *Eclogues, Georgics, Aeneid, Books I–VI.* Trans. H. R. Fairclough. Rev. ed. Cambridge, Mass., and London, 1978.

——. See also Alpers, Paul (in Part 2).

Vives, Juan Luis. *De disciplinis libri XX.* Antwerp, 1531.

Voltaire, François-Marie Arouet de. *Oeuvres.* 40 vols. [Geneva,] 1775.

Walton, Izaak. *The Compleat Angler.* Ed. Bryan Loughrey. Harmondsworth, 1985.

Winckelmann, Johann Joachim. *Writings on Art.* Ed. David Irwin. London, 1972.

Wolf, Friedrich August. *Prolegomena to Homer, 1795.* Trans. and ed. Anthony Grafton, Glenn W. Most, and James E. G. Zetzel. Princeton, 1985.

Wollstonecraft, Mary. *Collected Letters.* Ed. Ralph M. Wardle. Ithaca, N.Y., and London, 1979.

——. *An Historical and Moral View of the Origin and Progress of the French Revolution and the Effect It Has Produced in Europe (1794).* Intro. Janet M. Todd. Delmar, N.J., 1975.

——. *Letters Written During a Short Residence in Sweden, Norway, and Denmark.* Ed. Carol H. Poston. Lincoln, Neb., and London, 1976.

——. *Maria or The Wrongs of Woman.* Intro. Moira Ferguson. New York and London, 1975.

——. *Mary. A Fiction.* Ed. Janet Todd. New York, 1977.

——. *Mary, A Fiction* and *The Wrongs of Woman.* Ed. Gary Kelly. London, 1976.

——. *Thoughts on the Education of Daughters: With Reflections on Female Conduct, in the Important Duties of Life.* 1787; rpt. Clifton, N.J., 1972.

——. *A Vindication of the Rights of Men (1790).* Intro. Eleanor Louise Nicholes. Gainesville, Fla., 1960.

——. *A Vindication of the Rights of Woman.* Ed. Miriam Brody Kramnick. Harmondsworth, 1975.

——. *A Wollstonecraft Anthology.* Ed. Janet M. Todd. Bloomington, Ind., and London, 1977.

——, ed. *The Female Reader (1789).* Facs. ed. Intro. Moira Ferguson. Delmar, N.J., 1980.

Wood, Robert. *An Essay on the Original Genius of Homer, with a Comparative View of the Antient and Present State of the Troade.* Ed. J. Bryant. London, 1775.

Wordsworth, William. *The Prelude, or Growth of a Poet's Mind (Text of 1805).* Ed. Ernest de Selincourt. New ed. Stephen Gill. 1970; rpt. London, 1975.

——. *Selected Poetry.* Ed. Mark Van Doren. New York, 1956.

Young, Edward. *The Poetical Works of Edward Young.* 2 vols. London, n.d. [1834?].

Secondary Sources

Abrams, Meyer Howard. *The Mirror and the Lamp: Romantic Theory and the Critical Tradition.* 1953; rpt. New York, 1958.
———. *Natural Supernaturalism: Tradition and Revolution in Romantic Literature.* New York, 1971.
Adam, Antoine. *Histoire de la littérature française au xviie siècle.* 5 vols. Paris, 1968.
Allentuch, Harriet R. "Reflections on Women in the Theater of Corneille." *Kentucky Romance Quarterly,* 21, no. 1 (1974), 97–111.
Alpers, Paul. *The Singer of the Eclogues: A Study of Virgilian Pastoral.* With a New Translation of the *Eclogues.* Berkeley, Los Angeles, and London, 1979.
Apostolidès, Jean-Marie. *Le prince sacrifié: Théâtre et politique au temps de Louis XIV.* Paris, 1985.
———. *Le roi-machine: Spectacle et politique au temps de Louis XIV.* Paris, 1981.
Arendt, Hannah. *On Violence.* 1969; rpt. New York, 1970.
Arnold, Paul. *Histoire des Rose-Croix et les origines de la Franc-maçonnerie.* Paris, 1955.
Ashton, Robert. *The City and the Court, 1603–1643.* Cambridge, 1979.
———. *The English Civil War: Conservatism and Revolution, 1603–1649.* London, 1978.
Aston, H. T., ed. *Crisis in Europe, 1560–1660.* Cambridge, 1965.
Aston, H. T., and C. H. E. Philpin, eds. *The Brenner Debate: Agrarian Class Structure and Economic Development in Pre-Industrial Europe.* Cambridge, 1985.
Ayrault, Roger. *La genèse du romantisme allemand: Situation spirituelle de l'Allemagne dans la deuxième moitié du xviiie siècle.* 2 vols. Paris, 1961.
Backer, Dorothy Anne Liot. *Precious Women.* New York, 1974.
Badalo-Dulong, Claude. *Banquier du roi: Barthélemy Hervart (1606–1676).* Paris, 1951.
Baldwin, Charles Sears. *Renaissance Literary Theory and Practice.* Gloucester, Mass., 1959.
Baron, Hans. *The Crisis of the Early Italian Renaissance: Civic Humanism and Republican Liberty in an Age of Classicism and Tyranny.* Rev. in 1 vol. Princeton, 1966.
Barrell, John. *The Dark Side of the Landscape: The Rural Poor in English Painting, 1730–1840.* Cambridge, 1980.
———. *Poetry, Language, and Politics.* Manchester, 1988.
———. *The Political Theory of Painting from Reynolds to Hazlitt: "The Body of the Public."* New Haven, Conn., and London, 1986.
Bate, Frank. *The Declaration of Indulgence, 1672: A Study in the Rise of Organized Dissent.* London, 1908.
Bate, Jonathan. *Shakespearean Constitutions: Politics, Theatre, Criticism, 1730–1830.* Oxford, 1989.
Bate, Walter Jackson. *From Classic to Romantic: Premises of Taste in Eighteenth-Century England.* 1946; rpt. New York, 1961.
Beame, Edmond Morton. "The Limits of Toleration in Sixteenth-Century France." *Studies in the Renaissance,* 13 (1966), 250–65.
Beauvoir, Simone de. *The Second Sex.* Trans. H. M. Parshley. 1952; rpt. New York, 1971.
Beilin, Elaine V. *Redeeming Eve: Women Writers of the English Renaissance.* Princeton and Guildford, 1987.

Belsey, Catherine. *The Subject of Tragedy: Identity and Difference in Renaissance Drama.* London and New York, 1985.

Bénichou, Paul. *Le sacré de l'écrivain, 1750–1830: Essai sur l'avènement d'un pouvoir spirituel laïque dans la France moderne.* Paris, 1973.

Benjamin, Walter. *Illuminations.* Ed. Hannah Arendt. Trans. Harry Zohn. New York, 1969.

Bermingham, Ann. *Landscape and Ideology: The English Rustic Tradition, 1740–1860.* Berkeley and Los Angeles, 1986.

Bernal, Martin. *Black Athena: The Afroasiatic Roots of Classical Civilization. Vol. 1: The Fabrication of Ancient Greece, 1785–1985.* New Brunswick, N.J., 1987.

Berry, Philippa. *Of Chastity and Power: Elizabethan Literature and the Unmarried Queen.* London and New York, 1989.

Bersier, Eugène. *La révocation.* Discours prononcé dans le Temple de l'Oratoire de Paris, le 22 octobre 1885. Suivi de notes relatives aux jugements des contemporains sur l'édit de révocation. Paris, 1886.

Bert, Paul. *Histoire de la Révocation de l'Édit de Nantes à Bordeaux et dans le Bordelais. Diocèse de Bordeaux, 1653–1715.* 1908; rpt. Geneva, 1977.

Beverley, John R. *Aspects of Gongora's "Soledades."* Purdue University Monographs in Romance Languages, vol. 1. Amsterdam, 1980.

Bevington, David M. *Tudor Drama and Politics: A Critical Approach to Topical Meaning.* Cambridge, Mass., 1968.

Bleicher, Thomas. *Homer in der deutschen Literatur (1450–1740): Zur Rezeption der Antike und zur Poetologie der Neuzeit.* Stuttgart, 1972.

Bloom, Harold, ed. *John Dryden.* New York, 1987.

Blumenberg, Hans. *The Genesis of the Copernican World.* Trans. Robert M. Wallace. Cambridge, Mass., and London, 1987.

——. *The Legitimacy of the Modern Age.* Trans. Robert M. Wallace, Cambridge, Mass., and London, 1983.

——. *Work on Myth.* Trans. Robert M. Wallace. Cambridge, Mass., and London, 1985.

Borgerhoff, E. B. O. *The Freedom of French Classicism.* Princeton, 1950.

Bourgeon, Jean-Louis. *Les Colbert avant Colbert: Destin d'une famille marchande.* Paris, 1973.

Bouten, J. *Mary Wollstonecraft and the Beginnings of Female Emancipation in France and England.* Amsterdam, [1922].

Brandon, Ruth. *The New Women and the Old Men: Love, Sex, and the Woman Question.* London, 1990.

Brault, Pascale-Anne. "Prophetess Doomed: Cassandra and the Representation of Truth." Ph.D. diss., New York University, 1990.

Bray, René. *La formation de la doctrine classique en France.* Paris, 1927.

Bredvold, Louis I. *The Intellectual Milieu of John Dryden: Studies in Some Aspects of Seventeenth-Century Thought.* Ann Arbor, Mich., 1956.

Broadus, Edmund Kemper. *The Laureateship: A Study of the Office of Poet Laureate in England, with some Account of the Poets.* Oxford, 1921.

Brombert, Victor. *The Romantic Prison: The French Tradition.* Princeton, 1978.

Brown, Laura. "The Ideology of Restoration Poetic Form: John Dryden." In *John Dryden.* Ed. Harold Bloom. New York, 1987, pp. 101–19.

Bruford, W. H. *Germany in the Eighteenth Century: The Social Background of the Literary Revival.* 1935; rpt. Cambridge, 1968.

Brunschwig, Henri. *Enlightenment and Romanticism in Eighteenth-Century Prussia.* Trans. F. Jellinek. Chicago, 1974.

Buck, Philip W. *The Politics of Mercantilism.* New York, 1942.
Butler, Eliza Marian. *The Tyranny of Greece over Germany: A Study of the Influence Exercised by Greek Art and Poetry over the Great German Writers of the Eighteenth, Nineteenth, and Twentieth Centuries.* Cambridge, 1935.
Butler, Marilyn. *Romantics, Rebels, and Reactionaries: English Literature and Its Background, 1760–1830.* New York and Oxford, 1982.
Butler, Martin. *Theatre and Crisis, 1632–1642.* Cambridge, 1984.
Buxton, John. *Sir Philip Sidney and the English Renaissance.* 2d ed. London, 1964.
Bygrave, Stephen. *Coleridge and the Self: Romantic Egotism.* London, 1986.
Calvino, Italo. *The Castle of Crossed Destinies.* Trans. William Weaver. 1977; rpt. New York and London, 1979.
Camerlingo, Rosanna. "Matters of Honor: Knights and Courtiers in Sidney's Two *Arcadias.*" Ph.D. diss., New York University, 1991.
Canavaggio, Jean. *Cervantes.* Trans. J. R. Jones. New York and London, 1990.
Cannon, Mary Agnes. *The Education of Women in the Renaissance.* 1916; rpt. Westport, Conn., 1981.
Cassirer, Ernst. *The Individual and the Cosmos in Renaissance Philosophy.* Trans. Mario Domandi. 1963; rpt. Philadelphia, 1972.
———. *The Platonic Renaissance in England.* Trans. James P. Pettegrove. Austin, Tex., 1955.
Castor, Grahame. *Pléiade Poetics: A Study in Sixteenth-Century Thought and Terminology.* Cambridge, 1964.
Castor, Grahame, and Terence Cave, eds. *Neo-Latin and the Vernacular in Renaissance France.* Oxford, 1984.
Cave, Terence. *The Cornucopian Text: Problems of Writing in the French Renaissance.* Oxford, 1979.
———. "Recognition and the Reader." *Comparative Criticism: A Yearbook,* vol. 2. Ed. E. S. Shaffer. Cambridge, 1980, pp. 49–69.
———. *Recognitions: A Study in Poetics.* Oxford, 1988.
———. "Translating the Humanists: Erasmus and Rabelais." *Comparative Criticism: A Yearbook,* vol. 3. Ed. E. S. Shaffer. Cambridge, 1981, pp. 279–93.
———, ed. *Ronsard the Poet.* London, 1973.
Chartier, Roger. *Lectures et lecteurs dans la France d'ancien régime.* Paris, 1987.
Clark, Alexander Frederick Bruce. *Boileau and the French Classical Critics in England (1660–1830).* 1925; rpt. New York, 1965.
Clément, Pierre. *Histoire de Colbert et de son administration.* 2d ed. 2 vols. Paris, 1874.
Clements, Robert J. *Critical Theory and Practice of the Pléiade.* Cambridge, Mass., 1942.
Cohen, Ted, and Paul Guyer, eds. *Essays in Kant's Aesthetics.* 1982; rpt. Chicago and London, 1985.
Cohen, Walter. *Drama of a Nation: Public Theater in Renaissance England and Spain.* Ithaca, N.Y., and London, 1985.
Cole, Charles Woolsey. *Colbert and a Century of French Mercantilism.* 2 vols. New York, 1939.
———. *French Mercantilism, 1683–1700.* New York, 1943.
Coleman, Francis X. J. *The Aesthetic Thought of the French Enlightenment.* Pittsburgh, 1971.
Colley, Linda. *In Defiance of Oligarchy: The Tory Party, 1714–1760.* 1982; rpt. Cambridge, 1985.

Condé, Michel. "La genèse sociale de l'individualisme romantique." 3 vols. Ph.D. diss., Université de Liège, 1986.

———. *La genèse sociale de l'individualisme romantique en France: Esquisse historique de l'évolution du roman en France du dix-huitième au dix-neuvième siècle.* Tübingen, 1989.

Conley, Carey Herbert. *The First English Translations of the Classics.* Port Washington, N.Y., 1967.

Couton, Georges. *Corneille.* 2d ed. Paris, 1969.

———. *Corneille et la Fronde.* Clermont-Ferrand, 1951.

———. *Corneille et la tragédie politique.* Paris, 1984.

Crawford, Donald W. *Kant's Aesthetic Theory.* Madison, Wis., 1974.

Culture et pouvoir au temps de l'humanisme et de la renaissance. Geneva and Paris, 1978.

Davis, Natalie Zemon. "Gender and Genre: Women as Historical Writers, 1400–1820." In *Beyond Their Sex: Learned Women of the European Past.* Ed. Patricia H. Labalme. New York and London, 1980, pp. 153–82.

Davison, J. A. "The Homeric Question." In *A Companion to Homer.* Ed. Alan J. B. Wace and Frank H. Stubbings. London, 1962, pp. 234–66.

De Bolla, Peter. *The Discourse of the Sublime: Readings in History, Aesthetics, and the Subject.* Oxford, 1989.

DeJean, Joan. "Classical Reeducation: Decanonizing the Feminine." In *The Politics of Tradition: Placing Women in French Literature.* Ed. Joan DeJean and Nancy K. Miller. Yale French Studies, no. 75. New Haven, Conn., 1988, pp. 26–39.

———. *Fictions of Sappho, 1546–1937.* Chicago and London, 1989.

———. "*La Princesse de Clèves:* The Poetics of Suppression." *Papers in Seventeenth-Century French Literature,* 10, no. 18 (1983), 79–98.

———. *Tender Geographies: Women and the Origins of the Novel in France.* New York, 1991.

De Man, Paul. "Hegel on the Sublime." In *Displacement: Derrida and After.* Ed. Mark Krupnick. Bloomington, Ind., 1983, pp. 139–53.

———. "Reply to Raymond Geuss." *Critical Inquiry,* 10, no. 2 (Dec. 1983), 383–90.

———. "Sign and Symbol in Hegel's *Aesthetics.*" *Critical Inquiry,* 8, no. 4 (Summer 1982), 761–75.

DeMaria, Robert, Jr. *Johnson's Dictionary and the Language of Learning.* Chapel Hill, N.C., and London, 1986.

———. "The Politics of Johnson's *Dictionary.*" *PMLA,* 104, no. 1 (1989), 64–74.

De Mazan, J. *Les doctrines économiques de Colbert.* 1900; rpt. New York, 1972.

Dent, Julian. *Crisis in Finance: Crown, Financiers, and Society in Seventeenth-Century France.* New York, 1973.

Depping, Guillaume. "Un banquier protestant en France au xviie siècle: Barthélemy Herwarth, contrôleur général des finances (1607–1676)." *Revue Historique,* 10 (1879), 285–338; 11 (1879), 63–80.

Dessert, Daniel. *Argent, pouvoir et société au grand siècle.* Paris, 1984.

Dihle, Albrecht. *The Theory of Will in Classical Antiquity.* Berkeley, Los Angeles, and London, 1982.

Dobbs, Betty Jo Teeter. *The Foundations of Newton's Alchemy or "The Hunting of the Greene Lyon."* Cambridge, 1975.

Dollimore, Jonathan. *Radical Tragedy: Religion, Ideology, and Power in the Drama of Shakespeare and His Contemporaries.* Brighton, 1984.

Dollimore, Jonathan, and Alan Sinfield, eds. *Political Shakespeare: New Essays in Cultural Materialism.* Ithaca, N.Y., and London, 1985.

Donougho, Martin. "Art and Absolute Spirit or, the Anatomy of Aesthetics." *Revue de l'Université d'Ottawa,* 52, no. 4 (1982), 483–98.

Donovan, Josephine. "The Silence Is Broken." In *Women and Language in Literature and Society.* Ed. Sally McConnell-Ginet, Ruth Borker, and Nelly Furman. New York, 1980, pp. 205–18.

Dronke, Peter. *Fabula: Explorations into the Uses of Myth in Medieval Platonism.* Mittellateinische Studien und Texte, 9. Leiden and Cologne, 1974.

——. *The Medieval Poet and His World.* Rome, 1984.

——. *Women Writers of the Middle Ages: A Critical Study of Texts from Perpetua (*203) to Marguerite Porete (*1310).* Cambridge, 1984.

Dubois, Jacques. *L'institution de la littérature: Introduction à une sociologie.* Brussels, 1978.

Dunn, John Joseph. "The Role of Macpherson's *Ossian* in the Development of British Romanticism." Ph.D. diss., Duke University, 1966.

Ebin, Lois A. *John Lydgate.* Boston, 1985.

Edwards, Charles S. *Hugo Grotius, The Miracle of Holland: A Study of Political and Legal Thought.* Chicago, 1981.

Ehrmann, Jacques. *Un paradis désespéré: L'amour et l'illusion dans "l'Astrée."* New Haven, Conn., and Paris, 1963.

Eisenstein, Elizabeth L. *The Printing Press as an Agent of Change: Communication and Cultural Transformation in Early Modern Europe.* 2 vols. Cambridge, 1979.

——. *The Printing Revolution in Early Modern Europe.* Cambridge, 1983.

Eisenstein, Zillah. *The Radical Future of Liberal Feminism.* New York and London, 1981.

Ekberg, Carl J. *The Failure of Louis XIV's Dutch War.* Chapel Hill, N.C., 1979.

Elias, Norbert. *The Court Society.* Trans. Edmund Jephcott. New York, 1983.

Elliott, John H. *The Count-Duke of Olivares: The Statesman in an Age of Decline.* New Haven, Conn., and London, 1986.

——. "The Decline of Spain." *Past and Present,* 20 (1961), 52–75.

——. *Europe Divided, 1559–1598.* 1968; rpt. London, 1985.

——. *Imperial Spain, 1469–1716.* 1963; rpt. Harmondsworth, 1970.

——. *Richelieu and Olivares.* Cambridge, 1984.

——. "Self-Perception and Decline in Early Seventeenth-Century Spain." *Past and Present,* 74 (1977), 41–61.

——. "The Spanish Peninsula, 1598–1649." In *The New Cambridge Modern History IV: The Decline of Spain and the Thirty Years War, 1609–48/59.* Ed. J. P. Cooper. Cambridge, 1970, pp. 435–73.

Engell, James. *Forming the Critical Mind: Dryden to Coleridge.* Cambridge, Mass., and London, 1989.

Evans, Robert John Weston. *The Making of the Habsburg Monarchy, 1550–1700: An Interpretation.* Oxford, 1979.

——. *Rudolf II and His World: A Study in Intellectual History, 1576–1612.* Oxford, 1973.

Farnham, Fern. *Madame Dacier: Scholar and Humanist.* 1976; rpt. Monterey, Calif., 1980.

Fassiotto, Marie-Josée. *Madame de Lambert (1647–1733) ou le féminisme moral.* New York, Berne, and Frankfurt a/M, 1984.

Febvre, Lucien, and Henri-Jean Martin. *L'apparition du livre.* Avec . . . Anne Basanoff, Henri Bernard-Maitre, Moché Catane, Marie-Robert Guignard, et Marcel Thomas. 1958; rpt. Paris, 1971.

Ferguson, Frances. "Wollstonecraft Our Contemporary." In *Gender and Theory: Dialogues on Feminist Criticism*. Ed. Linda Kauffman. Oxford, 1989, pp. 51–60.

——. *Wordsworth: Language as Counter-Spirit*. New Haven, Conn., and London, 1977.

Ferguson, Margaret W. *Trials of Desire: Renaissance Defenses of Poetry*. New Haven, Conn., and London, 1983.

Ferguson, Margaret W., Maureen Quilligan, and Nancy J. Vickers, eds. *Rewriting the Renaissance: The Discourses of Sexual Difference in Early Modern Europe*. Chicago and London, 1986.

Ferguson, Moira, and Janet Todd. *Mary Wollstonecraft*. Boston, 1984.

Figgis, John Neville. *The Divine Right of Kings*. Cambridge, 1914.

Firestone, Shulamith. *The Dialectic of Sex*. New York, 1970.

Foot, Paul. *Red Shelley*. London, 1980.

Formaggio, Dino. *La "morte dell'arte" e l'estetica*. Bologna, 1983.

Foucault, Michel. *The Archaeology of Knowledge*. Trans. A. M. Sheridan Smith. New York, 1976.

——. *Histoire de la sexualité*. Vols. 2 and 3. Paris, 1984.

——. *L'ordre du discours*. Paris, 1971.

Fox, Alistair. *Politics and Literature in the Reigns of Henry VII and Henry VIII*. Oxford, 1989.

Franklin, Julian H. *John Locke and the Theory of Sovereignty: Mixed Monarchy and the Right of Resistance in the Political Thought of the English Revolution*. Cambridge, 1978.

Fraser, George. "Pope and Homer." In *Augustan Worlds*. Ed. J. C. Hilson, M. M. B. Jones, and J. R. Watson. Leicester, 1978, pp. 119–30.

Fröberg, Ingrid. *Une "histoire secrète" à matière nordique: "Gustave Vasa, histoire de Suède" (1697), roman attribué à Charlotte-Rose de Caumont La Force (vers 1650–1724)*. Acta Universitatis Upsaliensis: Studia Romanica Upsaliensia, 31. Uppsala, 1981.

Frye, Northrop. *The Critical Path: An Essay on the Social Context of Literary Criticism*. Bloomington, Ind., and London, 1971.

Fumaroli, Marc. *L'âge de l'éloquence: Rhétorique et 'res literaria' de la Renaissance au seuil de l'époque classique*. Geneva and Paris, 1980.

Gachon, Paul Jean Louis. *Quelques préliminaires de la Révocation de l'Édit de Nantes en Languedoc (1661–1685)*. Toulouse, 1899.

Garber, Frederick. "Pastoral Spaces." *Texas Studies in Literature and Language*, 30 (1988), 431–60.

Gellrich, Jesse M. *The Idea of the Book in the Middle Ages: Language Theory, Mythology, and Fiction*. Ithaca, N.Y., and London, 1985.

George, M. Dorothy. *England in Transition: Life and Work in the Eighteenth Century*. 1931; rpt. Harmondsworth, 1969.

——. *London Life in the Eighteenth Century*. London, 1925.

Geuss, Raymond. "A Response to Paul de Man." *Critical Inquiry*, 10, no. 2 (Dec. 1983), 375–82.

Giamatti, A. Bartlett. *The Earthly Paradise and the Renaissance Epic*. Princeton, 1966.

Gindely, Anton. *Geschichte des dreissigjährigen Krieges*. 4 vols. Prague, 1869–80.

Goldberg, Jonathan. *James I and the Politics of Literature: Jonson, Shakespeare, Donne, and Their Contemporaries*. Baltimore and London, 1983.

Gooch, G. P. *History of English Democratic Ideas in the Seventeenth Century*. London, 1898.

Gossman, Lionel. "Literature and Education." *New Literary History*, 13, no. 2 (Winter 1982), 341–71.

Gouhier, Henri Gaston. *Les premières pensées de Descartes: Contribution à l'histoire de l'anti-Renaissance.* Paris, 1958.

Grafton, Anthony, and Lisa Jardine. *From Humanism to the Humanities: Education and the Liberal Arts in Fifteenth- and Sixteenth-Century England.* London, 1986.

Grass, Günter. "The Business Blitzkrieg." *Weekend Guardian* (Oct. 20–21, 1990), pp. 4–7.

——. *Two States—One Nation?* Trans. Krishna Winston and A. S. Wensinger. London, 1990.

Green, Richard Firth. *Poets and Princepleasers: Literature and the English Court in the Late Middle Ages.* Toronto, Buffalo, N.Y., and London, 1980.

Greenblatt, Stephen Jay. *Renaissance Self-Fashioning: From More to Shakespeare.* Chicago and London, 1980.

——. *Shakespearean Negotiations: The Circulation of Social Energy in Renaissance England.* Berkeley, Los Angeles, and London, 1988.

Greene, Thomas M. *The Light in Troy: Imitation and Discovery in Renaissance Poetry.* New Haven, Conn., and London, 1982.

——. *The Vulnerable Text: Essays on Renaissance Literature.* New York, 1986.

Greenfield, Concetta Carestia. *Humanist and Scholastic Poetics, 1250–1500.* Lewisburg, Penna., 1981.

Guyer, Paul. *Kant and the Claims of Taste.* Cambridge, Mass., and London, 1979.

Habermas, Jürgen. *The Philosophical Discourse of Modernity: Twelve Lectures.* Trans. Frederick G. Lawrence, Cambridge, Mass., 1987.

Hall, Hugh Gaston. *Richelieu's Desmarets and the Century of Louis XIV.* Oxford, 1990.

Harth, Erica. *Ideology and Culture in Seventeenth-Century France.* Ithaca, N.Y., and London, 1983.

Hartman, Geoffrey H. *The Fate of Reading and Other Essays.* Chicago and London, 1975.

Hathaway, Baxter. *The Age of Criticism: The Late Renaissance in Italy.* Ithaca, N.Y., 1962.

Haywood, Ian. *The Making of History: A Study of the Literary Forgeries of James Macpherson and Thomas Chatterton in Relation to Eighteenth-Century Ideas of History and Fiction.* Rutherford, N.J., 1987.

Heinemann, Margot. *Puritanism and Theatre: Thomas Middleton and Opposition Drama under the Early Stuarts.* 1980; rpt. Cambridge, 1982.

Hepp, Noémi. *Homère en France au xviie siècle.* Paris, 1968.

Herrick, Marvin T. *The Fusion of Horatian and Aristotelian Literary Criticism, 1531–1555.* Illinois Studies in Language and Literature, 32, no. 1. Urbana, Ill., 1946.

Higman, Francis M. "Ronsard's Political and Polemical Poetry." In *Ronsard the Poet.* Ed. Terence Cave. London, 1973, pp. 241–85.

Hilden, Patricia J. *A Social History of Belgium: Women, Work, and Politics, 1830–1914.* Oxford, forthcoming.

——. "Women in Coal Mines: Belgium's *hiercheuses,* 1890–1914." Unpublished lecture, 1986–87.

——. *Women Workers and Socialist Politics in France, 1880–1914: A Regional Study.* Oxford, 1986.

Hill, Christopher. "Clarissa Harlowe and Her Times." In *Puritanism and Revolution: Studies in Interpretation of the English Revolution of the Seventeenth Century.* 1958; rpt. New York, 1964, pp. 367–94.

——. *Collected Essays.* 3 vols. Amherst, Mass., 1985–86.

Hilton, Rodney H., ed. *The Transition from Feudalism to Capitalism.* London, 1978.

Hinchman, Lewis P. *Hegel's Critique of the Enlightenment.* Gainesville, Fla., 1984.

Hinsley, Francis Harry. *Sovereignty.* 2d ed. Cambridge, 1986.

Hipple, Walter John, Jr. *The Beautiful, the Sublime, and the Picturesque in Eighteenth-Century British Aesthetic Theory.* Carbondale, Ill., 1957.

Hobby, Elaine. *Virtue of Necessity: English Women's Writing, 1649–88.* Ann Arbor, Mich., 1989.

Hobsbawm, Eric, and Terence Ranger, eds. *The Invention of Tradition.* Cambridge. 1983.

Hoffmann, Paul. "Le féminisme spirituel de Gabrielle Suchon." *XVIIe Siècle,* 121 (1978), 269–76.

Hogrefe, Pearl. *Tudor Women: Commoners and Queens.* Ames, Iowa, 1975.

Hohendahl, Peter Uwe. *Building a National Literature: The Case of Germany, 1830–1870.* Trans. Renate Baron Franciscono. Ithaca, N.Y., and London, 1989.

——. *The Institution of Criticism.* Ithaca, N.Y., and London, 1982.

——, ed. *A History of German Literary Criticism, 1730–1980.* With Contributions by Klaus L. Berghahn, Russell A. Berman, Peter Uwe Hohendahl, Jochen Schulte-Sasse, and Bernhard Zimmermann. Trans. Franz Blaha, John R. Blazek, Jeffrey S. Librett, and Simon Srebrny. Lincoln, Neb., and London, 1988.

Hollier, Denis. *La prise de la Concorde: Essais sur Georges Bataille.* Paris, 1974.

Holt, Mack P. *The Duke of Anjou and the Politique Struggle during the Wars of Religion.* Cambridge, 1986.

Horkheimer, Max. "Montaigne et la fonction du scepticisme." In *Théorie critique: Essais.* Paris, 1978.

Horn, András. *Kunst und Freiheit: Eine kritische Interpretation der Hegelschen Ästhetik.* The Hague, 1969.

Horner, Joyce M. *The English Women Novelists and Their Connection with the Feminist Movement (1688–1797).* Smith College Studies in Modern Languages, vol. 11, nos. 1–3. Northampton, Mass., 1929–30.

Houston, R. A. *Literacy in Early Modern Europe: Culture and Education, 1500–1800.* London and New York, 1988.

Howard, Michael. *Clausewitz.* Oxford and New York, 1983.

Howells, Robin J. "Dialogue and Speakers in the 'Parallèle des anciens et des modernes.'" *Modern Language Review,* 78, no. 4 (1983), 793–803.

——. "La religion des 'chefs' dans la querelle: Boileau, Perrault, Dacier, La Motte." In *D'un siècle à l'autre: Anciens et modernes. Xvie colloque (janvier 1986).* Ed. Louise Godard de Donville and Roger Duchêne. Marseille, 1987, pp. 53–62.

Hunter, George K. *John Lyly: The Humanist as Courtier.* Cambridge, Mass., 1962.

Hunter, Jean E. "The Eighteenth-Century Englishwoman: According to the Gentleman's Magazine." In *Women in the Eighteenth Century and Other Essays.* Ed. Paul Fritz and Richard Morton. Toronto, 1976, pp. 73–88.

Jardine, Lisa. *Still Harping on Daughters: Women and Drama in the Age of Shakespeare.* Brighton and Totawa, N.J., 1983.
——. See also Grafton, Anthony, and Lisa Jardine.
Javitch, Daniel. *"Il Cortegiano* and the Constraints of Despotism." In *Castiglione: The Ideal and the Real in Renaissance Culture.* Ed. Robert W. Hanning and David Rosand. New Haven, Conn., and London, 1983, pp. 17–28.
——. *Poetry and Courtliness in Renaissance England.* Princeton, 1978.
——. *Proclaiming a Classic: The Canonization of "Orlando Furioso."* Princeton, 1991.
Jehasse, Jean. *Guez de Balzac et le génie romain, 1597–1654.* Saint-Etienne, 1977.
——. *La renaissance de la critique: L'essor de l'humanisme érudit de 1560 à 1614.* Saint-Etienne, 1976.
Jondorf, Gillian. *Robert Garnier and the Themes of Political Tragedy in the Sixteenth Century.* Cambridge, 1969.
Jones, James Rees. *Country and Court: England, 1658–1714.* Cambridge, Mass., 1978.
——. *The First Whigs: The Politics of the Exclusion Crisis, 1678–1683.* 1961; rpt. London, 1966.
Jones, John. *The Egotistical Sublime: A History of Wordsworth's Imagination.* 2d ed. 1964; rpt. London, 1970.
Jones, Richard Foster. *Ancients and Moderns: A Study of the Rise of the Scientific Movement in Seventeenth-Century England.* 2d ed. St. Louis, Mo., 1961.
Jordan, Constance. "Feminism and the Humanists: The Case of Sir Thomas Elyot's *Defence of Good Women.*" In *Rewriting the Renaissance: The Discourses of Sexual Difference in Early Modern Europe.* Ed. Margaret W. Ferguson, Maureen Quilligan, and Nancy J. Vickers. Chicago and London, 1986, pp. 242–58.
——. "Woman's Rule in Sixteenth-Century British Political Thought." *Renaissance Quarterly,* 40 (1987), 421–51.
Kahler, Erich. *The Disintegration of Form in the Arts.* New York, 1968.
——. *The Inward Turn of Narrative.* Trans. Richard and Clara Winston. Foreword Joseph Frank. Princeton, 1973.
Kahn, Victoria. *Rhetoric, Prudence, and Skepticism in the Renaissance.* Ithaca, N.Y., and London, 1985.
Kaminsky, Jack. *Hegel on Art: An Interpretation of Hegel's Aesthetics.* 1962; rpt. Albany, N.Y., 1970.
Kantorowicz, Ernst H. *The King's Two Bodies: A Study in Medieval Political Theology.* Princeton, 1957.
Kay, Carol. *Political Constructions: Defoe, Richardson, and Sterne in Relation to Hobbes, Hume, and Burke.* Ithaca, N.Y., and London, 1988.
Kelley, Donald Reed. *The Beginning of Ideology: Consciousness and Society in the French Reformation.* Cambridge, 1981.
——. "Civil Science in the Renaissance: The Problem of Interpretation." In *The Languages of Political Theory in Early-Modern Europe.* Ed. Anthony Robin Pagden. Cambridge, 1987, pp. 57–78.
——. *Foundations of Modern Historical Scholarship: Language, Law, and History in the French Renaissance.* New York and London, 1970.
——. "Legal Humanism and the Sense of History." *Studies in the Renaissance,* 13 (1966), 184–99.

Kelso, Ruth. *Doctrine for the Lady of the Renaissance.* Urbana, Ill., 1956.
Kenney, E. J., ed. *The Cambridge History of Classical Literature. Vol. 2: Latin Literature.* Cambridge, 1982.
Kermode, John Frank. *The Classic.* London, 1975.
———. *Forms of Attention.* Chicago and London, 1985.
King, John N. "Queen Elizabeth I: Representations of the Virgin Queen." *Renaissance Quarterly,* 43, no. 1 (Spring 1990), 30–74.
Kirkham, Margaret. *Jane Austen, Feminism, and Fiction.* 1983; rpt. New York, 1986.
Kirkpatrick, Kathryn. "A Contextual Reading of Maria Edgeworth's *Castle Rackrent* and *Belinda.*" Ph.D. diss., Emory University, 1990.
Klaits, Joseph. *Printed Propaganda under Louis XIV: Absolute Monarchy and Public Opinion.* Princeton, 1976.
Knights, L. C. *Poetry, Politics, and the English Tradition.* London, 1954.
———. *Public Voices: Literature and Politics with Special Reference to the Seventeenth Century.* London, 1971.
Knox, Israel. *The Aesthetic Theories of Kant, Hegel, and Schopenhauer.* New York, 1936.
Knudsen, Jonathan B. *Justus Möser and the German Enlightenment.* Cambridge, 1986.
Kortian, Garbis. "L'art appartient-il au passé? La thèse hégélienne de la fin de l'art et la psychanalyse." *Critique,* 38, no. 416 (Jan. 1982), 72–83.
Krieger, Murray. *Words about Words about Words: Theory, Criticism, and the Literary Text.* Baltimore and London, 1988.
Labio, Catherine. "Enlightenment and the Epistemology of Origins." Ph.D. diss., New York University, 1991.
Labrousse, Elisabeth. *"Une foi, une loi, un roi?" Essai sur la révocation de l'Édit de Nantes.* Geneva and Paris, 1985.
Lachterman, David Rapport. *The Ethics of Geometry: A Genealogy of Modernity.* New York and London, 1989.
Lathrop, Henry Burrowes. *Translations from the Classics into English from Caxton to Chapman, 1477–1620.* [1933]; rpt. New York, 1967.
Lee, Sangsup. *Elizabethan Literary Opinion: A Study in Its Variety.* Seoul, 1971.
Lefebvre, Henri. *Contribution à l'esthétique.* Paris, 1953.
Legge, M. Dominica. *Anglo-Norman Literature and Its Background.* Oxford, 1963.
Levasseur, Émile. *Histoire des classes ouvrières et de l'industrie en France avant 1789.* 2d ed. 2 vols. Paris, 1900–1901.
Levin, Harry. *The Myth of the Golden Age in the Renaissance.* 1969; rpt. New York, 1972.
Levine, Joseph Martin. *Humanism and History: Origins of Modern English Historiography.* Ithaca, N.Y., and London, 1987.
Litman, Théodore A. *Le sublime en France (1660–1714).* Paris, 1971.
Loraux, Nicole. "La main d'Antigone." *Métis: Revue d'anthropologie du monde grec ancien,* 1, no. 2 (1986), 165–96.
Lord, George de F. "'Absalom and Achitophel' and Dryden's Political Cosmos." In *John Dryden.* Ed. Earl Miner. Athens, Ohio, 1972, pp. 156–90.
Lougee, Carolyn C. *"Le paradis des femmes": Women, Salons, and Social Stratification in Seventeenth-Century France.* Princeton, 1976.
Lowenthal, Leo. *Literature, Popular Culture, and Society.* Englewood Cliffs, N.J., 1961.

Lyons, John D., and Stephen G. Nichols, Jr., eds. *Mimesis: Mirror to Method, St. Augustine to Descartes.* Hanover, N.H., and London, 1982.

Lytle, Guy Fitch, and Stephen Orgel, eds. *Patronage in the Renaissance.* Princeton, 1981.

McCoy, Richard C. *Sir Philip Sidney: Rebellion in Arcadia.* New Brunswick, N.J., 1979.

McFadden, George. *Dryden: The Public Writer, 1660–1685.* Princeton, 1978.

McGann, Jerome J. *The Romantic Ideology: A Critical Investigation.* Chicago and London, 1983.

McGowan, Margaret. *L'art du ballet de cour en France (1581–1643).* Paris, 1964.

——. "The Presence of Rome in Some Plays of Robert Garnier." In *Myth and Its Making in the French Theatre: Studies Presented to W. D. Howarth.* Ed. E. Freeman, H. Mason, M. O'Regan, and S. W. Taylor. Cambridge, 1988, pp. 12–29.

McKeon, Michael. *The Origins of the English Novel, 1600–1740.* Baltimore and London, 1987.

——. *Politics and Poetry in Restoration England: The Case of Dryden's "Annus Mirabilis."* Cambridge, Mass., and London, 1975.

Maclean, Ian. *Woman Triumphant: Feminism in French Literature, 1610–1652.* Oxford, 1977.

Macpherson, Crawford Brough. *The Political Theory of Possessive Individualism: Hobbes to Locke.* 1962; rpt. Oxford, 1967.

Macpherson, Harriet D. *Censorship under Louis XIV, 1661–1715.* New York, 1929.

Magné, Bernard. *La crise de la littérature française sous Louis XIV: Humanisme et nationalisme.* 2 vols. Toulouse, 1976.

Mahoney, John L. *The Whole Internal Universe: Imitation and the New Defense of Poetry in British Criticism, 1660–1830.* New York, 1985.

Mandrou, Robert. *Magistrats et sorciers en France au XVIIe siècle: Une analyse de psychologie historique.* Paris, 1980.

Maravall, José Antonio. *Culture of the Baroque: Analysis of a Historical Structure.* Trans. Terry Cochran. Foreword Wlad Godzich and Nicholas Spadaccini. Minneapolis, 1986.

——. "From the Renaissance to the Baroque: The Diphasic Schema of a Social Crisis." Trans. Terry Cochran. In *Literature among Discourses: The Spanish Golden Age.* Ed. Wlad Godzich and Nicholas Spadaccini. Minneapolis, 1986, pp. 3–40.

Marin, Louis. *La critique du discours: Sur la "logique de Port-Royal" et les "pensées" de Pascal.* Paris, 1975.

——. *Le portrait du roi.* Paris, 1981.

——. *Le récit est un piège.* Paris, 1978.

Marks, R. Emerson. *Relativist and Absolute: The Early Neoclassical Debate in England.* New Brunswick, N.J., 1955.

Marsh, Robert Harrison. *Four Dialectical Theories of Poetry: An Aspect of English Neoclassical Criticism.* Chicago, 1965.

Marshall, Catherine, C. K. Ogden, and Mary Sargant Florence. *Militarism versus Feminism: Writings on Women and War.* Ed. Margaret Kamester and Jo Vellacott. London, 1987.

Martin, Germain. *La grande industrie sous le règne de Louis XIV (plus particulièrement de 1660 à 1715).* 1899; rpt. New York, 1971.

Martin, Henri-Jean. *Livre, pouvoirs et société à Paris au xviie siècle (1598–1701).* 2 vols. Geneva, 1969.

Martines, Lauro. *Power and Imagination: City-States in Renaissance Italy.* 1979; rpt. Harmondsworth, 1983.

——. *Society and History in English Renaissance Verse.* Oxford, 1985.

Maus, Katharine Eisaman. "Arcadia Lost: Politics and Revision in the Restoration *Tempest.*" In *Renaissance Drama as Cultural History: Essays from "Renaissance Drama," 1977–1987.* Ed. Mary Beth Rose. Evanston, Ill., 1990, pp. 127–47.

May, Georges. *Le dilemme du roman au xviiie siècle: Étude sur les rapports du roman et de la critique (1715–1761).* New Haven, Conn., 1963.

Mebane, John S. *Renaissance Magic and the Return of the Golden Age: The Occult Tradition and Marlowe, Jonson, and Shakespeare.* Lincoln, Neb., and London, 1989.

Meineke, Friedrich. *The Age of German Liberation, 1795–1815.* Trans. Peter Paret and Helmuth Fischer. Ed. Peter Paret. Berkeley, Los Angeles, and London, 1977.

Menendez y Pelayo, Marcelino. *Historia de las ideas estéticas en España.* Ed. D. Enrique Sánchez Reyes. 3d ed. 3 vols. Madrid, 1962.

Menhennet, Alan. *Order and Freedom: Literature and Society in Germany from 1720 to 1805.* New York, 1973.

Merleau-Ponty, Maurice. *Humanism and Terror: An Essay on the Communist Problem.* Trans. John O'Neill. Boston, 1969.

Mesnard, Pierre. *L'essor de la philosophie politique au xvie siècle.* 3d ed. Paris, 1969.

Miller, Jacqueline T. *Poetic License: Authority and Authorship in Medieval and Renaissance Contexts.* New York and Oxford, 1986.

Miner, Earl Roy. *The Restoration Mode from Milton to Dryden.* Princeton, 1974.

——, ed. *John Dryden.* Athens, Ohio, 1972.

Minnis, Alastair J. *Medieval Theory of Authorship: Scholastic Literary Attitudes in the Later Middle Ages.* London, 1984.

——, ed. *Gower's "Confessio amantis": Responses and Reassessments.* Cambridge, 1983.

Monk, Samuel H. *The Sublime: A Study of Critical Theories in XVIII-Century England.* 1935; rpt. Ann Arbor, Mich., 1960.

Moore, Leslie E. *Beautiful Sublime: The Making of "Paradise Lost," 1701–1734.* Stanford, Calif., 1990.

Moriarty, Michael. *Taste and Ideology in Seventeenth-Century France.* Cambridge, 1988.

Mousnier, Roland E. *The Institutions of France under the Absolute Monarchy, 1598–1789.* Trans. Arthur Goldhammer. 2 vols. Chicago and London, 1979–84.

Murat, Inès. *Colbert.* Paris, 1980.

Muratore, Mary Jo. *The Evolution of the Cornelian Heroine.* Potomac, Md., 1987.

Murphy, James Jerome. *Rhetoric in the Middle Ages: Rhetorical Theory from St. Augustine to the Renaissance.* Berkeley, Los Angeles, and London, 1974.

——, ed. *Renaissance Eloquence: Studies in the Theory and Practice of Renaissance Rhetoric.* Berkeley, Los Angeles, and London, 1983.

Mustoxidi, Théodore Mavroïdi. *Histoire de l'esthétique française, 1700–1900.* 1920; rpt. New York, 1968.

Myers, William. "Dryden's Shakespeare." In *Augustan Worlds.* Ed. J. C. Hilson, M. M. B. Jones, and J. R. Watson. Leicester, 1978, pp. 15–27.

Myres, Sir John L. *Homer and His Critics.* Ed. Dorothea Gray. London, 1958.

Nagler, Aloïs Maria. *Theatre Festivals of the Medici, 1539–1637.* Trans. George Hickenlooper. New Haven, Conn., 1964.

Navarrete, Ignacio. "Decentering Garcilaso: Herrera's Attack on the Canon." *PMLA*, 106, no. 1 (1991), 21–33.

Ngugi Wa Thiong'o. *Writers in Politics: Essays.* London, 1981.

Nicolson, Marjorie Hope. *Mountain Gloom and Mountain Glory: The Development of the Aesthetics of the Infinite.* 1959; rpt. New York, 1963.

Niderst, Alain. *Madeleine de Scudéry, Paul Pellisson et leur monde.* Paris, 1976.

Norbrook, David. *Poetry and Politics in the English Renaissance.* London, Boston, and Melbourne, 1984.

Olson, Glending. *Literature as Recreation in the Later Middle Ages.* Ithaca, N.Y., and London, 1982.

Orcibal, Jean. *La genèse d'Esther et d'Athalie.* Paris, 1950.

——. *Louis XIV et les protestants.* Paris, 1951.

Orgel, Stephen. *The Illusion of Power: Political Theater in the English Renaissance.* Berkeley, Los Angeles, and London, 1975.

Orgel, Stephen, and Roy Strong. *Inigo Jones: The Theatre of the Stuart Court.* 2 vols. London, 1973.

Owst, G. R. *Literature and Pulpit in Medieval England: A Neglected Chapter in the History of English Letters and of the English People.* Cambridge, 1933.

Pagès, Georges. *Les institutions monarchiques sous Louis XIII et Louis XIV.* Paris, 1962.

Parker, Geoffrey. *The Thirty Years' War.* 1984; rpt. London, 1987.

Parker, Geoffrey, and L. M. Smith, eds. *The General Crisis of the Seventeenth Century.* London, 1978.

Parker, Patricia. *Inescapable Romance: Studies in the Poetics of a Mode.* Princeton, 1979.

——. *Literary Fat Ladies: Rhetoric, Gender, Property.* London and New York, 1987.

Parker, Patricia, and David Quint, eds. *Literary Theory/Renaissance Texts.* Baltimore and London, 1986.

Parry, Adam. "The Making of Homeric Verse: An Introduction." In his *Language of Achilles and Other Papers.* [Ed. Hugh Lloyd-Jones.] Oxford, 1989, pp. 195–264.

Parry, Graham. *The Golden Age Restor'd: The Culture of the Stuart Court, 1603–42.* Manchester, 1981.

Patey, Douglas Lane. *Probability and Literary Form: Philosophic Theory and Literary Practice in the Augustan Age.* Cambridge, 1984.

Patterson, Annabel. *Censorship and Interpretation: The Conditions of Writing and Reading in Early Modern England.* Madison, Wis., 1984.

——. *Marvell and the Civic Crown.* Princeton, 1978.

——. *Pastoral and Ideology: Virgil to Valéry.* Berkeley, Los Angeles, and London, 1988.

Pearsall, Derek. *John Lydgate.* Charlottesville, Va., 1970.

Peck, Russell A. *Kingship and Common Pursuit in Gower's "Confessio amantis."* Carbondale and Edwardsville, Ill., 1984.

Perry, Elisabeth Israels. *From Theology to History: French Religious Controversy and the Revocation of the Edict of Nantes.* The Hague, 1973.

Perry, Ruth. *The Celebrated Mrs. Astell: An Early English Feminist.* Chicago, 1986.

——. *Women, Letters, and the Novel.* New York, 1980.

Picard, Raymond. *La carrière de Jean Racine*. Paris, 1961.

Picard, Roger. *Les salons littéraires et la société française, 1610–1789*. New York, 1943.

Pitkin, Hannah Fenichel. *Fortune Is a Woman: Gender and Politics in the Thought of Niccolò Machiavelli*. Berkeley, Los Angeles, and London, 1984.

Plumb, J. H. *The Origins of Political Stability in England, 1675–1725*. Boston, 1967.

Pocock, J. G. A. *The Machiavellian Moment: Florentine Political Thought and the Atlantic Republican Tradition*. Princeton, 1975.

Poirion, Daniel. *Le poète et le prince: L'évolution du lyrisme courtois de Guillaume de Machaut à Charles d'Orléans*. Grenoble, 1965.

Poovey, Mary. *The Proper Lady and the Woman Writer*. Chicago and London, 1984.

Pottinger, David T. *The French Book Trade in the Ancien Régime, 1500–1791*. Cambridge, Mass., 1958.

Price, Martin. *To the Palace of Wisdom: Studies in Order and Energy from Dryden to Blake*. Garden City, N.Y., 1964.

Prigent, Michel. *Le héros et l'état dans la tragédie de Pierre Corneille*. 1986; rpt. Paris, 1988.

Putnam, Hilary. *Reason, Truth, and History*. Cambridge, 1981.

Quint, David. *Origin and Originality in Renaissance Literature: Versions of the Source*. New Haven, Conn., and London, 1983.

Rabb, Theodore K. *The Struggle for Stability in Early Modern Europe*. New York, 1975.

Rajan, Tillotama. *Dark Interpreter: The Discourse of Romanticism*. Ithaca, N.Y., and London, 1980.

Ramsay, J. D. "The Foreign Policy of Elizabeth I." In *The Reign of Elizabeth I*. Ed. Christopher Haigh. Basingstoke, 1984, pp. 147–68.

Ranum, Orest. *Artisans of Glory: Writers and Historical Thought in Seventeenth-Century France*. Chapel Hill, N.C., 1980.

Rawson, Elizabeth. *The Spartan Tradition in European Thought*. Oxford, 1969.

Reed, T. J. *The Classical Centre: Goethe and Weimar, 1775–1832*. 1980; rpt. Oxford, 1986.

——. "Critical Consciousness and Creation: The Concept *Kritik* from Lessing to Hegel." In *Oxford German Studies*, 3. Ed. P. F. Ganz. Oxford, 1968, pp. 87–113.

Reiss, Erna. *Rights and Duties of Englishwomen: A Study in Law and Public Opinion*. Manchester, 1934.

Reiss, Timothy J. "The *concevoir* Motif in Descartes." In *La cohérence intérieure: Études sur la littérature française du xviie siècle, offertes à J.-D. Hubert*. Ed. J. van Baelen and D. L. Rubin. Paris, 1977, pp. 203–22.

——. "Descartes, the Palatinate, and the Thirty Years' War: Political Theory and Political Practice." In *Baroque Topologies: Literature/History/Philosophy*. Ed. Timothy Hampton. *Yale French Studies*, no. 80. New Haven, Conn., 1991, pp. 108–45.

——. *The Discourse of Modernism*. Ithaca, N.Y., and London, 1982.

——. "Du système de la critique classique." *XVIIe Siècle*, 116 (1977), 3–16.

——. "The Environment of Literature and the Imperatives of Criticism: The End of a Discipline." *Europa*, 4, no. 1 (1981), 29–64.

——. "Espaces de la pensée discursive: Le cas Galilée et la science classique." *Revue de Synthèse*, 85–86 (1977), 5–47.

——. "The Idea of Meaning and Practice of Method in Pierre de La Ramée,

Henri Estienne, and Others." In *Humanism in Crisis: The Decline of the French Renaissance.* Ed. Philippe Desan. Ann Arbor, Mich., 1991, pp. 125–51.

———. "Montaigne and the Subject of Polity." In *Literary Theory/Renaissance Texts.* Ed. Patricia Parker and David Quint. Baltimore and London, 1986, pp. 115–49.

———. "The Origin and Development of French Tragedy." In *A New History of French Literature.* Ed. Denis Hollier. Cambridge, Mass., 1989, pp. 205–9.

———. "Problems in Logic and Rhetoric." In *A New History of French Literature.* Ed. Denis Hollier. Cambridge, Mass., 1989, pp. 278–84.

———. "Racine and Political Thought: *Les Plaideurs* and Law." *Cahiers du Dix-Septième,* 1, no. 2 (Fall 1987), 1–19.

———. "Significs: The Analysis of Meaning as Critique of Modernist Culture." In *Essays in Significs.* Ed. Walter H. Schmitz. Amsterdam, 1990, pp. 63–82.

———. "Société, discours, littérature: De l'histoire discursive." *Texte,* no. 5/6 (1986–87), 151–79.

———. *Toward Dramatic Illusion: Theatrical Technique and Meaning from Hardy to "Horace."* New Haven, Conn., and London, 1971.

———. *Tragedy and Truth: Studies in the Development of a Renaissance and Neoclassical Discourse.* New Haven, Conn., and London, 1980.

———. *The Uncertainty of Analysis: Problems in Truth, Meaning, and Culture.* Ithaca, N.Y., and London, 1988.

———. "La voix royale: De la violence étatique ou, du privé à la souveraineté." In *Pierre Corneille: Ambiguïtés.* Ed. Michel Bareau. Edmonton, 1988, pp. 41–54.

Renoir, Alain. *The Poetry of John Lydgate.* London, 1967.

Reynolds, Siân, ed. *Women, State, and Revolution: Essays on Power and Gender in Europe since 1789.* Amherst, Mass., 1987.

Rigault, Henri. *Histoire de la querelle des anciens et des modernes.* 1859; rpt. New York, 1966.

Rochot, Bernard. "A propos des Rose-Croix, de Descartes et des rêves de 1619." *Revue de Synthèse* (July–Sept. 1956), 351–61.

Rodríguez, Juan Carlos. *Teoría e historia de la producción ideológica: Las primeras literaturas burguesas (siglo xvi).* Madrid, 1974.

Rogers, Pat. *The Augustan Vision.* London, 1978.

———. *Grub Street: Studies in a Subculture.* London, 1972.

———. *Literature and Popular Culture in Eighteenth-Century England.* Brighton, Sussex, and Totawa, N.J., 1985.

Ronzeaud, Pierre. "La femme au pouvoir ou le monde à l'envers." *XVIIe Siècle,* 108 (1975), 9–33.

———. "Note sur l'article de Paul Hoffmann." *XVIIe Siècle,* 121 (1978), 276–77.

Rose, Mary Beth. *The Expense of Spirit: Love and Sexuality in English Renaissance Drama.* Ithaca, N.Y., and London, 1988.

———, ed. *Renaissance Drama as Cultural History: Essays from "Renaissance Drama," 1977–1987.* Evanston, Ill., 1990.

———, ed. *Women in the Middle Ages and the Renaissance: Literary and Historical Perspectives.* Syracuse, N.Y., 1986.

Rothkrug, Lionel. *Opposition to Louis XIV: The Political and Social Origins of the French Enlightenment.* Princeton, 1965.

Rousset, Jean. *La littérature de l'âge baroque en France: Circé et le paon.* Paris, 1954.

Rozas, Juan Manuel. *Significado y doctrina del "Arte nuevo" de Lope de Vega.* Madrid, 1976.

Rubinstein, Nicolai. "The History of the Word *Politicus* in Early-Modern Europe." In *The Languages of Political Theory in Early-Modern Europe.* Ed. Anthony Robin Pagden. Cambridge, 1987, pp. 41–56.

Sales, Roger. *English Literature in History: 1780–1830, Pastoral and Politics.* London, 1983.

Salmon, John Hearsey McMillan. *The French Religious Wars in English Political Thought.* Oxford, 1959.

———. *Society in Crisis: France in the Sixteenth Century.* 1975; rpt. London, 1979.

Sandkühler, Bruno. *Die frühen Dantekommentare und ihr Verhältnis zur mittelalterlichen Kommentartradition.* Münchner Romanistische Arbeiten, no. 19. Munich, 1967.

Sankovitch, Tilde. "Inventing Authority of Origin: The Difficult Enterprise." In *Women in the Middle Ages and the Renaissance: Literary and Historical Perspectives.* Ed. Mary Beth Rose. Syracuse, N.Y., 1986, pp. 227–43.

Sarlet, Claudette Delhez-. "L'académie française du temps du Cardinal de Richelieu." *Marche Romane,* Cahiers de l'A.R.U. Liège, 29, nos. 1–2 (1979), 41–60.

———. "L'académie française et le mécenat." In *L'âge d'or du mécenat (1598–1661).* Colloque international C.N.R.S. (mars 1983). Paris, 1985, pp. 241–46.

Saunders, Bailey. *The Life and Letters of James Macpherson.* London and New York, 1894.

Scattergood, J. *Politics and Poetry in the Fifteenth Century.* London, 1971.

Schama, Simon. *The Embarrassment of Riches: An Interpretation of Dutch Culture in the Golden Age.* Berkeley, 1988.

Schaper, Eva. *Studies in Kant's Aesthetics.* Edinburgh, 1979.

Scheaper, Thomas J. *The Economy of France in the Second Half of the Reign of Louis XIV.* ICES Research Report/Cahiers de Recherche du CIEE, no. 2. Montreal, 1980.

Schérer, Jacques. *La dramaturgie classique en France.* Paris, 1962.

Schibanoff, Susan. "Taking the Gold out of Egypt: The Art of Reading as a Woman." In *Gender and Reading: Essays on Readers, Texts, and Contexts.* Ed. Elizabeth A. Flynn and Patrocinio P. Schweickart. Baltimore, 1986, pp. 83–106.

Schiebinger, Londa. *Mind Has No Sex? Women in the Origins of Modern Science.* Cambridge, Mass., and London, 1989.

———. "Skeletons in the Closet: The First Illustrations of the Female Skeleton in Eighteenth-Century Anatomy." *Representations,* 14 (Spring 1986), 42–82.

Schiff, Mario L. *La fille d'alliance de Montaigne: Marie de Gournay.* Essai suivi de "L'égalité des hommes et des femmes" et du "Grief des dames." Paris, 1910.

Schilling, Bernard Nicholas. *Dryden and the Conservative Myth: A Reading of "Absalom and Achitophel."* New Haven, Conn., and London, 1961.

Schmidt, Josephine A. *If There Are No More Heroes, There Are Heroines: A Feminist Critique of Corneille's Heroes, 1637–1643.* Lanham, Md., 1987.

Schoefer, Christine. "Germany Rewrites History: The Attack on Christa Wolf." *The Nation,* 251, no. 3 (Oct. 22, 1990), 446–49.

Schreiner, Olive. *Women and Labour* [1911]. Pref. Jane Graves. London, 1978.

Schwartz, Joel. *The Sexual Politics of Jean-Jacques Rousseau.* Chicago and London, 1984.

Scott, H. G., ed. *Problems of Soviet Literature: Reports and Speeches at the*

First Soviet Writers' Congress, by A. Zhdanov, Maxim Gorky, N. Bukharin, K. Radek, and A. Stetsky. New York, 1934.

Sharpe, Kevin. *Criticism and Compliment: The Politics of Literature in the England of Charles I.* Cambridge, 1987.

——. *Politics and Ideas in Early Stuart England: Essays and Studies.* London and New York, 1989.

Shevelow, Kathryn. "Fathers and Daughters: Women as Readers of *The Tatler.*" In *Gender and Reading: Essays, Texts, and Contexts.* Ed. Elizabeth A. Flynn and Patrocinio P. Schweickart. Baltimore, 1986, pp. 107–23.

Shils, Edward. *Tradition.* Chicago, 1981.

Shklovsky, Viktor. "Sterne's *Tristram Shandy:* Stylistic Commentary." In *Russian Formalist Criticism: Four Essays.* Trans. and ed. Lee T. Lemon and Marion J. Reis. Lincoln, Neb., and London, 1965, pp. 25–57.

Simone, Franco. *La coscienza della rinascita negli umanisti francesi.* Rome, 1949.

——. *Il rinascimento francese: Studi e ricerche.* Turin, 1961.

——. *Umanismo, rinascimento, barocco in Francia.* Milan, 1968.

——, ed. *Culture et politique en France à l'époque de l'humanisme et de la Renaissance.* Turin, 1974.

Simonsuuri, Kirsti. *Homer's Original Genius: Eighteenth-Century Notions of the Early Greek Epic (1688–1798).* Cambridge, 1979.

Skinner, Quentin. *The Foundations of Modern Political Thought.* 2 vols. Cambridge, 1978.

Smart, John Semple. *James Macpherson: An Episode in Literature.* 1905; rpt. New York, 1973.

Smith, Florence. *Mary Astell.* 1916; rpt. New York, 1966.

Smith, Hilda. *Reason's Disciples: Seventeenth-Century English Feminists.* Urbana, Ill., 1982.

Sonnino, Paul. *Louis XIV and the Origins of the Dutch War.* Cambridge, 1988.

Spencer, Jane. *The Rise of the Woman Novelist: From Aphra Behn to Jane Austen.* Oxford, 1986.

Spingarn, Joel E. *A History of Literary Criticism in the Renaissance.* 1899; rpt. New York and London, 1908.

Stafford, Fiona J. *The Sublime Savage: A Study of James Macpherson and the Poems of Ossian.* Edinburgh, 1988.

Stanton, Domna C. *The Aristocrat as Art: A Study of the "Honnête Homme" and the "Dandy" in Seventeenth- and Nineteenth-Century French Literature.* New York, 1980.

——. "The Fear of Women and the Fictions of *Préciosité.*" *Yale French Studies,* no. 62 (Fall 1981), 107–34.

——. "Woman as Object and Subject of Exchange: Marie de Gournay's Le *Proumenoir* (1594)." *Esprit Créateur,* 23, no. 2 (1983), 9–25.

Starobinski, Jean. *L'invention de la liberté, 1700–1789.* Geneva, 1964.

Steegman, John. *The Rule of Taste: From George I to George IV.* 1936; rpt. London, 1986.

Stegmann, André. *L'héroïsme cornélien: Genèse et signification.* 2 vols. Paris, 1968.

Steiner, George. *Real Presences.* Chicago, 1989.

Stephen, Leslie. *English Literature and Society in the Eighteenth Century.* 1904; rpt. London, 1963.

Stillman, Robert E. *Sidney's Poetic Justice: The Old Arcadia, Its Eclogues, and Renaissance Pastoral Traditions.* Lewisburg, Penna., 1986.

Stimpson, Catharine R. "Female Insubordination and the Text." In *Women in Culture and Politics: A Century of Change*. Ed. Judith Friedlander, Blanche Wiesen Cook, Alice Kessler-Harris, and Carroll Smith-Rosenberg. Bloomington, Ind., 1986, pp. 164–76.

Stock, Brian. *The Implications of Literacy: Written Language and Models of Interpretation in the Eleventh and Twelfth Centuries*. Princeton, 1983.

Strong, Roy. *Art and Power: Renaissance Festivals, 1450–1650*. 1973; rpt. Woodbridge, Suffolk, 1984.

——. *The Cult of Elizabeth*. London, 1977.

——. See also Orgel, Stephen.

Summers, David. *The Judgment of Sense: Renaissance Naturalism and the Rise of Aesthetics*. Cambridge, 1987.

Sutcliffe, Frank E. *Guez de Balzac et son temps: Littérature et politique*. Paris, 1959.

——. "Le pardon d'Auguste: Politique et morale dans *Cinna*." In *A Modern Miscellany*, presented to Eugène Vinaver. . . . Ed. T. E. Lawrenson, F. E. Sutcliffe, and G. F. A. Gadoffre. Manchester and New York, 1969, pp. 243–53.

——. *Politique et culture, 1560–1660*. Paris, 1973.

Sutton, Dana Ferrin. *The Lost Sophocles*. Lanham, Md., 1984.

Symcox, Geoffrey. *The Crisis of French Sea Power, 1688–1697: From the "Guerre d'Escadre" to the "Guerre de course."* The Hague, 1974.

Talmon, Jacob L. *The Origins of Totalitarian Democracy*. 1952; rpt. New York, 1960.

Tastevin, Maria. *Les héroïnes de Corneille*. Paris, 1924.

Tateo, Francesco. *Retorica e poetica fra Medioevo e Rinascimento*. Bari, 1960.

Taylor, Gary. *Reinventing Shakespeare: A Cultural History, from the Restoration to the Present*. New York, 1989.

Tenger, Zeynep. "Inventing the Reader and the Writer: Eighteenth-Century Literary Theory." Ph.D. diss., New York University, 1990.

Tennenhouse, Leonard. *Power on Display: The Politics of Shakespeare's Genres*. New York and London, 1986.

Thorpe, Clarence DeWitt. *The Aesthetic Theory of Thomas Hobbes*. Ann Arbor, Mich., and London, 1940.

Todd, Janet. *Sensibility: An Introduction*. London and New York, 1986.

——. *The Sign of Angellica: Women, Writing, and Fiction, 1660–1800*. London, 1989.

Tompkins, Joyce Marjorie Sanxter. *The Popular Novel in England, 1770–1800*. 1961; rpt. Westport, Conn., 1976.

Torrigiani, Ivo. *Lo specchio dei sistemi Batteux e Condillac*. Palermo, 1984.

Trevor-Roper, Hugh Redwald. *The European Witch Craze of the Sixteenth and Seventeenth Centuries and Other Essays*. New York, 1969.

Trout, Andrew. *Jean-Baptiste Colbert*. Boston, 1978.

Uildriks, Anne. *Les idées littéraires de Mlle de Gournay*. Groningen, 1962.

Vance, Eugene. *From Topic to Tale: Logic and Narrativity in the Middle Ages*. Foreword Wlad Godzich. Minneapolis, 1987.

——. *Mervelous Signals: Poetics and Sign Theory in the Middle Ages*. Lincoln, Neb., and London, 1986.

Van Tieghem, Paul. *Ossian en France*. Paris, 1917.

Védier, Georges. *Origine et évolution de la dramaturgie néo-classique*. Paris, 1955.

Venesoen, Constant. *Corneille apprenti féministe, de "Mélite" au "Cid."* Paris, 1986.

Viala, Alain. *Naissance de l'écrivain: Sociologie de la littérature à l'âge classique.* Paris, 1985.

Vierhaus, Rudolf. *Germany in the Age of Absolutism.* Trans. Jonathan B. Knudsen. Cambridge, 1988.

Vilar Berrogain, Jean. *Literatura y economía: La figura satírica del arbitrista en el Siglo de Oro.* Trans. Francisco Bustelo G.ª del Real. Madrid, 1973.

Vossler, Karl. *Poetische Theorien in der Italienische Frührenaissance.* 2 vols. Berlin, 1900.

Watson, J. N. P. *Captain-General and Rebel Chief: The Life of James, Duke of Monmouth.* London, 1979.

Wedgwood, Cecily Veronica. *The Trial of Charles I.* London, 1964.

——. *William the Silent: William of Nassau, Prince of Orange.* New Haven, Conn., 1944.

Weimann, Robert. *Shakespeare and the Popular Tradition in the Theater: Studies in the Social Dimensions of Dramatic Form and Function.* Ed. Robert Schwartz. Baltimore and London, 1978.

——. *Structure and Society in Literary History: Studies in the History and Theory of Historical Criticism.* Expanded ed. Baltimore and London, 1984.

Weinberg, Bernard. *A History of Literary Criticism in the Italian Renaissance.* 2 vols. 1961; rpt. Chicago, 1974.

Weinbrot, Howard D. *Augustus Caesar in "Augustan" England: The Decline of a Classical Norm.* Princeton, 1978.

Welby, Victoria, Lady. *What Is Meaning? Studies in the Development of Significance* (London, 1903). Facs. rpt. Intro. Gerrit Mannoury. Pref. Achim Eschbach. Amsterdam, 1983.

Wellek, René. *The Attack on Literature and Other Essays.* Chapel Hill, N.C., 1982.

——. *A History of Modern Criticism, 1750–1950.* 6 vols. New Haven, Conn., 1955–86.

Wheatley, Katherine E. *Racine and English Classicism.* Austin, Tex., 1956.

Wiesner, Merry E. "Women's Defense of Their Public Roles." In *Women in the Middle Ages and the Renaissance: Literary and Historical Perspectives.* Ed. Mary Beth Rose. Syracuse, N.Y., 1986, pp. 1–27.

Wilson, Diana De Armas. *Allegories of Love: Cervantes's "Persiles and Sigismunda."* Princeton, 1991.

——. "Cervantes's *Labors of Persiles:* 'Working (in) the In-Between.' " In *Literary Theory/Renaissance Texts.* Ed. Patricia Parker and David Quint. Baltimore and London, 1986, pp. 150–81.

Wilson, H. T. *Tradition and Innovation: The Idea of Civilization as Culture and Its Significance.* London, 1984.

Winn, James Anderson. *John Dryden and His World.* New Haven, Conn., and London, 1987.

Woodbridge, Linda. *Women and the English Renaissance: Literature and the Nature of Womankind, 1540–1620.* Urbana, Ill., and Chicago, 1984.

Woolf, Virginia. "The Countess of Pembroke's Arcadia." In *The Second Common Reader.* 1932; rpt. New York, 1960, pp. 32–41.

——. "On Not Knowing Greek." In *The Common Reader. First Series.* 1925; rpt. New York, 1953, pp. 24–39.

——. *Orlando: A Biography.* 1928; rpt. New York, 1946.

——. *Three Guineas.* 1938; rpt. New York, 1966.

Yates, Frances Amelia. *The Art of Memory.* 1966; rpt. Harmondsworth, 1969.
——. *Astraea: The Imperial Theme in the Sixteenth Century.* 1975; rpt. Harmondsworth, 1977.
——. *The French Academies of the Sixteenth Century.* Studies of the Warburg Institute, vol. 15. 1947; rpt. Nendeln (Liechtenstein), 1968.
——. *Giordano Bruno and the Hermetic Tradition.* 1964; rpt. New York, 1969.
——. *The Occult Philosophy in the Elizabethan Age.* London, 1979.
——. *The Rosicrucian Enlightenment.* 1972; rpt. St. Albans, 1975.
——. *The Valois Tapestries.* Studies of the Warburg Institute, vol. 23. London, 1959.
Youssef, Zobeidah. *Polémique et littérature chez Guez de Balzac.* Paris, 1972.
Zuber, Roger. *Les "Belles Infidèles" et la formation du goût classique: Perrot d'Ablancourt et Guez de Balzac.* Paris, 1968.
Zwicker, Steven N. *Dryden's Political Poetry: The Typology of King and Nation.* Providence, R.I., 1972.
——. *Politics and Language in Dryden's Poetry: The Arts of Disguise.* Princeton and Guildford, 1984.

Index

385

Library of Congress Cataloging-in-Publication Data

Reiss, Timothy J.
  The meaning of literature / Timothy J. Reiss.
    p. cm.
  Includes bibliographical references and index.
  ISBN 0–8014–2646–4 (cloth : alk. paper) ISBN 0–8014–9947–X (pbk : alk. paper)
  1. Literature—Philosophy. 2. Meaning (Philosophy) 3. Literature and history.
  4. Literature—History and criticism. I. Title.
PN49.R386 1992
801—dc20   91–23344